INIURIA AND THE COMMON LAW

The delict of *iniuria* is among the most sophisticated products of the Roman legal tradition. The original focus of the delict was assault, although *iniuria* – literally a wrong or unlawful act – indicated a very wide potential scope. Yet it quickly grew to include sexual harassment and defamation, and by the first century CE it had been re-oriented around the concept of *contumelia* so as to incorporate a range of new wrongs, including insult and invasion of privacy. In truth, it now comprised all attacks on personality.

It is the Roman delict of *iniuria* which forms the foundation of both the South African and – more controversially – Scots laws of injuries to personality. On the other hand, *iniuria* is a concept formally alien to English law. But as its title suggests, this book of essays is representative of a species of legal scholarship best described as 'oxymoronic comparative law', employing a concept peculiar to one legal tradition in order to interrogate another where, apparently, it does not belong. Addressing a series of doctrinal puzzles within the law of assault, defamation and breach of privacy, it considers in what respects the Roman delict of *iniuria* overlaps with its modern counterparts in England, Scotland and South Africa; the differences and similarities between the analytical frameworks employed in the ancient and modern law; and the degree to which the Roman proto-delict points the way to future developments in each of these three legal systems.

Volume 9 in the series Hart Studies in Private Law

Iniuria and the Common Law

Edited by
Eric Descheemaeker
and
Helen Scott

·HART·
PUBLISHING
OXFORD AND PORTLAND, OREGON
2013

Published in the United Kingdom by Hart Publishing Ltd
16C Worcester Place, Oxford, OX1 2JW
Telephone: +44 (0)1865 517530
Fax: +44 (0)1865 510710
E-mail: mail@hartpub.co.uk
Website: http://www.hartpub.co.uk

Published in North America (US and Canada) by
Hart Publishing
c/o International Specialized Book Services
920 NE 58th Avenue, Suite 300
Portland, OR 97213-3786
USA
Tel: +1 503 287 3093 or toll-free: (1) 800 944 6190
Fax: +1 503 280 8832
E-mail: orders@isbs.com
Website: http://www.isbs.com

British Library Cataloguing in Publication Data
Data Available

ISBN: 978-1-84946-503-8

Typeset by Hope Services, Abingdon
Printed and bound in Great Britain by
Lightning Source UK Ltd

PREFACE

The present volume contains ten papers originally presented at a seminar on '*Iniuria* and the Common Law' which took place on 9–10 September 2011 in the splendour of All Souls College, Oxford. The event was organised by the two editors under the auspices of the Institute of European and Comparative Law, University of Oxford. Diverse in their geographical origins (England, the civilian world and the mixed jurisdictions of Scotland and South Africa), the participants – listed overleaf – also represented a number of different intellectual traditions: Roman law, civilian and common law legal history, comparative law, and modern doctrinal scholarship. It was particularly gratifying to have three Regius Professors of Civil Law gathered together in the same room, the College's Old Library. Yet the absence of Alan Rodger made it impossible to escape a sense of sadness. Lord Rodger of Earlsferry, one of Britain's most distinguished Romanists, was to have presented a paper at the seminar but had died just a few months earlier. There was no-one in the room who had not strongly felt Alan's intellectual influence at some point, and to many of us he had been a dear friend also. This book is dedicated to his memory.

Eric Descheemaeker
Helen Scott
24 January 2013

CONFERENCE PARTICIPANTS

Iniuria and the Common Law
All Souls College, Oxford
9–10 September 2011

Professor John Blackie (University of Strathclyde)
Professor Jonathan Burchell (University of Cape Town)
Dr Eric Descheemaeker (University of Edinburgh)
Dr Simon Douglas (University of Oxford)
Professor François du Bois (University of Nottingham)
Professor Anton Fagan (University of Cape Town)
Dr Joshua Getzler (University of Oxford)
Professor Tony Honoré (University of Oxford)
Professor David Ibbetson (University of Cambridge)
Professor Yasunori Kasai (Otsuma University, Tokyo)
Mr James Lee (University of Birmingham)
Professor Paul Mitchell (University College London)
Professor Kenneth McKenzie Norrie (University of Strathclyde)
Dr Paul J du Plessis (University of Edinburgh)
Professor Geoffrey Samuel (University of Kent)
Professor Helen Scott (University of Cape Town)
Professor Boudewijn Sirks (University of Oxford)
Professor Robert Stevens (University College London)
Professor Stefan Vogenauer (University of Oxford)
Professor Reinhard Zimmermann (Max Planck Institute for Comparative and International Private Law, Hamburg)

ACKNOWLEDGEMENTS

We are grateful, first, to all the participants in the original '*Iniuria* and the Common Law' seminar for their enthusiastic engagement with our topic. They made this book possible. Not only did the South African contingent make the long journey from Cape Town; many of the other participants travelled to Oxford from outside England, in particular from Scotland and (in the case of Reinhard Zimmermann) Germany. Warm thanks are extended also to Robert Stevens, James Lee and Anton Fagan for providing structured responses during the concluding round table and to John Blackie for leading it; to Boudewijn Sirks for hosting the event at All Souls as well as the College staff for making it such a memorable occasion; and to Richard Hart, who embraced the project from the first day – his continued commitment to scholarship, even of the not readily marketable sort, spurs us on. Karen Baston, Jenny Dix and Jean Wilke offered highly valuable assistance in the organisation of the seminar and the production of the book. Finally, money is easy to despise only when one has enough of it; we wish gratefully to acknowledge the support provided by the Universities of Cape Town and Edinburgh and, especially, the *Modern Law Review*.

From left to right: Kenneth McKenzie Norrie, Robert Stevens, François du Bois, John Blackie, Reinhard Zimmermann, Helen Scott, Jonathan Burchell, Tony Honoré, David Ibbetson, Anton Fagan, Paul J du Plessis, Simon Douglas, Eric Descheemaeker, Joshua Getzler, Paul Mitchell, Yasunori Kasai, James Lee, Geoffrey Samuel.

CONTENTS

CONTRIBUTORS

John Blackie is Professor of Law Emeritus at the University of Strathclyde (Scotland)

Jonathan Burchell is Professor of Law in the Department of Public Law at the University of Cape Town (South Africa)

Eric Descheemaeker is Lecturer in European Private Law at the University of Edinburgh (Scotland)

François du Bois is Professor of Law at the University of Leicester (England) and Honorary Research Associate at the University of Cape Town (South Africa)

Anton Fagan is WP Schreiner Professor in the Department of Private Law at the University of Cape Town (South Africa)

David Ibbetson is Regius Professor of Civil Law in the University of Cambridge (England)

Paul Mitchell is Professor of Laws at University College London (England)

Kenneth McKenzie Norrie is Professor of Law at the University of Strathclyde (Scotland)

Paul du Plessis is Senior Lecturer in Civil Law and Legal History at the University of Edinburgh (Scotland)

Helen Scott is Associate Professor in the Department of Private Law at the University of Cape Town (South Africa)

TABLE OF CASES

France

New Zealand

Scotland

South Africa

TABLE OF LEGISLATION

Scotland (post-1999)

HISTORICAL SOURCES

ROMAN LEGAL SOURCES

Justinianic

Institutes

Digest

Non-Justinianic

Collatio legum Mosaicarum et Romanarum

Gaius, *Institutes*

ANCIENT NON-LEGAL SOURCES

Aulus Gellius, ***Noctes Atticae***

Seneca, ***De Ira***

1

Iniuria and the Common Law

ERIC DESCHEEMAEKER AND HELEN SCOTT

I. Introduction

Our title, *Iniuria* and the Common Law, reflects a type of legal scholarship which might be dubbed 'oxymoronic comparative law'. That is to say, it employs a concept from one legal tradition in order to interrogate another where, on the face of it, it does not belong. When the two terms of the oxymoron are properly chosen, such a comparison can turn out to be extremely fruitful. We hope that this book will serve to illustrate that point.

Iniuria, which is variously translated in English as 'insult', 'contempt',[1] 'affront', 'outrage' or 'contumely', has been the subject of much less enquiry than the *lex Aquilia* and the actions to which it gave rise. This is true both of the ancient delict and of its modern incarnations, and is most likely explained by the less than triumphant fate of the *actio iniuriarum* during the second life of Roman law.[2] Yet the delict of *iniuria* is one of the most sophisticated aspects of the Roman legal tradition, distinguished in particular by the high level of abstraction and generalisation achieved by the classical jurists. Nor is its relevance merely a matter of historical interest, for many features of the ancient delict strike us as remarkably modern, both in terms of the substance of the law and in view of the analytical framework employed.[3] Although the original, Republican focus of the delict was assault, it quickly grew to include sexual harassment and defamation, and by the classical period (ie from the first century CE) it had been entirely re-oriented around the concept of *contumelia*, contempt.[4] Under the influence of this productive generalisation, the delict was extended to cover a range of new wrongs: its scope came to comprise all attacks on dignity.[5]

[1] This was Peter Birks' favoured translation. See eg P Birks, 'Harassment and Hubris: The Right to an Equality of Respect' (1997) new ser 32 *Irish Jurist* 1, 8; P Birks and G McLeod (trans), *The Institutes of Justinian* (London, Duckworth, 1987) 151 (see: 'contempt').

[2] Below section V.

[3] Below section IV.

[4] Below section II.

[5] Below section III.

What of the 'common law' referred to in our title? The word *iniuria* might be familiar to many English lawyers, but with a very different meaning: it is generally used in the sense of 'injury', as in modern tort scholarship, to designate a wrong or a type of harm. As a concept, however, *iniuria* is alien to the common law, in the sense of the legal tradition rooted in medieval English law. This does not mean that it is not there, at least in the form of fragments, at a deeper level: this, indeed, is the major theme of this book; and it will be returned to later in this introductory chapter.[6] But our starting point must be that *iniuria* is an intruder. As a tort or delict, it simply does not feature in the landscape of the common law of civil wrongs. On the other hand, *iniuria* is a cause of action familiar in the civilian tradition, particularly in the mixed legal systems of South Africa and Scotland.[7] These, too, are comprised within the 'common law' of our title.

Of course, our decision to focus on England, Scotland and South Africa was due in part to our personal idiosyncrasies as the conference organisers and then editors of this book: each of us has one foot in England and the other in one of the 'crosses', northern or southern.[8] But it is our belief that our decision can also be defended on purely objective grounds: not only are Scotland and South Africa the two best-known mixed (in the sense of Anglo-Roman) jurisdictions; their more remarkable feature is that they are the two best examples of modern legal systems where contemporary private law proceeds, at least in part, from a Roman-law substrate which has evolved through an unbroken (ie uncodified) history. In that sense, they are both systems of 'living Roman law'. Although this is truer of South Africa than it is of Scotland, we have in both cases a modern law of delict which is still rooted in the principles of Roman law as they were revived and developed over the course of its 'second life'.[9] At the same time, the vagaries of history mean that they have also become part of the common law tradition.

Thus we are confronted with a remarkable paradox: the two most significant jurisdictions never to have broken their historical link with ancient Roman law through codification are part of the wider common law world. This provides a most intriguing vantage point from which to examine the significance of *iniuria* to the common law. To us it seemed eminently worthwhile to stimulate doctrinal scholarship around the modern law of tort in England, Scotland, and South Africa

[6] Below section VI.

[7] Remarkably, albeit for very different reasons that need not be pursued here, *iniuria* as an independent civil wrong has also disappeared from modern codified civilian legal systems such as France or Germany.

[8] See eg Reinhard Zimmermann and Daniel Visser, *Southern Cross: Civil Law and Common Law in South Africa* (Cape Town, Juta, 1996); Reinhard Zimmermann, Daniel Visser and Kenneth Reid, *Mixed Legal Systems in Comparative Perspective: Property and Obligations in Scotland and South Africa* (Oxford, Oxford University Press, 2004).

[9] Below section VI. See also, for South Africa: J Neethling, JM Potgieter and PJ Visser, *Neethling's Law of Personality*, 2nd edn (Durban, LexisNexis Butterworths, 2005) ch 2.1; Burchell, this volume, ch 10; Scott, this volume, ch 6. For Scotland: Niall Whitty and Reinhard Zimmermann, *Rights of Personality in Scots Law: A Comparative Perspective* (Dundee, Dundee University Press, 2009) esp 10, 15–18, 33–34, 143; Elspeth Reid, *Personality, Confidentiality and Privacy in Scots Law* (Edinburgh, W Green, 2010) §§ 1.03ff; David M Walker, *The Law of Delict in Scotland*, 2nd edn (Edinburgh, W Green & Son, 1981) 20, 22, 24–26.

from the perspective of the Roman delict. This is how the idea of a seminar, and then a book, on '*iniuria* and the common law' was born.

The structure of this chapter is roughly as follows. The next section, section II (Scott), seeks to provide a concise account of the Roman law of *iniuria*, both for its own sake and by way of general introduction to those essays which consider the Roman law in detail. Next, sections III to VI (Descheemaeker) seek to explore some of the conceptual issues arising from our attempt to examine *iniuria* from the outside perspective of the common law. These pertain, in particular, to the internal structure of the delict, the place of the *actio iniuriarum* within the broader context of the punitive and reipersecutory functions of the law, and the relationship of *iniuria* with the modern common law in the three jurisdictions under examination. Again, this is offered both for its own sake and by way of introduction to the essays that follow, in which these themes are examined more closely.

II. Roman *iniuria*[10]

A. Republican *iniuria*

The core of the classical delict is located in the Twelve Tables.[11] According to Table 1.13–15, there was to be *talio* in cases of *membrum ruptum* (the maiming of a limb or rendering useless of some part of the body), fixed penalties of 300 or 150 *asses* for the *os fractum* (broken bone) of a free person or a slave, and a penalty of 25 *asses* for 'any other *iniuria*.'[12] Yet as David Ibbetson says, the last of these is rather mysterious.[13] While '*iniuria*' here is often read as a noun ('*iniuriam*'), it could also be an adverb indicating that the conduct complained of was in some way wrongful;[14] both readings suggest a miscellaneous provision of wide scope. Assuming that this provision did contemplate a particular species of wrongdoing called *iniuria*, it is generally thought to have referred to minor personal injuries such as slapping, as distinct from the more serious assaults set out in the two preceding provisions.[15] Yet once again it is unclear whether the three provisions really can be understood to constitute a comprehensive regime regulating assaults in

[10] This section is by Helen Scott.

[11] Probably: *cf* Peter Birks, 'The Early History of Iniuria' (1969) 37 *Tijdschrift voor Rechtsgeschiedenis* 163; 'Lucius Veratius and the *lex Aebutia*' in WAJ Watson (ed), *Daube Noster: Essays in Legal History for David Daube* (Edinburgh, Scottish Academic Press, 1974) 39.

[12] Tab 1.13–15; Michael Crawford, *Roman Statutes* (2 vols, London, University of London, Institute of Classical Studies, 1996) vol 2, pp 604–8. cf Du Plessis, this volume, ch 7, pp 143–44.

[13] *cf* Ibbetson, this volume, ch 2, text to n 4.

[14] Crawford (n 12) 606. But see Birks, 'The Early History of Iniuria' (n 11) 188–90.

[15] eg Reinhard Zimmermann, *The Law of Obligations: Roman Foundations of the Civilian Tradition* (Oxford, Oxford University Press, 1996) 1051.

descending order of seriousness.[16] 'Right from the start of the Roman delict, therefore, there was seemingly a sense of open-endedness about it.'[17]

In the third century BCE or just afterwards some part of the delict created by the Twelve Tables was diverted into the *lex Aquilia*, which provided a compensatory remedy for injuries to slaves.[18] Thus *iniuria* now focused exclusively on injuries to free persons. By the beginning of the second century praetorian intervention had replaced the fixed penalties of the Twelve Tables with damages assessed at the discretion of the *iudex* or *recuperatores*.[19] The text of the General Edict (*Edictum generale de iniuriis aestumandis*) so introduced read as follows:

> He who brings the action for *iniuria* . . . let him specify for certain what *iniuria* he has suffered and place an upper limit on the damages (*vademonium*) set for the case.[20]

Although it is clear that in later law the scope of the General Edict was wide, certainly encompassing all physical assaults, there is dispute as to the original scope of the Edict and the *actio iniuriarum* which it created. The dominant view appears to be that it covered only minor personal injuries such as slapping etc – the *iniuriae* of the Twelve Tables.[21] Alternatively, it may have also comprised more serious assaults from the start – the *membrum ruptum* and *os fractum* of Tables 1.13 and 1.14. On either view, the developments brought about by the General Edict were primarily procedural ones: the fixed penalties of the Twelve Tables were abandoned in favour of more flexible aestimatory machinery.[22]

Unlike the General Edict, the so-called special edicts enacted during the course of the second and first centuries BCE undoubtedly imposed liability in new, previously unrecognised situations. Not confined to assaults, whether minor or major, these special edicts dealt with conduct which did not necessarily involve any physical contact between victim and wrongdoer. Indeed, it seems that there was originally no procedural relationship between the General Edict and the special edicts at all; that they began life as entirely independent wrongs.[23] Nevertheless, they do appear to have shared some of the central characteristics of the conduct penalised by the General Edict.

[16] *cf* eg Westbrook 'The Nature and Origins of the XII Tables' (1988) *Zeitschrift der Savigny-Stiftung für Rechtgeschichte* 74.

[17] Ibbetson, this volume, ch 2, p 33.

[18] eg Zimmermann (n 15) 953–61.

[19] These were judges with special powers who sat in cases of particular importance: see Birks, 'The Early History of Iniuria' (n 11) 197–200; JM Kelly, *Studies in the Civil Judicature of the Roman Republic* (Oxford, Clarendon Press, 1976) 40–70.

[20] Otto Lenel, *Das Edictum Perpetuum*, 3rd edn (Leipzig, Tauchnitz, 1927) 397–99 following *Collatio* 2.6.1 (Paul, *Liber singularis de iniuriis*).

[21] David Daube, '*Nocere* and *noxa*' (1939) 7 *Cambridge Law Journal* 23, 45–47; '*Ne quid infamandi causa fiat*: The Roman Law of Defamation' in David Cohen and Dieter Simon (eds), *David Daube: Collected Studies in Roman Law* (Frankfurt am Main, Vittorio Klostermann, 1991) 465, 467; Alan Watson, *The Law of Obligations in the Later Roman Republic* (Oxford, Clarendon Press, 1965) 248–50.

[22] Aulus Gellius, *Noctes Atticae* 20.1.12, 13.

[23] eg Daube, '*Ne quid infamandi causa fiat*' (n 21) 465. *cf* Peter Birks, '*Infamandi causa facta* in Disguise?' [1976] *Acta Juridica* 83 (=*Essays in honour of Ben Beinart*) and Birks, 'Harrassment and Hubris' (n 1) 12 fn 35.

The first of these was the edict *De convicio*. Ulpian gives the original wording of this edict in D 47.10.15.2 (57 *Ad edictum*):

> One who is said to have raised a clamour [*convicium*] at someone contrary to good morals [*contra bonos mores*] or one through whose efforts such a clamour is raised contrary to good morals, against him I will give an action [*iudicium dabo*].[24]

Note the edictal promise inherent in '*iudicium dabo*': if indeed the conditions set out in the edict were present, an action appeared to follow more-or-less as a matter of course.

Convicium is usually translated as 'clamour'. The situation envisaged in the edict appears to be that of a crowd gathering together to denounce someone. Ulpian tells us – in D 47.10.15.4 – that a *convicium* is literally a '*convocium*', a *collatio vocum* or combination of voices. This etymology suggests that the original gist of the delict was public abuse, and this is indeed how the edict is presented by Ulpian.[25] On the other hand, the further synonyms offered by Ulpian, *concitatio* and *conventus*, suggest something different: as David Daube argued, the term seems to have referred to a species of community action of 'warlike character', a gathering which threatened to explode into riot, rather than mere aggravated defamation.[26]

As appears from the wording of the edict itself, not every public demonstration attracted liability, but only those cases which were found to be have been raised contrary to good morals, *contra bonos mores*. This suggests that some forms of self-help would have been acceptable: Peter Birks imagines a case in which a group of friends assemble and shout outside the house of the debtor of one of their number that he ought to pay up.[27] But a clamour or demonstration would become actionable under this edict if it was in breach of prevailing standards: Birks gives the example of a demonstration mounted against a judge with a view to intimidating him.[28] The question remained an objective one, but whether or not the defendant had acted *contra bonos mores* and therefore unlawfully was to be flexibly assessed by the praetor in each case.

The second of the special edicts appeared under the rubric *De adtemptata pudicitia*: literally translated, this meant something like 'attacks on chastity', but Birks' 'sexual harassment' is perhaps closer to the gist of the wrong.[29] Although the text of the edict is nowhere recorded, it is paraphrased by Ulpian as follows:

[24] All translations of Digest texts in this section are based on those provided in T Mommsen and P Krueger (eds), A Watson (trans), *The Digest of Justinian* (Philadelphia, University of Pennsylvania Press, 1985).

[25] eg D 47.10.15.5, which clearly shows the influence of the special edict *ne quid infamandi causa fiat* (below pp 6–7). See Daube, '*Ne quid infamandi causa fiat*' (n 21) 491.

[26] Daube, '*Ne quid infamandi causa fiat*' (n 21) 466, 487–88: 'The recital of defamatory songs in a way likely to lead to a riot, *occentare*, was already a capital crime under the XII Tables and since, say, 200 B.C. when the rules of the XII Tables concerning insult were brought up to date, was actionable as *convicium*.' On *occentare* in the Twelve Tables see Crawford (n 12) 677–79. On the social origins of *convicium* and *occentatio* see Andrew Lintott, *Violence in Republican Rome*, 2nd edn (Oxford, Oxford University Press, 1999) 6–10.

[27] Birks (n 1) 12.

[28] ibid.

[29] ibid.

> If someone is alleged to have abducted the companion of a matron (*materfamilias*) or a boy or girl, or if someone has called out to them or followed them around contrary to good morals [*contra bonos mores*].[30]

A number of associated situations appears to be envisaged here. On the one hand, there is the relatively straightforward case in which the wrongdoer abducts the companion of his victim (later this came to include persuading the companions to desert his or her charge).[31] This might have been done in order to gain access to the victim, or perhaps to expose him or her to the censure involved in appearing in public without a chaperone. In any case, this conduct seems very close to the subject matter of the *Edictum Generale*, given that it would inevitably have involved some form of physical assault. Thus there was no difficulty in characterising this behaviour as prima facie unlawful, and no need for the flexibility offered by the rider *contra bonos mores*.[32] But the edict contemplated also the case in which the wrongdoer accosted his victim, addressing him or her in 'smooth words', *blanda oratio*,[33] or where he stalked the object of his affections, by following him or her around.[34] Here the wrongdoer's conduct is not prima facie unlawful.[35] However, as in the case of *convicium*, the criterion of *boni mores* allowed the praetor to penalise such approaches where appropriate, that is, where the behaviour in question was socially transgressive. 'Courtship had to go on', in Birks' phrase,[36] but equally there were some cases of accosting or following where a suitor crossed the line, and here the praetor would give an action.[37] Thus the edict dealt both with behaviour which was prima facie unlawful and conduct that became unlawful only when found to be *contra bonos mores*.

Third, perhaps as late as the end of the first century BCE,[38] the praetor introduced the edict *ne quid infamandi causa fiat*. Unlike *convicium*, this appears to have been aimed squarely at defamation, or perhaps (more broadly) 'shaming'. According to Ulpian – '*ait praetor*' – the edict said,

> Let nothing be done to bring *infamia* upon another. If anyone does anything to the contrary I will look into it according to the nature of the issue.[39]

Unlike in the case of the other special edicts, no particular factual situation is envisaged here: the question of which facts are capable of substantiating this edict is entirely open. What is more, no remedy is promised. The word *animadvertam*

[30] Lenel (n 20) 400.
[31] According to Daube, '*Ne quid infamandi causa fiat*' (n 21) 467, relying on D 47.10.15.18.
[32] Daube, '*Ne quid infamandi causa fiat*' (n 21) 467.
[33] D 47.10.15.20–21.
[34] Here again the influence of *ne quid infamandi causa fiat* is evident. See D 47.10.15.22. See further below pp 6–7.
[35] D 47.10.15.23.
[36] Birks (n 1) 12.
[37] Daube, '*Ne quid infamandi causa fiat*' (n 21) 467–68.
[38] For details of the debate regarding chronology see Helen Scott, '*Omnes unius aestimemus assis*: A Note on Liability for Defamation in Catullus V' (2006) 3 *Roman Legal Tradition* 95.
[39] Lenel (n 20) 401.

is key: the praetor simply says that he will 'look into' anything which has been done in order to bring *infamia* (shame or disgrace) upon another.[40]

In fact, when one considers the nature of defamation, the reasons for both these features become clear. Unlike the wrongs targeted by the other special edicts, it can find expression in almost any act apart from obvious cases like pamphleteering.[41] Indeed, as the stock example of Rich Man (*dives*) and Poor Man (*pauper*) shows, the conduct in question might be 'not only permissible but dutiful':[42] Poor Man follows Rich Man around the city in mourning in order to insinuate that he is responsible for Poor Man's father's death; when challenged, he replies that 'surely a son may mourn his father, a person in mourning may walk across the city, a cat may look at a king, and so on'.[43] The Roman solution to this perennial difficulty was to make liability turn exclusively on the subjective intention of the wrongdoer;[44] in Birks' words, 'some shades of intent could turn lawful conduct unlawful.'[45] Thus the praetor used the purposive construction *infamandi causa* in setting out the conditions of liability. As long as the wrongdoer's purpose was to bring his victim into disrepute, his conduct – whatever it was – was potentially actionable.

Again, this technique was different to that applied in the case of *convicium* and *adtemptata pudicitia*; indeed, as Daube says, to give the judge the power to label any conduct contrary to good morals would have been to make him a de facto censor.[46] At the same time, given the extraordinarily broad potential scope of the edict, it would have been going too far to promise an action in all cases where appropriate intention was present. Hence the wording of the formula: *animadvertam* gave the praetor the discretion to refuse an action on the facts stated even where the defendant had acted *infamandi causa*.

Finally, the fourth of the special edicts discussed by Ulpian in his edictal commentary can be briefly dealt with. This was *De iniuriis quae servis fiunt*,[47] and it created a new wrong of *servi (alieni) verberatio*, beating another's slave. According to Ulpian, the wording of this edict was as follows:

[40] Daube believed that *infamia* in this context referred to the institutionalised disgrace imposed by the praetor or censor which resulted in various legal disabilities and loss of status: '*Ne quid infamandi causa fiat*' (n 21) 468–84. According to Max Kaser, however, *infamia* was never a unitary, technical notion in this sense: M Kaser, 'Infamia und ignominia in den römischen Rechtsquellen' (1956) 73 *Zeitschrift der Savigny-Stiftung für Rechtgeschichte* 220. For a recent summary of the literature see Thomas AJ McGinn, *Prostitution, Sexuality and the Law in Ancient Rome* (Oxford, Oxford University Press, 1998) 65–69.

[41] Daube, '*Ne quid infamandi causa fiat*' (n 21) 468.

[42] Birks (n 1) 13, setting out the premise of Seneca's *Controversia* 10.1. Daube's imaginative reconstruction of the pattern formula associated with the edict assumes a similar situation: '*Collatio* 2.6.5.' in I Epstein et al, *Essays in Honour of JH Hertz* (London, Edward Goldston, 1942).

[43] Birks (n 1) 13.

[44] Daube, '*Ne quid infamandi causa fiat*' (n 21) 468–69.

[45] Birks (n 1) 13.

[46] Daube, '*Ne quid infamandi causa fiat*' (n 21) 468.

[47] Like the first three special edicts, *servi verberatio* is considered in detail by Ulpian in the long extract from Book 57 of his edictal commentary preserved in D 47.10.15: see D 47.10.15.34–49 and 17 pr 2.

> Where a man shall be said to have thrashed another's slave contrary to good morals [*contra bonos mores*] or to have submitted him to torture without the owner's consent, I will give an action. Equally, if it be said that something else be done, I will, having heard the circumstances [*causa cognita*], give an action.[48]

The praetor's strategy here was similar to that adopted in the context of *convicium* and *adtemptata pudicitia*: whereas torturing another's slave appears to have been prima facie unlawful, thrashing him gave rise to liability only if found to be *contra bonos mores*. As in the case of those earlier edicts, liability was objectively but flexibly determined.[49] It was of course the slave's owner who was to be the plaintiff in the action thus created, but it was not clear from the wording of the edict itself whether he sued *sui nomine* or *servi nomine*; whether it was the slave or his master who was thought to have suffered the primary wrong, and if the latter, of what kind exactly it was.[50]

B. Classical *iniuria*

By the first century CE a unified delict of *iniuria* had begun to emerge. According to Ulpian:

> Every *iniuria* is inflicted on the person or relates to one's dignity or involves disgrace.[51]

and,

> Labeo says that *convicium* is an *iniuria*.[52]

and,

> Labeo says that this particular edict [*ne quid infamandi causa fiat*] is superfluous since we can proceed under the general edict on *iniuria*.[53]

It is clear from these texts that by the beginning of the classical period the General Edict and special edicts had been welded together into a procedural unity: all wrongs falling within their scope were now actionable as *iniuriae* under the *actio iniuriarum*. Moreover, this procedural unity was matched by a substantive one, probably pioneered by the jurist Labeo: this was *contumelia*.[54] The importance of *contumelia* as a unifying principle in classical law emerges clearly from the contrast between the accounts of Gaius, on the one hand, and Ulpian, on the other.

48 Lenel (n 20) 401.

49 The final sentence of the edict appears to have given the praetor the discretion to investigate any other conduct, ie which might constitute *iniuria*.

50 Later this became the subject of debate: compare eg Gaius, *Institutes* (hereafter G) 3.222 with D 47.10.15.35 (Ulpian, 57 *Ad edictum*).

51 D 47.10.1.2 (Ulpian, 56 *Ad edictum*).

52 Ulpian D 47.10.15.3 (Ulpian, 57 *Ad edictum*).

53 Ulpian D 47.10.15.29.

54 On the role of Labeo in the construction of this general principle see Ibbetson, this volume, ch 2, text to n 38.

Gaius's treatment of *iniuria* in his *Institutes* begins with his merely running through the special edicts:

> *Iniuria* is committed not only by striking a man with a fist or a stick or by flogging him, but also by raising a clamour against him, or if, knowing that he owes one nothing, one advertises his property for sale as a debtor's, or by writing defamatory matter in prose or verse against him, or by following about a matron or a youth, and in short in many other ways.[55]

He appears to be holding to an older, more casuistic way of thinking about *iniuria*, one more directly influenced by the Edict itself. However, according to Ulpian,

> *Iniuria* is so called from that which happens *non iure*; for everything which does not come about *iure* is said to occur *iniuria*. This is general. But specifically, *iniuria* is said to be *contumelia*.[56]

This passage is echoed in Justinian's *Institutes*:

> *Iniuria*, in its general sense, signifies everything which happens *non iure*: specifically, it means sometimes *contumelia*, which is derived from *contemnere*, and is in Greek 'υβρις.[57]

What did *contumelia* mean? There appears to have been some connection with Greek thought, as the use of the word *hubris* in Justinian's *Institutes* indicates: it is 'highly likely that Labeo had the Greek idea in mind when he constructed the general principle which came to be accepted as underpinning the delict.'[58] Indeed, as Birks explains in his seminal article 'Harassment and Hubris: The Right to an Equality of Respect', hubris is key to understanding *contumelia* and thus classical *iniuria*.[59] Hubris/*contumelia* refers to, 'a kind of arrogance or pride, an over-confident exaltation of the self, manifested in violence or other misbehaviour towards others'.[60] The closest English analogue is contempt.[61] However, it denotes also the sort of act flowing from such a state of mind, best summed up as harassment. Thus as Birks explains, in naming the delict from the attitude of mind of the wrongdoer the classical jurists '[took] advantage of the easy transfer from the attitude of mind to the acts characterised by that attitude'.[62] Furthermore, the harm typically suffered by the victim of an act of hubris or *contumelia* is distress arising from injured feelings or self-esteem: here Birks uses the word 'belittlement'.[63] Yet such distress – the typical suffering caused by the wrongdoer's

[55] G 3.220. Francis de Zulueta (trans), *The Institutes of Gaius*, vol 1 (Oxford, Clarendon Press, 1946).

[56] D 47.10.1 pr (Ulpian, 56 *Ad edictum*).

[57] Justinian, *Institutes* (hereafter J) 4.4 pr.

[58] For the meaning of *hubris* in Greek law, see eg the account of a Greek criminal trial reported by Demosthenes in *Against Konon*. For Labeo's role in importing this idea, see Ibbetson, this volume, ch 2, text to n 38) and the works cited there.

[59] Birks (n 1) 5–14.

[60] ibid 8.

[61] ibid 8.

[62] ibid 9.

[63] ibid.

act – must in his view be distinguished from the interest or right which the delict protected: this was not an interest in happiness or tranquillity but rather a right to one's fair share of respect.[64] For Birks, then, the delict which the jurists called *iniuria* was in fact 'contemptuous harassment of another, calculated to cause distress in the nature of anger and humiliation . . . but violating, not an interest in emotional calm, but the victim's right to his or her proper share of respect'.[65]

The primacy of *contumelia* had two principal consequences. First, it appears to have played an important role in driving forward the boundaries of liability during the classical period: any form of behaviour, whether words or conduct (and potentially failure to speak or act) could be brought within the limits of the mature delict. Thus according to Ulpian, commenting on the edict *de adtemptata pudicitia*:

> One who uses base language does not make an attempt upon virtue but is liable to the *actio iniuriarum*.[66]

This was not an instance of *adtemptata pudicitia*, since that edict dealt with attempts at seduction rather than abuse, but that does not mean that it was not actionable as contempt under the *actio iniuriarum*. *Contumelia* is not specifically mentioned as the criterion driving forward liability, but it is close to the surface here. Turning to that portion of Ulpian's edictal commentary which addresses the General Edict itself,[67] here we find numerous examples of the same phenomenon: cases which would not have been actionable under any edict in the Republican period but which were drawn into the classical delict by virtue of the productive generalisation of *contumelia*.

> If someone prevents me from fishing in the sea . . . can I bring an action for *iniuria* against him? There are some who think that I can. And so Pomponius (and with him most jurists) says this is similar to the case of the man who is not allowed to wash in the public baths or sit in the public theatre or talk in some other place, or if someone does not allow me to use my own property; for he likewise can be sued for *iniuria*.[68]

This is a case remote from the content of the Republican *Edictum Generale*, although admittedly it is not difficult to see some prima facie unlawfulness in the defendant's actions.[69] Nor is it a case of defamation or shaming, although it could perhaps have been shoe-horned into the edict *ne quid*. Yet Ulpian, following Pomponius, concludes that these facts are actionable as *iniuria*. Again, it seems to be *contumelia* that is driving such expansion.[70] Similarly, D 47.10.9.4,

[64] ibid 10.

[65] ibid 11.

[66] D 47.10.15.21 (Ulpian, 57 *Ad edictum*).

[67] All but D 47.10.9.4 derive from the section of Ulpian's commentary on the General Edict which was *ad formulam*, on the formula itself. Otto Lenel, *Palingenesia Iuris Civilis* (2 vols, Leipzig, Bernhard Tauchnitz, 1889) vol 2, pp 770–71.

[68] D 47.10.13.7 (Ulpian, 57 *Ad edictum*).

[69] Birks (n 1) 11.

[70] *Contumelia* had been specifically addressed by Ulpian only a few lines earlier, in 13.4. Indeed, this section of Ulpian's *Edictal Commentary*, 13.1–6, treated as a block by Lenel (n 67), may have been devoted precisely to examining *contumelia* as an expansive criterion.

> If a person attempt to debauch another, whether male or female, freeborn or made free, he will be liable to the *actio iniuriarum*.

And D 47.10.15 pr,

> The question is raised by Labeo whether, if a person derange another's mind by a drug or some other means, the *actio iniuriarum* lies against him; and he says that it does.

The second consequence of the primacy of *contumelia* in the classical delict was that the defendant's state of mind, at least as presumed, became increasingly central. Of course *contumelia* functioned in the first instance as a unifying principle rather than a requirement for liability: it was not necessary to demonstrate its presence where the facts alleged fitted within one of the Republican special edicts.[71] Indeed, as David Ibbetson shows, even in the mature classical law the contours of these special edicts remained visible through the fabric of *iniuria*.[72] Thus the criterion of *boni mores* continued to be used in order to determine liability in cases falling within the rubric of *convicium*, *adtemptata pudicitia* and *servi verberatio*.[73] 'A purely subjective mental element was . . . not indispensable for purposes of liability, and it is quite in accordance with its rather limited function that many texts do not even mention it.'[74] Nevertheless, a delict of contempt is intrinsically tied to a contemptuous intention,[75] and the Republican components of the delict were increasingly reorganised and reanalysed to reflect the primacy of such intention.[76] It was in the very nature of *contumelia* that the wrongdoer acted deliberately and without taking into account the interests of the victim.[77] Indeed, it was only later that the mental element of the delict was identified, separated and generalised as '*animus iniuriandi*' (literally, the mind to insult, a post-classical expression), so tied up was it with the definition of the liability-creating event.

III. Mapping *iniuria*[78]

As a transversal wrong, not defined by reference to a particular type of wrongful conduct or a specific form of injury, but rather held together by a principle of liability almost as open-ended as negligence in modern English law, *iniuria* invited

[71] Birks (n 1) 13–14.

[72] Ibbetson, this volume, ch 2, p 35.

[73] Indeed, according to Paul *Collatio* 2.5.2 (*liber singularis de iniuriis*), 'it is common to all *iniuriae* that they occur contrary to good morals [*adversus bonos mores*]'. See further Zimmermann (n 15) 1059–61 and in particular the sources cited p 1059 fn 83 .

[74] ibid 1060.

[75] It is true that there can be difficult cases on the periphery. It is possible for conduct to be perceived as contemptuous without being intended as such.

[76] See further Ibbetson, this volume, ch 2, section III; Scott, this volume, ch 6, section IV.A.

[77] Ibbetson, this volume, ch 2, text after n 41.

[78] This section is by Eric Descheemaeker.

the internal mapping of its territory. Indeed, such a mapping was required if the delict was to remain intelligible as the law developed.

In the context of the Roman actional system, however, the cartography of *iniuria* remained crude. As was seen above,[79] the law thought in terms of the General Edict on *iniuria*, on the one hand, and on the other hand in terms of the four special edicts, which originated independently but came to be understood in the classical age as specific islands of liability within the general delict. With the possible exception of the edict *ne quid*, which can be (re)analysed straightforwardly enough[80] in terms of the protection of a particular right or interest, namely reputation, the clusters of factual situations they envisioned did not map on to any analytical framework, let alone divide up the broad field of *iniuriae* in a coherent order. This should not have been expected in a litigation-driven system, where causes of action are devised progressively to address new scenarios brought to the law by grievance-spurred individuals.

The mapping was bound to be left to the jurists. Historically, two main ways of ordering *iniuriae* emerged: one looked at the manner in which the *iniuria* was committed; the other at the type of interest it protected. The second is the one of primary relevance to us, both because it has historically been more influential and also because, in a law of civil wrongs which by its very nature looks first to the claimant, the sort of harm or legal injury complained of is of more significance than the process through which it was inflicted.

A. *Iniuriae re, verbis, litteris*

The first structure divided *iniuriae* according to whether they had been committed by words (*verbis*) or by another act (*re*).[81] As far as we can tell, this *summa divisio* is traceable to Labeo in the first century CE.[82] Early in the second life of Roman law, Azo added a third category: *iniuriae* committed in writing (*litteris*).[83] But neither in Roman law nor under the *ius commune* did the rules applicable to a dispute hang on the mode of infliction of the injury. It seems likely that the main reason why the division endured was because it was easier to grasp intuitively than one based on a purely legal construct such as a protected interest, yet approximated it in the sense that typically *iniuriae* committed *re* will result in a physical injury, whereas those committed *verbis* (or *verbis* and *litteris*) will cause a non-physical injury.[84]

[79] Above section II.

[80] Albeit not without some irritants: see below p 18.

[81] Literally, *re* means 'by a thing' or 'by a matter'; cf Birks and McLeod (n 1)13 fn 26, 154 (see: 'Obligation contracted by conduct').

[82] Du Plessis, this volume, ch 7, p 141; Zimmermann (n 15) 1064–65; Whitty and Zimmermann (n 9) 75–77, 151–52.

[83] Du Plessis, this volume, ch 7, p 150. On the relationship of this third class with the first two categories, see Zimmermann (n 15) 1064–65.

[84] Naturally this is not invariably the case. One can cause a physical injury by words, not only indirectly but in some cases directly as well (a modern example would be *Wilkinson v Downton* [1897] 2 QB 59). Conversely, one can cause a non-physical *iniuria*, like defamation, by acts other than the speaking or writing of words (see eg, again in an English context, *Monson v Tussauds Ltd* [1894] 1 QB 671).

B. *Corpus, fama, dignitas*

Of more significance, both historically and analytically, is the ordering of *iniuriae* according to the type of interest (to use a modern terminology) which they infringe, the violation of these different interests corresponding to different types of injuries or harms.[85]

What interest or interests did *iniuria* protect? At a high level of generality it would probably not be controversial to say that all *iniuriae* were offences against dignity in the broad sense of status or honour (*dignitas*).[86] The reason why the proposition, although not explicitly made in the sources,[87] is not a difficult one is because it is no more than the reverse side of the description of *iniuria* as a delict of *contumelia*: the contemptuous disregard for the plaintiff's personality, at the same time as it constitutes the wrong, also makes out the injury to his dignity. *Dignitas* is assailed, not when certain outcomes are made out, but precisely by the defendant's mind-attitude of disregarding the other party's status when it stands in their way.

Dignity, in that sense, might be too broad to be of much use as a legal category. It is easy to argue that it underpins whole swaths, if not the entirety, of the law and thus should not be pressed into service as a particular interest worthy of specific protection.[88] Whether or not this was his spur, Ulpian (who may have been following Labeo on this point) famously tried to unpack the (sub-)interests protected by *iniuria* when he distinguished between *corpus*, *fama* and *dignitas*.[89] How helpful the division is when it comes to understanding Roman law is not a straightforward question, but it is undeniable that the trichotomy became foundational in the later civilian tradition, being most visibly reflected today in South African law and legal scholarship.[90] It is also the framework around which the present book is structured.

[85] On the notion of an interest, see (succinctly) Eric Descheemaeker, 'Protecting Reputation: Defamation and Negligence' (2009) 29 *Oxford Journal of Legal Studies* 603, 605–6. This chapter is not the place to engage in a substantive or terminological controversy with, in particular, a rights-based approach; for a critical approach, see Robert Stevens, 'Rights and Other Things', in Donal Nolan and Andrew Robertson (eds), *Rights and Private Law* (Oxford, Hart Publishing, 2012) 115, 133ff.

[86] The meaning of Roman *dignitas* is returned to below p 19.

[87] It could however be regarded as implied by D 47.10.31 (Paul, 10 *Ad Sabinum*) read in conjunction with the immediately preceding D 47.10.30.1 (Ulpian, 42 *Ad Sabinum*).

[88] A similar reproach has been levelled against the use of a concept like 'autonomy' as an interest protected by the law of wrongs. See eg Johann Neethling, 'The Concept of Privacy in South African Law' (2005) 122 *South African Law Journal* 18, 25.

[89] D 47.10.1.2; see Du Plessis, this volume, ch 7, p 141; Zimmermann (n 15) 1083–85; Neethling, Potgieter and Visser (n 9) ch 1.1; Johannes Voet, 'Commentary on 47.10.7' in *The Selective Voet: Being the Commentary on the Pandects (Paris edn 1829),* trans Percival Gane (8 vols, Durban, Butterworth & Co, 1955–58) vol 7, pp 218.

[90] This can be seen easily, for example, from the structure of Neethling's authoritative work on personality rights, divided into 'physical integrity', 'good name' and 'dignitas' (untranslated), with a short section on 'data protection' added at the end (Neethling, Potgieter and Visser (n 9)).

Looking briefly at each of them in turn, the main meaning of *corpus* is simply the body:[91] in modern terms, the most likely candidate for translation, despite difficulties, would be 'physical integrity'.[92] Although earlier forms of *iniuriae* were quite clearly of a physical nature, Paul du Plessis highlights that it is not until the second century CE that we find the term *corpus* used in reference to *iniuria*.[93] Physical integrity is a more difficult concept than its intuitive nature might suggest: indeed, some key issues of modern tort law, like the redress of emotional or psychiatric harm in negligence, are intertwined with the question whether a violation of physical integrity occurred, which in turn can involve some difficult philosophical and medical issues. While the limits of bodily modifications are revisited by modern science on a level which the Romans would naturally have been incapable of reaching, the conceptual question has remained essentially the same: was there an infringement of the *corpus*? To take another example from English law, how we analyse the tort of assault and the underlying interest(s) it protects depends on how far we extend the scope of bodily integrity.[94]

Corpus is a paradoxical interest when it comes to the *actio iniuriarum*. Clearly, it was the primary object of protection of the delict in the sense that, as was mentioned, *iniuria* was originally developed for and around violations of physical integrity.[95] This is not surprising given that their tangible nature makes them much more intuitively wrongful (at least prima facie) than such non-tangible injuries as defamation or sexual harassment. Yet, when we think of personality rights today (analytically the reverse side of the wrong of *iniuria*),[96] we are unlikely to name physical integrity first. In fact, we might not list it at all,[97] at least not until prompted to consider what should happen if we do not include it on the side of patrimonial rights either, 'patrimony' and 'personality' being – rightly or wrongly – regarded as a *summa divisio* of the law of wrongs.

[91] *Oxford Latin Dictionary*, ed. PGW Glare (Oxford, Clarendon Press, 1982; hereafter *OLD*) entry for 'corpus'; Du Plessis, this volume, ch 7, pp 144ff.

[92] However, translating *corpus* with 'physical integrity' is probably too narrow. 'Personal integrity' in the sense of the integrity of the person of the claimant would be better, but the phrase would be understood very differently in modern English. What allows us to say that *corpus* is likely broader than physical integrity is that it is possible – as has been done historically – to identify corporeal (in the sense of *corpus*-related) sub-interests beyond physical or bodily integrity: for example life (a difficult interest since there is by definition no flesh-and-blood plaintiff left to claim once it has been violated), personal security and liberty. However, given that none of these categories has definite boundaries, it is difficult to say anything determinative on the question.

[93] Du Plessis, this volume, ch 7, text to n 16. The word first appears in a non-legal context in a play by Plautus in the second century BCE (idem).

[94] Assault is commonly characterised as protecting physical integrity, hand in hand with the tort of battery. But this is difficult to accept given that no contact need have occurred. Can we extend bodily integrity to include freedom from the (reasonable) fear of being battered? Or can this fear itself, and the observable consequences it has on the human body, be characterised as a violation of *corpus*? Neither option seems particularly attractive, but the question deserves closer attention.

[95] See above p 3.

[96] Below, text to n 106.

[97] For instance, it does not feature at all in the list provided in Gert Brüggemeier, Aurelia Colombi Ciacchi and Patrick O'Callaghan, *Personality Rights in European Tort Law* (Cambridge, Cambridge University Press, 2010) ch 21.

The reason is that *corpus* was, in many ways, a victim of its own strength as a legally protected interest. Its violation is so intuitively wrongful in the absence of countervailing factors (justifications or excuses)[98] that it hardly needs to be channelled through the – highly artificial – construct of *iniuria* for a remedy to be granted. Not only this, but one can easily see how the law might in fact positively want to give it a more accommodating home than *iniuria*, in particular one which would not restrict liability to cases of contemptuous injuries. The way in which the action on the *lex Aquilia*, despite its built-in insistence on patrimonial loss (*damnum*), gradually widened its scope to include injuries to *corpus* is indeed well known.[99] It could only have been made easier by the fact that, almost invariably, physical injuries involve some form of consequential economic loss, such as medical treatment or loss of earnings. (While there is scope for doubt, it does not seem that such losses would have been recoverable under the *actio iniuriarum*.)[100] Structurally, the move away from *iniuria* was, if not unavoidable, at the very least easy to understand.[101]

The common law provides a remarkably similar story in terms of treating *corpus* differently from other personality interests. In an English context, where the tort of negligence grew in the modern law to become a general and almost all-encompassing principle of liability, it is noteworthy in this respect that its ancestor, the action upon the case, never had any difficulty providing redress for physical injuries.[102] On the other hand, it has struggled considerably with – and, to the present day, has almost invariably refused to grant – compensation for injuries to other dignitary interests, such as reputation or privacy.[103] This struggle is difficult to explain from the common law's internal perspective,[104] in which there

[98] 'Justification' is taken here in the sense of a factor negating wrongfulness (or unlawfulness, depending on the terminology used) and 'excuse' in the sense of a factor negating fault, understood as a mental state: see Jonathan Burchell, *The Law of Defamation in South Africa* (Cape Town, Juta, 1985) 34.

[99] See eg Zimmermann (n 15) 1017ff; Margaret Hewett and Reinhard Zimmermann (trans and ed), *Larva legis Aquiliae: The Mask of the lex Aquilia Torn Off the Action for Damage Done* (Oxford, Hart Publishing, 2000) 60–64; see further below text to n 146.

[100] D 44.7.34 (Paul, 1 *Concurrent Actions*) and D 47.10.15.46 (Ulpian, 57 *Ad edictum*) show that the dominant view was that any such loss would have to be claimed under the *actio legis Aquiliae*. (Reading between the lines, the position appears to have been a matter of contention, although the basis of the controversy remains unclear from these passages.) Roman-Dutch law, and then South African law, maintained this dichotomy in principle (*cf* Melius de Villiers, *The Roman and Roman-Dutch Law of Injuries* (Cape Town, Juta, 1899) 184–85; and see most recently *Media 24 v SA Taxi Securitisation* (437/2010) [2011] ZASCA 117, [8]ff.)

[101] See further below text to n 146.

[102] See eg Ibbetson, this volume, ch 2, text to n 54.

[103] Descheemaeker (n 85). An interesting exception appears to be loss of liberty, which a number of cases have regarded as capable as grounding an action in negligence (see Donal Nolan, 'New Forms of Damage in Negligence' (2007) 70 *Modern Law Review* 59, 64–67 and references cited).

[104] Descheemaeker (n 85) esp 602–1. The argument commonly made, that fully fledged causes of action already exist, clearly does not work. For one thing, the same could be said of, say, trespass to the person in respect of *corpus*. More importantly, privacy provides a clear defeater: although there was no pre-existing nominate wrong, it is that route which English law chose in the twentieth century to grant it some measure of protection, not inclusion under the transversal wrong of negligence. Although this has never been completely true, it is difficult to escape the conclusion that, by and large, negligence behaves in English law as a form of *actio legis Aquiliae, as if* there also existed an *actio iniuriarum* constituting a second pillar of the law of wrongs.

does not seem to be any reason to rule out from this transversal action types of harm which are, in principle, recognised by the law. It makes more sense when examined from a civilian perspective, where a foundational divide exists between property rights (patrimony) and personality rights,[105] dovetailing with the distinction between the *actio legis Aquiliae* and the *actio iniuriarum*. However, the English division would be, not between property and patrimony, but between property plus *corpus* on the one hand and personality minus *corpus* on the other. This reflects a similar drift of bodily integrity from one pole of the law of wrongs to the other. Once the heart of personality rights (as they were not yet called), it now inhabits, at best, their periphery.

Moving to the second of the Ulpianic interests, *fama* is fame, renown, good name.[106] The best modern translation would be 'reputation'. As we have seen, there is scope for disagreement about the original meaning of the prohibition on making others 'in-famous', some suggesting that it should be read in the narrow sense of not subjecting them to the legal sanction of *infamia* (itself an open-textured concept);[107] but in the modern law it is clear that defamation is, at least prima facie, the taking away of another's *fama* in the sense of his reputation or, to use Grotius' words, the 'good esteem' in which others hold him.[108]

It remains to consider *dignitas*. If the above proposition is true, namely that *iniuria* as a whole protected dignity, then by construction *dignitas* must have assumed a narrower meaning in the context of the Ulpianic triad: *dignitas* (in the original sense of status or honour) minus *corpus* and *fama*. Linguistically this synecdochical use of the term would not be surprising, but the residual character of the definition explains why *dignitas* is very hard to understand or define when it is taken down one rung on the ladder of generality and contra-distinguished with the likes of *corpus* and *fama* – themselves dignitary interests in the wider and original sense of *dignitas*. In fact, a commonly held view, echoing the above wariness about the width of the concept, would be to say that it is unusable as an autonomous basis for the redress of wrongdoing. It functions merely as a label over an as-yet unmapped territory of residual dignitary

[105] I do not wish to suggest that 'property' is synonymous with 'patrimony', or 'property rights' with 'patrimonial rights'. This is a hugely difficult question, the complexity of which is compounded (not simply in a comparative perspective but within jurisdictional divides as well) by the fact that both terms have a shade of accepted meanings. The only point made here is that there exists a broad division, well grounded historically and analytically, between wealth and personhood, patrimonial loss and solatium (a *summa divisio* still foundational in Scots law), proprietary rights and personality rights, etc. As long as this broad division is true, which seems difficult to deny, the argument holds and there is no need for fine-tuning in the present context.

[106] *OLD*, entry for 'fama'; AHJ Greenidge, *Infamia: Its Place in Roman Republic and Private Law* (Oxford, Clarendon Press, 1894) ch 1; *cf* Descheemaeker (n 85) 608–9 for a more detailed terminological overview.

[107] The main proponent of this view was Daube. See Daube, '*Ne quid infamandi causa fiat*' (n 21) 470 and n 40 above.

[108] Hugo Grotius, *The Jurisprudence of Holland* (trans RW Lee, Oxford, Clarendon Press, 1926) 481. On the concept of reputation, with a particular emphasis on English law, see Lawrence McNamara, *Reputation and Defamation* (Oxford, Oxford University Press, 2007) esp chs 1–2.

interests.[109] It is hard to disagree with this view, no positive definition of *dignitas* in the narrower sense presenting itself to the mind.

The more important question would then become not, 'What is *dignitas* in this strict sense?', but, 'What (sub-)interests lie behind it?' Again, the question is much easier to ask than the answer to ascertain. Many candidates have been suggested in the course of time, but it remains fair to say in this early twenty-first century that no agreement has been reached, even in very broad terms. Today, privacy – often divided up into 'physical' (or 'personal') and 'informational' privacy, whether or not this is regarded as an exhaustive division – is the most likely candidate for extraction from the miscellany and inclusion on a par with the already established categories. Thus the series would run: bodily integrity, reputation, privacy, (residual) dignity. But, as is well known, very little is agreed upon concerning privacy, especially from a comparative perspective, besides the sheer existence of the category.

Historically, whether or not the link with the overarching category of *iniuria* was made clear, interests which were put forward as being dignitary, in this residual sense, include liberty, family relationships, sexual integrity, the protection of one's home, self-esteem, the freedom from wrongful prosecutions or from insults (in the modern, narrow sense of the term), honour (again, in a narrower sense than overall *dignitas*) as well as, more recently, identity and autonomy.[110] Little can be said about them which would not be controversial in any of the jurisdictions under consideration in this book, let alone across their divide. Indeed, other higher-level categories such as *corpus* or property might want to compete for the territory of some of these interests. More work will be needed before a sufficient degree of agreement, providing a safe basis on which to build up the law, can be said to have been reached. This is work of great importance, in particular insofar as it determines to a large extent the boundaries of liability in the law of civil wrongs; yet the ever-present temptation to add more elements to an already long list, with the correlative dangers of double-naming and of reinventing the wheel, must be warned against and resisted.

C. A Word of Caution

It might be helpful to finish this section with a note of caution: as historically influential as the Ulpianic trichotomy has proved (to the point where it would be

[109] See eg Niall Whitty, 'Overview of Rights of Personality in Scots Law' in Whitty and Zimmermann (n 9) 159–60 (incl references); Eric Descheemaeker, 'Reviews: Rights of Personality in Scots Law: A Comparative Perspective by Niall Whitty and Reinhard Zimmermann (eds)' (2010) 73 *Modern Law Review* 898, 899–900.

[110] The list has no claim to exhaustiveness, which probably would not mean much in the absence of a stable definition for these various categories anyway. See in particular Whitty (n 109) 164 (incl references); John Blackie, 'Unity in Diversity: The History of Personality Rights in Scots Law' in Whitty and Zimmermann (n 9) 31ff; John Blackie, 'Doctrinal History of the Protection of Personality Rights in Europe in the *Ius Commune*: General Actions or Specific Actions' (2009) 13 *Electronic Journal of Comparative Law* www.ejcl.org/131/art131-1.pdf, esp pt III.

difficult to consider the modern *actio iniuriarum* other than through its lens), it is important to remember that Roman law would not have thought of *iniuria* as a three-pronged cause of action, at least not in the sense of a delict dealing with three distinct types of injuries, each in their own particular way. In particular, in its classical age, it had no (sub-)delict akin to the battery of English law. If a violation of *corpus* was actionable, it was not *qua* battery but *qua* contempt;[111] more importantly, nothing in the outcome of the *actio iniuriarum* would have hinged on the characterisation of the allegedly wrongful conduct as *corpus*-infringing: this was simply one of the ways in which the general wrong could be committed.

While *ne quid* was, as mentioned, the one special form of *iniuria* which can be fitted into the Ulpianic scheme straightforwardly enough, even there the transition from the one overarching interest in *dignitas* to the three sub-interests runs into some difficulties. This can be seen by looking at a curious, if rarely highlighted, feature of the wrong. As far as we can tell, under the edict *ne quid*, a statement (or other form of conduct) did not have to actually *injure* the defendant's reputation to be actionable. Leaving aside the difficulty of the *animadvertam* clause, the wording of the Edict[112] does not appear, in effect, to have required any such harm for the cause of action to be complete. In the phrase '*Ne quid infamandi causa fiat. Si quis adversus ea fecerit*', the most plausible reading is that *causa* is in the ablative and *infamandi* a gerund. Thus the sentence would read 'Let nothing be done' (*ne quid . . . fiat*) 'on account of bringing disgrace' (*infamandi causa*). While *causa* imports purpose, it does not entail any outcome, and so grammatically there is no requirement that the attempt should have been successful and disgrace actually brought about. This is a feature of defamation, shared in fact by many modern legal systems,[113] which is very difficult to square with an analysis of the wrong in terms of an injury to reputation – for no such injury was in actual fact needed. That no-one might have believed the defamatory matter, and thus that the plaintiff's reputation would have remained untarnished, never appears to have negated liability. On the other hand, if one thinks of *ne quid* simply as an exemplification of a wrong of contempt (although, of course, the special edict would have historically predated the generalisation of *iniuria* as a delict of *contumelia*), this otherwise abnormal trait becomes much easier to understand: again, the gist of *iniuria* does not lie in any outcome, but in the external outworking of the defendant's hubristic state of mind. In the case of *ne quid*, this hubris can be characterised and made out regardless of whether the 'attack' on the plaintiff's *fama* was successful or not.[114]

[111] Birks (n 1) 18.

[112] D 47.10.15.25 (Ulpian, 77 *Ad edictum*); above, text to n 39.

[113] For English law, see eg *Hough v London Express Newspaper* [1940] 2 KB 507, 515 (Goddard LJ: 'If words are used which impute discreditable conduct to my friend, he has been defamed to me, although I do not believe the imputation, and may even know that it is untrue') and already *Russell's Case* (1537) Dyer 61; implicit in South African law in *SA Associated Newspapers Ltd v Yutar* 1969 (2) SA 442 (A).

[114] *cf* Anton Fagan's description of the gist of defamation in South African law as an 'attempt to do a particular kind of harm' (this volume, ch 9, p 169). It would be possible to say that a defamatory statement which was not believed by anyone did not injure the claimant's *fama* yet was still wrongful in

IV. The Asymmetry of *iniuria*[115]

Perhaps the odd fascination that, as modern common lawyers, we might feel towards the Roman delict of *iniuria* hinges on the fact that it is both so strikingly modern *and* anti-modern at one time. It is profoundly modern in the sense that the focus on the contemptuous intent of the defendant allowed Roman law to reach forms of conduct which we would intuitively regard as wrongful and yet do not fit with the established categories of the common law. Fifteen years ago, Peter Birks pointed out how the struggle of the English judiciary to find a peg on which to hang a tortious remedy in such cases as *Khorasandjian v Bush*[116] or *Kaye v Robertson*[117] evidenced the common law's implicit quest for an *iniuria*-like tort.[118] The Protection from Harassment Act 1997, while narrowing down the gap, highlights by its late enactment date the precocity, by contrast, of Roman law. The fact that the ancients would have had no difficulty, for example, redressing stalking – a very 'modern' type of conduct, in terms at least of society's sensitivity to its wrongfulness – whereas modern systems of civil liability have felt stretched to their limits by the need to respond to it, is indeed remarkable.

At the same time, if we turn to the underlying assumptions on which it rested, no head of wrongdoing could be described as more 'anti-modern' than the Roman *actio iniuriarum*. As was noted, *iniuria* can be analysed, at a high level of generality, as an injury to the *dignitas* of the claimant: *dignitas*, in that broader sense, meant the social rank, status or importance of its holder, along with the esteem that was due to him by virtue of his standing within society.[119] In modern English, the word 'honour' might be used to convey the same idea. Clearly, honour is a concept that we regard today with much greater suspicion than would have been the case in the past. Rather than evoking worthiness and excellence, it is likely to be immediately associated with ideas of pompousness and self-importance. Whether we would want such an interest to be protected by the law of wrongs in the first place is highly debateable. But there is worse: the idea of social rank is almost bound to carry with it all manner of distinctions and inequalities. Not everyone will have the same honour, rank, status or *dignitas*.

This has become highly unpalatable to our modern sensitivities; yet it is hard to strip the delict of *iniuria* from an idea of asymmetry between plaintiff and defendant: already present in Roman law, this dimension became a stronger focus of the law during the *ius commune* period. Central to the Roman *actio iniuriarum* was, in

that, by the very liberty it took, it injured his *dignitas*; but arguably this would only provide a further example of how versatile, and thus unhelpful, the concept of dignity is. At the very least, on this view, the wrong would have to be something else than defamation *qua* injury to *fama*.

115 This section is by Eric Descheemaeker.

116 *Khorasandjian v Bush* [1993] QB 727.

117 *Kaye v Robertson* [1991] FSR 62 (CA).

118 Birks (n 1) esp 4–5, 14–16, 20–23, 33–35.

119 *OLD*, see entry for 'dignitas'. This is the sense in which we might speak of a 'dignitary' today.

effect, the concept of *atrocitas* (aggravation, though literally 'dreadfulness'), which triggered damages that were calculated differently and would normally have been higher. One way in which contempt could be aggravated (*iniuria atrox*) was *ex persona*, that is to say, by virtue of the claimant's higher status in society: as Justinian put it, '[a] contempt can be aggravated . . . where a magistrate suffers a contempt, or a senator at the hands of a common person, or a parent or patron at the hands of children or freedmen. A contempt to a senator or to a parent or to a patron is differently valued from one committed against an outsider or a person of low degree'.[120] In that sense, it seems fair to say with Ibbetson that '[t]he Roman idea . . . was essentially upward-looking; it was concerned primarily with insolence from an inferior to a superior, if only a self-styled superior'.[121] Indeed, the very act of bringing the action would have been a way for the plaintiff to reassert a superiority that had been threatened by the hubris of the defendant.[122]

Admittedly, we must be careful not to press this point too far, especially in the context of the first life of Roman law, for the delict itself was not defined by disparities in social standing; and it seems that an *iniuria* could even be committed against a slave.[123] Nevertheless, the treatment of actions brought by a social inferior against a superior gives away the fact that they were regarded as somewhat anomalous, or at the very least uncharacteristic: for what we find is a series of attempts on the part of the law to bar them or reduce their significance. Thus, Roman law prohibited the bringing of an action by a freedman against a patron, or by a child not in power against his father, unless the contempt they had suffered was aggravated (on another ground, by construction, than the inequality of status between the parties).[124] If the child was in power, the action was never available, even if the *iniuria* was *atrox*.[125]

The *ius commune* exacerbated this idea. François Dareau's masterful *Traité des injures* (1775) contains extensive developments aiming to fine-tune the nature of the remedy according to the status of both defendant and claimant, Dareau dividing up society into no fewer than ten strata ranging from ecclesiastics at the top – the King being treated separately – to prostitutes (*personnes du sexe*) at the bottom. If we turn to his treatment of *iniuriae* committed by a superior against an inferior, for instance a master against his servant, we see that these are described by the author as being by nature 'insubstantial' (*légères*, the mirror image of *atrox*) and 'often' amounting to 'nothing' – whereas the very same insult committed the other way round would have been ipso facto aggravated.[126] Short of arguing that

120 J 4.4.9 (Birks & McLeod translation); cf. G 3.225.

121 D Ibbetson, *A Historical Introduction to the Law of Obligations* (Oxford, Oxford University Press, 1999) 16.

122 ibid.

123 D 47.10.9.4; D 47.10.15.35 (Ulpian, 57 *Ad edictum*).

124 D 47.10.7.2–3 (Ulpian, 57 *Ad edictum*).

125 D 47.10.7.3.

126 François Dareau, *Traité des injures dans l'ordre judiciaire* (Paris, Prault, 1775) 391; Hervé Piant, 'La justice au service des justiciables ? La régulation de l'injure à l'époque moderne' (2011) 40 *Rives méditerranéennes* 67, 73.

iniuria is definitionally upward-looking (which clearly never was the case), this is probably as far as the major *ius commune* treatise on the question could go in the recognition of the asymmetrical character of the wrong. While Roman law itself would not have gone as far, there already existed in it a clear undercurrent of dignitary asymmetry, which the second life of Roman law took over and built upon.

Now, it is hard to think of an idea more repellent to modern lawyers, at least on the level of discourse, than that of human beings having different degrees of worth in the eyes of the law and of society in general. Although we may not live this out, we are deeply committed to the idea that individuals are born and remain equal in their intrinsic worth, and that the law must reflect this equality. This evolution, the fruit of a long process drawing in particular on Christian ideas, Kantianism and a reaction against twentieth-century totalitarianisms,[127] can be seen with crystal clarity in the shift of meaning experienced by the word 'dignity'. Dignity, in modern parlance, is essentially the worth that individuals have by virtue of their being human. Because of the perceived oneness of humanity, all individuals are regarded as having dignity, and having it in equal measure. When we speak of an 'offence against (human) dignity', we typically mean a denial of the humane treatment that should be warranted by the recipient's belonging to the human race.[128] This is far removed from the *dignitas* which was violated by *iniuria*.

In that sense, the asymmetrical character of the Roman, and later civilian, delict is deeply antagonistic to our way of thinking as moderns. Yet this does not mean that the relevance of *iniuria* is tied to a hierarchical society, for the delict need not be understood as an attack on the plaintiff's dignity vis-a-vis the defendant's: it can perfectly exist as an attack on their dignity considered in and by itself, even if it is taken to be held in the same measure by all. As such, asymmetry cannot be regarded as constitutive of *iniuria*, even though it is undeniable that it has historically been entwined with it.

V. The *actio iniuriarum*: Between Private Punishment and Loss Compensation[129]

Before turning to the relationship of *iniuria* with the common law tradition, it is useful to say something about the fate of the *actio iniuriarum* in the later civilian tradition (excluding at this point, for the most part, the mixed jurisdictions of

[127] Michael Rosen, *Dignity: Its History and Meaning* (Cambridge, MA, Harvard University Press, 2012).

[128] On dignity and *dignitas*, see eg James Q Whitman, 'On Nazi "Honour" and the New European "Dignity"' in Christian Joerges and Navraj Singh Ghaleigh, *Darker Legacies of Law in Europe: The Shadow of National Socialism and Fascism over Europe and its Legal Traditions* (Oxford, Hart Publishing, 2003) 243, 245–46; David Feldman, 'Human Dignity as a Legal Value, pt I', [1999] *Public Law* 682, 687.

[129] This section is by Eric Descheemaeker.

Scotland and South Africa: these will be returned to as part of the next section). The aim is not to provide a general overview of what is an immense field of study, but simply to highlight one historical fact, of considerable importance when one tries to understand the *actio iniuriarum* as a principle of civil liability: namely, that its significance cannot be appreciated without broadening the perspective and observing that *iniuria* has been forced throughout the second life of Roman law to fight concurrently on two different fronts, with the *actio legis Aquiliae* on the one side and with criminal law on the other.

In order to understand this, we need to return to Roman law. The Roman law of delict rested on three main pillars: *furtum* (theft, although Roman theft had a significantly wider scope than our modern concept), *damnum iniuria* and *iniuria*.[130] There were a number of smaller causes of action which could be described as delictual, but these were clearly the three most important ones. *Furtum* and the *lex Aquilia* protected patrimonial rights; *iniuria* protected personality rights (including *corpus*).[131] To capture it pithily, we could say that the first two heads of wrongdoing protected the plaintiff's 'having' and the last one his 'being'.

At the same time, as is well known, the Roman law of civil wrongs mixed what modern lawyers would call compensatory and punitive responses. That is to say, the money award that was granted to the successful claimant could have as its aim to compensate them for a loss suffered, or to punish the defendant for their conduct, or a combination of the two. That both dimensions existed is transparent from the sources, but precisely how they fitted together is in fact a very difficult question. Part of the difficulty is terminological. To designate what we would call in English law 'loss', 'harm', 'damage' or 'injury',[132] the Romans only had one technical term, which was *damnum*. But *damnum* was very clearly our pecuniary loss, in the basic (and intuitive) sense of the claimant being 'out of pocket' as a result of the wrong.[133] The person whose chariot has been destroyed has suffered *damnum*, but the one whose good name has been violated has not.[134]

On this basis, analysing the legal response to *damnum iniuria* is, from a modern perspective, relatively straightforward: the money award granted to the claimant will be compensatory up to the value of the *damnum* caused, and punitive beyond. This was likely not the self-understanding of classical jurists,[135] but it appears to

[130] These were three of the institutional delicts mentioned by both Gaius and Justinian, the fourth (*rapina*) being an offshoot of *furtum*.

[131] Birks (n 1); *cf* above, text to n 105.

[132] These are four words which have the same core meaning. The edges of their acceptable uses are clearly different, but it is difficult to be more specific in the absence of a stable, single definition. They are simply taken as synonyms in the present context.

[133] David Daube, 'On the Use of the Term *damnum*' repr in Cohen and Simon (n 21) 279; Birks (n 1) 6; Descheemaeker, this volume, ch 4, n 82.

[134] At least not unless and until they can point to pecuniary effects of the original wrong, which are distinct from the wrong itself and would, in modern parlance, be called consequential economic loss.

[135] A good overview of the debate is provided in Boudewijn Sirks, 'The Delictual Origin, Penal Nature and Reipersecutory Object of the *actio damni iniuriae legis Aquiliae*' (2009) 77 *Tijdschrift voor Rechtsgeschiedenis* 303.

have been established by Justinian's time[136] and certainly strikes us as the most plausible interpretation of the remedy. However, things become rather more difficult when we cross the line between 'having' and 'being' and consider the *actio iniuriarum*. Leaving aside the question of consequential *damnum*, which as mentioned was probably not claimable under the action, what did the *actio iniuriarum* do when it granted a money award (the only possible form of redress) to the successful claimant?

The most common answer would be to say that it granted them a private penalty, the function of which was to assuage their wounded feelings. The term generally used in the modern law to describe this function is *solatium*.[137] On that reading, the *actio iniuriarum* was purely penal. This is an entirely plausible interpretation. But it is not the only one. In order to see this, we simply need to consider the law of a modern system like South Africa, where the *solatium* granted to the successful claimant under the very same *actio iniuriarum* has been seamlessly reinterpreted by at least one strand of legal scholarship as being exclusively compensatory in nature.[138]

Indeed, this is equally plausible. Provided we accept, as the modern law has no difficulty doing, that loss – in the above broader sense – need not be patrimonial, there is no reason why the injury suffered by the claimant whose dignity, reputation or bodily integrity has been violated in a contemptuous manner could not be described as a loss, for which compensation can be meaningfully granted. This loss, by nature non-pecuniary, could be characterised as an injury to the protected interest considered in and by itself, or to the claimant's feelings, or to both: this is a difficult but entirely separate question.[139] What matters for the present purpose is simply that the law should recognise it as an injury that can be redressed through the ordinary medium of compensatory damages.

Could we then retro-impose this interpretation onto Roman law itself? In terms of the substantive rules, the answer has to be yes: there is no difference between the ancient and the modern *actio iniuriarum* which would stop us from analysing Roman law in the same way. However, the terminology pressed into service by the Romans in the context of *iniuria* makes it all but certain that they would not have thought in such terms. In particular, their lack of a word for loss beyond *damnum*, ie for what we would call 'non-patrimonial' (or 'non-pecuniary') loss, suggests very strongly that the underlying concept did not exist either. From

[136] The interpretation is very strongly suggested, if not asserted in this exact form, by J 4.3.9; see also Descheemaeker, this volume, ch 4, text to nn 20–21. The alternative analysis, namely, that it would be all punitive without compensation being an aim at all, is rendered implausible by J 4.1.19(21) and J 4.2 pr. A difficulty is that an action could be described as penal (aiming at the imposition of a *poena*) while having a compensatory object, the *poena* being valued by reference to the *damnum* suffered.

[137] Descheemaeker, this volume, ch 4, section I.A and the sources cited therein.

[138] Descheemaeker, this volume, ch 4, text to n 28 and references cited. It is likely that this will become the sole orthodoxy if it is confirmed that punitive damages in delict have now been banned (a good recent discussion of the law can be found in Nugent JA's dissenting opinion in *Media 24 v SA Taxi Securitisation* [2011] ZASCA 117, [94]–[105]).

[139] This question is discussed at length in Descheemaeker, this volume, ch 4, section III, but the preferred approach is irrelevant in the present context.

a Roman perspective, extra-patrimonial loss or *damnum* would most likely have appeared as a contradiction in terms,[140] and therefore the idea that the *actio iniuriarum* could be compensatory for such loss as a non-sense.

Looking at Roman law, two propositions could thus be made: first, that the *actio iniuriarum* was in all likelihood exclusively penal in its aim; second, that compensation for loss was, within the law of civil wrongs, restricted to pecuniary loss (*damnum*).

Two things happened over the second life of Roman law which were of great consequence to the *actio iniuriarum*. The first is that the punitive function of the law was increasingly shifted from the law of delict to the law of criminal wrongs, leaving delict to deal with issues of loss-compensation. Naturally, both dimensions always co-existed at least to some extent. Already in Roman law, some forms of *iniuriae* were subjected to criminal redress (whether this was in addition to or instead of the *actio iniuriarum* is a disputed question).[141] Conversely, the punitive dimension of delict was probably never entirely abolished in the *ius commune* and the modern civilian tradition. Even in countries like France, where the rhetoric of the law came to settle emphatically against the very possibility, it is generally recognised that some features of the law cannot be understood without having recourse to an idea of private penalty;[142] and the (re?-)introduction of penal damages is openly discussed by legal scholars today.[143] Still, it is beyond doubt that, on the 'being' side of the law of civil wrongs, the law moved from being exclusively (or almost exclusively) punitive to being, if not solely at the very least predominantly, compensatory. Against such a background, an *actio iniuriarum* regarded as being in nature punitive, whether wholly or in part, was bound to become increasingly anomalous in the eyes of the law.

Of course, it could – as mentioned – be reinterpreted as being compensatory, but then it would run into another difficulty. For, at the same time as the above shift happened, the territory of the *actio legis Aquiliae* (perhaps best renamed in a modern context *actio de damno dato*, as resemblance with the original statute became increasingly flimsy) continued to grow steadily. The process of expansion had started in the first life of Roman law and is well documented:[144] one by one,

[140] Caution is required here because of the developments concerning injuries to the *corpus* of a free man (below text to n 146). However, although these suggest dissatisfaction with a state of the law where non-contumelious physical injuries to the claimant would not be compensatable, there is no evidence that the widening of the scope of liability (which occurred through *actiones utiles*) prompted any reconsideration of the concept of *damnum* itself.

[141] The *Lex Cornelia de iniuriis*, passed in the first century BCE, criminalised three specific forms of *iniuriae*, described as *pulsare* (striking), *verberare* (beating) and *domum introire* (forcible entry onto someone else's property); see WW Buckland, *A Text-Book of Roman Law from Augustus to Justinian*, 3rd edn, ed Peter Stein (Cambridge, Cambridge University Press, 1963) 590–91; *cf* Voet, 'Commentarius ad Pandectas 47.10 n 14–15' in Voet (n 89) vol 7, pp 232–34; de Villiers (n 100) 157–61.

[142] eg Geneviève Viney and Patrice Jourdain, *Introduction à la responsabilité*, 3rd edn (Paris, LGDJ, 2008) §§74–75 and references cited.

[143] eg Solène Rowan, 'Comparative Observations on the Introduction of Punitive Damages in French Law' in John Cartwright, Simon Whittaker and Stefan Vogenauer (eds), *Reforming the French Law of Obligations* (Oxford, Hart Publishing, 2009) 325.

[144] See eg Zimmermann (n 15) 1017ff; Hewett and Zimmermann (n 99) 60–64.

the requirements of liability were relaxed or abolished altogether, to the point where all that remained was essentially a general principle of liability for 'loss caused by fault'. The evolution culminated in the all-encompassing clause of Article 1382 of the French Civil Code in 1804.[145]

Crucial to the present argument is the meaning of 'loss' itself in that context. As long as it remains restricted to pecuniary loss, it cannot by construction redress the sort of losses which the *actio iniuriarum* concerned itself with. But the moment we accept the possibility that loss might be wider than *damnum*, the *actio de damno dato* is going to enter in a competition with *iniuria* to redress non-pecuniary harms. Given, in particular, the fact that the former action is dependent on a less restrictive standard of liability than *animus iniuriandi*, it will be a fierce competitor indeed.

This expansion of the scope of *damnum*, in other words of the types of harms or injuries which could be redressed under the *actio de damno dato*, is exactly what did in fact happen, along with the aforementioned consequences on the *actio iniuriarum*. The story is a complex one which cannot be narrated in detail here, but the broad picture is clear enough. Already in Roman law, moving by analogy from the body of a slave (an object of property) to the body of a free man, the *lex Aquilia* had come to be used, in some limited circumstances, for the redress of injuries to the claimant's *corpus*.[146] By the time Roman-French law was in the process of being codified in the early nineteenth century, no-one was seeing any difficulties with using the *actio de damno dato* (which would become art 1382 CC) in cases of physical injuries as well as damage to property. However, immaterial losses remained clearly (albeit not explicitly) out.[147] As in modern English negligence, the line was thus drawn between property plus *corpus* on the one hand and dignitary interests minus *corpus* on the other. For the reasons explained above, this expansion threatened the territory of *iniuria* by ushering in a competition between the *actio de damno* and the *actio iniuriarum* for the redress of dignitary injuries, the former having a structural competitive edge because of its reliance on *culpa*.

The competition played out in various ways across jurisdictional divides. South Africa, which retained the *actio iniuriarum* and guarded it against both the

[145] 'Tout fait quelconque de l'homme, qui cause à autrui un dommage, oblige celui par la faute duquel il est arrivé, à le réparer' (Any act whatever of man which causes damage to another obliges him by whose fault it occurred to make reparation; trans JH Crabb); for its basis in the works of Grotius and Domat, see Eric Descheemaeker, *The Division of Wrongs* (Oxford, Oxford University Press, 2009) ch 5; Robert Feenstra, 'Grotius' Doctrine of Liability for Negligence' in Eltjo JH Schrage (ed), *Negligence: The Comparative Legal History of the Law of Torts* (Berlin, Duncker & Humblot, 2001) 129.

[146] Zimmermann (n 15) 1014–17.

[147] No dignitary injuries other than those to *corpus* are mentioned in the *travaux préparatoires* of the Civil Code. While the treatment of the 'types of losses' (*genres de dommages*) covered by prospective art 1382 is flimsy at best, being only one short paragraph in length, the four examples given are all of damage to property (moveable and immoveable) or to *corpus* (life and bodily integrity). See PA Fenet, *Recueil complet des travaux préparatoires du Code civil* (15 vols, Paris, Videcoq, 1827–28) vol 13, p 488. It is unthinkable that non-tangible losses would have been meant to be included without being mentioned or discussed. Given how contested the issue would become 30 years later, when sentimental loss (*dommage moral*) was first recognised explicitly (in *Baget c Rosenweigh*, Chambres réunies, 25 June 1833, S. *1833.I.458*), this can only mean that they were at the time so evidently outside the scope of the proposed article as not to be worthy of discussion.

infiltration of Aquilian liability and the overtaking of its territory by criminal law, responded very differently from a country like France, where the *actio iniuriarum* was almost completely squeezed of its substance – though traces of it remain – under the combined 'stranglehold' of the general principle of liability for damage caused by fault and the rise of criminal responses to *iniuriae*.[148] The point which is true of all legal systems where the *actio iniuriarum* was received in principle is that its position in the modern law will be precarious. For, if its function is penal, it must justify why the penalty should be private rather than public (in a context where this is being increasingly at odds with the rest of the law) and, if it is reipersecutory, it must guard itself against the rise and rise of the *actio de damno dato*. It is only on a narrower understanding of loss-*damnum*, coupled with a clear appreciation of the fact that criminal law does not have a monopoly on punishment, that the distinctiveness of *iniuria* can be safeguarded. Failing this, the unattractive alternative is that it will either disappear or live on to fight constantly to retain a role within the territory which once was its own, but is now threatened by competitors. Such a fight is bound to disrupt the stability and coherence of the law.

VI. *Iniuria* in the Common Law[149]

We can now return to the oxymoron on which this chapter was opened: on the face of it, the concept of *iniuria* simply does not belong with common law. Of course, English law and the legal systems rooted in it have developed legal mechanisms to address factual situations and disputes which, in Roman law, would have come within the ambit of the *actio iniuriarum*; but this is a profoundly trivial remark. Unless, by some odd twist of fate, these situations did not arise in jurisdictions ruled by the common law, this was bound to be the case. What is of interest to the lawyer interested in law as law is *how* these factual situations are analysed and channelled through legal categories in order to reach a solution to the dispute; and here English law never received the Roman *actio iniuriarum* or developed its own equivalent action. It is impossible, historically, to find a head of wrongdoing in the common law which resembles either in scope or in purpose the ancient delict of *iniuria*. Yet, even in English law, the infiltration of *iniuria*-like

[148] In particular, defamation and insults – regarded as two separate categories – were criminalised in the early nineteenth century. In a French context, pecuniary damages can be sought in criminal courts by way of an *action civile* when loss (not necessarily of a pecuniary nature) has been suffered. As a result, by the time *dommage moral* became an established head of damages for the purpose of art 1382 CC, the field of both punishment *and* compensation had been pre-empted by the criminal law. This, however, does not mean that the provisions of the Civil Code could not be pressed into service. Indeed, their potential had been highlighted very early on by Aubry and Rau (Charles Aubry and Charles Rau, *Cours de droit civil français*, 3rd edn, vol 3 (Paris, Cosse, 1856) §445); and a residual role remained for them.

[149] This section is by Eric Descheemaeker.

forms of thinking (in the broader sense) is clearly discernible. These echoes of the ancient Roman delict in English law are a principal theme of this book.

The relationship between Roman *iniuria* and English tort was the subject-matter of an important lecture delivered by Peter Birks at University College Dublin in 1996, and already referred to several times in this chapter.[150] Its title, 'Harassment and Hubris', linked a Greek word, embodied in the Roman delict of *iniuria*,[151] with an English word which, to the common lawyer, evokes conduct that is prima facie wrongful but cannot easily, if at all, be straight-jacketed into any known cause of action. At the time the address was given, there was no wrong of harassment in English law. The year the written version was published, the British Parliament passed the Protection from Harassment Act 1997.[152] Birks, at the time, had argued that the existence of the remedies known to English lawyers as 'aggravated' or 'exemplary' damages demonstrated that English law was not unresponsive to the violation of what he dubbed the plaintiff's 'right to an equality of respect', the same interest which had underpinned Roman *iniuria*.[153] Thus, at the remedial stage, considerations apparently absent from the law crept back in.[154] However, as the argument continued, the fact that they were not allowed to inform the delineation of liability-creating events stopped English law from developing a tort of *iniuria*.[155] Contempt could aggravate the wrongfulness of conduct which was already wrongful on another basis, but it could not make it wrongful *qua* contemptuous. That this was, to his mind, a shortcoming of English law is transparent, even though he did not press the point very far.[156] Nor did he need to take a stance: this form of 'outside in' scholarship is primarily aimed at increasing our understanding of the law. While it does also give us an outside vantage point from which it is possible to pass a value judgement on it, this remains derivative and secondary.

Echoes in English law of *iniuria* and what we might want to call '*iniuria*-esque thinking'[157] are indeed manifold and not limited to those identified by Birks in his seminal piece. This book gives some examples, both within English law and further away in the common law tradition, although it too does not in any way claim

[150] Birks (n 1).

[151] J 4.4 pr (above, text to n 57).

[152] Du Bois, this volume, ch 11.

[153] Above, text to n 64.

[154] Birks (n 1) 14–18.

[155] ibid 18–28.

[156] The furthest he goes into this is to argue, at the very beginning, that '[t]here are large advantages in gathering all these interests together in one', 'these interests' referring to 'privacy, sexual propriety, reputation and so on' (Birks (n1) 4).

[157] This learning need not be historically rooted in Roman law. It is important to remember that similarities and chronological following are, of course, not enough to prove borrowing. But this is not a concern in the present context. Although historical influences are likely, if very difficult to demonstrate, in circumstances where Roman law was widely known, it is immaterial for our purpose whether the link can be proved to exist or not. What we are interested in is the superimposition onto a relatively stable grid (English law as it gradually evolved through the formulary system and ossified into forms of action) of an analysis carried out from the perspective of the Roman *actio iniuriarum*, ie of categories which prima facie do not fit on this grid.

exhaustiveness. The definition of what counts as an echo of *iniuria* in English law is too imprecise for this exercise to be even possible. This is not an issue: the aim is simply to provide examples of aspects of the common law which come into sharper focus when they are examined through the lens of an un-English category.

Similarities and dissimilarities between the analytical frameworks employed in the ancient and modern law are a common theme of the chapters looking more specifically at English law. David Ibbetson's examination of *Huth v Huth* provides a case in point, for this judgment is largely unintelligible from the internal perspective of the common law: as a defamation case, it is simply a trivial application of basic legal rules, based on a slightly odd pattern of facts. In order to understand it, we need to appreciate that it really is an attempt to obtain a court remedy for an instance of contemptuous behaviour: in Roman terms, an *iniuria*.[158] Paul Mitchell's chapter on *dissimulatio* provides a second example of such outside-in scholarship.[159] The doctrine of *dissimulatio* is a remarkable, if rarely studied, feature of the *actio iniuriarum*, according to which an affront overlooked at the time it was suffered could not be rekindled later to form the basis of a judicial action. As Mitchell shows, while *dissimulatio* does not on its face feature in the wrongs covering a similar ground to *iniuria* in English law, the principles which underpinned the Roman rule can be seen to exist on a deeper level.

Still concerning English law, Francois du Bois' chapter answers Birks' piece on 'Harassment and Hubris' fifteen years on. English (like Scots) law now has a statutory wrong of harassment: Du Bois' chapter explores the main similarity between the new tort and the Roman delict of *iniuria*, namely, that they both are transversal wrongs of acting *contra bonos mores*. Finally, Eric Descheemaeker's chapter looks at the concept of *solatium*.[160] Like *dissimulatio*, *solatium* appears at first sight not to exist in English law. However, the term (having detoured through Scots law) also made some inroads there, being pressed into service in respect of damages granted to indirect victims of a wrong who suffered emotionally from the death of a relative; from there, it was extended to various instances of injuries to feelings.[161] This is an evident, if not necessarily profitable, transplant in English law of a category originally belonging in the *actio iniuriarum*.

In all of these cases, by examining how the ancient delict overlaps with, falls short of or exceed its modern counterparts, we bring to the surface elements of analysis pertaining to English law which might have otherwise remained hidden. Many other examples could have been convoked, for example *iniuria* as an analytical framework for the perennially difficult case of *Wilkinson v Downton*,[162] or the resemblances and dissemblances between the concepts of malice and *animus iniuriandi* (and the way both have historically evolved). It must be stressed that none of this is to assert, or for that matter to suggest, that the absence of a wrong of *iniuria* in the

[158] Ibbetson, this volume, ch 2.
[159] Mitchell, this volume, ch 5.
[160] Descheemaeker, this volume, ch 4.
[161] ibid.
[162] *Wilkinson v Downton* [1897] 2 QB 59; see Birks (n 1) 1, 22, 42–44.

common law has historically been detrimental. Indeed, some of the chapters make specific claims in this respect, which go both ways. But the book as a whole has no other aim than to illustrate how an understanding of a concept essentially alien to the common law allows us to approach it from a different angle and, by so doing, to highlight features which had not been previously seen or noticed.

The above developments pertained to English law. Unsurprisingly, the picture changes significantly when, widening the scope of enquiry, we include within the common law tradition the two mixed legal systems of South African and Scots law. The major difference is that, in both instances, *iniuria* was part of the conceptual apparatus which was incorporated into the law in the early modern period. In Roman-Dutch and Roman-Scots law alike, the *actio iniuriarum* was received (and, importantly, has remained an essentially civil action, in contradistinction with some continental legal systems where the bulk of its materials was relocated to the criminal side of the law). However, the stories of the northern and southern crosses then forked off. While both are mixed legal systems in the original sense of being Romano-English in their substance and forms of reasoning, they are very different mixtures. In South Africa, the *actio iniuriarum* has remained a living reality as one of the two main pillars of the modern law of civil wrongs alongside the *actio legis Aquiliae*. Whereas many of the low-level rules are distinctly English in character, the big picture has remained avowedly Romanist. More importantly, *iniuria* as an overarching legal category is still part and parcel of the law of delict, and it is entirely trivial for judges and scholars, in the field of personality rights, to motivate solutions and innovations through direct recourse to the first principles of the *actio iniuriarum*.[163]

In this context, the significance of Roman *iniuria* will be markedly different from what it was from an English perspective. The question becomes that of the relevance of the ancient delict as a tool to analyse and assess (hence possibly prompt reform of) a modern body of law as it has evolved from a mixture of Romanist and common law sources. The short answer seems to be that returning to the original *actio iniuriarum* allows us to highlight the ways in which modern South African law has departed from its roots. At the very least, this calls for an exercise in accountability: can we justify these departures in a principled way?[164] Anton Fagan's chapter provides an example of such an exercise, arguing that the South African law of defamation, which has been considerably influenced on all levels by the English law of libel and slander, should return to its original conceptualisation as a delict of *contumelia* – where both the scope of the action and its principal rules can be derived by reference to its being a delict of hubristic conduct in respect of *fama* – in other words, a malicious attack on reputation.

[163] For a recent discussion of *iniuria* by the Constitutional Court, see *Le Roux and others v Dey* 2011 (3) SA 274 (CC).

[164] For example, in terms of a Constitutional right or protected interest. The common law *actio iniuriarum* has, however, generally been held to conform to the South African Bill of Rights. See eg *Khumalo and others v Holomisa* 2002 (5) SA 401 (CC); *M and others v Smith and others* 2007 (5) SA 250 (CC); *Le Roux and others v Dey* 2011 (3) SA 274 (CC).

The Scots law of delict has been, by contrast, much more profoundly anglicised than its South African counterpart. This is evident from even a cursory look at relevant textbooks: in one case, the main headings will be *actio legis Aquiliae* and *actio iniuriarum*; in the other, the likes of 'negligence', 'defamation', 'nuisance' or 'economic delicts'. After the Act of Union of 1707, but in particular over the course of the nineteenth century, the steady percolation of English law (which had become the new focal point of Scottish lawyers) changed the face of the Scots law of delict beyond recognition.[165] Anyone who needs persuading on this point need only read scholarship produced around 1900 and contrast it with works written on the same subject-matter a century earlier, ie on the tail of the withering institutional tradition.[166] This is not to say that older learning died entirely; but it tended to be contained in appendices complementing, if and when needed, the new rules of 'English-Scots' law. The example of verbal injuries, whose territory was essentially conquered by the common law of slander and libel, and which has survived as an appendage dealing with various forms of non-defamatory actionable words – and even this remnant was not unaffected by common law categories and thinking – provides a case in point.[167] This juxtaposition of largely different, and in part incompatible, analytical frameworks, which remained unexamined until recently, has been a significant cause of disorder.

It is a well-known and well-documented phenomenon that Scots law has been trying over the last few decades to reclaim its civilian past.[168] Within the field of delict, the dominant view seems to be that the negligence half of it is, and will remain, virtually identical to English law; but the 'everything but negligence' half is more open to differences and therefore to drawing inspiration from non-English sources. It is here that the *actio iniuriarum* might have a role to play, both *de lege lata* and *de lege ferenda*. Two structural difficulties, however, are that the non-negligence half of the law covers many bits which have no overlap with the *actio iniuriarum* of old; besides, the English-style action of negligence already straddles the divide between patrimony and personality. Thus the *actio iniuriarum* does not have a ready-made 'territory' to occupy which would be defined in contradiction from negligence; rather, it stands like a defeated former ruler whose realm has now been invaded and is governed, except perhaps for a few corners which have escaped their attention, by new masters. However, be it only because the defeat is incomplete, an understanding of the Roman and Roman-Scots *actio iniuriarum* remains a prerequisite to appreciate the fine-tuning of the modern law.

[165] See eg Walker (n 9) 30 (making the point less emphatically).

[166] Contrast for instance, in terms of both substance and form, FT Cooper, *A Handbook of the Law of Defamation and Verbal Injury* (Edinburgh, W Green and Sons, 1894) with John Erskine, *An Institute of the Law of Scotland* (Edinburgh, John Bell, 1773). While the latter reads like a typical work within the *ius commune* tradition, English lawyers would find themselves at home in the former, if slightly puzzled perhaps by a number of unfamiliar categories (such as 'verbal injuries', *rixa* or – only the terminology differs from English law – *veritas*).

[167] Cooper (n 166) ch 11; Reid (n 9) esp chs 7–8; Kenneth Norrie, *Defamation and Related Actions in Scots Law* (Edinburgh, Butterworths, 1995) esp ch 3.

[168] eg Reinhard Zimmermann, '"Double Cross": Comparing Scots and South African Law' in Zimmermann, Visser and Reid (n 8) 12.

Beyond this, the main question relating to *iniuria* in a Scottish context is whether it has a future in the jurisdiction as a cause of action, even a residual one. Niall Whitty has been a fervent supporter of this 'pro-*iniuria*' stance, using in particular a series of post-mortem cases as a basis for his argument.[169] In his chapter, Kenneth Norrie builds on Whitty's analysis to argue that *iniuria* does play a role in modern Scots law – if a very limited one – in the sense that the difference in outcomes between Scots and English law in these cases can be explained by the fact that the *actio iniuriarum* was received in the former but not the latter.[170] However, he goes on to argue that any attempt to revive a transversal delict of *iniuria* capable of protecting all aspects of personality ought to be resisted, in particular because some of them do not in fact deserve the protection that the *actio iniuriarum* has historically granted them. The argument, which will be controversial but deserves to be weighed carefully, is that widening the scope of liability is not necessarily (contrary to a common, if generally implicit, assumption) a step forward. On this point, like the others, while our understanding of the wider common-law tradition as it stands today can be considerably sharpened by examining it from the outside perspective of the civilian delict, this need not entail that we emulate the ancients in the way they determined the structure and boundaries of liability.

[169] Niall Whitty, 'Rights of Personality, Property Rights and the Human Body in Scots Law' (2005) 9 *Edinburgh Law Review* 216–19.

[170] Norrie, this volume, ch 3.

2

Iniuria, Roman and English

DAVID IBBETSON

It is easy to take an excessively simplistic view of the Roman delict of *iniuria*. If we approach it through the *Institutes* of Justinian, it can be thought of as being based on a general principle of *contumelia*,[1] perhaps best translated as insolence or disrespect, a principle which was then instantiated by certain typical fact-situations:[2] battery, defamation, sexual harassment and the like. Approach it through the texts in the Digest, though, and the picture is rather different, and rather more true to the history of the classical delict. Some analysis of this history is unavoidable therefore.

The core of the later delict is to be found in the provisions of the Twelve Tables imposing fixed penalties for the *os fractum* and *membrum ruptum* of a slave or free person, together with the penalty of 25 *asses* for any other *iniuria*.[3] The last of these is rather mysterious, and it is not at all clear whether *iniuria* here is a noun of somewhat indeterminate meaning or an adverb designating that the conduct complained of was in some way wrongful.[4] Right from the start of the Roman delict, therefore, there was seemingly a sense of open-endedness about it. In the third century BCE or just after, some parts of the Twelve Tables delict were sheared away, as the *lex Aquilia* provided a compensatory remedy for injuries to slaves;[5] it followed from this that the proto-delict of *iniuria* now had its focus on injuries to free person. Praetorian intervention, probably by the beginning of the second century BCE, replaced the Twelve Tables' fixed penalties for these injuries with damages assessed at the discretion of the *iudex* or *recuperatores*, judges with a particular function in cases with a public or constitutional dimension.[6]

[1] J 4.4 pr; Coll 2.5.1 (Paul). There is no equivalent text requiring *contumelia* in the *Institutes* of Gaius, but it is implicit in G 3.222. For the meaning of *contumelia*, see below section III, text to nn 38–50.

[2] G 3.220; J 4.4.1.

[3] Tab 1.13–15; Michael Crawford, *Roman Statutes* (2 vols, London, University of London, Institute of Classical Studies, 1996) vol 2, pp 604–8.

[4] ibid 606, with further references.

[5] Reinhard Zimmermann, *The Law of Obligations: Roman Foundations of the Civilian Tradition* (Oxford, Clarendon Press, 1996) 953–61. For the dating of the *lex*, discussing the previous theories and rightly sceptical of any certainty, MF Cursi, *Iniuria cum damno* (Milan, Giuffrè, 2002) 147–65.

[6] Otto Lenel, *Das Edictum perpetuum*, 3rd edn (Leipzig, Tauchnitz, 1927) 397–99; PBH Birks, 'The Early History of *Iniuria*' (1969) 37 *Tijdschrift voor Rechtsgeschiedenis* 163, 197–200. For the *recuperatores*, JM Kelly, *Studies in the Civil Judicature of the Roman Republic* (Oxford, Clarendon Press, 1976) 40–70.

Injuring free persons was just one wrong. In the course of the later Republic, a number of other wrongs were added alongside it in the praetors' edict: *convicium*, or the raising of a clamour against someone; *adtemptata pudicitia*, improperly following around or accosting a respectable woman or youth or luring away a companion chaperoning them; improperly shaming someone or making them *infamis*; and improperly thrashing or torturing another's slave without the consent of the owner.[7] All of these were distinct wrongs, and the only thing that they had in common was that they were actionable through the same formula, the action for wrongs or *actio iniuriarum*. Early English law had a parallel with its own action for wrongs, the action of trespass, covering a range of disparate situations with at first no common core.[8]

Early in the Roman Empire, a single idea behind all of these wrongs, the idea of *contumelia*, was identified, probably by the jurist Labeo.[9] More will need to be said about this in due course, but for the time being we need to note the effect that this had on the nature of liability. Instead of there being a number of disparate wrongs, as there had been before, there was now one single wrong, *iniuria*, though its earlier history continued visible in the name of the action, the plural *actio iniuriarum*.

I. The Structure of Liability

The classical Roman delict, approached through the Digest, reveals a fundamental tension between the levels of generality and specificity. This is most clear through Books 56 and 57 of Ulpian's commentary on the Edict, the most substantial source of D 47.10. Ulpian begins with the general principle of *contumelia*, defining this sort of wrong: *specialiter autem iniuria dicitur contumelia*.[10] After a treatment of the principles, he moves on to a discussion of the relationship between the delict of *iniuria* and liability under the *lex Cornelia de iniuriis*, and the more general question of when private actions are allowed, a topic with its own parallels with English law.[11] This is followed by more general principles relating, for example, to circumstances in which *iniuria* is said to be *atrox* and problems of multiple parties. Suddenly, though, the focus shifts, as Ulpian deals with the specific edictal wrongs: *convicium*,[12] or raising a clamour against someone; *adtemptata pudicitia*, improperly following or accosting;[13] making someone *infamis*, shaming them or

[7] Lenel (n 6) 400–1.

[8] David Ibbetson, *A Historical Introduction to the Law of Obligations* (Oxford, Oxford University Press, 1999) 13–17, 39–43, 63–70.

[9] D 47.10.15.46; Mario Bretone, 'Ricerche Labeoniane' (1975) 103 *Rivista di Filologia e di Istruzione Classica* 413, esp 416–18.

[10] D 47.10.1 pr.

[11] D 47.10.5.

[12] D 47.10.15.2–14; D 47.10.15.13 looks out of place.

[13] D 47.10.15.15–24.

lowering their reputation;[14] and thrashing or torturing another's slave.[15] Finally, presumably as a result of association with the last point, there is discussion of *iniuria* by slaves and the position of the *filiusfamilias*.

The four edictal wrongs lying within *iniuria* are not here treated simply as examples of the delict. Rather they are seen as edictal provisions in their own right. The discussions of *convicium*, shaming, and thrashing slaves begin with quotations of the edictal clauses; and it is likely that the discussion of *adtemptata pudicitia* did too, but that this has dropped out in the course of Justinian's compilation. Ulpian's discussion of each of them focuses not so much on how they relate to the general nature of *contumelia*, but on the interpretation of particular words in the edictal provisions. If we did not know that they were all constituent parts of the same delict, we might well think of them as being at least as independent of each other as were the four quasi-delicts.

One is reminded, inexorably, of St Exupéry's Little Prince. When presented by the boy with a drawing and asked if it frightened them, the adults asked why anyone should be frightened by a hat.[16]

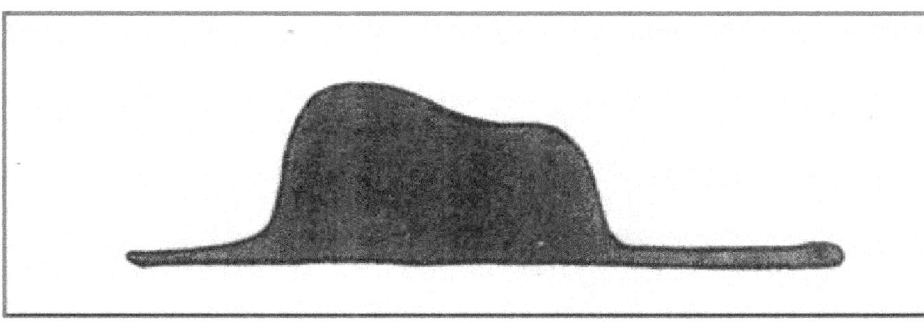

But it was not a hat, replied the prince, but rather a picture of a boa constrictor digesting an elephant. *Iniuria* is rather like this. The general principle of *contumelia* is of unquestioned importance, but the internal structure of the delict is strongly shaped by its component parts. To stick with the prince's metaphor, they had only been imperfectly digested. Where thrashing slaves was concerned, it might have been difficult to find *contumelia* in some specific situation, but if the case fitted into the edictal wording that was sufficient to establish liability. The problem, and a not wholly satisfactory solution to it, is palpable in Gaius' *Institutes*: where there had been a serious beating, of the sort which was covered by the edictal provision, an action would be granted, since it appeared to have been *aperte in contumeliam domini*, obviously to the disrespect of the master.[17]

[14] D 47.10.15.25–33.

[15] D 47.10.34–49; D 47.10.17 pr–2.

[16] Antoine de Saint-Exupéry, *Le petit prince*, avec dessins par l'auteur (New York, Reynal & Hitchcock, 1943). Image © Editions GALLIMARD.

[17] G 3.222.

English law is slightly different, though perhaps not quite so different as might have appeared at first sight. It has no general principle equivalent to the Romans' *contumelia*, but rather a list of separate torts covering much of the ground of *iniuria* and going beyond it. The component parts are there, but they have not begun to be digested into anything like a single whole. My list will almost certainly be incomplete, but it would include the following: assault and battery; breach of confidence; defamation; false imprisonment; harassment; invasion of privacy (?); malicious falsehood; malicious prosecution; misfeasance in public office; misuse of private information; slander of title; trespass to land; and wrongful interference with goods.

The structural difference between the two systems is reflected in the approach to formal rules. We may take the liability for making statements about a person as an example. In English law, the relevance of the truth of the statement depends on the tort in issue. In defamation it is a complete defence, in breach of confidence it is no defence at all. Roman law was more complex. Sometimes it would be relevant, sometimes not. Arguably it should have negatived liability where the action was based on the sub-delict of shaming someone. This was apparently the view of Paul: there was nothing wrong in saying such things since the sins of wrongdoers should be made public.[18] But the conclusion needed a reason to support it, and we might imagine circumstances in which the reason did not hold. Something shaming is not always sinful. Could the Roman equivalent of an Oxford tutor, having been told in confidence some embarrassing fact by a student, pass it on to others without any fear of being liable in *iniuria*? Still less could truth be an automatic defence elsewhere in *iniuria*. *Convicium* would be none the less improper and actionable even if what was shouted happened to be true. Roman law here had a much more open texture than the more sharply defined English law.

II. Legal Definition and the Manipulation of Facts

We have a difference in structure between the two systems, therefore. We also have a difference in technique. Roman law was jurists' law, so that unclear cases were discussed in terms of the specific sub-delicts and the general principle. Disrespect to a corpse is *iniuria* on general principles,[19] though it was not quite so obvious why the heir should have a claim. Giving a drug so that someone's mind is deranged counts as *iniuria*,[20] seemingly because it is on a par with causing physical injury by a blow. Raising a clamour against someone who is away from home counts as *convicium* and is therefore actionable as *iniuria*.[21] An action will, or perhaps will not, lie for improperly accosting a respectable woman even if she is not

[18] D 47.10.18 pr.
[19] D 47.10.1.4.
[20] D 47.10.15 pr.
[21] D 47.10.15.7.

dressed as one,[22] though this might have been controversial. Using foul language to a lady would not fall within *adtemptata pudicitia*, but was *iniuria* none the less.[23] Offering my property for sale as if it had been given as a pledge which has not been redeemed is *iniuria*:[24] it is shaming to me and brings me into disrepute. Mild intimidation of a slave does not fall within the boundaries of thrashing or torturing, and is not *iniuria*.[25] And so on.

English law, by contrast, has its focus on the courtroom and the decision in the lawsuit. We do need to know whether certain fact-situations fall within one tort or the other, of course, but it is equally important in practice to know whether they can be manipulated so as to appear to fall within an established tort. When the amateur golfer Cyril Tolley was featured in an advertisement for Fry's chocolate without his consent he was annoyed at what was described in the Court of Appeal as a piece of offensive vulgarity.[26] The defendants had, in the words of Greer LJ, 'acted in a manner inconsistent with the decencies of life, and in doing so they were guilty of an act for which there ought to be a legal remedy'.[27] However, using another's name without consent was not in itself a tort, and Tolley framed his claim in defamation, alleging that there was an innuendo that he had compromised his status as an amateur by accepting money for appearing in the advertisement.[28] At first instance, before Acton J, his claim was successful. The majority of the Court of Appeal held that the mere presence of his image in the advertisement could not bear this meaning, and the defendants' appeal was allowed. The House of Lords disagreed, and by a majority of four to one reversed the judgment of the Court of Appeal;[29] in the end damages were agreed in the not inconsiderable sum of £500,[30] rather more than the $500 which was the winner's prize money in the American Open Championship in the year that the advertisement appeared.[31] The dissenting speech of Lord Blanesborough is the most interesting. The real problem, as he saw it, was that the caricature of the golfer was so vulgar and so offensive that no reasonable person would ever suppose that he had consented to its use, all the more so since it would have imperilled his amateur status to have done so. Moreover, it was not at all obvious that the law should allow an action to Tolley when his image was used without permission, but not allow an action to a politician or professional sportsman in similar circumstances. But Tolley's problem, and that of the judges, was clear: the only way he could bring an action against the defendants, who had committed what would have been a clear case of

[22] D 47.10.15.15. See below, text to nn 46–50.

[23] D 47.10.15.21.

[24] D 47.10.15.32.

[25] D 47.10.15.41.

[26] *Tolley v Fry* [1930] 1 KB 467, 472 (Scrutton LJ).

[27] ibid 467, 478; similarly critical of the defendants, Slesser LJ at 491.

[28] At first instance Norman Birkett KC, counsel for the defendants, stressed that the nub of the plaintiff's case was not in truth any alleged defamation, 'The action was not really one for libel at all, but one for the unauthorized use of Mr. Tolley's name': *Tolley v Fry* The Times, 16 July 1929.

[29] *Tolley v Fry* [1931] AC 333.

[30] *Tolley v Fry* The Times, 15 July 1931. The jury had originally awarded £1,000.

[31] *American Golfer* (June 1928) 71.

iniuria in Roman law, was to squeeze his claim into the straitjacket of an existing English action and hope for the best.

Just on the other side of the line, but illustrating the same point, is the fact-situation behind *Huth v Huth*.[32] Mr and Mrs Huth had separated with some acrimony; Mrs Huth had left the family home, taking with her their children and their butler. At some time after this had happened, Captain Huth received a bill for saddlery supplied to Mrs Huth; he wrote on the back that Mrs Huth was not known, and that she should henceforth be known by her maiden name of Miss Edith Greaves. He then put the bill in an unsealed envelope, and sent it to 'Miss Greaves' at the address to which she had moved. We can imagine Mrs Huth's distress at opening the letter at the breakfast table, but that did not mean that she had a legal claim. At this time a wife could not sue her husband, so any action would founder from the start. Instead, therefore, an action was brought by the children; and as in *Tolley v Fry* it was framed in defamation, on the basis that there was an innuendo that the children were illegitimate.[33] Still, though, there was a problem. Leaving aside the question whether the wording of the letter could bear this meaning, there did not appear to have been any publication of it, as was required for an action in defamation to succeed: a communication between husband and wife, in the eyes of the law, was not a publication at all.[34] Enter the butler, who gave evidence that he had opened the unsealed letter and read it out of curiosity before placing it on the breakfast table for his mistress to read. Thus the basic elements of the claim in defamation were made out, though in the event the action failed on the basis that the butler's acts were not foreseeable so that there was no publication to him by the husband. For present purposes, this does not matter. What is important is that in order to find a way to get her own back on her husband, whose behaviour no doubt appeared to be intolerable, the whole matter had to be manipulated almost out of recognition. The action had to be brought by the children, whom we might well suspect to have been pawns in the struggle between their parents. The words of the letter had to be interpreted in such a way as to suggest that they were illegitimate, and even if this were possible (which it probably was not) it seems clear that neither they, nor Mrs Huth, nor the butler would have read them in that way. And we have to wonder whether the butler really did read the letter at all, except when shown it by Mrs Huth. At an earlier stage in the proceedings, where contempt proceedings were being brought against Captain Huth for breach of an order not further to harass Mrs Huth, it was said that there had only been a technical publication of the original letter since it had not been suggested that anybody but Mrs Huth had read it.[35] Do we genuinely believe that

[32] *Huth v Huth* [1915] 3 KB 32.

[33] The artificiality of the action was made quite explicit by counsel at first instance: The Times, 13 July 1914. The judges in the Court of Appeal were under no illusions: *Huth v Huth* (n 32) 32, 37, 42. The innuendo was rejected at first instance; it was not necessary to decide the point in the Court of Appeal.

[34] *Wennhak v Morgan* (1888) LR 20 QBD 635. The question was probably not wholly settled: George Spencer Bower, *A Code on the Law of Actionable Defamation* (London, Butterworth, 1923), 8, 262–63.

[35] *Huth v Huth* The Times, 6 March 1914.

the butler had indeed read it, and that he had subsequently confessed and put his employment at risk? Or is it more likely that he had been induced to lie on his mistress's behalf once Mrs Huth's legal adviser pointed out that there could have been no publication to her?

In defamation cases like these we see something like what Rodolfo Sacco has called a cryptotype,[36] an underlying framework of implicit liability rules separate from the formal rules which are being applied on the surface of the judges' reasoning. But only something like a cryptotype, for perhaps more simply we can see it as a pressure within English law for a remedy equivalent to the Romans' delict of *iniuria*, but without the tools to create that remedy openly. Something very similar occurred towards the end of the century in the attempts to deal with what we might characterise as invasions of privacy before the incorporation into English law of the European Convention of Human Rights, with litigants having recourse to claims in defamation, breach of confidence, nuisance, and under the Data Protection Act.

The presence of the generalised remedy in Roman law meant that new cases involving disrespect could easily be dealt with. In English law, without a generalised remedy, they could not be. As well, though, our modern perceptions of the two systems are different because of the different sources available to us. Jurists' law is concerned with the application of rules to sets of facts which can be stated as such. In courtroom law the facts themselves are controversial, and the interests of the plaintiff might well be better served by moulding the facts so that they fall within the generally accepted scope of the rules rather than arguing that the rule should be extended. D 47.10.15.1 is interesting in this regard. If one person raises his hand against another without striking him but putting him in fear of a beating, Ulpian tells us that this is not *iniuria* but that an *actio utilis* will lie, ie the court will treat it as if it were *iniuria* for convenience's sake. But if such facts had arisen just before Ulpian had said this, we might suspect that the plaintiff's lawyer would have preferred to stake his claim on the existence of some injury rather than trying to persuade the court that the *actio iniuriarum* should be given an equitable extension of this sort, especially if it was the case, as Labeo had argued, that mental injury counted as much as physical injury.[37]

III. The Nature of *iniuria*

While it is easy to see that cases falling within the praetorian sub-delicts would slip more or less straightforwardly into *iniuria*, it is necessary to look with some more precision into what *iniuria* was. Leaving aside the details of the sub-delicts within

[36] R Sacco, 'Legal Formants: A Dynamic Approach to Comparative Law' (1991) 39 *American Journal of Comparative Law* 1.

[37] D 47.10.15 pr.

it, we can treat it as having two principal elements, each of which demands some analysis. First was *contumelia*, second a principle that the defendant's act should have been *adversus bonos mores.*

There is something of a tendency amongst writers in English to translate *contumelia* as 'insult', thereby drawing the parallel with the tort of defamation. But the temptation to do this has to be resisted. The Romans themselves saw it as the equivalent of the Greek *hubris*, which had overtones of lack of an appropriate respect due from one person to another; indeed, it seems highly likely that Labeo had the Greek idea in mind when he constructed the general principle which came to be accepted as underpinning the delict.[38] I believe a better translation into English is something like 'disrespect'. Disrespect necessarily exists in the context of a relationship: an Oxford student throwing an egg at the Vice-Chancellor is clearly doing something different from another student throwing an egg at a friend in post-examination celebrations. The first can expect serious punishment, the second no more than a mild telling-off for youthful high jinks. The relative status of the parties is important, therefore. If we give appropriate weight to the parallel with *hubris*, this must have lain right at the heart of the Roman delict; but it comes out most clearly in Roman law in the treatment of what it is that makes an *iniuria atrox.* At first, probably, *atrocitas* was thought of in terms of particularly serious physical assaults, but Pomponius reoriented it in terms of the person affected and not simply the affecting act: hence *convicium* or *adtemptata pudicitia* could be *atrox* where the injured party was of particularly high status, and, inferentially, the wrongdoer was not.[39]

All that said, although the relationship between the parties was of importance in identifying whether conduct constituted *iniuria*, or whether it was *atrox*, the clear focus of the idea of *contumelia* was on the wrongdoer. This is well brought out in Ulpian's treatment of the relative importance of the mental states of wrongdoer and victim.[40] The wrongdoer must have an *animus*, so that a lunatic or a small child could not be guilty of it: *iniuria* lay *ex affectu facientis.* The victim, by contrast, needed no such mental competence, so that it might be suffered by the child or the lunatic; he or she need not even be aware of it.[41] It should be stressed too that the defendant's intentionality lay right at the heart of liability; it was not simply a rule, which might have been different, that this was the mental state that it was necessary to prove. It was in the very nature of *contumelia* that the wrongdoer was deliberately acting without taking into account the interests of the victim. We should not expect to find a rule requiring *animus iniurandi* distinct from the fact of *iniuria.*

[38] Bretone (n 9) 420–23; for claims of *hubris* in Greek law, see DM MacDowell, *The Law in Classical Athens* (London, Thames and Hudson, 1978) 129–32.

[39] D 47.10.9 pr.

[40] D 47.10.3 pr–2.

[41] That the delict might be suffered by a person unaware of it makes it difficult to accept the commonly stated view that he or she had to show resentment. *Dissimulatio* (D 47.10.11.1) might better be interpreted as a positive brushing off of the wrong.

It is this intentionality at the heart of *contumelia* that explains the absence of liability where the defendant was unaware of some centrally relevant fact. If, for example, he beat a free man in the belief that the victim was his slave no *actio iniuriarum* would lie;[42] similarly, there would be no liability where one beat a co-owned slave with the consent of one of the co-owners, if the actor believed that the person who had consented was the sole owner.[43] In both cases, on the facts as he believed them to be he was doing nothing which fell within the scope of the delict. The same principle applied where the defendant was unaware of some centrally relevant fact which would make his act disrespectful to some particular plaintiff. Hence, a master could not claim to be the victim of an *iniuria* by a person who beat his slave who was posing as a free man;[44] a *paterfamilias* could not complain of *iniuria* to him when his *filiusfamilias* was beaten by a person who believed the victim to be *sui iuris*, nor a husband where his wife was beaten by a person who believed her to be a widow.[45] The only text arguably going against this principle is one which suggests that an *actio iniuriarum* would lie when a man accosted a respectable woman who was dressed in such a way as to suggest that she was not:

> Si quis virgines appellasset, si tamen ancillari veste vestitas, minus peccare videtur: multo minus, si meretricia veste feminae, non matrum familiarum vestitae fuissent. Si igitur non matronali habitu femina fuerit et quis eam appellavit vel ei comitem abduxit, iniuriarum tenetur.[46]

> If someone accosts maidens, if they are clothed in slave's clothing, he seems to have committed only a slight wrong; and even less if the women are clothed in prostitute's clothing rather than that of a *materfamilias*. Therefore if the woman is not in the dress of a *materfamilias* and someone accosts her or abducts her companion, he will be liable to the *actio iniuriarum*.

The text presents two problems: its internal logic, and its consistency with the general principle that a relevant mistaken belief will relieve the defendant of liability. So far as the first of these is concerned, there is an apparent tension between the first and the second sentence: the thrust of the first sentence is towards the innocence of the accoster, and this looks quite at odds with the consequence – *igitur* – that he is guilty.[47] It is easy to get round the difficulty by supposing the text to have been altered. For Fritz Schulz it was so obvious as to be not worth arguing,[48] and already in the Byzantine world the text was being read as if the woman in the second

[42] D 47.10.3.4.

[43] D 47.10.17 pr.

[44] D 47.10.15.45.

[45] D 47.10.18.4.

[46] D 47.10.15.15.

[47] We cannot accept the solution of the Watson Digest, translating *igitur* as 'still'.

[48] Fritz Schulz, *Classical Roman Law* (Oxford, Clarendon Press, 1951), 597. For a survey of scholars' views, F Raber, 'Frauentracht und "Iniuria" durch "Appellare"', in *Studi in Onore di Edoardo Volterra* (6 vols, Milan, Giuffrè, 1971) vol 3, p 633. See also A Guarino, 'Ineptiae Iuris Romani', in *Daube Noster: Essays in Legal History for David Daube* (Edinburgh, Scottish Academic Press, 1974) 126.

sentence was (rather than was not) dressed as a *materfamilias*;[49] alternatively *non* could be inserted before the final *tenetur* to make it read that the accoster will *not* be liable to the action. We cannot rule out such a change to the text, though neither the supposed inclusion of the first *non* nor the supposed exclusion of a second *non* is an especially plausible scribal error or compilatorial alteration. It is not necessary to suppose any alteration, though. A slight wrong is still a wrong, and on that basis there is no formal contradiction between the first sentence and the second. The second problem, the conflict between this text and the other texts dealing with mistaken beliefs, is more difficult if we assume that it is concerned with the application of the sub-delict *de adtemptata pudicitia*. Ulpian is undoubtedly writing in the broad context of the sub-delicts, but he might not have been limiting himself slavishly to their content. His text here has clearly been abbreviated – there is no quotation of the edictal clause on *adtemptata pudicitia* as there is with the other sub-delicts – and we know from elsewhere that improperly accosting even a slave fell within the broad delict of *iniuria*.[50] The text of D 47.10.15.15 as it stands, therefore, need not be in conflict with what has already been said about the relevance of mistaken beliefs.

The other element of the delict was the defendant's acting *adversus bonos mores*. This is more complex, and it may be that Ulpian and Paul disagreed about its significance. That the defendant must have acted improperly, *adversus bonos mores*, was an explicit requirement of three of the praetorian sub-delicts: *convicium*, *adtemptata pudicitia* and thrashing slaves.[51] Ulpian comments on this requirement in his treatment of each of these sub-delicts, but makes no mention of it when dealing with physical injuries or shaming, where the relevant edictal provision made no mention of it. None of the texts of Ulpian surviving in the Digest would authorise us to say that he regarded impropriety as a general requirement of liability in *iniuria*. Paul, however, might have been different. A text from the Collatio attributed to him makes this explicit: 'Commune omnibus iniuriis est, quod semper adversus bonos mores fit'.[52] In D 47.10.33 too he appears to treat it as something necessary as well as *contumelia*:

> Quod rei publicae venerandae causa secundum bonos mores fit, etiamsi ad contumeliam alicuius pertinet, quia tamen non ea mente magistratus facit, ut iniuriam faciat, sed ad vindictam maiestatis publicae respiciat, actione iniuriarum non tenetur.
>
> Where something is done in the public interest according to sound morals, even though it is to the disrespect of someone, nevertheless, because the magistrate does it not with a mind to doing iniuria but to assert public maiestas, he is not liable to an actio iniuriarum.[53]

[49] Schol ad Bas 60.21.15 (ed Heimbach, 5.627; ed Scheltema, 3560).

[50] D 47.10.9.4.

[51] Lenel (n 6) 400–1. D 47.10.15.2, D 47.10.15.20, 23, D 47.10.15.34. We do not have the text of the edict on *adtemptata pudicitia*, but the inference from D 47.10.15.20 and 23 that the appropriate words were present seems secure.

[52] Coll 2.5.2.

[53] Translation based on the Watson Digest, with some amendment.

The Latin of the text is not good: the subject of the first clause is the thing that is done, of the second clause the person who has done it; and there is nothing in the first clause to explain the reference to the magistrate in the second. It is likely that it has undergone some abbreviation. None the less, the gist of the text is clear and there is little reason to doubt the genuineness of the substance. Something contumelious is done, but it is not *adversus bonos mores*; this is not an actionable *iniuria*. There is nothing to suggest that we are dealing with a situation in which the edictal formulation required a lack of *boni mores*: though it is not impossible that the magistrate had ordered the thrashing or torturing of another's slave, the opening *quod* is of more general application. This would suggest that for Paul the impropriety of the defendant's conduct was a requirement additional to his *contumelia*, and the absence of either requirement was fatal to liability. Another consideration, perhaps, points in the same direction, that the compilers took this point not from Ulpian's commentary on the Edict, which makes up the bulk of D 47.10. but as a single sentence from Paul's commentary on Sabinus. The inference is clear, if it is not overwhelmingly strong, that there was no equivalent text in Ulpian's commentary that could have been used to make the same point.

It is possible, of course, that the two jurists had very different ideas about the scope of the delict. More likely, though, is that for Ulpian the impropriety of the defendant's conduct was bundled up in his notion of *contumelia* and was commented on only when it appeared in the wording of the edictal text relating to the specific sub-delict, whereas for Paul the two requirements were treated as independent of each other, *contumelia* focusing on the subjective aspect of the defendant's conduct and *adversus bonos mores* on its social interpretation. But provided that *contumelia* invoked the idea of undue or inappropriate disrespect, Ulpian's approach becomes quite comprehensible: it was only by reference to the social interpretation that the question whether there had been a disrespect that was undue or inappropriate could be addressed.

IV. Orienting and Reorienting English Law

Historically, the structure of English law of torts has been very different from that of the Roman law of delicts. Within the latter the principal division was between *iniuria*, which covered wrongs to free men, and *damnum iniuria* based on the *lex Aquilia*, which covered damage to property. At the core of *iniuria* was *contumelia*, while by the time of Gaius at the latest the *lex Aquilia* was based on *culpa*, any blameworthy conduct. One consequence of this was that non-deliberate injuries to free persons were very problematic. There was no watering down of the liability rule of *iniuria* to cover such a case, and it was only very slowly that the *lex Aquilia* was extended to it. By contrast, as early as the fourteenth century English law had provided a remedy for the blameworthy causation of loss, whether through damage to property or injury to the person, in the form of the action of trespass on the case.[54] This existed alongside the action of trespass, the distinction between the two actions being formulated in the early years of the eighteenth century in terms of whether the injury had been caused directly or indirectly.[55] From the middle of the eighteenth century the law was coming to focus on negligence as a basic condition of legal liability, at first in the action on the case and then in trespass. English law therefore had no difficulty in providing a remedy for negligently caused personal injuries alongside property damage, and in the course of the nineteenth and twentieth centuries the tort of negligence expanded until it had taken over practically all of the law of torts.

The principal effect of this was that in English law little formal distinction could be drawn between deliberately causing injury and negligently doing so. The plaintiff could frame the action either as negligence or as trespass, and should succeed equally in both cases. Circumstances whose social interpretations were very different were characterised identically as a matter of tort law, for there was nothing equivalent to the Romans' counterpoise between *iniuria* and Aquilian liability.[56] Take this situation. An Oxford student goes into a bar on the town side of the town/gown divide and carelessly knocks over someone's drink. His friend goes into the same bar and deliberately pours someone's drink onto the floor. In the eyes of the law both situations would be analysed in the same way. Loss had been caused, and each student would have to compensate the drinker for the loss of his beer. But the social interpretation of these two situations would be very different indeed. So too with injury to the person: a slap across the face is not the same as having something carelessly dropped on one's toe.

The same trend towards negligence is seen too in other areas where the Roman lawyers would have thought in terms of *iniuria*. In the anomalous sub-species of liability based on the decision in *Wilkinson v Downton*,[57] where the defendant for a joke had told a married woman that her husband had been seriously injured in an accident as a result of which she suffered shock and fell ill, Wright J got very close to saying that the negligent infliction of harm in this way should be actionable. His language is somewhat ambiguous, but he may genuinely have been thinking in this way, refracting liability through the lens of what was at that time an emergent tort of negligence under which liability would arise for the negligent causation of injury by the failure to take reasonable care to avoid foreseeable harm. An alternative analysis based on the tort of deceit was rejected on the facts, and it as well to quote this so as not to miss its nuance:

> I am not sure that this would not be an extension of that doctrine, the real ground of which appears to be that a person who makes a false statement intended to be acted

[54] Ibbetson (n 8) 43–56.

[55] *Reynolds v Clarke* (1725) 1 Str 634, 2 Lord Raym 1399, 8 Mod 272, Fort 212. This distinction was already being drawn in the late fourteenth century: *Berden v Burton* (1382) YB T 6 Ric II, AF p 19.

[56] Criminal law, of course, might have been different.

[57] *Wilkinson v Downton* [1897] 2 QB 57.

upon must make good the damage naturally resulting from its being acted on. Here there is no *iniuria* of that kind.[58]

Iniuria here may, of course, mean no more than 'tort' or 'wrong'; but the overtones of the Roman delict – here said not to be established – could hardly have been missed.

Even in defamation some shift towards negligence was visible. Although the tort was, in terms of pleading, based on the defendant's malice, in practice by the start of the twentieth century liability was apparently strict subject to the defendant's ability to prove one of a number of defences;[59] in these actual malice did have a part to play as it destroyed what would otherwise be a good defence of qualified privilege or fair comment, thereby bringing about some limited tracking of *iniuria*. Another feature of *iniuria* which was still reflected in English law at the beginning of the twentieth century was the importance of context,[60] here typically that of popular newspapers;[61] it was thought simply wrong that they should be able to put into mass circulation untrue stories about innocent individuals, even though no-one who knew the individuals might have thought the story true.[62] But still the gravitational weight of the negligence principle came to play some part, and in 1952 the Defamation Act[63] provided that an innocent defamation – one that was made without knowledge of the reference to the plaintiff or of the relevant fact, and where the defendant had taken all reasonable care – would not be actionable provided the defendant made an appropriate offer of amends in the form of an apology and correction.

By the middle of the twentieth century, therefore, English tort law did not normally distinguish in substance between cases of deliberate wrongdoing and cases of negligence;[64] all was seen through the lens of negligence. Nonetheless, although there was no difference in substance, the distinction between deliberate and negligent misconduct was being made through the award of damages. Where the act was deliberate the plaintiff could receive exemplary or punitive damages as well as compensation for actual loss suffered. The analogy with *iniuria* here was clear. In *Loudon v Ryder*,[65] for example, Devlin J directed the jury that they might award

[58] ibid 57, 58.

[59] Paul Mitchell, *The Making of the Modern Law of Defamation* (Oxford, Hart Publishing, 2005) ch 5.

[60] D 47.10.15.6. Above, text after n 38.

[61] Mitchell (n 59) 117–20.

[62] *Hulton v Jones* [1910] AC 20; *Cassidy v Daily Mirror Newspapers Ltd* [1929] 2 KB 331; *Hough v London Express Newspapers Ltd* [1940] 2 KB 507. The statement of the facts in *Hough v London Express* is very revealing. The newspaper had published a story about the 'curly-headed wife' of a well-known boxer who attended all his fights. The wife was not in fact curly headed, and none of her neighbours who had read the article had leaped to the conclusion that she was not in fact the lawful wife of the boxer. Nonetheless, the friend who showed the article to the wife told her 'she would have to do something about it'. *Hough v London Express* 507, 508–9.

[63] s 4. See now Defamation Act 1996 s 4.

[64] The only significant situation where intention was relevant was the so-called economic torts giving a remedy in some cases where economic loss had been deliberately caused, but after *Hedley Byrne v Heller* [1964] AC 465 the negligence principle began to be operative here too.

[65] *Loudon v Ryder* [1953] 2 QB 202.

exemplary damages if they thought that an assault had been 'conducted in such a way as to insult the dignity of the person who is assaulted', so that it was 'an outrage against the plaintiff', language quite unmistakeably redolent of the Roman law. One of the standard tort textbooks of the time was completely explicit about this:

> The kind of wrongs to which [exemplary damages] are applicable are those which, besides the violation of a right or the actual damage, import insult or outrage, and so are not merely injuries but *iniuriae* in the strictest Roman sense of the term. The Greek *hubris* perhaps denotes with still greater exactness the quality of the acts.[66]

Similarly in defamation, it was only the power to sanction the award of aggravated damages that enabled the courts to distinguish between egregious cases of wanton defamation and less opprobrious situations.[67] This was the situation in *Tolley v Fry*, discussed above.[68] The defendants had acted with blatant disrespect to the plaintiff golfer in using a vulgar caricature of him in an advertisement for their chocolate without asking his permission. Equally, they had transparently infringed socially accepted norms by doing so. Clearly the jury assessing damages had thought so too in awarding a very substantial sum by way of damages without any evidence that the plaintiff had suffered any actual pecuniary loss.

Since the 1950s a further reorientation of English law has been visible, in terms both of the assessment of damages and the substantive law of torts. So far as the former is concerned, the turning point occurred with the decision of the House of Lords in *Rookes v Barnard* in 1964.[69] This case stressed the compensatory function of damage awards, and heralded a much more restricted role for exemplary or punitive damages whose role was to punish the defendant for egregious conduct; the decision in *Loudon v Ryder* was formally overruled. Exemplary damages were limited to two principal situations: where there had been outrageous conduct by an official or public body, and where the defendant had committed a tort with a view to make a gain in excess of what would be awarded by way of compensatory damages to the victim. A proposal by the Law Commission in 1997[70] to give a greater scope for this kind of damage award was rejected by the Government, and in *Kuddus v Chief Constable of Leicestershire*[71] the House of Lords showed no strong inclination to follow the lead of the Law Commission. This, however, was not the end of the matter, for in the wake of *Rookes v Barnard* the courts came to give greater weight to the separate head of 'aggravated' damages where the defendant's tortious conduct caused mental distress to the victim by an affront to his or her dignity or pride. Whether such damages should properly be seen as no more

[66] PA Landon, *Pollock's Law of Torts*, 15th edn (London, Stevens and Sons, 1951) 141–42.

[67] *Smith v Harrison* (1858) 1 F & F 565; George Spencer Bower, *A Code of the Law of Actionable Defamation*, 2nd edn (London, Butterworth, 1923) 160–62.

[68] Above, text to nn 26–31.

[69] *Rookes v Barnard* [1964] AC 1129.

[70] Law Commission, *Aggravated, Exemplary and Restitutionary Damages* (Law Com No 247, 1997).

[71] *Kuddus v Chief Constable of Leicestershire* [2002] 2 AC 122.

than compensatory, as suggested in *Richardson v Howie*,[72] is really little more than a semantic question; more important is the limitation that they should only be available where the defendant's behaviour had been intentional.[73] Two quotations will suffice to show the continued vitality of the *iniuria* principle behind these types of award. On exemplary damages:

> On occasion conscious wrongdoing by a defendant is so outrageous, his disregard of the plaintiff's rights so contumelious, that something more is needed to show that the law will not tolerate such behaviour.[74]

On aggravated damages:

> There seem to be two basic preconditions of an award of aggravated damages:
>
> (1) exceptional or contumelious conduct or motive on the part of a defendant in committing the wrong, or, in certain circumstances, subsequent to the wrong; and
> (2) mental distress sustained by the plaintiff as a result.[75]

This has been strengthened by the realignment of the substantive law which has taken place over the same period. Since the late 1950s, a wedge has been inserted between the tort of negligence and the tort of battery or trespass to the person, the former focusing on the harm done, whether carelessly or deliberately, and the latter on the intentionality of the wrongdoer's conduct even if no actual harm had been caused.[76] It is now clear that the action for battery can be used purely as a mechanism for vindicating the rights of the victim, parallelling the Roman *iniuria*,[77] and providing a framework within which the award of aggravated damages can be made. There has been a growth in the tort of misfeasance in public office, available in cases of the deliberate or reckless abuse of public power, one of the paradigm situations for the award of *iniuria*-like exemplary damages.[78] So too, the emergent protection of privacy through the law of torts has been justified in *iniuria*-like terms by reference to the 'autonomy, dignity and self-esteem' of the individual.[79]

English law does not have, and has never had, a tort equivalent to the Romans' *iniuria*. But if we disaggregate the elements of *iniuria* it is possible to see its component parts at work within English law: a special treatment of wrongs committed deliberately and with contempt for others' dignity, resulting in an injury to feelings. However, as things stand the claimant's action has to be fitted within some established tort, with the result that there is a palpable twisting of legal rules when

[72] *Richardson v Howie* [2005] PIQR Q3.

[73] Harvey McGregor, *McGregor on Damages*, 18th edn (London, Sweet and Maxwell, 2009) 7.009, fn 3.

[74] *Kuddus v Chief Constable of Leicestershire* (n 71) para [63], per Lord Nicholls. Later authority has stressed that this is not a *sufficient* condition for imposing liability: *Mosley v News Group Newspapers Ltd* [2008] EMLR 20, para [180].

[75] Law Com No 247 (n 70) para 2.4 (footnotes omitted).

[76] *Letang v Cooper* [1965] 1 QB 232, building on *Fowler v Lanning* [1959] 1 QB 426.

[77] *Ashley v Chief Constable of Sussex* [2008] 1 AC 962.

[78] See in particular *Three Rivers District Council v Bank of England* [2003] 2 AC 1.

[79] *Mosley v News Group Newspapers Ltd* (n 74) para [7].

attempts are made to squeeze some *iniuria*-like claim within the boundaries of that other tort. The restructuring of trespass as a deliberate tort, together with the development of other torts based on the abuse of power – a classical aspect of *hubris* and *contumelia* – makes it easier to see the *iniuria* typology within the framework of the substantive Common law, though as yet there are no signs of the linkages between the different torts being made explicit as a step towards the creation of a specific tort.

3

The *actio iniuriarum* in Scots Law: Romantic Romanism or Tool for Today?

KENNETH McKENZIE NORRIE

I. Introduction

Scots lawyers have always been fond of claiming that their system is one derived from principle rather than practice, that it has developed through the intellectual thought of our writers rather than through the piecemeal and arbitrary evolution of rules that is a defining characteristic of the common law. We tend to see ourselves as part of the civilian tradition, having received Roman law, or at least Roman-Dutch law, at the most crucial stage in the development of our modern legal system, that is to say the period between the Reformation and the Enlightenment. This reception was effected through the systematisation of Scots law achieved by the Institutional writers, who drew heavily on their Roman-Dutch training, rather than by the courts through case law. Yet notwithstanding that claimed love of principle, the treatment of one of Roman law's most significant contributions to legal thought, the *actio iniuriarum*, which was a central feature of the Scottish law of obligations during the Institutional period, was cavalier and even negligent throughout the nineteenth and for much of the twentieth centuries. It is only latterly that Scottish commentators, and even on occasion Scottish courts, are rediscovering our historical roots and we see once again the *actio iniuriarum* being called into aid – both as a means of achieving an appropriate result in particular cases, and as a means by which we can understand the structural underpinning of our law of obligations. This striking ambivalence towards the *actio iniuriarum* is probably explained by changing political imperatives. The Enlightenment Scots, Unionist to a man, exhibited a clear desire to associate themselves with the English and so participate in that great eighteenth- and nineteenth-century adventure, the British Empire; but as that empire recedes into history, legal nationalism reasserts itself once again by seeking a reconnection with our Romanist roots.

However that may be, Scottish judges and legal commentators are today comfortable once again in using concepts derived from Roman law to tackle new legal problems, but of course nowadays we also have other tools to drive the development of the law, none more important than the European Convention on Human Rights. This has had a profound effect on the development of the law of delict, both in the fields of personal injury[1] and of course privacy.[2] So the underlying question that I want to explore here is whether, in the modern world, Scots law gains anything by reactivating its long-neglected roots, over and above the tools that it unquestionably has. Would we be better striking out in a new direction, connecting with the new *ius commune* of European Human Rights law, instead of rediscovering, reviving, and seeking to apply the principles underpinning the *actio iniuriarum*? Should we regard it as no more than a romantic Romanism, useful for emphasising our difference from English law, or use it as an active driver of the development of our law in the modern world? It can be the latter only if it is able to serve some purpose other than or better than any other existing legal tool.

II. Characteristics of the *actio iniuriarum* in Scots Law

It was during the Institutional period that the *actio iniuriarum* was directly received into our law and 'injury', in its specialised Roman sense, became understood to be an actionable wrong in Scotland. Stair,[3] though he lists a number of the interests that the law of Scotland protects, and talks of a general obediential obligation of reparation, does not mention injury as a separate wrong and it is left to Bankton, as always the most accessible of the Scottish Institutional writers, to give it unequivocal recognition. He talks of 'injury' as a wrong independent of any other, though it is clear that he is finding this wrong in an anglicised *iniuria* – as something that is suffered – even although to the jurists of the *ius commune* that word more usually meant 'wrongfulness' as a judgment rather than injury as a loss.[4] 'Injury' (as a loss) was almost, but not quite, synonymous with insult, that is

[1] *Osman v United Kingdom* (1999) 29 EHRR 245 applied, for example, in *Chief Constable of Hertfordshire Police v Van Colle* [2008] UKHL 50.

[2] *Von Hannover v Germany* (2005) 40 EHRR 1 applied, for example, in *Douglas v Hello (No 3)* [2006] QB 125 and *Mosley v News Group Newspapers* [2008] EWHC 1777 (QB).

[3] Stair, James Dalrymple, Viscount of, 1619–1695, *The Institutions of the law of Scotland: deduced from its originals, and collated with the civil, canon and feudal laws, and with the customs of neighbouring nations, in 4 books*, 2nd edn, ed. David M. Walker (Edinburgh, University Presses of Edinburgh and Glasgow, 1981). Reprint of 2nd edn, originally published in 1693 (hereafter Stair, *Institutions*) 1.9.4.

[4] The ambiguity remains between injury as a loss and injury as an action. The maxim *volenti non fit iniuria* might be translated either as a defence that negatives loss or as a defence that negatives wrongfulness. The traditional formulation of a claim for damages in a Scottish court narrates that the pursuer has suffered 'loss, injury or damage'. Yet, in the phrase *damnum iniuria datum*, or damage wrongfully caused, *iniuria* unambiguously means wrongfulness, and this was the primary meaning Bankton gave it when he described injury as being committed 'either by Facts, as beating, or other attrocious usage of one's person; by Words, reproachful and slanderous, so far as they infer a damage to the state of the person or wound his character; by Consent, in giving warrant, command or authority to commit the injury; or by Writing, as by composing infamous libels and satires to one's disgrace'. Bankton, Andrew MacDowell, Lord, 1685–1760, *An institute of the laws of Scotland in civil rights: with*

to say an injury to dignity: it was an attack on a person's honour, dignity or status.[5] Now this was a 'high-level principle', to use the words of Lord Hoffmann in *Wainwright v Home Office*,[6] which of course as an analytical tool he rejected as being of no value to the development of the law. That rejection, however, reflects a peculiarly English mindset which has far less purchase in Scotland, for Scottish lawyers have never had a structural distrust for high-level principles from which we might extract particular rules of liability.[7] The phrase *actio iniuriarum* was able, therefore, to serve as a useful shorthand to mean an action raised in response to an attack on one of the interests protected by, and prohibited under, the concept of *iniuria*, or injury. Injury, in this sense, had at least three defining characteristics: affront, intent and the distinction between real and verbal injuries.

A. Affront

The first question is what interests were protected by the *actio iniuriarum*, so that their infringement gave rise to liability? Stair listed the interests that Scots law protected[8] without explicitly tracing any of them to the general wrong of *iniuria* but, following the Roman law more closely, Bankton[9] clearly envisaged a general wrong of which Stair's interests are merely examples. He made it clear that real injury included physical assault (if without using that precise term),[10] but revealingly the loss for which a monetary redress was due was less physical than emotional, and this gives us our first, and perhaps most important, defining characteristic of the action: damages were not awarded because the pursuer had suffered physical injury[11] but because he had suffered emotional disturbance.[12] It

observations upon the agreement or diversity between them and the laws of England : in four books after the general method of the Viscount of Stair's 'Institutions', Stair Society Series 41–43 (Edinburgh, Stair Society, 1993–1995). Facsimile reprint of the edn published: Edinburgh: Printed by R. Fleming, for A. Kincaid and A. Donaldson, 1751–1753. Andrew MacDowell, Lord Bankton (hereafter Bankton, *Institute*); 1.10.21.

[5] 'Injury according to Stair, Bankton, Erskine and other writers on the law of Scotland, who in that respect adopt the language of the civil law, "is an offence maliciously committed to the reproach and grievance of another, whereby his fame, dignity or reputation is hurt"'. *Newton v Fleming* (1846) 8 D 677 (Lord Murray) 694.

[6] *Wainwright v Home Office* [2004] 2 AC 406, 419.

[7] Stair's 'general obediential obligation', for example, is clearly a 'high-level principle' of a nature dismissed by Lord Hoffmann.

[8] Stair, *Insitutions* 1.9.4.

[9] Bankton, *Institute* 1.10.21–39.

[10] Bankton, *Institute* 1.10.22. See John Blackie, 'From *actio iniuriarum* to Rights of Personality: The Historical Background in Scots Law' in Niall Whitty and Reinhard Zimmermann (eds), *Rights of Personality in Scots Law* (Dundee, Dundee University Press, 2009) 104–8 for the emergence of 'assault' as a nominate wrong.

[11] Indeed, none may be suffered since the concept of assault has always included threats of assault.

[12] For cases involving real injury but no physical harm, see for example *Gordon v Stewart* (1842) 5 D 8 (an attempt to touch the pursuer's nose 'in an insulting manner') and *Ewing v Earl of Mar* (1851) 14 D 314 (riding a horse at the pursuer). For the modern law concerning the emotional aspects of assault, see Elspeth Reid, *Personality, Confidentiality and Privacy in Scots Law* (Edinburgh, SULI, 2010) paras 2.19–23.

was the affront at the insult to his honour that demanded redress rather than the corporeal effects on the pursuer of the wrongful act. The protected interest was honour, or *dignitas*, and the loss suffered through its infringement was affront.[13] Given the very incorporeality of such a loss, compensatory damages were not appropriate, for no true (commercial) value can be placed on affront, and instead monetary redress in the form of *solatium* was the appropriate remedy (remembering that punitive or exemplary damages have no place in the law of Scotland). A *solatium* acted both as a solace to the affronted victim and an acknowledgement by the law that a wrong had been committed (*iniuria*, in the wider sense of wrongfulness). Other infringements of interests that came within this high-level principle included wrongful imprisonment, defamation, and interference with family relationships: in all of these it was the element of affront that was the loss attracting monetary redress, and for this reason many of the modern forms of liability traced to the *actio iniuriarum* may conveniently be referred to as the 'affront-based delicts'.[14]

B. Intent

The second definitional characteristic of *iniuria* concerns the nature of fault (or wrongfulness) that it was (or is) necessary for a pursuer to establish. Now to a large extent this is explained by the jurisdictional rules of the Scottish courts in the Institutional period. Insofar as it concerned *dignitas*, that is to say the place of a person in society (the person's honour, dignity and status), 'injury' jurisdictionally belonged to the Commissary court, which had taken over the Consistorial jurisdiction of the Courts of the Official (the papal courts) at the Reformation.[15] With those injuries that led to death or physical harm, the Justiciary Court had jurisdiction. There was some overlap between the Commissary and the criminal court, and even between these courts and the civil courts, but the remaining dividing lines were removed entirely when the Court of Session took over jurisdiction for all delictual (as opposed to criminal) liability, which it had done by 1830.[16] The flavour of criminality remained, however, even when redress for the wrong was sought only in the civil courts, and this fact, together with the historical influence of the church courts which focused on matters of conscience, meant that the nature of fault with *iniuria* in Scotland was always intent. It follows that

[13] In Roman law an attack on *dignitas* was likely thought wrongful because of its potential to distrupt the stability of a highly stratified society, but in Scotland the loss always was a more personal affront.

[14] Bankton explicitly sees injury as an 'affront': *Institute* 1.10.38. According to John Erskine, *An Institute of the Law of Scotland*, new edn bringing down the law to the present time by Alexander Macallan (Edinburgh, 1838; hereafter Erskine, *Insitute*) 4.4.80, 'the crime of injury, in a strict acceptation, consists in the reproaching or affronting our neighbours'.

[15] Simon Ollivant, *The Court of the Official in Pre-Reformation Scotland* (Edinburgh, Stair Society, 1982).

[16] Blackie (n 10) 35–40.

the affront-based delicts were and are intentional delicts. As the Court of Session put it in 1765:

> An *actio iniuriarum*, where there is no patrimonial loss, and where the damages awarded are only *in solatium*, must be founded upon *dolus malus*, according to the opinions of all writers upon law; and so far it differs from damages awarded to repair patrimonial loss, in which it is sufficient to specify even *culpa levissima*.[17]

This remains the case today and it is this fact that justifies recovery for a wider range of losses than is possible with Aquilian liability. Negligence, or the unintentional causing of injury, does not found liability for mere mental disturbance unless that disturbance amounts to a recognised psychiatric illness, but the matter is very different when the harm has been caused intentionally.[18] While it is good social policy to accept that distress and upset are part and parcel of life itself and therefore have to be borne without redress, it is also good legal policy to discourage people from acting with the intention of causing such upset.[19] Remember that *solatium* not only provides a solace but it also acts as an acknowledgement that some legal wrong has been committed and so it is peculiarly appropriate that redress should be available for intentional wrongfulness, even when that does not lead to physical and quantifiable loss, injury or damage. We need to be clear, however, as to the exact nature of 'intent' that is necessary to found liability. It would seem that there is no requirement to intend to cause emotional distress and that it is sufficient for liability that the defender intended to do the wrongful act.[20] However, because this rather contradicts the policy basis that justifies recognising liability for affront in the first place (discouraging people from acting in a manner designed to cause affront), something additional to the intent to do the act is necessary before liability is established. In English law[21] this additional element is the concept of imputed malice. Intentionally doing an act that leads to an unintended (or, perhaps better, a non-intended) injury may impute 'malice' in the English sense.[22] But Scots law seems to take a different approach to justify imposing liability on someone for an intentional act when they did not specifically intend the harmful result of the act. Scots law betrays very clearly its civilian roots here, for it imposes liability for harmful consequences when there is no lawful justification

[17] *Graeme and Skene v Cunningham* (1765) Mor 13923. See also *Newton v Fleming* (1846) 8 D 677 (Lord Murray) 694: 'But in order to make out injury, it must be shown in the outset that there is an offence committed and malice'.

[18] Lord Hoffman in *Hunter v Canary Wharf Ltd* [1997] AC 655, 707 pointed out that there was no reason why a tort of intention should be subjected to the same limitations to compensation as the tort of negligence, in particular the rule that excludes damages for distress short of psychiatric injuries: 'The policy considerations are quite different'.

[19] An example I gave some years ago (*Stair Memorial Encyclopaedia*, vol 15 (1996), para 437) was of a person locking a building with someone inside. If this is done intentionally to imprison the person damages for emotional upset might be recoverable, but if it is merely negligent there is no *animus iniuriandi* and emotional upset is not enough to sound in damages – though the negligent act might lead to damages if it causes patrimonial loss.

[20] See further Kenneth Norrie, 'Actions for Verbal Injury' (2003) 7 *Edinburgh Law Review* 390.

[21] See discussion in *Wainwright* (n 6) 424–26.

[22] *Wilkinson v Downton* [1897] 2 QB 57, as explained by Lord Hoffmann in *Wainwright* (n 6).

for doing the intentional act.[23] Wrongfulness is found not in the intention to do an act which injures, but in the intention to do an injurious act without having lawful authority to do it. This has long been the justification for giving damages for assault, in the sense of physical touching without the lawful authority of consent[24] and the same thinking can be seen in quite different aspects of the law of obligations, such as unjustified enrichment, where it is now clear that enrichments will be reversed where there is no legal authority to keep the enrichment.[25] We see this again in real injury cases such as wrongful imprisonment and wrongful prosecution where fault is typically found in 'malice and want of probable cause'. Affront is therefore not enough to found liability under the *actio iniuriarum* in Scotland: it must be affront caused by an intentional act done without lawful justification, and it is for the pursuer to aver and show this lack of lawful justification.

C. Real and Verbal Injuries

Affront was the basis of *iniuria* in Roman law as it is in Scots law; intent was part of the Roman law too, if only by default since the distinction between intent, recklessness and negligence was never truly drawn by the Romans. The third defining characteristic of the Scots law of *iniuria* is also taken directly from Roman law:[26] this is the structural distinction that we make between real injuries and verbal injuries. Now, it is a common mistake to interpret this as referring to the losses suffered (using 'injury' in its sense of loss rather than its sense of wrongfulness). In fact, the distinction is between the methods of causing the loss. Real injuries are injuries caused by physical acts (subdivided into wrongs such as assault, mutilation, killing and rape) while verbal injuries are those caused by the use of words (originally this class was not subdivided, but it later became divided into defamation and other verbal injuries[27]). The legal distinction between these two categories in Scotland was, however, jurisdictional rather than substantive, with the Justiciary Court dealing with real injuries (in both the criminal and the civil

[23] *Barratt International Resorts Ltd v Barratt Owners Group* 2003 GWD 1–19 (OH). I had earlier suggested that (at least in the context of a requirement for malice in cases of qualified privilege in defamation) 'malice does not in this context connote bad intent, but more lack of good intent': *Defamation and Related Actions in Scots Law* (Edinburgh, Butterworths, 1995) 120. Privilege in defamation is based on presumed good intent, and malice in that context is therefore the lack of good intent.

[24] See Hector McKechnie in *Green's Encyclopaedia* (1931) vol 12, para 1124: 'The essence of assault is insult rather than actual physical hurt . . . In its civil aspect it consists of an overt physical act intended to insult another and committed without lawful justification or excuse'.

[25] *Morgan Guaranty Trust Co of New York v Lothian Regional Council* 1995 SC 151; *Shilliday v Smith* 1998 SC 725.

[26] D 47.10.1.1: Ulpian reports that Labeo (who was alive at the very end of the Republic) distinguishes between *iniuriam . . . aut re aut verbis*, though Paul du Plessis (this volume, ch 7) concludes that the distinction was in reality that of Ulpian and no earlier.

[27] Scots law never distinguished between the different methods of communicating words, whether for example spoken or written and so has never distinguished between what in English law is called libel and slander.

sense) and the Commissary Court dealing with verbal injuries.[28] However, once jurisdiction had been transferred from both of these courts to the civil courts,[29] the continuing relevance of the distinction becomes open to question, except insofar as it indicates a factual difference with wrongful imprisonment (for example) being a real injury because it is effected by physical acts, and defamation being a verbal injury because it is effected by words. In truth it was never a particularly helpful distinction even in a classificatory sense because it is easy to imagine cases in which it is difficult or impossible to say whether it is physical acts or words that have caused the loss. For example if I have in my possession a compromising letter that you wrote, or that someone wrote to you, is my giving it to a third party to see and to read a verbal or a real injury? If it is a breach of confidence, or is defamatory, it is clearly an injury, but given the unified jurisdiction of the civil courts today there really is little if any point in classifying it one way or the other.[30]

III. Change of Focus in the Nineteenth Century

In the nineteenth century, there were three crucial developments in the law of obligations that substantially changed the focus of *iniuria* and moved Scots law some distance away from its civilian roots. First, as happened elsewhere, the action for negligence came to dominate the law of delict in Scotland: peripheral at the start of the nineteenth century, negligence was ubiquitous by the end. Yet the modern ubiquity of the action for negligence obscures to our contemporary eyes the exceptionality of a legal remedy pronounced against an individual who did not intend to cause any harm. Liability in negligence lends itself well to losses of a physical nature, patrimonial in the case of damage to property and personal in the case of damage to human body or mind, and it does have a deontological attractiveness in its provision of redress against persons who neglected to do what they ought to have done. But affront is not and never has been a justifiable human reaction to unintended acts. We are affronted at insult not because of its effect but because of the intent with which it is done. Our dignity is not – cannot be – harmed by accident, but by the knowledge (of ourselves, and of others) that there has been a deliberate effort to undermine it. We may feel emotional distress at

[28] Blackie (n 10) 76

[29] The Commissary Court was abolished in 1830, its jurisdiction being taken over by the Court of Session, as was the Jury Court which had been created in 1815 with jurisdiction to hear 'all actions on account of injury to the person, whether real or verbal, as assault and battery, libel or defamation' (actions listed in the Court of Session Act 1825, s 28).

[30] In *Continental Tyre Group Ltd v Robertson* [2011] GWD 14–321 (Sheriff Principal Bowen) it was held that it mattered little whether the claim was one for defamation or for verbal injury: but that was in the context of the remedy of interdict, where all that is necessary to show is a legal wrong (as opposed to the particular legal wrong). The opportunity was, thereby, lost to examine the parameters of verbal injury (in that case as an economic, as opposed to personality, loss).

accidental injury, but that distress cannot truly be characterised as affront, which is properly a reaction to a deliberate assault on one's sense of worth.

The second nineteenth-century development was that in Scottish court practice the very phrase *actio iniuriarum* began to be misused, and it took on a meaning that none of the Institutional writers, nor the civilian writers of the *ius commune*, would ever have given it. Perhaps because Aquilian liability, as manifested in the action for negligence, expanded from patrimonial to all physical losses, including bodily injury, the word 'injury' came to be used in a far wider sense than Bankton had used it: the word became, and indeed remains, the denominator of a central aspect of the law of negligence – personal injury. Of course physical injury leads to damages, while *solatium* remains the appropriate remedy covering monetary redress given as solace for emotional injury, but one particular type of solace came, for reasons that are yet obscure,[31] to be seen as so peculiarly associated with the *actio iniuriarum* that the very term became synonymous with the claim. This was the *solatium* awarded to a surviving relative on the death of a person wrongfully killed – a bereavement award, in other words.[32] By the mid-nineteenth century most people who were wrongfully killed were killed negligently and the continuation of the long-established practice of awarding *solatium* to the relatives of those wrongfully killed had the effect of blurring the distinction between *iniuria* and negligence,[33] so much so that by the mid-twentieth century, judges (though not writers) were describing the method of attaining any damages for non-patrimonial (and so non-quantifiable) losses caused through negligence as an *actio iniuriarum*.[34] It took Lord Kilbrandon in the House of Lords decision of *McKendrick v Sinclair*[35] to remind Scottish court practitioners what writers had been saying for some decades[36] that the action for negligence, whoever the pursuer is and whatever the physical loss suffered, is traced to the *lex Aquilia* while the *actio iniuriarum* is properly concerned with cases of intentional insult or affront. However, the crucial effect of seeing bereavement awards as the major application of the *actio iniuriarum* was that it shifted the focus of the loss away from affront to dignity, and towards hurt to feelings. Emotional distress, upset and sadness are the natural consequences of bereavement in the way that affront,

[31] The error is traced by TB Smith (n 36 below) to Lord President Inglis in *Eisten v North British Railway Co* (1870) 8 M 980.

[32] Now governed by the Damages (Scotland) Act 2011.

[33] In *Black v North British Railway Co* 1908 SC 444, 453, Lord President Dunedin may be found saying: 'The end of it all is that I think *solatium* borrowed from the action of assythment, has in the *actio iniuriarum* come to mean reparation for feelings – in short all reparation which is not comprehended under the heading of actual patrimonial loss.'

[34] See eg Lord Avonside's first instance judgment in *McKendrick v Sinclair* 1972 SC(HL) 25.

[35] *McKendrick v Sinclair* 1972 SC (HL) 25. See also Lord Fraser of Tullybelton in *Robertson v Turnbull* 1982 SC(HL) 1, 8.

[36] Hector McKechnie, 'Scottish Legal History' in *An Introduction to Scottish Legal History* (Edinburgh, Stair Society, 1958) 276–77 and *Green's Encyclopaedia of the Laws of Scotland* (1931) vol 12, paras 1088–90; TB Smith, *Short Commentary on the Law of Scotland* (Edinburgh, Green, 1962) 653–63 and 'Designation of Delictual Actions: Damn *iniuria* damn' 1972 *Scots Law Times* (News) 125 and 'Damn *iniuria* Again' 1984 *Scots Law Times* (News) 85.

or insult, or the taking of offence, is not. This opened the way for the *actio iniuriarum* to expand its parameters beyond insult and towards hurt feelings, and it is this that gives the action its potential in the modern age.

The third crucial development in the nineteenth century was the response of the law to a hardening of the rules applicable to the wrong of defamation. This was and is in Scotland an archetypical affront-based delict, even if there was always the possibility of claiming for patrimonial loss caused through damage to the economic worth of one's reputation in the same action.[37] That affront founds the action explains why, unlike in English law, it has always been possible in Scotland to sue for defamation even if no-one other than the pursuer hears the words used by the defender – there is no need for 'communication' in the English sense.[38] However, after some decades of doubt, it was conclusively settled in 1859 that truth is an absolute defence to an action for defamation.[39] In itself a perfectly sound rule[40] – even with a civilian conception of defamation being an *iniuria*, or an affront to dignity,[41] on the basis that a person has no business being affronted by having his true character revealed – the rule nevertheless seems right away to have been assumed to apply to all injuries caused through words and not only the form of verbal injury that we call defamation. So other types of verbal injury took on truth as an absolute defence even when they are non-defamatory. But since it is defamatoriness that justifies the court in presuming falsity (so that truth in defamation is properly a defence for the defender to prove), in non-defamatory cases of verbal injury falsity became part of the definition of the wrong (and so for the pursuer to prove).[42] Now, requiring falsity to be established in non-defamatory cases of verbal injury is actually very odd if the essence of the wrong is affront caused without legal justification. Clearly a person may legitimately be affronted in circumstances in which truth or falsehood really is neither here nor there. This did not really matter before 1859 where there was no real need to distinguish between defamation and other forms of verbal injury, but there have long been

[37] I describe defamation as a 'Janus-headed delict protecting [the] personality right to honour (dignity) and [the] patrimonial right to reputation': Kenneth Norrie, 'The Scots Law of Defamation: Is There a Need for Reform?' in Whitty and Zimmermann (n 10) 435.

[38] *Mackay v McCankie* (1883) 10 R 537. Lord Kilbrandon said, in 'The Law of Privacy in Scotland' (1971) 2 *Cambrian Law Review* 31, 38: 'In such a case the damage is done neither to the man's patrimony nor to his reputation, which remain respectively undiminished and untarnished. The damage is done to his dignity, and is thus actionable under the old law'.

[39] *Mackellar v Duke of Sutherland* (1859) 21 D 222. The same is true in England and the history and continuing justification of the rule in English law is explained by Eric Descheemaeker in '"*Veritas non est defamatio*"? Truth as a Defence in the Law of Defamation' (2011) 31 *Legal Studies* 1.

[40] See Descheemaeker (n 39). His argument, alluded to in the article's very title, is that in English law defamation is *by definition* false because the interest being protected is deserved reputation.

[41] Putting it at its simplest, the Scottish approach to defamation is that it protects *dignitas*, the third of Ulpian's bases of *iniuria*, before *fama*, which was the second: D 47.10.1.2.

[42] This is probably why pursuers have long preferred to squeeze their actions into defamation where they get the benefit of the presumption of truth, rather than raise their case in a more natural way under another action for verbal injury where they would have themselves to prove falsity. It is interesting to note that in 1936 a claim for what was effectively breach of privacy by unwarranted surveillance was raised as an action for defamation in *Robertson v Keith* 1936 SC 29 while in 2003 it was argued in privacy in *Martin v McGuiness* 2003 Scots Law Times 1424.

two particular types of allegation which, though clearly harmful, do not come within the modern definition of what is 'defamatory' in the *Sim v Stretch*[43] sense. With neither can falsehood be the essence of the wrong, and yet they have both, almost by default, been swept into the wrong of defamation. First there are allegations of bankruptcy. These might or might not be defamatory depending on whether any fraud or business incompetence or impropriety is implied but damages have long been recoverable under defamation even when no such innuendo is drawn:[44] the only explanation is that the pursuer has been affronted,[45] but affront does not make the statement defamatory, and truth may not diminish the affront. Secondly the drawing attention to disease or deformity[46] (in particular the socially unmentionable impotency)[47] is clearly a matter of informational privacy, and its breach may well be a civil wrong, yet again it is constantly cited in the literature as an example of defamation.[48] In reality, both of these are affront-based verbal injuries that have been sucked into defamation when the category of non-defamatory verbal injury was squeezed almost out of existence.

The residual category of non-defamatory verbal injury was effectively limited to what we call the public hatred, contempt and ridicule cases[49] (or, again following Ulpian,[50] *convicium*). Yet even here from the nineteenth century the law focused on truth and falsity, which hardly arises and explains why so few public hatred cases are successful – and those that are[51] are really actions for defamation argued a slightly peculiar way. There is some evidence that more recently the Scottish courts are beginning to refocus their enquiry in this direction.[52] If, however, truth as a defence is limited (as it should be) to the action based on lie-mongering (defamation) then the *actio iniuriarum* can much more comfortably be utilised to provide

[43] *Sim v Stretch* [1936] 2 All ER 1237, 1240 (Lord Atkin): 'Would the words tend to lower the plaintiff in the estimation of right-thinking members of society generally?'

[44] *Outram & Co v Reid* (1852) 14 D 577; *Anderson v Drummond and Graham* (1887) 14 R 568, *Barr v Musselburgh Merchants' Association* 1912 SC 174; *Russell v Stubbs* 1913 SC(HL) 14; *Mazure v Stubbs Ltd* 1919 SC(HL) 112.

[45] In *Murray v Bonn* (1913) 29 Sh Ct Rep 62 affront was the express basis of the award of *solatium*.

[46] Bankton included within defamation cases where a person charged the pursuer 'with a foul disease, whereby his character is blemished': *Institute* I.10.24. Erskine, however, explicitly held it wrongful even when 'the infirmities of that sort imply no real reproach, either in themselves or in the just opinion of mankind': *Institute* IV.4.80.

[47] 'That peculiar defect in respect of which marriage may be annulled' as Lord Deas archly put it in *Cunningham v Phillips* (1868) 6 M 926, 928.

[48] Though, in truth, no case has been identified in which an action for defamation has been raised on this point alone. A false allegation that a person had contracted a sexually transmitted disease may amount to an allegation of sexual misconduct: *A v B* 1907 SC 1154. The allegation of insanity in *Mackintosh v Weir* (1875) 2 R 877 may be taken, in that different age, to impute moral fault.

[49] *Sheriff v Wilson* (1855) 17 D 528; *Cunningham v Phillips* (1868) 6 M 926; *Macfarlane v Black and Co* (1887) 14 R 870; *Paterson v Welch* (1893) 20 R 744; *Andrew v Macara* 1917 SC 247; *Lamond v Daily Record (Glasgow) Ltd* 1923 SLT 512; *Caldwell v Bayne* (1936) 52 Sh Ct Rep 334; *Steele v Scottish Daily Record* 1970 SLT 53.

[50] D 47.10.15.15.

[51] Such as *Lamond v Daily Record (Glasgow) Ltd* 1923 SLT 512.

[52] See *Barratt International Resorts Ltd v Barratt Owners' Group* 2003 GWD 1–19, and comment thereon by K Norrie in 'Actions for Verbal Injury' (2003) 7 *Edinburgh Law Review* 390.

redress for hurt feelings when the truth is being broadcast in a way that has no legal justification.

IV. The *actio iniuriarum* in Modern Scots Law

So what of the *actio iniuriarum* in the modern law? Does it remain useful as a 'high-level principle' in the way that was disapproved by Lord Hoffmann in *Wainwright*? The concept continues to receive occasional, possibly increasing, judicial mention in the Scottish law reports, though in no modern case is it possible to say definitively that the judge decided the matter before him by application of the *actio iniuriarum* in a manner that would not have been possible had the *actio* never been received into our law. Perhaps, however, that is too strict a test for the continued relevance of the *actio* in Scotland today, because Scots law has traditionally eschewed any reliance on name-based classifications. It is possible to identify a number of cases that illustrate a willingness on the part of the Scottish courts to award monetary redress through the recognition of sometimes unarticulated notions of honour, dignity or esteem as legally protected interests that have been infringed by deliberate act done without legal justification. A starting point might be to compare the Scottish and English approaches to similar claimed wrongs where the two jurisdictions produce different results.

Wainwright v Home Office[53] is the well-known and important House of Lords decision that denied the existence of a 'high level right to privacy' from which different actions may emerge. The case involved the strip-searching of visitors to a prison, which was carried out in a manner contrary to prison regulations. The claimants were affronted at this indignity, but they failed in their action, the Court holding that there was no common law tort of invasion of privacy and that any gap between that proposition and article 8 of the European Convention on Human Rights could be filled by judicial development of existing actions. Interestingly, however, the judges did not entirely exclude the possibility that an action based on the intentional causing of distress that fell short of psychiatric harm might be actionable, though Lord Hoffman was clear to the effect that if such an action were to be successful it would have to be shown that the defendant actually intended to cause emotional distress, rather than simply intentionally doing an act that caused emotional distress. Imputed malice of the sort that founded liability in *Wilkinson v Downton*[54] would never, he made plain, be sufficient.

[53] *Wainwright v Home Office* [2003] UKHL 53.

[54] *Wilkinson v Downton* [1897] 2 QB 57. Here the defendant had intended to do the act but not to cause the injury, but damages were still awarded on the theory of imputed intention (doing such a dangerous act imputes an intention to cause the harm that directly arises from it). In *Wainwright* Lord Hoffman said that 'imputed intention will not do' for injuries short of psychiatric illness, such as affront. 'The defendant must actually have acted in a way which he knew to be unjustifiable and either intended to cause harm or at least acted without caring whether he caused harm or not'. [2003] UKHL 53, [45].

That English case may be compared with a similar Scottish decision, *Henderson v Chief Constable of Fife*,[55] where a woman who had been arrested during the course of an industrial dispute was required, on being placed in a police cell, to remove her bra. Now, this was a correct application of police procedure (unlike, be it noted, the strip-search in *Wainwright*) but nevertheless Lord Jauncey in the Outer House of the Court of Session (in one of his last judgments there before his elevation to the House of Lords) held that the unthinking and unjustifiable application of police procedure when it was unnecessary (for there was no possibility of this woman being a suicide risk, or using her bra to attack policemen) amounted to a wrong for which damages could be claimed. He made no explicit mention of the *actio iniuriarum* but the wrong suffered was clearly an affront:

> I consider that Mrs Henderson has established that the request to remove her brassiere was an interference with her liberty which was not justified in law, from which it follows that she has a remedy in damages . . . I consider that a figure of £300 would fairly reflect the invasion of privacy and liberty which Mrs Henderson suffered as a result of having to remove her brassiere.[56]

Now, in neither *Wainwright* nor *Henderson* was there any deliberate intent on the part of the police or prison service to humiliate or affront anyone and while that was enough to bring the case to an end in England, it was not enough in Scotland: in the English case fault was required to be found in direct intent to inflict emotional harm (which did not exist) while in the Scottish case fault was located in the lack of legal justification for the actions which caused the affront. Following correct procedure was not in itself a justification.

We again see fault being constructed as lack of legal justification for the act in question in the Scottish post-mortem cases.[57] In each of these three cases, decided in the early years of the twentieth century, the bodies of deceased persons had been interfered with for medical reasons without the knowledge or consent of the deceased's relatives, and while the discussion of actionability was for the most part obiter, the judges in each were willing to contemplate that damages might be awarded to the relatives for the distress that they suffered. They belong to the same group of cases as *Henderson*, since it was the lack of legal authority to act that rendered the post-mortems actionable. Whitty has argued, persuasively, that the only explanation for these cases is that the remedy applicable was *solatium* for affront which derives directly from the *actio iniuriarum*.[58] He quotes Bankton (who claims authority from the *Digest*) that 'Injury, may not only be done to the Living, but also in a manner to the Dead, by reproaching their memory, detaining their bodies from burial, lifting their bodies out of their graves, or defacing their

55 *Henderson v Chief Constable of Fife* 1988 SLT 361.

56 *Henderson* (n 55) 367.

57 *Pollok v Workman* (1900) 7 SLT 338; *Conway v Dalziel* (1901) 9 SLT 86; *Hughes v Robertson* 1913 SC 394.

58 Niall Whitty, 'Rights of Personality, Property Rights and the Human Body in Scots Law' (2005) 9 *Edinburgh Law Review* 194, 216.

monuments. The children or next of kin may prosecute the injuries done to the remains of their parent or relation'.[59]

The matter was discussed in a more modern case, and one that provides the most direct affirmation of the continuing authority in twenty-first century Scotland of the *actio iniuriarum*. In *Stevens v Yorkhill NHS Trust*[60] an action for damages was raised by a bereaved mother against a health board who had removed and retained the organs of her deceased baby without her knowledge or consent. The action was explicitly based upon the mother's right not to be exposed to injury to her emotional health. The defence was that there was no doctor–patient relationship between the hospital and the mother such as would give rise to a duty of care. The temporary judge held that that defence might have been appropriate in an action for negligence, traced to the *lex Aquilia*, but the claim at hand was in contrast one traced to the *actio iniuriarum*. He held that Scots law recognised as a legal wrong, for which damages by way of *solatium* could be claimed, the unauthorised removal and retention of organs from a dead body. It was the judge's view that the earlier post-mortem cases were not explained as an extended application of assythment (the native Scottish remedy for wrongfully inflicted death)[61] but as an aspect of the *actio iniuriarum*, in particular because the damage being sued upon was the emotional distress suffered by the pursuers. Again, actionability is clearly founded on the lack of legal authority to do the act.[62]

Stevens might usefully be compared with the factually similar English case of *A v Leeds Teaching Hospital NHS Trust*,[63] where damages were denied, though that action was explicitly raised in negligence, and explicitly decided on the basis of the hospital's legal right to remove the organs. So there was no discussion of affront as the basis of the action, or of the nature of intent. But if the hospital did have legal authority to remove the organs the action is likely to have failed in Scotland too.

V. Future Developments

There is little doubt, then, that the Scottish courts, if they are so minded, could build upon the concept of *iniuria* in order to provide monetary redress in the form of *solatium* in appropriate contexts. The question is, in what contexts today would it be appropriate to do so? There are clearly some interests, historically

[59] Bankton, *Institute* 1.10.29. This suggests, however, more a representational than a direct liability. In fact, the post-mortem cases, if based on injury as Whitty suggests, are examples of injury to feelings as opposed to affront to dignity.

[60] *Stevens v Yorkhill NHS Trust* 2006 SLT 889 (OH).

[61] See Kenneth Norrie, 'The Intentional Delicts' in Kenneth Reid and Reinhard Zimmermann (eds), *A History of Scottish Private Law* (Oxford, Oxford University Press, 2000) 484–88.

[62] While the post-mortem examination of the dead child was not in this case unauthorised, the removal and retention of her brain tissue was.

[63] *A v Leeds Teaching Hospital NHS Trust* [2005] QB 506.

protected by the *actio iniuriarum*, which if they are interfered with today would not, in the eyes of the modern world, justify an award of *solatium*. Interference with family relations is an example. Rape[64] or sexual abuse was and is clearly a direct *iniuria* against the victim, and not just for the physical injury involved.[65] But the *actio iniuriarum*, protecting the family relationship as in itself a value, recognised more than one victim to rape. When a married woman was raped, the *actio iniuriarum* gave the husband a claim:[66] in Walker's words,

> It is also a wrong to her husband, justifying an *actio iniuriarum* at his instance; the wrong consists in the gross affront to the husband, the hurt to his feelings, the violation of the husband's right to the exclusive possession of his wife's person, and the dishonour done to his marriage-bed by the other man.[67]

It is difficult to believe that such an action would succeed, on this basis, today. The state has an obligation under the European Convention on Human Rights to protect citizens from sexual attack[68] but that obligation is amply fulfilled through the criminal law, and an argument that there is something missing with the lack of civil remedy available to the husband of a rape victim will get nowhere under article 8 of the European Convention on Human Rights.[69] We simply do not see the husband and wife relationship today in terms that would found any action based on his affront at her rape (however real his emotional distress might be and however clearly there is a lack of legal justification for the act).

Adultery too was an actionable wrong[70] because it was an affront against the husband's honour (though not, revealingly, the wife's).[71] Again, the abolition of that action[72] involves no incompatibility with the European Convention. I see no gap in the law if we say today that, however much a man is genuinely affronted by

[64] In the modern sense, as well as the older sense of 'rapt', which included an element of abduction see John Blackie (this volume) ch 8, p 160.

[65] In *G v Glasgow City Council* 2011 SC 1, [30] the Inner House of the Court of Session said this: 'Sexual abuse is not really about physical injury. It is more about affront and degradation'. A more old-fashioned way of seeing the matter, but still clearly as an aspect of *iniuria*, is shown in *A v C* (1919) 35 Sh Ct Rep 166 where a married woman's claim was held competent as a means of vindicating her character. (The competency of the action had been challenged by the defender on the ground that he had paid £20 'damages' to the husband and that the wife had no independent right of action).

[66] See *Black v Duncan* 1924 SC 738.

[67] David M Walker, *The Law of Delict in Scotland*, 2nd edn (Edinburgh, SULI, 1981) 714.

[68] Art 3 ('No one shall be subjected to torture or to inhuman or degrading treatment or punishment') imposes positive obligations on the state to ensure that its criminal law provides sufficient protection to its citizens: *A v United Kingdom* [1998] 2 FLR 959.

[69] For similar reasons the husbands in *CR v United Kingdom, SW v United Kingdom* (1996) 23 EHRR 363 had no claim when the English courts moved away from the proposition that no man may rape his wife on the basis that her consent to marriage carries with it, for all time coming, consent to sexual intercourse. The Scottish courts had come to that conclusion a few years earlier: *S v HM Adv* 1989 SLT 469.

[70] Interestingly, this was recognised only relatively late in the development of the law: Hume *Lectures* III, 130.

[71] *Steedman v Coupar* (1743) Mor 7337; *Kirk v Guthrie* (1817) 1 Mur 271.

[72] Divorce (Scotland) Act 1976 s 10(1).

his wife being unfaithful, or leaving him,[73] he cannot recover a monetary solace for his damaged self-esteem, or even for his hurt feelings. Our concepts of loss and damage can surely change to such an extent that what was once regarded as an affront ought no longer to be so.[74] Breach of promise of marriage, which was only recognised as giving rise to delictual liability in the early nineteenth century,[75] was explicitly abolished by s 1(1) of the Law Reform (Husband and Wife) (Scotland) Act 1984, and the affront and indignity of such a breach is no longer regarded by modern society as requiring monetary redress. Even if we cannot deny that (in some circumstances at least) breaking off an engagement might be personally devastating, it does not follow that we should see our personal relationships as part of our dignity and self-esteem: they are consensual relationships of equals, not enhancements of our honour and status.

At a broader level, it also seems to me that the very concept of 'honour' as a personal interest needs to be regarded with deep suspicion. In a society with virtually unanimity in its moral outlook (which is, surely, a hugely unattractive society) it might be possible to regard an attack on a person's honour as an 'injury', but today honour is an entirely self-defined notion with no generally accepted social content. Putting it at its most benign, 'honour' is characterised by pomposity and self-regard; at its most malign, we are too distressingly used to hearing about 'honour killings' and the like to be much attracted to 'honour' as a legally protected interest. Some men probably are genuinely affronted by their sisters and daughters wanting to lead a life of social and sexual freedom, and their sense of religious duty might well compel them to attempt to force their wills upon their sisters and daughters by harsh physical means, but the modern law cannot give any value to 'honour' in this sense. Nor is there much attraction in expanding liability for hurt feelings beyond the narrow bounds set for it in negligence and

[73] Enticing a woman to leave her husband amounted to a civil wrong against the husband and examples are found well into the twentieth century: *Adamson v Gillibrand* 1923 SLT 328 (mother incited her daughter to leave her husband); *McGeever v McFarlane* (1951) 67 Sh Ct Rep 48 (husband's lover induced him to leave his wife). The action for enticement was abolished by s 2(2) of the Law Reform (Husband and Wife) (Scotland) Act 1984.

[74] Other wrongs against family relationships have been recognised by the law of Scotland. *Plagium*, or child-stealing, might well have been regarded in the Institutional period as a real injury, but it has survived only in its criminal aspects today. Damages do not lie in negligence for wrongful interference with the parent–child relationship (*McKeen v Chief Constable, Lothian and Borders Police* 1994 SLT 93) and, even if this is done with intent, it is difficult today to accept that the real harm done when one's child is kidnapped is an affront to one's dignity.

[75] *Hogg v Gow* 27 May 1812 FC. Previously, as Blackie points out (n 10, 125) the simple withdrawal from an engagement, if not done in particularly egregious circumstances or in a particularly hurtful way, was not in itself regarded as an injury: *Johnston v Pasley* (1770) Mor 13916. He suggests (126) that the recognition of breach of promise in itself was a result of a growing sentimentality in the early nineteenth century, and a softening of the ideal of femininity. The judges in *Hogg v Gow* recognised that they were reflecting views of society that had not been held generally in Scotland in a (not much) earlier and rougher age. Another explanation for the historical absence from Scots law of breach of promise as an actionable wrong is the fact that, if the promise were followed by sexual intercourse, the parties became married in any case through operation of the Canon law doctrine of marriage *per verba de futuro subsequente copula*, which survived in Scotland until the Marriage (Scotland) Act 1939.

the long-established, but ultimately peculiar,[76] claim for bereavement awards. However, it may be that hurt feelings combined with a social necessity for the law to give some recognition that a wrong has been committed is (just) enough to allow for the recognition of a claim based on breach of informational privacy, which is clearly an interest that is gaining in importance – but has not yet been fully accepted – in the modern world.[77]

Niall Whitty[78] has argued that the most obvious use of *iniuria* in the modern world is to provide a remedy for breach of personal privacy and he argues, surely rightly, that it would be far better to develop the law in this way than to require pursuers to attempt to squeeze breach of privacy into another action like defamation, breach of confidence or even breach of copyright.[79] The danger, as always, is that policy considerations applicable to one action might be inappropriately applied to the other action. What Whitty does not do, however, is to explain why it is better to use the traditional concept of injury rather than other, more contemporary, sources of privacy rights as the driver of this potential legal development. Elspeth Reid is doubtful whether an expanded concept of *iniuria* would really serve this purpose and she is much more attracted to the idea of using the European Convention on Human Rights to drive the development of the law of privacy.[80] Her primary argument is that modern concerns, in particular informational privacy, can only be effectively protected if liability extends beyond intentional infringement.[81] This may well be true, but given that the true basis of liability in Scotland is lack of legal justification for doing the intentional act, the criticism does not really explain why the *actio iniuriarum* should not be used in addition to, or as foundational of rights developed in light of, the ECHR. The question in *Von Hannover v Germany*[82] or even in *Mosley v News Group Newspapers*[83] can as easily be structured as whether the newspapers had any legal justification for printing the stories about the celebrated personages in these cases. The answer to such a question would invariably require an assessment of the value of the right to free speech and whether that is truly interfered with by prohibiting publication – a similar analysis to that required under the European Convention. So I am not convinced that we face a stark choice, between looking back to the

[76] The true explanation for bereavement awards is that they serve the valuable policy purpose of ensuring that causing death is not cheaper to the wrongdoer than causing injury. No other general principle can be extracted, it is submitted, from the existence of bereavement awards.

[77] No-one now believes the statement of Lord Hoffmann in *R v Central Independent Television, plc* [1994] 3 All ER 641, 652 that there is no question of balancing free speech with any other interest, because freedom of speech is 'a trump card which always wins.'

[78] Whitty (n 10) 174 f.

[79] The use of copyright to protect privacy is evidenced in cases like *Prince Albert v Strange* (1849) 1 H&W 1 (LC) and *Prince of Wales v Associated Newspapers* [2007] 2 All ER 139. Ibbetson (this volume, ch 2) explores the artificiality involved when claims are construed as defamation when, in reality, they are no such thing.

[80] Elspeth Reid (n 12) para 17.12.

[81] Elspeth Reid (n 12) para 17.13.

[82] *Von Hannover v Germany* (2005) 40 EHRR 1.

[83] *Mosley v News Group Newspapers* [2008] EMLR 20.

actio iniuriarum or looking forward to the European Convention on Human Rights, for the appropriate way of protecting privacy: the focus of enquiry in both is the search for the legal justification for the publication.

And there are other drivers to the development of the law of privacy, particularly the social need and growing desire to control an unruly press.[84] There is, for example, much to be gained by expanding and adapting the 'responsible journalism' defence from the law of defamation[85] as a useful way of balancing privacy and free speech.[86] The concept of publication in the public interest[87] might also lend itself as a defence to an action based on an otherwise unjustifable infringement of personal privacy, by providing legal justification. It is true that, in Scotland, that concept never caught on as a defence in the law of defamation[88] when truthful allegations were at issue,[89] but the policy considerations are so different when dealing with privacy that I think that there is some attraction in developing a public interest defence. In other words, existing notions of public interest, responsible journalism and a whole jurisprudence from the European Court are likely to act as drivers to the developing law of privacy, building upon the protection that *iniuria* affords to the individual's feelings.

VI. Conclusion

If the above analysis is correct, then the *actio iniuriarum* is certainly more than a romantic Romanism in Scots law, in that it serves to identify emotional hurt as a loss worthy, in some limited circumstances, of monetary redress by way of *solatium*. However, the law's general resistance to regarding emotional hurt as a loss is sound, and the identification of the circumstances in which that redress is justified is and should be driven by other forces than the ghosts of the past. A combination of the European Convention on Human Rights and domestic developments in the control of unbridled journalism (which we are likely to see more of) may

[84] The 'phone-hacking' scandal that hit the UK press in the summer of 2011 reminded us that many journalistic practices, wide-spread and accepted, are anything but responsible.

[85] *Reynolds v Times Newspapers* [2001] 2 AC 127; *Bonnick v Morris* [2003] 1 AC 300; *Jameel v Wall Street Journal Europe (No. 3)* [2007] 1 AC 359; *Flood v Times Newspapers Ltd* [2012] UKSC 11.

[86] Admittedly, the European Court of Human Rights resisted importing one aspect of 'responsible journalism' (notification to the subject of an intention to publish material about them) into the art 8 right of privacy in *Mosley v United Kingdom* (2011) 53 EHRR 30.

[87] Which is the test in some jurisdictions: see for example Jonathan Burchell, 'Personality Rights in South Africa: Re-affirming Dignity' in Niall Whitty and Reinhard Zimmermann (eds), *Personality Rights in Scotland* (Dundee, Dundee University Press, 2009).

[88] Bankton has not been followed when he said that truth is a defence to verbal injury (that is to say, not limited to defamation) 'if it concerned the good of the commonwealth to have the crime known, and is not said with design of reproach, otherwise the general rule is *veritas convitii non excusat a calumnia*': *Insitute* I.10.31 (citing Voet).

[89] Unlike in South Africa and elsewhere: see Descheemaeker (n 39).

well be the way of the future. That future will also face challenges unimagined by the Institutional writers as contemporary society grapples with the evermore urgent need to control privacy-devouring social networking and information sharing sites on the internet. Freedom from affront is no longer seen as a fundamental human interest. Privacy, on the other hand, is a fundamental human interest, like liberty, with which it has in common that it is an essential precondition for the development of our personality and talents: that is why we protect it. How protection of privacy develops will depend upon the modern imperatives of our contemporary society and not upon the extent to which it can be accommodated in our old law.

4

Solatium and Injury to Feelings: Roman Law, English Law and Modern Tort Scholarship

ERIC DESCHEEMAEKER

In legal systems which have received the *actio iniuriarum*, the word *solatium* is routinely used to characterise the monetary award granted as a remedy to successful claimants in the action. This award is described as providing solace for 'injured' (or 'wounded' or 'outraged') 'feelings'. English law, which, despite some trickling in of Romanist ideas, never received the action on *iniuria*, also makes use of the term – if in a more sparse, and apparently haphazard way – typically in the context of what is called 'injured feelings' (or 'emotional distress').

Behind legal words lie, of course, legal categories. Terminology is particularly important in a discipline such as law because law is part of culture not nature. As such, the words we use to think as lawyers do not simply describe a pre-existing reality; to a very large extent at least, they create this reality. The importance of words and of their underlying meaning (which naturally need not be either stable or even clearly defined simply on account of a word having come into existence) is difficult to overstate. No study of the term *solatium* having been conducted in the context of either Roman or English law, it seemed worthwhile to spend some time on it. This is all the more true because, as often is the case, a careful study of both systems reveals some striking similarities and echoes between the two. Roman law, in this context, can be used as a way of bringing the modern law into sharper focus (whether or not that modern law can historically be traced back to *iniuria*, which is not essential).

Hence the present study is not meant to be primarily semantic or terminological; rather, the study in words (or, in this case, in *a* word) aims at contributing some new insights into important modern debates. Foremost among these is the question of the redress of emotional distress in the law of civil wrongs and also the question of how this province of the law is and ought to be structured. These two issues are highly topical; what is perhaps less obvious is that they are closely related. The main intention of this chapter is to use the word *solatium* and the study of its underlying substance as a springboard from which to make one basic, but arguably fundamental, point to both debates: namely, that there should never be any direct compensation (or, generally, redress) of emotional distress in the law of civil wrongs. To put the same point using a different perspective, the argument is that emotional wellbeing is not and should not be one of the interests that this province of the law aims to protect. Awarding such redress is committing a category mistake: because *solatium*, as a word, works powerfully towards concealing this reality, its use ought to be discontinued.

The focus of the study is on Roman and English law; but the law of the two leading uncodified jurisdictions of Scotland and South Africa will also be considered. Because the concept is not intuitively intelligible to the English lawyer, greater care must, however, be taken to introduce the word and its meaning(s) than would be necessary if the main audience were lawyers from the Northern or Southern Cross.

I. *Solatium* in Roman Law

A. The Word and its Use in Sources

The noun *solatium* (or *solacium*) derives from the verb *solor*, meaning to 'comfort', 'console', 'soothe', 'lighten', 'relieve', 'assuage', 'mitigate'. Accordingly, a *solatium* – anglicised into 'solace' – is a 'relief', a 'comfort', a 'consolation' hence, by extension, a 'compensation' or 'indemnification'.[1]

The word is routinely used by writers of modern legal systems that have received the *actio iniuriarum*, particularly Scotland and South Africa. It is also used, to a lesser extent, by modern writers on Roman law to describe the nature of the remedy granted under the *actio iniuriarum*.[2] It might therefore come as a surprise to the modern enquirer that nowhere do the surviving Roman sources use the word in that context. The term *solatium* appears five times in the *Digest* and twice in Justinian's *Institutes*.[3] An examination of these various occurrences indicates clearly that the word had no technical meaning and could be used across the whole spectrum covered by the general idea of assuagement implied by its etymology. Thus, it may refer to:

[1] *Oxford Latin Dictionary*, ed. PGW Glare (Oxford, Clarendon Press, 1982) (hereafter *OLD*) entries for *solatium*, *solor*; Charlton T Lewis and Charles Short, *A Latin Dictionary* (Oxford, Oxford University Press, 1900), entries for *solatium*, *solor*.

[2] eg Barry Nicholas, *An Introduction to Roman Law* (Oxford, Clarendon Press, 1962) 217 ('solace for injured feelings').

[3] It also appears a number of times in imperial constitutions as 'stipend' or 'salary' (Adolf Berger, *Encyclopedic Dictionary of Roman Law* (Philadelphia, American Philosophical Society, [1953]) entry for *solacium*), a meaning that can be traced back to D 8.4.13.1 (below n 4).

- the grant of a pecuniary benefit as indemnification for a non-wrong (D 8.4.13.1: a form of *quantum meruit*;[4] D 26.7.33: a form of *quantum valebat*);[5]
- a moral consolation for a misfortune (D 23.3.6 pr;[6] J 1.11.10;[7] J 3.3.1[8] – no wrong committed in any of these cases, and the consolation may or may not be pecuniary); or
- the 'solace' the punishment of murdering brigands is deemed to bring to the relatives of their victims (D 48.19.28.15).[9]

The closest use we find to the modern idea of comfort brought to the victim of a wrong through the grant of a monetary award to the claimant is the reference in D 44.6.3 to the possible payment of a penalty to a mishandled adversary in a lawsuit.[10] If Roman law used a word to express the modern idea of the 'comforting'

[4] (Ulpian, 6 *Opinions*) 'Si constat in tuo agro lapidicinas esse, invito te nec privato nec publico nomine quisquam lapidem caedere potest, cui id faciendi ius non est: nisi talis consuetudo in illis lapidicinis consistat, ut si quis voluerit ex his caedere, non aliter hoc faciat, nisi prius solitum solacium pro hoc domino praestat.' (If it is established that there are stone quarries on your land, then, without your permission, no one who does not have a right to do so can quarry stone, either in a private capacity or in the name of the state, that is, unless a custom exists in respect of those quarries to the effect that if anyone wishes to quarry stone from them, he may do so, providing he first of all gives the owner the usual indemnification in consideration thereof.) Alan Watson (trans), *The Digest of Justinian* (Philadelphia, University of Pennsylvania Press, 1998).

[5] (Callistratus, 4 *Judicial Examinations*) 'Sumptuum, qui bona fide in tutelam, non qui in ipsos tutores fiunt, ratio haberi solet, nisi ab eo qui eum dat certum solacium ei constitutum est.' (It is usual to draw up an account of expenses which are incurred in good faith for the benefit of the tutelage, not that of the tutors themselves, unless the person who appointed the tutor decided upon a certain compensation for him.) ibid.

[6] (Pomponius, 14 *Sabinus*) 'Iure succursum est patri, ut filia amissa solacii loco cederet, si redderetur ei dos ab ipso profecta, ne et filiae amissae et pecuniae damnum sentiret. (The law assists a father who has lost his daughter by returning the dowry which he provided so as to comfort him and not let him suffer the loss of his daughter and his money.) ibid. This is the oldest surviving use of the term in a legal source.

[7] 'Feminae quoque adoptare non possunt, quia nec naturales liberos in potestate sua habent: sed ex indulgentia principis ad solatium liberorum amissorum adoptare possunt.' (Women cannot adopt. They do not hold family authority even over their real children. But by imperial favour they are allowed to adopt to make up for the loss of their own children.) Peter Birks and Grant McLeod (trans), *The Institutes of Justinian* (London, Duckworth, 1987).

[8] 'Et primus quidem divus Claudius matri ad solatium liberorum amissorum legitimam eorum detulit hereditatem.' (The Emperor Claudius was the first to console a mother's loss by giving her the estates of her children.) ibid.

[9] (Callistratus, 6 *Judicial Examinations*) 'Famosos latrones in his locis, ubi grassati sunt, furca figendos compluribus placuit, ut et conspectu deterreantur alii ab isdem facinoribus et solacio sit cognatis et adfinibus interemptorum eodem loco poena reddita, in quo latrones homicidia fecissent: nonnulli etiam ad bestias hos damnaverunt.' (The practice approved by most authorities has been to hang notorious brigands on a gallows in the place which they used to haunt, so that by the spectacle others may be deterred from the same crimes, and so that it may, when the penalty has been carried out, bring comfort to the relatives and kin of those killed in the place where the brigands committed their murders; but some have condemned these [criminals] to the beasts.) Watson (n 4).

[10] (Gaius, 6 *Twelve Tables*): 'Rem de qua controversia est prohibemur in sacrum dedicare: alioquin dupli poenam patimur, nec immerito, ne liceat eo modo duriorem adversarii condicionem facere. Sed duplum utrum fisco an adversario praestandum sit, nihil exprimitur: fortassis autem magis adversario, ut id veluti solacium habeat pro eo, quod potentiori adversario traditus est.' (We are prohibited from dedicating property about which there is a suit as sacred property; if we act to the contrary, we suffer a penalty of double, and rightly so, lest by such conduct we be allowed to make the position of our adversary harder. But nothing is stated as to whether the double penalty ought to be

purpose of the *actio iniuriarum*, it would rather have been the noun *satisfactio*[11] or the verb *vindicare* – from which we derived our modern 'vindication' and the Romans the action of *rei vindicatio*, but which originally meant no more than 'avenging' a wrong: a 'retribution' (cf. English 'vindict').[12]

The Roman roots of the modern concept of *solatium* are therefore flimsy. Nor does the second life of Roman law yield more than a couple of occurrences of the word in the sense we use it today. The greatly increased mass of materials makes it difficult to make more than provisional conclusions in this respect, but a thorough search in the legal literature of the *ius commune* – a manual search for some leading writers and an electronic search across the board – suggests that the first use in the context of the victim of a wrong would have been by Gentili in his *De iure belli* (1598). Describing the retribution visited by the victor in a war, the author lists 'consolation for the injured party' (*solatium affecti iniuria*) as one of the functions of punishment as well as vengeance.[13] Remarkably, the word is used by Thomasius in 1703 in the context of the *lex Aquilia*;[14] but it does not appear to be until 1751 and the first volume of Bankton's *Institute of the Laws of Scotland* that it was used in respect of the *actio iniuriarum*.[15] Through Scots law, the word would later make its way into English law.[16] It was also picked up by the German

paid to the imperial treasury or to the adversary; perhaps, however, it should preferably be paid to the adversary so that he may, so to speak, derive solace from the fact that he has been treated as the more powerful adversary.) ibid.

[11] D 47.10.17.4, 6 (Ulpian, 57 *Ad edictum*): if a slave commits an *iniuria*, his master can present him for a thrashing in order to 'mollify' the insulted party (*ut satisfiat*; Watson (n 4)), following which the victim can no longer bring the *actio iniuriarum* as he has already 'receive[d] satisfaction' (*accepit satisfactionem*; idem). *Satisfactio* here has a meaning close to our modern *solatium*, even though the 'satisfaction' is not a monetary award.

[12] *OLD* (n 1) entry for *uindico* (ss 5–6); Berger (n 3), entry for *vindicatio* (etymologically, 'to assert strength'). See D 37.6.2.4: 'Emancipatus filius si iniuriarum habet actionem, nihil conferre debet: magis enim vindictae quam pecuniae habet persecutionem: sed si furti habeat actionem, conferre debebit.' (If the emancipated son has an action for insult, he should contribute nothing; for he has a claim for redress rather than money.) Watson (n 4); another translation would be 'retribution'. Also D 47.10.7.1, referring to the criminal action under the *lex Cornelia* and contrasting the Cornelian action with the Aquilian action: 'at in actione iniuriarum de ipsa caede vel veneno ut vindicetur, non ut damnum sarciatur' (In the action of injury the action relates to retribution and not to compensation of the actual loss sustained). Joannes Voet, *The Roman and Roman-Dutch Law of Injuries: A Translation of Book 47, Title 10 (De Injuriis), of Voet's Commentary on the Pandects*, trans Melius De Villiers (Cape Town, Juta, 1899–1915).

[13] Alberico Gentili, *De iure belli libri tres*, vol 1 (Oxford, Oxford University Press and Humphrey Milford, 1933) 481; vol 2 (trans John C Rolfe) 295 [1st edn 1598]. The *solatium* would not normally have been of a pecuniary nature here. For a use reminiscent of D 48.19.28.15 (above n 9), the *solatium* being for the relatives of the wrong's victim, see Samuel Pufendorf, *Elementorum jurisprudentiae universalis libri duo*, vol 2, trans WA Oldfather (Oxford, Oxford University Press and Humphrey Milford, 1933) 201 ('as if it be proper for a man to be slain, not as an example, but to assuage the grief of the murdered man's kinsmen') [1st edn 1660].

[14] Margaret Hewett and Reinhard Zimmermann (trans and ed), *Larva legis Aquiliae: The Mask of the lex Aquilia Torn Off the Action for Damage Done* (Oxford, Hart Publishing, 2000) para 1: 'It is not only equitable but even just that I should make good damage done by accident. It is equitable . . . to give something as a *solatium* (consolation) for their loss of property') [1st edn 1703].

[15] Below n 42.

[16] Below section II.A.

tradition, where the word *solatium* has become of common usage in the modern law to refer to damages for non-patrimonial loss.[17]

B. Uncertainties

One principal argument that this chapter aims to make is that the use of the word *solatium* in respect of *iniuria*, whether in the context of Roman law or the modern *actio iniuriarum* (or, to use the reverse perspective, to characterise the redress of injured feeling in the law of civil wrongs), breeds ambiguity if not confusion. The present section will explore this idea in the context of Roman law (with some references to Roman-Dutch and Roman-Scots law). What adds to the interest of the topic, however, is that the very same difficulties can be seen to surface in the context of modern English law, which difficulties can be directly related to Roman law and Roman legal terminology: this will be explored in the next section.

i. First Ambiguity: Between Compensation and Punishment

The first uncertainty that the term *solatium* fosters is between compensation and punishment as aims of the monetary awarded granted in redress of the wrong suffered under the *actio iniuriarum*. That the Roman law of civil wrongs had what we would call in modern parlance both compensatory and punitive goals is transparent. But these were also markedly intertwined. This should not come as a surprise given that the dichotomy is much less self-evident than modern law, where it has become foundational, generally takes it to be.[18] It is remarkable how many of the words of Latin origin that we use to denote forms of redress in the law of wrongs are defined in terms encompassing ideas of both compensation and punishment (in the modern sense). These words bind the two strands up under a very broad idea of making up for an equilibrium that has been unsettled: commutative justice in its barest form.[19] How could the ideas be expected to be clearly differentiated when the very words we use to think about them are not?

[17] Reinhard Zimmermann, *The Law of Obligations: Roman Foundations of the Civilian Tradition* (Oxford, Oxford University Press, 1996) 1093.

[18] For example, it is possible to consider, and has in fact been argued, that compensation is a form of punishment and vice versa (below n 81).

[19] A few examples taken from the *Oxford English Dictionary* include (the etymology of the word appears first, then terms used to define it):

> 'amends' = fine, penalties/reparation, retribution, restitution, compensation, satisfaction;
> 'compensate' and 'compensation' = to counterbalance/remuneration, amends, recompense;
> 'recompense' = to compensate, make up for/reparation, atonement, satisfaction;
> 'retribute' and 'retribution' = to hand back duly/repayment, recompense, restitution, punishment, redress)

(*OED*, entries for 'amends', 'compensate', 'compensation', 'recompense (n.)', 'recompense (v.)', 'retribute', 'retribution').

Even the word *poena*, from which we derived 'punish', 'punishment', 'penal' and 'penalty', has an etymology which simply refers to an idea of a price to pay as a consequence of one's actions (citing the *OED* entry: '< classical Latin *poena* penalty, punishment, satisfaction, revenge, unpleasant consequence,

This, however, does not mean that attempts could not and were not made at disentangling them. For instance, an important snippet in J 4.3.9 suggests very strongly, in the context of the *lex Aquilia*, that the part of the money award which goes up to the value of the loss (*damnum*) suffered by the claimant is compensatory, while whatever lies in excess of it is punitive.[20] But, in itself, a money award is essentially aim-neutral: it does not tell us what it purposes to achieve. There might naturally be pointers; but, in principle, information will need to be inputted. If the loss is patrimonial, in the untechnical sense of the claimant being 'out of pocket', then the pointers are strong. Thus, if the defendant who destroyed property is required to pay say twice the 'value' of the thing, then – unless some loss distinct from and additional to the damage to property can be identified, and the second helping of damages be regarded as making up for it – the award can plausibly be assumed to be punitive in aim. This is why, independently of the fact that Justinian explicitly tells us so,[21] it is easy to regard the actions on *furtum* or *damnum iniuria*, where damages were openly calculated in such a way that they might (and generally would) exceed the loss suffered, as punitive at least in part.

But what about the *actio iniuriarum*? Whether we say that the claimant's loss is intangible or that there is no loss at all,[22] what is clear is that the wrong – the punching, the clamour raised, the defamatory poem or the stalking in the street[23] – will have no immediate patrimonial consequences[24] and often no tangible consequences at all. Consequently, it is plausible from a modern perspective to see the award of the *poena* as a private punishment visited on the wrongdoer. But then it is also plausible to see the award as making up for – compensating – the non-patrimonial (tangible or intangible) injury suffered. A combination of the two, along the lines of the *actio legis Aquiliae*, is conceivable as well. Different views might be entertained as to whether these hypotheses are equally plausible; but it seems difficult to argue that any is unsustainable, either on first principles or against the background of the sources. The pointers are weak and external input is therefore required.[25] But this is the very thing that the use of the word *solatium*

in post-classical Latin also suffering, affliction (4th cent.) < ancient Greek ποινή blood-money, fine, penalty, satisfaction, reward < the same Indo-European base as Avestan *kaenā* vengeance, reparation and, with a different ablaut grade, Old Church Slavonic *cěna*, Russian *cena*, and Lithuanian *kaina* all in sense "price"'. [*OED* entries for 'penal', 'penalty', 'poena', 'punish', 'punishment']). Lewis and Short define *poena* as 'indemnification, *compensation*, satisfaction, expiation, punishment, penalty' (Lewis and Short (n 1) entry for *poena*; emphasis added).

[20] 'The statutory words "the highest value which the thing had in that year"... is the basis for saying that the statutory action is penal, since a defendant is not liable merely for the loss he has inflicted but sometimes for a much larger sum'. Birks and McLeod (n 7). The alternative reading, that the action is entirely penal because of this feature, is implausible, especially in the light of J 4.1.19(21) and J 4.2 pr.

[21] J 4.3.9 (n 20); J 4.1.19(21).

[22] This important point will be returned to below, n 82.

[23] The examples are taken, of course, from G 3.220.

[24] There might be, to use a modern phrase, some consequential loss of a pecuniary nature (in particular for violations of *corpus*), but this is an altogether distinct issue.

[25] The main pointer is the statement, found in J 4.4.7, that '[t]he valuation of contempts rises and falls according to the victim's social standing and honour'. Birks and McLeod (n 7). It can easily be read

does not do. Like its perhaps closest equivalent 'satisfaction', 'solace' is among the most neutral, hence least informative, words that can be used to describe the redress provided by the law. That the aim of any remedy in a private lawsuit is to make the aggrieved party feel better after than before is almost tautological.[26] The interesting question is how it seeks to achieve that purpose: this is what needs to be unpacked. It could be by aiming to compensate the loss suffered, or by giving the victim the satisfaction of seeing the offender receive his comeuppance, or something else, or a combination of these aims. 'Solace' does not tell us. It acts like a black box, which has an appearance of being informative but in reality is not.

This can be seen most clearly by looking, not at Roman law (where, as mentioned, the word was not utilised in the context of *iniuria*), but at the modern *actio iniuriarum*. Thus, in Scots law, the *solatium* awarded by courts to the successful claimant under *iniuria*, in redress of his wounded feelings, was originally regarded as being entirely penal. Yet, it was effortlessly reinterpreted as being purely compensatory when the time came for legal writers to fit the *actio iniuriarum* into the modern theory of Scots delict law.[27] Again, the South African debate shows how it is quite possible for delict scholars to interpret the same awards made by courts under that heading on a spectrum that goes from an almost exclusively punitive to an almost entirely compensatory reading.[28] The intrinsic normative content of *solatium* is so weak in that respect that all views can legitimately be argued for.

ii. Second Ambiguity: Between Injury to Feelings and Injury to Personality Interests[29]

More important for the present purpose is a second ambiguity that hides behind the use of the word *solatium*. If we accept a modern analytical framework according to which civil wrongs aim to redress the violation of one or more protected interests,[30] – and, given this, there is no reason why *iniuria* cannot prima facie be

either way. Either the money award is larger because the *dignitas* infringed is greater, or because it is a more heinous offence to insult a dignitary than a common man.

[26] We will come back in the next section to the idea of soothed feelings as the general aim of the law of civil wrongs.

[27] Niall Whitty, 'Overview of Rights of Personality in Scots Law' in Niall Whitty and Reinhard Zimmermann (eds), *Rights of Personality in Scots Law: A Comparative Perspective* (Dundee, Dundee University Press, 2009) 147, 217, 236–37.

[28] Johann Neethling, 'Punitive Damages in South Africa' in Helmut Koziol and Vanessa Wilcox (eds), *Punitive Damages: Common Law and Civil Law Perspectives* (New York, Springer, 2009) 123, 131–34.

[29] On the use of the word 'personality', see below section III.A and Eric Descheemaeker, book review of Niall Whitty and Reinhard Zimmermann (eds), *Rights of Personality in Scots Law: A Comparative Perspective*, 73 *Modern Law Review* (2010) 898, 898–900.

[30] On the notion of an interest and the interest-based classification of the law of civil wrongs, see Eric Descheemaeker, *The Division of Wrong* (Oxford, Oxford University Press, 2009) 27–28, 219–24. The redress may be through compensation of loss caused or any other legal response: it is important to keep this question distinct from the one addressed in the previous section.

understood within that framework – then the question immediately arises as to what interest or interests the *actio iniuriarum* aimed to protect. In the context of Roman law (but also of the *usus modernus* of the action), it seems that two answers are possible.

The first one would simply be to say that *iniuria* protected the interest in 'emotional' or 'mental' 'tranquillity' (or 'wellbeing', 'stability', 'calm', 'peace' etc). This seems to follow logically from the above developments on the remedy under the *actio iniuriarum* being a *solatium* for injured feelings. On that reading, wounded feelings are the loss or injury; emotional tranquillity, the corresponding interest; and the monetary award granted as solace, the response of the law – whatever the nature, compensatory, punitive or otherwise of that response.

However, an altogether different answer is suggested by Ulpian in D 47.10.1.2 when he writes, trying (in modern terms) to unpack the *actio iniuriarum* along the lines of protected interests, that

> [o]mnemque iniuriam aut in corpus inferri aut ad dignitatem aut ad infamiam pertinere
>
> [e]very *iniuria* pertains either to *corpus* or to *dignitas* or to *fama*
>
> Every insult pertains to physical integrity or to rank (status) or to reputation.[31]

So, does *iniuria* protect feelings; or does it protect bodily integrity, reputation and dignity (*corpus*, *fama* and *dignitas*); or both? It seems to me that the only possible answer is both, but on two different levels. The former interest we can, for want of a better term, describe as 'internal'. The latter three, on the other hand, are 'external' interests. On that logic, the money award directly redresses the injury to the external interests and thus, indirectly, provides satisfaction for the claimant's feelings that were wounded by the injury. Both are true, but not in the same way. The same phenomenon is being described on two separate levels, which ought not to be mixed and matched.[32] The question of how the two levels relate to one another, and which one is preferable, will be returned to; but one remark that can be made immediately is that the internal level is evidently less informative, because there only is one interest at play to cover the same ground.

When we speak of *solatium*, what happens is that we undo Ulpian's work of serialisation of the loss or injury suffered (into separate injuries to external interests) by jumping back to the internal, indiscriminate tier of feelings. The *solatium* for wounded feelings does not tell us what sort of encroachments on protected (external) interests, having caused wounded feelings, are being redressed. Again, it acts as a black box. It disguises, under an informative-looking word, the fact that an important question has been left unaddressed.

We will come back to these questions in the final part, after the corresponding experience of the English common law has been surveyed.

[31] D 47.10.1.2 (Ulpian, 56 *Ad edictum*); Du Plessis, this volume, ch 7.

[32] Below section III.A.

II. *Solatium* in English Law

A study in modern English law reveals striking echoes to the issues encountered in the previous section, making Roman law a fertile outside vantage point from which to analyse and evaluate the law.

A. Use of the Word in Sources

As with Roman law, it is helpful to start with an examination of the occurrences of the word *solatium* in English law (which will involve a detour through Scots law).[33] Thanks to increasingly exhaustive databases, it is possible to trace the usage of the word in English legal discourse with a good degree of precision, first and foremost the judgments of courts, but also legislation, parliamentary debates and scholarly literature. In English cases concerning the law of England, both the timing and the reason for the appearance of the word can be easily pinpointed: it happened in the 1850s in the context of interpretative debates surrounding the Fatal Accidents Act 1846.[34]

The Act for Compensating the Families of Persons Killed by Accidents of 1846 allowed,[35] for the first time in English law, family members of a person who had died as the direct consequence of a wrong to claim under the Act, in cases where the person would have had a tortious action had they survived. The Act referred to the remedy sought simply as 'damages';[36] and thus the question arose in court as to what these 'damages' encompassed. In particular, did they extend beyond patrimonial loss – loss of the financial support provided by the defunct before his death – to what was termed 'injury to feelings' – the emotional upheaval caused by the death of a close relative? The argument was made by counsel for claimants that the answer should be similarly positive as that of the neighbouring law of Scotland, which had deliberately been excluded from the scope of application of the 1846 Act on account of its already possessing a legal mechanism for carrying

[33] The word does not appear in most English-language law dictionaries of either the present or the past. It it is mentioned in a few, for example *Jowitt's Dictionary* (Daniel Greenberg, *Jowitt's Dictionary of English Law*, 3rd edn (London, Sweet & Maxwell, 2010) entry for *solatium*). *Solatium* is one of these many words or concepts which inhabit the Marches of English law.

[34] The word surfaces in House of Lords decisions on appeal from the Scottish Court of Session before that date (eg *Hughes and Dalrymple-Hamilton v Gordon* (1819) I Bligh 287, 295; 4 ER 109, 113). By the time of the 1846 Act, *solatium* had been part of Scottish legal terminology for a century (see para immediately below). The search on *solatium* was extended to the Anglicised form 'solace', which turned out not to be used at all in the specialised sense(s) of the Latin word.

[35] For the historical background to the Act, see Richard Kidner, 'A History of the Fatal Accident Acts' (1999) 50 *Northern Ireland Legal Quarterly* 318.

[36] An Act for Compensating the Families of Persons killed by Accidents 1846 (9 & 10 Vic c 93). The Act is commonly referred to as the Fatal Accidents Act 1846 or the Lord Campbell's Act (even though it was introduced, not by him, but by Lord Lyttleton. Kidner (n 35) 318, 323–26). In an interesting echo of the Roman *actio iniuriarum*, the action was barred after 'twelve calendar months'.

out the function of redressing third-party losses in the event of wrongful death. Following what had become settled Scottish terminology (on which see immediately below), the award for non-pecuniary loss was termed *solatium*; and thus the term entered the lexicon of English law.

By the time it made its way into English law, *solatium* had been part of the Scottish toolbox for over a century. While the immediate temptation is to link its appearance to the reception into Scots law of the *actio iniuriarum* of Roman law – which undoubtedly happened, if in a disorderly and comparatively tardy fashion – the above remarks should warn us that there is not necessarily a connection between the two. It is in fact to a customary Scots action, upon which the conceptual apparatus of *iniuria* and Roman law was later superimposed, after centuries of independent existence, that the first occurrences of the term have been traced: the action for assythment.[37] Assythment,[38] an institution with no equivalent in either Roman or pre-nineteenth-century English law, provided monetary redress to the relatives of a person who had been killed (or wounded) by the defendant; and this award clearly aimed at assuaging the family's grief as well as any pecuniary loss they might have suffered.[39] It was granted, in the untechnical sense of Roman law, *in solatium*;[40] and this is the sense in which Scots courts pressed the term into service.[41] With the rise of Romanist scholarship, and in particular of the modern *actio iniuriarum* with which the action of assythment came to be linked, the word jumped from assythment to *iniuria*, albeit in a factual scenario in which the Roman action would have provided no redress. The term proved very successful, and gradually its scope of application grew to encompass an entire side of the Roman foundational dichotomy between *damnum iniuria* and *iniuria*.[42] The

[37] The question of the relationship between the action of assythment and the *actio iniuriarum* in Scots law is a difficult one, compounded by definitional uncertainties on both sides. What is undoubted is that the Roman action was gradually interpreted as occupying much, if not all, of the territory of the old customary remedy; and as a result the conceptual apparatus of the two actions underwent reciprocal influences. The best point of entry on this question is DM Walker, 'Solatium' (1950) 62 *Juridical Review* 144, 157–59. Much of the change, Walker remarks, was prompted by the growth of railways, the very same force behind Lord Campbell's Act of 1846.

[38] Stair defined the doctrine as follows: 'the life of any person being taken away, the damage of those who were entertained and maintained by his life, as his wife and children, may be repaired' (cited by Walker (n 37) 149).

[39] *Moodie v Sir James Stuart* (1741) 5 Brown's Supplement (1826) 709 (Court of Session): 'The question here was about the quantity of an assythment, whether it contained only the expenses laid out by the relations of the defunct in the prosecution of his death, together with an aliment to those of his relations who stood in need of being alimented, and whom the defunct would have been obliged to aliment; or whether it did not likewise contain something *in solatium* to the relations for the loss they had sustained. This last the Lords found'. Even though the fact is not spelt out, the 'loss' suffered by the relatives transparently means the emotional loss, contrasted with the patrimonial 'aliment'.

[40] Above nn 6 and 9.

[41] According to Walker (n 38) 161, the first occurrence of the word was in *Moodie* (n 39).

[42] The first usage in legal literature was, according to Blackie, in Bankton's *Institute* 1.10.35. John Blackie, 'Unity in Diversity: The History of Personality Rights in Scots Law', in Whitty and Zimmermann (n 27) 31, 90; *cf* 135 for use of the term in cases of deprivation of liberty. Speaking of 'real injuries', Bankton writes: 'in all cases of injury, full reparation ought to be made to the party aggrieved, and even a consideration given him *in solatium*'. As in *Moodie* above, the reference to injured feelings is transparent even if it is implicit. This might well be the oldest occurrence of the word

distinction between the award of 'damages for injury to property' and '*solatium* for injury to feelings' became most solidly established in the Scots law of delict, and has remained unchallenged to the present day.[43]

Returning south of the Border, the argument of counsel in the 1850s was that, because the new Act provided for an English-style action of assythment, the 'damages' referred to included – against the common's law settled position on the question[44] – a *solatium* for the 'injury to feelings' of the defunct's dependants. The argument was rejected but the word remained. In the first instance, *solatium* took on the same narrow meaning it had had in the context of Scots assythment. The word cannot be said to have enjoyed nearly the same success as it had north of the border, but it did take roots. Although there was no English *actio iniuriarum* to extend its use to, the range of circumstances in which it has been used mirrors at least in part that of the civilian tradition.

Similarly to Roman law, the word *solatium* has been used by English judges with different shades of meaning around the same broad idea of comfort or consolation conveyed by the Latin term. From its original usage, it has retained a close association with the idea of assuagement of wounded feelings, particularly in the context of the wrong-induced death of a relative. This is the one situation in which it has become common to speak of *solatium* or 'solace', if only to deny the availability of a remedy under English law.[45] Beyond this core, other contexts can be identified. From the injury to feelings caused by the death of a family member on which the claimant depended,[46] the use of the term was extended to other types

solatium in the explicit context of the action on *iniuria*. Blackie (p 85) uses a case from 1707 to link the idea of what was then called 'smart money' to Matthaeus, and thus to Roman-Dutch law; but the word *solatium* is not used either in the case or in Matthaeus' *De criminibus* (1644).

[43] See the definition provided by Lord President Clyde in *Duffy v Kinneil*: 'Solatium in the law of Scotland properly means reparation for the pain inflicted on anyone in consequence of the commission of a delict against him. The pain may consist in physical suffering, or it may consist in wounded feelings. But, as a competent element in the assessment of damages, it is in contrast with patrimonial loss. Cases occur in which the element of solatium so greatly preponderates over that of patrimonial loss that it is common to speak of the whole reparation due in them as solatium' (cited by Walker (n 37) 145).

[44] *Baker v Bolton* (1808) 1 Campbell 493, 170 ER 1033. The claimant, who had lost his wife in a coaching accident, sought damages for 'great grief, vexation, and anguish of mind' but also, apparently, economic loss. He lost on both counts on the basis that 'the death of a human being could not be complained of as an injury' (Lord Ellenborough).

[45] eg *Chaplin v Boys* [1971] AC 356, 382: 'The law of England gives no right to solatium in respect of the death of a near relative, as Scots law does' (Lord Guest); Law Commission, *Report on Personal Injury Litigation: Assessment of Damages* (Law Com No 56, 1973) para 100.

[46] Starting the series: *Blake v Midland Railway Co* (1852) 18 QB 93, 108; 118 ER 35, 42 ('This case turns entirely upon the construction of the recent statute, 9 & 10 Vict. c. 93; and the important question is, whether the jury, in giving damages apportioned to the injury resulting from the death of the deceased to the parties for whose benefit the action is brought, are confined to injuries of which a pecuniary estimate may be made, or may add a solatium to those parties in respect of the mental sufferings occasioned by such death?' (Coleridge J)); *Franklin v South Eastern Railway* (1858) 3 H&N 211, 214; 157 ER 448, 450; *Pym v Great Northern Railway* (1863) 4 B&S 396, 401 and 404; 122 ER 508, 511 and 512; *Duckworth v Johnson* (1859) 4 H&N 653, 658; 157 ER 997, 1001.

A modern example of the use of the word in that context is provided by *McLoughlin v O'Brian* [1981] QB 599 (CA) 624: 'We speak of people being grief-stricken, and time being the only healer. Would it really be wise to introduce into this common experience of mankind the possibility of some

of injured feelings,[47] or even injuries to feelings generally.[48] Unsurprisingly, the word came to be linked to the idea of aggravated damages, which themselves have been explicitly analysed as compensating the claimant for the sense of outrage caused by the insulting, humiliating or high-handed manner in which he was wronged.[49] *Solatium* was also pressed into service, using the external perspective this time, in reference to specific rights or interests which have as a common characteristic that the injury caused by their violation is not patrimonial (typically not tangible either) and therefore not susceptible of immediate valuation in money. These include honour,[50] physical injury,[51] reputation,[52] a patient's 'right to choose',[53] privacy,[54] and some – probably non-existent – right to remain in one's familiar environment.[55,56] The link with *iniuria* is evident here: we are dealing with the protection of personality not patrimony.[57] Finally, along rather

monetary solatium for their suffering if they are able to persuade a judge that the suffering is due in part to shock, not grief.' (Griffiths LJ).

[47] eg *Berry v Da Costa* (1865–66) LR 1 CP 331, 333 ('outraged feelings of the mother and family of the plaintiff' consecutive to the breach of a promise of marriage); *Cassell & Co Ltd v Broome* [1972] AC 1027 (HL) 1070–71 (*solatium* for injury to feelings in a defamation action); *Angel v Stainton & Another* [2006] EWHC 637 (QB) [23] ('*solatium* for distress and hurt feelings' in an action for defamation).

[48] *Dunnachie v Kingston-upon-Hull City Council* [2004] UKHL 36, [2004] IRLR 727 [21].

[49] Below, section III.C.ii. For a more recent approval of these views, see *Collins Stewart v The Financial Times* [2005] EWHC 262 (QB), [2006] EMLR 100 [30]: 'It appears to me from those authorities that Mr Browne is right when he says that the defining characteristic of an award of aggravated damages is that its function is to provide a claimant with compensation ('solatium') for injury to his or her feelings caused by some conduct on the part of the defendant or for which the defendant is responsible' (Gray J).

[50] HL Deb 20 May 1856, vol 142, col 410 (Divorce and Matrimonial Causes Bill): 'Another branch of this question that demands particular attention, [sic] is the prosecution for alleged criminal conversation. The husband brings an action against a supposed paramour, to recover damages as a solatium for what is described as his "loss of honour".' (Lord Lyndhurst).

[51] *Lancashire Insurance Company v Commissioners of Inland Revenue* [1899] 1 QB 353, 360: 'Those words surely must mean a sum agreed to be paid as some solatium or recompense for personal injury' (Wills J).

[52] *Uren v John Fairfax & Sons Pty Ltd* (1966) 117 CLR 118, 150 (Windeyer J), approved in *Cassell* (n 47) 1071 (Lord Hailsham LC).

[53] *Chester v Afshar* [2004] UKHL 41, [2005] 1 AC 134 [33] (Lord Hoffmann), [56] (Lord Hope); compare [18] (Lord Steyn: 'the autonomy and dignity of each patient'). Lord Hoffmann's suggestion that the *solatium* should be 'modest', echoed in other cases, is remarkably at odds with the historical roots of the notion: far from evoking aggravated or punitive damages, it links the Romanist idea with nominal damages.

[54] *Mosley v News Group Newspapers* [2008] EWHC 1777 (QB), [2008] EMLR 20 [231]: 'Notwithstanding all this, it has to be accepted that an infringement of privacy cannot ever be effectively compensated by a monetary award. Judges cannot achieve what is, in the nature of things, impossible. That unpalatable fact cannot be mitigated by simply adding a few noughts to the number first thought of. Accordingly, it seems to me that the only realistic course is to select a figure which marks the fact that an unlawful intrusion has taken place while affording some degree of *solatium* to the injured party.' (Eady J).

[55] *Wakeman v Quick Corp* [1999] IRLR 424 (CA): 'any "solatium" for being uprooted from a home environment, friends, schooling etc which would otherwise act as a disincentive to secondees'.

[56] As early as 1819, in an appeal from the Court of Session, the House of Lords had spoken of a *solatium* for the infringement of a right to vote (*Hughes v Gordon* (1819) I Bligh 287, 295; 4 ER 109, 113: '*in solatium* of the detriment arising from the loss of the pursuer's vote and right of electing').

[57] Below section III.A.

different lines, the term *solatium* was used in *Chaplin v Hicks* to denote the award of pecuniary redress (in contract) for what was not yet termed loss of a chance.[58,59]

Legal literature followed a similar pattern. A search on *The Making of Modern Law* reveals that, Scottish literature and references to Scots law in English literature apart, the first occurrence of the word in English legal scholarship was in Addison's *Wrongs and their Remedies* (1860) in the context of the 1846 Act.[60] It was later to be found in respect of the redress of 'wounded feelings' for breach of promise of marriage,[61] of nominal – or perhaps contemptuous – damages in an action for defamation,[62] of the redress of physical injury[63] and of an action for seduction.[64]

B. Uncertainties

The relevant question for the present purpose is how the use of the word *solatium* in the common law relates to the two uncertainties that were mentioned earlier in the context of Roman law. The argument to be made is that both ambiguities have also had a significant, and detrimental, impact on modern English law; and that the use of the word *solatium*, along with its underlying idea of soothing of wounded feelings, has played a key role in this. The primary reason is, as in Roman law, that the concept of *solatium* acts as a black box. This is what the present section will examine.

i. Back to the Second Ambiguity: Between Injury to Feelings and Injury to Personality Interests

Starting with the second of the above ambiguities, that which pertains to injury to feelings ('internal' interest) as opposed to injury to personality rights ('external' interests), an examination of the use of the word in English legal discourse shows transparently that, whenever the perspective of solace for wounded feelings is resorted to, the corresponding external interest is either left unidentified or implicitly regarded as insufficiently secure to ground the award of damages.[65] A comparison between property rights (where the injury is patrimonial hence

58 *Chaplin v Hicks* [1911] 2 KB 786, 794.

59 As to statutes, according to the very extensive database on legislation.gov.uk, no occurrence of the word *solatium* can be found in British primary legislation outside the specific context of Scotland. On the other hand, the Wrongs Act 1936 of South Australia provides an example of the word being taken up in the legislation of other common law jurisdictions (also in the core sense of monetary compensation for the injury to feelings caused by the loss of a parent).

60 Charles G Addison, *Wrongs and their Remedies* (London, Stevens & Son, 1860) 266. Addison was the first English textbook on the law of civil wrongs.

61 Charles MacColla, *Breach of Promise* (London, Pickering, 1879) 28, 55–56.

62 John CH Flood, *A Treatise on the Law concerning Libel and Slander* (London, Maxwell & Son, 1880) 202.

63 Walter Shirley, *Leading Cases Made Easy* (London, Stevens and Sons, 1880) 183.

64 John Indermaur, *Principles of the Common Law*, 2nd edn (London, Stevens & Haynes, 1880) 328.

65 See cases above at nn 46–55.

directly valuable in money, although it may or may not be tangible), physical integrity (where the injury is non-patrimonial but tangible),[66] and those interests other than *corpus* which would have been protected under the Roman *actio iniuriarum* (ie *fama* and *dignitas*, where the injury is both non-patrimonial and intangible)[67] shows that it is primarily with the last class of rights that English law encounters difficulty. Because the interests in question are, to use Melius de Villiers' phrase, perceived as 'purely ethical',[68] and therefore provide an insecure basis from which to derive a legal remedy, the law is tempted to switch over – or back – to a different perspective: namely, the internal perspective of wounded feelings, outrage and *solatium*, which intuitively appears more secure because the loss (or detriment) can be immediately and intuitively apprehended. Even more than *fama*, it is *dignitas* – or perhaps the myriad of as yet unmapped dignitary interests[69] – which constitutes *terra incognita* (or at least *male cognita*) for the law; and it is in respect of these that, as shown above, the notion of *solatium* is being implemented. Consciously or not (and most likely it would be unconscious) the use of the word becomes a way either of deflating the importance of the protected external interest – the suggestion being that it is not its violation that is compensated but the injured feelings of the claimant – or of bypassing the question of its existence and identification altogether.

ii. Back to the First Ambiguity: Between Compensation and Punishment

It was mentioned in the context of Roman law that, because injuries to 'being' are incapable of being immediately valued in money, we need external information to know what aim or aims the monetary award granted to the claimant pursues. On the face of it, we cannot know whether the £100 or £100,000 awarded to the defamed party are meant as compensation for a lost reputation or punish the defendant or some *tertium quid*.[70] Describing it as a solace for the claimant's wounded feelings does not allow us to decide, and thus using the concept of *solatium* structurally perpetuates the ambiguity as to the aim or aims of the award.

By and large, resolving this ambiguity is not a problem that English law has been confronted with because, by the time a self-reflective discourse emerged on the law of civil wrongs, the compensatory aim of money awards granted by courts had assumed an ultra-dominant position. Besides, this predominance straddled

[66] English law has long been happy to compensate what is called, in the context of personal (ie physical or psychiatric) injuries, 'pain and suffering' and 'loss of amenities'. Terminology is highly unstable, and the various heads of losses are often not clearly distinguished, but this appears to be at least in part a form of *solatium* for physical injuries, ie compensation for the wounded feelings caused by the infringement of *corpus*. However, save for one isolated example (above n 51), this is not a word that English law will use in that context. The better view, in my mind, is that this is part of the valuation of the injury to *corpus*. Separating the internal loss from the external would amount to counting the same injury twice (see further section III.C.iii below).

[67] Consequential economic loss is an altogether separate issue.

[68] De Villiers (n 12) 25. Birks spoke of interests that are 'subtle, abstract and elusive'. Peter Birks, 'Harassment and Hubris: The Right to an Equality of Respect' (1997) new ser, 32 *Irish Jurist* 1, 8.

[69] Below, section III.D.

[70] Again, possible consequential economic loss is ignored here.

the old Roman divide between *damnum iniuria* and *iniuria*, ie between injuries to 'having' and injuries to 'being'. We do not have in a modern English context to ask ourselves whether the defamed claimant's substantial money award is (or at least is meant to be) compensatory or punitive or something else, because we assume – and rightly so – that it is compensatory, unless and until we hear reason from the law to believe otherwise.

Yet, it is striking to see something of the Roman ambiguity appearing in the context of English law; and what makes it interesting for our purpose is the way this modern metastasis relates to the Romanist concept of *solatium*. As was mentioned, one principal context in which the word *solatium* and the underlying idea of the assuagement of wounded feelings has been used in English law is within this class of monetary awards that has been variously described as 'exemplary', 'aggravated' or 'punitive',[71] and whose explicit recognition in English law dates from the late eighteenth century.[72] This is a class of damages where, at least on the face of it, the sum awarded did more than compensate for the claimant's loss.[73]

As is well known, these monetary awards were reclassified by Lord Devlin in *Rookes v Barnard* (1964) in a way which is still regarded today as authoritative. Splitting the category in two, Devlin described one sub-class, of a narrow scope, as being truly punitive in nature while another, larger, sub-part was in actual fact compensatory for a further loss suffered by the claimant due to the manner in which the wrong was committed.[74] This loss was identified – using the internal perspective – as the 'mental distress' suffered by the claimant.[75] In turn, Birks argued that the underlying (external) interest protected by the award of such 'aggravated' damages (in the newer and narrower sense of the term) was the right to a 'proper share of respect',[76] which he argued provided the basis for an English-style *actio iniuriarum*. In other words, the greater part of these damages thought of hitherto as 'more than compensatory' was reinterpreted as compensatory on the basis of a wider understanding of loss. As a result, we now have a class of clearly punitive awards and a class of clearly compensatory awards, which is no different in nature from 'ordinary' damages, even though the identification of the loss suffered – or the underlying protected right – undoubtedly remains more

[71] The terminology used also included the phrases 'at large', 'retributory' and 'vindictive': *Cassell* (n 47) 1069 (Lord Hailsham LC citing Halsbury's *Laws of England*).

[72] Harry Street, *Principles of the Law of Damages* (London, Sweet & Maxwell, 1962) 28.

[73] Here, it is difficult to use a terminology which is not question-begging when it comes to the scope of 'loss': below n 81.

[74] *Rookes v Barnard* [1964] UKHL 1; [1964] AC 1129, 1221: 'the manner of committing the wrong may be such as to injure the plaintiff's proper feelings of dignity or pride' (Lord Devlin).

[75] The view that aggravated damages are compensating the claimant for his 'mental distress' (which John Murphy, 'The Nature and Domain of Aggravated Damages' (2010) *Cambridge Law Journal* 353, 355–56 denies was Lord Devlin's view) was endorsed by the Law Commission and also by Professors Burrows and Stevens. Law Commission, *Aggravated, Exemplary and Restitutionary Damages* (Law Com No 247, 1997) para 2.1; Andrew Burrows, *Remedies for Torts and Breach of Contract*, 3rd edn (Oxford, Oxford University Press, 2004) 339; Robert Stevens, *Torts and Rights* (Oxford, Oxford University Press, 2007) 85.

[76] Birks (n 68) 14, a view endorsed among others by Alan Beever, 'The Structure of Aggravated and Exemplary Damages', 23 *Oxford Journal of Legal Studies* (2003) 87, 89 and Murphy (n 75) 358.

troublesome than that of more intuitive, and historically better mapped, types of injuries.

The significant part of the story for the present purpose is the period between the late eighteenth century and 1964. It is absolutely transparent that, as implied by the oft-used label 'punitive', there was in that period an idea that the (apparently) more-than-compensatory award served to punish the wrongdoer for his high-handed conduct.[77] But it is equally clear that there also was an idea of assuaging the claimant's sense of outrage at the way he had been handled.[78] In that sense, aggravated damages closely resemble the Roman *actio iniuriarum*, where, in a similar fashion, both strands were evidently present and so closely intertwined as to be hardly separable. Unsurprisingly perhaps, the idea of solace for wounded feelings showed itself to be as normatively weak in English as in Roman law, straddling anew the divide between compensation and punishment, and breeding fresh ambiguity in that respect. Before 1964, as illustrated by *Knuppfer v London Express Newspapers*, where the word was used by Goddard LJ to describe punitive damages 'old style',[79] *solatium* sat comfortably within a class of monetary awards where the dominant if not exclusive avowed aim was to punish the defendant. After 1964, however, it was effortlessly reclassified as being compensatory (whether the compensation be for wounded feelings, on the internal level, or for the violation of a right to respect, on the external level), as shown by Lord Hailsham LC in *Cassell v Broome*.[80] *Solatium* shows itself again to be too vague and flexible to lack any determinative content about the function or functions it is deemed to serve, thereby perpetuating in English law an ambiguity which had already plagued Roman law two thousand years earlier.[81]

[77] eg *Tullidge v Wade* (1769) 3 Wils KB 18, 19; 95 ER 909, 909.

[78] eg *Benson v Frederick* (1766) 3 Burr 1845, 1846; 97 ER 1130, 1130.

[79] *Knuppfer v London Express Newspapers* [1943] KB 80 (CA) 91.

[80] *Cassell* (n 47) 1073, 1076.

[81] There are two distinct, if related, threads to the argument concerning the relationship between, on the one hand, punishment and compensation and, on the other hand, external interests and internal interest. The argument developed in this section is that the perspective of injured feelings is intrinsically ambiguous as to where the remedy stands on the question of the aim or aims of the award: whether compensation, punishment or other. By contrast, for reasons to be mentioned immediately below, if we move to the perspective of external interests, it becomes much more difficult to bind these aims together and therefore we are naturally drawn to confront the question of what aim(s) the monetary award given in redress of the interest – for example the injury to reputation – serves.

At no point is the argument saying that the perspective of injuries to feelings leads to punishment and that of injuries to external interests to compensation. In principle, these two levels of interest could lead to any response of the law: there could be a compensatory or punitive response to the injury to the external interests, just as well as a compensatory or punitive response to injured feelings. At the same time, it is undeniable that there is a correlation between the two in our perceptions. The link is intuitive: if the injury caused to the defamed person is analysed as an injury to his reputation, possibly coupled with another external interest like his right to an equal share of respect, then a compensatory response seems natural. Punishing the wrongdoer is not going to restore the claimant's reputation or respected position. A punitive answer is possible but it appears immediately implausible. On the other hand, if the injury is characterised, on the internal level, as an injury to feelings, then – while the compensatory answer remains entirely possible – the punitive response acquires an attraction that it previously lacked. Punishing the wrongdoer is an immediately plausible way of making the claimant feel better. The punishment becomes the reparation. At the same time as it ties together punishment

III. Disease and Illness in the Law of Wrongs

The main point that appears from the above examination of Roman and English law is that these two great legal systems have both experienced difficulties of a similar nature concerning the way their law of civil wrongs understands – to use a loose phrase – the protection of 'being', as contradistinguished from the protection of 'having'. That injuries to personhood can be equally wrongful as injuries to wealth does not seem to have been ever doubted by either system; but whether they amount to loss,[82] and either way what the response of the law should be, has

and reparation, the internal perspective of feelings leads the law away from the latter and towards the former. By contrast, the perspective of external interests, by removing the – imperfect and ambiguous, but intuitive – assimilation of reparation with punishment, both forces the law to make an explicit choice and pulls it, away from punishment, towards compensation.

[82] This question has proved consistently troublesome. The root of the problem lies in the difficulty of regarding an injury to feelings (internal level), or injuries to *fama*, *dignitas* and – to a lesser extent – *corpus* (external level) as real losses. These seem too intangible and abstract: in what sense are the lady who was followed about in the streets by her suitor, or the man against whom a clamour was raised, or even who was slapped in the face, 'worse off' after the wrong than before? The Romans organised their law of civil wrongs around a fundamental, and intuitive, divide between *damnum iniuria* and *iniuria*, 'wrongful loss' and 'insult'. What we would regard today as a distinction between essentially patrimonial and non-patrimonial loss, they appear to have seen as a distinction between loss and non-loss. *Damnum* concerned the economic consequences of damage; it was by nature patrimonial. David Daube, 'On the Use of the Term *damnum*' in *Studi in onore di Siro Solazzi* (Naples, 1948) 93, repr in David Daube, *Collected Studies in Roman Law*, vol 1, ed David Cohen and Dieter Simon (Frankfurt am Main, Vittorio Klostermann, 1991) 279; *cf* Birks (n 68) 8. Injuries to being caused no immediate *damnum* (although they might cause consequential patrimonial loss). They were obviously still wrongful – otherwise the law would not have stepped in – and might be regarded as no less or even more serious; but they were fundamentally distinct: there is loss (= patrimonial loss) on the one hand and insult on the other. The Romans did not press into service any specific word to designate non-patrimonial loss, the counterpart of *damnum* on the other side of the having/being divide. This, however, does not mean that it did not implicitly exist underneath the concept of insult. Given the way the monetary award under the *actio iniuriarum* was calculated, there would have been no need to bring out.

Even though the line was blurred from the very beginning by the fact that whatever redress was given would boil down to a money award, the divide is deep and runs through history. What we first see when we turn to English law is that, by and large, it has always been happy to extend money awards to the redress of losses which are not financial or, to use the terminology typically employed, 'special'. Thus, Ibbetson describes how, from the origins, the notion of loss inherent in the actions of trespass was broad enough to encompass physical injury or verbal insults (David Ibbetson, *A Historical Introduction to the Law of Obligations* (Oxford, Oxford University Press, 1999) 14–15). Yet the old Roman divide between *damnum* and insult can be seen to resurface time and again throughout history, an idea of dishonour being brought up to be contrasted with loss, even loss so broadly understood in the first place (see Frederick Pollock and Frederic William Maitland, *The History of English Law*, vol 2 (Cambridge, Cambridge University Press, 1968) 537–38: 'Shame was keenly felt. In almost every action before an English court of the thirtieth century the plaintiff will claim compensation, not only for the damage (*damnum*) but also for the shame (*huntage, hontage, dedecus, pudor, vituperium*)'; *cf* in modern law the contrast drawn in *Emblen v Myers* (1860) 6 H&N 54, 59; 158 ER 23, 25 between 'insult' and 'actual loss' or 'injury': 'As soon as it is admitted that the plaintiff may recover more than the actual loss . . . that principle applies . . . Suppose a person caused a nuisance in front of another's man house, damages might be given for the insult as well as the actual injury' (Bramwell J)).

Still today, the line between loss and what we call 'special' loss – which is essentially financial, even though the boundaries of the category are unclear – is so thin as to be routinely crossed. Even

been a cause a perennial difficulties. It was illustrated how, in both systems, the word *solatium* and the underlying idea of assuagement of wounded feelings have played key roles in the institutionalisation of these difficulties by creating a convenient legal black hole. In this final section, the study in words across the two systems is used as a springboard towards more general remarks concerning the redress of emotional distress and the structure of the law of wrongs. This extension and generalisation is done in the context of the English law of wrongs; but the ideas developed have at least prima facie wider applicability.

A. Two Levels of Protection

As was seen, a principal dichotomy that underpins the law of wrongs in both systems is that between 'having' and 'being', between personhood and wealth, between personality rights and property rights and (at least in Roman law and the civilian tradition) between the *actio legis Aquiliae* and the *actio iniuriarum*.[83] *Solatium*, as was noted, (a) was and is being used, almost invariably, in the context of the protection of 'being' not 'having'; and (b) adopts an internal not external approach to the consequences of a wrong: it is concerned with the disruption of the emotional wellbeing caused by the injury, the assault, or the insult.[84] This can be contrasted with an external approach, which concerns itself with the individual's rights, the sphere of legal protection created around him by the law.[85] The latter approach was brought to the fore in the early modern period by writers such as Donellus and Grotius, but it was already implicit – and to some extent explicit – in Roman law. In the context of the *actio legis Aquiliae*, it is what the law clearly focused on: the violation of the claimant's proprietary right in his thing (*res*), and the way this injury would be valued by the legal system. (As noted, the action had according to its own rhetoric – at least by Justinian's time – both compensatory and punitive aims, and the valuation did not purport necessarily to reflect the value of the *damnum*; but this is an entirely separate issue).

very senior judges will happily describe a wrong actionable without proof of special loss as a wrong actionable without proof of loss *simpliciter* (eg *Watkins v Secretary of State for the Home Department* [2006] UKHL 17, [2006] 2 AC 395 [41], [45], [47] (Lord Rodger); *Watkins v Secretary of State for the Home Department* [2004] EWCA Civ 966, [2005] QB 883 [67] (Laws LJ)). Birks seems to have been after a similar distinction when he argued that mental distress constituted 'harm' but not 'loss' (Birks (n 68) 30 n 82): even though neither term is defined, the strong suggestion is that loss is restricted to *damnum*, ie patrimonial loss. In turn, this forced Birks to turn to punishment to justify the award of money damages when harm which is not loss has been caused.

[83] In order not to be distracted by endless definitional difficulties which are not relevant in this context, I will take these four pairs to be expressions of the same basic and essentially intuitive divide.

[84] The words 'assault' and 'insult' have a remarkably similar etymology. To 'insult' is to jump or leap (*saltare*) in, while to 'assault' is to jump towards (*OED*, entries for 'assault', 'insult'). In both cases, the idea is that of a forcible attack against a territory or, in the present context, person.

[85] For a very brief overview of historical developments around the notion of an interest, see Eric Descheemaeker, 'Protecting Reputation: Defamation and Negligence' (2009) 29 *Oxford Journal of Legal Studies* 603, 606–8.

These two perspectives, internal as far as *iniuria* is concerned, and external in the case of loss wrongfully caused,[86] are summarised in Figure 1:

		'HAVING'		'BEING'
internal level				*solatium* for wounded feelings
				⇧
wrong		*DAMNUM INIURIA*		*INIURIA*
		⇩		
external level		property (= patrimonial) rights		

Figure 1

The basic but important point that the final section of this chapter aims to make is that this approach is illogical. There is no reason why the law should jump from one level to the other, from one perspective to another, when it crosses the line between the protection of 'having' and that of 'being'. While it is easy to understand why it would be tempted to do so, the fact of the matter is that both approaches can be applied across the board. A principled choice needs to be made between them, and then applied to the entire law of wrongs.

It had already been pointed out that it is quite possible to approach the protection of personhood in terms of external rights. This is what Ulpian did when he described the interests protected by the *actio iniuriarum* as *corpus*, *fama* and *dignitas*.[87] In the civilian tradition as well as the common law, later legal developments in the field of what we would now call 'personality rights' have attempted to map out and explore these interests, along with the legal consequences that their violation should lead to.[88]

[86] Or 'loss and unlawful injury', as Alan Rodger translated it (Alan Rodger, 'What Did *damnum iniuria* Actually Mean?' in Andrew Burrows and Alan Rodger (eds), *Mapping the Law: Essays in Memory of Peter Birks* (Oxford, Oxford University Press, 2006) 421, 437.

[87] Above n 31. This is why Buckland and McNair were wrong to draw a – false – dichotomy between the two when, contrasting the Roman law of *iniuria* with the common law of defamation, they argued that 'the basis of the liability is different. It rests not on loss of reputation but on outrage to the feelings (William W Buckland and Arnold D McNair, *Roman Law and Common Law: A Comparison in Outline* 2nd edn (Cambridge, Cambridge University Press, 1965) 380).

[88] Descheemaeker and Scott, this volume, ch 1.

Figure 2 shows the unravelling of the protection of 'being' on the level of external interests:

		'HAVING'		'BEING'
internal level				*solatium* for wounded feelings
				⇧
wrong		*DAMNUM INIURIA*		*INIURIA*
		⇩		⇩
external level		property rights		personality rights (*corpus*, *fama*, *dignitas*)

Figure 2

What has not yet been mentioned, and might be less intuitive, is that it is also possible to approach the protection of 'having' in terms of internal interests. The reason is that, in the final analysis, the violation of all protected, external interests – including property rights – boils down to an injury to emotional wellbeing, ie to injured feelings. The translation process might be more or less direct; but by reason of our human nature the point where the chain ends is always the same.

It is true, of course, of these rights that we straightforwardly describe as personality rights, like reputation or dignity. If you are defamed, or your privacy is violated, you – normally – feel terrible about it. You feel embarrassed, ashamed, outraged, humiliated, grieved, hurt, violated; your mind is in turmoil. To put it in the mundane language of the law, which might not do justice to the possible depth of the experience, your feelings are injured; you are mentally distressed; your emotional wellbeing is violated. The word 'normally' reflects the fact that this is what will typically happen. Of course, it is possible that you might not have been aware at the time that a wrong was being committed, or that it is in your temperament to care very little, or not at all, about what others know or think of you. This discrepancy is ordinarily ignored by the law.[89] Subject to this irritant, the link between the violation of

[89] Occasionally, a 'subjective' assessment is carried out, for example in respect of what is called 'pain and suffering' in the context of personal injuries (Burrows (n 75) 272; above n 66) to the effect that, in particular, no award will be made if the claimant is unable to feel any pain. There does not seem to be any principled reason while this should be the case when, for instance, damages for 'loss of amenities' are assessed objectively. This simply appears to be a consequence of a switch of approaches between the external and the internal level whenever an – ill-defined – line is crossed (see also Burrows (n 75) 30–31; below section III.B.iii esp n 103).

the external interest – reputation or dignity – and the disruption of the inner tranquillity is fairly obvious, because the chain is a short one.

But the same is true of the violation of an interest like physical integrity (which was also covered by the *actio iniuriarum* but which we tend to cut off from the list of personality rights and treat as a law unto itself, probably because there is something tangible to hold to). A slap in the face, a broken leg, a chopped arm or any perceptible sickness will also – normally – cause emotional distress. More importantly, despite a longer chain, it is also true of injuries to 'having' which, to simplify, we can describe as violations of property (or patrimonial) rights. To take one example, your car is damaged, or destroyed. Your property right in it has been encroached upon, reducing or taking away its value. What do you feel? The answer is the same: emotional distress – ordinarily. It might be rather direct a chain, because you cared in a particular way about the thing; or it might be less direct, because it fulfilled a function which it no longer does, and this affects your emotional wellbeing – you can no longer go to a family event, or only at the cost of much greater hassle; or because it costs you money to repair or replace the thing, and this in turn will stop you from using your assets in the way you wanted, which again will affect your emotional wellbeing in a more or less direct fashion. Whatever the length of the chain, the subjective syndrome of the violation of the protected interest is always the same: emotional distress. You feel bad: a little bad, very bad, awful. The loss might be that of a loved one, of an arm, of your psychiatric integrity, freedom of movement, car, job, autonomy or savings: in the final analysis, the loss suffered is always emotional. The quantum of the loss will naturally vary, and perhaps its properties as well; but its nature remains the same. Arguably, it is precisely because we – normally – feel terrible about the violation of any of these interests that we consider ourselves wronged when they are violated and that we will want the law to intervene to protect them.

As perhaps surprising, or even provocative, as the argument might sound at first sight – for we do not like to think of the death of a parent and a scratch to our car as being losses of a remotely similar nature[90] – it should not in fact come as a surprise. It stems directly from human nature. There is no need to make any deep inquiry into the nature of humankind to say that we are a stream of consciousness.[91] Any injury that we experience is bound to translate into an unpleasant disruption of that stream.[92] If it was not a disruption we would not experience it,

[90] The paradox here is that it is the former which has historically had a tendency not to be compensated at all, on the basis of its being either too great or incapable by nature of being redressed.

[91] Again, a discrepancy may arise. We can lose our consciousness and few would argue that we lose our humanity when this happens. So we can be human without being conscious. Naturally, on a purely internal approach, there should be no redress in such a case. But if we carry out the process of 'externalisation' of the injury to feelings into protected interests, whose violation can be observed and assessed from the outside, then lack of consciousness should not matter any more – provided the law is still willing in principle to hear an action on behalf of the person – than the fact the claimant actually happened to feel no grief at the destruction of his car.

[92] This is why the contrast drawn by Roscoe Pound between 'the immunity of the body from direct and indirect injury' and 'the immunity of the mind and the nervous system from direct and indirect injury' is a false dichotomy. Injuries to physical integrity, as to any other external interest, will translate

and presumably there is no reason why the law would then take an interest in it. If it was not unpleasant, we would not characterise it as an injury for which we would seek redress.

Figure 3 completes the picture on the level of the internal interest in emotional wellbeing:

		'HAVING'		'BEING'
internal level		*solatium* for wounded feelings	⇔	*solatium* for wounded feelings
		⇧		⇧
wrong		*DAMNUM INIURIA*		*INIURIA*
		⇩		⇩
external level		property rights	⇔	personality rights (*corpus, fama, dignitas*)

Figure 3

What appears from Figure 3 is that we have two levels of inquiry, which both cut across the whole spectrum of the law of civil wrongs. They are both coherent, although not perhaps equally so. What is incoherent is to jump from one level to the other between one side of the law of wrongs and the other. The use of the word *solatium* is doubly problematic, not simply, as we have seen, because it hides the underlying interests, but because it does so over only a part of the spectrum, as if there was something specific about the sphere to which it is applies – whether the protection of being in general or a narrower segment – which made it appropriate, or even necessary, to think in terms of a different analytical framework. In reality, the whole of the law of civil wrongs provides a *solatium* for wounded feelings caused by the violation of an external interest. There might be a difference of degree between the protection of 'having' and that of 'being', but there is no difference of nature.[93]

into an injury to the 'mind and nervous system' (Roscoe Pound, 'Interests of Personality' (1914–15) 28 *Harvard Law Review* 343 and 445, 356; *cf* Peter Handford, *Mullany and Handford's Tort Liability for Psychiatric Damage*, 2nd edn (Sydney, Lawbook Co, 2006) 73.

[93] This argument does not appear to have been made before, although it does have a fascinating forerunner in Thomasius' early remark in the context of the *lex Aquilia* (n 14). Burrows suggested that 'ultimately all non-pecuniary loss is concerned with the claimant's distress or loss of happiness', going beyond the residual categories directly identified as such, but remaining on the 'being' side of the law.

B. The Parallel with Clinical Medicine

A comparison with clinical medicine helps illustrate this point. One principal way in which sickness is analysed by medical science is by drawing a distinction between 'illness' and 'disease'. In the particular sense in which the words are pressed into service when this dichotomy is drawn, a disease refers to a pathological transformation of the body, and an illness to the patient's experience of a process that he finds detrimental. Disease is a matter of physics and chemistry, while illness is a matter of perceptions.[94] What clinical medicine is interested in is diseases: even in the field of psychiatry, where the pathological transformation directly affects the brain and thus is closest to perceptions, what distinguishes medical from non-medical approaches to the condition (like psychotherapy) is that they regard it as a biological matter capable of being dealt with through the ordinary means of transforming the body, like drugs or surgery.

Injury to feelings is to the violation of external rights as illness is to disease. It is uniquely internal (to the stream of consciousness constituting the claimant-patient's perceptions) and is standing on its own, to be contrasted with the potentially myriad of rights constituting the claimant's sphere of legal protection, which can be encroached upon in the same way as diseases deteriorate the patient's tissues.

C. Three Questions

The analogy with clinical medicine can be helpfully pressed further to address three questions raised by the distinction drawn between injury to feelings on an internal level and protected interests on an external level, namely: (1) What difference does it make to use one approach rather than the other?; (2) Which should be favoured?; (3) Why does it have to be either one or the other?

i. The Difference

Illness and disease ordinarily coincide. A patient experiences a negative disruption of his stream of consciousness because of some pathological transformation in his body. Illness and disease are two facets of the same reality: the patient is ill because diseased; being diseased he feels ill. However, it is possible to be diseased without being ill or ill without being diseased.[95] In the same way, it is possible to suffer an injury to one's protected interests without being injured in one's feelings and vice versa; but ordinarily the two will co-exist.

Burrows (n 75) 31; *cf* Law Commission, *Aggravated, Exemplary and Restitutionary Damages* (Law Com CP No 132, 1993) 20.

[94] David Jennings, 'The Confusion between Disease and Illness in Clinical Medicine' (1986) 135 *Canadian Medical Association Journal* 865, 866.

[95] ibid. The latter limb might be a matter of controversy but this need not concern us here. In the field of law, one can clearly feel terrible without having had any protected interest wrongfully violated.

Possible differences in the redress provided by the law on either approach could pertain either to the availability of monetary redress in the first place or, if such redress is granted, to the quantum of damages. The latter point will be returned to below. As to the former, the difference between both approaches will not be so great as one might assume at first because the internal approach is always, if implicitly, dependent on the external level. No-one would suggest that any behaviour which distresses another should even prima facie give rise to liability. Sooner rather than later the enquiry into whether it should is bound to hit upon notions of protected interests and wrongfulness (though these might be disguised under very broad labels like an idea of the behaviour being '*contra bonos mores*', ie against prevailing standards). Only violations of such protected 'goods', and only such violations that are characterised as wrongful, will give rise to redress.

In spite of this, it is easy to think of a number of typical situations where the difference in approach will lead to a principled difference when it comes to the very availability of damages. The case of juridical persons, who obviously do not have feelings but own such rights as a right to reputation, is an obvious example.[96] Birks' example of *Fan Club Two*, a factual variation of *Kaye v Robertson* where the would-be claimant (in whose name the action is brought) is permanently unconscious,[97] is another one.

ii. The Choice

It seems entirely obvious that the external approach should be favoured. Just as clinical medicine is interested in pathological processes which can be observed, rather than the patients' perception thereof, so the law should be concerned with protected rights, not the claimant's disposition as to their violation. Because there is unlikely to be any serious disagreement on this, it is not necessary to mount a systematic defence. The most important reason is likely to be the sheer degree of arbitrariness and unaccountability that would be bred by any general attempt to compensate injured feelings directly. Not only does the category act as a black box for all manner of considerations, worthy of consideration or not; it also seems to be so dependent on the individual claimant's idiosyncrasies as seriously to endanger our sense of both justice and legal certainty. As we try to objectify and stabilise the quantum of damages, we are almost bound to fall back on the external level of enquiry. (This, however, is not to deny that both levels will lead to a degree of arbitrariness: no-one can deduce from observation how much an injured reputation is worth, no more than injured feelings. For the same reason, it is impossible to say whether an internal approach would ordinarily yield greater or smaller awards.[98] But it seems clear that it is only on an external approach, where the vio-

[96] This issue is explored in Eric Descheemaeker, 'Three Keys to Defamation: *Media 24* in a Comparative Perspective' (forthcoming) *South African Law Journal*, section 'A Juridical Person's Title to Sue in Defamation'.

[97] Birks (n 68) 6–7. The reference is to *Kaye v Robertson* [1991] FSR 62 (CA).

[98] Subject to what was explained in n 81 above.

lation of the interests is considered in itself, based on observable circumstances rather than subjective implications, that we can hope to achieve consistency – and therefore accountability – in the quantum of awards.)

The external approach is evidently preferable, and is in fact the approach that the modern law has favoured. What it entails, if we want to follow it consistently, is that there should never be any direct attempt to compensate wounded feelings. To the (limited) extent that modern English law does that, it should abandon this approach. The key word here is 'direct'. The point is emphatically not that the law of wrongs should not care about grief, pain, suffering, distress, humiliation, anxiety or the like.[99] It is not that these things do not matter. In a sense, quite the opposite: what this chapter has tried to argue is that they are the only type of loss which, ultimately, individuals can *suffer*. It is because the law of wrongs is concerned through and through with emotional loss that it should never care directly about it. The way in which the law has historically (and rightly) decided to address it, by and large, is by compensating – or, generally, redressing – it indirectly, through the valuation of the external rights whose violation led to the inner turmoil. It is the sum of these which provides the claimant's *solatium* for all the losses he has suffered. Just as medicine seeks to alleviate pain by operating on the bone, removing the tumour or dealing with the underlying mental disorder, so the law should address emotional distress on the level of its external causes not internal manifestations.[100,101]

When we reintroduce an idea of emotional loss as a distinct category of loss alongside such other classes as physical injury or damage to property, we bring distortion into the law. For, either we compensate something that is not worthy of compensation because there is no underlying right protected by the law, or we short-circuit the redress of that right in a way which, at best, duplicates the analysis in terms of protected interests.

[99] An interesting attempt at classifying 'unpleasant' emotions is provided by Handford (n 92) 56–57, who divides them into seven categories: '1. Fear or apprehension. 2. Horror. 3. Grief, sorrow and loneliness. 4. Shame, humiliation and embarrassment. 5. Anger, annoyance and vexation. 6. Disappointment and frustration. 7. Worry and anxiety'.

[100] The analogy can be pressed further to make two additional points. One is that we – rightly – seek to remove the tumour even if the patient has no negative perception of it. The law should likewise aim to redress injuries independently of their perception. This is the reverse side of its refusal to redress a subjective sense of having been wronged when no right has in fact been infringed. The second point is that, even if we have drugs which allow the patient not to feel at all the pain of the broken bone and to walk normally, it is obviously better to remove the pain indirectly by dealing with the fracture. In the same way, emotional distress is better compensated indirectly even if it is possible to compensate it directly.

[101] An important question that is in need of further consideration is the relationship between injury to feelings and physical injury. To what extent a disruption of emotional wellbeing does or does not have any physical underpinning, at what point any possible disruption can be described as pathological and therefore injurious, and how this relates to the protection of *corpus* are all difficult questions. If the distinction between psychiatric injuries and 'mere distress' ties in with the line separating injuries to *corpus* from non-injuries, then psychiatric integrity can be regarded as an 'external' interest capable of direct redress if it is infringed; and the present chapter would have no impact on the way they are currently dealt with by the law.

iii. The Alternative

The most difficult question is the third one. Why does emotional wellbeing have to sit on its own rather than – as would ordinarily be the case when the question is considered in the literature – be added to the list of interests protected by the law of wrongs?[102] The reason is that, if it was, we would start counting every injury twice, once as a disease and a second time as an illness. This chapter has focused on the illogicality of looking at injuries-sicknesses now as a disease and now as an illness. Examining them all from both perspectives would not be illogical in that sense, but it would lead to over-compensation (or redress) – at least on the basis of our current understanding of redressable loss – as the law addresses each injury twice.[103] While it would not be unintelligible to do so, it would need to be done

[102] Examples include Calvert Magruder, 'Mental Disturbance in Tort' (1936) 49 *Harvard Law Review* 1033, 1055 (speaking of an 'interest in mental and emotional peace' standing alongside the 'interest in reputation'; JW Wade, 'Tort Liability for Abusive and Insulting Language' (1950–51) 4 *Vanderbilt Law Review* 63, 92 (speaking of a 'new legally protected right, the right to emotional equanimity and freedom from mental disturbance'); Johann Neethling and others, *Neethling's Law of Personality* (London, Butterworths, 1996) 219 (arguing that a 'right to feelings' ought to be 'appreciated fully and thus protected'); Harvey McGregor, *McGregor on Damages*, 18th edn (London, Thomson Reuters, 2009) listing, in the context of defamation, 'injury to feelings' alongside 'injury to reputation' and other as heads of damages apart from 'special damage'; MA Jones and others, *Clerk & Lindsell on Torts*, 20th edn (London, Thomson Reuters, 2010) paras 1–30 (listing 'distress' among the 'personal interests' 'protected by the law of torts'). Using the reverse perspective of damages, Burrows (n 75) puzzlingly divides non-pecuniary loss into, on the one hand, 'loss of reputation' and 'personal injury losses' (using the external perspective) and, on the other hand, 'mental distress or physical inconvenience' (using the internal perspective). To a large extent, the latter perspective is used to deal with infringements of 'being' (personality rights) other than the well-established heads of *corpus* and *fama*.

On the other hand, rare suggestions that the redress of mental distress has to be regarded as alternative to that of protected (external) interests can be found in AI Ogus, 'Damages for Lost Amenities: for a Foot, a Feeling or a Function?' (1972) 35 *Modern Law Review* 1, 2–3 (contrasting a 'conceptual approach' – 'so much for a foot' and a 'personal approach' – 'so much for a feeling'); Whitty (n 27) 207 (who explains that 'an award of solatium for affront is traditionally explained as compensation for wounded feelings' but that 'it may be better understood as compensation for the infringement *per se*', adding that the latter view would be a 'novel' theory) and Denise G Réaume, 'Indignities: Making a Place for Dignity in Modern Legal Thought' (2002–03) 28 *Queen's Law Journal* 61, 74–75, 90.

[103] It is extremely difficult to assess to what extent this double-counting is happening in actuality because courts, even in the post-jury age, rarely itemise heads of loss with sufficient precision. Even if they do, it is impossible to know whether they do not award more or less to a claimant depending on how affected he appears to be on a personal level (it is difficult not to suspect that they take this factor into account). It is undeniable that courts do award damages for mental distress in a number of torts as well as statutory schemes of civil liability, either explicitly under that head or as 'aggravated damages' (Burrows (n 75) 334ff). Whether this is double-counting is nigh impossible to determine since, in order to do so, one would need to value the sum awarded for each external interest – keeping in mind that it might remain implicit or unidentified, as in the case of aggravated damages – and then see whether anything has been awarded on top of that, which cannot be linked to any interest protected (whether explicitly or implicitly) but is still part of a compensatory response of the law – as opposed to, for example, punitive. This would be the element of 'double-counting'. It seems clear that in the majority of cases, what is happening is not double-counting but a switch from an external to an internal perspective, the compensation of injured feelings acting as indirect redress for the infringed protected interest (compare n 89 above). Thus, the problem with the practice of courts is not so much overcompensation as it inconsistency between heads of wrongdoing as to whether, and if so how, they grant such damages (when, as has been said, all wrongs will in the final analysis – normally – cause emotional loss). The inconsistency also lies in the way courts relate the monetary award to the external interests which the cause of action is openly meant to protect (if any).

consistently, which has never been the case; and it would also entail a radical transformation of the law of wrongs. No-one appears to have ever suggested that we should go down this road. From Roman times the internal and external approaches have been regarded, if implicitly, as alternatives. Save for occasional overlaps, the law – rightly – considers the injury-sickness either as a disease or an illness. Thus, when Ulpian tried to unravel the interest protected by *iniuria*, he did not add emotional tranquillity to physical integrity, reputation and dignity. He saw that 'vindication' of *corpus*, *fama* and *dignitas* was the way in which a *solatium* (as later writers would characterise the monetary award) was provided to the claimant. The two operate on different levels.[104] The principal reason why mental distress is so difficult to analyse is because, in reality, and although this is not acknowledged, we use it as a residual category for such emotional losses which have not already been dealt with under established heads of injuries. The law should consistently be interested in legal sicknesses either as legal diseases or legal illnesses, but not both. Because only the former approach is arguably sustainable, the perspective of illness must be abandoned altogether.

D. Exploring Unmapped Interests

If this is true, then why is the perspective of injured feelings, along which the concept of *solatium* (which is used to name a segment of this category) still used? The answer, as alluded to above, is simply that it is easier. Pain, under whatever guise, might not be tangible; but it is certainly very real and thus provides a ready-made peg for any remedy: we are in no doubt that we suffer, and we naturally empathise with others whose suffering is impossible to deny. On the other hand, the perspective of protected interests can run into identification difficulties, especially within the ill-mapped dignitary segment of the Ulpianic triad. The temptation is then strong to 'jump back' to the level of perceptions.

Indeed, there is no consensus on the taxonomy of interests which the law of wrongs seeks to protect – a question that is much more commonly ignored than addressed. If we adopt the Roman classification as a starting point,[105] it is clear that what Ulpian calls *dignitas* is the most troublesome one. Few people would want to deny that it is or ought to be given at least a degree of legal protection; but beyond this there is virtually no agreement as to the scope of that protection. In

[104] Birks drew a different, but parallel, distinction in the context of *iniuria*, contrasting 'distress arising from injured feelings or injured self-esteem' as the typical loss suffered (he uses the word 'harm') with the 'right to one's fair share of respect' as the protected interest. Birks (n 68) 12–13.

[105] An intriguing question is to what extent we could come up with a new classification from scratch. It is remarkable how different eg John Finnis' list of 'basic goods' appears. John Finnis, *Natural Law and Natural Rights*, 2nd edn (Oxford, Oxford University Press, 2011) 86–90: 'life', 'knowledge', 'play', 'aesthetic experience', 'sociability (friendship)', 'practical reasonableness' and '"religion"' [original inverted commas].) There are also some 'goods' which seem to be well-qualified candidates for protection as legal interests yet never appear to have been given consideration, like time. At any rate, if we want to avoid turning the exercise in gradual improvement of the law into an exercise in law-fiction, we have no choice but to start with what has been bequeathed to us and is commonly accepted.

fact, there is no agreement as to what the word even means. In a Roman context, *dignitas* very much meant rank or status.[106] Individuals were endowed with different degrees of *dignitas*, and the delict *iniuria* could be said to have had at its core the disruption of this hierarchy: *iniuria* was committed whenever the defendant wilfully raised himself above, or brought the claimant below, the status granted to either of them by society. In that sense, as some writers have remarked, *dignitas* could be seen as the one overarching interest protected by the *actio iniuriarum*; and the *dignitas* of the Ulpianic triad as a residual category: *dignitas* in the wider sense minus *corpus* and *fama*.[107]

In modern societies where we are deeply committed – at least idealistically – to the equal intrinsic worth of all human beings, the idea of dignity has assumed a very different meaning; yet the Roman perspective remains useful. If we are all equal in this intrinsic worth which we still call dignity, two things follow. The first one is that the wrong is no longer relational: what matters is to have demeaned the plaintiff, independently of the defendant's own position. The second is that 'dignity' has assumed a meaning akin to 'humanity'. This raises more problems than it solves. One is the sheer uncertainty of the term: it is difficult to find a label which can be more readily used to justify any position and its opposite than our modern 'dignity'. The second is the position of the right to dignity on the map of protected interests. If dignity is common humanity, it seems that it is the entirety of the law, including the law of wrongs, which should be geared at protecting it – albeit typically in an indirect way. So what we are tempted to call 'dignity' would, like Ulpian's *dignitas*, be a residual category. It is unclear that it has any unity in that residual form. If not, then we need to bypass the unhelpful label and continue the work of identification of dignitary interests, or sub-interests, which can be aligned with the likes of *corpus* and *fama*. Privacy seems to be the only candidate currently having a sufficient degree of recognition. Beyond this are as yet unchartered waters.[108] Self-esteem,

[106] Descheemaeker and Scott, this volume ch 1, pp 16, 19.

[107] Descheemaeker and Scott, this volume ch 1, p 13.

[108] Neither the existence nor the scope of these rights, or the level of generality at which they should be pitched, is widely agreed upon. Compare for example the list drawn by Niall Whitty (n 27) 147–48: 'right to life', 'rights to bodily integrity and to personal security', 'right to physical liberty', 'right to honour and reputation'; 'right to dignity (in the narrow sense)', 'right to privacy', 'right to informational privacy', 'right to identity or image', 'right to publicity', 'moral right to copyright', 'right to autonomy' (with a question mark), 'personality rights in family relationships' (the author adds a final section on 'personality rights after death') – with that of Neethling (n 102) vii–viii: 'right to body (and right to life)', 'right to physical liberty', 'right to good name (reputation)', 'right to dignity or honour', 'right to feelings', 'right to privacy', 'right to identity'. In a French context, Jean Carbonnier mentioned five '*droits de la personnalité*'. Jean Carbonnier, *Droit civil*, vol 1, rev edn (Paris, Presses universitaires de France, 2004) para 274: '*droit à la vie*' (right to life), '*droit au nom*' (right to one's name), '*droit à la propre image*' (right to one's own image), '*droit à l'honneur*' (right to honour) and '*droit à la dignité*' (right to dignity). '*Le respect de la vie privée*' (respect for private life; privacy) and '*la présomption d'innocence*' ('presumption of innocence') are classified by the author as '*libertés individuelles*' (individual freedoms) rather than '*droits de la personnalité*' (personality rights), even though they are routinely spoken of as 'rights'. For a 'down–up' view of personality rights rooted in the writings of sixteenth and seventeenth century scholars, see John Blackie, 'Doctrinal History of the Protection of Personality Rights in Europe in the *Ius commune*: General Actions or Specific Actions?' (2009) 13 *Electronic Journal of Comparative Law* (2009) www.ejcl.org/131/art131-1.pdf.

often placed there, might fall foul of the same problem as feelings. Autonomy, as Neethling remarked, is a general value which – like dignity – underpins the entirety of the law. For the same reason, it should not be another item on the list of interests protected by the law of wrongs.[109] The danger is real to use overly broad concepts whose relationship with the already mapped-out areas of the law has not been sufficiently thought through. But real as the difficulties are, there is no alternative if we believe in accountability, rationality and the fact that one role of legal scholars is to open the black boxes which, like *solatium*, connect more or less intuitively factual situations to legal remedies.

Conclusion

In English as in Roman law, the remedy granted to the successful claimant in an action based on a civil wrong is typically a money award which, in modern law, we describe (perhaps misleadingly) as 'damages'. It is difficult not to agree with Lord Hailsham's remark in *Cassell v Broome* that 'the language of damages is more than usually confused'.[110] If anything, the issue has become more rather than less acute over the past forty years. A growing number of labels is being used to describe these awards. Each new label creates a new concept whose relationship with existing doctrines is rarely explored in any depth. Whenever this is the case, confusion increases.

The concept of *solatium* is part of the problem. As a word, it straddles the divide and therefore complicates the distinction between compensatory and punitive awards; more importantly, it acts as a black box concealing the true nature of the interest for whose invasion redress is sought. It suggests that, if there is one, it would be something akin to emotional wellbeing rather than the underlying external interest. By doing so, it confuses two levels of enquiry. Besides, because the black box only operates within one section of the law of wrongs, the word – and its underlying idea of soothing for wounded feelings – have done much to stifle the emergence of a coherent body of law pertaining to the protection of 'being', that is to say, to the redress of personality rights, which Roman law entrusted to the *actio iniuriarum*. It has nothing to commend itself and should be dropped from the conceptual apparatus of the modern lawyer. Instead, it should be accepted that interests in 'being' (personality rights) are of a same nature as interests in 'having' (proprietary rights); that their violation is a real wrong which causes real loss. This loss is significant whether or not it is tangible; and it can be redressed by a substantial award of damages even though it is not immediately valuable in money. There is no need for the law, in order to reach this position, to convoke ideas of punishment, aggravated damages, injured feelings or *solatium*.

[109] Johann Neethling, 'The Concept of Privacy in South African Law' (2005) 122 *South African Law Journal* 18, 25.

[110] *Cassell* (n 47) 1073.

5

Dissimulatio

PAUL MITCHELL*

I. Introduction

When a person behaves in a way that does not accurately reflect his or her true state of mind, any legal system has difficult choices to make. Legal principles might be formulated in such a way that appearances are disregarded, and the person is assessed according to their 'true' mental state. Alternatively, legal principles might require that the misleading appearance is to be taken at face value, and the 'true' position ignored. Intermediate solutions are also possible, which could require an investigation into the reasons behind the misleading appearance, or only permit a person to act inconsistently with a misleading appearance under certain conditions. Furthermore, different legal doctrines might well call for different approaches: a rigorous instance on objective manifestations of intention in the law of contract, for instance, would not be equally appropriate for criminal law.[1]

This chapter focuses on the problem of dissimulation in the Roman delict of *iniuria* and in parallel doctrines of the English common law. It argues (in section II) that, behind the Roman solution to the problem of misleading appearances there lies a sophisticated philosophical debate about the nature of emotions and our ability to control them. The same difficult questions lie behind the English common law approach (discussed in section III), but, as will be shown, the range of English law doctrines on the issue bring out different dimensions of the problem, and solve it – not entirely consistently – in several different ways.

* I gratefully acknowledge the insightful comments of participants at the conference, and of Maria Lee.

[1] Compare *L'Estrange v F Graucob Ltd* [1934] 2 KB 394 (contract) with *R v Hancock and Shankland* [1986] AC 455 (murder).

II. Roman Law

In the final sentence of his analysis of the delict *iniuria*, the author of Justinian's *Institutes* states:[2]

> Haec actio dissimulatione aboletur: et ideo, si quis iniuriam dereliquerit, hoc est statim passus ad animum suum non revocaverit, postea ex paenitentia remissam iniuriam non poterit recolere.
>
> This action is extinguished by dissimulation. If someone lets a contempt pass – having suffered it dismisses it from his mind – he cannot later change his mind and rekindle the contempt he overlooked.[3]

There is no equivalent statement in Gaius. The source of this proposition is, however, easily traced. In D 47.10.11.1, the following passage from Ulpian's *Ad edictum* is set out:

> Iniuriarum actio ex bono et aequo est et dissimulatione aboletur. si quis enim iniuriam dereliquerit, hoc est statim passus ad animum suum non revocaverit, postea ex paenitentia remissam iniuriam non poterit recolere. secundum haec ergo aequitas actionis omnem metum eius abolere videtur, ubicumque contra aequum quis venit. proinde et si pactum de iniuria intercessit et si transactum et si iusiurandum exactum erit, actio iniuriarum non tenebit.
>
> The action for insult both arises from what is good and equitable, and is destroyed by dissimulation. For if someone shall have disregarded the affront, that is, as soon as he suffers it, he does not direct his mind to it, he cannot, on second thoughts, renew the affront which he let pass. In consequence, the equitable nature of the action removes all fear of it being granted whenever a plaintiff does not come forward in circumstances of equity. In the same way, if there has been any agreement of the parties over the affront or if they have made a *transactio* or if the alleged insulter has sworn that he was not guilty, the action for insult will not lie.[4]

From these texts one might be led to conclude that, in order for there to be liability for *iniuria*, it was never enough for a claimant merely to show that he was the victim of a deliberate affront. He would also have to show that he reacted to that affront immediately.

However, the position is not quite so straightforward. A closer examination of the two texts set out above reveals that they are not saying exactly the same thing. The *Institutes* presents the rule more starkly than Ulpian, and omits the illustrative examples. Ulpian also hints at a general justification for the rule – that the claim is based on what is good and just – which has been excised from the *Institutes*. The author of the *Institutes* may simply have wanted to shorten the exposition of the rule

[2] Inst 4.4.12.

[3] Peter Birks and Grant McLeod (trans), *The Institutes of Justinian* (London, Duckworth, 1987) 127–29.

[4] Translation based on Alan Watson, *The Digest of Justinian* (Philadelphia, PA, University of Pennsylvania Press, 1985).

for use in an introductory work, but the result is a less flexible legal proposition than Ulpian's original statement. Whilst Ulpian's formulation would have the potential to allow a claim to proceed, despite *dissimulatio*, where countervailing factors of justice and fairness were present, the formulation in the *Institutes* appears to be more dogmatic. The sense that Ulpian had in mind only a general rule, which could be displaced in unusual circumstances, is reinforced by his assertion, in D 47.10.3.1, that lunatics and *impubes* could sue for *iniuria*. 'Itaque pati quis iniuriam,' he comments, 'etiamsi non sentiat, potest'.[5] Clearly such claimants were not required to respond immediately, on pain of losing their action.

A second complicating factor is that the *dissimulatio* rule is not mentioned by Gaius. Gaius may, of course, have omitted it from his institutional work for reasons of space, or because he thought that it was unimportant. But the rule hardly requires a lengthy exposition, and it seems to cut down liability significantly. A more likely explanation, which will be developed in the next section, is that the *dissimulatio* principle was only elaborated at some point after the mid-second century CE (when Gaius was writing), because it was only at that later stage that the broader reasons behind the doctrine were established.

The texts on *dissimulatio*, therefore, raise two inter-related questions: why was the requirement introduced?, and what, exactly, was its content and rationale?

A. The Development of *iniuria*

At least part of the explanation for the introduction of the requirement of immediate response can be found in the development of *iniuria* itself. The delict in classical law was held together by the conceptual framework of *contumelia* (insult), from which flowed the requirement of intention, and also – since insults can be inflicted in diverse ways – the ability to impose liability in a broad range of circumstances.[6] In a delict whose conceptual centre of gravity is insult, it makes some sense to insist on the claimant actually being insulted.

Earlier approaches to *iniuria*, however, were less elegant. The Twelve Tables specified particular wrongs and their penalties, making no attempt at conceptual unification.[7] These provisions were superseded by the praetor's edicts dealing with specific wrongs[8] such as *convicium* (raising a clamour) and *adtemptata pudicitia* (which included following an honest young woman around), but these edicts also lacked any conceptual unity. The praetor's *Edictum Generale*, although widely acknowledged as the origin of the classical delict, simply provided the opportunity for juristic elaboration, rather than specifying what the structure or content of the delict should be. The first jurists to engage in such elaboration

[5] D 47.10.3.2. 'Thus, someone can suffer an insult, even though unaware' (Watson translation).

[6] Hence Helmholz's description of *iniuria* as 'large and in many ways shapeless'. Richard Helmholz, 'The Roman Law of Blackmail' (2001) 30 *Journal of Legal Studies* 33, 37.

[7] Peter Birks, 'The Early History of *Iniuria*' (1969) 37 *Tijdschrift voor Rechtsgeschiedenis* 163.

[8] Reinhard Zimmermann, *The Law of Obligations: Roman Foundations of the Civilian Tradition* (Oxford, Clarendon Press, 1996) 1053ff.

adopted a classification based on the method by which the insult was inflicted. Thus, in D 47.10.1.1 Ulpian reports that Labeo drew a distinction between *iniuria manus* (by hand) and *iniuria verbis* (by words). The *manus* category was self-explanatory; *verbis*, however, was less straightforward – 'verbis autem, quotiens non manus inferuntur, convicium fit'. Here Labeo seems to regard the *verbis* category as a residual classification ('quotiens non manus inferuntur'), and – read literally – as containing only *convicium*. Certainly there is no sense of an over-arching unifying concept of *contumelia*.

Classification into *iniuria manus* and *verbis*, however, was not to last. Immediately after setting out Labeo's view, Ulpian continued:

> omnemque iniuriam aut in corpus inferri aut ad dignitatem aut ad infamiam pertinere: in corpus fit, cum quis pulsatur: ad dignitatem, cum comes matronae abducitur: ad infamiam, cum pudicitia adtemptatur.
>
> Every contumely is inflicted on the person or relates to one's dignity or involves disgrace: It is to the person when someone is struck; it pertains to dignity when a lady's companion is led astray; and to disgrace when an attempt is made upon a person's chastity.[9]

It is not immediately obvious whether this passage is continuing the quotation from Labeo, or introducing Ulpian's own view.[10] However, the latter interpretation seems to be more plausible, since it would be rather odd for Labeo to introduce one classification only to replace it immediately with another one (unless Labeo was, perhaps, stating that *manus* and *verbis* were categories favoured by earlier jurists). In any case, in the new categorisation of *iniuriae* the focus has shifted from method to result.[11] The elaboration of rules concerned with the effect of an *iniuria* – of which the *dissimulatio* rule is one example – would flow naturally from adopting such a classification.

Given the compilers' practice of using Ulpian as their primary source, and referrring to other jurists only for additional material,[12] it is impossible for us to know now whether any earlier jurist had raised the issue of *dissimulatio*. However, it seems unlikely. The general conceptual structure of *iniuria* based on contumely was only emerging slowly – indeed Ulpian himself seems to have been very cautious, taking his illustrations of situations in the categories of *dignitas* and *fama* directly from the specific edicts.[13] Furthermore, the absence of any discussion of the point in Gaius is surely significant. The rule that an immediate reaction is needed is simple, striking, and cuts down the scope of recovery in an interesting way. It is exactly the kind of point that a student text should make (as the author of

[9] Translation from Watson (n 4).

[10] Contrast Paul du Plessis, this volume, ch 7, pp 141–142, (continuing quotation) with A Lewis, 'Trespass and *iniuria*' in William Butler (ed), *Anglo-Polish Legal Essays* (Dobbs Ferry, Transnational Publishers, 1982) 98–100 (shifting to Ulpian's own view).

[11] Lewis (n 10) 98–100.

[12] Alan Rodger, 'Introducing *iniuria*' (1991) 59 *Tijdschrift voor Rechtsgeschiedenis* 1, 5 (making the general point in the context of *iniuria*).

[13] See further, David Ibbetson, this volume, ch 2, p 35.

Justinian's *Institutes* realised), but it is not there. Both the nature of the *dissimulatio* rule, and its omission from Gaius' *Institutes* suggest that it was not formulated until Ulpian's time.

B. The Content of the *dissimulatio* Principle

As the previous section has shown, for Ulpian to be making a point about the consequences necessary for liability in *iniuria* is not entirely surprising. What is surprising, though, is that the point he makes seems to be at odds with the underlying general principle of *iniuria*. For in his illustration of dissimulation, the claimant has been the victim of a deliberate insult and has felt insulted. The allusion to dissimulation does not seem to offer much help. In the example there is no pretence or insincerity on the part of the claimant: he simply reacts more slowly than other people might do in similar circumstances. We might also be troubled by the underlying policy preference apparently manifested by the rule: is it really the case that Roman law gave special protection to people with short tempers?

Four possible explanations may be suggested. First, it may be that Ulpian was making a point about the inherent triviality of an affront that the claimant was initially able to dismiss from his mind. The adjective *remissam*, which Ulpian uses to describe the affront in such a situation, can mean 'forgotten', and is translated as such by Watson; but it can also mean 'small'. Ulpian may perhaps have been playing on the ambiguity.

A second possible explanation is that Ulpian saw the remedy for *iniuria* as a way of preserving public order; where a claimant was not provoked by the insult, there was no risk of retaliation and, therefore, no need for an action.[14] Some support for this interpretation might be found in the latter part of D 47.10.11.1, where Ulpian discusses settlements entered into between the parties. Historically, the rules governing affronts by violence had been aimed at curtailing private revenge, and settlements had been a very significant part of this strategy. For instance, the Twelve Tables provided for the remedy of retaliation for *membrum ruptum* unless the parties had agreed otherwise, and specified the maximum payment needed to buy off retaliation for broken bones.[15] It may be that Ulpian intended to hint at this historical role of actions for wrongs as a justification for denying an action where the claimant's response was not immediate.

A third possibility is that Ulpian regarded feelings of insult generated by the claimant turning over the matter in his mind, after the event, as being different in nature to an instantaneous response, and, therefore, as calling for different legal treatment. Ulpian's choice of language certainly suggests that he regarded a

[14] Chittharanjan Amerasinghe, *Defamation and other Aspects of the actio iniuriarum in Roman-Dutch Law in Ceylon & South Africa* (Colombo, Lake House Investments, 1968) 348 asserts that 'the reason for [the dissimulation] rule is probably that the action was *vindictam spirans*'.

[15] Birks (n 7) 178–88; Alan Watson, 'Personal Injuries in the XII Tables' in Alan Watson, *Studies in Roman Private Law* (London, Hambledon Press, 1991) 253.

delayed response as the result of the claimant's own voluntary processes. Thus, *dereliquerit*, *revocaverit*[16] and *recolere* all connote deliberate acts: putting aside, calling back, turning over in one's mind. *Recolere* is particularly interesting. It has strong connotations of deliberate action – in other contexts it means 'to recultivate' land, or 'rework' a mine. Literally it means 'to reheat', which both hints at Aristotelian physiological accounts of anger in terms of the boiling of blood around the heart, and also suggests that the claimant has had to put some energy into reaching his current state of indignation. We might even translate *recolere* in our texts as 'stoking' a grievance.

In drawing a distinction between the involuntary initial reaction to an insult, and the considered response generated by brooding on the matter, Ulpian was analysing the situation in a way that had deep philosophical roots. Indeed, behind Ulpian's simple factual situation lay a sophisticated philosophical controversy about the nature of emotions.[17] On one side of the controversy were the Greek Stoics, whose basic position was that emotions consisted in reasoned judgments. Taken to its logical extreme (as Chrysippus famously did), it followed that children incapable of reason were also incapable of true emotions. There was also strong support for the diametrically opposed view, which saw emotions as a kind of irresistible force to which individuals (including children and animals) were temporarily subjected.[18] Ulpian's famous contemporary, the physician Galen, for instance, described emotions as 'unreasoning movement'.[19] Between these two extremes, more subtle intermediate positions were possible, which contained more realistic, nuanced accounts of emotional experience. The most important of these accounts, for our purposes, is given by Seneca in *De ira*. There he put forward a three-stage model of emotions.[20] The first stage ('first movement') was the initial jolt, or shock (*ictus*, *agitatio*), which was independent of emotion properly so called.[21] It included things like sudden pallor, or eyes flashing at a perceived injustice. The second stage was a voluntary response, including a reasoned judgment that one's reaction was appropriate.[22] This stage corresponded to the Stoics' emotion properly so called. The third stage consisted of uncontrolled will, unaccompanied by any assessment of appropriateness.[23]

Ulpian's distinction between initial and considered responses to *iniuriae* echoes Seneca's distinction between the first and second movements of emotion. Indeed,

[16] 'Hoc est statim passus ad animum suum non revocaverit' may, perhaps, be an interpolation (or later gloss), but it seems to be an accurate paraphrase of *dereliquerit*. See further Ernst Levy and Ernst Rabel, *Index interpolationum*, vol 3 (Weimar, Böhlaus Nachfolger, 1935) 515.

[17] Richard Sorabji, *Emotion and Peace of Mind* (Oxford, Oxford University Press, 2000).

[18] Dan Kahan and Martha Nussbaum, 'Two Conceptions of Emotion in Criminal Law' (1996) 96 *Columbia Law Review* 269, 275–84.

[19] Galen, *On the Doctrines of Hippocrates and Plato*, ed and trans Phillip de Lacy (Berlin, Akademie-Verlag, 1984) 332.

[20] Sorabji (n 17) ch 4.

[21] Seneca, *De ira* 2.2.2.

[22] Seneca, *De ira* 2.4.1.

[23] ibid.

Ulpian's analysis may even have been picking up on Seneca's allusion to *iniuria* in the following passage:[24]

> Ergo prima illa agitatio animi quam species iniuriae incussit non magis ira est quam ipsa iniuriae species; ille sequens impetus, qui speciem iniuriae non tantum accepit sed adprobauit, ira est, concitatio animi ad ultionem uoluntate et iudicio pergentis.
>
> Therefore that first shock which the appearance of *iniuria* inflicts is no more anger than the appearance of *iniuria* is *iniuria*; it is the subsequent impulse, which not only received but also approved the appearance of injustice, that is anger; the rousing of a mind that prosecutes vengeance with will and judgment.[25]

However, the relationship between Seneca's analysis and Ulpian's rule was not straightforward. Indeed, Seneca's view might even be taken as indicating that the emotional response produced by a voluntary reasoned judgment should be taken more seriously than a mere instinctive reaction, since it was a true emotion. That would suggest a legal result exactly the opposite of Ulpian's. A broader reading of Seneca, though, suggested that the law should not indulge those who voluntarily worked themselves up into a state of indignation. It seems that Seneca's underlying philosophical purpose was to defend the Greek Stoics against their detractors, thereby reasserting the centrality of reasoned judgment in understanding the emotions.[26] Since emotions were the product of reason, it followed that they could and should be controlled by reason. It was a short step from that philosophical position to a legal rule that denied a claim to an emotionally undisciplined claimant.

These three possible explanations for the legal rule provide important contextual material, but none of them can be said to be entirely satisfactory, because none of them directly engage with what Ulpian saw as the underlying issue, namely the abuse of the action by the claimant's dissimulation. Why exactly did Ulpian think that a person whose reaction to an insult was delayed was guilty of dissimulation? Certainly the defendant could not claim to have been the victim of a misrepresentation about whether a claim would be brought. Nor had the claimant's initial reaction been feigned or insincere. It seems that what must be meant is a broader sense of dissimulation, which can be gathered from the situation as a whole. When he did not react to the insult at all, the claimant appeared to the outside world to be a person of admirable calmness and self-control. He had, apparently, managed to master the universal human tendency to respond instinctively. As Seneca put it in *De ira*, such instinctive responses were outside the control of reason ('Primum illum animi ictum effugere ratione non possumus')[27]. The best that a person could hope to do would be to weaken such instinctive responses (or 'first movements') by familiarity and constant attention ('consuetudo fortasse et adsidua obseruatio extenuat')[28]. Reportedly even Socrates could

[24] Seneca, *De ira* 2.3.5.
[25] Translation from Sorabji (n 17) 74.
[26] Sorabji (n 17).
[27] Seneca, *De ira* 2.4.2.
[28] ibid.

only manage this feat occasionally.[29] Hence, the Roman who did not react instinctively to an insult had reached an exceptionally high standard of *decorum*. When he subsequently attempted to prosecute his claim for *iniuria*, however, that appearance was belied. The essence of the dissimulation, in other words, was that people witnessing the claimant's exemplary response to the insult got a false impression of his true nature.

This interpretation of dissimulation allows us to explain why the rule did not apply to children or those with mental illnesses that made them unaware of what was happening around them. The failure of such claimants to react to an insult would not be put down to superior powers of self-control; their mental condition supplied the obvious explanation. Interpreting dissimulation in this way also demonstrates that there was no policy favouring claimants who were easily upset. The policy behind the rule is actually concerned with claimants who try to take the benefit of being thought calm and dignified, and then seek compensation because the opposite is true. It is not unlike the vice of *calliditas* (craftiness), of which Ulpian was particularly critical.[30] To put it slightly differently, using an analytical tool that Ulpian employed elsewhere in his work,[31] the individual who takes the benefit of being esteemed as a person of self-control and moderation must also bear the burden of not being able to sue for *iniuria* in circumstances where other, less moderate, individuals, would have claims.

This explanation for the *dissimulatio* rule would also harmonise very well with what can be discerned of Ulpian's broader philosophy. As Tony Honoré has argued, there is evidence of the influence of stoicism in some of Ulpian's writings, particularly those acknowledging the dignity and humanity of slaves.[32] D 47.10.11.1 could well be another example of Stoic influence, mediated by Seneca's theory of emotional behaviour. It may even be that Seneca's discussion of *iniuria* in the passage in *De ira* quoted above,[33] with its point about the misleading appearance of anger and the appearance of *iniuria* prompted Ulpian to think of the misleading appearance of *decorum* as the key to the legal analysis of the situation. But, in any event, the text on *dissimulatio* shows Ulpian characteristically pulling together threads of philosophy, morality, and principled legal analysis, to produce an original and elegant legal solution.

[29] Sorabji (n 17) ch 4 esp 69.

[30] Tony Honoré, *Ulpian: Pioneer of Human Rights*, 2nd edn (Oxford, Oxford University Press, 2002) 69, 93.

[31] ibid 93.

[32] Honoré, *Ulpian* (n 30) ch 3 esp 80ff. See also Tony Honoré, 'Ulpian, Natural Law and Stoic Influence' (2010) 78 *Tijdschrift voor Rechtsgeschiedenis* 199. *Cf* the 'more sceptical' approach to deducing jurists' beliefs from their writings in Alan Rodger, 'Behind the Scenes of Roman Law' (1983) 3 *Oxford Journal of Legal Studies* 382, 388–90.

[33] Text at n 24.

III. Common Law

The *dissimulatio* principle was taken to apply in jurisdictions that directly adopted *iniuria*.[34] Thus, in the South African case of *R v Makeke*[35] the defendant was a houseboy at an establishment where European girls lived as boarders. He was convicted of criminal *iniuria* for making remarks such as 'I want to make a baby with you' to three of the girls. Two of the girls, who were aged ten and eleven, were clearly insulted by the words, and the defendant's conviction for the offence against them was upheld. The third girl, however, aged thirteen, responded differently: 'far from being insulted, she was pleased at being addressed as she was'.[36] In giving evidence at the trial, the third girl had claimed to feel insulted later, but the High Court of Southern Rhodesia set aside the defendant's conviction for the words he had addressed to her. Hudson ACJ commented that 'one of the essentials of the crime of *injuria* is that the complainant should be aggrieved by the conduct complained of'.[37] It was implicit in the court's decision that an immediate reaction was required.

In the English common law, by contrast, none of the torts covering similar ground to the Roman delict of *iniuria* (such as defamation, trespass to the person, false imprisonment or breach of confidence) require an immediate outraged reaction from the claimant. Nor is there a consistent policy of imposing a short limitation period to ensure that grievances are not nurtured and litigated long after the event: whilst the one year limitation period for defamation prevents claimants from being able to brood on allegations for too long,[38] the period for trespass to the person is a generous six years.[39] Nor has there been any attempt to incorporate anything like the dissimulation principle into statutory wrongs involving *iniuria*-like conduct. Thus, under the Protection from Harassment Act 1997, liability is imposed in respect of a course of conduct which the defendant 'knows or ought to know' amounts to harassment.[40] The victim's immediate outraged reaction might well be powerful evidence to show that a defendant who did not know that he was committing harassment should have appreciated that fact, but the statute does not require such a reaction. Similarly, discrimination on grounds such as sex, age, race or religion does not require an outraged response on the part of the victim.[41] For instance, in one leading case it was no bar to the claim being brought that the

[34] Amerasinghe (n 14) 298, 312, 348 and 378–79.

[35] *R v Makeke* 1942 SR 47.

[36] *Makeke* (n 35) 48.

[37] ibid.

[38] Limitation Act 1980 s 4A (introduced by Defamation Act 1996 s 5). It should be noted, however, that prior to the Defamation Act 2013 s 8, every publication gave rise to a cause of action; it was therefore possible for claimants to seize on republications by a defendant so as effectively to extend the time limit: *The Duke of Brunswick and Luneberg v Harmer* (1849) 14 QB 185, 117 ER 75.

[39] Limitation Act 1980 s 2.

[40] Protection from Harassment Act 1997 s 1(1).

[41] Equality Act 2010.

interview in which the allegedly discriminatory act took place was conducted amicably by both parties.[42]

At first glance, therefore, it might seem that the principle of dissimulation has not found its way directly into English law. Perhaps part of the explanation for that is that, unlike the Roman delict, neither the English common law torts nor the English statutory wrongs are conceived in terms of insult or disrespect. Of course, remedies for those torts and wrongs often compensate a claimant for the hurt feelings and wounded dignity which we would typically associate with claims for *iniuria*, but that is a merely incidental feature, rather than being a unifying characteristic.[43] However, on closer inspection, there are principles and doctrines in the common law which, although they are not exact replicas of *dissimulatio*, echo *dissimulatio* or perform an equivalent function. These doctrines and principles, which both illuminate and are illuminated by the Roman rule, shall now be examined.

A. Manifestations of Consent

The closest direct parallel to the *dissimulatio* principle in common law can be found in the case law on misleading manifestations of consent to intentional torts. The leading case is *Freeman v Home Office (no 2)*,[44] in which a prisoner sought damages for medical treatment that had been administered to him whilst he was in prison. McCowan J, with whom the Court of Appeal agreed, held that the claim failed because, on the facts of the case, consent had been present. Sir John Donaldson MR, however, discussed what the legal analysis would have been where a claimant misled the defendant into believing that he had consented. 'The maxim "volenti non fit injuria"', he explained,[45]

> can be roughly translated as 'You cannot claim damages if you have asked for it', and 'it' is something which is and remains a tort. The maxim, where it applies, provides a bar to enforcing a cause of action. It does not negative the cause of action itself. This is a wholly different concept from consent which, in this context, deprives the act of its tortious character. 'Volenti' would be a defence in the unlikely scenario of a patient being held not to have in fact consented to treatment, but having by his conduct caused the doctor to believe that he had consented.

Taken on its own terms this passage is difficult to reconcile with well-established doctrines of the English law of tort. Of course, the defence of *volenti non fit iniuria* is a very well-known defence, but its application has traditionally been limited to

[42] *Crown Suppliers (Property Services Agency) v Dawkins* [1993] ICR 517, 518. For the current law on discrimination see Equality Act 2010.

[43] eg *Sutcliffe v Pressdram Ltd* [1991] 1 QB 153 (defamation); *Rowlands v Chief Constable of Merseyside Police* [2006] EWCA Civ 1773, [2007] 1 WLR 1065 (false imprisonment); Protection from Harassment Act 1997 s 3(2) (expressly including the recovery of damages for anxiety caused by the harassing conduct).

[44] *Freeman v Home Office (no 2)* [1984] QB 524 (QB), 548 (CA).

[45] ibid 548, 557.

situations where claimants were suing for negligence, after having either expressly waived their right to sue, or having deliberately placed themselves at the risk of injury by the defendant's carelessness.[46] The idea of consenting to a risk could possibly be extended to claimants suing for an intentional tort: for example, we could say that the patient has, by his conduct, voluntarily exposed himself to the risk that his wishes would be misunderstood by the defendant doctor, who would then act on that mistaken understanding. However, to extend the defence to intentional torts in this way would conflict with the fundamental principle that a defendant's belief that the claimant has consented is not sufficient to provide a defence to an intentional tort.[47] It would, in effect, be to change the basis of the test for consent from its current subjective basis (where the claimant's actual state of mind is decisive) to an objective basis (where the appearance of consent is what matters).

In the analysis put forward by Sir John Donaldson MR, however, the full implications of recognising a defence of *volenti non fit iniuria* in intentional torts is not acknowledged. On the contrary, it is asserted that consent and *volenti* are entirely separate doctrines, operating in different ways. Whilst that might be technically correct – a person who voluntarily creates the risk of being touched does not necessarily consent to the touching – the analysis fails to acknowledge the interrelationship between the two concepts, and thereby obscures the larger issues at stake. There may well be an argument for reforming the law so that a defence becomes available whenever the defendant reasonably (though mistakenly) believes that the conditions for a successful defence to an intentional tort are present. The recent statutory reforms relating to necessity take precisely that approach, conferring a defence on a person who reasonably believes both that the claimant lacks the capacity to make a decision and that the treatment in question will be in the claimant's best interests.[48] The courts may even be considering a similar development in relation to consent.[49] But it is vital that the decision about whether to adjust the basis of consent from subjectivity to objectivity should be made with a clear appreciation of the significance of the decision. To bring about a fundamental change by invoking Latin maxims, whilst simultaneously claiming that everything is as it was, can only result in confusion.

It also seems rather unfortunate that Sir John Donaldson MR did not consider other bases on which liability could be denied. He might, for example, have emphasised the claimant's moral wrongdoing in deliberately misleading the doctor, and applied the more apposite Latin maxim 'ex turpi causa non oritur actio'. He might also have taken the approach that, even if the fundamentally subjective approach to consent meant that an action was technically available, it would be an obvious case for the award of contemptuous damages, and for denying the claimant his

[46] *Dann v Hamilton* [1939] 1 KB 509; *Nettleship v Weston* [1971] 2 QB 691.

[47] *Chatterton v Gerson* [1981] QB 432, 443.

[48] Mental Capacity Act 2005 s 5.

[49] *Ashley v Chief Constable of Sussex Police* [2008] UKHL 25, [2008] 1 AC 962, [19]–[20] (Lord Bingham).

costs.[50] However, given his readiness to invoke propositions from Roman law, it seems a particular pity that he was not invited to make use of a principle that would not have required a 'rough' translation, and was focused precisely on the claimant's misleading conduct: *actio dissimulatione aboletur.*

B. Protests

A second parallel to the dissimulation principle in English law can be found in the cases on the role of protest in duress. The current position is that the making of a protest at the time of payment is merely evidence that the payment was not voluntary.[51] However, earlier cases seem to have taken a stricter approach.[52] Thus, in *Pratt v Vizard*[53] Parke J observed that 'The plaintiff, having been obliged to pay this money and, having done so under protest, may recover it back'.[54] In *Valpy v Manley*[55] Tindal CJ consciously set out a general rule:[56]

> I am not aware that there is any difficulty or impropriety in laying it down, that, where money is voluntarily paid, with full knowledge of all the circumstances, the party intending to give up his right, he cannot afterwards bring an action for money had and received; but that it is otherwise, where, at the time of paying the money, the party gives notice that he intends to resist the claim, and that he yields to it merely for the purpose of relieving himself from the inconvenience of having his goods sold.

Whether protest was always necessary, or merely evidence that the payment was involuntary was resolved, to some extent, in *Maskell v Horner.*[57] There it was alleged that a long series of periodical payments had been made under duress. Threats against the claimant's property had clearly been made, and each payment was accompanied by a protest, although there was some evidence that, as time went on, the protests had become something of a joke. At first instance Rowlatt J seemed to insist on the need for protest, saying that the claimant 'can only recover if he does not intend to give up his right and gives notice that that is his position at the time'.[58] He then subjected the facts relating to the claimant's conduct to close analysis, and concluded that it was very significant that the protests had become a joke. '[T]he protests passing into a standing joke', he said[59]

[50] See section III.D below.

[51] Hugh Beale (ed), *Chitty on Contracts*, 31st edn (London, Sweet & Maxwell, 2012) 7.035; eg *Deacon v Transport Regulation Board* [1958] VR 458.

[52] Robert Goff and Gareth Jones, *The Law of Restitution* (London, Sweet & Maxwell, 1966) 159–60; Gareth Jones (ed), *Goff and Jones; The Law of Restitution*, 7th edn (London, Sweet & Maxwell, 2007) 10.055. In South Africa, protest has been held to be a necessary ingredient of a claim for the return of payments on the ground of duress: Graham Glover, '"Methinks He Doth Protest too Much"? Recovering Unjustified Payments Made under Duress and Protest' (2006) *Journal of South African Law* 135.

[53] *Pratt v Vizard* (1833) 5 B & Ad 808, 110 ER 989.

[54] ibid 812, 991.

[55] *Valpy v Manley* (1845) 1 CB 594, 135 ER 673.

[56] ibid 603, 677.

[57] *Maskell v Horner* [1915] 3 KB 106.

[58] ibid 109.

[59] *Maskell v Horner* (n 57) 111.

> passed out of the sphere of effective protests; they came to indicate a grumbling acquiescence, and were not what they must be to satisfy the rule that there must be a declaration that the transaction was not closed but that the payment, which was only made for the relief of a deadlock, was not to be reclaimed. There is no magic in the use of a protest.

The Court of Appeal adopted a very different approach. For Lord Reading CJ, who gave the leading judgment, the fundamental question was whether the payment was made under compulsion. He doubted whether Rowlatt J had intended to find 'that there must be anything in the shape of an express notice or declaration to the defendant of the plaintiff's intention to keep alive his right to recover'.[60] However, the party making the payment should not remain entirely passive. 'It is clear', he explained,[61]

> that no express words are necessary and that the circumstances attending the payments and the conduct of the plaintiff when making them may be a sufficient indication to the defendant that the payments were not made with the intention of closing the transactions.

Lord Reading CJ also differed from Rowlatt J in his analysis of the facts. For Lord Reading CJ the claimant's protests were effective to communicate the payer's lack of consent, despite being accompanied by a laugh or jest. In the most recent authorities on duress, this insistence on some response has been watered down, and the claimant's response, if any, is merely part of the evidence of coercion.

There is clearly a parallel here between the Roman law of *iniuria* and the relatively recent English law of duress.[62] It seems unlikely that the parallel is the result of direct influence – although one early duress case expressly drew on *volenti non fit iniuria*[63] – but the similarity of approach is surely more than coincidence. In both systems a crucial feature of the claim is the claimant's state of mind: has he been affronted (*iniuria*) or coerced (duress)? A legal rule turning purely on a party's state of mind, however, is open to obvious abuse – hence the need for some external, corroborating evidence. Both the English and Roman rules require such external evidence, but they also go further. In the English rules the indications of involuntariness are directed towards the defendant; in the same way, the Roman requirement of instantaneous reaction means that, except in very unusual circumstances, the defendant will be aware that he has given offence. In other words, both rules give the defendant the opportunity to do something about the problem that he has created – to apologise, retract, and seek to achieve his ends through some other, legitimate, means. This built-in opportunity to retrieve the situation is highly appropriate for legal rules addressing what are essentially breaches of civility – in duress the defendant has exceeded the scope of legitimate bargaining,

[60] *Maskell v Horner* (n 57) 119.

[61] *Maskell v Horner* (n 57) 119–20.

[62] For exploration of a different parallel between the two subjects see Peter Birks, 'Harassment and Hubris: The Right to an Equality of Respect' (1997) 32 *Irish Jurist*, new series, 1, 35–36.

[63] *Astley v Reynolds* (1731) 2 Str 915, 916; 93 ER 939, 939.

in *iniuria* there is a breach of manners. It reflects the fact that often the parties themselves are best-placed to eliminate, or at least to minimise, the loss.

C. Immediacy of Reaction

One consequence of the principle of dissimulation was that delayed, brooding reactions to events were not legally acknowledged. As shown above, it is unlikely that the Romans meant to encourage people immediately to take offence, but the fact remained that only immediate reactions attracted liability. English law has adopted a similar position in relation to the criminal law on provocation, and the tortious infliction of psychiatric injury.

In the law of provocation it was, until relatively recently, crucial to examine the lapse of time between the provocation and the killing.[64] Devlin J's 'impeccable'[65] direction in *R v Duffy*,[66] having defined provocation in terms of 'a sudden and temporary loss of self-control, rendering the accused so subject to passion as to make him or her for the moment not master of his mind', went on to say that 'the further removed an incident is from the crime, the less it counts'.[67] In case the jury had missed the point, he reiterated that 'the first' of two 'matters of great importance' was 'whether there was . . . time for cooling, that is for passion to cool and for reason to regain dominion over the mind'.[68]

Devlin J was not the first judge to emphasise the importance of the time for cooling – the same point was being elaborated in the 1830s[69] – but his direction proved to be highly influential. In particular, the emphasis on 'sudden' loss of self-control and the importance of time for cooling excluded slow-burn reactions to provocation, such as were often experienced by spouses in abusive relationships. Indeed, *R v Duffy* itself was such a case.[70] Eventually, in *R v Ahluwalia*,[71] the Court of Appeal acknowledged that a significant lapse of time between the provocation and the killing was not inconsistent with loss of self-control, although it left some ambiguity over whether that loss of self-control was still required to be 'sudden'.[72]

The law relating to negligently inflicted psychiatric injury shows a similar concern with immediacy, particularly where claims are brought by witnesses of traumatic events. The House of Lords in *Alcock v Chief Constable of the South Yorkshire*

[64] For the current law see Coroners and Justice Act 2009 ss 54–56, in particular s 54(2): 'it does not matter whether or not the loss of control was sudden'.

[65] *R v Duffy* [1949] 1 All ER 932n (Lord Goddard CJ).

[66] *R v Duffy* [1949] 1 All ER 932n.

[67] *Duffy* (n 65) 932.

[68] *Duffy* (n 65) 933.

[69] *R v Hayward* (1833) 6 C & P 157, 172 ER 1188; *R v Fisher* (1837) 8 C & P 182, 173 ER 452.

[70] S Edwards, 'Justice Devlin's Legacy: Duffy – A Battered Woman "Caught" in Time' [2009] *Criminal Law Review* 851.

[71] *R v Ahluwalia* [1992] 4 All ER 889.

[72] Edwards (n 70) 856.

Police[73] set out several prerequisites for a duty of care including, most importantly for our purposes, that the injury must be shock-induced. Lord Ackner gave the fullest explanation of this test, commenting that there must be 'the sudden appreciation by sight or sound of a horrifying event that violently agitates the mind'.[74] Lord Keith referred to the need for 'a sudden assault on the nervous system'[75], and Lord Oliver to a 'sudden and unexpected shock to the plaintiff's nervous system'.[76] Their Lordships also approved the test set out by Brennan J in the Australian High Court case of *Jaensch v Coffey*:[77]

> sudden, sensory perception – that is by seeing hearing or touching – of a person, thing or event, which is so distressing that the perception of the phenomenon affronts or insults the plaintiff's mind and causes a recognizable psychiatric illness.

The shock requirement has been applied rigorously by the Court of Appeal,[78] although more recent cases have indicated that a flexible approach can be taken to identifying both the event,[79] and its aftermath,[80] by which the shock must have been inflicted.

In what is a competitive field, the shock requirement has a good claim to be the most highly criticised aspect of the law of negligence. Its detractors point out that 'shock' is not clinically significant, that there is no good reason to exclude claims by claimants who suffer psychiatric injuries as the result of an accumulation of experiences, and that the Australian High Court has now rejected a shock requirement.[81] The courts themselves now seem to have a more ambivalent attitude to the shock requirement. Whilst the *Alcock* criteria remain good law, they have not been extended to situations where psychiatric injury has been suffered in breach of a pre-existing relationship, for instance through stress at work, or through being inadequately defended by legal representatives at a criminal trial.[82] In these situations, the courts have said that the fundamental test is, simply, whether the psychiatric illness was reasonably foreseeable. The main explanation for the shock

[73] *Alcock v Chief Constable of the South Yorkshire Police* [1992] 1 AC 310.

[74] ibid 401. The requirement of sudden shock had not previously been expressly articulated, but it was consistent with the decisions in earlier cases on psychiatric injury: Donal Nolan, '*Alcock v Chief Constable of South Yorkshire Police* (1991)' in Charles Mitchell and Paul Mitchell (eds), *Landmark Cases in the Law of Tort* (Oxford, Hart Publishing, 2010) 273, 305.

[75] *Alcock* (n73) 398.

[76] *Alcock* (n73) 411.

[77] *Jaensch v Coffey* (1984) 54 ALR 417, 430.

[78] *Taylorson v Shieldness Produce Ltd* [1994] PIQR 329; *Sion v Hampstead Health Authority* (Court of Appeal, 27th May 1994).

[79] *North Glamorgan NHS Trust v Walters* [2002] EWCA Civ 1792, [2003] PIQR P16.

[80] *Galli-Atkinson v Seghal* [2003] EWCA Civ 697.

[81] See, eg Law Commission, *Liability for Psychiatric Injury* (Law Com No 249, 1998) 5.28–5.29; R Mulheron, 'Secondary Victim Psychiatric Illness Claims' (2003) 14 *King's College Law Journal* 213; Pat McInerney, 'Negligently Inflicted Psychological Harm and the "Sudden Shock" Requirement: A Comparative Analysis' (2009) 13(3) *Electronic Journal of Comparative Law*.

[82] Stress at work: *Walker v Northumberland County Council* [1995] ICR 702; *Hatton v Sutherland* [2002] EWCA Civ 76, [2002] ICR 613 affirmed in *Barber v Somerset County Council* [2004] UKHL 13, [2004] 1 WLR 1089. Legal representation: *McLoughlin v Jones* [2001] EWCA Civ 1743, [2002] QB 1312. See further Peter Handford, 'Psychiatric Injury in Breach of a Relationship' (2007) 27 LS 26.

requirement remains, as expressed in *Alcock v Chief Constable of the South Yorkshire Police* and other cases,[83] essentially defensive: some restrictions on claims are necessary, and the current restrictions do not entirely rule out incremental development in the future.[84]

A comparison of the psychiatric injury rules with the development of the law of provocation, and the Roman principle of *dissimulatio*, suggests that the use of immediacy as a control device is not merely a convenient place to draw the line. Just as the law of provocation required immediacy, the law of negligence demands shock; just as negligence requires the direct witnessing of the traumatic event, the law of provocation formerly required direct perception of the provocative event (for instance, a spouse had to be actually seen committing adultery). These restrictions are surely not imposed because the law cannot conceive of people losing their self control as the result of information received, or suffering psychiatric injury through caring for an injured spouse. Fear of fraudulent claims may provide part of the explanation, but, more fundamentally, the law is imposing certain normative behavioural expectations.[85] Thus, for instance, it was said in *R v Fisher*[86] that whether there had been sufficient cooling time between the event and the killing was a question of law, not fact.[87] A defendant who had had sufficient cooling time (as a matter of law), but was still unable to regain his self-control would fail in his defence of provocation. Similarly, the Roman who was able to dismiss an affront from his mind was expected to be able to continue to be in control of his passions. By the same kind of reasoning, the claimant suffering a psychiatric injury through a gradual accumulation of experiences has the opportunity to adjust to the evolving situation, unlike the victim of a single 'insult to the mind', to quote Brennan J's phrase. Of course, the time to adjust may be inadequate to enable the claimant to avoid injury, just as the cooling time for provocation might be inadequate, or the brooding Roman be unable to suppress his outrage. At that point, the law has a choice: it could insist on normative behavioural expectations being met, or it could say – 'you take your victim as you find him or her'. The modern preference for the latter solution in the new statutory defence of loss of control (subject to the objective criteria being met),[88] and in personal injury more generally,[89] does not mean that the alternative approach of insisting on behavioural expectations being met is necessarily inappropriate elsewhere.

Indeed, it may well be the case that, behind the restrictive rules on duties of care owed to secondary victims, lies a fundamental unresolved ambiguity about what

[83] *Sion v Hampstead Health Authority* (Court of Appeal, 27 May 1994) per Staughton LJ.

[84] For instance, in *North Glamorgan NHS Trust v Walters* [2002] EWCA Civ 1792, [2003] PIQR P16 at [52] Clarke LJ emphasised that this was a developing area of the law, and saw it as significant that in *Alcock* Lord Ackner had commented that 'shock' was '*yet*' to include psychiatric illnesses caused by an accumulation of gradual assaults.

[85] AJ Ashworth, 'The Doctrine of Provocation' [1976] CLJ 292, 295.

[86] *R v Fisher* (1837) 8 C & P 182, 173 ER 452.

[87] ibid 186, 454 (Park J).

[88] Coroners and Justice Act 2009 ss 54–55. For the objective criterion see s 54 (1)(c).

[89] eg *Smith v Leech Brain* [1962] 2 QB 405.

the courts (and society more generally) understand the essence of psychiatric illness to be. Some psychiatric injuries have physiological manifestations, but it is generally accepted that psychiatric injury is distinct from physical injury. It is difficult (and incautious) to generalise, but at least some psychiatric injuries seem most accurately identified in terms of an extreme emotional reaction – for instance, pathological grief disorder,[90] or gambling addiction.[91] Classifying psychiatric injuries in terms of emotional damage, however, raises a further problem. As Dan Kahan and Martha Nussbaum have demonstrated in the context of criminal law, assumptions about the nature of emotions are rarely examined (or even articulated) in the analysis of legal rules, but those assumptions fundamentally influence the content of legal doctrine.

Taking a lead from Kahan and Nussbaum's compelling account, a distinction should be drawn, (which corresponds to the opposing approaches taken by the Stoics and their critics),[92] between the mechanistic model of emotions and the evaluative model. The mechanistic model regards emotions as forces devoid of cognitive content, which impel actions; the evaluative concept, by contrast, treats emotions as thoughts that appraise or evaluate a particular object. The House of Lords' treatment of secondary victims in *Alcock v Chief Constable of the South Yorkshire Police*[93] suggests that they adopted the mechanistic model of emotional harm, since the restrictions on liability which they devised emphasised a sudden, overwhelming emotional experience. In the cases on psychiatric injury suffered in breach of a relationship, by contrast, a more evaluative conception of psychiatric injury is being assumed. That evaluative conception does not regard the involuntary, overwhelming nature of the experience as decisive, but focuses instead on the claimant's appraisal of the situation with which he or she was presented. If that appraisal is found to be within the range of what is reasonably foreseeable in the circumstances, legal liability is imposed. If this evaluative conception were applied to the situations concerning secondary victims, very different results would be reached. For instance, whether a claimant who suffered depression as a result of caring for her injured spouse was entitled to recover damages would not turn on the need for the claimant to have been involuntarily overwhelmed by the experience. It would turn on whether the claimant's response to the situation was appropriate, as judged by societal standards. In other words, different parts of the law on negligently inflicted psychiatric injury are adopting different conceptions of what psychiatric injury essentially is, and those conceptions are governing the outcomes of cases.

This inability of the courts to agree among themselves about the nature of psychiatric injury corresponds closely to the inability of the ancient philosophers to agree about the nature of emotions. As we have seen, Ulpian had to consider a similar problem in D 47.10.11.1, which he resolved by committing himself to a

[90] *Vernon v Bosley (no 1)* [1997] RTR 1.
[91] *Calvert v William Hill Credit Limited* [2008] EWHC 454 (Ch), [2008] EWCA Civ 1427.
[92] See above, text following n 18.
[93] *Alcock* (n 73).

particular model of emotional behaviour espoused by Seneca. In English law, unfortunately, a consistent commitment to one conception of psychiatric injury has not been made. Undoubtedly, as the philosophical disputes indicate, the question is a difficult one. But until it is addressed, English law is unlikely to develop consistent principles on liability for psychiatric injury.

D. Doctrines Concerned with Dissimulation

The previous three sections have dealt with aspects of the common law that bear obvious similarities to the principle of dissimulation set out by Ulpian in D 47.10.11.1. In this section the focus broadens, to give an overview of doctrines which, although they lack detailed similarity to the dissimulation principle, serve the same broad purpose, namely, to prevent claimants profiting by double standards. These doctrines can be divided into two categories. The first concerns the principles of justification and mitigation of damage in defamation. The second concerns the court's general discretion over the size of damages awards and the award of costs.

The principles governing justification and mitigation of damage in defamation frequently prevent claimants from using the legal process to appear better than they really are. Thus, the defence of justification will not fail by reason only of the defendant's failure to justify a trivial allegation if more serious allegations have been proved true.[94] Furthermore, the non-technical approach to ascertaining the sting of defamatory words[95] has enabled courts to allow pleas of justification that seek to prove a general allegation, as opposed to the specific instance of it made in the defamatory words.[96] The principles governing mitigation of damage show a similar underlying concern, by permitting defendants to adduce evidence of the claimant's prior bad reputation in the broad area to which the defamatory allegation related.[97]

More generally, the courts have the power to award contemptuous damages where they take the view that, although a claim has technically been made out, it should never have been brought in the first place. Such an award is of very low value – in pre-decimal currency it was typically a farthing (¼ d).[98] The most prominent examples of contemptuous damages can be found in defamation cases, perhaps because until recently defamation cases tended to be tried by juries, and juries may have felt less compunction than judges about expressing their moral disapproval of claimants. The circumstances in which contemptuous damages are appropriate are not limited, but one of the most common examples of their use is

[94] Defamation Act 2013 s 2.

[95] *Lewis v Daily Telegraph* [1964] AC 234.

[96] *Williams v Reason* [1988] 1 All ER 262; for the limits of this approach see *Bookbinder v Tebbit* [1989] 1 All ER 1169.

[97] *Plato Films Ltd v Speidel* [1961] AC 1090.

[98] eg *Newstead v London Express Newspaper Ltd* [1940] 1 KB 377.

particularly relevant to this chapter. It occurs where a plea of justification has fallen short, but the evidence adduced has shown egregious misconduct.

One of the most high-profile recent uses of contemptuous damages occurred in in *Grobbelaar v News Group Newspapers Ltd*,[99] where the defendant alleged that the claimant, a professional goalkeeper, had taken bribes to let in goals during matches, and then performed his side of the bargain. The defendant sought to justify the allegation, and proved that the claimant had indeed accepted a bribe. However, the jury found that the defamatory sting of the allegation extended to fixing matches (or attempting to fix them) by letting in goals. The defendant was unable to substantiate that allegation, and the plea of justification therefore failed. The House of Lords replaced the jury's award of £85,000 with a 'derisory'[100] award of £1, emphasising that the claimant's conduct in accepting a bribe had drastically diminished his reputation as a sportsman. Lord Scott of Foscote added a second reason for the award, which focused on the fact that the claimant had been recorded saying that he had previously fixed matches. Lord Scott said that:[101]

> If an individual makes damaging admissions about himself which come to the attention of a third party who has no reason to doubt their credibility and who repeats them in public, the notion that the individual can then, by successfully denying the truth of his admissions, succeed in extracting defamation damages from the third party seems to me inconsistent with justice as well as with common sense. It has not been suggested to your Lordships that the Law Reform (Contributory Negligence) Act 1945 might have a part to play in such a scenario but it seems to me that it might.

The use of the 1945 Act in this situation would be problematic, as it has now been established that the Act's provisions only apply where contributory negligence had been available as a defence prior to 1945.[102] Contributory negligence seems never to have been available in defamation. Lord Scott's broader point, however, seems compelling. His invocation of 'justice as well as . . . common sense' as the reason for denying substantial damages to a dissimulating claimant echoes Ulpian's emphasis on what is 'good and equitable' when reaching the same conclusion in relation to the same kind of claimant.

Grobbelaar's case also highlights a further feature of the common law principles on double standards: the claimant, despite having won the case, had to pay his own costs. Costs generally follow the event, but the courts have the discretion to depart from this presumption, and it is interesting to note that one of the longest established grounds for doing so in a defamation case is where the claimant's

[99] *Grobbelaar v News Group Newspapers Ltd* [2002] UKHL 40, [2002] 1 WLR 3024.

[100] ibid [36] (Lord Steyn). For an insight into some of the difficulties that would have faced a court had it been necessary to assess loss of future managerial earnings, see the description of Grobbelaar's training methods in Simon Kuper, *Soccer Men* (New York, Nation Books, 2011) 9–12. One player, given the protection of anonymity, comments with some understatement that 'He's still got a way to go as a coach'.

[101] *Grobbelaar* [86].

[102] *Reeves v Commissioner of the Police of the Metropolis* [2000] 1 AC 360; *Standard Chartered Bank v Pakistan National Shipping Corporation* [2003] 1 AC 959; *Co-Operative Group (CWS) Ltd v Pritchard* [2011] EWCA Civ 329.

conduct showed that he had brought the defamation on himself.[103] The inconsistency between the claimant's acts and his stance in litigation effectively deprives him of his action (and literally makes him pay for having pursued it).

The common law principles governing justification, mitigation, contemptuous damages and costs awards are concerned with the same broad mischief that Ulpian was concerned with in D 47.10.11.1. The situations are not precisely identical of course. In the English cases the claimant is trying to use the legal process to give himself a better reputation than his prior actions entitle him to; in Ulpian it is the claimant's public conduct that has given him an undeservedly good reputation (for calmness and magnanimity), which his recourse to law belies. In both cases, however, the legal rules are trying to eliminate the discrepancy between the moral significance of events in the outside world and their legal significance in the courts. That such corrective legal rules are necessary, both in England and in Rome, highlights the ever-present potential for legal rules to be over-inclusive, by imposing liabilities which, whilst accurate according to law, are in conflict with the expectations of the society that the law is supposed to be serving.

IV. Conclusion

As befits a doctrine dealing with misleading appearances, there is more to the dissimulation principle than meets the eye. Its appearance in Roman law may well have been a consequence of the new juristic approach to *iniuria* associated with Ulpian, which emphasised the consequences of the delict as opposed to the manner of its infliction. But the precise form of the principle went beyond what an emphasis on outcomes required, because it deprived claimants of an action even where they had genuinely felt outraged by the defendant's insult. The reason for this principle must, therefore, be sought elsewhere. The most compelling explanation seems to be that a claimant who was able to dismiss an affront from his mind when the affront was given, but on further thought became insulted by it, should not be allowed to have the best of both worlds: his immediate reaction irrebuttably showed that he was a person of exceptional dignity and moderation, and, as such, he had no need of an action for *iniuria*.

None of the forms of tortious liability in the common law exactly replicated the delict of *iniuria* and, as a result, the dissimulation principle has not been directly transplanted into the common law. However, several instances can be seen where something like the dissimulation principle has been in play. The Court of Appeal's involved analysis of the position where a patient misleads a doctor into believing that the patient consents to treatment would have been a lot more straightforward had the dissimulation principle been adopted. Similarly, the concern that the

[103] *Harnett v Vise* (1880) 5 Ex D 307; *Martin v Benson* [1927] 1 KB 771. See also *Bostock v Ramsey Urban District Council* [1900] 2 QB 616 (malicious prosecution).

claimant should not be able to dissociate himself from his own previous conduct can be seen in the rules on justification and mitigation of damage in defamation, and in the principles permitting the award of contemptuous damages and costs more generally. The controversy over the role of protests in duress, the role of delay in provocation, and the role of shock in negligence claims for psychiatric injury suffered by secondary victims illustrate that problems with features similar to the difficulty that Ulpian addressed in D 47.10.11.1 continue to trouble the courts. In the final analysis, that should not be surprising, because the underlying oppositions that Ulpian had to reconcile – between external and internal, objective and subjective, and, ultimately, legal doctrine and social expectation – are never likely to be neatly resolved in any legal system.

6

Contumelia and the South African Law of Defamation

HELEN SCOTT

I. *Animus iniuriandi* in South African Law

The case of *Le Roux v Dey*[1] arose from a schoolboy prank. The three defendants (all between the ages of 15 and 17) had between them manufactured and disseminated an image of their school principal and vice-principal naked and locked in an intimate embrace. It appeared that the first defendant had simply pasted images of his teachers' faces over the heads of the two people depicted in the original photograph. It was sufficiently crudely executed to be an obvious fake.

The boys having been found out and punished, the school principal was prepared to dismiss the episode. Not so Dr Dey, the vice-principal. He pursued the matter in the courts by means of an action that in South African law is still called the *actio iniuriarum*. More specifically, he claimed sentimental damages for the infringement of both his dignity (*dignitas*) and his reputation (*fama*). The High Court found for the plaintiff on both counts, awarding a composite amount of R45,000 (about £3,000) as damages with costs on the magistrate's court scale. Both sides appealed to the Supreme Court of Appeal, the boys against the judgment and Dr Dey against the damages award. The boys' appeal was dismissed, while the cross-appeal was upheld. On appeal to the Constitutional Court, the orders granted in the High Court and Supreme Court of Appeal were set aside and the defendants ordered, jointly and severally, to pay the plaintiff R25,000 (about £1,600) as compensation and to tender an unconditional apology to the plaintiff for the injury they caused him.[2]

The case raised a number of important issues, both constitutional and otherwise: these included whether the image was defamatory, and whether infringements of

[1] *Le Roux and others v Dey* 2010 (4) SA 210 (SCA); *Le Roux and others v Dey (Freedom of Expression Institute and Restorative Justice Centre as Amici Curiae)* 2011 (3) SA 274 (CC).

[2] The defendants were ordered pay the plaintiff's costs in the High Court but no order was made as to costs in the Constitutional Court or in the Supreme Court of Appeal.

dignity and reputation were separate wrongs for the purposes of the *actio iniuriarum*; in other words, whether the same act could give rise to two actions. However, this essay addresses only one further issue, namely, the precise character of the requirement of *animus iniuriandi*, intention to injure. Assuming the image to be defamatory, the three schoolboy defendants attempted to rebut the presumption of *animus iniuriandi* generated by its publication by arguing that they had not known that their conduct was unlawful – indeed, that they had not known that there was such a thing as defamation – and that they had intended the publication as a joke. These defences were rejected by a majority of both the Supreme Court of Appeal and the Constitutional Court. Giving the judgment of the SCA, Harms DP held as follows:

> [27] To assess the defence of lack of *animus injuriandi* it is necessary once again to visit the issue as to its meaning and application in the context of the *actio injuriarum* in its different forms . . . *[A]nimus injuriandi* means the intention to injure.
>
> . . .
>
> [29] The Continental Pandectists of the 19th century analysed the concept of *dolus* and added another element to the intention to injure, namely consciousness of the wrongfulness of the act (coloured intent or 'wederregtelikheidsbewussyn'). In spite of my high regard for them it has to be conceded that by systematising the Roman-law concepts they did not necessarily state the Roman-Dutch law. This means that an adherence to the roots of our law does not necessarily require an adoption of Pandectist theories.
>
> . . .
>
> [37] A purely Pandectist approach does get one into a bind . . . It appears to me to be incongruous that a defendant who, for example, cannot establish truth and public benefit to justify defamation, can nevertheless escape liability by relying on a belief in either the truth or public benefit.
>
> . . .
>
> [39] . . . I therefore conclude, especially in view of precedent and the constitutional emphasis on the protection of personality rights, that the *animus injuriandi* requirement generally does not require consciousness of wrongfulness (*wederregtelikheidsbewussyn*).
>
> [40] In addition . . . I do not believe that jest excludes the intention to injure. It goes to motive and . . . if a joke is degrading the defendant's motive does not matter.[3]

Speaking for the majority in the Constitutional Court, Brand J upheld Harms DP's finding regarding the defendants' argument that they had intended the publication as a joke:

[3] Footnotes omitted. *cf* also para 10: 'It appears to me that if a publication is objectively and in the circumstances in jest it may not be defamatory. But there is a clear line. A joke at the expense of someone – making someone the butt of a degrading joke – is likely to be interpreted as defamatory. A joke at which the subject can laugh will usually be inoffensive.'

> [131] . . . [E]stablished principles of our law dictate that motive to raise a laugh and not to injure, in itself, would not exclude *animus iniuriandi.* This is so because in our law motive does not necessarily correlate with intent. A defendant who foresaw the possibility that his attempt at humour might be defamatory of the plaintiff, but nonetheless proceeds with the attempt, will have *animus iniuriandi* or intent in the form of *dolus eventualis.*[4]

Regarding the defendants' argument that they did not know that their conduct was unlawful,

> [134] I must admit that, in the circumstances I found their reliance on this basis rather peculiar. Lack of knowledge of wrongfulness is generally advanced in the context of a subjective belief in some ground of justification which is then found, objectively, not to exist. So, for example, it would be contended by a defendant that he or she thought the defamatory statement was privileged, or that the defamatory statement was true and its publication for the public benefit, or that the plaintiff had consented to publication. But this was not the defence raised by the applicants. Nor did they contend that they were unaccountable or *culpae incapax* because their emotional and intellectual development had not reached the stage that enabled them to distinguish between right and wrong and to act accordingly. They simply denied that they were aware that what they were doing was wrong.
>
> . . .
>
> [137] I do not believe that knowledge of wrongfulness requires familiarity with the existence of a particular delict . . . Ultimately, it must be borne in mind that the applicants bore the onus to establish their defence of absence of knowledge of wrongfulness on a preponderance of probabilities. In my view, they simply failed to rebut this onus. It was therefore not necessary for the Supreme Court of Appeal to embark upon the enquiry as to whether our law should still require knowledge of wrongfulness as part of *animus iniuriandi.* Nor do I find it necessary for this Court to do so.[5]

Thus Brand J distanced himself from the finding of Harms DP that, 'the *animus injuriandi* requirement generally does not require consciousness of wrongfulness'. On the other hand, he upheld his finding that jest goes only to motive and is thus incapable of excluding *animus iniuriandi.*

These conclusions rest on hundreds of years of legal development. In the South African context, the meaning of *animus iniuriandi* in the original Roman sources and in the later civilian tradition has been the subject of contention for at least a century.[6] It may well be that a concept of *animus iniuriandi* that incorporates

[4] *cf* also para 110: 'The concept of a joke or jest is usually cast in the role of a defence excluding *animus iniuriandi*, an instance in which the defendant bears the onus. In this case the applicants also sought to assign it to that role. I will come to that. But the concept of a joke may also come in at the earlier stage of determining whether a statement is defamatory. If the conclusion is that the reasonable observer would understand the statement as good clean fun which simply caused amusement, it will not be regarded as defamatory'.

[5] Footnotes omitted.

[6] eg Melius De Villiers, *The Roman and Roman-Dutch Law of Injuries* (Cape Town, Juta, 1899); 'Malice in the English and Roman Law of Defamation' (1901) 17 *Law Quarterly Review* 288; RG McKerron, 'Fact and Fiction in the Law of Defamation' (1931) 48 *South African Law Journal* 154; Melius De Villiers,

consciousness of wrongfulness is incompatible with the analytical structure of the modern South African law of defamation: that a defamation regime that recognises (as South African law has done since the nineteenth century) the stereotyped defences of English law – truth (in the public interest), fair comment and privilege – and that conceives of these defences (as South African law now does) as defences to wrongfulness, cannot also accommodate a fault regime that allows liability to be defeated by proof of the absence of wrongful intention.[7] Yet it is not the purpose of this paper to rehearse or contribute to that important debate. All that it seeks to do is to consider the propositions set out above: that advanced by Harms DP, that consciousness of wrongfulness is a Pandectist invention, and that adherence to the roots of our law does not therefore require that we recognise such coloured intent as an element of liability under the modern *actio iniuriarum*;[8] and that accepted by both Harms DP and Brand J, that jest goes only to motive and is thus incapable of excluding *animus iniuriandi*.

In this respect Reinhard Zimmermann's warning regarding the role of subjective considerations in classical Roman law is salutory:

> Objective and subjective ingredients were inextricably interwoven within the concept of *iniuria*, and the relative weight attached to each depended, furthermore, on the type of injury in question. This makes it impossible to generalize. The most one can probably say is that here, as in many other instances, the Roman lawyers did not think in terms of specific, isolated requirements for liability that had to be satisfied, but tended to look at the typicality of the situation.[9]

'*Animus Injuriandi*: An Essential Element in Defamation' (1931) 48 *South African Law Journal* 308; RG McKerron, *The Law of Delict* (Cape Town, Juta, 1933); TW Price, '*Animus Injuriandi* in Defamation' (1949) 66 *South African Law Journal* 4; TW Price, 'The Basis of the South African Law of Defamation' [1960] *Acta Juridica* 254. Much of this literature was cited by De Villiers AJ (not Melius) in *Maisel v Van Naeren* [1960] 4 All SA 447 (C), in which a mistaken belief in the existence of a privilege on the part of the defendant was taken to exclude *animus iniurandi* and thus liability. For a more recent view see J Neethling and JM Potgieter, *Neethling-Potgieter-Visser: Law of Delict*, 6th edn (JC Knobel (trans), Durban, LexisNexis, 2010) 128–30. Regarding the fault standard to be applied to the press see *Suid-Afrikaanse Uitsaaikorporasie v O'Malley* 1977 (3) SA 394 (A); *National Media Ltd v Bogoshi* 1998 (4) SA 1196 (SCA); *Khumalo v Holomisa* 2002 (5) SA 401 (CC); *NM and Others v Smith and Others (Freedom of Expression Institute as Amicus Curiae)* 2007 (5) SA 250 (CC).

[7] It is clear that these defences were originally (ie in the nineteenth and early twentieth centuries) conceived of as defences to *animus iniuriandi*: see eg *Crawford v Albu* 1917 AD 102 (dealing with fair comment). For the modern South African position regarding the nature of these defences, see eg *Suid-Afrikaanse Uitsaaikorporasie v O'Malley* 1977 (3) SA 394 (A); *Pakendorf v De Flamingh* 1982 (3) SA 146 (A); *Khumalo v Holomisa* 2002 (5) SA 401 (CC) and *Le Roux v Dey* 2011 (3) SA 274 (CC) itself. For a masterful account of this paradigm shift and its doctrinal implications see Fagan, this volume, ch 9.

[8] As authority for this proposition Harms DP cited R Midgley and JC van der Walt 'Delict' in *The Law of South Africa* 8(1), 2nd edn (Durban, LexisNexis, 2005) para 105 fn 3: 'Although there are indications that Roman and Roman-Dutch law acknowledged the relevance of consciousness of the wrongfulness of the act as an element of *dolus* (see, in particular, *D* 47 10 3 2–4; Voet 47 10 20; De Villiers *Injuries* 28–29, 193–99), the constituent elements of the concept *dolus* were only formulated during the nineteenth century by the Pandectists.'

[9] Reinhard Zimmermann, *The Law of Obligations: Roman Foundations of the Civilian Tradition* (Cape Town, Juta, 1990) 1061. This is essentially the view of Raber. See Fritz Raber, *Grundlagen Klassischer Injurienansprüche* (Wien, Böhlaus, 1969) ch 3, summarised on p 174.

Indeed, it is anachronistic to speak of a requirement of *animus iniuriandi* in Roman law: certainly the term itself is not used in *Digest* 47.10.[10] Nevertheless, it will be argued below that the Roman delict of *iniuria* was in fact overwhelmingly subjective in focus. Not only was it extremely sensitive to shades of intent on the part of the defendant (including what the judges in *Le Roux v Dey* called motive); by the end of the classical period it was approaching the position that the defendant's injurious or contemptuous intent – the fact that he had acted in order to perpetrate an *iniuria* or out of *contumelia* – was determinative of liability.[11]

II. Roman *iniuria*: The Edictal Delict

The relationship between the *iniuria* of the Twelve Tables and that of the praetorian General Edict *de iniuriis aestumandis* is obscure.[12] Equally, the meaning of *iniuria* in each context is unclear. According to Table 1.13–15, there was to be *talio* in cases of *membrum ruptum* (the maiming of a limb or rendering useless of some part of the body), fixed penalties of 300 or 150 *asses* for the *os fractum* (broken bone) of a free person or a slave, and a penalty of 25 *asses* for 'any other *iniuria*'.[13] Assuming that this provision did contemplate a particular species of wrongdoing called *iniuria*, it is generally thought to have referred to minor personal injuries such as slapping, as distinct from the more serious assaults set out in the two preceding provisions.[14] On the other hand, the text of the General Edict *de iniuriis aestumandis*, enacted around the turn of the second century BCE, read as follows:

> He who brings the action for *iniuria* . . . let him specify for certain what *iniuria* he has suffered and place an upper limit on the damages (*vademonium*) set for the case.[15]

[10] The closest we come is *corrigendi animo aut . . . emendandi* (used by Ulpian in D 47.10.15.38) and *animus iniuriae faciendae* in D 47.10.26. *cf* Fritz Schulz, *Classical Roman Law* (Oxford, Clarendon Press, 1951) 597.

[11] *cf* Ibbetson, this volume, ch 2, text after n 41: 'It should be stressed too that the defendant's intentionality lay right at the heart of liability; it was not simply a rule, which might have been different, that this was the mental state that it was necessary to prove. It was in the very nature of *contumelia* that the wrongdoer was deliberately acting without taking into account the interests of the victim. We should not expect to find a rule requiring *animus iniurandi* distinct from the fact of *iniuria*.'

[12] In particular, Peter Birks has suggested that the classical delict had its origin in the praetor's edict rather than the Twelve Tables: 'The Early History of Iniuria' (1969) 37 *Tijdschrift voor Rechtsgeschiedenis* 163; P Birks, 'Lucius Veratius and the lex Aebutia' in WAJ Watson (ed), *Daube Noster: Essays in Legal History for David Daube* (Edinburgh, Scottish Academic Press, 1974) 39. See generally Descheemaeker and Scott, this volume, ch 1, section II.

[13] Tab 1.13–15; Michael Crawford, *Roman Statutes* (2 vols, London, University of London, Institute of Classical Studies, 1996) vol 2, pp 604–8. *cf* Du Plessis, this volume, ch 7, text to nn 5–6.

[14] eg Zimmermann (n 9) 1051.

[15] *Collatio* 2.6.1. (*Paul libro sing. [de iniuriis] sub titulo quemadmodum iniuriarum agatur*). See Otto Lenel, *Das Edictum Perpetuum*, 3rd edn (Leipzig, Tauchnitz, 1927) 398.

The Edict did not specify any actionable conduct at all, referring simply to *iniuria* and leaving it to the claimant to particularise the harm suffered. The dominant view appears to be that it covered only minor personal injuries such as slapping – ie the *iniuriae* of Table 1.15[16] – but it may have comprised also more serious assaults from the start – the *membrum ruptum* and *os fractum* of Tables 1.13 and 1.14.[17] On either view, the only developments brought about by the Edict were procedural ones: the fixed penalties of the Twelve Tables were abandoned in favour of damages assessed at the discretion of the *iudex* or *recuperatores*.[18] Thus it appears that liability under the Edict was originally strict, as it had been under the Twelve Tables themselves. Proof that the defendant had smashed a limb, broken a bone etc gave rise to prima facie liability.

Unlike the General Edict, the so-called special edicts enacted during the course of the second and first centuries BCE undoubtedly imposed liability in new, previously unrecognised situations. Yet the conduct which they identified appeared to share some of the central characteristics of *iniuria*, namely a latent insulting character. The first of these was the edict *De convicio*, creating a delict of *convicium*, usually translated as clamour. Ulpian gives the original wording of this edict in D 47.10.15.2 (57 *Ad edictum*):[19]

> One who is said to have raised a clamour [*convicium*] at someone contrary to good morals [*contra bonos mores*] or one through whose efforts such a clamour is raised contrary to good morals, against him I will give an action [*iudicium dabo*].

The nature of *convicium* – the situation envisaged in the edict appears to be that of a crowd gathering together to denounce someone – and the conditions of liability under this edict were discussed in detail in the Introduction and will not be repeated here.[20] However, it is important to note that the criterion of *boni mores* – prevailing standards – used by the praetor to distinguish public demonstrations which were socially permissible and therefore lawful from those which were not, while flexible, remained objective. The intention or purpose of the defendant was not specified. Deliberate conduct – which would invariably have been present – was apparently sufficient.

[16] David Daube, '*Nocere* and *noxa*' (1939) 7 *Cambridge Law Journal* 23, 45–47; '*Ne quid infamandi causa fiat*: The Roman Law of Defamation' in David Cohen and Dieter Simon (eds), *David Daube: Collected Studies in Roman Law* (Frankfurt, Klostermann, 1991) 465, 467; Zimmermann (n 9) 1052.

[17] See eg the authors listed by Birks in 'The Early History of Iniuria' (1969) 37 *Tijdschrift voor Rechtsgeschiedenis* 163, 194. A third view is that of Birks, that the *Edictum Generale* originally comprised all unlawful conduct. See eg '*Infamandi causa facta* in Disguise' [1976] *Acta Juridica* 83; 'Harassment and Hubris: The Right to an Equality of Respect' (1997) 32 *Irish Jurist* 1, 12 fn 35. The account of Daube in '*Ne quid infamandi causa fiat*' according to which the special edicts created new delicts outside an originally narrow *Edictum Generale* is preferred here.

[18] These were judges with special powers who sat in cases of particular importance: see Birks, 'Early History' (n 17) 197–200; JM Kelly, *Studies in the Civil Judicature of the Roman Republic* (Oxford, Clarendon Press, 1976) 40–70.

[19] Not Book 77: Otto Lenel, *Palingenesia Iuris Civilis* (2 vols, Leipzig, Bernhard Tauchnitz, 1889) vol 2, p 772. All translations of Digest texts are based on those provided in T Mommsen and P Krueger (eds), A Watson (trans), *The Digest of Justinian* (Philadelphia, University of Pennsylvania Press, 1985).

[20] Descheemaeker and Scott, this volume, ch 1, section II.A.

The second of the special edicts appeared under the rubric *De adtemptata pudicitia*: literally translated this meant something like 'attacks on chastity', ie sexual harassment. Although the text of the edict is nowhere recorded, it is paraphrased by Ulpian as follows:

> If someone is alleged to have abducted the companion of a matron (*materfamilias*) or a boy or girl, or if someone has called out to them or followed them around contrary to good morals [*contra bonos mores*].[21]

Again, the factual complexes comprised within this edict are discussed in detail in the Introduction.[22] In short, the edict addressed both behaviour that was prima facie *iniuria* (abduction) and behaviour that was *iniuria* only where found to be in breach of prevailing standards, *contra bonos mores* (accosting or following); thus the first sub-delict corresponded to the assaults comprised within the General Edict, the latter to *convicium*.

Similar again was the last of the special edicts to be discussed by Ulpian in his edictal commentary: this was *De iniuriis quae servis fiunt*,[23] which created a new wrong of *servi alieni verberatio*, beating another's slave.[24] According to Ulpian, the wording of this edict was as follows:

> Where a man shall be said to have beaten another's slave contrary to good morals [*contra bonos mores*] or to have submitted him to torture without the owner's consent, I will give an action. Equally, if it be said that something else be done, I will, having heard the circumstances [*causa cognita*], give an action.[25]

Whereas torturing another's slave appears to have been prima facie *iniuria*, beating him gave rise to liability only if found to be *contra bonos mores*. As in the case of those earlier edicts, liability was objectively but flexibly determined.

Yet the third of the special edicts to be introduced by the praetor relied on an entirely different technique for determining liability: this was the edict *ne quid infamandi causa fiat*.[26] According to Ulpian, apparently quoting verbatim (*ait praetor*) the edict ran,

> Let nothing be done to bring *infamia* upon another. If anyone does anything to the contrary I will look into it according to the nature of the issue.[27]

Unlike in the case of the other special edicts, no particular wrongful conduct was envisaged: the question of which facts were capable of substantiating this edict was left entirely open.[28] Instead, liability under the edict turned exclusively on the

[21] Lenel, *Das Edictum Perpetuum* (n 15) 400.

[22] Descheemaeker and Scott, this volume, ch 1, section II.A.

[23] Like the first three special edicts, *servi verberatio* is considered in detail by Ulpian in the long extract from his edictal commentary preserved in D 47.10.15. See D 47.10.15.34–49 and D 47.10.17 pr 2.

[24] For details see Descheemaeker and Scott, this volume, ch 1, section II.A.

[25] Lenel, *Das Edictum Perpetuum* (n 15) 401.

[26] For details see Descheemaeker and Scott, this volume, ch 1, section II.A.

[27] Lenel, *Das Edictum Perpetuum* (n 15) 401.

[28] eg D 47.10.15.27.

subjective intention of the wrongdoer.[29] As long as the wrongdoer's purpose was to shame his victim, his conduct – whatever it was – was deemed to be actionable. This technique for determining unlawfulness, while also extremely flexible, was of course quite distinct from that applied in the case of *convicium*, *adtemptata pudicitia* and *servi verberatio*.[30] Indeed, it was astonishingly sophisticated – even revolutionary – in the context of a legal system which seems otherwise to have dealt exclusively in objectively framed forms of action.[31]

III. Roman *iniuria*: Harassment and Hubris

What emerges clearly from this brief summary of the development of *iniuria* is that it began life as a particularised or fragmented delict. Indeed, during its edictal phase it does not seem that there was any unitary *iniuria* delict at all.[32] It follows that there could be no standardised approach to intention during this period. However, by the first century CE the General Edict and special edicts had been welded together into a single procedural unity: all wrongs falling within their scope were now actionable as *iniuriae* under the *actio iniuriarum*.[33] Moreover, this procedural unity was matched by a substantive one: the mature delict of *iniuria* was organised around the principle of *contumelia*.[34]

What did *contumelia* mean?[35] There appears to have been a strong connection with the Greek concept of *hubris*, as indicated by the fact that Justinian in his *Institutes* treats the two words as virtual synonyms.[36] This state of mind – the Greek *hubris* or Roman *contumelia*, best rendered in English as 'contempt'[37] – is key to understanding the nature of the classical *iniuria* delict. It refers to, 'a kind of arrogance or pride, an over-confident exaltation of the self, manifested in violence or other misbehaviour towards others'.[38] In fact, the word *contumelia* refers not only to a particular attitude of mind but also to the conduct flowing from it: in this sense it is best translated as 'harassment'.[39] Thus it combines the attitude of mind of one who harasses with the acts that derive from that mental

[29] Daube, '*Ne quid infamandi causa fiat*' (n 16) 469.

[30] '[S]ome shades of intent could in themselves turn lawful conduct unlawful.' Birks, 'Harassment and Hubris' (n 17) 13.

[31] Daube, '*Ne quid infamandi causa fiat*' (n 16) 469.

[32] *cf* n 17 above.

[33] For further details see Descheemaeker and Scott, this volume, ch 1, section II.

[34] ibid.

[35] *cf* Descheemaeker and Scott, this volume, ch 1, section II.A.

[36] Re the meaning of *hubris* in Greek law, see eg the account of a Greek criminal trial reported by Demosthenes in *Against Konon*. Re Labeo's role in importing this idea, see Ibbetson, this volume, ch 2, text to n 38 and the works cited there.

[37] Birks, 'Harassment and Hubris' (n 17) 8.

[38] ibid, relying on the *OED*.

[39] Birks, 'Harassment and Hubris' (n 17) 8–9.

attitude.[40] It was this flexibility that made *contumelia* such a suitable unifying idea. The Roman jurists saw it as capable of integrating the many different manifestations of the mature delict.[41]

For Birks, then, the delict *iniuria*, which 'by specialization of the sense of that word, [the jurists] in effect called "contempt"', was in fact 'contemptuous harassment of another, calculated to cause distress in the nature of anger and humiliation . . . but violating, not an interest in emotional calm, but the victim's right to his or her proper share of respect'.[42] Yet Birks' definition of classical *iniuria* as *contumelia* is subject to several 'important riders', one of which pertains to the interaction between *contumelia* and objective unlawfulness. According to Birks, in practice *contumelia* played 'a surprisingly unobtrusive role'.[43] It was a principle, not a requirement: the big idea without which this synthetic tort stitched together from the fabric of the Republic edicts would have fallen apart.[44] Rather than requiring to be distinctly proved in each case, it was an inference drawn from other facts. Thus if A assaulted B – deliberately attacked him with an axe – or raised a clamour (*convicium*) against him or sexually harassed him, it did not need to be demonstrated that A had acted with a specifically contemptuous intention towards B. The mere fact that A had intentionally committed those acts of harassment showed his contempt for his victim.

That rider is itself qualified in Birks' account. The inference of contemptuous intention generated by the intentional committing of prima facie or demonstrably injurious acts could be rebutted. Birks gives the famous example discussed by the jurist Julian in D 9.2.5.3 (Ulpian, 18 *Ad edictum*):

> If a teacher in the course of instruction wounds or kills a slave, is he liable under the *lex Aquilia* as having done unlawful damage? Julian writes that a man was held liable under the *lex Aquilia* who had put a pupil's eye out in the course of instruction: much more therefore must the same view be taken if he kills him. Now he puts the following case: a shoemaker, he says, when a boy who was learning under him, a freeborn *filiusfamilias*, did rather badly what he gave him to do, struck at his neck with a last, so that the boy's eye was put out. Accordingly Julian says that the *actio iniuriarum* does not lie, because he struck the blow not in order to perpetrate an *iniuria* [*quia non faciendae iniuriae causa percusserit*] but to correct and instruct: he inclines to think that the *actio ex locato* lies, since only slight punishment is permitted to a teacher: but I have no doubt that an action can be brought on the *lex Aquilia*.

A teacher, in the course of chastising a pupil, hits him too hard, causing serious harm. The shoemaker's conduct (inflicting a serious injury) appears to be prima facie *iniuria*. Yet the teacher escapes liability under the *actio iniuriarum*. The reason: the hitting was done without contempt, in order to correct and teach the

[40] ibid and see further Descheemaeker and Scott, this volume, ch 1, section II.A
[41] Birks, 'Harassment and Hubris' (n 17) 9.
[42] ibid 11. *cf* Descheemaeker and Scott, this volume, ch 1, section II.B.
[43] Birks, 'Harassment and Hubris' (n 17) 11.
[44] ibid 13.

pupil [*monendi et docendi causa*].[45] 'The intention to admonish in the interests of instruction rebutted the inference of contempt normally drawn from intentional hitting.'[46]

Both propositions are indisputably correct. In particular, Birks is clearly right in arguing that a specific demonstration of *contumelia* or contempt was often not required in order to found liability under the mature delict.[47] Nevertheless, this paper seeks to qualify these propositions on two grounds. First, it appears that there were at least two techniques for driving forward the boundaries of the classical *iniuria* delict that relied on wholly subjective considerations. In part this was due also to the survival of the Republican edicts in the classical delict: the special edict *ne quid*, like the older *convicium* and *adtemptata pudicitia*, continued to play a prominent role in the context of the classical delict.[48] As a result, in certain cases contemptuous (or strictly shaming) intention functioned as a sufficient condition for liability, provided of course that it issued in conduct of some kind. Indeed, there is evidence that the elements of *convicium* were influenced by the subjective focus of *ne quid*.[49] Furthermore, it appears that *contumelia* itself frequently drove the expansion of liability under the classical delict.[50] In such cases the contemptuous character of the defendant's conduct did have to be specifically demonstrated. While contemptuous intention could often be inferred from the intentional commission of a contemptuous act, the matter was by no means always presented in this way. In fact, there are a number of cases preserved in *Digest* 47.10 where the contemptuous intention of the defendant appears to constitute the primary

[45] *cf* D 19.2.13.4 (Ulpian, 32 *Ad edictum*), in which Ulpian discusses the same case, as well as Julian's view, in the context of *locatio conductio*. Here the *actio iniuriarum* is said to be denied by Julian 'quia non iniuriae faciendae causa hoc fecerit, sed praecipiendi'. See also D 48.19.16.2 (Claudius Saturninus, *Penalties of Civilians*): 'emendationis non iniuriae gratiae'. Alternatively we could say that the beating would have been lawful if confined to reasonable chastisement but was in danger of becoming *contra bonos mores* and therefore actionable if excessive. The subjective intention of the teacher was then simply one of the factors leading to the conclusion that the beating was not in fact contrary to good morals. This is the analysis of Zimmermann (n 9) 1060–61, relying on Ulpian's own view in D 47.10.15.38: 'The words *contra bonos mores* are inserted in order that not everyone who beats a slave but only he who beats him contrary to good morals is made liable. One who does so by way of correction or reform [*corrigendi animo aut . . . emendandi*] is not liable.' However, the difficulty here is that D 47.10.15.38 forms part of Ulpian's commentary on the edict *De iniuriis quae servis fiunt*: Lenel, *Palingenesia* (n 19) vol 2, pp 773–74. As the passage shows, the words *contra bonos mores* appeared in the text of the edict. It is not clear that this criterion would have been applied to cases falling outside the scope of that edict, ie in a case like Julian's, which involved a freeborn boy.

[46] Birks, 'Harassment and Hubris' (n 17) 14.

[47] See also Zimmermann (n 9) 1059–61.

[48] Ibbetson, this volume, ch 2, p 35: 'The general principle of *contumelia* is of unquestioned importance, but the internal structure of the delict is strongly shaped by its component parts.' As we have seen, the edicts of the Republic survive more-or-less intact in the edictal commentary of Ulpian. Thus instances of conduct actionable either by virtue of prima facie unlawfulness (like hitting) or by virtue of being contrary to objectively-determined prevailing standards (like *convicium*) are well represented in *Digest* 47.10. *cf* Descheemaeker and Scott, this volume, ch 1, section II.B.

[49] *cf* D 47.10.15.5, which clearly shows the influence of the special edict *ne quid infamandi causa fiat*. See Daube, '*Ne quid infamandi causa fiat*' (n 16) 491 and Descheemaeker and Scott, this volume, ch 1, section II.A.

[50] For details see Descheemaeker and Scott, this volume, ch 1, section II.B.

reason for liability. Section IV.A below addresses each of these expansive techniques in turn.

Second, regarding Birks' rider about mistake, the example he gives from D 9.2.5.3 suggests too limited a role for intention in rebutting the presumption of contempt generated by prima facie or demonstrably injurious conduct. It is true that the outcome in Julian's case is specifically justified with reference to the shoemaker's innocent intention: again, he struck the boy not to perpetrate an *iniuria* (*non faciendae iniuriae causa*) but in order to correct and teach him. But it is not difficult to see that this is not in fact a case of intentional conduct at all. We are told that the shoemaker knocked out the boy's eye by striking at his neck with a last; if indeed his intention was to correct and teach, it seems that he cannot have intended to inflict that injury, or indeed any injury at all beyond perhaps a bruise. Thus the example shows only that no contempt could be presumed from unintentional conduct. But there are a number of other cases of mistaken *iniuria* in *Digest* 47.10 in which defendants are exonerated on grounds of far lesser mistakes: mistakes that do not displace intention itself, but merely show that the defendant's intention was not a contemptuous one. Section 4(B) below considers these cases in detail.

IV. Subjective Considerations in Roman *iniuria*

A. The Defendant's Intention as the Reason for Liability

i. The Continuing Role of the Edict ne quid

As we have seen, even in the mature classical law the contours of the special edicts remained visible through the fabric of *iniuria*. This is evident from Ulpian's extensive commentary on the special edicts preserved at D 47.10.15.25 to D 47.10.17.2.[51] Again, liability under the special edict *ne quid* depended exclusively on the demonstration of an intention on the part of the defendant to bring disgrace or shame upon the plaintiff, coupled with some (unspecified) conduct – simply, that he had acted *infamandi causa*. The defendant's purpose in so acting rendered what might otherwise have been lawful conduct, unlawful. Thus as in the special edict itself, in the classical law the fact that the defendant had acted *infamandi causa* was treated as a sufficient condition for liability in milder cases of defamation not falling within *convicium*.

We find several such cases in *Digest* 47.10, not only in those sections that derive from Ulpian's edictal commentary on the edict *ne quid* but also elsewhere. Thus beginning with Ulpian's edictal commentary, D 47.10.15.31:

[51] Lenel, *Palingenesia* (n 19) vol 2, pp 771–73.

> If someone appropriates another's assets or only one of them for the sake of perpetrating an *iniuria* [*per iniuriam*], he is liable to the *actio iniuriarum.*

15.32:

> Similarly, if someone announce that he is selling a pledge *infamandi mei causa* [in order to bring shame upon me], as though he had received it from me, Servius says that I can bring the *actio iniuriarum.*

Finally, 15.33:

> If someone summon a non-debtor as if he were a debtor, in order to perpetrate an *iniuria* [*iniuriae faciendi causa*], he is liable to the *actio iniuriarum.*

In the first case the defendant's conduct (appropriating another's assets) appears unlawful on its face, although the act in question is not a typically injurious one. This would presumably have strengthened the case for liability under *ne quid.* Indeed, in the second and third cases too it is arguable that the defendant's conduct is extrinsically unlawful, that is, unlawful by virtue of law external to the delict.[52] Nevertheless in all three cases liability under the *actio iniuriarum* is made to turn on the intention or purpose of the defendant: on the fact that he acted *infamandi* or *iniuriae faciendi causa.*

Stepping outside the context of Ulpian's commentary on *ne quid,* D 47.10.19 records Gaius (22 *On the Provincial Edict*) as follows:

> If my creditor, whom I am ready to pay, should call upon my verbal guarantors *in iniuriam meam* [in order to discredit me?], he will be liable to me under the *actio iniuriarum.*

While the case closely resembles those discussed in D 47.10.15.32 and 33, the role of the defendant's subjective intention here is obscure.[53] However, the very next fragment, D 47.10.20, attributed to Modestinus (12 *Replies*) is clearer:

> If, without the authority of the person who has the right and power to permit such a course, Seia seal up the house of her absent debtor *iniuriae faciendae gratia* [for the sake of perpetrating an *iniuria*], she can be sued by means of the *actio iniuriarum.*

As in D 47.10.15.31, Seia's conduct appears extrinsically unlawful. However, what makes her conduct actionable under the *actio iniuriarum* is her injurious intention.

Finally, as Daube noted,[54] there is evidence of the reorientation of certain of the other special edicts under the influence of *ne quid,* specifically *convicium,* to which it was of course closely related. According to Ulpian, the special edict on *convicium* concerned 'loud calling after a person' (*vociferatio*) which is

[52] For this concept see Birks, 'Harassment and Hubris' (n 17) 11–12. Re D 47.10.15.32 in particular see Birks, '*Infamandi causa facta*' (n 17) 95–97.

[53] So Raber (n 9) 151.

[54] Daube, '*Ne quid infamandi causa fiat*' (n 16) 491.

> both contrary to good morals (*contra bonos mores*) and directed to the disgrace and unpopularity of an individual (*quaeque ad infamiam vel invidiam alicuius spectaret*).[55]

Thus while *convicium* preserved its original edictal criterion – *contra bonos mores* – it had clearly been assimilated to *ne quid* in some degree, as evidenced by Ulpian's additional requirement that the defendant be seeking to bring shame or hatred upon the plaintiff.

ii. Contumelia *as an expansive criterion*

As we have seen, *contumelia* – contempt – functioned in the first instance as a unifying principle rather than a requirement for liability. A contemptuous intention on the part of the defendant did not have to be independently demonstrated in each case; rather, *contumelia* was an inference drawn from other facts, specifically those facts necessary to constitute liability under the Republican edicts. Yet in addition to its synthetic function, *contumelia* played an important role in driving forward the boundaries of liability. Because it could encompass almost any conduct characterised as contemptuous, it had the potential to expand liability far beyond the delict's Republican scope, to encompass almost any form of behaviour, whether words or conduct.[56] In fact, there are a number of texts preserved in *Digest* 47.10 in which a specifically contemptuous (or injurious) intention appears to have been the criterion used to determine the boundaries of liability.

First, a tranche of four texts, a sustained analysis taken from Ulpian's commentary on the General Edict, specifically his commentary *Ad formulam*.[57] According to D 47.10.13.1–2:

> A person who does something under the public law [*qui iure publico utitur*] does not appear to have done it in order to perpetrate an *iniuria* [*iniuriae faciendae causa*]; for there is no *iniuria* in the administration of the law [*iuris enim executio non habet iniuriam*]. 2. If someone be led away for failing to comply with a decree of the praetor, the case is not such that he can bring the *actio iniuriarum* by reason of the praetorian order.

Here subjective (*iniuriae faciendae causa*) and objective (*iure publico utitur*/*iuris executio*) criteria appear to be pulling in the same direction, against liability: one who exercises a public function or public right will be presumed to act without injurious intention. This conclusion is unremarkable, although it is noteworthy that the defendant's intention is specified. But according to the next text, D 47.10.13.3:

> If, in order to annoy me [*vexandi mei causa*], someone interrupt me when speaking before court for the sake of perpetrating an *iniuria* [*per iniuriam*], I can bring the *actio iniuriarum*.

[55] Ulpian, 57 *Ad edictum*, D 47.10.15.5.
[56] For further details see Descheemaeker and Scott, this volume, ch 1, section II.B.
[57] Lenel, *Palingenesia* (n 19) vol 2, pp 770–71.

Here there is clearly no extrinsic unlawfulness in the defendant's conduct. The only possible basis for liability is the intention of the interrupter (*vexandi mei causa*). Indeed, Ulpian may have repeated this point in order to drive it home: *per iniuriam* likewise appears to express purpose.

In neither of the texts just considered is *contumelia* specifically mentioned. It is, however, referred to in the next text, 13.4:

> If, in a matter of decreeing honours for someone, a person be unwilling that they should be decreed, for example, a statue or the like, can proceedings for *iniuria* be brought against him? Labeo says that he is not liable, even though he did it for the purpose of *contumelia* [*quamvis hoc contumeliae causa faciet*]. He says that there is a great distinction between whether a thing be done for the purpose of *contumelia* [*contumeliae causa*] and whether a person will not tolerate the honouring of another.[58]

The analysis in this case is difficult, perhaps because the text is corrupt.[59] One explanation for the decision is the fact that the defendant's unwillingness to confer honours on the plaintiff amounts to a mere failure to act. More likely it has to do with the fact that he is acting in an official capacity, as in D 47.10.13.1–2; the context favours that explanation. Nevertheless, it is striking that Labeo (and Ulpian?) regards the defendant's contemptuous purpose as central. The arguments against liability may be compelling, but the argument in favour is obviously that the defendant acted *contumeliae causa* in refusing to confer the honours in question.

Moving outside the context of Ulpian's edictal commentary, here again we find a number of texts in which the dominant criterion for liability appears to be the contemptuous intention of the defendant. D 47.10.33 contains the following fragment from Paul, Book 10, *Ad Sabinum*:

> When something is done in the public interest [*rei publicae venerandae causa*] according to good morals [*secundum bonos mores*], even though it effects *contumelia* to someone [*ad contumeliam alicuius pertinent*], nevertheless, because the magistrate does not intend to perpetrate an *iniuria* [*non ea mente facit . . . ut iniuriam faciat*], but to assert public *maiestas*, he will not be liable to the *actio iniuriarum*.

Here, as in 13.1, but unlike in the previous case, subjective and objective criteria appear to be working together: a magistrate who acts in the public interest and according to *boni mores* also acts without injurious intention. Nevertheless, it seems that this text identifies the intention of the magistrate as determinative: because he does not act in order to perpetrate an *iniuria* there is no liability under the *actio*, despite the fact that the action is objectively contumelious.[60]

[58] In the Watson Digest, *contumelia* is translated as 'contumely'.

[59] Lenel, *Palingenesia* (n 19) vol 2, p 771. See Raber (n 9) 148–50.

[60] *cf* Ibbetson's analysis: this volume, ch 2, pp 42–43. See here also the peculiar case described in D 25.4.1.8 (Ulpian, 24 *Ad edictum*): a husband who requests that his wife be officially examined for signs of pregnancy is liable if he acted *iniuriae faciendae causa/animo*, but not if he genuinely believed her to be pregnant.

Finally, a text of Javolenus preserved in D 47.10.44[61] states that:

> If the owner of lower premises create smoke in order to smoke out [*fumigandi causa*] his upstairs neighbour, or if the owner of upper premises throw or pour anything on to the building below, Labeo says that the *actio iniuriarum* does not lie. I think this is wrong, if it were done with the intention to perpetrate an *iniuria* [*iniuriae faciendae causa inmittitur*].

The conduct described here may well have been actionable under the law of neighbours (eg by means of an *actio negatoria*) and in terms of the quasi delict *de effusis vel deiectis*.[62] Nevertheless, for Javolenus at least, it gave rise to liability under the *actio iniuriarum* also provided that it was done *iniuriae faciendae causa*. As in D 47.10.15.31 and D 47.10.20, the defendant's conduct appears extrinsically unlawful. But as in those cases, it is the injurious intention of the defendant – *iniuriae faciendae causa* – that renders his conduct actionable as an *iniuria*.[63]

B. Mistaken *iniuria*

It remains to address the second reservation raised with respect to Birks' account of classical *iniuria*, namely, his treatment of mistaken *iniuriae*. Here we are concerned with a different body of cases from that addressed in the first half of this section: not those new instances of the classical *actio iniuriarum* generated by the *contumelia* principle, but rather those which constituted the original subject-matter of the earlier Republican edicts. In these cases – and in particular those cases covered by the General Edict, *convicium*, *adtemptata pudicitia* and *servi alieni verberatio* – the defendant's conduct was either prima facie *iniuria* (hitting, abducting the companion of a matron or child, torturing another's slave) or demonstrably *iniuria*, ie *contra bonos mores* (raising a clamour against someone, calling out at someone or following them around, beating another's slave). Here, *contumelia* – contumelious intention or contempt – did not have to be specifically demonstrated. Rather, it could be readily presumed from fact that the defendant had intentionally carried out such injurious conduct. This was Birks' rider to his claim regarding the centrality of *contumelia* to the mature delict.

This presumption was not, of course, an irrebutable one. As Birks himself maintains, the defendant in such a case could escape liability by showing that he had in fact acted without contempt. However, the example Birks gives – the case of the shoemaker who put out his apprentice's eye, discussed in D 9.2.5.3 – appears to show only that no *contumelia* would be presumed from wholly unin-

[61] *From the Posthumous Works of Labeo*, Book 9.

[62] For a detailed discussion of the situations envisaged here see Raber (n 9) 145–48.

[63] *cf* D 9.2.41 pr (Ulpian, 41 *On Sabinus*): '[I]f someone who is looking after another's will makes an erasure or reads it out with other people present, it is better to bring an *actio in factum* [modelled on the *lex Aquilia*] or *actio iniuriarum*, if he published the secrets of one's legal affairs *iniuriae faciendae causa*.' See here also D 16.3.1.38 (Ulpian, 30 *Ad edictum*): 'Labeo says that the *actio depositi* can rightly be brought.'

tentional conduct.[64] In fact, there are a number of cases recorded in D 47.10 in which defendants appear to escape liability on grounds of far lesser mistakes. These cases illuminate the particular shade of intent that formed the gist of classical *iniuria*. In the language of the *ius commune*, they reveal the precise character of the requirement of *animus iniuriandi*.

We begin with D 47.10.3, taken from Ulpian, Book 56 *Ad edictum*. This forms part of the jurist's general introduction to *iniuria* before the start of the specific edictal commentary in Book 57.[65] In the fragment preserved in D 47.10.1 (with which Ulpian's general account of *iniuria* begins) he sets out the definition of the delict (D 47.10 pr–2), before going on to discuss the issue of standing (who can sue). He continues in 3.pr–1 as follows:

> We are told that those who can suffer can equally commit *iniuria*. 1 Of course, there are some who cannot commit it, such as the deranged [*furiosus*] and the *inpubes* [child below the age of puberty] who is not capable of wrongful intent [*doli capax*]; they can suffer *iniuria* but cannot commit it. For since *iniuria* consists in the mental state of the one committing it [*ex affectu facientis*], it follows that these classes, even if they do strike people or shout abuse, will not be regarded as having committed an *iniuria*.

The issue of standing leads on to the question of who can commit *iniuria*. Ulpian maintains that because *iniuria* consists in the will or mental state of the one who commits it, one who is incapable of forming any wrongful intention (*dolus*) cannot commit *iniuria*, even if he commits an injurious act, ie an act that would ordinarily amount to an *iniuria*.[66] Ulpian goes on,

> 2 Thus, someone can suffer *iniuria*, even though he be unaware [*non sentiat*], but no-one can commit *iniuria* unless he knows that he commits it [*nisi qui scit se iniuriam facere*], although he may not know against whom he commits it.

The use of 'thus' (*itaque*) at the start of the fragment shows the continuation of Ulpian's train of thought. Having discussed what we would call capacity – the inability of certain classes of person to commit the delict – Ulpian attempts to formulate a general rule about the sort of intention that is required to commit it. In order to be liable, a defendant must know – *scit* – that he is committing an *iniuria*. Only then, we infer, will he have the appropriate mental state (*affectus*), namely *dolus* (as in 3.1) or indeed *contumelia*.

Next, Ulpian discusses several of cases of mistaken *iniuria*:

> 3 Hence, if someone strike another in jest [*per iocum*] or during a contest, he will not be liable to the *actio iniuriarum*. 4 If someone beat a freeman, thinking that he is his slave, the position is that he is not liable to the *actio iniuriarum*.

[64] See above section III.

[65] Lenel, *Palingenesia* (n 19) vol 2, pp 766–67.

[66] *cf* D 44.7.34 pr (Paul, 1 *On the Praetor's Edict*), where Paul uses the word *affectus* in the same way. For a survey of the textual criticism to which this passage has been subject see Raber (n 9) 108–10.

Again, the use of *quare* (hence) shows that these cases are understood to follow directly from the general propositions above. The first two examples are clearly cases in which *dolus* or intention to commit *iniuria* is lacking. The defendant intentionally committed an injurious act – he hit the other – but still he lacked the intention necessary to constitute *iniuria*, since he did it in jest or in the course of a sporting contest. However, the third case, 3.4, is less clear. If you intended to hit your slave (which is not an *iniuria*) and you actually hit a free man (which is a *prima facie* injurious act), the difficulty is not that you lacked *dolus* or the intention to commit *iniuria* (as per 3.1 and 3.2); in fact you never meant to commit the injurious act in question – the act of beating a free man – at all. In other words, the case is closer to D 9.2.5.3 than to D 47.10.3.3.

Following D 47.10.3 the compilers of the Digest have inserted into Ulpian's text a fragment from Book 55 (not 50)[67] of Paul's commentary *Ad edictum*. According to Paul,

> If, when I wish to punch my slave, I involuntarily [*invitus*] hit you standing next to him, I will not be liable to the *actio iniuriarum*.

Again, this text is more like D 9.2.5.3 than the two examples given in D 9.2.3.3: if your intention was to punch your slave (a lawful act), and you involuntarily – *invitus* – hit the person standing next to him, your punching him was wholly unintentional, not merely lacking in injurious intention.

At this point the evidence is not conclusive. The general statements in D 47.10.3 pr 2 suggest that *iniuria* was constituted by *dolus* or *contumelia*. The same is true of the treatment of blows inflicted in jest or in the course of a contest: note again that we are clearly meant to see these cases as illustrations of the general points that precede them. On the other hand, the two examples of mistaken *iniuria* given in 3.4 (Ulpian) and 4 (Paul) are consistent also with the much weaker proposition that an inadvertent act could never amount to *iniuria*.

Furthermore, there is at least one case discussed in D 47.10 that actively militates against the view that the prima facie liability arising from the intentional commission of an injurious act could be rebutted by evidence of the absence of *contumelia*.

In the context of his commentary on the special edict *De adtemptata pudicitia*, a text preserved in D 47.10.15.15 (57 *Ad edictum*),[68] Ulpian discusses the following case:

> If someone accosts [*appellasset*] maidens who are however dressed in slave's clothing [*ancillari veste*] his offence is rather minor; even more so if a woman be in prostitute's dress [*meretricia veste*] and not that of a matron. If, therefore, a woman be not in the dress of a matron [*matronali habitu*] and someone accost her [*appellavit*] or abduct her attendant [*comitem abduxit*], he will be liable to the *actio iniuriarum*.

[67] Lenel, *Palingenesia* (n 19) vol 1, pp 1060–61 and 1072. See, however, Alan Rodger, 'Introducing *iniuria*' (1991) 59 *Tijdschrift voor Rechtsgeschiedenis* 1.

[68] Not Book 77: Lenel, *Palingenesia* (n 19) vol 2, p 772.

Admittedly there is some difficulty with the text: in particular, something appears to have dropped out between the two sentences.[69] Nevertheless, it is possible to make out the gist of what Ulpian is saying. Where an act of *appellare* that was *contra bonos mores* had been intentionally committed, liability arose, even if the defendant had believed himself to be acting lawfully. Thus Ulpian's analysis of this case appears at odds with his analysis in D 47.10.3.2–3.

However, that view of the text rests on the assumption that accosting a slave could not amount to *appellare contra bonos mores. Appellare* in respect of prostitutes must invariably have been lawful, but D 47.10.9.4 suggests that this was not the case with respect to slave women:

> If a person attempt to debauch another, whether male or female, freeborn or made free, he will be liable under the *actio iniuriarum*. So also if an attempt be made upon the chastity of a slave [*si servi pudicitia adtemptata sit*].

While this text appears in the context of Ulpian's commentary on the General Edict, his language unmistakably evokes the special edict *de adtemptata pudicitia*. This suggests that the case was seen as a narrow extension of liability under the special edict. Thus it seems that the defendant in D 47.10.15.15 may have realised that he was committing *iniuria* after all, at least insofar as the text deals with the *appellare* of a matron dressed as a slave woman. That explains his liability despite his mistake as to the identity of the victim. Yet the *iniuria* he sought to effect – the harassment of a slave – was less serious than that which he did effect. His damages were presumably calculated accordingly.[70]

Moreover, if we turn our attention to a portion of Ulpian's commentary on the edict *De iniuriis quae servis fiunt*, excerpted at D 47.10.15.45–49 and 17 pr,[71] we find a sustained analysis of standing under the *actio iniuriarum*, and in particular of the effect of mistaken identity, which seems to turn directly on *contumelia*. As we have seen, the original wording of this edict appears from Ulpian's edictal commentary itself, in a text preserved at D 47.10.15.34–35. 'Where a man shall be said to have beaten another's slave contrary to good morals [*contra bonos mores*] or to have submitted him to torture without the owner's consent, I will give an action.'[72] It is clear from the wording of the edict itself that the determinative criterion in respect of beatings, as in the case of *convicium* and *adtemptata pudicitia*, was *boni mores*, good morals. Yet in the analysis below we find evidence of the almost total reorientation of *servi alieni verberatio* around *contumelia*.

[69] Schultz dismisses the text as interpolated: *Classical Roman Law* (n 10) 597. See also Ibbetson, this volume, ch 2, pp 41–42: 'the thrust of the first sentence is towards the innocence of the accoster, and this looks quite at odds with the consequence – *igitur* – that he is guilty'. Raber does not discuss this text in the context of his account of *animus iniuriandi* ((n 9) ch 3). But see 'Frauentracht und "Iniuria" durch "Appellare"' in *Studi in Onore di Edoardo Volterra* (6 vols, Milan, Giuffrè, 1971) vol 3, p 633 and the sources there cited: 'Ulpian kann die Stelle, so wie wir sie kenne, nicht geschrieben haben' (p 646).

[70] *cf* Ibbetson's view: this volume, ch 2, pp 41–42.

[71] Lenel, *Palingenesia* (n 19) vol 2, pp 773–75.

[72] *cf* section II above.

45 An *iniuria* to a slave sometimes affects the master also, sometimes not; for if the slave is posing as a freeman or if the person who beats him thinks that he belongs to someone else and would not have done it if he knew that the slave was mine, Mela writes that the striker cannot be sued for having done an *iniuria* to me.

46 If, when his slave has been beaten, a master bring the *actio iniuriarum* and subsequently sues for *damnum iniuria*, Labeo says that the causes of action are not the same, for the second action pertains to loss culpably inflicted, the first to *contumelia*.

47 If I have a usufruct in a slave and you own him and slave is beaten or tortured, you as owner rather than I have the *actio iniuriarum*.

48 Again, if someone beat a freeman who is in good faith acting as my slave, a distinction must be made; if he was beaten to express contempt [towards me] [*in contumeliam*], I will have the *actio iniuriarum*. The same applies in respect of someone else's slave serving me in good faith, so that we allow the *actio iniuriarum* whenever the *iniuria* is committed against him in order to express contempt towards me [*in meam contumeliam iniuria ei facta sit*]. Indeed, we do give a master the *actio iniuriarum* in the name of the slave. But if the slave is beaten to get at me, I also have my own action. And the same distinction can be made in respect of the usufructuary.

49 If is more than obvious that if I beat a slave with several owners, each of them has the *actio iniuriarum*.

17 pr But if I did it with the permission of one owner, thinking the slave to belong to him alone, none would have the *actio iniuriarum*. Clearly, if I know that there are several owners, no action will be available to the one who gives me permission, but the others can sue me.

With respect to the cases discussed in D 47.10.15.45, despite the fact that the potential plaintiff is really the owner of the slave, if it appears that the defendant was entirely ignorant of the plaintiff's existence (thinking the slave to be free), or if he believed the slave to belong to someone else against whom he specifically wished to express *contumelia*, no action on the part of the owner will lie. Conversely, in 48 an attack on a *liber homo bona fide serviens* (a free man who believes himself to be a slave), or on A's slave serving B in good faith, gives rise to an action on behalf of the slave's putative owner provided that the assault was perpetrated in order to express *contumelia* towards him. Thus it emerges from 45–48 that whereas only the actual owner of a slave can bring an action in respect of *iniuria* to the slave, *servi nomine*, a putative owner or usufructuary can sue in his own right in respect of an assault on a slave, provided that the assault was perpetrated in order to express contempt for him.

Regarding the case of a slave with several owners, the general rule (given in 49) is that each co-owner has an action in his own right against one who beats the slave. However, where the defendant is ignorant of the existence of some of the co-owners and thus neglects to ask their permission to beat the slave, they cannot sue him for *iniuria* (17 pr). The reason for the absence of liability must be inferred from 48: it is the absence of any *contumelia* with respect to those co-owners.

We appear to encounter a different approach to problems of mistaken identity in D 47.10.18.3–5, excerpted from Book 55 of Paul's edictal commentary *De iniuriis*, specifically that portion of it devoted to *iniuria* through those in the power of the plaintiff:[73]

> 3 If an *iniuria* be perpetrated against me by someone to whom I am unknown or who thinks me to be Lucius Titius when I am in fact Gaius Seius, the thing that really matters is that he wishes to commit *iniuria* against me; for I am a definite person although he thinks me someone other than I am; and therefore I have the *actio iniuriarum*.
>
> 4 But when someone thinks a son-in-power to be a head of household, he cannot be regarded as perpetrating an *iniuria* against the son's father any more than he perpetrates an *iniuria* against her husband when he thinks a woman to be a widow; for no *iniuria* is directed towards their persons [*neque in personam eorum confertur iniuria*], and there can be no transferring of the imputation to them from the person of the son since the will of he who commits the *iniuria* [*affectus iniuriam facientis*] is directed to the son as being a head of household.
>
> 5 But if the wrongdoer knows that his victim is a son-in-power, although he does not know whose power, I would say, says Pomponius, that the father should be given the *actio iniuriarum* in his own right, so also the husband, if he knows his victim to be a married woman. For one who is not unaware of these facts wishes to inflict an *iniuria* [*vult facere iniuriam*] on the father, whoever he may be, through the son and likewise the husband through the wife.

At first glance, 18.3 suggests a more robust analysis than Ulpian's since the defendant is held liable for *iniuria* even against an unknown plaintiff. Yet it is clear from the passage as a whole that Paul's view is the same as that expressed by Ulpian in D 47.10.3.2: 'no-one can commit *iniuria* unless he knows that he commits it [*nisi qui scit se iniuriam facere*], although he may not know against whom he commits it'. Thus where the defendant mistakes Gaius Seius for Lucius Titius, he nevertheless commits *iniuria* against Gaius Seius. The same is true if the identity of his primary victim's father or husband is unknown to him: nevertheless he wishes to inflict an *iniuria* on those persons, whomever they may be. On the other hand, if the defendant commits *iniuria* against someone in ignorance of the very existence of their father or husband he incurs no liability to those persons, since he intends no *iniuria* towards them. As for Ulpian in D 47.10.3.1, for Paul *iniuria* consists in the mental state of the one committing it [*ex affectu facientis*].

V. Conclusion

In the mature law *contumelia* functioned chiefly as a unifying principle, drawing together the existing Republican cases. Yet it seems that the *infamandi causa* of

[73] Lenel, *Palingenesia* (n 19) vol 1, p 1073.

the special edict *ne quid* – the defendant's subjective purpose – continued to play an important role in the context of the classical delict. Moreover, it appears that in many new cases the criterion driving forward liability was indeed the defendant's contemptuous or injurious intention: the fact that he acted in order to perpetrate an *iniuria* (*iniuriae faciendae causa*) or for the purpose of *contumelia* (*contumeliae causa*). Turning to mistaken *iniuria*, some of the best-known cases turn out on closer examination to be inconclusive. However, it seems clear that for Ulpian jokes excluded liability specifically because they excluded wrongful intention. Indeed, there are a number of general statements attributed to Ulpian in *Digest* 47.10.3 that are difficult to reconcile with the view that liability under the *actio iniuriarum* required only intentional conduct – the intention to commit the act in question – rather than the intention to commit an *iniuria*. Simply, 'no-one can commit *iniuria* unless he knows that he commits it (*nisi qui scit se iniuriam facere*)'. Ulpian and Paul's analyses of cases involving *iniuria* through slaves, preserved in *Digest* 47.10.15.45–49, 17 pr and 18.3–5, are likewise incompatible with that view, turning as they do on a specifically contemptuous intention towards the plaintiff.

What has all this to do with *animus iniuriandi* in the modern South African law of defamation? The disclaimer made at the beginning of this essay stands: it has not attempted to address the development of Roman *iniuria* in the *ius commune*, nor the process by which the Roman delict has been converted in modern South African law into one that deals almost exclusively in wrongfulness.[74] Rather, it has simply sought to show that whatever the origins of the term 'consciousness of wrongfulness', the concept itself is Roman. Indeed, by the end of the classical period Roman law was approaching the position that contemptuous or injurious intention on the part of the defendant was determinative of liability under the *actio iniuriarum*. That said, it is undoubtedly the case that a system organised around *contumelia* in this way was bound to become unworkable once combined with the specific defences of the English law of defamation.[75] Succinctly, in the words of Harms DP, such a double analysis 'gets one into a bind'.[76] Sometimes, even mixed legal systems must choose between competing paradigms. The modern South African law of defamation is increasingly 'common law' rather than *iniuria*.

[74] *cf* section I above.

[75] Classical Roman law may have recognised a narrow version of justification (see D 47.10.18 pr, Paul, 55 *Ad edictum*), but it knew nothing of fair comment or privilege. See further Fagan, this volume, ch 9.

[76] See *Maisel v Van Naeren* 1960 (4) SA 836 (C), in which mistaken belief in privilege was treated as having in law the same effect as privilege itself.

7

An Infringement of the *corpus* as a Form of *iniuria*: Roman and Medieval Reflections

PAUL J DU PLESSIS

Generations of law students have been taught that the Roman delict of *iniuria* had a threefold subdivision based on the object of the civil wrong. In classical Roman law, it is said, *iniuria* could be inflicted upon the *corpus*, the *fama* or the *dignitas*. This threefold subdivision originates from a single text by the late-classical jurist, Domitius Ulpianus (D 47.10.1.2; Ulpian, 56 *Ad edictum*):

> Omnemque iniuriam aut in corpus inferri aut ad dignitatem aut ad infamiam pertinere: in corpus fit, cum quis pulsatur: ad dignitatem cum comes matronae abducitur: ad infamiam cum pudicitia adtemptatur.
>
> Every contumely is inflicted on the person or relates to one's dignity or involves disgrace: It is to the person when someone is struck; it pertains to dignity when a lady's companion is led astray; and to disgrace when an attempt is made upon a person's chastity. (Watson's translation)[1]

The Latin text contains a standard *accusativus cum infinitivo* (ACI) construction which is dependent on the main verb in D 47.10.1.1 (*Labeo ait*) where Ulpian reports the views of the Augustan jurist Labeo with approval (D 47.10.1.1; Ulpian, 56 *Ad edictum*):

> Iniuriam autem fieri Labeo ait aut re aut verbis: re, quotiens manus inferuntur: verbis autem, quotiens non manus inferuntur: convicium fit . . .
>
> Labeo says that contumely can be perpetrated by act or by words: by act when an assault is made; by words, there is insult whenever there is no physical attack. (Watson's translation)

The origins of the threefold division can therefore seemingly be traced back to Labeo, a jurist who flourished at the start of the classical period of Roman law. One fact which immediately piques the reader's interest is that within the space of two consecutive text fragments, two separate classifications of *iniuria* are attributed to Labeo. In D 47.10.1.1 Labeo states that *iniuria* could be inflicted *aut re aut verbis*,

[1] Alan Watson (ed), *The Digest of Justinian* (2 vols, Philadelphia, University of Pennsylvania Press, 1985).

while in D 47.10.1.2 Ulpian reports that Labeo stated that *iniuria* could be inflicted *aut in corpus* or pertains *aut ad dignitatem aut ad infamiam.* Given the apparent disparity, it is tempting to suggest that the threefold subdivision in D 47.10.1.2 is a reworking by Ulpian of Labeo's original twofold distinction. Let us see whether the texts support such a claim.

Labeo's division of *iniuria* into two forms, *re* and *verbis*, is manifestly an attempt to structure the late Republican law on *iniuria* into two broad categories, physical and non-physical *iniuria.* That Labeo mentions a *convicium* (one of the praetorian forms of *iniuria* created during the first century BCE) is an indication that he is also taking the specific forms of non-physical *iniuria* created through praetorian innovation into account in his classification.

Roughly 150 years later, even though Gaius (*Institutes*; hereafter G) does not explicitly use Labeo's twofold division (*re et verbis*) it does seem to be present in the way in which he structures his examples. For ease of reference I have divided the text into three sections using numbers (G 3.220):

> Iniuria autem committitur [1] non solum, cum quis pugno puta aut fuste percussus vel etiam verberatus erit, [2] sed etiam si cui convicium factum fuerit, sive quis bona alicuius quasi debitoris sciens eum nihil sibi debere proscripserit sive quis ad infamiam alicuius libellum aut carmen scripserit sive quis matrem familias aut praetextatum adsecatus fuerit [3] et denique aliis pluribus modis.
>
> Now contempt is committed [1] not only when someone is struck with a fist or with clubs, or even flogged, [2] but also when a vocal attack is made on him, when his goods are advertised for sale as a debtor's by someone who knows he owes him nothing, when someone writes a defamatory book or poem about someone, or when someone harasses a lady or a youth; [3] and finally in many other ways. (Gordon and Robinson's translation)[2]

Using Labeo as his starting point, Gaius opted for a threefold division, *re, verbis et aliis pluribus modis.* Gaius is well known for this threefold division which famously also appears in his division of obligations by source.[3] Looking at his examples of *iniuria* committed *re*, it is clear that there has been little change from those envisaged by Labeo. If anything, the number of examples of violent acts has merely increased. There is a slight change in nuance though. As in the case of juristic discussion of the *lex Aquilia,* it may be pointed out that the examples of physical *iniuria* in Gaius not only include assault with hands, but also with an 'extension' of your hands – a whip. As far as the other two categories are concerned, Gaius' text clearly shows the evolution from *iniuria* committed *verbis* to a more subtle distinction which also takes into account verbal *iniuria* committed *ad infamiam.*

[2] William M Gordon and Olivia F Robinson (eds), *The Institutes of Gaius* (London, Duckworth, 1988).

[3] On the influence of Gaius, see Donald R Kelly, 'Gaius Noster: Substructures of Western Social Thought' (1979) 84-3 *The American Historical Review* 619; Obrad Stanojević, *Gaius Noster: Plaidoyer pour Gaius* (Amsterdam, JC Gieben, 1989) 15–63. On the person of Gaius, see also Tony Honoré, *Gaius* (Oxford, Clarendon Press, 1962) generally and Stanojević, *Gaius* (above) 99–115. It has been suggested that the scheme of classification employed by Gaius arose out of a 'school dispute' between the Proculians and the Sabinians. Gaius is known to have been a Sabinian, see Klaus-Peter Nanz, *Die Entstehung des Allgemeinen Vertragsbegriffs im 16. bis 18. Jahrhundert* (Munich, J Schweitzer, 1985) 12–13 and the literature cited there.

The final stage in the evolution of this threefold division is visible in a text by a contemporary of Ulpian, the jurist Paul. This text was not included in the *Corpus iuris civilis* and only exists in the *Collatio* (*Coll* 2.5.4). It shows the transition from the earlier scheme of Labeo *re et verbis* to the scheme eventually adopted by Ulpian, *corpus, fama et dignitas.*

> Fit autem iniuria vel in corpore, dum caedimur, vel verbis, dum convicium patimur, vel cum dignitas laeditur, ut cum matronae vel praetextatae comites abducuntur.
>
> We suffer injury either in body, when we are beaten, or in words, when we suffer verbal abuse, or when dignity is violated, as when the companions of a matron or of a girl are abducted. (Frakes's translation)[4]

Here, for the first time, we see the presence of the terms *corpus* and *dignitas* in the text of Paul. Labeo's original category *verbis* would shortly be transformed by Ulpian into *iniuria ad infamiam pertinere* in D 47.10.1.2.

Given that Ulpian cites Labeo's twofold division with approval, it seems safe to assume that the two forms of classification may be reconciled. This is evident from the examples provided. *Iniuria* is committed *re, quotiens manus inferuntur* (whenever a hand is involved). Similarly, *iniuria* is perpetrated *in corpus . . ., cum quis pulsatur . . .* (when someone is struck/beaten). Thus, while these attempts at classification approach the matter from different angles, it is clear that they were complementary: *iniuria* committed *re* referred to an unlawful physical act such as a beating inflicted upon the *corpus.* That the *corpus* is the passive recipient of the unlawful physical act is also reflected in the Latin: all *iniuria inferri* (passive verb) *in corpus* (accusative), whereas it *pertinere* (active verb) *ad dignitatem* or *ad infamiam.*

But what does *corpus* mean in this context? Does it merely refer to the body of the victim of the *iniuria*? To assess the range of meaning of this term, a brief overview of the history of this delict is required.

Iniuria as a delict first appears in the Twelve Tables which contains three provisions traditionally viewed as the historical foundations of this delict: for *membrum ruptum* ('the permanent disablement of a limb'), *talio* unless the wrongdoer could persuade the victim to accept monetary compensation in lieu;[5] for *os fractum* (the breaking of a bone), a fixed monetary penalty determined by status; 300 *asses* for a free person, 150 for a slave and finally for any other (less serious) form of *iniuria,* a fixed penalty of 25 *asses.*[6] Much ink has been spilt over the meaning of these provisions and they need not detain us here. A few observations will suffice. Physical *iniuria* seems to have been pre-eminent during this period. This adds (some, but not much) weight to the view expressed by modern scholars that the

[4] Robert M Frakes, *Compiling the 'Collatio legum Mosaicarum et Romanarum' in Late Antiquity* (Oxford, Oxford University Press, 2011).

[5] Robert Feenstra, *The Law of Delict from Roman Law to Modern Times: Lectures Delivered in the Department of Civil Law, University of Edinburgh, Summer Term 1961,* 38. The phrase 'permanent disablement of a limb' is that of De Zulueta as quoted by Feenstra.

[6] Reinhard Zimmermann, *The Law of Obligations: Roman Foundations of the Civilian Tradition* (Oxford, Clarendon Press, 1996) 1050–51.

Twelve Tables was a product of a class struggle aggravated by Rome's many skirmishes with her Italian neighbours in an attempt to dominate the Italian mainland.[7] Whether one accepts this hypothesis or not, it would seem that physical *iniuria* was the oldest form of the delict. Furthermore, there is a curious correlation between the 'harm verbs' used in relation to *iniuria* (*membrum ruptum, os fractum*) in the Twelve Tables and that of the *lex Aquilia* chapter 3 (*urere, frangere, rumpere*) enacted roughly two centuries later.[8] This, together with the combination of general and specific rules in relation to *iniuria* which also feature in chapters 1 and 3 of the *lex Aquilia* later on, lends support to the idea, popular in recent scholarly literature, that all of the Roman delicts originated from one common ancestor. Finally, it is worth noting that intent is not mentioned in any of the provisions of the Twelve Tables in relation to *iniuria* and seems to have been implied in these provisions.[9] This is consistent with modern scholarly research on the rise of notions of liability in Roman law.[10]

How does this contribute to our understanding of the meaning of the term *corpus*? Although evidence is scarce for this early period, it is worth noting that none of the provisions of the Twelve Tables in relation to *iniuria* mention the term *corpus*. Instead, the existing provisions focus, in the way in which early legal systems often do, upon the consequence of a violent act upon a specific part of the body (a limb, a bone). The absence of this term is also visible elsewhere in the Twelve Tables, for example, in the famous reference to the 'cutting up' of the body of the condemned debtor (if this is what the phrase *partes secanto* really means),[11] no reference to *corpus* may be found. Although the evidence is slight, this suggests that the term *corpus*, either in relation to *iniuria* or more generally as a concept, most likely did not exist in the time of the Twelve Tables and that it must therefore be the product of a later period.

To establish the likely period in which this term first appeared, we must return to the history of the delict. During the course of the Republic, the fixed penalty system of the Twelve Tables became inadequate.[12] According to the traditional account, based on a rather gossipy story related by Aulus Gellius, one Lucius Veratius, sometime in the early second century BCE, went around the forum deliberately slapping random bystanders and instructing his slave, who carried his purse, to hand over the 25 *asses* as prescribed by the Twelve Tables for cases of less serious *iniuria*.[13] This allegedly caused such outrage that it precipitated law reform and the praetors intervened to create the *actio de iniuriis aestimandis*, a new action whereby the *quantum* of the claim was assessed with reference to the facts

[7] Arrigo D Manfredini, *Istituzioni di diritto romano*, 3rd edn (Turin, G Giappichelli, 2007) 18–19.

[8] Feenstra (n 5) 37.

[9] Michael Crawford (ed), *Roman Statutes* (2 vols, London, Institute of Classical Studies, 1996) vol 2, 607–8.

[10] Imre Molnár, *Die Haftungsordnung des römischen Privatrechts* (Szeged, Diligens, 1998) 11–29.

[11] Geoffrey MacCormack, 'Partes secanto' (1968) 36 *Tijdschrift voor rechtsgeschiedenis* 509.

[12] Fritz Schulz, *Classical Roman Law* (Oxford, Clarendon Press, 1954) 594, Zimmermann (n 6) 1052.

[13] Aulus Gellius, *Noctes Atticae* 20.1.13 as quoted by Feenstra (n 5) 39 who is sceptical about the veracity of this account.

of the case rather than as a fixed penalty as prescribed by law.[14] The story of Lucius Veratius, while entertaining, is likely fictional as Peter Birks has shown.[15] In his view, it is far more likely that the praetorian changes to the law were precipitated by economic instability and the devaluation of the Roman currency, a recurring theme of the mid-Republic as well as by legal developments elsewhere, such as the enactment of the *lex Aquilia* which separated assaults on slaves from *iniuria* and relegated it to the sphere of wrongful damage to property.

The earliest references to the term *corpus* in the Latin language appear in the comedies of Plautus during the late-third century BCE.[16] Given Plautus' penchant for legalistic language, it would be tempting to suggest that the appearance of this term is in some way connected to praetorian changes in the law, but there is too little legal evidence to support such an inference. It is worth pointing out though that the introduction of the *actio de iniuriis aestimandis*, most likely in the second century BCE, which heralded a new mode of assessing the *quantum* of claim with reference to the facts of the case, would not be incompatible with the rise of an abstract concept of *corpus*, but more research needs to be done to confirm this.

During the course of the first century BCE, the praetorian action on *iniuria* was supplemented by a number of ad hoc actions for specific cases. It is commonly said that these actions were not initially regarded as forms of *iniuria* and that their recognition as such only occurred during the classical period. Of these four, the only one that has a physical element is the one involving the *iniuria* perpetrated upon slaves. The others are mostly concerned with non-physical *iniuria*. This has led to the suggestion that the physical aspect of *iniuria* declined during the late Republic and was overtaken in importance by non-physical *iniuria*. While this reading is certainly plausible, it seems rather strange that there should be less law about physical violence during one of the most turbulent periods in Roman history. In my view, the evidence should be seen from a different angle. It should not be forgotten that the praetorian regulation of *iniuria* was augmented during the first century BCE (81 BCE) by a statute, the *lex Cornelia de iniuriis* specifically aimed at examples of physical *iniuria* (assault, battery and violent home invasion). Unfortunately, the text of this statute has not been preserved and we are largely reliant on secondary references to assess its function. The relationship between the praetorian regulation of *iniuria* and this statute has long been a matter of controversy.[17] In my view, however, following Dalla and Lambertini, the *lex Cornelia* should be viewed as emergency legislation which created an alternative 'fast-track' process to deal with the effects of the civil war which gripped large

[14] Schulz (n 12) 593. And on *iniuria* more generally see Fritz Raber, *Grundlagen klassischer Iniurienansprüche* (Vienna, Böhlau, 1969) and Marco Balzarini, *De iniuria extra ordinem statui* (Padua, CEDAM, 1983).

[15] Peter Birks, 'Lucius Veratius and the *lex Aebutia*' in Alan Watson (ed), *Daube Noster: Essays in Legal History for David Daube* (Edinburgh, Scottish Academic Press, 1974) 39.

[16] For a survey of the occurrence of this term in the works of Plautus, see Charlton T Lewis and Charles Short (eds), *A Latin Dictionary* (Oxford, Clarendon Press, 1962) entry on *corpus* (B.4).

[17] Schulz (n 12) 594.

parts of Italy in 82 BCE.[18] The *lex Cornelia* stipulated that assault, battery and home invasions should be dealt with in a swift fashion via the court of the recoverers (*recuperatores*). It therefore did not replace the praetorian action *de iniuriis aestimandis* which could still be brought for physical *iniuria*, it merely permitted victims to obtain swift justice in an unsettled political period. Since the text of this law has not been preserved, we cannot be sure how it dealt with these forms of physical *iniuria*.

So what does this mean for physical *iniuria* and the concept of *corpus*? The great innovation of this praetorian action was that *quantum* of *iniuria* would now be assessed according to the formula of the action for 'whatever is fair and reasonable according to the circumstances'. Such an assessment was made with reference to the physical act which caused the *iniuria* and, as this text by Gaius shows, the law required that the plaintiff describe in the *demonstratio* in quite specific detail which part of his body (*pars corporis*) had been injured. Misrepresenting the extent of an injury led to the dismissal of the case (G 4.60):

> Sed nos apud quosdam scriptum invenimus in actione depositi et denique in ceteris omnibus, ex quibus damnatus unusquisque ignominia notatur, eum, qui plus quam oporteret demonstraverit, litem perdere, . . . aut si is, cui pugno mala percussa est, in actione iniuriarum etiam aliam partem corporis percussam sibi demonstraverit; quod an debeamus credere verius esse, diligentius requiremus.
>
> We find in the writings of some authorities that in an action on deposit, and, in brief, in all other actions in which anyone who is condemned is branded with ignominy,[19] someone who alleges more than there should be, loses his suit, . . . or if, in an action for contempt, someone struck on the cheek in a brawl states that some other part of his body was struck as well. Let us inquire carefully into whether we should regard this as the truer view (Gordon and Robinson's translation)

A similar physical meaning of the term can be seen from his discussion of noxal liability (G 4.75):

> Ex maleficio filiorum familias servorumque, veluti si furtum fecerint aut iniuriam commiserint, noxales actiones proditae sunt, uti liceret patri dominove aut litis aestimationem sufferre aut noxae dedere. Erat enim iniquum nequitiam eorum ultra ipsorum corpora parentibus dominisve damnosam esse.
>
> Noxal actions lie when sons in power and slaves commit a delict, for instance, theft or contempt. These actions allow the father or owner either to pay the damages as assessed in money or to make noxal surrender. For it would be unjust to allow the wickedness of sons or slaves to inflict on fathers or owners any loss beyond their own value. (Gordon and Robinson's translation)

As these two texts show, by the mid-second century, the term *corpus* clearly had both a physical meaning (as part of the body), but also a more figurative meaning

[18] Danilo Dalla and Renzo Lambertini, *Istituzioni di diritto romano*, 3rd edn (Turin, G Giappichelli, 2006) 402.

[19] On *infamia* here, see Abel HJ Greenidge, *Infamia: Its Place in Roman Public and Private Law* (Oxford, Clarendon Press, 1894) 154–70.

(as the value of an asset). The physical meaning can be traced back to the classical period as the following reference by Ulpian to the mid-classical jurist L Neratius Priscus shows (D 17.2.52.16; Ulpian, 31 *Ad edictum*):

> Socium universa in societatem conferre debere Neratius ait, si omnium bonorum socius sit: et ideo sive ob iniuriam sibi factam vel ex lege Aquilia, sive ipsius sive filii corpori nocitum sit, conferre debere respondit.
>
> Neratius says that a partner is obliged to make over all his goods to the partnership if he is a partner in all goods. Thus, he gave an opinion to the effect that the partner pay in anything he has received as compensation for injury or as damages under the *Lex Aquilia*, whether the injury was done to his own person or to that of his son. (Watson's translation)

But even though the term can be traced back to the early second century CE, it is evident from the following text that it was not used by Labeo (D 11.7.8 pr; Ulpian, 25 *Ad edictum*):

> Ossa quae ab alio illata sunt vel corpus an liceat domino loci effodere vel eruere sine decreto pontificum seu iussu principis, quaestionis est: et ait Labeo expectandum vel permissum pontificale seu iussionem principis, alioquin iniuriarum fore actionem adversus eum qui eiecit.
>
> If someone has carried bones or a corpse for burial to a place belonging to somebody else, is the owner permitted to dig up or remove these remains without a decree by the priests or an order from the emperor? Labeo says he must wait to receive either the permission of the priests or the command of the emperor; otherwise, an action for insult will lie against the person who removes the remains. (Watson's translation)

It is clear from this text that the reference to *corpus* (in this case a corpse) is that of Ulpian rather than of Labeo. Having established that the term *corpus* comes to be used with reference to *iniuria* in the period between the early second and third centuries CE, let us assess the use of the term *corpus* with reference to *iniuria* in a number of other Roman law texts from this period.

D 47.10.1.6 (Ulpian, 56 *Ad edictum*):

> Quotiens autem funeri testatoris vel cadaveri fit iniuria, si quidem post aditam hereditatem fiat, dicendum est heredi quodammodo factam (semper enim heredis interest defuncti existimationem purgare): quotiens autem ante aditam hereditatem, magis hereditari, et sic heredi per hereditatem adquiri. Denique Iulianus scribit, si corpus testatoris ante aditam hereditatem detentum est, adquiri hereditati actiones dubium non esse.
>
> Now whenever there be any affront at the testator's funeral or to his corpse, if it occur after the inheritance has been accepted, it must be said that in a sense, the insult is to the heir (for it is always the heir's obligation to vindicate the reputation of the deceased); but if it be before acceptance, the insult is rather to the inheritance itself and it is thus through the inheritance that the heir will acquire the action. Then Julian writes that if a testator's corpse be detained by someone before acceptance of the inheritance, there is no doubt that the action vests in the inheritance. (Watson's translation)

D 9.2.27.17 (Ulpian, 18 *Ad edictum*):

> Rupisse eum utique accipiemus, qui vulneraverit, vel virgis vel loris vel pugnis cecidit, vel telo vel quo alio, ut scinderet alicui corpus, vel tumorem fecerit, sed ita demum, si damnum iniuria datum est: ceterum si nullo servum pretio viliorem deterioremve fecerit, Aquilia cessat iniuriarumque erit agendum dumtaxat . . .
>
> We accepted that 'to rend asunder' includes the case of him who wounds a slave either with a rod or a whip or fist or strikes him with a weapon or in any other way that cuts him or makes a bruise, but only if wrongful damage is caused thereby. However, if he makes the slave in no way less valuable or less useful, the Aquilian action will not lie, and the action for insult will have to be brought so far as this matter is concerned . . .

D 47.10.9 pr (Ulpian, 57 *Ad edictum*):

> Sed est quaestionis, quod dicimus re iniuriam atrocem fieri, utrum, si corpori inferatur, atrox sit, an et si non corpori . . .
>
> But it is a matter of discussion, in talking of an affront being aggravated by its very nature, whether that applies only where it is inflicted upon the person or also when it is not a physical assault . . .

Having surveyed the use of the term *corpus* in relation to the delict of *iniuria* in the second and third centuries CE, it seems clear that it predominantly referred to the body of the victim. As the survey of meanings in Lewis and Short's *Latin Dictionary* shows, this was the primary (literal) meaning of the term which can be traced with great frequency both in legal sources and in Latin literature of the classical period.[20] While there is evidence of the secondary (metonymic) meaning 'a whole comprised of its parts' both in legal and literary sources of this period, this does not appear to have been the sense in which it was used in relation to *iniuria*.

One further question which needs to be addressed in relation to the use of the term *corpus* in relation to *iniuria* is the motivation for its introduction. In my view, a number of factors contributed to this. The introduction of the *actio de iniuriis aestimandis* in the first century BCE brought about a shift in the mode of assessment from the act (*membrum ruptum, os fractum*) to its impact on the victim. This, combined with an increase in the use of the term *corpus* in philosophical works, such as those of Cicero, most likely led over time to the rise of an abstract concept of the body (as opposed to parts of the body as in early Roman law). Furthermore, the interdependence of the delicts of *iniuria* and *damnum iniuria datum*, a subject of much juristic controversy during the classical period, undoubtedly played a role. There is ample evidence, for example, from the *lex Aquilia* that the jurists were interested in the terms (*corpori corpore*). Finally, the gradual refining of the category of *iniuria* committed *verbis* through the recognition of *dignitas* and *infamia* undoubtedly led to a solidifying of the term *corpus* around the body of the victim.

[20] See Lewis and Short (n 16) entry on *corpus* (I–II).

A few questions remain. Is there a philosophical angle to the term *corpus*? Quite possibly, but the extent to which Greek philosophy impacted upon Roman legal thought is disputed.[21] The metonymic meaning of the term appears in the Digest and also in the works of Cicero, but there is no evidence from the existing Roman law texts that the term ever had a philosophical meaning in relation the delict of *iniuria*.[22] Why did Ulpian attribute the threefold subdivision of *iniuria* to Labeo when it would seem that it was his own creation? Apart from the fact that the Labeonic and Ulpianic divisions of *iniuria* are compatible, it was, in all likelihood, an attempt by Ulpian to give due prominence to the importance of Labeo in the structuring of the delict of *iniuria* around the central concept of *contumelia*.[23]

* * *

As a postscript I wish to examine very briefly the manner in which the idea of the *corpus* was understood in medieval learned law. For this period, one should examine both legal dogmatics, based on the legacy of Roman law texts, as was expounded in the works of the medieval jurists and legal practice as is visible in the statutes of the medieval city states.[24] The picture which emerges from this brief overview is a complex one. A certain ambiguity of terminology relating to delicts (*delicta*) and crimes (*crimina*) is visible both in works on medieval learned law and in the city statutes. The reasons for this are twofold. First, the Roman law texts on which medieval learned law was based often discussed a 'criminal law' penalty alongside reference to a delictual penalty.[25] This, combined with the growth of criminal law during the late medieval period as an aspect of 'public law' enforced by city authorities and deriving its power from the rule of the state,

[21] For a recent assessment of the impact of Greek philosophy of Roman law, see Peter G Stein, 'The Roman Jurists' Conception of Law' in Andrea Padovani and Peter G Stein (eds) *The Jurists' Philosophy of Law from Rome to the Seventeenth Century* (Dordrecht, Springer, 2007) 1.

[22] See Lewis and Short (n 16) entry on *corpus* (II). The explicit comparison drawn between the Roman term *contumelia* and the Greek term *hubris* in Justinian, *Institutes* 4.4 pr does suggest some philosophical influence, especially since Labeo, credited with the conceptual reorganisation of *iniuria* around the central notion of *contumelia*, is known to have been influenced by Aristotelian thought.

[23] It is also worth mentioning that the term *iniuria corporalis*, while not present in the Digest, appears regularly in the Codex and even more frequently in the Theodosian Code. For an interesting seventh-century definition of *corpus*, see Isidore of Seville, *Etymologiae* 11.1.14: 'The body (*corpus*) is so called, because it 'perishes when it disintegrates' (*corruptum perire*). It can be dissolved and it is mortal, and at some point has to be dissolved . . . [17] However, what is meant by flesh and what is meant by a body (*corpus*) are different; in flesh there is always a body, but in a body there is not always flesh, for flesh is what is alive, and this a body. A body that is not alive is not flesh. The word 'body' is applied to what is dead after life has departed, or to what has been brought forth without life. Sometimes also there is a body that is alive yet lacks flesh, like grass or trees.' Stephen A Barney and others (eds), *The Etymologies of Isidore of Seville*, new edn (Cambridge, Cambridge University Press, 2010) 232.

[24] Andrea Errera, 'The Role of Logic in the Legal Science of the Glossators and Commentators: Distinction, Dialectical Syllogism and Apodictic Syllogism: An Investigation into the Epistemological Roots of Legal Science in the Later Middle Ages' in Andrea Padovani and Peter G Stein (eds), *The Jurists' Philosophy of Law from Rome to the Seventeenth Century* (Dordrecht, Springer, 2007) 79.

[25] Helmut Coing, *Europäisches Privatrecht*, vol 1 (Munich, CH Beck, 1985) 504–5. The question as to whether these different actions could be brought together was a source of great controversy in the medieval and early modern period, see, for example Wilhelm Höpfner, *Einheit und Mehrheit der Verbrechen: Eine strafrechtliche Untersuchung*, vol 1 (Berlin, F Vahlen, 1901) 30–47.

contributed to a complex picture where *iniuria*, as a delict, is sometimes also discussed as a crime.[26] This distinction is particularly visible in the distinction between physical *iniuria* such as assault which is often dealt with under criminal law and non-physical *iniuria* which continues to be dealt with under the law of delict as Feenstra has shown.[27]

Let us examine the textual evidence relating to medieval learned law. One of the anonymous twelfth-century summaries of Roman law, the *Brachylogus* (*Corpus legum*) employs a threefold division of *iniuria*:

> Iniuria autem fit, non solum cum mala alicuius pugno percutitur: sed etiam cum convicium ei fit: vel cum quis carmen, vel libellum ad infamiam alicuius scripsit ediditve, vel edi fecit, aut scribi dolo malo.[28]
>
> But there is *iniuria*, not only when someone's cheek is forcibly struck with a fist, but also when a clamour is raised against him: either when he wrote or edited a song or a book with the intention to defame someone, or made a poem or allowed it to be written or edited in bad faith. (My translation)

This text shows a familiarity with the Labeonic distinction between physical and non-physical *iniuria*. Whereas the examples of non-physical *iniuria* are in a sense more colourful, those representing physical *iniuria* are quite similar to the Roman examples. It is worth noting that this text makes no mention of the term *corpus*.

Nearly a century later, the glossator Azo († *c*1230) classified *iniuria* in the following manner:

> [3] Fit autem iniuria tribus modis: re, verbis, litteris. Re quotiens manus inferuntur . . . [5–6] Item sciendum est quod omnis iniuria aut infertur in corpus, aut ad dignitatem, aut ad infamiam pertinet. In corpus fit cum quis pulsatur, verberatur, vel domus alicuius vi est introita et in his tribus casibus agitur iniuriarum ex lege Cornelia.[29]
>
> But *iniuria* is inflicted in three ways: *re, verbis, litteris*. It is inflicted *re* whenever a hand is involved . . . It should also be noted that all *iniuria* is committed either with reference to the *corpus*, the *dignitas* or pertains to *infamia*. It is inflicted with reference to the *corpus* whenever someone is pushed, beaten or his home is entered with force and in these cases suit can be brought with the *actio iniuriarum ex lege cornelia*. (My translation)

Azo's threefold division of *iniuria* (*re, verbis, litteris*) again shows some similarity to the Labeonic division, but with an added category. His use of the Ulpianic distinction (*corpus, dignitas, infamia*) later in the same passage suggest that he regarded these two forms of division as compatible. The reference in this text to *corpus*, one of the earliest in medieval learned law, clearly means body of the victim as the examples illustrate, but the inclusion of violent home invasion under

[26] See Michele Pifferi, *Generalia delictorum: il tractatus criminalis di Tiberio Deciano e la 'parte generale' di diritto penale* (Milan, Giuffrè, 2006) 8–9, 370–75. The author argues (at 3–4) in favour of a conceptual break between the late medieval concept of 'criminal law' and the emergence of the first systematic works on criminal law as an autonomous subject during the sixteenth century.

[27] Feenstra (n 5) 44.

[28] *Brachylogus iuris civilis sive corpus legum* (Frankfurt, 1743) bk 3, c 22, *De iniuria* (fol 178).

[29] *Summa Azonis locuples iuris civilis thesaurus* (Venice, 1566) *Summa super Institutionibus* (*De iniuriis* fol 914).

the *lex Cornelia* suggests an attempt at synthesis. This is also visible in the Accursian gloss created by the glossator Accursius (†1263):

> Gl. on [omnem] – Pulsatur ut infra eodem lege l. cornelia in princip. et § 1. Acc.[30]
>
> Gloss on the word 'omnem' – [that is] when anyone is struck as below in the same law (citation to the provisions of the *lex Cornelia*). (My translation)

The threefold division of *iniuria* continues to prevail in works of medieval learned law throughout the late medieval period. Thus, Cinus de Pistoia (†1336/1337) states:

> Iniuria sumitur in tribus modis . . .[31]
>
> There is recourse to *iniuria* in three ways . . . (My translation)

Baldus de Ubaldis (?1327–†1400), on the other hand, seems to prefer the twofold Labeonic distinction:

> Infert quis iniuriarum non solum verbo; sed etiam facto hoc dicit.[32]
>
> Someone commits *iniuria* not only through word, but also deed. This is the meaning of this text. (My translation)

Finally, Angelus (Gambilionibus) de Aretinus (15th cent.), who produced an influential treatise on delicts, states the following:

> [1] Multis modis et diversis iniuria irrogatur. Sed altero de tribus modis fit iniuria, videlicet aut facto, aut verbis aut litteris. Facto dicitur fieri iniuria quotiens quis pulsatur et verberatur, vel domus eius introitur animo iniuriandi . . . [3] Et generaliter quocumque iniuria inferatur in corpus, vel in re alterius animo vulnerandi dicitur facto fieri et non solum si fiat in tua persona propria, vel re sua, sed etiam si fiat in persona uxoris, vel sponsae tuae, vel filii, vel nepotis tui, qui est in potestate, vel servi tui ad tuam contumeliam.[33]
>
> *Iniuria* is understood in many and different ways. But an *iniuria* [is inflicted] upon another in three ways, namely either through deed, through words, or in writing. *Iniuria* is said to be committed through deed whenever someone is struck or beaten or his house is entered with injurious intent . . . And generally *iniuria* in whatsoever way, which is committed with reference to the body, or *in re* with the intention to wound another, is said to have been committed through deed, not only if it is done to your own person, or yours, but also if it is done to the body of your wife, your betrothed, or your son or your grandson who is in your power, or your slave with the intention to injure you. (My translation)

This summary of the understanding of physical *iniuria* according to medieval learned law demonstrates a number of interesting points. First, the threefold distinction (*re, verbis, litteris*) continues to prevail. In second place, the examples of

[30] *Corpus iuris civilis (Digestum novum)* [mit der Glossa Ordinaria von Accursius Florentinus] (Venice 1477) on D 47.10.1.2 (fol 1103).

[31] *Lectura super Codice* (Venice, 1493) fol 391 *verso.*

[32] *Lectura super Institutionibus* (Venice, 1500) *De iniuriis* fol 44 *verso.*

[33] *Tractatus de maleficiis* (Venice, 1578) *De iniuriis* fol 449 *verso.*

physical *iniuria* taken from Roman legal sources are blended with those from the *lex Cornelia* (violent home invasion) to form one concept. But perhaps the most interesting aspect of Aretinus' discussion is his blending of the two Roman classifications (*res* and *corpus*) into one. This is done to reinforce the point that physical *iniuria* may be committed not only with reference to your own body, but also with reference to those who are in your power. This is a novel interpretation which is not visible in other medieval works. It is worth noting that Aretinus uses the term *corpus* literally to mean the physical body of the victim. He also employs the term *persona* with reference to physical integrity of other members of the *familia* which can be subject to physical *iniuria*.

It remains to speak briefly about medieval canon law. The contribution of medieval canon law to the development of *iniuria* is complex. In the standard works of medieval learned law such as the Decretals of Gregory IX, which were given the force of law in 1234, *iniuria* and *damnum iniuria datum* are discussed together and at times fuse into one.[34] The main reason for this is the spectacular development of *damnum iniuria datum* with reference to the body of the free person in medieval learned law. This had two consequences. First, physical *iniuria* became intertwined with *damnum iniuria datum* and was treated as an aspect of criminal law which was enforced by state authority. In second place, since one of the basic tenets of canon law was that no one could benefit financially from a wrong,[35] the only redress possible for physical *iniuria* under canon law was a financial penalty enforced through criminal prosecution.[36] As for the threefold division of *iniuria* (*re, verbis, litteris*), it is visible in the works of medieval canonists such as Henricus de Segusio (*c* 1200–1271).[37]

As for examples of legal practice regarding physical and non-physical *iniuria* in medieval city states, Dean provides a particularly vivid overview. In his chapter on insult, he paints a wonderfully colourful picture of the types of verbal insult which came before the courts most frequently and the approaches taken by the lawmakers of various city states towards the prosecution of insults.[38] His chapter on physical *iniuria* (violence) gives a particularly detailed account of the various legislative approaches in the late medieval Italian city states to the criminal prosecution of physical violence.[39] Through an analysis of these legislative measures, Dean shows that physical assault is almost exclusively prosecuted under criminal law and that, in keeping with late medieval criminal law, is dealt with through a system of monetary fines. Such fines were carefully calculated with reference to factors such as citizenship, status, type of weapon used and the place on the body where the

[34] Decretals 5.34.1 (On duels).

[35] Coing (n 25) 504.

[36] Robert Feenstra, *Vergelding en vergoeding: enkele grepen uit de geschiedenis van de onrechtmatige daad*, 3rd edn, ed LC Winkel (Deventer, Kluwer, 2002) 15–16.

[37] Henricus de Segusio, *Summa aurea* (Venice, 1570) 448.

[38] Trevor Dean, *Crime and Justice in Late Medieval Italy* (Cambridge, Cambridge University Press, 2007) 113–32. This chapter also carefully discusses vengeance in the context of insult and the approaches taken by law-makers and the jurists towards this notion.

[39] ibid 168–81.

injury occurred.

* * *

By focusing on an infringement of the *corpus* as a form of *iniuria* in both Roman and medieval learned law, this contribution has merely scratched the surface of a much larger topic which is in desperate need of further research. The Roman law of *iniuria* is a much neglected topic compared to the other named delicts which existed in Roman law and more research is needed on a variety of topics such as the interplay between delict and crime and the relationship between non-physical *iniuria* (*ad dignitatem aut infamiam pertinere*) and the Roman conception of virtues such as *dignitas*, *virtus*, *pietas* and *auctoritas*. Furthermore, in medieval learned law, the conceptual interaction between delict and crime and the relationship between legal doctrine in works on medieval learned law and legal practice as visible in the statutes of medieval Italian city states requires much work. With that said, initial investigations suggest that *corpus* seems to have had a largely literal meaning in both Roman and medieval learned law.

8

The Protection of *corpus* in Modern and Early Modern Scots Law

JOHN BLACKIE

I. Introduction

The protection in the Scots law of delict of a person's interest in his or her bodily integrity and physical freedom from the early modern period on has been in different ways separated from the protection of other specific interests relating to the person. This has had consequences not only for the details of the law protecting these interests, but also for determining what are the fundamental principles and the doctrinal theoretical structure of the law of delict as a whole. In particular this phenomenon provides much of the explanation why the Scots common law of delict is not today structured clearly under two broad heads, Aquilian liability and *iniuria* (adapted and modified by human and rights law and statute law).

II. Early Modern Analysis: Crime/Delict

It is now clear beyond a peradventure that the early modern Scots law of delict protecting personality rights was, as throughout Europe at the time, the application of the general law of delict as understood, elaborated and, with some different approaches to detailed points, debated in *ius commune* treatises, with the courts, taking particular positions on them for Scotland. Both that literature and that local Scots case law were then reflected in Scottish juristic writing, from Stair[1] and Mackenzie[2] and Pitmedden[3] in the seventeenth century on through the leading

[1] Stair, *Institutions of the Law of Scotland* (1693).

[2] George Mackenzie, *The Institutions of the Law of Scotland* (first published Edinburgh, 1684); George Mackenzie, *The Laws and Customs of Scotland in Matters Criminal* (first published Edinburgh, 1678; 2nd edn, Edinburgh, 1699; 3rd edn, ed OF Robinson, Edinburgh, Stair Society, 2012); henceforth Mackenzie, *Matters Criminal*.

[3] Alexander Seton of Pitmedden, *A Treatise of Mutilation and Demembration* (Edinburgh, 1699) published as an appendix to Mackenzie, *Matters Criminal* (1699).

eighteenth century jurists Bankton,[4] Erskine[5] and Hume.[6] This being so, Scotland did recognise the basic grammar of Aquilian liability and of *iniuria*. However, treating the protection of a person's interests in his or her bodily integrity and physical freedom with rarely any reference to that basic grammar had ultimately as one of its effects that one of the central aspects of that grammar was obscured, namely that patrimonial consequences gave rise to Aquilian liability as much where there was *iniuria*, ie in cases of intentional invasion of these interests,[7] as in situations where there was a non-intentional invasion. In so far as Aquilian liability is recognised at all as an organising category in modern Scots law, which is debateable, it is conceived solely as being concerned with non-intentional invasion of rights, in today's language 'negligence', and the protection of a person's interest in bodily integrity as protected by that area of law is completely distinct from the law where the invasion is by intentional conduct. It is not certain that negligent (de facto) deprivation of a person's freedom of movement without any physical harm resulting is actionable. But if it is, it would likewise be treated as distinct from intentional deprivations of physical liberty.

The word *corpus* is familiar from the standard tripartite classification of interests stemming from a text of Ulpian, *corpus*, *fama*, *dignitas*.[8] However, it is used in this essay simply because it provides a convenient single-word term for the rights in bodily integrity, and by extension in physical liberty, and possibly for what today may additionally be a right to sexual integrity.[9] The only specific citation of this Ulpian text in Scottish published material until recent times is in the work of Lord Bankton published in the middle of the eighteenth century.[10] The somewhat more lengthy formulations of protected rights or interests that appear in Scottish juristic writing from Stair in the late seventeenth century through to Hume[11] at the turn of the eighteenth to the nineteenth century confirm that analytically the law at that high level of analysis was correctly focused in this way. They also drew on wider philosophical and theological thought in the European tradition. So, for

[4] Bankton, *An Institute of the Laws of Scotland in Civil Rights: With Observations upon the Agreement of Diversity between them and the Laws of England* (first published Edinburgh, 1751–53; Edinburgh, Stair Society, vols 41–43, 1993–95).

[5] Erskine, *An Institute of the Law of Scotland* (first published Edinburgh, 1773).

[6] David Hume, *Commentaries on the Law of Scotland Respecting Crimes* (first published Edinburgh, 1797); Hume, *Commentaries on the Law of Scotland Respecting Crimes*, 4th (posthumous) edn, ed BR Bell (Edinburgh, 1844) – henceforth Hume, *Commentaries*; and David Hume, *Baron David Hume's Lectures 1786–1822*, ed GCH Paton, 3 vols (Stair Society, vols 5, 13, 17–19, 1939–58) – henceforth Hume, *Lectures*.

[7] Clear in the seventeenth century in case law on quantum of patrimonial loss in invasions of bodily integrity. *Dewar v Baxter* (1662) WG Scott-Moncrieff, *The Records of the Proceedings of the Justiciary Court Edinburgh 1661–1678*, vol 1 (Edinburgh, Scottish History Society, 1905) 53; J Blackie, 'Unity in Diversity: The History of Personality Rights in Scots Law' in NR Whitty and R Zimmerman (eds), *Rights of Personality in Scots Law: A Comparative Perspective* (Dundee, Dundee University Press, 2009) 87.

[8] Justinian, *Institutes* (hereafter J) 4.4.1; D 47.1.2: (Ulpian): 'omnem iniuriam aut in corpus inferri aut ad dignitatem aut ad infamiam pertinere'.

[9] For whether there is such a distinct personality right see below text to nn 72–74.

[10] Bankton, *Institute* 1.10.21.

[11] Hume, *Commentaries*, vol 1, pp 327, 332 and 333, vol 2, p 121.

instance, Stair's 'life, members and health' may be at least in part inspired by a similar, though shorter, formulation in Grotius: '*corpus, membra*',[12] and is clearly within the approach also of earlier Calvinist jurists of the northern natural law school.[13] Stair's listing of 'liberty' as a specific interest mirrors the approach by for example Donellus.[14] The next level of categorisation by way of the mechanism used in the invasion of the right in question, ie whether by words (verbal injury/*iniuria verbalis*) or physical acts (real injury/*iniuria realis*) was also understood and referred to in Scottish juristic writing[15] in the early modern period. But, as invasions of the right to bodily integrity etc in the nature of things in virtually all instances that arise in practice are through a physical act, courts never needed in such cases to refer to that.[16] What is more, and crucially for the development of the law, cases were decided by courts applying a set of specific sub-categories that were used by courts all over Europe. What brought these sub-categories into existence were variously particular Roman texts, canonist approaches (founded on Christian theology) to the nature of the bodily aspect of human personality, and probably for some categories some influence from customary law. Broadly, whatever the original impetus for them individually, they were primarily ways of considering by category a hierarchy of seriousness of the invasion of the right. For the invasions of bodily integrity in descending order of seriousness they were: (1) mutilation, the making useless a distinct functioning part of the body, sometimes subdivided with a specific further sub-category demembration (otherwise dismembration) where the part was actually severed from the body, (2) invasion of bodily integrity in a person's home ('Hamesucken'), (3) drawing blood ('effusion of blood') (4) other impacts on the body, 'invasion', 'hurting', 'wounding' etc. For invasions of physical liberty the sub-categories, all built on Roman texts, and the boundaries of which were subject to considerable debate in Scotland as elsewhere, were abduction, ravishment (*raptus*), *plagium*, and *crimen privati carceris.* The debates about these covered in particular whether ravishment had to be *libidinis causa*, and whether for ravishment and *plagium* the victim had to be female or not (Scotland till the late seventeenth century taking the latter view). The debates on the requirements *crimen privati carceris*, for instance whether it required that the victim was held in a building do not appear in Scottish published material, but exist in European juristic writing. Modern day descendants of some of these sub-categories exist in criminal codes in a number of European

[12] Grotius, *De iure belli ac pacis* (first published, 1625) 2.17.2.1.

[13] eg Donellus, *Commentarii de iure civile* (1589–97) lib 2 c 8: '*vita, corporis incolumnitas*'.

[14] ibid.

[15] Mackenzie, *Laws and Customs of Scotland* (1699) 30.1.1. Mackenzie, *Laws and Customs of Scotland* (2012) 222; A Bayne, *Institutions of the Criminal Law of Scotland* (1730) 175; Bankton, *Institute* 1.10.22 and 24.

[16] Contrast the distinction used in determining what courts had jurisdiction in cases of *iniuria* by written words, and one unsuccessful attempt to argue that the High Court of Justiciary had jurisdiction in cases of *iniuria* by oral words where the status of the victim was exceptionally high, discussed in Blackie, 'Unity in Diversity' (n 7) 75–77.

jurisdictions.[17] That this is the case is a consequence of the forcible breaking in the era of codification of the intertwined relationship of delictual and criminal law doctrine, a relationship which in Scotland and in some other jurisdictions was in the early modern period additionally strengthened by the criminal courts being the forum where parties sought their 'civil remedies' in cases of infringement of bodily integrity, and in cases of deprivation of physical liberty.

In connexion with the protection of these personality rights in Scotland in the early modern period the relationship of criminal law and delict in fact amounts to a complete identification of doctrine, as it would have in at least in those jurisdictions elsewhere in Europe where civil remedies were sought within the criminal process. There was a single body of crime/delict doctrine. That contrasted with the position with respect to the protection of property rights and the protection of pure economic rights. Scottish courts, therefore, in applying the sub-categories and in deciding what approach to take to debateable points utilised continental European (often contemporary or relatively recent) juristic writing on criminal law and criminal evidence. It appears that it is precisely this literature that was used in courts all over Europe,[18] although it has not figured as largely in modern scholarship on the doctrinal history of the law of delict. Of course Scotland never codified either its private or its criminal law. But nevertheless a process occurred from the eighteenth century onwards whereby even with respect to the protection of bodily integrity and physical liberty delictual doctrine came to have a life of its own separated from criminal law.

III. The Separation of Delict and Crime

There are several reasons why criminal law and delictual doctrine came to be separated in the protection of *corpus*. The old sub-categories for the protection of bodily integrity were abandoned by the nineteenth century. The protection of physical liberty became definitively separated a hundred years earlier.

The disappearance by the nineteenth century of the old sub-categories for the protection of bodily integrity meant that the old learning based on continental European juristic writing on them simply became irrelevant. However, that in itself cannot be the explanation for the breaking of the identity of civil and criminal law which then occurred in this context. The old sub-categories disappeared for the criminal law, too at that time. Hume, who provided what in many ways was a new taxonomy for criminal law at the turn of the eighteenth to the nineteenth century, patently assumed that it would be applicable as much to where the

[17] J Blackie, 'Doctrinal History of the Protection of Personality Rights in Europe in the *ius commune*: General Actions or Specific Actions?' (2009) 13 *Electronic Journal of Comparative Law* www.ejcl.org/art131-1.pdf.

[18] For a preliminary consideration see ibid.

victim sought damages.[19] Also in his contemporaneous *Lectures* on private law, though he gives as a specific example a claim by a 'tradesman who has been assaulted',[20] and he discusses *inter alia* in the context of bodily injury the approach to be taken to patrimonial and non-patrimonial damages,[21] to solidary liability as contrasted with potentially different levels of criminal punishment for the participants,[22] and to the question of transmissibility, he does not provide any analysis of the basis of liability. He simply refers to it as a 'wrong or criminal act'.[23] The term 'assault' was used for a new category in both civil and criminal law. Other English law terms and concepts, notably trespass to the person were not imported. Though 'battery' sometimes can be found in early nineteenth-century Scottish civil jury cases in an omnibus phrase 'assault and battery' it did not have any particular significance doctrinally.[24] Notwithstanding this, however, the adoption of the category 'assault' was crucially important, because ever since it has in Scots law had the effect of removing or largely removing the protection of the interest in bodily integrity by the law of delict from *iniuria*, and, as discussed further below, to what is in effect a body of rules developed anew from the start of the nineteenth century up to the present time by way of a rather thin case law, and till recently[25] a very limited literature. However, at the time that 'assault' began to develop in Scottish private law in the first third of the nineteenth century it was sometimes at least formally connected to *iniuria*.[26] There is still a possible debate about whether in some respects at least that connexion may be a source of ideas in the modern law.[27]

With respect to the protection of rights to physical liberty the separation of delict from crime had occurred by the beginning of the eighteenth century. The old sub-categories, and so again the old learning based on continental European juristic writing, had since that time in this connexion been obsolete in Scotland. As far as civil cases were concerned there developed completely new sub-categories which did not apply in criminal law, while criminal law lost most of the old sub-categories and changed the nature of two that survived. These developments meant as has remained that physical liberty and bodily integrity are not linked at

[19] By this time the remedy of seeking an expression of repentance survived only in the form of the 'palinode' in verbal injury cases.

[20] Hume, *Lectures* vol 3.

[21] ibid, pp 120–22.

[22] Hume, *Lectures* vol 3, pp 124–25.

[23] Hume, *Lectures* vol 3, pp 120 and 122.

[24] Blackie, 'Unity in Diversity' (n 7) 105; See though EC Reid, *Personality, Confidentiality and Privacy in Scots Law* (London, W Green, 2010) 2.04 for Adam Smith's distinguishing between a 'person put to bodily fear' as 'assault' and 'actualy [*sic*] beat' as 'battery'.

[25] Reid, *Personality* (n 24) is the indispensable treatment of the civil law of assault in modern Scots law.

[26] Notably in the statutory provision listing actions of this type amongst those where proof of facts would now be in the form of a civil jury trial: Judicature Act 1925 s 28: 'Actions . . . on account of Injuries to the Person, whether real or verbal, as Assault or Battery, Libel or Defamation'.

[27] As argued for generally in NR Whitty, 'Overview of Rights of Personality in Scots Law' in NR Whitty and R Zimmerman (eds), *Rights of Personality in Scots Law: A Comparative Perspective* (Dundee, Dundee University Press, 2009) 167 and 205.

all for legal analysis. In the criminal law two of the old physical liberty sub-categories, *plagium* and ravishment/*raptus* changed completely. In the process of disappearing from the general law of deprivation of liberty, the former came to be the term for the crime of the abduction only of children,[28] and the latter as 'rapt' and then 'rape' for the most serious type of sexual offence committed against women,[29] which till then had been where there was no abduction of the victim classified as 'deforcement'. In the now unconnected civil law, the paradigm case of wrongful invasion of liberty became one concerning the citizen and the state, not that of the taking and holding against his or her will of an individual by another acting in a private capacity. The result was that the new delictual sub-category of the seventeenth century, 'wrongous imprisonment', the name being very possibly influenced by the English law term, 'false imprisonment',[30] was applied to deal with a state officer or body, whether acting on his or its own initiative, or stimulated to do so by an accusation against the victim by another, which was by definition not covered by the sub-category, *crimen privati carceris*, nor readily covered by any of the other sub-categories. The development of the category, 'wrongous imprisonment', then was further stimulated by what can be seen a conscious Scottish response just before the Union of the Parliaments to awareness of *habeas corpus* in English law,[31] the Act anent Wrongous Imprisonment 1701 with its own scheme for assessment of damages, depending on social status and the length of time detained, even though a common law claim was alternatively possible. By the nineteenth century the law became largely identical to English law and has remained so.

IV. The Nominate Delict of Assault

Today the rules of a nominate delict of assault, that has grown from the apparently nominate delict that emerged in the early nineteenth century, is the source of the protection in private law of *corpus*. The law has been comprehensively stated in detail and exhaustively analysed by Elspeth Reid.[32] As a result of her work it is now apparent that the questions of greatest difficulty today are precisely ones which earlier law glossed over or did not consider at all. Further (just as happened with the protection of physical liberty from the eighteenth century on) the law today has to reflect the reality that civil assault actions are most likely to be raised 'to call to account individuals alleged to have overstepped the power which their

[28] Hume, *Commentaries*, vol 1, 83–84.

[29] Mackenzie, *Matters Criminal* (2012) (n2) 16.2 (p 124).

[30] *Oliphant v Wemyss* (1661) WG Scott-Moncrieff, *The Records of the Proceedings of the Justiciary Court Edinburgh 1661–1678*, vol 1 (Edinburgh, Scottish History Society, 1905) 5. 'Persuit [*sic*] . . . for false imprisonment continued' discussed in Blackie, 'Unity in Diversity' 63–64.

[31] *Mackenzie v Earl of Marchmont* (1704) 4 BS 595 (Fountainhall) 596.

[32] Reid, *Personality* (n 24) 2.01–2.41.

status gives to use force against others', and in particular the police. Apart from these it is contexts of consensual physical interaction, medical treatment and sport[33] that are the prominent concerns of the law in this area. These latter, of course, existed in even the farther past but were not a source of litigation until the twentieth century. Thus, as Elspeth Reid emphasises, actions now are not likely to be raised against private individuals for minor physical injury such as in the context of being spat or having one's nose tapped or hat tilted.

Since the late nineteenth century a number of writers have used for the taxonomy of the whole law of delict a division based in conduct, distinguishing therefore fundamentally negligence law from the law of 'intentional delicts'.[34] However, at least in the context of the protection of bodily integrity, what was meant by intention, or earlier *animus iniuriandi*, or 'malice' as a synonym for these was never analysed. Further, in the context of assault there is connected with that the question as to whether some further quality of the conduct is required, such as that the act was hostile, for which there is some English authority although the pertinence of that idea has been strongly doubted there too.[35] Elspeth Reid has now provided a structured analysis of intention in the civil law of assault:

> Assault is an intentional delict, first of all, in the sense that the conduct which precipitated the harm must have been deliberate . . . But intentional conduct is not enough: assault also requires some measure of intention with regard to the infliction of harm. Thus liability may be found if and only if: (a) the defender acted deliberately; and (b) (i) with the purpose of causing harm; or (ii) knowing that harm of some kind was likely to occur, even if he or she did not positively desire that outcome; or (iii) with reckless disregard to the possibility of causing harm. It is important to consider the scope of harm in this context.[36]

Most of this mirrors the concept of intention in the criminal law. But the conduct showing a reckless disregard and the need to consider the 'scope of the harm' demonstrate that civil assault is a body of distinct rules, not just being concerned with providing a remedy of damages where on the lower civil standard of proof the requirements for the crime of assault are satisfied. Also it is likely that a different approach is taken in the civil law of assault to the question of capacity of the defender.[37] Ever since the emergence in the early nineteenth century of the then apparently nominate delict of assault the law has been that assault, as in modern Scots criminal law, can take the form of the threat of a physical injury. Before that time with a generalised idea of *iniuria* it was not necessary to spell that out. However classifying that as coming under 'assault' led to a need to have some rules to draw a line more clearly as to when such would be actionable and when

[33] Reid, *Personality* (n 24) 2.02.

[34] From AT Glegg, *A Practical Treatise on the Law of Reparation* (Edinburgh, William Green & Sons, 1892) Part II Malice – Breaches of Duty in which there is Wrongful Intention; Part III Negligence.

[35] *Re F (Mental Patient Sterilisation)* [1990] 2 AC 1, 73.

[36] Reid, *Personality* (n 24) 2.10.

[37] There is also the possibility that a defender whose capacity is impaired could be civilly liable on the basis of negligence if he or she ought to have known that consciousness was impaired. (Reid, *Personality* (n24) 2.14).

not. That line was drawn in the nineteenth century case law by a requirement of credible fear on the part of the pursuer, and it has been argued[38] that now an extended interpretation as applied in England in the criminal law of assault covering silent phone calls may be correct and so cover also fear of 'the *possibility* of immediate personal violence'.[39] Applying these tests relating to fear provides a way of setting a boundary that in the old law of *iniuria* would have been set by way of the consideration what could count as an affront. But as rude gestures were a category well-recognised as actionable without needing to draw on general theory,[40] in effect the law lacked sharp-edged tools to draw a boundary.

There remains then a question whether there is any role left for *iniuria* as a concept that can still contribute to the law protecting *corpus*. It has been argued in effect that there is really none, though, of course, the non-patrimonial aspect of an award for damages can reflect 'the element of indignity, humiliation or distress suffered in an assault'.[41] Then it is consistently argued acts such as the taking away of a person's clothes or strip searching are more logically categorised as infringing privacy alone[42] and (additionally) in some cases through the law protecting the separate personality right of physical liberty. Further, the statutory delict of harassment, an innovation in 1997,[43] is often applicable, and provides a much wider basis of actionability, since the impact element extends to 'causing the person alarm or distress',[44] and the conduct element does not require intention but is satisfied alternatively if in the circumstances 'it would appear to a reasonable person that it would amount to harassment'.[45] In the nineteenth century a new delict was invented called 'molestation' of the person which covered the vexatious conduct generally affecting the person. Its functional role was to enable interdict[46] to be obtained, and in the twentieth century was principally used in cases of marital breakdown. It is difficult to see that it has any longer any role in the law, although in theory as the delict it could found an action for damages.

V. Cases with a Sexual Element

There is a need for further consideration of the law in cases with a sexual element. The question is whether in the law of delict these are to be categorised as just a

[38] Reid, *Personality* (n 24) 2.16.
[39] *R v Ireland* [1998] AC 147 (Steyn) 162.
[40] Discussed in Blackie, 'Unity in Diversity' (n 7) 79.
[41] Reid, *Personality* (n 24) 2.02.
[42] Reid, *Personality* (n 24) 2.20.
[43] Protection from Harassment Act 1997.
[44] S 8(3).
[45] S 8(1)(b).
[46] The notion of a distinct category does not obviously pre-date its use in H Burn Murdoch, *Interdict in the Law of Scotland* (Edinburgh, W Hodge, 1933). (See *Ward v Scotrail Railways* 1999 SC 255, 259 (Reed)).

form of assault. In early modern law it certainly was the case that these situations were treated as requiring the application of legal rules that were not just directed at the protection of bodily integrity, and but also at what in the society and culture of that period may be described as a right in moral sexual relations[47] (and associated aspects of rights in family life).[48] To understand how it came about that there has been little consideration today of whether a civil case with a sexual element may need distinct consideration as involving the protection of a personality right in addition to that of bodily integrity, it is necessary to see how the categories built on early modern understanding changed, and how the criminal law developed from the late eighteenth century on, i.e. the time when delict came to be treated separately from crime in the literature and in the courts. The early modern law was in its origins the product of canonists, though they elaborated on Roman texts. The canonist approaches were taken over directly by European jurists of the sixteenth and seventeenth centuries analysing the criminal law (including its associated 'civil' remedies). As already discussed above, from the time of Mackenzie in the second half of the seventeenth century the crime of rape took on the role of being the most serious sexual offence, and was divorced entirely from the law relating to protection of physical liberty. Until modified by judicial decision in the later twentieth century, as now changed again by a new statutory definition,[49] its *actus reus* consisted of penetrative sexual intercourse, a lack of consent by the victim and an overbearing of that victim's will by the perpetrator. These requirements were adjusted and changed to reflect the goals of criminal law as society and cultural attitudes changed.[50] Over the same period new categories of sexual offence emerged in Scots criminal law, notably 'clandestine injury to women', and 'lewd and libidinous' conduct, which were not classifications found in early modern law. The opposite process happened with the mediaeval and early modern sub-category, *stuprum*, the alluring of a virgin or widow into having sexual intercourse with the perpetrator. As it was dealt with in Scotland in the Commissary Courts, which following the Reformation took over the jurisdiction of the courts of the bishops' Officials, in Scotland it never became part of criminal law doctrine, and by the eighteenth century was actionable in the Court of Session as an ordinary civil case. At some point the standard late mediaeval remedy recognised by the canonists that the wronged woman was entitled to an order that the defender marry her or provide her with a sum of money appropriate in the light

[47] See generally Blackie, 'Unity in Diversity' (n 7) 64ff.

[48] Claims by the innocent spouse against a party committing adultery, or for what became known as 'enticement' of a wife ie (eg by a parent) to leave her husband (eg against a parent) or the equivalent with enticing children to leave their homes though in origin associated with the interest in moral sexual relations as they are not claims by the person with whom adultery etc took place are about a different personality right to family life. See for details of the mid-twentieth century law DM Walker, *The Law of Delict in Scotland*, 2nd edn (Edinburgh, W Green, 1981) 711 ff and for the law today K McKenzie Norrie, 'Obligations', *Stair Memorial Encyclopaedia of the Laws of Scotland* vol 15, para 596.

[49] Sexual Offences (Scotland) Act 2009 s 1.

[50] For the social and cultural perception today and the goals of the criminal law in Scotland see PR Ferguson and C McDiarmid, *Scots Criminal Law: A Critical Analysis* (Dundee, Dundee University Press, 2009) 11.2.7.

of her status for her to bring as a dowry in marriage with someone else, ceased to be available in Scotland. Instead the remedy was damages, with the quantum reflecting the social status of the pursuer. In the eighteenth century *stuprum* became renamed as the delict of 'seduction'. Just exactly what conduct in alluring the victim is necessary was never fully clarified, as, indeed, it was not in the old law of *stuprum*. The delict of seduction has not been abolished by statute. It is taken in one textbook as still existing, and the absence of modern cases and changes in sexual mores not commented on this connexion.[51] But its continuing existence seems doubtful. The opinion has been expressed that 'female virginity doubtless remains a protected interest in the law today'.[52] However, if that is so it raises a more fundamental issue, as opposed to the narrow question whether there is still a delict seduction, namely whether the law of delict today recognises in sex cases a distinct personality right classifiable separately from the general right to bodily integrity, and accordingly what are the applicable rules and principles if it does that.

Given the change of social mores with respect to sex it is certainly not meaningful to denote any such separate personality right as it can be for the early modern period as a right in moral sexual relations. There is a case, however, for considering, nonetheless, that there is a right in addition to the right to bodily integrity which should be reflected in the approach law of delict. There are four possible views. The first is that this is unnecessary as sexual cases can be dealt with by the nominate delict of assault, and that there is a sexual element is reflected in the quantum of any award. The second is that cases with a sexual element are 'aggravated assault'. The third is that the law of delict is an application of the criminal law of sexual offences. The fourth is that by drawing on the concept of *iniuria* it is possible to recognise that a further right than that to bodily integrity is infringed, and that then would require further detailed rules to be developed.

The first approach is expressly taken in one modern text[53] and it can also be found expressed *obiter* in a case recognising a husband's claim where his wife was raped.[54] The same approach is implied in Elspeth Reid's treatment of the protection of personality rights, in not dealing specifically with sexual cases, and likewise is implied in the standard late nineteenth-century and early twentieth-century work on delict,[55] though it includes 'seduction', and contemplates an action by a married woman against a man with whom she had committed adultery 'if she could show that her virtue had been overcome by his seductive arts',[56] a ground of liability invented by the author, without any historical precedent.

[51] J Thomson, *Delictual Liability*, 3rd edn (Edinburgh, LexisNexis UK, 2004) 16.

[52] K McKenzie Norrie, 'The Intentional Delicts' in K Reid and R Zimmermann (eds), *A History of Private Law in Scotland*, vol 2 (Oxford, Oxford University Press, 2000) 513.

[53] Thomson, *Delictual Liability* (n 51) 16.

[54] *Black v Duncan* 1924 SC 738 (Anderson) 748.

[55] AT Glegg, *A Practical Treatise on the Law of Reparation*, 2nd (and last by the author) edn (Edinburgh, W Green, 1905) – seduction is dealt with in a separate chapter 7; in the first edn of 1892 it is dealt with under a separated heading in the same chapter as assault at 95–98.

[56] Glegg, *Practical Treatise*, 2nd edn (n 55) 139.

The second approach, 'aggravated assault', but combined with a nod in the direction the fourth, drawing on *iniuria* and then applying the third, the criminal law, can be found in Walker on *Delict*, (in addition to 'seduction') dealing specifically with rape,[57] and in a footnote mentioning also 'assault with intent to rape'.[58] Rape is classified by him as 'aggravated assault . . . a pure *actio injuriarum* the conduct being a gross affront to the pursuer'. The elements of the delict are then stated as 'thought to be the same as the crime of rape'. Resulting pregnancy (which is not an element in the crime of rape, nor an 'aggravation' of it) is stated to 'enhance' 'the gravity of the wrong'. It is not clear that the concept of 'aggravation' in the sense understood in criminal law, where it not only serves to classify a crime within a wider genus but which has a particular procedural consequence that a party tried for aggravated assault can be convicted either of the offence as charged or of it without the aggravation.[59] 'Aggravated', however, might rather be just another way of referring to the wider concept of *iniuria* as affront in considering quantum, which was done occasionally in Scottish material in the early modern period in using that term in taking account of the social status of the victim, and the nature of the environment in which an invasion of bodily integrity occurred.[60] If this is the position, it should be made clear. Otherwise the concept of 'aggravation' might be assumed to be the same as in criminal law under in the law of delict. Moreover, the criminal law of sexual offences in the Sexual Offences (Scotland) Act 2009 no longer uses the concept of 'aggravation' and specifically the crime of 'indecent assault', which was classified as an instance of 'aggravated assault' has been abolished and superseded by new specific free-standing sexual offences, as detailed further in the next paragraph.

The third approach, treating civil cases with a sexual element as simply the application of criminal law doctrine for actions for civil actions is unsatisfactory, since the criminal law of sexual offences now takes the form it does because of the particular goals of criminal justice in our society. These goals may overlap with the goals of the law of delict, but both areas of law have some goals distinctive to them. It is a trite observation that to reflect these goals the criminal law has in modern times come to work with a distinct category 'Sexual Offences'. As far as Scotland is concerned that has been clearly so since the work of Gordon, the first edition of which appeared in 1967.[61] The original author of the previous standard text of criminal law, dating from the late nineteenth century treated sexual offences, at least other than rape, as falling into the category of assault.[62] The 2009

[57] DM Walker, *The Law of Delict in Scotland*, 2nd edn (Edinburgh, W Green, 1981) 498–99.

[58] ibid, 498 fn 55 citing *Hill v Fletcher* (1847) 10 D 7.

[59] Criminal Procedure (Scotland) Act 1995 Sched 3 para 9(3).

[60] See Blackie, 'Unity and Diversity' (n 7) 107 (the principal use of the term in Scotland before the nineteenth century was descriptive to denote that a lesser crime/delict was committed along with a more serious one).

[61] GH Gordon, *The Criminal Law of Scotland* (Edinburgh, W Green. 1967) pt 3, pp 823–901.

[62] JHA Macdonald, *A Practical Treatise on the Criminal Law of Scotland*, 3rd (and last by the author) edn (Edinburgh, W Green, 1894) 158ff.

Act[63] has reformed the whole of the criminal law of sexual offences with new offences being created in some cases replacing slightly different older offences, and in other cases extending the range of offences and in the case of rape changing the requirements for the offence. The offences now include rape,[64] sexual assault by penetration,[65] sexual assault,[66] sexual coercion,[67] and administering a substance for sexual purposes. Prominently there are also many specific categories of offence where the victim is a child under thirteen[68] and other specific categories where the victim is a child aged fourteen or fifteen.[69] The background work by the Scottish Law Commission to this legislation was not concerned with delictual liability.[70] The offences that have been created are manifestly, therefore, to seek to achieve goals of criminal justice, not civil justice. The starting point for consideration in the work of the Scottish Law Commission that resulted in the 2009 Act was to identify the field of sexual offences as: (1) 'offences which are concerned with promoting or protecting a person's sexual autonomy', (2) 'offences which seek to provide protection to persons who are vulnerable to sexual exploitation or about whom there are doubts concerning their capacity to engage in consenting sexual conduct', and (3) 'offences which seek to promote a social or moral goal other than those in the previous two categories (that is, autonomy and protection)'.[71]

It may be argued that the fourth approach, drawing on the concept *iniuria* could be the best approach for the civil law of delict but only if that is accompanied by a clear analysis of what the additional protected interest is, in addition to that of bodily integrity, and then is accompanied by further rules to give precision to the concept in this concept. 'Sexual autonomy' may not be adequate as a way of characterising the interest. There has been real difficulty in the law of delict generally in seeing autonomy as a free-standing protected interest in its own right.[72] More appropriate could be to recognise that in civil sexual cases there is a right to sexual integrity[73] infringed at the same time as the right to bodily integrity. One of the principles of criminal law is that to achieve its goals there has to be 'fair

[63] Sexual Offences (Scotland) Act 2009.

[64] s 1.

[65] s 2.

[66] s 3.

[67] s 4.

[68] ss 18–27.

[69] ss 28–39.

[70] The only mention of delict is in Scottish Law Commission, *Rape and Other Sexual Offences* (Scot Law Com No 131, 2006) 4.53 where the SLC in discussing non-penile penetration and other touching in the context of healthcare states, 'we not concerned with the question of any delictual liability which might follow as a consequence of a medical intervention done without a person's consent'.

[71] ibid 1.28. See also Scottish Law Commission, *Report on Rape and Other Sexual Offences* (Scot Law Com No 209, 2007) 1.18.

[72] For the view that in Scotland at least the right to determine the size of one's family, and the right to take an autonomous decision to undergo medical treatment even where the individual would have undergone it can be classified in this way see Whitty, 'Overview' (n 27) 311.

[73] I have adopted this phrase from C Gane, *Sexual Offences* (Edinburgh, Butterworths, 1992) 1–6, cited in Scottish Law Commission, *Rape and Other Sexual Offences* (n 70) 126.

labelling' of crimes.[74] In the law of delict the equivalent issue may arise with the expectations of victims. To have a sexual case classified just as 'assault' or 'aggravated assault' does not meet those expectations even if the sexual dimension is reflected in the size of an award of damages. If this is correct and the law should make clear that the law of delict considers sexual integrity an interest worthy of legal protection in addition to the interest in bodily integrity, then the task is a creative one as to how to develop the general concept of *iniuria* to do that effectively, since that can no longer be done, as it was in early modern times, just by riding on the criminal law rules.

[74] For this from a Scottish standpoint see J Chalmers and F Leverick, 'Fair Labelling in Criminal Law' (2008) 71 *Modern Law Review* 217; Ferguson and McDiarmid, *Scots Criminal Law* (n 50) 4.61. For the application of this in the Sexual Offences (Scotland) Act 2009 see Scottish Law Commission, *Report on Rape* (n 71) 3.5–3.6.

9

The Gist of Defamation in South African Law

ANTON FAGAN

I. Introduction

For 150 years, the South African courts understood the *iniuria* of defamation as a particular kind of attempt to do a particular kind of harm. It was the attempt, by making an assertion about another's character or conduct to one or more third parties, to get them to think less of him than they ought. As a result, there were two conditions for a person to commit the *iniuria* of defamation: that he published matter referring to another; and that he did so *animo iniuriandi*. The presence or absence of *animus iniuriandi* could only be inferred from external circumstances. It was to be presumed that a defendant had acted *animo iniuriandi* in publishing matter referring to a plaintiff if the matter was defamatory: that is, if possession of the character or performance of the conduct which the defendant had attributed to the plaintiff diminishes a person's worth. But this presumption was rebuttable. It would be rebutted if the defendant succeeded in raising any of three well-defined defences: truth and public interest, privileged occasion, and fair comment.

Around about 1980, the South African Appellate Division rejected this understanding of defamation in favour of a new one, most aspects of which are still accepted today. According to the new understanding, a person committed the *iniuria* of defamation if and only if he satisfied three conditions: he published matter referring to another; it was wrong of him to do so; and he intended his wrongdoing. Whether a person acted wrongfully in publishing matter referring to another is an objective question independent of, and logically anterior to, the subjective question whether he intended to act wrongfully. Moreover, where a defendant published defamatory matter referring to a plaintiff, two presumptions arise: that he acted wrongfully and that he intended to do so. Both of these presumptions are rebuttable. However, the standard defences – truth and public interest, privilege, and fair comment – cannot be used to rebut the presumption of intent. Instead, they are to be regarded as justification grounds rebutting the presumption of wrongfulness.

The new conceptualisation of defamation was not invented by the Appellate Division. It had been proposed by a number of South African delict scholars in the early and mid 1960s, and some of its key ideas had appeared in two much earlier treatises on the South African law of delict. The scholars acknowledged that the conceptualisation which they were advocating did not fit the cases. They also knew that it was not supported by Roman-Dutch authority. Why, then, did they insist upon it? Mainly, it seems, because they believed the original conceptualisation to be analytically flawed. In particular, the scholars thought that it was 'illogical' and 'unscientific' to see the standard defences (truth and public interest, privilege, and fair comment) as concerned with a defendant's intentions rather than with the wrongfulness of his conduct.

These historical developments are presented in greater detail in section II below. However, the main point of the historical discussion is to provide the background for what follows in section III. There it will be argued that the scholars' criticism of the original conceptualisation was unfounded and the courts' subsequent abandonment of it therefore unwarranted. Contrary to the scholars' claims, there was nothing 'unscientific' or 'illogical' about the original conceptualisation. It made no less, and perhaps even better, sense of the law of defamation – including the standard defences – than does the new conceptualisation which replaced it.

II. The Two Conceptualisations

Here, in point form, are the South African courts' original and new conceptualisations of defamation:

Original conceptualisation:

(1) A person commits the *iniuria* of defamation in so far as he attempts, by making an assertion about another's character or conduct, to get one or more third parties to think less of him than they ought.
(2) It follows that a defendant committed the *iniuria* of defamation vis-à-vis a plaintiff if and only if: (a) he published matter referring to the plaintiff (ie he made an assertion about the plaintiff's character or conduct to one or more third parties) and (b) he did so *animo iniuriandi* (ie he did so with the intention of getting the third parties to think less of the plaintiff than they ought).
(3) The presence or absence of *animus iniuriandi* is to be inferred from objective and external circumstances.
(4) Its presence will be presumed if the matter published by the defendant was defamatory (ie if possession of the character or performance of the conduct which the defendant attributed to the plaintiff diminishes a person's worth).

(5) This presumption will be rebutted if the defendant successfully raises any of the standard defences: justification and public interest, privileged occasion, and fair comment.

New conceptualisation:

(1) A defendant committed the *iniuria* of defamation vis-à-vis a plaintiff if and only if: (a) he published matter referring to the plaintiff, (b) he acted wrongfully, and (c) he acted *animo iniuriandi.*
(2) Wrongfulness is objective – it depends on public policy, reasonableness and the community's legal convictions.
(3) *Animus iniuriandi* is subjective – it requires that the will be directed at injury and that there be consciousness of wrongfulness.
(4) When a defendant has published defamatory matter referring to a plaintiff, both wrongfulness and *animus iniuriandi* will be presumed.
(5) The standard defences, ie truth and public interest, privileged occasion, and fair comment, serve to rebut the presumption of wrongfulness rather than of *animus iniuriandi.*

From 1830 through to 1977, the South African courts repeatedly endorsed propositions (2) to (5) in the original conceptualisation. The evidence for that is provided in the first sub-section below, which deals with the cases up to the establishment of the South African Appellate Division in 1910, and the second sub-section, which discusses the cases thereafter. There is, admittedly, no direct evidence for the courts' acceptance of proposition (1). But it can be inferred from their acceptance of propositions (2) to (5). For it is impossible to make sense of propositions (2) to (5) other than on the assumption that the *iniuria* of defamation is constituted by the kind of attempt which proposition (1) describes.

The new conceptualisation of defamation was adopted by the South African Appellate Division in five judgments in the late 1970s and early 1980s. But the Appellate Division was following the lead of a provincial division judgment which a decade earlier had rejected the original conceptualisation as mistaken, at least in respect of the defence of privilege. That judgment, in turn, was relying on several academic publications which had appeared in the early and mid 1960s, and which had been written by the likes of Paul Boberg, Nico van der Merwe and Johannes van der Walt. However, it is possible that the origins of the new conceptualisation lay further back. Most of the propositions constituting it had been endorsed by Melius de Villiers at the end of the nineteenth century and some of them had been accepted by Robin McKerron in the early 1930s. Sub-section (3) discusses the cases which ushered in the new conceptualisation and provides some evidence for its persistence until today. Sub-section (4) discusses the academic writing which provided the impetus for this conceptualisation's judicial adoption.

A. Pre-1910 Cases Endorsing the Original Conceptualisation

It is best to start the discussion of this period in the middle, with two judgments from 1878, both by De Villiers CJ, namely *Botha v Brink* and *Dippenaar v Hauman*. The following two passages are from those judgments:

> In an action for defamation, the law presumes the existence of the *animus injuriandi*, or, as I would rather call it, of malice, from the mere fact that the defamatory words were published; and it lies on the defendant to disprove malice. If he shows that the words were used on a privileged occasion, he so far rebuts the presumption of malice as to throw on the plaintiff the burden of proving express malice. If he proves that the words were true he does not completely rebut the presumption of malice unless it appears from the pleadings, or unless the defendant avers and shows, that some public benefit was to be derived from the publication.[1]
>
> Every man is presumed to intend the consequences of his own acts, and there is good reason for it, otherwise it would be necessary to dive into the depths of every man's heart and thoughts in order to discover what his intentions were. The simple rule is that we judge of a man's intentions by what he does and says, and if the necessary consequences of what he does and says are to injure another, the law presumes he intended it.[2]

These passages represent an almost complete statement of the original conceptualisation. All that is missing from them are the requirement of publication (in proposition (2) above) and the defence of fair comment (in proposition (5) above). Significant for present purposes is the fact that De Villiers CJ did not purport to be breaking new ground, but only to be summarising principles which had previously been accepted by the Court. And that was so. The principles set out by De Villiers CJ can be traced back to 1830, to *Mackay v Philip*, one of the earliest reported cases on defamation in South Africa. In that case it was accepted that a defendant in a defamation case will escape liability if 'there is no proof . . . of any *animus injuriandi*'.[3] And it was held that '[b]oth common sense and the law . . . dictate that the existence or absence of *animus injuriandi* must be gathered from the circumstances of each particular case'.[4] As to how such inference is to be drawn, the Court said the following:

> [T]he falsehood of the statements injurious to the character of a plaintiff, which have been published by a defendant, is . . . sufficient to prove such an *animus injuriandi*, direct or indirect, as is required to render the defendant liable in damages, unless he shall be able to prove some special circumstance sufficient to negative the presumption of the existence of such *animus injuriandi*, and to prove that, in publishing injurious statements, not consistent with truth, he was actuated by some motive, which is in law held sufficient to excuse the error into which the defendant has fallen.[5]

[1] *Botha v Brink* (1878) Buchanan 118, 123–24; see also 130.
[2] *Dippenaar v Hauman* (1878) Buchanan 135, 143; see also 139.
[3] *Mackay v Philip* (1830) 1 Menzies 455, 462.
[4] ibid 463.
[5] ibid.

Other early cases in which these principles had been accepted were *Sparks v Hart*,[6] *Norden v Oppenheim*,[7] and *White v Pilkington*.[8] Here is what Menzies and Musgrave JJ said in the second of them:

> [I]t is sufficient in the first instance for the plaintiff to prove that the defendant uttered the injurious words complained of. The law presumes the injurious words to be false until the defendant, under a plea of justification, shall have proved them to be true, and it presumes that they were uttered by the defendant maliciously until he shall have proved circumstances sufficient in law to rebut this presumption of malice.[9]

And here is how Wylde CJ began his judgment in the third: 'The action for slander is given by the Roman-Dutch law in case of words uttered *dolo malo* for the purpose of traducing the character and estimation of another'.[10]

The principles which De Villiers CJ set out in *Botha* and *Dippenaar* were confirmed in a number of subsequent pre-1910 judgments: *Meurant v Raubenheimer*,[11] *Michaelis v Braun*,[12] *Bennett v Morris*,[13] *Gladwyn v Sunde*,[14] *Botha v Pretoria Printing Works Ltd*,[15] *Smith & Co v SA Newspaper Co*,[16] and *Wyndham v Wallachs' Printing and Publishing Co Ltd*.[17] Two extracts – the second from a judgment by Innes CJ in 1907 – suffice to demonstrate that.

> Any one who either utters, writes, or in any way publishes language calculated to injure another in his fair fame and reputation, or to bring him into hatred, contempt or ridicule, is liable to an action for any damages which the subject of the defamation may have thereby sustained. For the defendant to be so liable the words must have been used by him maliciously or, as the civilians put it, *animo iniuriandi*; but if the natural effect of the words, when in their ordinary sense, is defamatory, the law in this, as in other cases, presumes that a man intends to produce the natural consequences of his own language and conduct, and infers the existence of malice or *animus*, unless circumstances can be shown to exist rebutting such inference or presumption.[18]
>
> [The words] are upon the face of them defamatory. That being so, the law presumes the existence of what we call *animus injuriandi*, and what the English law calls malice. And all the defences to an action of this kind which are known to our law will be found to be based upon the absence, presumed or proved, of this *animus*.[19]

What about the doctrines omitted from De Villiers CJ's summaries? What, in other words, about the requirement of publication and the defence of fair comment? The

[6] *Sparks v Hart* (1833) 3 Menzies 3.
[7] *Norden v Oppenheim* (1846) 3 Menzies 42.
[8] *White v Pilkington* (1851) 1 Searle 107.
[9] *Norden* (n 7) 53.
[10] *White* (n 8) 119.
[11] *Meurant v Raubenheimer* (1882) 1 Buchanan AC 87.
[12] *Michaelis v Braun* (1887) 4 SC 205.
[13] *Bennett v Morris* (1893) 10 SC 223.
[14] *Gladwyn v Sunde* (1897) 8 HCG 137.
[15] *Botha v Pretoria Printing Works Ltd* (1906) TS 710.
[16] *Smith & Co v SA Newspaper Co* (1906) 23 SC 310.
[17] *Wyndham v Wallachs' Printing and Publishing Co Ltd* (1907) TS 385.
[18] *Gladwyn* (n 14) 143.
[19] *Wyndham* (n 17) 386.

position as regards the latter is straightforward. Three years before *Botha* and *Dippenaar*, De Villiers CJ, in the case of *De Jager v Bryant*, had already acknowledged a limited fair-comment defence rebutting the presumption of *animus iniuriandi*.[20] Subsequent to *Botha* and *Dippenaar*, the existence of a fair-comment defence negating *animus iniuriandi* was again accepted, and its ambit widened, in several more cases.[21] In fact, the extract from Innes CJ's judgment in the *Wyndham* case (the second extract immediately above) goes straight on to say:

> Under the old Roman-Dutch law there would have been no defence to the present action, save justification. But the defence relied upon here is that of fair comment upon a matter of public interest. It is a defence originally elaborated by English decisions . . . The doctrine which it embodies is in itself not inconsistent with the principles of the Roman-Dutch law; and it has been freely adopted, and applied over and over again by courts not only in this country, but in other parts of South Africa.[22]

In respect of the requirement that the defendant published matter referring to the plaintiff, the position is more complicated. There is no doubt that the South African courts, during the period under discussion, never took the wrong of defamation to be constituted by *animus iniuriandi* alone. For a defendant to have committed the wrong of defamation, it was necessary that he had the intention of getting one or more third parties to think less of the plaintiff than they ought – but it was not sufficient. In addition, the defendant had to have performed some conduct. He had to have done something in order to carry out his intention. But not anything would do. According to the courts, the conduct had to have a particular form. It had to be an assertion to a third party about the plaintiff's character or conduct. And the word 'assertion', here, implies a degree of success. In other words, it was not enough that the defendant said or wrote certain words (or performed some non-verbal symbolic act) with the intention of making an assertion about the plaintiff to a third party. The words must actually have been heard or seen – and understood to convey that assertion – by the third party.

That the wrong of defamation was conditional not merely upon the presence of *animus iniuriandi*, but also upon conduct of this particular form, is not indicated by the extracts from *Botha* and *Dippenaar* with which this sub-section started. But other cases provide evidence for it:

> [N]one of the judges had any doubt that an action for damages could not be supported for writing or composing a libel which had not been published.[23]
>
> A libel requires publication, and there is no proof of publication in this case. The letter was not shown to have come into anybody's hands but Wheeler's [ie the plaintiff's].[24]

[20] *De Jager v Bryant* (1875) Buchanan 145.

[21] eg *Upington v Saul Solomon & Co; Upington v Dormer* (1879) Buchanan 240; *Wyndham* (n 17); *Roos v Stent and Pretoria Printing Works Ltd* (1909) TS 988.

[22] *Wyndham* (n 17) 386.

[23] *De Lettre v Kiener* (1835) 3 Menzies 12, 14 (Wylde CJ).

[24] *Kearns v Wheeler* (1889) 3 South African Republic 89, 90 (Kotzé CJ).

When defamatory words are spoken in a foreign language they must be set out in that language, and a translation must be appended, together with an averment that the person or persons to whom they were uttered understood their meaning.[25]

[T]he fact that there were defamatory statements in this letter cannot expose defendant to an action for libel. It is essential to such an action that there should be some allegation of publication before plaintiff can succeed.[26]

B. Post-1910 Cases Endorsing the Original Conceptualisation

The previous sub-section showed that propositions (2) to (5) in the original conceptualisation were expressly – and repeatedly – endorsed by the South African courts in the period 1830 to 1910. This sub-section shows that, in the years 1910 to 1977, all these propositions were again endorsed by the South African courts. In fact, by 1930, every one of propositions (2) to (5) had been expressly accepted by the South African Appellate Division. And, for the next 47 years, its commitment to them never wavered. The evidence for this is presented in schematic form. Each of the propositions is taken in turn, except that the requirement of publication is again discussed separately at the end.

Proposition (2) – in so far as it deals with *animus iniuriandi*:

> [I]t would be essential as in all cases of *injuria* to prove that there was the *animus injuriandi*.[27]

Proposition (3):

> It is for the Court to judge from all the surrounding circumstances whether this *animus injuriandi* existed or not: the mere word of the wrongdoer that he had no such intention is not conclusive.[28]

Proposition (4):

> In the case of libel or slander the *animus injuriandi* is presumed from the mere use of words which in themselves are defamatory.[29]

Proposition (5):

> Now the plea of fair comment is one which has been adopted in our practice from that of England as being entirely consistent with the principles of our law, and it has accordingly been recognised by our courts as affording a defence to an action of defamation. It is based, in my opinion, upon the ground that where there is fair comment

[25] *Chadwick v Faku* (1890) 11 Natal Law Reports 174, 174–75 (Gallwey CJ).

[26] *Hall v Zietsman* (1899) 16 SC 213. 215–16 (De Villiers CJ). See also *Konigsberg v Stanislaus* (1904) 21 SC 663, 664; *Gray v Tosh* (1908) TS 76; *Martin v Kemlo* (1909) 26 SC 457, 460.

[27] *GA Fichardt Ltd v The Friend Newspapers Ltd* 1916 AD 1, 11 (Solomon JA). See also *Nasionale Pers Bpkt v Long* 1930 AD 87, 99; *Monckten v British South Africa Co* 1920 AD 324, 332.

[28] *Nasionale Pers* (n 27) 99 (Wessels JA). See also *De Graaf and Viljoen v Viljoen* 1916 AD 539, 542–43; *Sutter v Brown* 1926 AD 155, 163.

[29] *Fichardt* (n 27) 11, see also 7. See also *Nasionale Pers* (n 27) 99; *Kleinhans v Usmar* 1929 AD 121, 126.

> there is an absence of that *animus injuriandi* which is of the essence of a libel or slander.[30]
>
> [The document] was therefore defamatory, and being so, the law presumed the existence of *animus injuriandi* – a presumption which it is for the defendant to rebut if he desires to escape the consequences. Such rebuttal might be effected in various ways. In this instance he has elected to plead privilege.[31]
>
> [T]he presumption of *animus injuriandi* which arises from the use of the defamatory language is conclusively rebutted by proving justification, ie, that the charge was true and that its publication was in the public interest.[32]

What about publication? Did it remain a necessary condition for a defendant to have committed the wrong of defamation that he succeeded in making an assertion about the plaintiff to one or more third parties? The only Appellate Division judgment to touch on publication, namely that of Innes CJ in *Sutter v Brown*, suggests that it did:

> [T]he way in which matter alleged to be defamatory was understood by the communicatee may nevertheless under certain circumstances become important. It is of course always open to the defendant to show that the words used made no impression on the mind of the person addressed, because he was deaf or ignorant of the language, or for other reasons, so that there was no publication to the prejudice of the plaintiff.[33]

This was just a passing remark. However, a string of provincial division decisions from 1910 to 1977 leaves no doubt but that publication – in the sense described – continued to be a requirement. So, for example, in *Parshotam v Lallu*, it was held that 'the plaintiff must in order to succeed prove the publication, which he can only do by proving that the bystanders understood the words spoken in their presence'.[34] In *Whittington v Bowles* it was held not only that 'there can be no defamation . . . in the absence of publication to some person other than the two parties, by and [of] whom the statement is made', but also that 'if persons, though hearing words and understanding them in a defamatory sense, do not identify the plaintiff as the person referred to, there is no publication'.[35] And, in *African Life Assurance Society Ltd v Robinson & Co Ltd and Central News Agency Ltd*, it was said that '[t]here is no publication of a libel unless the defamatory sense of the words complained of is conveyed to those who read them' and thus that '[i]n the case . . . of words written in a foreign language or in a secret cipher there is no publication to readers who do not understand such language or cipher.'[36]

As the evidence so far presented in this sub-section has shown, the South African Appellate Division had firmly entrenched the original conceptualisation

[30] *Crawford v Albu* 1917 AD 102, 124 (Solomon JA). See also 114 (Innes CJ). See also *Hertzog v Ward* 1912 AD 62, 71.

[31] *Tromp v McDonald* 1920 AD 1, 2 (Innes CJ). See also *Monckten* (n 27) 332.

[32] *Kleinhans* (n 29) 126 (De Villiers ACJ).

[33] *Sutter* (n 28) 164.

[34] *Parshotam v Lallu* (1917) CPD 288, 290.

[35] *Whittington v Bowles* (1934) EDL 142, 145, 147.

[36] *African Life Assurance Society Ltd v Robinson & Co Ltd and Central News Agency Ltd* 1938 NPD 277, 295.

of defamation by 1930. And it remained faithful to this conceptualisation for the next half-century. So for example, in 1940, in *Young v Kemsley*, Tindall JA had the following to say about the South African law's conceptualisation of defamation:

> Our decisions have laid down that the defamatory nature of the words used raises a presumption of *animus injuriandi* but that, if it is shown that the words were spoken on a privileged occasion, the *onus* is shifted back on to the plaintiff to prove affirmatively the existence of *animus injuriandi.* As the Court cannot look into the mind of the speaker, it starts with the principle that a man is presumed to intend the natural consequences of his acts and, therefore, that a person who uses defamatory language of another is presumed to intend to injure. The variety of circumstances, however, under which defamatory words may be spoken shows that in many cases the speaker is not moved to say the objectionable words through *animus injuriandi.* As reported cases multiply, an attempt to classify the decisions and to use concise and convenient terminology for the purposes of classification is only to be expected. Thus the term 'privileged occasion' has been adopted as a comprehensive term for denoting a certain class of case where the special circumstances in which the words are spoken *prima facie* negative existence of malice.[37]

More significant, perhaps, is the fact that the Appellate Division unambiguously affirmed its commitment to this conceptualisation in four judgments in the 1960s, namely *Jordaan v Van Biljon*,[38] *Craig v Voortrekkerspers Bpk*,[39] *Nydoo v Vengtas*,[40] and *Benson v Robinson & Co (Pty) Ltd*.[41] Curiously, the Court's judgment in all four of these cases was delivered by Rumpff JA. Only a decade later, as Rumpff CJ, he would play a key role in the original conceptualisation's destruction.

C. Cases Endorsing the New Conceptualisation

In 1967, in the case of *Wentzel v SA Yster en Staalbedryfsvereniging, Wentzel v Blanke Motorwerkersvereniging*, Jansen J (as he then was) said the following:

> Notwithstanding the conventional and stereotyped approach that a privileged occasion . . . rebuts the presumption of *animus iniuriandi*, there appears to be little doubt that, jurisprudentially viewed, it is a justification ground which excludes wrongfulness and not intention or *animus iniuriandi*.[42]
>
> As against the conventional, stereotyped use of *animus iniuriandi* as something which is 'rebutted' by, for example, the presence of privilege, there is the scientifically more precise use thereof as the label for the subjective fault element of the delict.[43]

[37] *Young v Kemsley* 1940 AD 258, 277–78. See also *Gluckman v Schneider* 1936 AD 151; *De Waal v Ziervogel* 1938 AD 112; *Basner v Trigger* 1946 AD 83; *Naude v Whittle* 1958 (1) SA 594 (A).

[38] *Jordaan v Van Biljon* 1962 (1) SA 286 (A).

[39] *Craig v Voortrekkerspers Bpk* 1963 (1) SA 149 (A).

[40] *Nydoo v Vengtas* 1965 (1) SA 1 (A).

[41] *Benson v Robinson & Co (Pty) Ltd* 1967 (1) SA 420 (A).

[42] *Wentzel v SA Yster en Staalbedryfsvereniging, Wentzel v Blanke Motorwerkersvereniging* 1967 (3) SA 91 (TPD), 98A–B (my translation).

[43] ibid 98F–G (my translation).

This was a provincial division decision. And it dealt with only one of the three defences, namely privileged occasion. Yet, with hindsight, it must be regarded as a curtain-raiser for the Appellate Division's abandonment of the original conceptualisation, and adoption of the new conceptualisation, ten years later.

The turning point in the Appellate Division's understanding of defamation undoubtedly was the case of *Suid-Afrikaanse Uitsaaikorporasie v O'Malley*, decided in 1977. Judgment was given by Rumpff CJ. But one of the concurring judges was Jansen JA (as he had meanwhile become) and one can only wonder whether his presence on the Bench may not have had some influence. Here are the key passages from the judgment:

> It must be accepted that in our law publication of defamatory words creates a presumption that the words were published intentionally and that the publication is wrongful. As a result of the adoption of English terminology in our law of defamation, the two essential elements of defamation as a delict, namely wrongfulness and fault, were not always clearly distinguished and a fair amount of confusion ensued.[44]
>
> [W]hen the question arises whether the publication of defamatory words was lawful or wrongful, it is the task of this Court to determine . . . whether public policy requires that the publication be regarded as justified and thus be found to have been lawful.[45]
>
> The circumstances which give rise to the so-called 'privileges' of English law count in our law as examples of circumstances which exclude wrongfulness.[46]
>
> At this stage it can be accepted that the intention to defame is the mental state of willing the particular result . . . with the knowledge that the willed result will be wrongful.[47]

The *O'Malley* analysis was entrenched and expanded by four judgments in the early 1980s. In *Borgin v De Villiers*, Corbett JA reiterated most of what Rumpff CJ had said.[48] So, in *May v Udwin*, did Joubert JA. But he added the claim that wrongfulness was 'the objective element of defamation' – as opposed to *animus iniuriandi*, which was 'the subjective element'.[49] Of much greater importance is the case of *Marais v Richard*. In this case Jansen JA (with Rumpff CJ concurring) held that not only the defence of privileged occasion, but also the defences of fair comment and truth and public interest, relate to the wrongfulness element of defamation and should be regarded as grounds of justification rather than as grounds rebutting the presumption of *animus iniuriandi*.[50] That truth and public interest negates wrongfulness rather than *animus iniuriandi* was again stated (by necessary implication) in *Pakendorf v De Flamingh* (judgment by Rumpff CJ, Jansen JA concurring).[51]

[44] *Suid-Afrikaanse Uitsaaikorporasie v O'Malley* 1977 (3) SA 394 (A) 401–2 (my translation).
[45] ibid 402–3 (my translation).
[46] ibid 403A–B (my translation).
[47] ibid 403C–D (my translation).
[48] *Borgin v De Villiers* 1980 (3) SA 556 (A) 571D–G.
[49] *May v Udwin* 1981 (1) SA 1 (A) 10C–G 13C–D.
[50] *Marais v Richard* 1981 (1) SA 1157 (A) 1166–67.
[51] *Pakendorf v De Flamingh* 1982 (3) SA 146 (A) 156C.

By and large, the conceptualisation of defamation that was developed in these judgments has continued to enjoy judicial support. A quote from a Constitutional Court judgment in 2002 shows this:

> Once a plaintiff establishes that a defendant has published a defamatory statement concerning the plaintiff, it is presumed that the publication was both unlawful and intentional. A defendant wishing to avoid liability for defamation must then raise a defence which rebuts unlawfulness or intention. Although not a closed list, the most commonly raised defences to rebut unlawfulness are that the publication was true and in the public benefit, that the publication constituted fair comment and that the publication was made on a privileged occasion.[52]

Only in one respect has there been a deviation – and it is a very recent one – from the conceptualisation of defamation which was adopted in *O'Malley*, *Borgin*, *May*, *Marais*, and *Pakendorf*. According to this conceptualisation, *animus iniuriandi* has two aspects, namely the will to injure and the knowledge that this is wrongful. That the second of these, namely knowledge or consciousness of wrongfulness, was not a requirement for *animus iniuriandi* in respect of certain *iniuriae* (such as wrongful arrest and detention) was established (or, more accurately perhaps, re-affirmed) in 1993, in the case of *Minister of Justice v Hofmeyr*.[53] However, it remained possible, even subsequent to that case, that consciousness of wrongfulness was still a requirement for *animus iniuriandi* in the context of defamation. In 2010, in the case of *Le Roux v Dey*, the Supreme Court of Appeal closed the door on this possibility. The notion that *animus iniuriandi* in the context of defamation required 'coloured intent' was rejected as a Pandectist import which created more difficulties than it solved.[54]

D. Academic Support for the New Conceptualisation

As was acknowledged by Jansen J in the *Wentzel* case, the inspiration for his adoption of the new conceptualisation of defamation was a number of academic publications appearing in the early and mid 1960s. Jansen J credited Boberg, Van der Walt, Van der Merwe, Olivier and Van der Vyver, among others.[55] The following extracts, from publications by three of these scholars, suggest that Jansen J

[52] *Khumalo v Holomisa* 2002 (5) SA 401 (CC) 414A–C. See also *Argus Printing and Publishing Co Ltd v Inkatha Freedom Party* 1992 (3) SA 579 (A) 588G–I; *Argus Printing & Publishing Co Ltd v Esselen's Estate* 1994 (2) SA 1 (A) 25C–E; *Le Roux v Dey* 2011 (3) SA 274 (CC) 314–15, 317F–G.

[53] *Minister of Justice v Hofmeyr* 1993 (3) SA 131 (A) 154–56.

[54] *Le Roux v Dey* 2010 (4) SA 210 (A) 219–25.

[55] *Wentzel* (n 42) 98B–C, G–H. The references are to PQR Boberg, 'The Mental Element in Defamation' (1961) 78 *South African Law Journal* 171; JD van der Vyver, '*Animus iniuriandi* en die Afwesigheid van Wederregtelikheidsbewussyn [Pt 1]' (1966) 29 *Tydskrif vir Hedendaagse Romeins-Hollandse Reg* 336; NJ van der Merwe, 'Vonnisbespreking: Hassen v Post Newspapers (Pty.) Ltd and Others, 1965 (3) S.A. 562 (W)' (1966) 29 *Tydskrif vir Hedendaagse Romeins-Hollandse Reg* 76; NJ van der Merwe and PJJ Olivier, *Die Onregmatige Daad in die Suid-Afrikaanse Reg* (Pretoria, JP van der Walt, 1966); SA Strauss and others, *Die Perswese en die Reg* (Pretoria, JL van Schaik,1964).

in *Wentzel*, and subsequently the Appellate Division in *O'Malley*, *Borgin*, *May*, *Marais* and *Pakendorf*, did little more than replicate the academics' views.

> Defamation is the wrongful, intentional publication of words or conduct concerning a specific person which impairs his good name or reputation in the community.[56]
>
> Wrongfulness, I say, is an objective qualification of the act.[57]
>
> Fault, by contrast, is a . . . subjective attitude of the agent, which in the case of defamation must take the form of *animus iniuriandi*, that is to say, the intention to impair the *fama* of the plaintiff.[58]
>
> It is said that when one of the well-known justification grounds is raised and proved in a defamation action, the action fails because the defence cancels out *animus iniuriandi* (intent). The fallacy resides therein that a justification ground which is relevant to the question of wrongfulness suddenly is seen as a ground excluding fault. In so doing, wrongfulness and fault are hopelessly confused with each other.[59]
>
> One of the recognised ways in which a defendant in a defamation action can rebut the presumption of *animus iniuriandi*, is by proving that he made a mistake concerning the wrongfulness of the statement or conduct. If the defendant can prove that he made such an error, then consciousness of wrongfulness is lacking and he cannot be regarded as having acted with intent.[60]

The analysis of defamation advanced in these publications was at odds with that in several earlier academic works. In Maasdorp's *Institutes of Cape Law*,[61] Nathan's *Law of Defamation in South Africa*,[62] and Wille's *Principles of South African Law*,[63] the original conceptualisation was faithfully reproduced, without departure or criticism. The original conceptualisation was set out again, and vigorously defended, by TW Price in articles appearing in 1949 and 1960.[64] Even so, the analysis of defamation which Van der Vyver, Van der Merwe, and the others were proposing was not a novel one. All its key elements had already been expounded in Melius De Villiers's *The Roman and Roman-Dutch Law of Injuries*, which appeared in 1899, and RG McKerron's *The Law of Delicts in South Africa*, which was published in 1933.

According to De Villiers, there are 'three essential requisites to establish an action of injury [ie an *iniuria*]'.[65] The third is not of present concern. But the first

[56] NJ van der Merwe and PJJ Olivier, *Die Onregmatige Daad in die Suid-Afrikaanse Reg*, 2nd edn (Pretoria, JP van der Walt, 1970) 336 (my translation).

[57] Van der Vyver (n 55) 346 (my translation). See also Van der Merwe and Olivier (n 56) 340.

[58] Van der Vyver (n 55) 346 (my translation). See also Van der Merwe and Olivier (n 56) 375.

[59] Van der Merwe and Olivier (n 56) 349 (my translation). See also Van der Vyver (n 55) 346.

[60] Van der Merwe and Olivier (n 56) 381 (my translation). See also JD van der Vyver, '*Animus iniurandi* en die Afwesigheid van Wederregteliksbewussyn [Pt 2]' (1967) 30 *Tydskrif vir Hedendaagse Romeins-Hollandse Reg* 15, 26.

[61] AFS Maasdorp, *The Institutes of Cape Law, Book III The Law of Obligations, Part II Actionable Wrongs* (1909) 89–90, 93–94, 99–100.

[62] Manfred Nathan, *The Law of Defamation in South Africa* (Johannesburg, Hortors, 1933) 82–129.

[63] George Wille, *Principles of South African Law* (Cape Town, Juta, 1937) 382–87.

[64] TW Price, '*Animus Injuriandi* in Defamation' (1949) 66 *South African Law Journal* 4; TW Price, 'The Basis of the South African Law of Defamation' (1960) *Acta Juridica* 254.

[65] Melius De Villiers, *The Roman and Roman-Dutch Law of Injuries* (Cape Town, Juta, 1899) 27.

and second are. They are '[t]he intention to produce the consequences of one's act' (ie *animus iniuriandi*) and 'some overt act, and one which is unlawful in its nature'.[66] It is not the requirement that there be an overt act, but rather the requirement that it be unlawful in nature, which aligns De Villiers's understanding of defamation with the new, rather than the old, conceptualisation thereof. That De Villiers's understanding represents an early version of the conceptualisation that would emerge in the 1960s is also shown by his insistence that the unlawfulness of an act is to be determined independently of, and prior to, the determination of whether the act was performed with the intention to injure:

> The first question for the determination of the existence or non-existence of an injury must always be, not whether there exists *animus injuriandi*, but whether the act in question is lawful or unlawful. Only when it has been settled that it is unlawful can further inquiry be raised as to the presence or absence of *animus injuriandi*.[67]

Further confirmation of the similarity between De Villiers's understanding of defamation and the new conceptualisation thereof is provided by his treatment of truth, privilege and fair comment. According to De Villiers, a defendant who succeeds with one of these defences avoids liability by showing, not that he lacked *animus iniuriandi*, but rather that his conduct was lawful. Only in the case of a defendant who fails successfully to raise any of these defences (in response to a prima facie case against him), and whose conduct is thus unlawful, does the question of *animus iniuriandi* become relevant.[68]

In one obvious and significant respect, McKerron's analysis of defamation differs from the new conceptualisation. The new conceptualisation (like the original one, and like that of De Villiers) regards *animus iniuriandi* as an essential element for liability for defamation. McKerron, by contrast, did not.[69] However, in other important respects, McKerron's analysis and the new conceptualisation converge. First, like the new conceptualisation (and like De Villiers before him), McKerron took unlawfulness to be a necessary condition for liability.[70] Secondly, like the new conceptualisation (and again like De Villiers), McKerron believed that truth and public interest, privileged occasion and fair comment rendered conduct lawful, rather than showed it to be performed without *animus iniuriandi*.[71] Thirdly, even though McKerron's analysis differs from the new conceptualisation on the question whether *animus iniuriandi* is essential for defamation, it agrees with the new conceptualisation as to how *animus iniuriandi* is to be understood. According to McKerron, *animus iniuriandi* has two elements: '(1) an intention to produce the consequences of the act complained of; and (2) an accompanying wrongful state of mind.'[72] In fact, it was partly because McKerron took *animus iniuriandi* to

[66] ibid 27, 37.
[67] ibid 105. See also pp 37, 200.
[68] ibid 105, 200, 202–3, 208–29, 224, 227.
[69] RG McKerron, *The Law of Delicts in South Africa* (Cape Town, Juta, 1933) 113.
[70] ibid 48.
[71] ibid 124 fn 75, 132 fn 119.
[72] ibid 49.

comprise the second element, namely consciousness of wrongfulness, that he concluded that *animus iniuriandi* was not a necessary condition for defamation.[73]

III. A Defence of the Old Against The New

It is understandable that the courts should have buckled under the weight of the scholarly consensus which emerged in the 1960s. But it is harder to grasp why that consensus should have emerged in the first place. As has been explained, and as the scholars in fact acknowledged, their analysis directly contradicted more than 130 years of South African case law.[74] It also seems to have been in conflict with the Roman-Dutch law.

Consider, for example, the scholars' contention that the defence of truth and public interest does not rebut the presumption of *animus iniuriandi*, but rather is a justification ground negating wrongfulness. Voet clearly held the opposite view. In the case of *iniuriae verbis*, said Voet, the truth of a statement avoids liability if it was 'to the interest of the commonwealth'.[75] Why? Because, in that event, '[i]t is not to be presumed that [the speaker] meant to do it with the evil purpose of doing a wrong'.[76] However, if the statement, though true, was not in 'the interest of the commonwealth', liability is not avoided – and '[t]he reason for that is that in such a case no inference of good purpose can be drawn, so that there remains therefore no other presumption than one of wreaking a wrong'.[77] That Voet saw the defence of truth and public interest as avoiding liability, if at all, by negating *animus iniuriandi* is confirmed by the distinction he drew between *iniuriae verbis* (spoken wrongs) and *iniuriae litteris* (written wrongs). In the case of the latter, said Voet, truth (even if in the interest of the commonwealth) does not avoid liability. The reason which Voet gave for this is a purely subjective one: while a person may say something defamatory 'in sudden heat, and because the tongue often outstrips the mind', 'defamatory screeds . . . require a stretch of time for the composition of them, and they proceed rather from a settled and persistent purpose to do harm.'[78]

That Voet and other Roman-Dutch authorities took truth and public interest to exclude *animus iniuriandi* (and not wrongfulness) was admitted by De Villiers.[79] In fact, De Villiers acknowledged that the old authorities viewed the defences *in*

[73] ibid 50.

[74] Boberg (n 55) 186; Van der Vyver (n 55) 346; Van der Merwe and Olivier (n 56) 349, 380.

[75] Johannes Voet, 'Commentary on Book 47 Title 10 of the Digest, dealing with wrongs and defamatory screeds' in *The Selective Voet: Being the Commentary on the Pandects*, translated by Percival Gane (Durban: Butterworth, 1955–58) s 9.

[76] Voet, 'Commentary' (n 75) s 9.

[77] ibid.

[78] ibid s 10.

[79] De Villiers (n 65) 105.

general as grounds pertaining to *animus iniuriandi* rather than lawfulness.[80] Boberg, similarly, conceded that his proposed approach to privilege, rejecting as it did the idea that this defence negated *animus iniuriandi*, was inconsistent with Roman-Dutch law.[81] Other scholars responsible for the new conceptualisation, such as Van der Vyver, Van der Merwe and Olivier, did not make similar concessions. But neither did they justify any aspect of their analysis by referring to the Roman-Dutch authorities.

Given that the scholarly consensus of the 1960s was at odds with the cases and unsupported by the Roman-Dutch law, and that the scholars knew this to be so, how is its emergence to be explained? There is no evidence that any of the scholars was motivated by moral concerns. Instead, their motivation appears to have been purely analytical. According to Boberg, the old conceptualisation had to be rejected, at least in respect of privilege, because it failed 'to make sense' of, was 'logically irreconcilable' with, and could not give 'the dignity of logical symmetry and predictability' to, the rules pertaining to privilege (most of which had been taken over from English law).[82] According to Van der Vyver, Van der Merwe and Olivier, the old conceptualisation had to be rejected, in respect of all three defences, because it was a necessary truth that *animus iniuriandi* (as a species of fault) was subjective, whereas wrongfulness was objective, and because all three defences turned on objective facts.[83] To hold otherwise, according to these scholars, was 'unscientific' and 'illogical'.[84] Similar conceptual concerns appear to have motivated, at least in part, De Villiers's and McKerron's earlier disagreement with the original conceptualisation.[85]

This section defends the original conceptualisation against these analytical objections. It shows that the original conceptualisation is perfectly intelligible and that it makes good sense of the various rules constituting the law of defamation. In order to do this, the section deals with each of the three defences – truth and public interest, fair comment, and privileged occasion – in turn.

A. Truth and Public Interest

The place to start, if one is trying to render intelligible the original conceptualisation's claim that the defence of truth and public interest avoids liability by rebutting the presumption of *animus iniuriandi*, is with the presumption itself. To presume that a defendant published matter about a plaintiff *animo iniuriandi* is to presume that he did so with the intention of getting others to think less of the plaintiff than they ought. What objective and external circumstances or facts could justify the inference that a defendant, in publishing matter about a plaintiff,

[80] ibid 200, 202 n 43.
[81] Boberg (n 55) 187.
[82] ibid 186.
[83] Van der Vyver (n 55) 346; Van der Merwe and Olivier (n 56) 349–50, 380.
[84] Van der Vyver (n 55) 336; Van der Merwe and Olivier (n 56) 349, 350.
[85] De Villiers (n 65) 200; McKerron (n 69) 124 fn 75, 132 fn 119.

acted with such an intention? In response to this question, the cases in which the original conceptualisation was developed or accepted invariably answer: 'the fact that the published matter was defamatory'. This is not wrong. But it is only half the answer. Moreover, it is in fact the other half of the answer that holds the key to the explanation which this sub-section aims to provide, that is, an explanation of how truth and public interest could avoid liability by negating *animus iniuriandi.*

To understand why a defendant's publication of defamatory matter concerning a plaintiff is insufficient to warrant the inference that the defendant did so *animo iniuriandi*, one must fully grasp the concept (or, at least, the South African courts' concept) of defamatoriness. In this regard, the early cases are of little assistance. Though applying the concept of defamatoriness, they made no effort to analyse it. Only in the twentieth century does one begin to see cases in which some attempt at explanation is made. From them one can glean the following. First, the question of defamatoriness is distinct from (though obviously dependent upon) the question of meaning. That is to say, it is distinct from the necessarily prior question: what assertion about the plaintiff did the defendant succeed in making to others?[86] Secondly, the question of defamatoriness concerns the worth of persons. Unlike the question of meaning, it thus is value-dependent. Thirdly, the values to be applied in determining defamatoriness are objective rather than subjective. They are not the values of the third parties to whom the publication was made, or of any other sector of society. The second and third of these features are implied by the courts' acceptance of the idea that the defamatoriness of an assertion is to be determined by asking whether 'it tended [or was calculated] to lower the plaintiff in the estimation of right-thinking [or reasonable] members of society generally'.[87] They also are implied by several judgments in which the courts drew a clear distinction between the question whether an assertion about someone was defamatory and the question whether it would diminish the willingness of others to associate with him.[88]

The observations about defamatoriness in the cases, though instructive, are inexact. It is possible to do better. Here is a definition of defamatoriness which, while remaining true to the comments concerning defamatoriness in the cases, more precisely explains its nature:

> The assertion that a plaintiff possesses some characteristic or performed some conduct is defamatory if and only if possession of that characteristic or performance of that conduct diminishes a person's worth – in other words, if and only if a person who possesses that characteristic or performs that conduct is, all other things being equal, of less worth than a person who does not.

[86] See eg *De Graaf* (n 28) 544. See also *SA Associated Newspapers Ltd v Samuels* 1980 (1) SA 24 (A) 30F–G; *Demmers v Willie* 1980 (1) SA 835 (A) 840A–C.

[87] See *Smith v Elmore* 1938 TPD 18, 21; *Gluckmann v Holford* 1940 TPD 336, 339; *Conroy v Stewart Printing Co Ltd* 1946 AD 1015, 1018; *Conroy v Nicol* 1951 (1) SA 653 (A) 660H; *SA Associated Newspapers Ltd v Schoeman* 1962 (2) SA 613 (A) 616G; *Samuels* (n 86) 30G–H; *Demmers* (n 86) 840A–C.

[88] See *Fichardt* (n 27) 6, 9, 12, 13; *Wallachs Ltd v Marsh* 1928 TPD 531, 545; *Unie Volkspers Bpk v Rossouw* 1943 AD 519, 524; *Schoeman* (n 87) 616H–617D.

This definition explains why it is defamatory to say that a person assaulted someone, or stole something, or is corrupt, or is a liar. It is defamatory because a person who did or is any of these things is, all other things being equal, of less worth than a person who did or is not. It also explains two otherwise puzzling features of defamatoriness that have not yet been mentioned. First, the defamatoriness of an assertion is independent of (and thus can be established prior to determining) its truth or falsity. For example, to say of a thug that he is a thug is no less defamatory than to say that of a saint. Secondly, the defamatoriness of an assertion is unaffected by its impact on the beliefs of those to whom it is made. Thus it may well be that case that, if I tell a group of ANC stalwarts that Jacob Zuma received a personal kick-back from the so-called 'arms-deal', none of them will believe me. But my assertion will be no less defamatory because of that. As it was put in the case of *Nasionale Pers Bpkt v Long*, 'a libel is none the less a libel because the people who read it do not believe that the person libelled did in fact do what he is charged with.'[89] Conversely, it may be that if I make the same remark to a group of right-wing businessmen, I will only confirm what they already believe. Again, that does not mean that my remark is not defamatory.

'All true,' it may be said, 'but how does it show that mere publication of defamatory matter is insufficient to justify the inference of *animus iniuriandi*?' It does so like this. To publish matter about someone *animo iniuriandi* is to do so with the intention of getting third parties to think less of him *than they ought*. The italicised three words at the end are critical: not 'than they do', but 'than they ought'. Now, if I say that you are a thief, though believing that you are not (or not believing that you are), I clearly do intend to get my listeners to think less of you than they ought. I do, therefore, act *animo iniuriandi*. However, if I say that you are a thief, in the belief that you really are one, I do not act *animo iniuriandi*. I do not do so because, even though I may intend to get my listeners to think less of you than they do (because they presently think you a person of impeccable virtue), I do not intend to get them to think less of you than they ought. On the contrary, my intention is to get them to think of you exactly what they should. It is to get them to estimate you at your real or true worth.

So, the mere fact that a defendant published defamatory matter about a plaintiff is as compatible with his having done so with the intention of getting others to think as much of the plaintiff as they should, as it is with his having done so with the intention of getting them to think less of the plaintiff than they ought. This has an important implication. In order for the fact that a defendant published defamatory matter about a plaintiff to justify the inference that he acted *animo iniuriandi*, it has to be supplemented with an additional fact – a fact indicating that the defendant did not believe that the plaintiff possessed the characteristic or performed the conduct which the defendant attributed to him (and possession of which diminishes a person's worth). More simply put, what is required is an additional fact showing that, more likely than not, the defendant

[89] *Nasionale Pers* (n 27) 97.

did not believe his defamatory statement to be true (or even that he believed it to be false).

What fact would show this? Most obviously, it would be shown by the fact that the plaintiff in truth did not possess the characteristic or had not performed the conduct in question. That is, it would be shown by the fact that the defamatory statement actually was false. It may be thought that this additional fact (or, to put it differently, the falsity of the defendant's defamatory assertion) would have to be proved by the plaintiff. But that is not so. As was stated by Menzies and Musgrave JJ way back in 1846, in the case of *Norden*, that the plaintiff in a defamation dispute does not possess the characteristic or did not perform the conduct attributed to him by the defendant (ie that the defamatory statement was false) may, indeed must, simply be assumed.[90] Remember, the characteristic or conduct attributed to the plaintiff is such that possession or performance of it diminishes a person's worth. All other things being equal, a person who possesses that characteristic or performs that conduct is of less worth than one who does not. However, as De Villiers CJ put it in 1874, in the case of *Fick v Watermeyer*, 'the legal presumption is in favour of a man's good character'.[91] And that has to be correct. The default position, in respect of everyone, has to be that he does not possess any characteristic and did not perform any conduct that would diminish his worth. It has to be that he did not assault anyone, that he stole nothing, that he is not corrupt and that he does not lie.

Everything is in place to explain why a defendant, by proving the truth of his defamatory statement, rebuts the presumption that he acted *animo iniuriandi*. The presumption rests on two pillars. One is a fact that has to be proved by the plaintiff, namely that the defendant published defamatory matter concerning him – in other words, the defendant asserted that the plaintiff possesses some characteristic or performed some conduct, possession or performance of which diminishes a person's worth. The other is a fact which has to be, and is, assumed in the plaintiff's favour, namely that the plaintiff actually does not possess that characteristic or did not perform that conduct – in other words, the defendant's defamatory assertion is false. If either of these two pillars is knocked over, the presumption which they support will inevitably come tumbling down too. And that, according to the original conceptualisation, is the effect and the point of the defence of truth and public interest. By proving that the defamatory matter which he published is true, a defendant shows that the assumption as to the second fact is mistaken. He destroys the second of the two pillars supporting the presumption of *animus iniuriandi* and, by doing so, causes the presumption itself to come crashing down.

The discussion of the defence of truth and public interest in this section so far is incomplete. In South African law (unlike in English law) truth alone is no defence. For a defendant to escape liability on the ground that his defamatory statement was true, it in addition has to be the case that the statement was 'in the

[90] *Norden* (n 7) 53.
[91] *Fick v Watermeyer* 1874 Buchanan 86, 89.

public interest' or 'for the public benefit'.[92] On the face of it, the requirement that the publication of the defamatory matter was in the public interest poses a difficulty for the original conceptualisation. For it is not obvious why the question whether a defendant acted *animo iniuriandi*, when publishing defamatory matter, should be affected by whether the publication of that matter was in the public interest or not. But the public interest requirement can in fact be reconciled with the original conceptualisation. Recall, once more, what it means to say that a defendant has published defamatory matter about a plaintiff *animo iniuriandi*. It means that he did so with the intention of getting others to think less of the plaintiff *than they ought*. The italicised words are, again, critical. What others *ought* to think of one need not – and in fact usually should not – reflect everything he is, does, or has done. To put it differently, it is not so that every one of a person's character traits and acts (and omissions) has a bearing on, or is relevant to, how others should estimate his worth.

An example illustrates this. Assume that I am a pornography addict. A colleague, having stumbled upon this fact during a visit to my home, mentions it to the LLB class that we both teach. Assume further that, all other things being equal, a person who is addicted to pornography is of less worth than one who is not. In this scenario, my colleague has published defamatory matter about me. But the defamatory matter which he published is true. It follows that, if my students now think less of me than they did before, my colleague will have gotten them to estimate me at my true worth (or at least to estimate my worth more accurately than they did before). Does it also follow that my colleague could not have gotten my students to think less of me *than they ought*? It surely does not. My pornography addiction is my business not theirs. It is wholly irrelevant to my dealings with them. It is, as between us, a fact private to me. What my students *ought* to think of me should not, therefore, be in any way affected by it.[93]

How does this make sense of the idea that, for a defendant who published defamatory matter about another to rebut the resultant presumption of *animus iniuriandi* on the ground of truth, he also has to prove public interest? It does so because it means that the 'additional fact' discussed earlier – the fact which has to be added to the fact that the defendant published defamatory matter about the plaintiff, in order to justify the presumption of *animus iniuriandi* – has to be re-described:

> *Either* the plaintiff does not possess the characteristic or did not perform the conduct attributed to him by the defendant (ie the defamatory statement is false) *or* the plaintiff's possession of that characteristic or performance of that conduct is a private fact.

[92] See *Sparks* (n 6); *Botha* (n 1); *Michaelis* (n 12); *Williams v Shaw* (1884) 4 EDC 105; *Graham v Ker* (1891) 9 SC 185; *Kernick v Fitzpatrick* 1907 TS 389; *Sutter* (n 28) 161.

[93] For a real example not altogether dissimilar to this hypothetical one, see *Groenewald v Hornsby* 1917 TPD 81, in which Mason J rejected the proposition that 'if adultery has been committed lately you are entitled to enlighten the whole community as to the misconduct of the adulterer' (83).

Moreover, it is this more complex fact (rather than simply the fact that the defamatory matter is false) which has to be, and is, assumed, and which forms the second pillar on which the presumption of *animus iniuriandi* rests. Consequently, if a defendant wishes to topple that presumption by knocking over the second of the pillars supporting it, he has to prove both that his defamatory statement was true and that it was not a private fact – or, as the South African courts put it, that his statement was 'in the public interest' or 'for the public benefit'.[94]

Admittedly, the distinction between public and private facts is a vague one. That I tried to seduce my colleague, though both she and I are married to others, presumably is a private fact. But how is the fact that I seduced several of my students to be classified? And does it matter that I last did this 20 years ago, at another institution which I consequently had to leave? The vagueness in the public–private distinction is a real difficulty. It may even be reason enough to prefer a defence of truth only over a defence of truth and public interest. However, that is irrelevant to the analysis in this sub-section. Its aim was not to vindicate the public interest requirement. It was only to show that, if the public interest requirement is justified, it is not at odds with the original conceptualisation's claim that the defence of truth and public interest avoids liability by rebutting the presumption of *animus iniuriandi.*

B. Fair Comment

To make sense of the original conceptualisation's claim that the defence of fair comment negates *animus iniuriandi*, one has to understand three things. First, one has to grasp the distinction between assertions that are intended as authoritative and assertions that are intended as non-authoritative. Secondly, one has to understand that a person acts *animo iniuriandi* in making a defamatory assertion only if he has the former intention, that is, the intention that the assertion be authoritative. Thirdly, one has to realise that – in South African law at any rate – proof that a defamatory assertion constitutes fair comment is really just proof that (contrary to first appearances) it was made with the latter intention, that is, the intention that it be non-authoritative. This sub-section deals with each of these three points in turn.

Most assertions are intended to be authoritative. While conversing with the stranger sitting next to me on a 12-hour plane trip, I say the following: 'My name is Anton Fagan'; 'I have three children'; 'I am on my way to a conference about *iniuria* and the common law'. In respect of every one of these assertions, I intend my neighbour simply to take my word for it. I intend him to believe what I have said, just because I have said it. To put it another way, in making each of these assertions, my intention is not only that my neighbour will believe what I assert, but also that the assertion itself will be his reason for believing it. And, chances are, that is exactly what will happen. For, in respect of the evidence for each of

[94] The relationship between 'public interest' and 'private facts' was acknowledged in *Independent Newspaper Holdings Ltd v Suliman* [2004] 3 All SA 137 (SCA) para 71 (Nugent JA).

these assertions – that is, the facts or reasons upon which its truth depends – I am, relative to my neighbour, in a privileged position. And, absent unusual circumstances, he will know and accept that.

But not all assertions are like this. In an argument with a creationist I may, having set out all the contrary evidence, conclude by saying: 'There you have it, human beings are the product of evolution'. This assertion, unlike those in the previous paragraph, is not intended to be authoritative. I do of course intend the creationist to believe what I have asserted, namely that humans evolved. But I do not intend him to believe it just because I said they did. On the contrary, I intend him to believe it only because he is persuaded by the evidence that I marshalled in its support. Indeed, if he were to respond by saying, 'I did not understand any of your arguments, but if you say humans evolved, I believe it', I would regard myself as having failed. The same holds for a lawyer arguing a matter in court: he may intend the judge to believe that his client did no wrong, as he has asserted, but he does not intend the judge to take his word for it – rather, he hopes that the judge will have been convinced by the evidence that he led and the arguments which he presented to support that assertion. Likewise an academic writing a paper in which it is claimed that *animus iniuriandi* is the gist of defamation: he intends his readers to accept his claim, not because he has claimed it, but rather because they find his evidence and arguments persuasive.

Whether a person has made an assertion with the intention that it be authoritative or not is a matter of inference. But there may be strong indicators one way or the other. For example, it would be a rare occasion when a person could assert 'I have a headache' without intending the assertion to be authoritative, since the evidence for (or against) it is uniquely his. Similarly, an assertion like 'chocolate ice cream is more delicious than strawberry ice cream' is typically made with the intention that it be non-authoritative, because neither the speaker nor anyone else can claim a privileged position in respect of the evidence that would make the assertion true (or false). The fact that a person makes a claim only after having set out the evidence that supports it, points – though not conclusively – to an intention that the claim be non-authoritative. And the converse applies to a claim baldly made, without any supporting evidence.

That concludes the first of the three points to be made in this sub-section. The second point is that it is a necessary condition, for a defendant to have acted with *animus iniuriandi* in making a defamatory assertion about a plaintiff, that he intended the assertion to be authoritative rather than non-authoritative. In other words, it is necessary that he intended his hearers or readers to believe that the plaintiff possesses the character or performed the conduct which his assertion attributed to him, *just because he asserted it.* It is easy enough to see why this must be so. For it to be said that a person, in publishing an assertion about someone, intended to do him harm, it must be that he intended his publication of that assertion to make a difference: he must have intended the assertion itself to change others' beliefs about that person. But it is precisely that condition which is not met when a person publishes an assertion (defamatory or otherwise) with the intention that it be non-authoritative. For example: facts a, b and c justify the conclusion that X is a thief; having described these facts to you, I add the conclusion which inevitably follows; however, I do so with a non-authoritative rather than an authoritative intention. In that case, while I intend my assertion that 'X is a thief' to reflect facts a, b and c, I do not intend it have any additional weight of its own. I do not intend it to have an independent impact on your beliefs. Thus, I cannot be said to have made the assertion *animo iniuriandi*.

Now for the third point, namely that – in South African law – assertions qualifying as fair comment are in reality just assertions made with the intention that they be non-authoritative. Admittedly, most contemporary South African lawyers probably do not know this. That would be, in part, because of Jansen JA's altogether unhelpful (and question-begging) claim, in *Marais*, that the 'primary question' in determining whether an assertion qualifies as comment is 'how the ordinary reader (with the usual characteristics of reasonableness, and so on) would understand it'.[95] It may also be because the South African courts, confusingly, contrast 'comments' with 'statements of fact'. However, a few judgments in the early twentieth century show that there was a time when fair comment's nature was better understood. Here are some extracts from them:

> Now it is not always easy to disentangle a statement of the facts from the comment made upon those facts. A statement does not necessarily cease to be a comment because it appears in the form of a statement of fact. It may be a deduction from the facts and *intended* as a comment upon those facts, and yet appear in the guise of a statement of fact. (emphasis added)[96]

> It is often not at all an easy matter to decide as to what is comment and what is an assertion of fact. As the Court pointed out in *Van Gorkom's* case, comment may appear in the guise of a statement of fact, but it will not cease to be comment if it is clearly *intended* as such. (emphasis added)[97]

> If a writer chooses to publish an expression of opinion which has no relation, by way of criticism, to any fact before the reader, then such an expression of opinion *depends upon nothing but the writer's own authority*, and stands in the same position as an allegation of fact. (emphasis added)[98]

> It [the defamatory statement] *rests upon the mere authority of the writer* who made it, and therefore to my mind it does not come within the protection of the defence of fair comment. (emphasis added)[99]

> [I]f he had been understood by his audience to be stating the bare fact that these men had actually committed crimes [as opposed to making a comment], they would probably have accepted the statement *on his authority*, believing naturally that he had adequate grounds for making so serious a charge. (emphasis added)[100]

[95] *Marais* (n 50) 1168G (my translation).
[96] *Hultzer & Das v Van Gorkom* 1909 TS 232, 241.
[97] *Roos* (n 21) 1009.
[98] *Roos* (n 21) 998 (Innes CJ).
[99] *Roos* (n 21) 1000 (Innes CJ).
[100] *Crawford* (n 30) 129.

In these extracts one sees explicitly recognised, first, that whether an assertion amounts to a comment or not turns, critically, on the intention with which it was made and, secondly, that the relevant intention is the intention that the assertion be authoritative ('rest upon the mere authority of the writer'). And it goes beyond that. Further conditions for an assertion to be covered by the defence of fair comment – such as that the facts upon which the assertion is based be either stated or readily accessible, and that the assertion be a reasonable inference from those facts – are often understood as requirements additional to (and independent from) the requirement that the assertion qualify as a comment. But they are better understood as conditions justifying precisely that qualification, that is, as conditions justifying the inference that the assertion in question was made with the intention that it be non-authoritative. That Innes CJ took the first of these conditions to have this role is suggested by the third extract above, and the extract immediately below:

> [I]n my opinion there must be some reference in the article which indicates clearly what facts are being commented upon. If there is no such reference, then the comment rests merely upon the writer's own authority.[101]

C. Privileged Occasion

Textbooks on the South African law of defamation generally divide the defence of privilege into two kinds, namely absolute privilege and qualified privilege. Absolute privilege is enjoyed by Members of Parliament and the provincial legislatures. It means that a parliamentarian or provincial legislator who makes a false defamatory statement about someone, knowing it to be both false and defamatory, cannot be held civilly liable – provided the statement was made to the body of which he is a member or to one of its committees.[102] Since a person who knowingly makes a false defamatory statement about another to one or more third parties undeniably does so with the intention of getting them to think less of him than they ought, the basis for this defence – the reason it avoids liability – cannot possibly be that it negates *animus iniuriandi*. It follows that this defence, that is the defence of absolute privilege, cannot be accommodated by the original conceptualisation. That is hardly surprising. The defence was neither recognised by Roman-Dutch law nor created by the South African courts, but was instead imported from English law by statute.[103] Moreover, no court subscribing to the original conceptualisation ever claimed that it could accommodate absolute privilege. And at least one of the original conceptualisation's academic defenders was perspicacious enough to see that absolute privilege had to be treated as an exception.[104]

[101] *Roos* (n 21) 999–1000.

[102] The Constitution of the Republic of South Africa, Act 108 of 1996, ss 58(1), 71(1) and 117(1).

[103] See *Poovalingham v Rajbansi* 1992 (1) SA 283 (A) 286–91; De Villiers (n 65) 201 n 38.

[104] Price, '*Animus Iniuriandi* in Defamation' (n 64) 29–30.

What about qualified privilege? The textbooks invariably distinguish three instances of qualified privilege: (1) statements made in the discharge of a duty or the exercise of a legitimate interest; (2) statements made in the course of judicial or quasi-judicial proceedings; and (3) reports on the proceedings of parliament, the courts and certain public bodies. The question for this sub-section is whether it makes sense to claim, as the original conceptualisation does, that a defendant who successfully raises a defence of qualified privilege escapes liability by rebutting the presumption of *animus iniuriandi*. As will be seen below, it certainly does make sense in the case of instances (1) and (2): that is, in the case of statements made in the discharge of a duty or the exercise of a legitimate interest, and statements made in the course of judicial or quasi-judicial proceedings. In respect of instance (3), the position is more complex. For it may be that the privilege pertaining to reports on the proceedings of parliament, the courts and public bodies is best understood as an extended (and diluted) form of absolute privilege, and thus as a further exception to the original conceptualisation.

There is, perhaps, no better way to start the explanation of why qualified privilege (in respect of instances (1) and (2) at any rate) rebuts the presumption of *animus iniuriandi*, than with the following passage from the judgment of Menzies and Musgrave JJ in *Norden*:

> The law . . . recognizes several cases in which the situation of the person who has uttered the injurious words, or the circumstances under which they have been uttered, are held to make his case a privileged one, and to remove to a greater or less degree the legal presumption of *animus injuriandi*, which would otherwise arise from the injurious nature of the expressions which have been used; for example, the case of judges, while engaged in the discharge of their office, and of parties to a cause as to observations made on the adverse party or his witnesses. (*Voet*, 47, 10, 20.) Now, the claim of a witness to privilege for what he has stated under oath, and while under examination, is much stronger than that of either a judge or a party. The law forces him, whether he will or not, to attend the Court, to take an oath to speak the truth to the best of his belief, and to answer the questions put to him. If asked, he must state not only what he knows, but what he believes, and what are the grounds of his belief. He is under a compulsion which leaves him no discretion. He is forced to state his own impressions on the subject, no matter how formed . . . That the statements he has made were made on oath is a legal ground for presuming that they were true, or, at least, believed by the witness to be true. That they were made under legal compulsion is a legal ground for presuming that they were not made *animo injuriandi*.[105]

An important implication of this passage is that the description – in the sub-section on truth and public interest – of the grounds upon which the presumption of *animus iniuriandi* rests requires further refinement. To the proven fact that the defendant published defamatory matter about the plaintiff and the assumed fact that defamatory matter was false (to keep things simple, public interest will be ignored here), needs to be added a further assumed fact, namely that the defamatory matter was *gratuitously* published. This is an additional, not

[105] *Norden* (n 7) 54.

an alternative, ground. If, therefore, a defendant can show that this assumption, that is the assumption that the defamatory matter was gratuitously published, is mistaken, he brings about the collapse of the presumption that he acted *animo iniuriandi*. How does the defendant do that? He does so by showing that he had good reason to speak (or write) about the aspect of the plaintiff's character or conduct which he did speak about. In *Norden*, the reason was an obligatory one imposed by the law. But it could be an obligatory reason, moral in nature. And it could be a non-obligatory reason, based on the interests of the defendant and his audience.[106]

There is a great deal of common sense in this. Remember, again, that to presume *animus iniuriandi* on the part of a defendant is to presume that he had an intention to get others to think less of the plaintiff *than they ought*. If a defendant had valid reason to speak about some aspect of the plaintiff's character, for example his competence in his job, and confines himself to speaking just about that, the reasonable inference to draw surely is, not that he intended to get his listeners to think less of the plaintiff than they ought, but rather that he intended to get them to think of the plaintiff exactly what they should. The reasonable inference to draw, in other words, is that the defendant was simply trying to do what he was obliged or had reason to do, namely accurately to assess the relevant aspect of the plaintiff's character (in our example, how well the plaintiff does his job). As Voet put it (albeit in the context of truth and public interest rather than privilege): 'It is not to be presumed that he who does something which he could have done without meaning well and without [a] good intention . . . meant to do it with the evil purpose of doing a wrong, since every person is in doubt regarded as a good man until the contrary has been proved.'[107]

It may be objected that this analysis of qualified privilege, as a defence aimed at negating *animus iniuriandi*, is incompatible with the fact that some of the conditions for the defence are objective. Now, that some of the conditions for the defence of qualified privilege are objective cannot be denied. Consider first the condition that the defendant had valid reason to speak about an aspect of the plaintiff's character or conduct (or, as it is usually put, that the occasion was a privileged one). This, said Watermeyer AJA in *De Waal v Ziervogel*, is to be determined either by application of the law (where the reason is alleged to be a legal duty) or by asking: 'did the circumstances in the eyes of a reasonable man create a duty or an interest which entitles the defendant to speak' (where the reason is alleged to be a moral duty or legitimate interest).[108] Consider next the condition that the defendant confined himself to speaking about that aspect of the plaintiff's character or conduct which he had valid reason to speak about (or, as it is usually put, that the defamatory matter was relevant or germane to the occasion). Though the point is not altogether settled, this probably is to be determined by asking

[106] *De Waal* (n 37) 121, 123.

[107] Voet, 'Commentary' (n 75) s 9.

[108] *De Waal* (n 37) 121–23. See also *Borgin* (n 48) 577E–G; *Mohamed v Jassiem* 1996 (1) SA 673 (A) 711A–D.

whether 'the defamatory matter could fairly be regarded as reasonably necessary to protect the interest or discharge the duty which was the foundation of the privilege'.[109] However, there is no incompatibility here. The presumption as to *animus iniuriandi* may be a presumption as to a subjective state of affairs. But it is based on objective and external facts. It is only to be expected, therefore, that a defence aimed at its rebuttal could involve objective conditions – for an obvious way to attack the subjective presumption is to attack the objective grounds supporting it.

IV. Conclusion

The previous section investigated the analytical objection to the original conceptualisation and found it wanting. Contrary to what was claimed by South African delict scholars in the 1960s and by the South African courts thereafter, the original conceptualisation has no difficulty making sense of the standard defences: truth and public interest, fair comment and privileged occasion. The only clear exception is absolute privilege. However, there is one more challenge which the original conceptualisation's detractors are likely to raise. Borrowing a well-known phrase, one could call it 'rights as the trump'. This conclusion offers a brief explanation of, and response to, that challenge.

Several of the Appellate Division judgments which developed, or subsequently applied, the new conceptualisation of defamation describe wrongfulness in general as concerned with, and the defences in particular as founded upon, public policy.[110] Some judgments go one step further and acknowledge that the primary policy concern here is freedom of expression.[111] Moreover, it would appear that public policy – and thus also the right to freedom of expression – is taken not only to justify the existence of the defences, but also to determine their content. Consistent with this, it has been held that a court may, on the basis that public policy (specifically the right to freedom of expression) requires it, recognise further defences in addition to the existing ones.[112] Precisely that was done in the case of *National Media Ltd v Bogoshi.*[113]

The fact that the new conceptualisation so closely connects the defences to the right to freedom of expression may seem sufficient reason to prefer it over the original one. For, it may be thought, it means that the new conceptualisation fits

[109] *Van der Berg v Coopers & Lybrand Trust (Pty) Ltd* 2001 (2) SA 242 (SCA) 254I. See also *Molepo v Achterberg* 1943 AD 85, 97–98; *Rhodes University College v Field* 1947 (3) SA 437 (A), 464; *Herselman NO v Botha* 1994 (1) SA 28 (A), 36.

[110] *O'Malley* (n 44) 402–3; *Borgin* (n 48) 571F–G; *Marais* (n 50) 1168C–E; *Neethling v The Weekly Mail* 1994 (1) SA 708 (A) 777E; *National Media Ltd v Bogoshi* 1998 (4) SA 1196 (SCA) 1204D–F.

[111] *May* (n 49) 19H; *Inkatha Freedom Party* (n 52) 588G-591G; *Esselen's Estate* (n 52) 25D–E; *Modiri v Minister of Safety and Security* 2011 (6) SA 370 (SCA) 379D–G.

[112] *Inkatha Freedom Party* (n 52) 588I–J, 590C–D; *Neethling* (n 110) 777E–F.

[113] *National Media* (n 110). 1

with the relatively modern realisation that the law of delict is in large part about balancing competing rights, and that the law of defamation in particular is about balancing the right to reputation and the right to freedom of expression. By contrast, it may be said, the original conceptualisation provides no location for this balancing of rights to take place or, if it does, unhelpfully hides it from view. Thus, it may be concluded, to defend the original conceptualisation – as this chapter has done – is anachronistic and retrogressive.

This attack misses its target. The original conceptualisation did not entail that the South African law of defamation failed to strike a balance between the rights to reputation and freedom of expression. Indeed, it is impossible for the law not to strike this balance in one way or another. What the original conceptualisation did entail, however, was that the South African law of defamation struck that balance once only – when it endorsed the second of the propositions constituting the original conceptualisation: that is, the proposition that a person commits the *iniuria* of defamation if and only if he publishes matter referring to another and does so *animo iniuriandi.*

Why does acceptance of this proposition entail a once-off balancing of reputation and expression? Because, while the proposition itself (inevitably) reflects a particular balancing of the two rights, application and further elaboration of the proposition can be done without again balancing them. The proposition stipulates two conditions. One is that the defendant succeeded in making an assertion about the plaintiff to a third party. This condition may have a normative basis, but it is itself purely factual in nature. Its application, its development, requires no evaluative argument – let alone a balancing of rights. The other condition is that the defendant intended to get others to think less of the plaintiff than they ought. Application and elaboration of this condition probably does require some resort to values (because of the 'ought' in it) – but freedom of expression is not one of them.

In respect of the rights to reputation and freedom of expression, the difference between the two conceptualisations thus boils down to this. According to the new conceptualisation, the rights directly justify the defences. According to the original conceptualisation, by contrast, the rights ultimately – but indirectly – justify the defences. For the original conceptualisation interposes, between the rights and the defences, the proposition (or rule) that the *iniuria* of defamation requires publication and *animus iniuriandi.* The rights justify the proposition, and the proposition in turn justifies the defences.

That raises the question whether there are any reasons to prefer the three-tier justificatory structure of the original conceptualisation to the two-tier structure of the new one. There are. But a discussion of them lies beyond the scope of this chapter.

10

Retraction, Apology and Reply as Responses to *iniuriae*

JONATHAN BURCHELL

I. Introduction

A recent article in a popular magazine referred to a celebrity as having a 'narcissistic personality disorder'. The magazine later retracted and apologised for the hurt to the celebrity's dignity saying that the dominant symptoms of narcissistic personality did not apply to the celebrity, but adding that the celebrity actually suffered from a 'histrionic personality disorder'. Without determining whether the imputation is defamatory, whether there could be any truthfulness in this assertion or whether, if the assertion constituted a comment on the celebrity, it was fair, it is nevertheless self-evident that the purported retraction and apology merely served to sprinkle salt on the original wound.

How many times have we heard an apology like this: 'I apologise for whatever I may have said that could have caused you hurt. If mistakes were made and you felt upset because of what I said, then I'm sorry for any hurt that you may have experienced'. The person making this so-called 'apology' might just as well have said 'I deny saying what you allege I said but, if I did happen to say something that offended you, you're merely hyper-sensitive in feeling hurt by it'. But, what is an adequate apology and in what way should the law take such an apology into account in a civil claim for impairment of reputation or infringement of some other personality right?

One also frequently hears the retort: 'If only I'd been given a chance to reply to the allegations made against me, then I could immediately have set the record straight'. In what way can the law facilitate the continuing of debate through replies or responses to injurious allegations? A 'right of reply', as it is sometimes called, is of relatively recent origin,[1] and possibly has less contentious relevance[2]

[1] Linked most probably to the advent of mass publication through the development of printing.

[2] As will be seen later, a number of judicial decisions have acknowledged that providing an opportunity for 'reply' to a person whose reputation has been impaired by the media is part of the examination into the 'reasonableness' of the publication and even of journalistic integrity.

to striking a balance between freedom of expression and protection of reputation, so I will first examine 'retractions and apologies' and then turn to 'replies'.

The initial part of this chapter is on the origin, true meaning and contemporary relevance of retraction and apology ('palinode' as it is sometimes called) in cases of impairment of reputation and other instances of personality *iniuriae*? The vexed issues of whether apologies may or may not amount to admissions of guilt, may adversely affect the cover of insurance policies or serve to confirm a cause of action,[3] do not form part of this chapter. However, the view propounded by Vines that 'the most effective apologies are those which include an admission of fault'[4] is endorsed.

Furthermore, this chapter does not seek to confront the value of public apologies on a much grander scale, sometimes by successor governments apologising for human rights abuses perpetrated by a previous regime on its citizens. Although the underlying reasons for all apologies may be the same, the focus of this chapter is on the meaning and role of retraction, apology and reply as methods of assisting in resolving private disputes relating to individual reputation and dignity.

In conclusion, a modern, common law way of giving weight to retractions and apologies and continuing the debate by giving an opportunity to the aggrieved party to respond to injurious imputations will be examined.

II. Origins and Development of Retraction and Apology as a Response to Insults and Defamation

Borthwick[5] points out that although the *actio ad palinodiam* was unknown to Roman law it was derived from Roman and Greek practice. Although the essence of the Roman *actio iniuriarum* for impairment of reputation was the payment of pecuniary damages, the Roman-Dutch law provided two actions: *amende profitable* and *amende honorable*. *Amende profitable* bore a distinct resemblance to the Roman law action for the recovery of pecuniary damages. *Amende honorable* took two forms: (a) a declaration by the wrongdoer retracting his words and acknowledging that they were false (*palinodia*, *retractio* or *recantio*); and (b) an apology or acknowledgement of guilt and prayer for forgiveness (*deprecatio*).[6] Although there was some dispute on this matter amongst the authorities, it seems that the correct view was that *amende honorable* was a remedy additional, rather than alternative, to damages.[7] The recantation, which applied to oral and written words, could be

[3] These matters are comprehensively examined by Prue Vines, 'Apologies and Civil Liability in the UK: A View from Elsewhere' (2008) 12 *Edinburgh Law Review* 200.

[4] ibid 222.

[5] John Borthwick, *A Treatise on the Law of Libel and Slander* (Edinburgh, 1826) 181.

[6] See Jonathan Burchell, *The Law of Defamation in South Africa* (Cape Town, Juta, 1985) 11–12.

[7] See the authorities cited in ibid 12.

made in court and, if the defendant refused to make honourable amends, he or she could render himself or herself liable to fine or imprisonment.[8]

Leaving aside the fact that, at times, humiliating forms of apologies were sought, that the retraction and apology did not always reach the desired audience and that it was enforced by threat of punishment, the concept of retracting the offensive words and apologising for their use nevertheless still has some attraction from the perspective of the legal and practical resolution of disputes or the striking of an effective balance between protection of reputation and free speech.

In older Scottish practice, palinode (or public retraction with acceptance that the words were untrue) could be a remedy for insult before the commissary courts where *solatium* was sought.[9] Borthwick concludes that palinode appeared in commissary court records and reflected a practice adopted in Scotland. For instance, the defamer could be required to stand at 'church doors, and other places, clothed in sack cloth, and say, "False tongue, I lied"'. [10] The palinode was in addition to a fine and damages, but was awarded with caution.[11] Borthwick perspicaciously points to the

> [v]alue of this expedient in reconciling animosities, shortening law-suits, and saving litigants from expenses which may often prove ruinous to both parties engaged in actions of defamation.[12]

The United Kingdom Defamation Act of 1996[13] refers to a 'suitable correction' of, and a 'sufficient apology' for, a defamatory statement as integral parts of an offer of amends. The offer of amends in ss 2–4 of the Defamation Act[14] (which Gatley describes as a 'means of settlement provided by statute'[15]) allows an innocent[16]

[8] Burchell, *Law of Defamation* (n 6) 12.

[9] Kenneth McKenzie Norrie, *Defamation and Related Actions in Scots Law* (Edinburgh, Butterworths, 1995) 2, 125 and 164. John Blackie (in 'The Protection of *corpus* in Modern and Early Scots Law', this volume, ch 9, n 19) has pointed out that an expression of repentance could form part of the criminal process in injury cases until approximately 1800 in Scots law.

[10] Borthwick (n 5) 181 (chapter on palinode). See also *Deanes v Bothwel* (1669) Mor 7577 (where having alleged that a procurator was a 'false knave', the wrongdoer was required to stand at the church door of Glencourse, acknowledge his fault and pay money to the poor and the party) and *Symmond v Williamson* (1752) Mor 3435. I am indebted to Elspeth Reid for drawing my attention to these Scottish authorities.

[11] Borthwick (n 5) 181–82.

[12] Borthwick (n 5) 183.

[13] The Defamation Act 1996 applies to Scotland (with the exception of s 3(8) by s 18 of the Act): see *Moore v The Scottish Daily Record and Sunday Mail Ltd* 2007 SLT 217.

[14] These provisions came into operation in England and Wales on 28 Feb 2000 and in Scotland on 31 March 2001: Matthew Collins, *The Law of Defamation and the Internet*, 3rd edn (Oxford, Oxford University Press, 2010) para 18.01.

[15] Partrick Milmo and WVH Rogers (eds), *Gatley on Libel and Slander*, 11th edn (London, Sweet & Maxwell 2008) para 31.28. See also Eady J in *Milne v Express Newspapers* [2003] 1 WLR 927 [41]: 'The main purpose of the statutory regime is to provide an exit route for journalists who have made a mistake and are willing to put their hands up and make amends'.

[16] Someone who did not know and had no reason to believe (it is presumed that the offeror did not know or had no reason to believe) that the statement was likely to be understood as referring to the aggrieved party, or that the statement was both false and defamatory of that person. The scope given for innocent defamation plus an offer of amends which has been rejected to become a defence is a way of alleviating the general rule of strict liability under the United Kingdom defamation law.

publisher to rely on an exclusive defence that an offer of amends has been made but rejected. If the offeree accepts the offer,[17] then the offer may be enforced and no further defamation proceedings taken. Where the offer of amends is accepted, a judge may decide on the extent of compensation to be paid where the parties do not agree on the measure of compensation and apparently there is no ceiling on the amount of compensation a judge may award for serious defamation.[18]

The precursor to the offer of amends (s 4 of the Defamation Act of 1952) seemed to be 'hardly, if ever, used'[19] and, because the procedure is essentially one of settlement without a full-blown trial, the frequency with which the 1996 version is, or may be, invoked will also be difficult to trace.

The defence under s 4(3) of the 1996 Act will only be lost where the plaintiff can prove that the defendant knew or had reason to believe[20] that the statement referred to the plaintiff and was both false and defamatory. There is a strong presumption that the defendant did not know or have reason to believe these matters.[21] Furthermore, Eady J in *Milne v Express Newspapers*[22] has interpreted the words 'no reason to believe' to mean proof of 'bad faith' or 'reckless indifference to the truth' ie recklessness that the words referred to the plaintiff and that they were both false and defamatory must be proved. According to Eady J in *Milne*, proof of negligence on the part of the media would not be sufficient and, in fact, allowing proof of negligence to lead to a forfeiture of the defence available to the journalist would, according to Eady J, be 'self-defeating'.[23] In other words, proof of either malice or recklessness on the part of the defendant (usually the media) would be required in order to further freedom of expression by making the forfeiture of the defence less likely, even though the plaintiff loses his or her right to a jury trial by agreeing to the offer of amends.

III. A South African Analogy

The South African law relies on the principles of the South African common law, derived from the Roman *actio iniuriarum*, to regulate defamation. Apart from the

[17] The legislation does not set a time limit for acceptance or stipulate acceptance in a reasonable time: See *Craig Moore v Scottish Daily Record and Sunday Mail Ltd* 2007 CSOH 24. In terms of the Defamation Act 2005 of South Australia, if the offer is not accepted, but is later found to have been 'reasonable', then the fact that an offer was made in an appropriate form and within an appropriate time provides the publisher with a defence to an action.

[18] See, however, n 76 below on the £10,000 cap for *minor* defamation under the 1996 Act. The Court of Appeal in *John v MGN Ltd* [1997] QB 586, 621A–C capped *jury awards* in *serious* defamation cases to £200,000.

[19] See Sir Brian Neill's *Committee on Practice and Procedure in Defamation* (1991) para VII.1.

[20] Which was interpreted by Eady J in *Milne* (n 15) [41] to mean 'recklessness' that the words referred to the plaintiff were both false and defamatory must be proved.

[21] Defamation Act 1996, s 4(3) and Elspeth Reid, *Personality, Confidentiality and Privacy in Scots Law* (Edinburgh, W Green, 2010) para 11.64.

[22] *Milne* (n 15) para 41.

[23] *Milne* (n 15) para 41.

traditional approach regarding retraction and apology as something affecting only the extent of damages, there appears to be a resurgence of interest in the *amende honorable* on the part of the South African courts, prompted to some extent by indigenous emphasis on restorative justice and *ubuntu*, despite the fact that *amende honorable* was thought to have been abrogated by disuse.[24]

In *Mineworkers Investment Co (Pty) Ltd v Modimane*,[25] Willis J described the *amende honorable* as a forgotten 'little treasure lost in a nook of our legal attic'. The majority of the Constitutional Court in *Dikoko v Mokhatlala*[26] did not make a finding on the relevance of the *amende honorable* in current law, but Mokgoro J dissenting, took the view that whether or not the *amende honorable* did still form part of our law, it was important that once an apology was forthcoming it be 'sincere and adequate'.[27] Le Grange J in *Manuel v Crawford-Browne*[28] held that the apology would, on the facts, not be 'sincere and adequate' and that freedom of expression did not cover 'the right to falsely attack the integrity of a fellow citizen for selfish reasons or for reasons which have nothing to do with public benefit'.[29]

In *Le Roux v Dey*[30] the majority of the Constitutional Court ordered an unconditional apology, in addition to the payment of damages, for the injury caused by a defamatory composite, digital picture. Cameron and Froneman JJ, regarding the wrong as an impairment of dignity rather than reputation, considered it time the South African law recognised the value of restorative justice implicit in an apology and retraction. The justices urged that the law should be developed in this direction.[31] In fact, there was some evidence of an unsuccessful attempt at apology in *Dey* and, if the apology by the schoolchildren to their aggrieved teachers had been sincere, adequate and accepted, this would have been an ideal and educational way of resolving the dispute in an amicable fashion.

The issue of apology also arose in *McBride*'s case, but Cameron J (for the majority of the Constitutional Court) considered the factual scenario in *McBride* as different from *Dey*, especially because no personal relationship needed restoring in *McBride*,[32] the media defendant in *McBride* displayed 'no remorse', and the plaintiff asserted that an apology was 'inappropriate'. According to Cameron J, 'the question of an apology where a media defendant has defamed another must await another day'.[33]

[24] On the history of *amende honorable* in the South African law and the reasons for its falling into desuetude, see Burchell, *Law of Defamation* (n 6) 315. The resurgence of interest in apology, possibly encouraged by a broader ethos of reconciliation, has also found some support in the range of rehabilitative options available to child offenders who are diverted from the criminal justice process under s 53(3)(a) of the Child Justice Act 75 of 2008. Australian administrative law has also added 'apology and explanation' to the range of remedies against governmental abuse.

[25] *Mineworkers Investment Co (Pty) Ltd v Modimane* 2002 (6) SA 512 (W) 525E.

[26] *Dikoko v Mokhatlala* 2006 (6) SA 235 (CC).

[27] *Mokhatlala* (n 26) 260F.

[28] *Manuel v Crawford-Browne* [2008] ZAWCHC 13; [2008] 3 All SA 468 (C).

[29] *Crawford-Browne* (n 28) [28].

[30] *Le Roux v Dey* [2011] ZACC 4; 2011 (3) SA 274 (CC).

[31] *Dey* [197] (rather than re-instating the old *amende honorable*: [199]).

[32] *The Citizen 1978 (Pty) Ltd v McBride* [2011] ZACC 11; 2011 (4) SA 191 (CC), [133].

[33] *McBride* (n 32) [134].

South African law allows greater common law scope for innocent defamation in a situation where a non-media defendant is (i) *genuinely* ignorant or mistaken regarding the defamatory nature of a communication, its publication or its reference to the plaintiff and (ii) *genuinely and reasonably* ignorant or mistaken as to a ground of justification (ie truth for the public benefit, fair comment, privileged occasion etc).[34] In terms of *National Media Ltd v Bogoshi*[35] the media are also entitled, in addition to the defence of 'reasonable publication' and the standard grounds of justification, to a defence of absence of fault in the form of negligence (ie a defence of reasonable ignorance of, or mistake in relation to, any of the basic elements of defamation or the existence of any justificatory defences).[36] These defences of absence of intention or negligence exist, in terms of South African law, irrespective of an offer of amends having been made.

It has been argued that honourable amends implies a form of 'interpersonal repair' linked to a personal relationship between the parties, which is often absent where the media has impaired the reputation of another.[37] In reaching this conclusion, Visser defines the media as including not just the press, radio and television, but also 'internet publishers'.[38] Visser rightly regards an impersonal relationship between publisher and the plaintiff as diminishing the full restorative value of retraction and apology for defamatory imputations. However, the advent of interactive websites, blogs and social networking appear to be restoring a measure of a 'personal relationship' to what might otherwise have been seen as the 'faceless' dissemination of information and opinion. (Of course, the same cannot be said of anonymous publication on the internet.) Visser also sees the role of apology as disregarding the part played by the community's right to be informed in the balancing of reputation and freedom of expression. Apart from the fact that retraction of incorrect factual statements has, and still is, a major part of journalistic integrity, Visser has focused solely on the role and potential disadvantages of an apology as a complete defence or remedy. Merely by retracting and apologising, the media publisher may seldom satisfy a person whose reputation is severely impaired without also recognising the availability of an opportunity to recover tangible damages as well. Visser does not examine the arguably beneficial role that a genuine retraction and apology could play, not as a complete defence or exclu-

[34] These principles emerge from the Supreme Court of Appeal judgment of Harms DP *Le Roux v Dey* 2010 (4) SA 210 (SCA) [34] as Brand J in the Constitutional Court judgment in this case preferred not to consider the matter of knowledge of unlawfulness in defamation ([2011] ZACC [137]). However, on a strict interpretation of the 1977 judgment of Rumpff CJ in the Appellate Division in *SAUK v O'Malley* 1977 (3) SA 394 (A) a distinction between a mistake or ignorance relating to an element of defamation and mistake or ignorance relating to the purported existence of a ground of justification was not drawn. Rumpff CJ would seem to have given free rein to *every* genuine lack of knowledge of unlawfulness.

[35] *National Media Ltd v Bogoshi* 1998 (4) SA 1196 (SCA).

[36] ibid 1214F–I, 1215B, 1215H–J; *Khumalo v Holomisa* 2002 (5) SA 401 (CC) [20]; *S v Hoho* 2009 (1) SACR 276 (SCA) [33].

[37] CJ Visser 'The Revival of the *amende honorable* as Applied to Defamation by the Media' (2011) 128 *South African Law Journal* 327, 347.

[38] Visser (n 37) 337.

sive remedy, but merely as part of the factual scenario relevant to assessing the 'reasonableness' of a publication.

As was realised by Cameron J and Froneman J in the South African case of *Le Roux v Dey*,[39] an apology may be particularly apt in providing a restorative justice solution for an impairment of dignity as well as an infringement of reputation.

Aaron Lazare, an American Professor of Psychiatry, suggests that an effective apology must satisfy at least one of seven psychological needs of an offended person in order to heal and, it would seem, most if not all of the seven psychological needs would particularly apply to insult or injury to dignity:

- restoration of self-respect and dignity
- assurance that both parties have shared values
- assurance that the offenses were not their fault
- assurance of safety in their relationships
- seeing the offender suffer
- reparation for harm caused by the offense
- having meaningful dialogues with the offenders.[40]

The South African law of delict, through the modern *actio iniuriarum*, provides a remedy for impairment of dignity[41] and South African courts have regarded the test for determining dignity as both subjective and objective – objective in the sense that a reasonable person in the position of the plaintiff would have felt insulted or considered their dignity impaired.[42] The offering of a satisfactory and prompt apology might not erase the entire hurt, but could be regarded as a factor affecting the reasonableness of the defendant's conduct. Of course, English law does not specifically regard dignity *eo nomine*, as opposed to reputation, as the subject of a claim in tort, although some might see a nascent protection of privacy as emerging, whether by means of a wrong of breach of confidence or by the development of a specific concept of privacy.[43]

In the past, a potential practical difficulty in the use of retraction and apology as a defence or a remedy would have been that the retraction and apology might never reach the readers or hearers of the original defamatory statement. Internet

[39] *Le Roux* (n 30). See also Aaron Lazare, *On Apology* (Oxford, Oxford University Press, 2004).

[40] Lazare, *On Apology* (n 39) 44.

[41] See Jonathan Burchell, 'Personality Rights in South Africa: Re-affirming Dignity' in Niall Whitty and Reinhard Zimmermann (eds), *Rights of Personality in Scots Law: A Comparative Perspective* (Dundee, Dundee University Press, 2009). The origin of *dignitas* lay in the concept of 'status' (see Eric Descheemaeker, '*Solatium* and Injury to Feelings' this volume, ch 4, text to nn 105–7) but has now been given a broader meaning in the South African pre- and post-Constitution jurisprudence.

[42] *De Lange v Costa* 1989 (2) SA 857 (A) 860 and *Le Roux* (n 30) [70], [143], [175]–[180].

[43] Jonathan Burchell, 'The Protection of Privacy in South African Law: A Transplantable Hybrid' (2009) 13.1 EJCL<www.ejcl.org>. Burchell is of the view that the *actio iniuriarum* could become the vehicle for the Scots law extending its protection for privacy (ibid) and dignity (above n 41). However, according to Elspeth Reid, *Personality, Confidentiality and Privacy in Scots Law* (Edinburgh, W Green, 2010) there is less chance of the *actio iniuriarum* being recognised as a method for introducing the protection of privacy as such into the Scots law (paras 17.11 and 17.12) and she suggests that if Scots law requires inspiration, then this could be found in English law or European jurisprudence (para 17.18).

communication and extensive e-news coverage, with its immediacy and its ability to reach as wide, if not wider, an audience than that which might have read, seen or heard the original defamatory publication might encourage a re-evaluation of the merits of retraction and apology.

IV. Reply

An 1881 French Law established a right of reply – the so-called *droit de réponse*[44] – which traditionally applied to press reports.[45] Under French law, once a party is referred to by name or indirectly by the press, the right of reply comes into play even regarding true reports, whether of fact or opinion[46] and even artistic or scientific criticism. Furthermore, designated persons may reply with the object of defending the reputation of a deceased person.[47] The only restriction on the content of the reply under French law is that it does not infringe the legitimate interest of a third party or embody an attack on the journalist's reputation.[48] The aggrieved party is given 'opportunity to express himself in the same fashion and before the same forum [in] which the publication occurred'.[49] The remedy was originally enforced through the criminal law, but enforcement by civil proceedings is gaining ground.[50] It is argued, in those European countries [51] that followed the French-style right of reply, that the right was a corollary of media freedom.[52] Anglo-American jurisdictions have, however, not found a formal right of reply attractive.

Although a reply is a most effective way of continuing the debate and furthering freedom of expression, like retraction and apology, there are potential problems of inhibiting editorial discretion and in determining means of enforcing a 'right of reply'.[53] If the phrase 'right of reply' is used then, as 'right' implies 'duty',

[44] See Hans Stoll, 'Consequences of Liability: Remedies' in *International Encyclopedia of Comparative Law*, vol 11 (Tübingen, JCB Mohr, 1986) 164.

[45] In 1933 and 1967 it was argued that the right should also apply to other media.

[46] Stoll, 'Consequences' (n 44) 164.

[47] Stoll (n 44) 164. For most systems of defamation, the personal nature of the action precludes protecting the reputation of the dead. See, however, Kenneth McKenzie Norrie's reference to *Stevens v Yorkhill NHS Trust* 2006 SLT 889 regarding the *actio iniuriarum* for *solatium* for relatives for unauthorised removal and retention of organs from a dead relative. See also Neill Whitty, 'Rights of Personality, Property Rights and the Human Body in Scots Law' (2005) 9 *Edinburgh Law Review* 194, 216.

[48] Stoll (n 44) 164.

[49] Stoll (n 44) 162.

[50] Stoll (n 44) 162. Some countries prefer administrative law remedies.

[51] For instance, Germany, Holland, Denmark, Hungary, Yugoslavia and Portugal: Stoll (n 44) 162.

[52] Stoll (n 44) 162.

[53] For instance, the *droit de réponse* in France requires a newspaper that refers to a person, even in a non-defamatory way, on pain of a fine, to allow that person a right of reply. The interference with editorial discretion impelled the United States Supreme Court to hold that a right of reply infringed the first amendment: *Rosenbloom v Metromedia Inc* 403 US 29 (1971) and *Miami Herald Publishing Co v Tornillo* 418 US 241 (1974).

a problem of enforcement of the duty arises. It is, therefore, preferable to use the wording 'opportunity to reply'.

V. A commonwealth and common law solution: 'reasonable publication' or 'responsible publication on matters of public interest'

An obvious and ideal way of giving appropriate weight to the provision of an opportunity to reply to injurious imputations and to making amends (in the form of retraction and apology) in the context of media publication leading to infringement of personality rights, lies within the common law concepts of 'reasonable publication' and 'responsible publication on matters of public interest' that have recently emerged in jurisdictions within the Commonwealth of Nations.[54]

In determining whether the media (and this includes internet publishers) acted reasonably or responsibly, a major factor will be whether an opportunity to rebut allegations was provided. While absence of a retraction or apology could be a factor affecting the unreasonableness of a publication, absence of an opportunity to reply or respond is already a factor affecting the conclusion that the media have acted unreasonably or irresponsibly in Australia, South Africa and Canada. A defence of 'publication on a matter of public interest' has recently been introduced in the United Kingdom by s 4 of the Defamation Act of 2013.

This emphasis on 'reasonable publication' or 'responsible publication on matters of public interest' avoids the need to decide whether an offer of amends, including retraction and apology, or offer of an opportunity to reply, should be regarded as remedies or defences. They are neither. Their presence or absence are simply factors which need to be weighed in the balance in reaching a conclusion whether the publication is reasonable or the journalist/reporter acted responsibly in compiling the injurious report. Unlike the French-style right of reply (which in Europe extends beyond injurious imputations and which has to be enforced in some way) the approach which is favoured in this chapter is to regard retractions, apologies and replies as significant, although on their own not necessarily decisive, parts of the existing modern defence of 'reasonable publication' or 'responsible publication on matters of public interest'.

[54] *Lange v Australian Broadcasting Corp* (1997) 189 CLR 520 (Australia); *Lange v Atkinson* [1998] 3 NZLR 424 (New Zealand); *National Media Ltd v Bogoshi* 1998 (4) SA 1196 (SCA) (South Africa); and *Grant v Torstar Corp* 2009 SCC 61 (Canada). In *Jameel v Wall Street Journal Europe sprl* [2007] 1 AC 359, [46], Lord Hoffmann accurately referred to the expanded privilege defence in *Reynolds* [2001] 2 AC 127 (HL) as more of a 'public interest' defence. An expanded public interest defence could well be interpreted to include the relevance of the presence or absence of an offer of amends (in the form of retraction and apology). The common law defence known as the *Reynolds* defence has been abolished by s 4(6) of the United Kingdom Defamation Act of 2013.

This suggested approach is easily adapted (and, in fact, ideally suited) to new forms of electronic publication. One of the features of internet communication is that an almost immediate reply, which can reach a similar (or perhaps even wider) audience, could be forthcoming. Moreover, growing opportunities are being given to ordinary persons, who do not form part of the organised media, to become 'self-publishers' of their own views by utilising modern forms of electronic social-networking and blogs. While opportunities for impairing the reputations and dignities of others are compounded by electronic communication, so are the opportunities for redressing the *iniuria*.

Retractions and apologies (especially for factual inaccuracies, but also potentially extending to expression of opinion) are a common part of journalistic integrity.[55] Failure to pursue, or even offer, the option of amends may, in certain circumstances, point towards 'unreasonable' or 'irresponsible journalism'. A prompt retraction and apology would be facilitated by access of both defendant and plaintiff to electronic means of communication. Where an individual rather than a media defendant is involved and the publication takes place in some electronic form (as in *Dey* where a mobile phone was used), then it may also be adjudged 'unreasonable' conduct to fail to offer to make amends for inaccuracies or misrepresentations.[56] Thus the line between media and individual defendant may, in the end, become blurred.[57]

The High Court of Australia in *Lange*[58] referred to the following factors as relevant in determining the 'reasonableness' of a publication; absence of belief that the imputation was untrue and reasonable grounds for believing that the imputation was true; that the defendant took 'proper steps, so far as they were reasonably open, to verify the accuracy of the material'; and that the defendant offered an opportunity to the defamed person to respond to the imputation where practicable and necessary and published this response.

The Court of Appeal in *Reynolds v Times Newspapers Ltd*,[59] delivering its judgment on 8 July 1998 (just in time to be cited by the Supreme Court of Appeal in South Africa in *Bogoshi*[60]) in distinguishing the 'circumstantial' from the 'duty' and 'interest' inquiry in the case of a defence of privileged occasion, referred to the 'nature, status and source of the material, and the circumstances of the publication, such that the publication should in the public interest be protected in the absence of proof of express malice'.[61] Hefer JA in *Bogoshi* commented on this formulation in *Reynolds*:

[55] One might have to be more cautious, in the light of recent allegations of 'hacking' in the United Kingdom, in assuming journalistic integrity.

[56] See above text after n 31.

[57] Emphasis on the 'organisational' aspect of the media might serve to re-instate the distinction, though.

[58] *Lange* (1997) 189 CLR 520, 574.

[59] *Reynolds v Times Newspapers Ltd* [1998] 3 All ER 961 (CA) 994–95.

[60] *Bogoshi* (n 54).

[61] *Reynolds* (n 59) 994–95.

> 'Status' was used to denote the degree to which the information on a matter of public concern may, because of its character and known provenance, command respect. This test is more concise than, but does not differ materially from, the test of 'reasonableness of conduct' as expounded in Australia.[62]

Based on these comments, Hefer JA, although acknowledging that the list was not exhaustive, went on the set out factors relevant to determining the 'reasonableness' of a publication in South Africa:[63]

- The nature, extent and tone of the allegations
- The nature of the information on which the allegations are based, the reliability of their source, as well as the steps taken to verify the information
- Greater latitude is given to political discussion
- The need to publish before establishing the truth in a positive manner
- The opportunity given to the person concerned to respond

Shortly after *Bogoshi* was decided in South Africa, the House of Lords delivered judgments in the appeal in *Reynolds.*[64] Lord Nicholls set out ten factors which the House of Lords later in *Jameel v Wall Street Journal Europe sprl*[65] confirmed as constituting an illustrative (not exhaustive) guide to what would render a publication in the public interest:[66]

> (1) The seriousness of the allegation . . . (2) The nature of the information, and the extent to which the subject matter is a matter of public concern. (3) The source of the information . . . (4) The steps taken to verify the information. (5) The status of the information . . . (6) The urgency of the matter . . . (7) Whether comment was sought from the plaintiff [although Lord Nicholls recognised that this will not always be necessary] . . . (8) Whether the article contained the gist of the plaintiff's side of the story. (9) The tone of the article . . . (10) The circumstances of the publication including the timing.

In *Grant* the Canadian Supreme Court referred to the following factors[67] as part of a non-exhaustive list for determining what constitutes responsible journalism on a matter of public interest: (1) The seriousness of the allegation; (2) The public importance of the matter; (3) The urgency of the matter; (4) The status and reliability of the source; (5) Whether the plaintiff's side of the story was sought and accurately reported; (6) Whether the inclusion of the defamatory statement was justifiable; and (7) Whether the defamatory statement's public interest lay in the fact that it was made rather than in its truth (reportage).

There appears to be a strong commonality in the factors mentioned in all the above cases, although it is only the *Grant* judgment that specifically distinguishes between reportage (simply reporting that something was actually said by someone) and reporting matter the truth of which is relied upon. A clear common

[62] *Bogoshi* (n 54) 1212A–B.
[63] *Bogoshi* (n 54) 1212H–1213C.
[64] *Reynolds v Times Newspapers Ltd* [2001] 2 AC 127.
[65] *Jameel v Wall Street Journal Europe sprl* [2006] UKHL 44; [2007] 1 AC 359.
[66] *Reynolds* (n 64) 205A–D.
[67] *Grant* (n 54) [110–19].

factor in *Lange*, *Bogoshi*, *Reynolds* and *Grant* is the emphasis on an 'opportunity to respond' to defamatory allegations.

The listed factors in the Australian, South African, English and Canadian jurisprudence (with the exception of the opportunity to respond) relate essentially to the reasonableness of the publication determined by factors present at the time of, and during, the publication process and so would also have a role in determining whether the publisher had taken due care (ie was not negligent) in publishing the material.

However, examination into the unreasonableness of a publication (and the inquiry into the reasonableness or unreasonableness of imposing liability for this publication) is broader than that into alleged 'negligence' on the part of the publisher and, rightly, takes account of the lack of remedial action taken by the publisher to alleviate the harm done. If the failure to offer an opportunity to reply is rightly considered a factor to be added to the broad mix, then a retraction and offer of amends (in the form of apology) could equally be part of the assessment of the 'reasonableness' of a publication. Although the concept of 'unreasonableness' used in its fault sense overlaps with the concept of 'unreasonableness' used in its unlawfulness sense, a clear distinction should be drawn between the unreasonableness of a publication (absence of a defence excluding unlawfulness), the unreasonableness of a belief (fault in the form of negligence) and the overall reasonableness or unreasonableness of imposing liability (the unlawfulness inquiry).

How would this inclusion of retraction, apology and reply under the inquiry into the reasonableness of the publication (or, in the United Kingdom, whether the publication is in the public interest) differ from a traditional approach which sees the absence of these factors as affecting only the extent of damages awarded? Under the traditional approach, the offering of a retraction, apology and/or reply could not contribute to a defence, but only serve to mitigate the award of damages. Under the suggested approach, the existence of an offer to retract and apologise and/or opportunity given for a reply could, in consideration with the totality of the factual scenario, contribute ultimately to a defence of 'reasonable' publication.

How does the suggested common law approach differ from the statutory offer of amends procedure as it applies in the United Kingdom? A practical example might help. Say a daily newspaper has based a news item (containing a defamatory imputation against the plaintiff, a respected medical doctor) on a confidential source that has hitherto been reliable. As a result of information supplied by the source, the newspaper genuinely believes that the factual allegation against the plaintiff doctor that he has had an 'intimate relationship with one of his young patients' is true and that the comment published in the newspaper that the plaintiff is thus 'lacking moral scruples' is 'fair' and 'in the public interest'. The newspaper has tried unsuccessfully to verify the information (probably because the doctor has himself tried to keep the information secret). In fact, the newspaper sends an email to the doctor setting out the allegations against him, asking him if he wishes to respond and agreeing to publish any such response in the same issue of the newspaper as the report is due to appear. The doctor's secretary, who is also unaware of the liaison and fiercely believes in the doctor's integrity, receives the email from the newspaper setting out the allegation and offering the doctor a chance of replying. However, the secretary regards the newspaper's letter as a hoax and deletes it without referring it to the doctor. After two weeks, the newspaper runs the report about the plaintiff doctor. It transpires that the allegation is substantially incorrect as the person the doctor is having an 'intimate relationship' with is not a patient of his, and is, in fact, a person to whom he, as a single person, has recently become engaged. The newspaper immediately contacts the doctor and offers to publish an unqualified retraction and apology.

In the United Kingdom, if the offer of amends procedure as set out ss 2–4 of the 1996 Defamation Act has been complied with and the newspaper's offer accepted, then the newspaper can avoid a trial, but would still have to pay compensation to the plaintiff (subject to a court assessing reasonable compensation if the parties cannot agree on the amount). Incidentally, this payment, depending on the level of financial compensation, could itself have a chilling effect on future reporting. If the offer of amends is not accepted and the newspaper seeks to rely on the offer of amends as a defence, it would lose its right to rely on any other defence (for instance, fair comment or public interest). Unless the plaintiff could prove bad faith or recklessness on the part of the newspaper in publishing the report about the plaintiff, the defence that an offer of amends was made could succeed in a defamation action. Built into the legislation is a presumption in favour of the publication being made without bad faith or recklessness and so it would be extremely unlikely that the plaintiff would be able to prove that the defence was forfeited.

However, under the common law in jurisdictions that accept a 'reasonable publication' defence, the newspaper could lead evidence to support a defence of 'reasonable publication', emphasising the record of reliability (although not necessarily the identity) of the source, the steps taken to verify the factual basis of the article, the opportunity given to the doctor to reply and the offer of amends. The formalities of a statutory offer of amends would not apply and, of course, if the defence succeeded, no compensation would have to be paid. If the defence did not succeed, the damages awarded to the plaintiff could be considerably reduced taking into account all of the above factors. Even if the answer regarding the non-liability of the media might possibly be the same whether a common law or statutory route were adopted, the common law approach to the issue of damages/compensation would appear more flexible in striking a balance between freedom of expression and protection of reputation.

Suppose that the same facts arose, except that the newspaper ought to have suspected the error about the doctor's relationship (say because, in a recent previous interview with the doctor broadcast on television, he had let slip a reference to his 'fiancé'). Any defence under legislation (such as the 1996 Defamation Act in the United Kingdom) that an offer of amends had been made would not necessarily fail because negligence on the part of the defendant would apparently not be sufficient to lead to the forfeiture of the defence. In post-*Bogoshi* South African law, the aggrieved doctor might (and perhaps should) be able to recover damages for defamation based on the negligence of the newspaper, weighing all the factors in the balance. This would currently seem not to be possible in the United Kingdom in terms of the Defamation Act of 1996 (or perhaps in terms of the common law in the United Kingdom as well) unless an inference of 'bad faith' or 'recklessness' could be drawn.

It is true (as Eady J in *Milne v Express Newspapers*[68] stated) that greater freedom of expression is conferred by allowing a genuinely contrite (or non-reckless) media to avoid protracted litigation by a plaintiff who alleges that his or her reputation has been impaired by their publication. But, allowing a genuine/ non-reckless belief plus an offer of amends to trump protection of individual personality rights where there has been an unreasonable (albeit genuine/non reckless) mistake regarding the truth of the allegations would seem to undermine the emphasis on reasonable publication or responsible journalism developed in commonwealth jurisdictions.[69] Admittedly, a person who is injuriously referred to in the press might well be able to allege (with relative ease) that the journalist who compiled the offending report could have taken further steps to verify its accuracy, but this allegation could always be met by the journalist, who would have more intimate knowledge of journalistic standards, refuting this by relying on these standards of reasonable journalism. How can this be 'self-defeating'? If anything, allowing proof of presence of negligence (as fault) on the part of the journalist leading to the forfeiture of a defence, merely re-affirms accepted standards of reasonable journalism, which have been endorsed in recent commonwealth jurisprudence.[70]

It is perhaps instructive that the definition of 'innocent dissemination' in s 1 of the Defamation Act of 1996 not only refers to the identical phrase (ie 'no reason to believe') but also requires the disseminator (who is not the author, editor or publisher) to establish that he or she took 'reasonable care' in relation to the publication. An absence of 'reasonable care' means that the disseminator would be 'negligent'. The disseminator who is not the author, editor or publisher would have to prove that reasonable care was taken. Surely the author, editor and publisher should not be accorded greater freedom of expression than the mere disseminator who may not have the same means and opportunity as the author, editor and publisher of verifying the information disseminated?

Eady J in *Milne v Express Newspapers*[71] has argued that regarding proof of journalistic negligence (as opposed to bad faith or recklessness) would simply return the statutory law in England to its 1952 form, which had proved so unattractive to the media that it was not used at all. If one merely compares the scope of the 1952

[68] *Milne v Express Newspapers* (n 15) para 41.The claimant's appeal from Eady J's judgment was unsuccessful and the court of Appeal agreed with Eady J's interpretation of s 4(3) ([2004] EWCA Civ 664; [2005] 1 WLR 772). Eady J's approach carries additional weight as he was part of Sir Brian Neill's Committee (n 19) which provided the impetus for the 1996 offer of amends procedure.

[69] See n 54.

[70] ibid.

[71] *Milne v Express Newspapers* (n 15).

and 1996 legislative interventions in the law of defamation, there might be some substance in this argument, but the broad fair comment (honest opinion) defence[72] and the new defence of 'responsible publication on a matter of public interest' in sections 3 and 4 of the Defamation Act of 2013 have changed the perspective dramatically in favour of media freedom and made these defences rather more attractive than a statutory offer of amends that, even if accepted, will lead to the payment of (possibly uncapped) compensation.

The potential benefits of the current United Kingdom statutory form of offer of amends in resolving matters expeditiously and avoiding lengthy and costly civil suits have not yet been fully realised.[73] However, restricting the statutory offer of amends to 'innocent' defamation, as defined in the Defamation Act of 1996, may lead to the following adverse consequences for both media defendant and plaintiff:

(i) A defence of innocent/non-reckless publication, confined as it is solely to errors regarding the identity of the plaintiff and to falsity and defamatory content of words, is unduly restrictive since disputes about genuine (and possibly reasonable) mistakes on the part of the media regarding the 'fairness' of comment or a perceived duty to report (or correlative right of the public to be informed) are rather more likely to occur than mistakes regarding identification of the plaintiff, defamatory content and falsity of words. The South African Supreme Court of Appeal in *Le Roux v Dey*[74] has rightly recognised that a genuine and reasonable mistake regarding the existence of any defence to a defamation (or impairment of dignity) claim should excuse. Linking the amends procedure to cases of 'innocent' (or non-reckless) defamation both limits the scope for a defence of a genuine mistake and neglects the importance of the standard of reasonable care in publishing information and comment.[75]

(ii) Where the offer of amends is accepted, the plaintiff is deprived of his or her right to a jury trial and the defendant exposed to pay compensation[76] in a situation where the potential availability of the general defences to a defamation action, including a broad *Reynolds*/*Jameel*-type defence, have not yet been factually and legally tested;

(iii) Where the offer of amends is not accepted and litigation results, if the defendant relies on the offer of amends, he or she loses the right to rely on any other defence; and

[72] Section 3 of the Defamation Act 2013 defines the defence of 'honest opinion' and abolishes the common law defence of fair comment (s 3(8)). For broad approaches to the common law defence of fair comment, see Lord Phillips in *Joseph v Spiller* [2010] UKSC 53; [2010] 3 WLR 1791 and Justice Cameron in *The Citizen 1978 (Pty) Ltd v McBride* [2011] ZACC 11; 2011 (4) SA 191 (CC), [83] and [84].

[73] Eady J in *Abu v MGN Ltd (Practice Note)* [2003] 1 WLR 2201 (QB); [2002] EWHC 2345 (QB) [21] acknowledged that the offer of amends 'is by no means always going to lead to speedy and cheap resolution in any ordinary sense'. See also Milmo and Rogers (n 15) para 31.33 who cites a passage from *Rigg v Associated Newspapers Ltd* [2003] EWHC 710 (QB) [21] to the same effect.

[74] *Le Roux v Dey* 2010 (4) SA 210 (SCA) [34].

[75] Clause 21(2) of the Irish Defamation Bill reads 'knew or ought reasonably to have known': See Milmo and Rogers (n 15) para 19.6 fn 45.

[76] For which there is apparently no cap, except in the case of minor libel where there is a cap of £10,000 under ss 8 to 10 (summary disposal regime) of the 1996 Act.

(iv) A statutory offer of amends confined to defamation cases is unduly restrictive as the use of suitable amends could potentially apply to the infringements of other personality rights (such as impairments of dignity) as well.[77]

The Press Complaints Commission (PCC) in the United Kingdom, a self-regulating body set up by the newspaper industry, uses corrections and apologies as a method of facilitating a settlement between complainant and publisher.[78] The PCC, however, has no mechanism for enforcing its rulings or awarding compensation[79] and so, if retractions, apologies and/or replies are perceived as ways of assuaging wounded reputations and dignity, then they must be integrated into the legal process in some way.

Retraction and apology provides one of the remedies in South Africa which can be obtained from the Press Council, but the availability of this remedy is conditional upon the aggrieved person waiving his or her civil remedy and it is debateable whether this waiving of common law rights is constitutional.

VI. Conclusion

On the one hand, it is debatable whether a civil action for monetary compensation, even in a capitalist society, can on its own provide adequate redress for impairment of personality rights or even offer appropriate *solatium* for wounded feelings.[80] A rejuvenation of options, arguably more (or at least equally) suited to redressing sentimental loss, needs to be investigated and encouraged.

On the other hand, neither an effective, prompt retraction and apology nor a viable opportunity to reply can necessarily, or perhaps even fully, provide adequate redress for a wrong to a personality right. Furthermore, a rigorously enforced retraction, apology or opportunity for reply will clearly interfere with editorial freedom.

However, regarding retraction, apology and reply as facets of the common law inquiry into determining whether the author, publisher or editor of an injurious imputation should have a valid defence to the perpetration of what would otherwise constitute an *iniuria* and as factors relating to the culpability (ie negligence) of the author, publisher or editor for such an *iniuria*, would seem to be viable ways of underscoring the appropriate balance between media freedom and media responsibility.

[77] As noted above (text to n 39), retraction and apology may be particularly pertinent in cases of insult or impairment of dignity.

[78] See Reid (n 21) paras 16.09–16.15.

[79] Reid (n 21) para 16.15.

[80] Although, as Eric Descheemaeker, '*Solatium* and Injury to Feelings' (this volume, ch 4, section I.B) has indicated, one needs to be aware of the ambiguity and confusion implicit in the concept of *solatium*.

The development of defences of 'reasonable publication', 'responsible communication on matters of public interest', which have recently emerged in commonwealth jurisdictions[81] and which can be used to accord due weight to retractions, apologies and replies under the *common law*, are arguably preferable to restrictive and rigid statutory options of amends.[82]

The current broad-based 'public interest' *Reynolds/Jameel* defence[83] even linked, as it initially appears to be, to the rather restrictive mould of 'qualified privilege' could also become a common law vehicle for accommodating this renewed interest in retractions, apologies and replies.

The chance of this happening[84] would, however, be considerably increased if an independent defence of 'reasonable publication/communication' (preferably separate from qualified privilege occasion) were developed along the lines of contemporary commonwealth jurisprudence. If this approach were adopted, then the common law could reclaim from the legislature its historic ability to accommodate retractions, apologies and replies. *Reynolds* and *Jameel*[85] have laid the foundation of a 'public interest' defence in defamation. What is now needed is the further step of consolidating this defence under the rubric of 'reasonable publication/communication' (inspired by Commonwealth jurisprudence) and extending the scope of the defence to include an investigation into retraction and apology as well as opportunity for reply, rather than invoking restrictive statutory provisions along the lines of the 1996 Defamation Act. This change could be effected with little, if any, disruption in the common law.

Furthermore, a clear recognition that a 'due diligence' or 'reasonable care' standard for the media is simply another way of reinforcing a *negligence fault criterion* for defamation (at least perpetrated by the media in both their traditional and web-based forms) would go a long way to striking a more effective balance between freedom of expression and protection of reputation,[86] especially in an electronic era.

But, of course, this final step would involve a fundamental shift away from the common law emphasis on 'strict liability' for defamation in the United Kingdom. Similarly, if a *statutory* regime of amends were still retained, the taking of the suggested final step would require a change to the current interpretation of the words 'no reason to believe' under the 1996 English Defamation Act or else an amendment to the Act along the lines of the Irish Defamation Bill[87] which prefers the wording 'knew or ought reasonably to have known'.

[81] See n 54.

[82] Kenneth McKenzie Norrie suggests that the 'responsible journalism' defence could usefully apply to balancing privacy and free speech, in addition to the development of a 'public interest' defence ('The *actio iniuriarum* in Scots Law: Romantic Romanism or Tool for Today', this volume, ch 3, text to n 83).

[83] See n 54.

[84] Incidentally, the 'public interest' defence, even as formulated by Lord Hoffmann in *Jameel* (n 54) could provide one of the ways of resolving future invasion of privacy cases which would, in the past, have foundered on the mere 'truthfulness' of the disclosure.

[85] See (n 54).

[86] See *Bogoshi* (n 54) at 1206G–H. On the distinction between negligence as a fault element of a tort and the tort of negligence, see (n 88) below.

[87] See (n 75) above.

In the end, though, the policy objectives underlying a standard of 'reasonable care' are not completely incompatible with those underpinning no-fault (or strict) liability. Furthermore, negligence-based liability is well entrenched in the common law.[88] It also provides an ideal half-way house between subjectively assessed, intention-based liability and somewhat antiquated liability devoid of any emphasis on blameworthiness, whether subjectively or objectively assessed. A middle course of negligence-based liability is particularly appropriate where the right to reputation and dignity must be balanced against freedom of expression and, especially, where the information communicated is distributed for profit by an organised media.

[88] As David Ibbetson has observed, the role of media was not only important in establishing strict liability for defamation in the English law, but also for emphasising the requirement that reasonable steps to check information must be taken. He also refers to the 'gravitational weight' given to the negligence principle in English tort of defamation (see Ibbetson, '*Iniuria*, Roman and English' (this volume, ch 2, text to n 63)). The concept of 'negligence-based liability' as an aspect of *fault* is used in this article as distinct from the English concept of the 'tort of negligence' which has a much broader meaning extending beyond a negligence fault element of liability and including, for instance, the element of causation. In the tort of defamation in England and the delict of defamation in South Africa, a *presumption* that an impairment of reputation has been caused is sufficient for liability. Actual causing of such harm does not have to be proved: see Lord Steyn in *Berezovsky v Michaels* [2000] 1 WLR 1004. In the South African law of defamation, on the publication of defamatory matter referring to the plaintiff, the plaintiff is presumed to have suffered injury to reputation. The effect of this presumption is that the plaintiff is considerably assisted in the task of proving that the conduct of the defendant caused loss (see Jonathan Burchell, *Personality Rights and Freedom of Expression: The Modern Actio Injuriarum* (Kenwyn, Juta, 1998) 204). Theoretically, it is possible, however, for the defendant to show that this presumption is rebutted (ibid).

11

Harassment: A Wrong without a Right?

FRANÇOIS DU BOIS

I. Introduction

The Protection from Harassment Act 1997 (PHA) appears to return English law to a path left behind more than seven hundred years ago. Once the common law in the second half of the thirteenth century had shed its earlier concern with affronts to honour, causation of loss – more accurately, infringement of rights[1] – 'became the central feature of the action of trespass, and it has remained the central feature of the English law of tort'.[2] A number of cases before the courts in the 1980s and 1990s highlighted some unpalatable consequences of this development, however, and so the PHA was enacted to create a new wrong – one that could be committed regardless of whether a right was being infringed, attacked or even threatened.[3] Section 1 of the PHA made it wrongful for anyone to pursue a course of conduct which amounts to harassment of another and which he knows or ought to know amounts to harassment of the other. Contravention of this prohibition may lead to civil as well as criminal liability,[4] and injunctions may be granted to restrain contraventions.[5]

[1] See especially Robert Stevens, *Torts and Rights* (Oxford, Oxford University Press, 2007) and Allan Beever, *Rediscovering the Law of Negligence* (Oxford, Hart Publishing, 2009). I do not mean to endorse these authors' specific arguments. For a convincing critique of their 'rights fundamentalism', see Peter Cane, 'Rights in Private Law' in Donal Nolan and Andrew Robertson (eds), *Rights and Private Law* (Oxford, Hart Publishing, 2012) 35. See further section IV below.

[2] David Ibbetson, *A Historical Introduction to the Law of Obligations* (Oxford, Oxford University Press, 1999) 17.

[3] The PHA deals separately with harassment in Scotland in ss 8–11. Because the provisions on civil liability in s 8 are fundamentally similar to those obtaining in England, I shall focus on the latter, referring to the position in Scottish law only where there is a relevant difference.

[4] PHA ss 2(1) and 3(1). Section 4 also creates an aggravated criminal offence of putting people in fear of violence.

[5] PHA s 3(3). Breach of such an injunction without reasonable excuse is rendered a criminal offence by s 3(6). A court sentencing someone for an offence under the Act may also impose a restraining order under s 5.

Since then, harassment has emerged as a wrong of astonishing versatility, covering not only stalking, the primary target behind its enactment,[6] but also workplace disputes,[7] conflicts among neighbours[8] and family members,[9] debt collection[10] and litigation practices,[11] the pursuit of private grievances[12] and campaigns,[13] public protests,[14] blackmail attempts via threatened disclosures of information,[15] and, increasingly, press activities and publications[16] as well as the dissemination of images, opinions and information on the web.[17] As such, the PHA frequently offers tort claimants a way round the strict requirements of torts such as trespass to the person,[18] nuisance,[19] negligence,[20] and defamation,[21] as well as the more targeted rules contained in anti-discrimination legislation.[22]

This remarkable development deserves critical scrutiny. Significantly, the Calcutt Committee Report on Privacy and Related Matters of June 1990 rejected

[6] *KD v Chief Constable of Hampshire* [2005] EWHC 2550 (QB), [2005] *Police Law Reports* 253 (QBD) (inappropriate questioning and frequent phone calls made by a police officer during a rape investigation).

[7] *Majrowski v Guy's and St Thomas's NHS Trust* [2006] UKHL 34, [2007] 1 AC 224.

[8] *Mitton v Benefield* [2012] EWCA Civ 304; *Jones v Ruth* [2011] EWCA Civ 804, [2012] 1 All ER 490 (CA).

[9] *Singh v Bhakar* [2007] 1 FLR 880 (CC (Nottingham)); *Andresen v Lovell* [2009] EWHC 3397 (QB), [2009] All ER (D) 196 (Dec).

[10] *Ferguson v British Gas Trading Ltd* [2009] EWCA Civ 46, [2010] 1 WLR 785 (CA).

[11] *Iqbal v Dean Mason Solicitors* [2011] EWCA Civ 123, [2011] IRLR 428.

[12] *Law Society v Kordowski* [2011] EWHC 3185 (QB) (defendant running a website listing 'solicitors from hell'); *Chelsea and Westminster Healthcare NHS Trust v Redmond* [2003] All ER (D) 87 (Jun) (threatening behaviour to persuade the claimant and its staff to apply a different course of medical treatment to defendant's daughter).

[13] *Hayes v Willoughby* [2011] EWCA Civ 1541, [2012] 1 WLR 1510 (a seven-year long campaign by the defendant against the claimant in the form of allegations of fraud and embezzlement communicated to the Inland Revenue, Customs & Excise, the Criminal Investigation Branch of the DTI, Companies House, the Official Receiver and several different police forces).

[14] *Masters and Scholars of the University of Oxford v Broughton* [2006] EWHC 1233 (QB), [2006] All ER (D) 387 (May); *Heathrow Airport Ltd v Garman* [2007] All ER (D) 28 (Aug) (protests respectively targeting animal experimentation and airport expansion).

[15] *CC v AB* [2006] EWHC 3083 (QB), [2006] All ER (D) 39 (Dec); *ZAM v CFW* [2011] EWHC 476 (QB), [2011] All ER (D) 69 (Mar); *SKA v CRH* [2012] EWHC 766 (QB), [2012] All ER (D) 216 (Mar).

[16] *Thomas v News Group Newspapers Ltd* [2001] EWCA Civ 1233, [2001] All ER (D) 246 (Jul); *Hong v XYZ* [2011] EWHC 2995 (QB), [2011] All ER (D) 132 (Nov) (journalists 'doorstepping' the mother of the actor Hugh Grant's daughter).

[17] *Cray v Hancock* [2005] All ER (D) 66 (remarks on internet forums) in *Petros v Chaudhari* [2004] All ER (D) 173 (internet-based campaign against hospital believed responsible for child's death); *S v Director of Public Prosecutions* [2008] EWHC 438 (Admin), [2008] 1 WLR 2847 (picture placed online with an offensive caption); *AMP v Persons Unknown* [2011] EWHC 3454 (TCC), [2012] All ER (D) 178 (Jan) (explicit pictures of claimant uploaded from her lost or stolen phone).

[18] It requires neither physical contact nor a threat or apprehension of force.

[19] No interest in land is required as for private nuisance, nor is it necessary that there be an interference with a class of the public as in the case of public nuisance.

[20] There is no need for personal injury or psychiatric harm; there is no need for any harm at all, as pointed out by Baroness Hale in *Majrowski* (n 7) [66].

[21] Justification – the truth of a statement – is no defence to a claim for harassment. The attractiveness of harassment claims is likely to increase greatly in the wake of the Defamation Act 2013 with its requirement that claimants must show serious harm to reputation.

[22] The Equality Act 2010 only covers harassment in defined circumstances and on the ground of specified protected characteristics. See n 64.

the idea of a general wrong of harassment partly because of the difficulty of devising a satisfactory definition.[23] Can this statutory wrong, as developed through judicial interpretation of the PHA, withstand such misgivings? Or does it compromise the integrity of tort law and is thus best repealed at the earliest opportunity?[24] In the context of this book, these questions gain added interest from the possibility of viewing the PHA as a modern home-grown equivalent of the Roman delict of *iniuria*. After all, 'harassment' is, according to Peter Birks, 'the best generic description of the act involved in any example of *iniuria*'.[25] To be sure, the triad of protected interests identified in Ulpian's first-century account of *iniuria* – *corpus*, *fama* and *dignitas*[26] – already find an echo in trespass to the person, defamation, and the extension of breach of confidence to cover misuse of private information. But, as Birks also points out, 'the English torts in themselves protect only the narrower interests in physical integrity and reputation [and, we would today add, private information], not . . . the interest in equality of respect' that he believes lay at the core of the Roman delict.[27] It is precisely this characteristic of the common law that the PHA is designed to counteract.

How the PHA does so and whether the law should do so are the principal themes of this chapter. As will become evident, the PHA itself contains only a sketchy outline of this new wrong. Judicial interpretation has brought sharper definition, but, as I show below, it has done so by moving a considerable distance from the text as well as the immediate purpose behind its enactment. For that reason this chapter offers what one might call a constructive interpretation of the law of harassment as jointly crafted by Parliament and the courts – an attempt to establish the meaning of harassment by undertaking both an analysis (section III) and an evaluation (section IV) of the judicial application of the PHA. Section III shows harassment law to discriminate among harms on the basis of whether they result from reprehensible flouting of 'civility rules', even though it accommodates harms that are widely divergent in nature and seriousness. Section IV compares this feature of harassment to the standard approach of the common law of torts, which makes the wrongfulness of an act turn on whether it has infringed an interest sufficiently important to be the object of a right. Here I argue that the test produced by the courts represents a viable alternative to this standard approach. Harassment is concerned with duties of manner, a species of duties which not only can be distinguished from rights-based duties, but in this instance also should be kept separate from rights. For that reason this statutory tort is a defensible supplement to the common law. Section V concludes that harassment therefore not only forges a connection between the common law and Roman law, but

[23] *Report of the Committee on Privacy and Related Matters* (Cm 1102, 1991).

[24] Note the clear distaste for the PHA in Baroness Hale's speech in *Majrowski* (n 7).

[25] Peter Birks, 'Harassment and Hubris: The Rights to an Equality of Respect' (1997) 32 *Irish Jurist* 1, 7.

[26] D.47.10.2.

[27] Birks (n 25) 18. Not everyone agrees with this characterisation of *iniuria*. According to Ibbetson (n 2) 16, 'the Roman idea . . . was essentially upward looking: it was concerned with insolence from an inferior to a superior'.

also constitutes an important element in the relationship between the common law and contemporary civilian systems via the Principles of European Tort Law (PETL) and the Draft Common Frame of Reference (DCFR). In a legal environment where the protection of human dignity is increasing in prominence[28] as well as controversy,[29] critical reflection on the PHA thus also has wider ramifications for the development of the law. But I must start by justifying my claim that the PHA was designed to open up a pathway for liability long regarded as closed.

II. Genesis of the PHA

In moving the Protection from Harassment Bill for second reading in the House of Lords, Lord Mackay, the Lord Chancellor, stated that: 'The Government believe that it would be right to provide greater certainty through the creation of a statutory tort'.[30] Lord Mackay explained that, although 'some court decisions have extended existing civil law provisions to protect the victims of harassment, the extent to which the courts are prepared, or are able, to provide relief in these circumstances remains unclear.'[31] This uncertainty is readily apparent from the law reports. On the one hand, cases such as *Thomas v National Union of Mineworkers (South Wales Area)*[32] and *Burris v Azadani*[33] appeared to treat harassment as in principle tortious. On the other hand, a number of decisions emphatically rejected the notion that the law had developed to the point of recognising a tort of unreasonable harassment.[34] This notably included *Khorasandjian v Bush*,[35] where the Court of Appeal nevertheless proved willing to expand the scope of nuisance in order to accommodate harassment within the existing array of torts.[36] The prob-

[28] See PETL Art 2:102(2) and DCFR VI.2:203; *Reynolds v Times Newspapers* [1999] 4 All ER 609, 622; *Campbell v MGN Ltd* [2004] UKHL 22, [2004] AC 457 [50]–[56]; *OBG Ltd v Allan* [2007] UKHL 21, [2008] 1 AC 1 [275].

[29] See James Q Whitman 'The Two Western Cultures of Privacy: Dignity versus Liberty' (2003–04) 113 *Yale Law Journal* 1151; Stephanie Henette-Vauchez, 'A Human Dignitas? Remnants of the Ancient Legal Concept in Contemporary Dignity Jurisprudence' (2011) 9 *International Journal of Constitutional Law* 32.

[30] HL Deb 24 January 1997, vol 577, col 917. The same was said in the Commons by the Home Secretary: HC Deb 17 December 1996, vol 287, cols 781–862.

[31] HL Deb 24 January 1997, vol 577, col 917.

[32] *Thomas v National Union of Mineworkers (South Wales Area)* [1986] Ch 20. Scott J concluded (at 64) that: 'Unreasonable harassment' of miners while using the highway to return to work during the 1984 strike 'would, in my judgment, be tortious'.

[33] *Burris v Azadani* [1995] 4 All ER 802. Sir Thomas Bingham MR leading a unanimous bench stated (at 809) that 'the view [cannot] be upheld that there is no tort of harassment'.

[34] See *News Group Newspapers Ltd v Society of Graphical and Allied Trades 1982 (No 2)* [1987] ICR 181, 206; *Burnett v George* [1992] 1 FLR 525 (decided in 1986); and *Patel v Patel* [1988] 2 FLR 179, 182 where Waterhouse J stated that 'in the present state of the law there is no tort of harassment'.

[35] *Khorasandjian v Bush* [1993] 3 All ER 669 (CA) 683.

[36] *Khorasandjian* (n 35) 657–56. The other possibility, favoured in this case by Peter Gibson J as well as by *Burnett v George* (n 34), was to adopt a relaxed attitude to the requirements for liability under *Wilkinson v Downton* [1897] 2 QB 57 and *Janvier v Sweeney* [1919] 2 KB 316.

lem thrown up by these cases was that the defendants' behaviour appeared to merit a civil sanction despite failing to infringe rights protected by statute or the common law. The judgments represented two strategies for resolving this tension: the creation of a new tort of harassment or the stretching of existing tort principles.

Subsequent judicial developments have borne out Lord Mackay's doubts about the ability of the common law to reach interferences that fall short of the infringement of established rights. In *Hunter and others v Canary Wharf Ltd*,[37] which was being considered by the law lords at the very time that the Protection from Harassment Bill was being debated in Parliament, the *Khorasandjian* approach was eventually held to *over*stretch the existing torts. This among other authorities led the Court of Appeal to conclude in *Wong v Parkside Health NHS Trust* that: 'Until that Act [ie the PHA] came into force, there was power to restrain by injunction conduct which might result in the tort of intentional infliction of harm or otherwise threaten the claimant's right of access to the courts, but there was no right to damages for conduct falling short of an actual tort.'[38] Most importantly, in *Wainwright v Home Office*[39] the House of Lords held, in the words of Lord Scott of Foscote, that 'the infliction of humiliation and distress by conduct calculated to humiliate and cause distress, is [not] without more, tortious at common law'. Their lordships' stance appears clearly from the following remarks in Lord Hoffmann's leading speech:

> Even on the basis of a genuine intention to cause distress, I would wish, as in *Hunter v Canary Wharf Ltd*, to reserve my opinion on whether compensation should be recoverable. In institutions and workplaces all over the country, people constantly do and say things with the intention of causing distress and humiliation to others. This shows lack of consideration and appalling manners but I am not sure that the right way to deal with it is always by litigation.[40]

The direct spur to the enactment of the PHA was, however, a Member's Bill on stalking introduced in the Commons on International Women's Day 1996 by Janet Anderson MP.[41] The Calcutt Committee Report had declined to recommend a general wrong of harassment in 1990,[42] but the issue revived in the wake of concerns about stalking. In 1995, Lord Mackay himself indicated in a debate on domestic violence legislation that he considered the development of a new branch of tort to be important in order to deal with incidents that did not fall within the

[37] *Hunter and others v Canary Wharf Ltd* [1997] AC 655.

[38] *Wong v Parkside Health NHS Trust* [2001] EWCA Civ 1721, [2003] 3 All ER 932 (CA) [30]. See also *Mbasogo v Logo Ltd* [2006] EWCA Civ 1370, [2007] 2 WLR 1062 (CA) [90]–[100].

[39] *Wainwright v Home Office* [2003] UKHL 53, [2004] 2 AC 406 [62].

[40] *Wainwright* (n 39) [46]. The significance of these remarks is accentuated by the fact that in *Hunter v Canary Wharf* (n 37) Lord Hoffmann had suggested that *Khorasandjian* (n 35) could be saved if it were 'seen as a case on intentional harassment, not nuisance' and had left open the possibility that a tort of intention might appropriately provide compensation for 'mere distress, inconvenience and discomfort'. All that is left of this in *Wainwright* is the description of *Canary Wharf* as another case in which he had reserved his opinion on this issue.

[41] Stalking Bill [Bill 78 of 1995–96]. See HC Deb 6 March 1996, vol 273, cols 370–71.

[42] *Report* (n 23).

proper remit of such legislation.[43] A few months later, a Home Office minister stated in a parliamentary written answer that the government was examining anti-stalking laws of the US and Canada and would consider, in light of this examination and of other evidence provided by campaigners, whether there was a need for a formal review of existing legislative provisions.[44] But it was an opposition MP who eventually introduced the first Stalking Bill.

Janet Anderson's immediate concern arose from perceived gaps in the criminal law, similar to those revealed by the tort cases surveyed above. Although the House of Lords had adopted a more expansive interpretation of the Offences Against the Person Act 1861 in *R v Ireland*; *R v Burstow*,[45] conviction still required proof of a clinically recognised psychiatric disorder or at least fear of bodily harm. The Stalking Bill accordingly set out to criminalise stalking as such and proposed a non-exhaustive definition covering activities such as shadowing another person, making repeated telephone calls to someone, interfering with property and leaving offensive material.[46] It required such behaviour to be persistent, to constitute a course of conduct over a reasonable period of time *and* to amount to harassment or molestation. It also proposed giving Magistrates' Courts power to issue prohibitory orders against respondents on the civil burden of proof without making formal criminal findings. But the Bill failed to get a second reading,[47] the government refusing to support it. Despite the government announcing that its own 'proposals to combat the menace of stalkers will be published by the Government at the earliest opportunity',[48] an opposition peer soon after introduced an identical Bill in the Lords.[49] This not only managed to receive a second reading, but was passed by the Lords at third reading and sent to the Commons.[50] It failed to progress further, however, again due to lack of government support. A Home Office Consultation Paper entitled *Stalking – The Solutions* was nevertheless published at around the same time as the third reading of the Lords' Bill.[51] As was to be expected in the context of a looming general election and positive press coverage for the private Bills, these were soon overtaken by the government's own Protection from Harassment Bill. This gave effect to the essential thrust of these Bills, but, equally unsurprisingly in a period where government and opposition were vying with each other to appear tough on anti-social behaviour, it also extended their reach – notably as far as tort liability is concerned.

[43] HL Deb 24 April 1995, vol 563, cols 1–26GC.

[44] HC Deb 17 July 1995, vol 263, col 934W.

[45] *R v Ireland*; *R v Burstow* [1998] AC 147. Prior to this, it had been thought that ss 47 and 20 of the 1861 Act required proof of physical harm and that the 'immediacy' necessary before a threat of such harm would constitute an assault was absent in cases involving, for instance, silent phone calls. Both interpretations inhibited use of the 1861 Act in stalking cases.

[46] For a description of the Bill, see Tim Lawson-Cruttenden, 'Stalking Farce – The Way the Government Acted to Kill off the Bill to Outlaw Stalking' (1996) *Law Society Gazette* 15 May, 93 (15).

[47] HC Deb 10 May 1996, vol 277, col 609 and 12 July 1996, vol 281, col 753.

[48] HC Deb 13 March 1996, vol 273, col 603(W).

[49] Stalking (No. 2) Bill [HL Bill 92 of 1995–96]. See HL Deb 13 May 1996, vol 572, col 325.

[50] HL Deb 9 July 1996, vol 574, cols 175–76.

[51] Home Office, *Stalking – The Solutions: A Consultation Paper* (11 July 1996).

The government objected to the Members' Bills for three principal reasons.[52] Firstly, they were considered too widely drafted, threatening to turn behaviour which would ordinarily be lawful into unlawful acts. Secondly, it was feared that by defining 'stalking' the Bills risked excluding some types of behaviour and encouraging stalkers to evade the law by simply adopting a type of conduct not listed in the definition. Finally, the government opposed the mixing of criminal and civil jurisdictions that would take place if magistrates were authorised to issue what amounted to civil injunctions. Importantly, the last two of these were eventually taken up in the Lords' Stalking (No.2) Bill, the promoter, Lord McIntosh, introducing several amendments during the committee stage which removed the criminal element from the Bill and simplified the definition of 'stalking' to 'engaging in a course of conduct whereby a person molests another person so as to be reasonably likely to cause that other person to feel harassed, alarmed, distressed or to fear for his safety or for that of one or more third persons'.[53] Indeed, Lord McIntosh went so far as to describe the Bill as now serving to create 'a civil tort of molestation',[54] although his Bill did not in fact make provision for damages. In terminology and approach this closely followed the recommendations contained in the Home Office Consultation Paper.

The government's own Bill re-introduced the criminal dimension, although it took care to maintain the established division between the civil and the criminal jurisdictions by confining the issuing of civil orders to the civil courts. But it also extended the civil remedies, empowering the courts to award compensation for distress. Both private Bills as well as the Consultation Paper had envisaged only a civil order in the nature of an injunction, most likely because cases such as *Khorasandjian v Bush* and *Burris v Azadani* had highlighted the restriction of the existing statutory non-molestation orders to the domestic and family context. The government's Bill was therefore the first to propose the creation of a fully fledged statutory tort alongside new statutory offences. Crucially, the Protection from Harassment Bill was specifically drafted to overcome the common law's centuries-long insistence on personal injury, providing for damages to be available for any anxiety caused by the harassment. It also provided that any financial loss resulting from the harassment would be recoverable.

As envisaged in the Home Office Consultation Paper, the Bill was drafted so as to target the harm caused to the victim rather than the constitutive elements of stalking.[55] However, the terminology favoured by the government differed from that employed in both the Consultation Paper and the Lords Bill. Whereas these had targeted 'molestation', the government's Bill focused on 'harassment'. This shifted the Bill's terminological connections with other statutes out of the civil into the criminal realm. 'Molestation' had been derived from the civil non-molestation

[52] See the Home Secretary's remarks during the PHA second reading debate: HC Deb 17 December 1996, vol 287, cols 781–862.

[53] HL Deb 28 June 1996, vol 573, cols 1194–1206.

[54] ibid.

[55] See the remarks of the Home Secretary HC Deb 17 Dec 1996, vol 287, col 817.

orders made available by a series of family law measures,[56] but 'harassment' had its roots in section 4A of the Public Order Act 1986, introduced in 1996, which had created the criminal offence of intentional harassment by threatening, abusive or insulting words or behaviour. While the Consultation Paper proposal could therefore be described as 'bolting new criminal sanctions onto old civil remedies',[57] the government's Bill extended the reach of a criminal measure into the civil field.

One possible explanation for this terminological shift is that 'harassment' appeared to be the real nub of the issue. After all, the Consultation Paper itself had answered the question 'What is stalking?' by stating that 'It can be broadly described as a series of acts which are intended to, or in fact, cause harassment to another person.'[58] Another is that several responses to the Consultation Paper, including that of the Law Society, had criticised the term 'molestation' as lacking certainty of definition.[59] This explanation derives support from the insistence by the government's parliamentary spokesmen that their Bill had the virtue of being drafted in a manner that would enable its interpretation to draw on case law dealing with the Public Order Act 1986.[60] However, plumping for 'harassment' hardly improved matters, especially as the Law Society had also objected that imposing liability wherever someone 'realised or should have realised that his conduct was likely to cause a plaintiff distress or harassment' was too widely drawn.[61] But whatever the reason for this terminological shift, choosing 'harassment' also established a significant terminological linkage between the Bill and the contemporary common law debates in the cases outlined above, placing beyond doubt the aim of overcoming the pressures and limitations which these had revealed.

Most importantly, this seemingly technical difference between the style of legislative drafting employed in the original Stalking Bill with its convoluted definition of the wrong and in the government's own Bill which simply forbade harassment, expanded the reach of the PHA far beyond the anti-stalking objectives of the original Bill. This consequence was already flagged up in the Consultation Paper.[62] It was also emphasised in the second reading speeches of the Lord Chancellor and the Home Secretary, no doubt because of the political

[56] The Domestic Violence and Matrimonial Proceedings Act 1976, the Domestic Proceedings and Magistrates' Courts' Act 1978, the Matrimonial. Homes Act 1983, and the Family Law Act 1996. See Consultation Paper (n 51) paras 2.1 and 2.2.

[57] Neil Rose, 'Stalking Question – The Problem of Finding a Workable Legal Definition of Stalking' (1996) *Law Society Gazette*, 9 Oct, 93 (12).

[58] Consultation Paper (n 51) para 1.2. Similarly, Ormrod LJ in *Horner v Horner* [1982] 2 All ER 495 (CA) 497: 'For my part I have no doubt that the word "molesting" . . . does not imply necessarily either violence or threats of violence. It applies to any conduct which can properly be regarded as such a degree of harassment as to call for the intervention of the court.'

[59] House of Commons Library, *Stalking, Harassment and Intimidation and the Protection from Harassment Bill* (Parliamentary Research Paper 96/115) 35.

[60] See the second reading speeches of the Lord Chancellor and the Home Secretary (n 30).

[61] HC Library (n 59).

[62] Consultation Paper (n 51) para 5.15: 'A general tort of molestation on these lines might also catch a wider range of activities than those of stalkers, such as harassment in disputes between neighbours or at work. The provision of remedies to deter stalkers may therefore give further protection to people in these wider areas.'

hay that could be made out of this in the upcoming general election. Both boasted that, as the latter put it, the government's 'Bill covers not only stalkers, but disruptive neighbours and those who target people because of the colour of their skin'.[63]

In fact, the PHA reached further still. In freeing the concept of harassment from its moorings in the Public Order Act's requirement that it be caused by threatening, abusive or insulting words or behaviour, or at least disruptive behaviour, the PHA created a free-floating wrong that could seemingly be committed in unlimited ways. And unlike the statutory civil remedies for molestation, this new wrong could be committed against anyone at all. The PHA's remarkably broad scope emerges even more vividly from a comparison with the anti-harassment provisions incorporated in more recent equality legislation, which not only circumscribes what qualifies as harassment in the manner of the Public Order Act, but also limits its remit to defined relationships.[64]

Whether this was a wise strategy to adopt is certainly a question worth asking. The Calcutt Committee took the view that it would be necessary to limit the scope of an harassment tort, and favoured proscribing a number of specific acts such as persistently following someone about from place to place and watching or besetting a person's house, place of work or the route to and from them.[65] The Committee feared a wide-ranging tort of harassment to have potential implications for civil liberties, in particular for the right to demonstrate peacefully. But this is best assessed in light of the fate of the PHA in the hands of the judiciary.

III. The Meaning of 'Harassment'

Strikingly, the PHA refrains from defining 'harassment'. The reason for this is plain from the history surveyed in the preceding section. The legislative commitment to creating a wrong that would reach where the existing law could not, produced a text which not only imposed liability irrespective of whether the rights to bodily integrity and property had been infringed, attacked or threatened – as required by the common law – but also was specifically designed to confound

[63] HC Deb 17 December 1996, vol 287, cols 781–862; HL Deb 24 January 1997, vol 577, col 917.

[64] The Equality Act 2010 now gathers together the protection against harassment formerly conferred by the Sex Discrimination Act 1975, the Race Relations Act 1976, the Disability Discrimination Act 1995, the Employment Equality (Religion or Belief) Regulations 2003, the Employment Equality (Sexual Orientation) Regulations 2003 and the Employment Equality (Age) Regulations 2006. The 2010 Act creates statutory torts of harassment in defined circumstances where the harassment is on the ground of protected characteristics listed as: age; disability; gender reassignment; marriage and civil partnership; pregnancy and maternity; race; religion or belief; sex; sexual orientation. The Act does not make harassment on the grounds of protected characteristics unlawful in general terms but only in specific contexts: services and public functions; premises; work; education; and associations. There are also some subject-specific Acts which provide protection against harassment in particular areas, especially the Protection from Eviction Act 1977, s 3 and the Housing Act 1988, s 27.

[65] *Report* (n 51) paras 6.30–6.39.

those who might seek to avoid its strictures by adapting their conduct to the contours of the wrong. Thus the PHA offers no more than that: 'References to harassing a person *include* alarming the person or causing the person distress'; 'A "course of conduct" must involve conduct on at least two occasions'; and '"Conduct" *includes* speech' (emphasis added).[66] Apart from this, only indirect guidance is provided by way of the exclusion from the ambit of the PHA of a course of conduct that a defendant shows –

(a) was pursued for the purpose of preventing or detecting crime,
(b) was pursued under any enactment or rule of law or to comply with any condition or requirement imposed by any person under any enactment, or
(c) was reasonable to pursue in the particular circumstances.[67]

It is of course a vital question whether such a deliberate crafting of a statutory text in order to *minimise* the guidance offered to its addressees is compatible with the rule of law and associated human rights values. It has been said that: 'Such legislation, which may be politely described as "open textured", is wholly unsatisfactory.'[68] But I wish to put this to one side for the moment and concentrate first on establishing, in so far as this is possible, the meaning that 'harassment' has acquired in judicial practice. Only then will we be in a position to give adequate consideration to this important question of general principle.

The following summary of the authorities by Mr Justice Simon in *Dowson v Chief Constable of Northumbria Police*[69] is regularly cited as the test of what must be proven in order for a claim in harassment to succeed:

(1) There must be conduct which occurs on at least two occasions,
(2) which is targeted at the claimant,
(3) which is calculated in an objective sense to cause alarm or distress, and
(4) which is objectively judged to be oppressive and unacceptable.
(5) What is oppressive and unacceptable may depend on the social or working context in which the conduct occurs.
(6) A line is to be drawn between conduct which is unattractive and unreasonable, and conduct which has been described in various ways: 'torment' of the victim, 'of an order which would sustain criminal liability'.

To this one must add that in terms of PHA s 1(1)(b) a harasser only commits a wrong if s/he 'knows or ought to know [the course of conduct] amounts to harassment of the other'. Section 1(2) explains that 'the person whose course of conduct is in question ought to know that it amounts to harassment of another if a reasonable person in possession of the same information would think the course of conduct amounted to harassment of the other'.

[66] PHA s 7.
[67] PHA s 1(2). During the second reading debate the Home Secretary gave the following examples of the last of these items: a course of conduct pursued by journalists, salesmen, religious activists, debt collectors, private investigators or political canvassers. (HC Deb 17 December 1996, vol 287, col 784).
[68] Stevens (n 1) 53.
[69] *Dowson v Chief Constable of Northumbria Police* [2010] EWHC 2612 [142].

There is a noticeable gap between the *Dowson* test and the wording of the PHA. The Act does not state that alarm or distress is a requirement; it merely *includes* this under the umbrella of harassment, in the same way as it accommodates speech under the heading of conduct. Nor does the PHA stipulate an objective test for harassment, and it is not inconceivable that a legislature might wish to cover all conduct that is subjectively experienced as harassing, especially if, as here, a distinct defence of reasonable conduct is provided. And not a word of items (2) or (4) to (6) can be found in the PHA. Thus the bulk of the test is the product of judicial elaboration of the PHA. It represents a series of choices made by the courts.

As importantly, these choices follow the same general direction. They pursue a tightening up of the notion of harassment that not only is not required by the original aim of attacking stalking, but in fact runs counter to that purpose. The very point of the PHA was to get at stalkers' conduct which, even when innocent and lawful, adds up to a pattern placing another at risk.[70] This is no longer fully achievable if the course of conduct itself must be such that it torments the victim or be so reprehensible that it merits criminal liability. Significantly, the courts' strict construction of harassment has already led to new anti-stalking legislation, calculated precisely to escape what critics saw as the PHA's overly narrow coverage in practice.[71] This is not to say that the courts' interpretation of the PHA is inappropriate. To the contrary, and as I explain in the next section, there is good reason for narrowing down the meaning of harassment in exactly the way the judiciary has done. Moreover, the new anti-stalking provisions themselves reflect a drafting strategy that is designed to replace the open-endedness of the PHA with a more precisely targeted formulation.[72] But it is highly significant that the courts have opted for such a strict approach and their interpretive choices merit closer investigation.

The PHA does not state that the conduct must be targeted at the claimant. This requirement was first introduced in *Thomas v News Group Newspapers Ltd*,[73] where Lord Philips MR derived it from what he described as the 'generally understood' meaning of harassment. In his view, that meaning covered only a subset of all actions that would foreseeably alarm or cause a person distress.[74] The point of emphasising this by spelling out that the conduct must be targeted at the claimant is readily apparent from *Thomas* itself. This case concerned a harassment claim

[70] See Consultation Paper (n 51) para 1.6 as well as the opinions expressed by various participants in the pertinent Parliamentary debates cited in n 30.

[71] Protection of Freedoms Act 2012, s 111, introducing new stalking offences into the PHA. For critiques of the PHA leading up to this development, see Harry Fletcher and Laura Richards, 'Not Fit for Purpose' (2012) 176 *Criminal Law & Justice Weekly* 82; Tim Lawson-Cruttenden, 'Stalking' (2012) 176 *Criminal Law & Justice Weekly* 103; Laura Richards and Harry Fletcher, 'Stalking and Harassment – The Need for Law Reform' (2012) 68(2) *Magistrate* 2–3; Home Office *Consultation on Stalking* (November 2011).

[72] Ironically, this involves reverting to the approach used in drafting the 1996 Stalking Bill but rejected when it came to the PHA – see the new PHA s 2A(3) and Lawson-Cruttenden, 'Stalking' (n 71).

[73] *Thomas* (n 16) [30], Jonathan Parker LJ and Lord Mustill agreeing.

[74] *Thomas* (n 16) [29].

brought against a newspaper on the ground that it had published a series of articles (and associated readers' online comments) which, in disapproving of a black police station clerk's complaint about the use of racist language by police officers, had made repeated gratuitous references to the complainant's race. Having observed that, prior to the PHA, '[s]ubject to the law of defamation, the press was entitled to publish an article, or series of articles, about an individual, notwithstanding that it could be foreseen that such conduct was likely to cause distress to the subject of the article', Lord Philips was anxious to maintain the freedom of the press to do so.[75] By requiring (inter alia) that the conduct must be targeted at the claimant, he avoided outlawing conduct whenever it is foreseeable that the claimant would find it alarming or distressing – including, for example, because he belongs to a religious grouping or nationality that considers the conduct to be blasphemous or to ridicule a treasured national symbol or leader. On the facts of this case, however, the claimant had been the specific target of the articles and so her claim succeeded.

The effect of this requirement is to treat the prohibition of harassment as concrete rather than abstract: it is not obnoxious behaviour in general that is covered but only such behaviour in relation to a particular person. This might at first sight appear puzzling, for, as Baroness Hale pointed out in *Majrowski*, 'conduct might be harassment even if no harm or distress was in fact caused' and there is accordingly no requirement that harm, or even alarm or distress, be actually foreseeable'.[76] However, Baroness Hale's list does not exhaust the possibilities of interference with another. As I explain in section IV below, the prohibition of harassment serves to protect a more general interest of individuals in a reasonably civil social environment. This can be compromised even if none of the listed interferences takes place. The targeting requirement serves to ensure that at least this general interest is interfered with.

As Thomas itself makes clear, requiring the targeting of the claimant does not mean that the defendant has to interact directly with the claimant. Although in many harassment cases the defendant 'forced himself physically into the presence of the claimant, or . . . bombarded the claimant with messages or letters of a threatening nature', claims have also been successful where the conduct took the form of publications to the world at large which the claimant found out about through friends or associates and chose to read by using internet search engines and alerts.[77] Nevertheless, it is not sufficient that the alleged harasser knew or ought to have known that his conduct was of a kind that constitutes harassment in the abstract; he must have known, or at least ought to have known that it would harass the concrete individual who brings the claim to court.[78] *Trimingham v*

[75] *Thomas* (n 16) [33]–[34].

[76] *Majrowski* (n 7) [66]–[67].

[77] *Trimingham v Associated Newspapers Ltd* [2012] EWHC 1296 (QB) [98], [100]. See eg *Law Society* (n 12). Similarly in *James v DPP* [2009] EWHC 2925, [2010] Crim LR 580 it was held irrelevant that that the victim had initiated the series of telephone calls alleged to constitute the harassment.

[78] *Kellett v DPP* [2001] EWHC Admin 107 held harassment to have taken place where the victim was informed of the contents of two telephone calls to her employer by a third party rather than by the

Associated Newspapers Ltd[79] provides a good illustration of this aspect of the courts' approach. Here Mr Justice Tugendhat accepted that 'the repeated publication in the media of offensive or insulting words about a person's appearance can ... [in principle] amount to harassment'[80] and found on the facts that the defendants had indeed on several occasions published 'insulting and offensive' descriptions of the claimant's appearance and clothing.[81] Her claim nevertheless failed because he also concluded that none of the authors of the articles in question 'ought to have known that what he or she was writing amounted to harassment of Ms Trimingham'.[82] The reason for this was that, 'in considering whether journalists ought to know their articles amount to harassment of a person referred to, the court is entitled to, and should, consider the characteristics of that person which are known to the journalist'.[83] In light of Ms Trimingham's job as a leading politician's press officer and her past career as a journalist, a reasonable person would have come to the conclusion 'that she was tough, a woman of strong character, not likely to be upset by comments or offensive language, a woman who was known to give as good as she got'.[84]

Thomas is also the source of the further requirement that the conduct must be *objectively* calculated to cause harm and distress as well as judged oppressive and unacceptable. The subjective presence of these elements will not do; the claimant's own experience and evaluation of the conduct is insufficient to give rise to harassment. According to Lord Philips the reason for this is that '[t]here are many actions that foreseeably alarm or cause a person distress that could not possibly be described as harassment'.[85] Thus this requirement, too, is designed to restrict the occasions on which actually alarming and distressing conduct is legally treated as wrong. Lord Philips distinguished between two elements of the wrong: The (subjective) *effect* of the conduct, dealt with in the reference in PHA s 7 to 'alarming the person or causing the person distress'.[86] And the (objective) *type* of conduct, which is not defined in the PHA but is supplied by the 'generally understood' meaning of 'harassment', according to which it 'describes conduct . . . which is calculated to produce the consequences described in section 7 and which is oppressive and unreasonable'.[87] On the facts of the case both elements were held to be satisfied.

defendant himself even though the defendant had asked that she should not be so informed, provided there was evidence on the basis of which the court could properly conclude that the defendant was pursuing a course of conduct which he knew or ought to have known amounted to harassment of the victim.

[79] *Trimingham* (n 77).
[80] *Trimingham* (n 77) [70].
[81] *Trimingham* (n 77) [254] and [255].
[82] *Trimingham* (n 77) [251].
[83] *Trimingham* (n 77) [89].
[84] *Trimingham* (n 77) [89]. The quotation is from *Banks v Ablex Ltd* [2005] EWCA Civ 173, [2005] ICR 819 [26] (Kennedy LJ).
[85] *Thomas* (n 16) [29].
[86] *Thomas* (n 16) [29].
[87] *Thomas* (n 16) [30].

Since it was not disputed in *Thomas* that publishing articles calculated to incite racial hatred of an individual is capable of amounting to harassment, Lord Philips did not have occasion to elaborate on the degree of seriousness required before conduct would be regarded as meeting this objective test. However, the opportunity to do so presented itself in *Majrowski v Guy's and St Thomas's NHS Trust*,[88] the only PHA case so far to reach the House of Lords or the Supreme Court. In holding that an employer is vicariously liable under the PHA when one employee harasses another, Lord Nicholls observed that:

> Where . . . the quality of the conduct said to constitute harassment is being examined, courts will have in mind that irritations, annoyances, even a measure of upset, arise at times in everybody's day-to-day dealings with other people. Courts are well able to recognise the boundary between conduct which is unattractive, even unreasonable, and conduct which is oppressive and unacceptable. To cross the boundary from the regrettable to the unacceptable the gravity of the misconduct must be of an order which would sustain criminal liability under section 2.[89]

The objective character of the test therefore has a dual significance. It functions, firstly, to prevent people from imposing their own preferences regarding the social environment on others. Just as no-one is permitted to act without restraint, so everyone must put up with some degree of irritation, annoyance and upset. Hence in *Conn v City of Sunderland*,[90] a harassment claim failed where two out of three employees subjected to a foreman's aggressive tirades and the threat of 'a good hiding' regarded these as empty threats and had not felt intimidated. The claimant was undone by his exceptional sensitivity. On the other hand, a claim based on what has been described as 'the kind of allegations that are commonplace in many workplaces and could, perhaps, best be categorised as poor management',[91] succeeded in *Veakins v Kier Islington Ltd*[92] where the court judged the claimant to be a 'substantially reasonable and usually robust woman'.

The contrasting outcomes of these two cases also highlights the context-bound normative character of the objective test. Whether the course of conduct is 'objectively judged to be oppressive and unacceptable' is not simply a question of the extent of the impact on the claimant but turns on the court's assessment of how much upset the claimant *should* put up with in the circumstances. Thus in *King v Medical Services International Ltd*[93] one reason why an executive manager failed to obtain compensation for psychiatric illness allegedly resulting from harassment at the hands of her chief executive officer, was that '[e]xecutives are expected to withstand the demands and criticisms of their CEOs'. Similarly, in *Dowson* 'insensitive, belittling and overbearing' conduct by a senior police officer to his subordinates was not considered harassment in 'a stressful working environment in

88 *Majrowski* (n 7).
89 *Majrowski* (n 7) [30].
90 *Conn v City of Sunderland* [2007] EWCA Civ 1492, [2008] IRLR 324 [18].
91 Keith Patten, 'Employment: Defining Harassment' [160] *New Law Journal* 331, 332.
92 *Veakins v Kier Islington Ltd* [2009] EWCA Civ 1288, [2010] IRLR 132, [15].
93 *King v Medical Services International Ltd* [2012] All ER (D) 27 (Apr).

which case-hardened officers were dealing with career-hardened criminals'.[94] In this way, as explained by Gage LJ in *Conn*[95] (and reiterated in the *Dowson* test), what crosses the boundary 'may well depend on the context in which the conduct occurs'. This aspect of the concept of harassment is particularly prominent in cases concerning allegations of harassment by protestors. In one of the earliest cases of this kind, *Huntingdon Life Sciences Ltd v Curtin*,[96] Eady J said that the PHA was not intended to clamp down on the discussion of matters of public interest or upon the rights of political protest and public demonstration, and added that the courts would resist any wide interpretation of the Act. In cases involving the press as defendants the courts likewise pay careful attention to the need to balance the claimant's interests against Article 10 of the ECHR.[97]

Of course, it remains necessary to determine the content of the test. The clearest indication of how this is done is provided by Lord Philip's reference to the *generally understood* meaning of harassment.[98] Since harassment features in general discourse as a morally loaded description of conduct, expressing clear disapproval of the manner in which one individual has treated another,[99] Lord Philips is here pointing to social criteria for evaluating interpersonal conduct. Such 'generally accepted standards of decency and morality that define for us the meaning of life in a civilized community' and 'represent the special claims which members [of a community] have on each other' have usefully been labelled 'civility rules' by Robert Post.[100] These rules, Post points out, help constitute both individual and community identity, and their enforcement accordingly safeguards individual claims that members of a society have against each other as much as a community's particular character.[101] Using this terminology, the courts can be said to draw on society's civility rules when giving effect to the generally understood meaning of harassment, and harassment can be described as a targeted violation of the obligations individuals owe each other by virtue of the civility rules governing the context of their interaction.

Secondly, the objective test sets a threshold of seriousness. The course of conduct must cross the boundary delineated by Lord Nicholls in *Majrowski*. The references in the *Dowson* test to alarm, distress, oppressiveness, torment, and the sustaining of criminal liability, combine to emphasise that not every breach of

[94] *Dowson* (n 69) [277]–[278].

[95] *Conn* (n 90) [12].

[96] *Huntingdon Life Sciences Ltd v Curtin* (1997) *Times* (11 December) (QB).

[97] See *Thomas* (n 16) [32]–[37]; *Trimingham* (n 77).

[98] *Thomas* (n 16) [30].

[99] According to *The Concise Oxford Dictionary*, 10th edn (Oxford, Oxford University Press, 1999), to harass is to 'torment by subjecting to constant interference or intimidation'. This definition was cited and applied by Pill LJ in *R v Curtis (James Daniel)* [2010] EWCA Crim 123, [2010] 3 All ER 849 (CA).

[100] Robert C Post, 'The Constitutional Concept of Public Discourse: Outrageous Opinion, Democratic Deliberation, and *Hustler Magazine v Falwell*' (1989–90) 103 *Harvard Law Review* 602, 624 (internal quotations omitted). See also Robert C Post, 'The Social Foundations of Privacy: Community and Self in the Common Law Tort' (1989) 77 *California Law Review* 957.

[101] Post, 'The Constitutional Concept' (n 100) 624. Significantly, only natural persons can be victims of harassment under the PHA: *Daiichi UK Ltd v Stop Huntington Animal Cruelty* [2003] EWHC 2337 (QB), [2004] 1 WLR 1503.

civility rules qualifies as harassment. This is further underscored by the express requirement in the PHA that the conduct must occur on at least two occasions,[102] since repetition typically aggravates the effects of uncivil behaviour.[103] Significantly, the courts take the view that the fewer and the wider apart the incidents are, the less likely they are to amount to harassment and the more severe each is likely to have to be.[104] Moreover, the Court of Appeal has interpreted this requirement to exclude sporadic outbursts of temper and bad behaviour interspersed with considerable periods of affectionate life in a generally volatile relationship.[105]

The location of this boundary is not easy to determine, however. Although it is clear that the defendant's conduct need not sustain criminal or civil liability independently of the PHA, it is not self-evident how serious it must be before it would be 'of an order which would sustain criminal liability under section 2', as required in *Majrowski*.[106] Section 2 itself is silent on the point, stipulating merely that someone 'who pursues a course of conduct in breach of section 1 is guilty of an offence'. The Court of Appeal's application of the *Majrowski* test fails to take this much further. On the one hand, in *Conn v City of Sunderland*[107] Gage LJ took *Majrowski* to mean that 'the touchstone for recognising what is not harassment . . . will be whether the conduct is of such gravity as to justify the sanctions of the criminal law'.[108] Echoing this, Buxton LJ rejected the claim in *Conn* on the ground that the conduct in question was 'a very long way away from anything that, in a sensible criminal regime, would lead to a prosecution, much less to a conviction'.[109] On the other hand, Maurice Kay LJ in *Veakins v Kier Islington Ltd*[110] regarded the likely willingness of a prosecutor to prosecute as irrelevant,[111] and considered instead whether, 'in a criminal court, the proceedings would properly be stayed as an abuse of process'.

To this one must add judicial recognition of harassment in a range of cases where criminal sanctions would seem out of place. In *Allen v Southwark London Borough Council*,[112] for example, a council tenant who refused to pay rent into an account at the post office because he preferred paying in cash at the Council's

[102] PHA s 7(3).

[103] As Lord Hoffmann explains in *Wainwright* (n 39) [46]: 'The requirement of a course of conduct shows that Parliament was conscious that it might not be in the public interest to allow the law to be set in motion for one boorish incident.'

[104] *Lau v DPP* [2000] 1 FLR 799, [2000] Crim LR 580 (DC); *Jones v DPP* [2010] EWHC 523 (Admin), [2011] 1 WLR 833.

[105] *R v Curtis* [2010] EWCA Crim 123, [2010] 1 WLR 2770; cf *Pratt v DPP* [2001] EWHC Admin 483.

[106] *Majrowski* (n 7).

[107] *Conn* (n 90).

[108] *Conn* (n 90) [12].

[109] *Conn* (n 90) [18].

[110] *Veakins* (n 92) [15].

[111] Similarly, *Trimingham* (n 77), Tugendhat J declined an invitation to take note of the Crown Prosecution Service's published Policy for Prosecuting Cases with a Homophobic Element because: 'The question for me to decide is not whether the CPS would or should prosecute the Defendant, but whether Ms Trimingham has proved her claim that the Defendant has committed the statutory tort created by the PHA.'

[112] *Allen v Southwark London Borough Council* [2008] EWCA Civ 1478, [2008] All ER (D) 113 (Nov).

housing office (which had been closed down), was allowed to proceed with a harassment claim based on five sets of possession proceedings as well as some letters of demand for the unpaid rent. A claim was allowed to proceed in *Ferguson v British Gas Trading Ltd*[113] on the basis that the defendants had repeatedly unjustifiably billed the claimant, their former customer, and threatened her with legal proceedings for the supply of gas she was obtaining from a different supplier. The court, whilst accepting that a course of conduct must be grave before the offence or tort of harassment could be made out, said it was strongly arguable that the impugned conduct was on the wrong side of the line as being 'oppressive and unacceptable'.[114] In *Henriksen v Pires*[115] again, the claimants successfully contended that being bombarded over a period of years with unjustifiable demands by a joint freeholder for the payment of money to use a driveway amounted to harassment. And in *Bloom v Robinson-Millar*[116] the sending of seriously defamatory letters was held to be enough to constitute harassment.

The criminal liability test is rooted in the wording of the PHA, which creates a single wrong in section 1 for which it then provides apparently parallel criminal and civil sanctions in sections 2 and 3 respectively.[117] Lord Nicholl's guidance in *Majrowski* gives effect to this, but the other cases outlined above suggest that it is followed in spirit rather than to the letter. As in the *Dowson* test quoted above, the emphasis in the cases falls on drawing a line between the merely unattractive and the unreasonable, and references to the appropriateness of criminal sanctions serve simply to underline that the court must judge the defendant's course of conduct to have crossed that line. Indeed, in *Dowson* Mr Justice Simon warns against 'confining civil claims only to those cases where a criminal case would succeed'.[118]

This looser approach is nevertheless in keeping with the statute. Even as formulated in *Dowson*, the practical effect of the test is that civil remedies for harassment will only be made available if the defendant crossed a line that is normally of no concern to the civil law. Unlike the criminal law, civil liability does not censure a perpetrator through punishment. At least not automatically. Absent exceptional factors that would justify the imposition of aggravated damages,[119] a civil remedy does no more than instruct the defendant either, in the case of injunctions, to comply with his primary obligation, or, in the case of damages, to do the next best thing to complying with his primary obligation.[120] For that reason, civil liability does not normally require the defendant's conduct to have been worthy of

[113] *Ferguson* (n 10).
[114] *Ferguson* (n 10) [19].
[115] *Henriksen v Pires* [2011] EWCA Civ 1720, [2012] All ER (D) 76 (Feb).
[116] *Bloom v Robinson-Millar* [2009] All ER (D) 75 (Oct).
[117] This is true of harassment in England only, as the PHA does not render harassment a criminal offence in Scotland (see PHA ss 8–11).
[118] *Dowson* (n 67) [134].
[119] See generally, John Murphy, 'The Nature and Domain of Aggravated Damages' (2010) 69 *Cambridge Law Journal* 353.
[120] See John Gardner, 'What is Tort Law For? Part 1: The Place of Corrective Justice' (2011) 30 *Law and Philosophy* 1.

censure, ie reprehensible.[121] Yet precisely this is what the courts insist on in the case of harassment, including in *Dowson*. The function of the criminal liability test in judicial practice is therefore not so much to treat civil liability for harassment as an adjunct of criminal liability as it is to ensure that the statutory tort of harassment meets the same general criteria as apply to the criminalisation of conduct.[122] The purpose of the references to criminal liability is to place the spotlight – unusually among torts – on the moral quality of the defendant's conduct, requiring that it constitutes a reprehensible flouting of civility rules.

IV. Harassment, Civility and the Justification of Tort Liability

Ever since causation of loss has grown into 'the central feature of the English law of tort',[123] liability is normally imposed only if harm has been suffered. This is true also in the case of torts actionable per se. Although torts falling into this category are actionable without proof of consequential loss, they do give rise to remote harms.[124] The infringement of the regime of property law by a trespass to land, for example, compromises the general benefits to human flourishing – including to the claimant – that flow from having such a regime.[125] The various forms of trespass to the person likewise inflict (at least) remote harm by depriving the affected individuals (and others) of the many advantages that security of one's person and freedom of movement hold in addition to the avoidance of pain, suffering and financial harm.

This feature is crucial to the justification of tort liability, at least in a context where moralistic justifications, whether traditionalist or religious, no longer hold sway. For it means that tort law complies with the Harm Principle, famously formulated by John Stuart Mill in 1859 as stipulating that 'the only purpose for which power can be rightfully exercised over any member of a civilised community, against his will, is to prevent harm to others'.[126] This principle is a key requirement for the legitimacy of coercive measures since it serves to ensure, as Mill was at pains to explain, that the law respects the status of persons as moral agents. Although perhaps more familiar in the context of discussions of criminal law, the Harm Principle applies equally to the exercise of power through the imposition of

[121] *Ashley v Chief Constable of Sussex Police* [2008] UKHL 25, [2008] AC 962 [17]–[18].

[122] For a leading account of the prerequisites for justified criminalisation, see AP Simester and Andreas Von Hirsch, *Crimes, Harms and Wrong: On the Principles of Criminalisation* (Oxford, Hart Publishing, 2011).

[123] Ibbetson (n 2) 17.

[124] On remote harms, see Simester and Von Hirsch (n 122) 46–50.

[125] Simester and Von Hirsch (n 122) 40–43.

[126] John Stuart Mill, *On Liberty* (repr. Oxford, Oxford University Press, 2008) 21.

coercive civil sanctions.[127] That tort law complies with the Harm Principle is accordingly an essential component of its justifiability.

But not every loss or harm results in tort liability. This, too, is vital to its justification. It is not just that more than a fleeting impact is required, ie that there must be a genuine set-back to someone's (welfare) interests before it is appropriate to speak of harm,[128] although this is of course essential. It is also, and as importantly, the case that the harm must be one which it is fitting for tort law to involve itself with as a state-sponsored system of civil recourse.[129] This is because such a system has specific institutional features that are relevant to the way in which it deals with harms. It is, firstly, maintained at public expense and in the interest of all members of society. This means that it should not overextend itself; society's available material and symbolic capital must be husbanded with care in the general interest. The most important implication for present purposes is that tort law should only concern itself with protecting resources that are generally valuable in the relevant society as means for pursuing varied conceptions of a good life. Secondly, a state-run system that has such wide coverage is inevitably incapable of fine discriminations, liable to at least occasional human error, and, with only a limited range of sanctions at its disposal, will often risk unintended secondary consequences. For this reason the harms it concerns itself with must be of sufficient importance to justify the costs produced by enforcing obligations in a comparatively rough and ready way. And thirdly, the prevention and remedying of harm is not the only obligation of the state. It must also, as the Harm Principle itself indicates, uphold important general freedoms. Hence the obligations imposed by the law must not unduly restrict such freedoms. Only harms meeting all of these criteria are suited to the system of civil recourse provided by tort law.[130] This is why the common law torts do not extend to cover all harms but, broadly speaking, are confined to harms to the physical (including psychological) integrity of persons, their reputations and private information, and property (including its use and enjoyment). These are the harms (currently) judged to satisfy these requirements.

If, then, we use the term 'rights' to denote protected relationships between persons and certain of their interests, all this can be summed up by saying that tort liability is and should be founded on the violation of rights – the harming of interests considered suitable for grounding civil redress.[131] That is, the arguments just

[127] Stephen Smith, 'Towards a Theory of Contract' in Jeremy Horder (ed), *Oxford Essays in Jurisprudence*, 4th ser (Oxford, Oxford University Press, 2000) 107.

[128] This is emphasised by Simester and Von Hirsch (n 122) 46–47.

[129] On the importance of understanding tort law as such a system, see John CP Goldberg and Benjamin Zipursky, 'Rights and Responsibility in the Law of Torts' in Nolan and Robertson (eds) (n 1) 251.

[130] See also François du Bois, 'Getting Wrongfulness Right: A Ciceronian Attempt' 2000 *Acta Juridica* 1–48.

[131] This presupposes either that interest theories of rights are preferable to will theories, or (at least) that interest is an indispensible component of a pluralistic theory of rights. For the issues, see Matthew Kramer, Nigel Simmonds, and Hillel Steiner, *A Debate over Rights* (Oxford, Oxford University Press, 2000); Leif Wenar, 'The Nature of Rights' (2005) 33 *Philosophy and Public Affairs* 223. I cannot here engage in that debate.

set out explain why rights-based analyses of tort law are to be preferred.[132] As importantly, they explain when and why the imposition of tort liability is in principle justified.

But they simultaneously pose a challenge to the statutory tort of harassment. The previous sections have shown the PHA to be designed precisely to extend civil recourse to circumstances where insistence on the centrality of rights would result in the denial of common law tort remedies. How can this be justified if the protection of rights is key to the justification of tort liability? True, Parliament has the power to create new legal rights, and the PHA can certainly be described as having '*introduced* a . . . right not to be harassed'.[133] In fact, the Scottish provisions expressly lay down that '[e]very individual has a right to be free from harassment'.[134] But the exercise of all authority, including that of legislatures, is only justified if it produces instructions that reflect reasons which already independently apply to their addressees and should govern their conduct.[135] Does the PHA do so?

The answer lies in the significance of the most prominent characteristic of harassment to have emerged from the judicial interpretation of the PHA. This is that it requires of the courts, as Baroness Hale put it, 'to draw sensible lines between the ordinary banter and badinage of life and genuinely offensive and unacceptable behaviour'.[136] As the previous section showed, harassment under the PHA accordingly takes place when someone flouts society's civility rules in a manner so seriously reprehensible that it merits legal censure. This marks out a clear boundary between harassment and the main common law torts. None of these require conduct to cross this threshold. To the contrary: they ignore what harassment makes pivotal. It is entirely irrelevant to a tort claim for trespass, defamation, negligence or nuisance whether the defendant's conduct deserves condemnation as 'offensive and unacceptable' or 'oppressive'. A tortious battery can be committed by someone judged to have a valid defence to a criminal charge,[137] defamation is a tort of strict liability requiring no more than an unjustified injury to someone's reputation,[138] liability for negligence is imposed regardless of the efforts made by the defendant to meet the required standard of conduct,[139] and a

[132] The analysis put forward here nevertheless differs in many ways from the rights theories made prominent by Stevens (n 1) and Beever (n 1).

[133] Stevens (n 1) 53.

[134] PHA s 8.

[135] This is a simplified paraphrase Raz's 'normal justification thesis' of authority: see Joseph Raz, *The Morality of Freedom* (Oxford, Oxford University Press, 1986) 53–57.

[136] *Majrowski* (n 7) [66].

[137] *Ashley* (n 121).

[138] This is its most basic characteristic; there are of course defences other than justification. The defence of 'responsible journalism' created in *Reynolds v Times Newspapers Ltd* [2001] 2 AC 127 does not detract from the point made in the text since the relevant standard is an objective one that can be infringed by a well-meaning journalist.

[139] Even learners (*Nettleship v Weston* [1971] 2 QB 691) and the less experienced (*Wilsher v Essex Area Health Authority* [1987] QB 730) will be held liable if they fail to meet the standard required by the activity engaged in.

nuisance may be committed by someone who has taken all reasonable care to avoid the interference complained of.[140]

Crucially, this very distinction enables harassment to meet the conditions for justified provision of civil recourse outlined above. A targeted reprehensible flouting of society's civility rules – as required by the courts – turns an interference that would otherwise be of limited significance into a serious setback in much the same way as an apparently harmless trespass in fact harms the right-holder. Such a course of conduct is not merely displeasing, offensive or insulting, but gives rise to remote harm, largely by compromising the advantages flowing from general social compliance with such civility rules. These rules 'provide a normative framework for the development of individual personality':[141] 'By following these rules, individuals not only confirm the social order in which they live, but they also establish and affirm "ritual" and "sacred" aspects of their own and others' identities.'[142] Violation of these rules may therefore harm a person not only directly 'by discrediting his identity and injuring his personality',[143] but also indirectly by eroding the framework on which the integrity of individual personality depends. In this way, harassment interferes with the victim's interest in a reasonably civil social environment by compromising 'the "ritual idiom" through which . . . respect [for individual personality] finds social expression'.[144] This is why the courts describe harassing conduct as 'oppressive', and also why it is appropriate to provide a remedy even in the absence of alarm or distress.[145] Moreover, it means that the PHA vindicates an important element of individual well-being and cannot be dismissed as simply a vehicle for enforcing conventional mores. Since members of society generally gain in this way from compliance with civility rules, it is also appropriate to employ public resources to provide civil recourse to individual victims of harassment. Indeed, these rules: 'when taken together, give normative shape and substance to the society that shares them . . . [and] create for a community "its distinctive shape, its unique identity".'[146] Hence 'the law . . . endows such plaintiffs with the capacity to bring suit, thereby upholding the normative identity of the community'.[147] In the practical application of the PHA this

[140] *Rapier v London Tramways Co* [1893] 2 Ch 588. So baldly stated this is of course a simplification of the law (eg cases involving a 'continuation' of a nuisance created by a third party or nature involve a 'sort of condominium' with the law of negligence: *Transco Plc v Stockport MBC* [2003] UKHL 61, [2004] 2 AC 1 [96]).

[141] Post, 'Social Foundations' (n 100) 985.

[142] Post, 'Social Foundations' (n 100) 962.

[143] Post, 'Social Foundations' (n 100) 963.

[144] Post, 'Social Foundations' (n 100) 986. See also Joseph Raz, *Value, Respect and Attachment* (Cambridge, Cambridge University Press, 2001) 171–75 on the importance and complexity of conventional and symbolic expressions of respect for persons, and Joseph Raz, *Ethics in the Public Domain* (Oxford, Oxford University Press, 1994) Part I on the ethical relationship between individual well-being and group membership.

[145] Compare the explanation by Raz, *The Morality of Freedom* (n 135) 175 of the binding character of promises the performance of which do not hold any specific advantage for the promisee.

[146] Post, 'Social Foundations' (n 100) 964.

[147] Post, 'Social Foundations' (n 100) 964. On rights and the interests of persons other than the right-holder, see Joseph Raz, *Ethics in the Public Domain* (Oxford, Oxford University Press, 1994) ch 3.

finds expression especially in judicial references to the criminal liability test, as there is a close connection between criminalisation and moral communication between a community and its citizens.[148]

The translation of civility rules into judicial orders is certainly no straightforward matter. A liability test as broad as that contained in the definition of harassment is bound to result in considerable variation in practice as well as mistakes. The institutional needs of the law also give rise to an unavoidable gap between the law and social norms, and in pluralistic societies there is the equally inescapable risk of civility rules being 'hegemonically imposed by one dominant cultural group onto others'.[149] But as long as the threshold for a legally relevant flouting is usually set high enough, the benefits flowing from the maintenance of civility rules are sufficiently weighty to compensate for the costs flowing from the rough and ready ways of the law.[150] A social environment in which interactions are routinely seriously un-civil is likely to be experienced as a hostile one and thus to discourage social participation and to stymie the various dimensions of individual and communal development that are fostered by the lubrication of social interaction through civility rules. As the comparatively long history of racial and sexual harassment measures indicates,[151] this is perhaps most obvious when specific groups are targeted and/or specific environments such as schools or places of employment are affected, but there is no reason to think that this phenomenon is restricted in either of these ways. Finally, general freedoms are safeguarded by the conception of harassment as targeted reprehensible flouting of society's civility rules. Conduct that qualifies as harassment generally has no significant value[152] and must, in any case according to the courts, be objectively oppressive and cross the requisite threshold of seriousness.

It is tempting to conclude from this that the PHA simply gives expression to an underlying right not to be harassed. But this temptation should be resisted. The concept of a right occupies a distinctive place in normative discourse. As Robert Audi puts it, 'even if there are normative statements that are necessarily equivalent to rights ascriptions, they differ both in conceptual content and in pragmatic role'.[153] Dworkin's portrayal of rights as trumps is a vivid depiction of the specific function of this concept in our moral and legal usage: it serves to signal that the right-holder's interest is prima facie worthy of protection against competing

[148] See Anthony Duff, *Punishment, Communication, and Community* (Oxford, Oxford University Press, 2003).

[149] Post, 'Social Foundations' (n 100) 977. See also Leslie Green, 'Two Worries about Respect for Persons' (2010) 120 *Ethics* 212, 228–30.

[150] I agree with Green (n 149) 230 that 'we should resist joining those who are equally confident in the causal powers of law and legal institutions when it comes to doing harm and their causal impotence when it comes to doing good'.

[151] See n 64.

[152] The defences provided in PHA, s 1(3) protect various socially valuable activities, as does the approach of the courts in cases involving the press and public protests – see *Thomas* (n 16), *Trimingham* (n 77), *Heathrow* (n 14), *Daiichi* (n 101) and *Astellas Pharma Ltd v Stop Huntingdon Animal Cruelty* [2011] EWCA Civ 752.

[153] Robert Audi, 'Wrongs within Rights' (2005) 15 *Philosophical Issues* 122, 136.

considerations.[154] It also makes clear why it is inappropriate to speak of a right not to be harassed. The interest protected by this alleged right is, as we saw, the interest in a reasonably civil social environment. Important as it is, this interest cannot be treated as one that is prima facie worthy of protection against competing considerations. It is far too broad to qualify for such generalised special protection.[155] It is not only capable of being infringed to degrees of widely diverging seriousness, but, most importantly, is liable to infringement by appropriate, or at least tolerable, self-expression: hostility, anger, rudeness, offensiveness and so on may on occasion be no less apt than civility.[156] Indeed, the transgression of civility rules is itself a means whereby individual characters are formed and social identities evolved.[157] It is crucial to bear in mind Joseph Raz's observation that 'the fact that rights are sufficient to ground duties limits the rights one has'.[158] Given the peremptory character of duties, this helps to explain why there cannot be right to civil treatment. For these reasons, a fully flexible case-by-case assessment is needed, one which considers any claim to civility without the pre-endorsement that is built into the very nature of rights. And this is exactly how the courts approach harassment.

Our normative vocabulary must contain more than rights if this concept is to convey something distinctive about the moral or legal relationship between persons. The benefits of precision that flow from using 'right' to convey a particular conceptual content and to play a specific role in our normative discourse and practices come at the price of accepting that 'our moral conduct cannot be adequately described, appraised, and guided without appeal to obligations, virtues, and moral ideals'.[159] One situation calling for the supplementation of rights exists when someone may justifiably be criticised for acting within his rights, ie for the manner in which he exercises his rights. Audi gives the example of someone who, despite wearing a sweater heavy enough to keep him warm, refuses to lend his coat to a freezing friend who has neither. As he points out, 'the [first] friend's right to keep his coat is compatible with an obligation of friendship that calls for lending it'.[160] To take the coat from him against his will would be a violation of his property right even though he ought to lend it. Here the wrong that is done by the refusal to lend the coat cannot be expressed in the language of rights violations. The selfish friend is acting within his rights and the freezing friend does not have

[154] Ronald Dworkin, 'Rights as Trumps' in Jeremy Waldron (ed), *Theories of Rights* (Oxford, Oxford University Press, 1984) 153. There are of course also further important dimensions to the role of rights in normative thought: see Raz, *The Morality of Freedom* (n 135) 180–92.

[155] This is the principal reason why the House of Lords rejected a common law right along these lines in *Wainwright* (n 39). See the speeches of Lord Hoffmann at [46] and Lord Scott at [62].

[156] Concerns along these lines lead some to reject the legal protection of civility rules altogether: see eg James Q Whitman, 'Enforcing Civility and Respect: Three Societies' (1999–2000) 109 *Yale Law Journal* 1279; Whitman, 'Two western Cultures' (n 29).

[157] See the Hart–Devlin debate: HLA Hart, *Law, Liberty and Morality* (Oxford, Oxford University Press, 1963) and Patrick Devlin, *The Enforcement of Morals* (Oxford, Oxford University Press, 1965).

[158] Raz (n 135) 183.

[159] Audi (n 153) 136.

[160] Audi (n 153) 129.

a right to the coat: however much he may need it, and should get it, it does not belong to him. The selfish friend commits what Audi calls a 'wrong within a right'.[161]

This example is on all fours with the circumstances the PHA is meant to deal with. As we saw, the PHA is in origin as well as implementation a response to objectionable conduct that falls short of interfering with legally recognised rights. Moreover, there is good reason for denying the existence of a right to civil treatment. The PHA's core concern is therefore the manner in which people exercise what one might call their residual general right to freedom of action and self-actualisation – the freedom that is left over after due account has been taken of the obligations imposed by the rights of others. The civility rules by means of which the courts pursue this concern are, like the duties of friendship, special claims generated by a relationship involving mutual commitment and concern.[162] They reflect justified expectations arising from the bonds of 'civic friendship' about the manner in which members of society are to exercise this residual general right. A violation of such expectations is wrong even though it takes place 'within' this right.

For this reason, the vindication of rights does not exhaust the range of possibilities for justifying the imposition of tort liability. It provides at most the standard justification. With its case-bound moral evaluation of the defendant's conduct, the test for harassment developed by the courts provides a sound alternative to the approach of the common law torts for meeting the conditions for civil recourse. Together, Parliament and the courts have therefore crafted a perfectly viable statutory tort.

V. Conclusion

The PHA was enacted to provide remedies in circumstances where the courts had concluded that the common law could not do so. Lord Scott captured the courts' view pithily in answering his own question in *Wainright*:

> [W]hy, absent any of the traditional nominate torts such as assault, battery, negligent causing of harm etc, should the law of tort intrude? If a shop assistant or a bouncer or barman at a club is publicly offensive to a customer, the customer may well be humiliated and distressed. But that is no sufficient reason why the law of tort should be fashioned and developed with a view to providing compensation in money to the victim.[163]

This chapter has defended a different answer, the one that Parliament adopted in enacting the PHA. Civil recourse – ie tort remedies – should indeed be available in the event of serious breaches of the social rules of civility. These rules straddle

[161] Audi (n 153) 129. See also Jeremy Waldron, 'A Right to Do Wrong' (1983) 93 *Ethics* 320.
[162] See Post (n 100) and the text and quotations accompanying nn 100–1 and 146–47 above.
[163] *Wainright* (n 39) [62].

individual and social interests, providing conditions as essential for the development and protection of individual personality and communal identity as those safeguarded by the rights already protected by tort law. There is admittedly no underlying right to be free from harassment. To that extent the common law position cannot be faulted.[164] But our normative arsenal does not consist of rights alone, and the analysis in this chapter has shown that the courts have interpreted the concept of harassment in the PHA in a way that provides a viable alternative to the rights-based approach of the common law torts.[165] Harassment stands out because it discriminates among harms not on the basis of their nature and seriousness, but by focusing on the moral quality of the manner in which the defendant exercised his general liberty of action in the concrete circumstances of each case, so confining the law's involvement to egregious transgressions of civility rules. That is the way in which the law of harassment, as jointly crafted by Parliament and the courts, gives expression to this fundamental truth articulated by Lord Justice Jacobs:

> What makes the wrong of harassment different and special is . . . [that] in life one has to put up with a certain amount of annoyance: things have got to be fairly severe before the law, civil or criminal, will intervene.[166]

An integral part of this development is the courts' recourse to what they take to be the generally understood meaning of harassment. This provides the necessary link between judicial practice and society's civility rules. Importantly, this is made possible by the very aspect of the PHA for which it has been most severely criticised: the absence of a definition of harassment.[167] Some may consider the courts in this way to have made a virtue out of a rather lame attempt to evade the definitional difficulty that had persuaded the Calcutt Committee against a harassment tort. But to me this development appears the fitting outcome of a feature of the PHA that is anything but regrettable. There is often good reason for the law to draw on social norms and to stabilise these rather than to seek to displace them by precise directives of its own. How people should behave is frequently best settled outside the institutions through which law is generated and maintained.[168] The state should not – indeed cannot – have authority over every corner of people's lives.[169] Individual conscience and civil society have indispensable roles to play in

[164] I do not mean to suggest that the absence of such an underlying right prevented the courts from developing a tort of harassment. I don't share the rights fundamentalists' view that judicial development of the law is confined to working out existing rights – see the critical discussion of their views in Cane (n 1). The general issue of judicial law-making competence is complex and cannot be canvassed here.

[165] It may well be that the courts could for this reason have undertaken such a development themselves, as was foreseen in *Burris v Azadani* (n 33).

[166] *Ferguson* (n 10) [18].

[167] Stevens (n 1) 53; Baroness Hale (n 24); the Law Society in HC Library (n 59).

[168] In the context of Tort law, consider for example the *Bolam* test for determining the standard to be met by medical professionals.

[169] See generally Raz (n 135) Ch 4; idem (n 144) Ch 14; Leslie Green, *The Authority of the State* (Oxford, Oxford University Press, 1988).

shaping human lives. This is what the open texture of the PHA gives effect to, entirely properly. It enables the PHA to complement and support social processes of community formation which should not, and probably cannot, be taken over by the state and its institutions.

The relationship between the PHA and civility rules affirms the parallel with the Roman delict of *iniuria* noted at the start of this chapter. Birks' description of *iniuria* as turning on whether someone had been deprived of his or her 'fair share of respect' by behaviour *contra bonos mores huius civitatis*,[170] can without distortion be applied to the former as well. Both protect the social 'rules [that] enable individuals to receive and to express respect, and to that extent are constitutive of human dignity'.[171] This connection with the civilian tradition is interesting in its own right, but also, and importantly, means that the PHA is a valuable element in the approximation of English and Scots law to the protection of dignity as foreseen in the Principles of European Tort Law and the Draft Common Frame of Reference.[172]

[170] Birks (n 25) 10, 12.

[171] Post, 'Social Foundations' (n 100) 1008. The content of the civility rules of contemporary Britain and ancient Rome is, of course, very different. But this does not detract from their functional similarity.

[172] See PETL Art 2:102(2) and DCFR VI.2:203.

INDEX

www.ingramcontent.com/pod-product-compliance
Ingram Content Group UK Ltd.
Pitfield, Milton Keynes, MK11 3LW, UK
UKHW020250290926
15470UKWH00002B/843

9 781849 465038

THE SOCIO-POLITICS OF LEGAL DESIGN AND ITS EPISTEMIC CONSEQUENCES

This book brings together diverse perspectives from researchers working in the fields of law, justice, and design to interrogate the emergence of vocabularies and methods of legal design and unpack their epistemic consequences.

Legal design has emerged in the last decade as an interdisciplinary practice, at the intersection of law and justice, and initially human-centred design. Despite the short history of legal design as a discipline, its foundations in human-centred design have been questioned. Justifying all sorts of innovation for the universal needs of users is even more problematic for human-centred design due to its large adoption in industry and the public sector. Placing a market type of human-consumer at the centre of the legal design activity justifies the reproduction of capitalist and oppressive systems by placing the inspiration for new products and services on the human-user-consumer. The adoption of such practices in policy and legal design can be seen as a tool to impose the market values over democracy, justice, and equality.

This book offers a wide array of alternatives and reference points for making sense of legal design. It critically addresses issues of epistemic injustice in the designing of legal services and systems, bringing together the tradition of socio-legal studies in dialogue with new concepts and frameworks from critical design approaches.

Oñati International Series in Law and Society

A SERIES PUBLISHED FOR THE OÑATI INSTITUTE FOR THE SOCIOLOGY OF LAW

Recent titles in this series

Gender and Careers in the Legal Academy
Edited by Ulrike Schultz, Gisela Shaw, Margaret Thornton and Rosemary Auchmuty

Contesting Austerity: A Socio-Legal Inquiry
Edited by Anuscheh Farahat and Xabier Arzoz

The Right to the Continuous Improvement of Living Conditions: Responding to Complex Global Challenges
Edited by Jessie Hohmann and Beth Goldblatt

Supporting Legal Capacity in Socio-Legal Context
Edited by Mary Donnelly, Rosie Harding and Ezgi Tascioglu

What Is a Family Justice System For?
Edited by Mavis Maclean, Rachel Treloar and Bregje Dijksterhuis

Combining the Legal and the Social in Sociology of Law: An Homage to Reza Banakar
Edited by Håkan Hydén, Roger Cotterrell, David Nelken and Ulrike Schultz

Criminal Justice and The Ideal Defendant in the Making of Remorse and Responsibility
Edited by Stewart Field and Cyrus Tata

Socio-Legal Trajectories Across Europe: Comparative Perspectives
Edited by Christian Boulanger, Naomi Creutzfeldt and Jennifer Hendry

Parole Futures: Rationalities, Institutions and Practices
Edited by Harry Annison, Nicola Carr and Thomas Guiney

The Socio-Politics of Legal Design and its Epistemic Consequences
Edited by Siddharth Peter de Souza and Joaquín Santuber

For the complete list of titles in this series
see www.bloomsbury.com/uk/series/oñati-international-series-in-law-and-society

The Socio-Politics of Legal Design and its Epistemic Consequences

Edited by
Siddharth Peter de Souza
and
Joaquín Santuber

Oñati International Series in Law and Society

A SERIES PUBLISHED FOR THE OÑATI INSTITUTE
FOR THE SOCIOLOGY OF LAW

•HART•
OXFORD • LONDON • NEW YORK • NEW DELHI • SYDNEY

HART PUBLISHING

Bloomsbury Publishing Plc

Kemp House, Chawley Park, Cumnor Hill, Oxford, OX2 9PH, UK

1385 Broadway, New York, NY 10018, USA

Bloomsbury Publishing Ireland Limited, 29 Earlsfort Terrace, Dublin 2, D02 AY28, Ireland

HART PUBLISHING, the Hart/Stag logo, BLOOMSBURY and the Diana logo are trademarks of Bloomsbury Publishing Plc

First published in Great Britain 2026

A catalogue record for this book is available from the British Library.

A catalogue record for this book is available from the Library of Congress.

Library of Congress Control Number: 2026936269

ISBN: HB: 978-1-50999-006-1
ePDF: 978-1-50999-008-5
ePub: 978-1-50999-007-8

Typeset by Compuscript Ltd, Shannon

For product safety related questions contact productsafety@bloomsbury.com

To find out more about our authors and books visit www.hartpublishing.co.uk. Here you will find extracts, author information, details of forthcoming events and the option to sign up for our newsletters.

Acknowledgements

WE WOULD LIKE to thank the Oñati International Institute for the Sociology of Law for providing us with the opportunity to host a workshop at the institute in July 2024, and especially to Malen Gordoa and Manttoni Kortabarria for their partnership in developing the project and making it a wonderful experience. We would also like to thank Leire Kortabarria, Sasha Jawed, Tom Adams and Rachit Sharma for their work in ensuring the publication of the volume. The workshop was made possible thanks to a grant from Tilburg University Fund.

The main issue this book addresses is that of knowledge generation, and how we can develop alternative ways to open up the possibilities for plural voices, perspectives, and attitudes in the practice of designing for the law and justice. The rich collection we are able to present in the following chapters was possible thanks to the commitment of the authors of these chapters who came from a range of latitudes to Onati, generously participating in the discussion, supporting each other's contributions, and creating a safe and caring space for exchange of experiences and hopes. Both at the workshop in Onati and throughout these pages, this wonderful group of academics and practitioners gift us a renewed commitment and belief in the law as a powerful tool to bring social transformation. For that, we are deeply thankful.

Contents

Notes on Contributors

Abdul Rehman Khan is an Assistant Clinical Professor at Seton Hall Law School's Center for Social Justice. He directs the Housing & Legal Design Clinic and founded the New Jersey Legal Design Lab, a social change laboratory that shifts power into local movements through co-creation design methods, understanding law as a source of its own design. His interests encompass racial and economic justice, appellate strategy, and the right to an adequate standard of living, particularly focusing on tenant conditions. Abdul Rehman sits on the Board of Directors for Essex-Newark Legal Services and previously served as the inaugural Pro Bono Fellow for the City of Newark with McCarter & English.

Ade Mabogunje is a Senior Research Engineer at Stanford University's Mechanical Engineering Department. He specializes in design thinking, measuring its processes, and providing feedback to enhance team performance. Previously, he was Associate Director at Stanford's Center for Design Research and led the Real-time Venture Design Lab. His industry experience includes work at Elf (now Total) and research with NASA Ames. Collaborating with educators, designers, and investors, he fosters innovation ecosystems. His research spans design theory, knowledge management, engineering education, and AI applications in design. He has published extensively on design methodology and emotions in engineering.

Amanda Perry-Kessaris is Professor of Law at Kent Law School. She specialises in empirically grounded, theoretically informed, inter-disciplinary approaches to law. She is Fellow of the Design Research Society, elected in recognition of her pioneering application of design-based methods to enhance legal research, education and practice; and Fellow of the Academy of Social Sciences, elected in recognition of her development of an integrated 'econo-socio-legal' approach to understanding the economic lives of law. Her publications include *Doing Sociolegal Research in Design Mode* (2021) and *Design in Legal Education* (with Emily Allbon, 2022). She has postgraduate qualifications in law, economics and design.

Bader Alnoaimi is an Independent researcher focusing on law, political economy and technology. In previous research, Bader has examined the use of sovereign wealth funds as key intermediary institutions in privatisation law; local court jurisdiction over foreign cloud data; and the political economy of delivery apps and immigration policies.

Bhawna Parmar is a researcher-designer leading human-centred research and social innovation projects across education, climate action, and digital rights.

Her expertise lies in conducting ethnographic research, designing participatory and co-design methodologies, and translating insights into actionable strategies for social impact. Currently she is leading the Youth Futures Studio at Quest Alliance where she works at the intersection of youth engagement, learning design, futures thinking, and systems thinking. Additionally, she is also the founder of Gustakhi Lab, an experimental social design lab that creates good trouble by challenging the status quo. She moonlights as a political illustrator and holds a Masters in Social Design from Ambedkar University Delhi.

Dorra Harrar, a pioneering Tunisian business attorney, is the founder of Legal.D – the first legal design firm in Tunisia and the MENA region. As the region's first certified legal design expert, she transforms complex legal systems into accessible, human-centred solutions. In 2019, she made history by applying legal design in a Tunisian court case, setting a regional precedent. Honoured with the WorldCC Excellence Award in 2022, Dorra also collaborates with NGOs like UNDP to simplify legal aid for vulnerable communities. A global speaker, including at the 2023 Legal Design Summit in Helsinki, she champions clarity, inclusion, and justice for all.

Ebru Metin is an early-stage researcher at Tallinn University of Technology. Her research explores how legal design can reduce regulatory complexity, making corporate sustainability frameworks more accessible, actionable, and effective for businesses, policymakers, and stakeholders. She holds an LL.M. from King's College London (2014) as a Jean Monnet Scholar, another LL.M. from Istanbul Bilgi University (2013) and LL.B. from Bilkent University (2009). She was previously awarded by Fortune-US Department of State (2022), British Council (2022), International Legal Technology Association (2022), Euclid Network (2022) and UNDP Turkey (2021) for her work at Legal Design Turkey.

Elena Kuran is staff attorney in the Civil Action Practice at the Bronx Defenders in New York City. She graduated from Northeastern University School of Law in May 2025. Her research and practice focus on liberatory legal designing and exploring the ways that design can help shift power to movements and democratize freedom practices. Elena previously interned at the U.S. District Court for the District of Massachusetts, the Amsterdam Law Hub, and the Surveillance Technology Oversight Project.

Hallie Jay Pope is a legal information designer, educator, and cartoonist. She is the Director of the New Jersey Legal Design Lab, a social transformation laboratory at Seton Hall Law School's Center for Social Justice. Hallie's work focuses on using participatory design processes and visual storytelling to share legal knowledge and build movement power. Before joining Seton Hall, Hallie taught the Creative Advocacy Lab at the University of Utah S.J. Quinney College of Law and directed the Graphic Advocacy Project.

Jaana Kovalainen (LL.M., eMBA) is a doctoral researcher at the Faculty of Law, University of Lapland. Her research combines health law, public law, and legal design to explore whether legal design can improve access to justice in healthcare and affect the interpretation of good administration principles. She is also interested in the role of AI, legal informatics, and information design in public services. Prior to working as a researcher, she has worked for years in the banking business, mainly in risk management and business management.

Joaquín Santuber is a lawyer and obtained his PhD in Design and IT-Systems on the topic of designing for digital justice, studying public innovation in courts. He is a Univ.-Assist. (Assistant Professor) and research-group lead at the Metaverse Lab, Johannes Kepler University Linz, Austria and works with art-based and design approaches to legality in digital environments. Joaquín has been Assistant Professor at Universidad de Los Andes, Colombia, Fellow of the HIIG, Humboldt University, Berlin, and Guest Researcher at the Center for Social Studies (CES), University of Coimbra, Portugal. Currently he serves as editor of the Legal Design Journal and is a visiting professor at the School of Design of the Pontificia Universidad Católica de Chile.

Jules Rochielle Sievert has served as the Creative Director of NuLawLab since 2013. They are a Ph.D. candidate in the Interdisciplinary Doctoral Program at Northeastern University's College of Art, Media, and Design, where their dissertation develops a transformative and transdisciplinary framework for legal design. Sievert is the Primary Investigator of NuLawLab's National Endowment for the Arts Research Lab on Spatial Justice in East Boston and a Co-Principal Investigator on a special initiative funded by the Mellon Foundation. In the past, Jules has held positions such as Ambassador for Health Equity at PolicyLink and Creative Placemaking Policy Fellow at Arizona State University through the Herberger Institute for Design and the Arts.

Kanan Dhru is a three-times founder in legal innovation, having launched Lawtoons, LawForMe and Research Foundation for Governance in India. With expertise at the crossroads of law, design, and technology, she advises and investing in scaling justice startups globally. Most recently, she has worked on researching and coordinating courses around European technology regulations at The Hague University of Applied Sciences. She is passionate about blending human-centred design with emerging technologies to transform the access to justice space.

Nina Toivonen is a doctoral researcher in law at the University of Helsinki, Finland. Her dissertation develops the legal-theoretical foundations of systemic design of law, drawing on insights from systems sciences, critical design research and design for policy research, particularly to address regulatory challenges related to sustainability. Toivonen holds a master's degree in legal design and legal expertise from Laurea University of Applied Sciences. She has previously worked as a legal designer and legal counsel.

Pablo Hermansen is a designer who holds a PhD in Architecture and Urban Studies from Pontificia Universidad Católica de Chile. Dr. Hermansen's research and publications focus on the material conditions of interspecies coexistence, prototyping as a more-than-human research device, and performative strategies for the political visibility of counter-hegemonic groups in public space. He works in the field of digital museography and interactive installation and provides consulting services in the area of critical service design for public institutions.

Michael Doherty is Professor of Legal Design and Associate Head of the Law School, Lancaster University, UK. He is co-author of *Public Law* (3rd edn, Routledge 2023) and *Transforming Higher Education Through Human-Centred Design* (Routledge, 2024), co-founder of the *Connecting Legal Education* online community and a former Chair of the Association of Law Teachers. His legal design work encompasses education, disciplinarity, and access to justice. He is the founding editor-in-chief of the *Legal Design Journal.*

Saumya Varma is a public policy professional with extensive experience in politics, legislative research, industry-government engagement, and strategic policy advisory. She holds a Master's in Modern Indian History from Jawaharlal Nehru University and a Master's in Public Policy from the University of Oxford. She spent five years leading legislative and policy research for a national political party in India. More recently, she has been working in the strategic advisory space, operating at the intersection of government, policy, and industry. She is also Senior Consultant, Parliament and Policy Research at Justice Adda, a social enterprise specializing in legal access through design and tech, and was part of the team that created 'Sabha', a board game that educates players about India's parliamentary process through interactive learning.

Siddharth Peter de Souza is an Assistant Professor in AI & Society and the Centre for Interdisciplinary Methodologies, Warwick University. His work explores how data is governed globally in contested and plural settings, and he is interested in the role that social movements and civil society can play in shaping digital transformations. He is also the founder of Justice Adda, a law and design social venture in India where he works on matters related to access to justice, and legal empowerment. Siddharth has worked as a digital policy consultant with UNDP and IDLO and was previously a post-doctoral researcher at the Global Data Justice Project at Tilburg Institute for Law, Technology and Society. He is a research associate at the African Centre for Epistemology and Philosophy of Science, University of Johannesburg.

Siddhi Gupta is a designer and educator with a decade of experience leading projects in equity design and digital storytelling with global stakeholders. Her work has been published in Amsterdam University Press, Teacher Plus Magazine, and AD Magazine. She has been nominated as a Games for Peace UNESCO MGIEP fellow and comes with a Masters degree in Visual Communication from Royal College of Art, London.

Varsha Aithala is an assistant professor and doctoral candidate at the National Law School of India University. She is Operations Lead at Justice Adda, a law and design thinking social enterprise. Her teaching and research interests cover social investment, law and technology, access to justice and legal system reform. Varsha is qualified as a solicitor in England and Wales and as an advocate in India. She has a Master's degree in corporate law from the University of Cambridge and a Bachelor's degree in law from NALSAR University of Law.

List of Illustrations

LIST OF FIGURES

LIST OF TABLES

From Legal Design to Legal Designing: Opening Up the Field of Possibilities

JOAQUÍN SANTUBER AND SIDDHARTH PETER DE SOUZA

INTRODUCTION

ADDRESSING LEGAL PROBLEMS is multifaceted, involving various social, cultural, and political considerations. Because of the interconnected nature of these considerations, dealing with them is complex, especially in pluralistic and contested settings. Against this backdrop, legal design (LD) has emerged as a practice that demonstrates the entanglements between law and design. It offers ways of examining how society is structured through unpacking its hierarchies, cultures, relations, and objects, and through these interactions affords tools to study and analyse how structures emerge.

Legal Design has been variously described as a movement,[1] as a series of methods,[2] as a thing,[3] and as a framework.[4] In defining what it is, a helpful starting point is the kind of questions that can be asked. These include lawyerly questions, for instance, about rights, rules, or risks, as well as designerly questions about how things feel, how they systematise, and how they interact.[5] Underlying these different questions is a focus on aspects of relationality between people, institutions, and the non-human environment around us.

In this book, we take LD as communities of practice(s) that encompass values of participation, exploration, and interrogation. We recognise that there is a plurality in its emergence in terms of missions (research, practice, business), methods (grounded, reflexive, iterative), and movements (local, global); however, we also recognise that there is a convergence in terms of what it ought

[1] Doherty, M and others (2021) 'A New Attitude to Law's Empire: The Potentialities of Legal Design' in Marcelo Corrales Compagnucci and others (eds), Legal Design: Integrating Business, Design and Legal Thinking with Technology (Cheltenham, Edward Elgar Publishing).

[2] Perry-Kessaris, P (2019) 'Legal Design for Practice, Activism, Policy, and Research' *Journal of Law and Society* 46, 185–210.

[3] Hagan, M (2020) 'Legal Design as a Thing: A Theory of Change and a Set of Methods to Craft a Human-Centered Legal System' *Design Issues* 36, 3.

[4] Legal Design practitioners, This is Legal Design, Justice Adda, etc.

[5] Hagan, M (2021) 'Legal Design', *Law By Design*, www.lawbydesign.co/legal-design/; Perry-Kessaris, A (2021) *Doing Sociolegal Research in Design Mode* (London, Routledge).

to be. We reflect on developments not just of legal design as a practice but also in interrogating what kinds of practice(s) of legal design are gaining prominence. This includes thinking about what kinds of ideologies, vocabularies, methods, as well as projects, are visible, and in turn, influencing the shaping of the field. We are concerned with exploring the social dynamics that underpin how knowledge is being created around the dynamics of law and design, as well as the epistemic responsibility of recognising the implications of one's knowledge and the impacts on others, and how this emerges in a situated context.[6]

We are interested in the epistemologies of the everyday that emerge through routine practice, decisions, experiences, and lifeworlds. This involves paying special attention to voices that are included and excluded, both in terms of their testimonial capacity and also in a hermeneutical sense, where vocabularies may not exist to be able to conceptually engage with people's experiences.[7]

Having this epistemic reflection is important because it enables us to reflect on the *What*, *Who*, *Where*, and *How* of LD. Although there has been emphasis in literature on LD on the 'what,' the questions of *who* and *for whom*, as well as *where* and *from where*, have received little to no attention thus far. Keeping this in mind, this book aims to contribute to pluralising the discourse in the field by asking questions about what kind of narratives have emerged, and what stories need to be made more prominent and visible.

This book has emerged from a dialogue between the authors and the editors. Our collaborations first began in January 2023 through a proposal that the editors convened with the authors to the International Institute for the Sociology of Law (IISL), Onati, to host a workshop in 2024. Upon the successful application, we engaged in discussions around initial ideas of how to frame the discussion on LD, which took place online and subsequently in person at IISL in July 2024. The book brings together academics, practitioners, and activists who view LD through their locations of place, work, and identity. We aim to surface this plurality of perspectives while at the same time grounding the discussions in each chapter around the following questions:

- How far does the contribution challenge/address/highlight promises or limitations in the field of LD? What do these conclusions mean for legal research and practice generally?
- What consequences of LD – political, pedagogical, epistemic, methodological – are addressed?
- Is the chapter
  a. A call to action to build community?

[6] Haraway, D (1988) 'Situated Knowledges: The Science Question in Feminism and the Privilege of Partial Perspective' *Feminist Studies* 14, 575–599; Code, L (1987) *Epistemic Responsibility* (Hanover, NH, Published for Brown University Press by University Press of New England).

[7] Fricker, M (2007) 'Introduction' in Miranda Fricker (ed), *Epistemic Injustice: Power and the Ethics of Knowing* (Oxford, Oxford University Press).

b. A methodological contribution?
c. A practice contribution?
d. A teaching/training resource?

We are pleased to have a variety of contributions that traverse these different questions, and in their own unique ways, aim to address these pressing questions.

As Editors, we have experienced LD in different modes; we have both been researchers, entrepreneurs, and activists. Though originally from countries in the Global Majority, much of our education and academic practice has been in countries in the Global Minority. Our activist and entrepreneurial practice is more distributed and includes different locations. As a result, we bring a multiplicity of perspectives to viewing LD from being a method of inquiry, an instrument of practice, as well as a field of study.

In the next sections of this introductory chapter, we will discuss some of the ways in which LD can be conceptualised otherwise, exploring whether it serves communities, whether it has priorities, and what kinds of legal systems it aims to influence. It will discuss the many windows of LD as demonstrated in this book. We will then discuss the motivations behind LD practice, exploring what elements are important, as well as what alternatives are not included. In doing so, this chapter will next discuss how to move from LD to *legal designing* before the final section, which offers an alternative agenda/commitment/manifesto for LD as a practice going forward.

LEGAL DESIGNING: MANY FACES, MANY WINDOWS

The question of epistemic consequences is not about which epistemological standpoint should prevail, in the sense of finding or agreeing on one, totalising, way of knowing and producing knowledge[8] applied to LD. Instead, the discussions in this book reveal LD as a field ripe for a plurality of approaches to doing and knowing. The diversity of issues being addressed through LD demands from the community a rich repertoire of possibilities for action, forms in which those actions take place and actors who are driving these changes.

Therefore, to think of the socio-politics of LD is to acknowledge that, in the face of multiple approaches to change or renewal in the legal system, the decision of which approach we take is a political one and defines the possibilities and limits of the transformation we want to make in the world. Put differently, LD practitioners are equipped with tools to make change in the world, but determining which tools to use for which challenge lies at the core of a committed and responsible practice.

[8] Escobar, A (2018) 'Introduction', *Designs for the Pluriverse: Radical Interdependence, Autonomy, and the Making of Worlds* (Durham, NC, Duke University Press).

The contributions to this workshop highlight both a plurality of societal challenges and a plurality of ways to deal with them – within and beyond the traditional designerly and lawyerly ways of doing and knowing. The contributions remind us that different types of challenges, different contexts, and different times require different answers.

The first theme that emerges from the collection is exploring the tensions between the emergence of stable and dominant vocabularies around LD, which affirm the status quo, as well as critiques that challenge this process of stabilisation and interrogate the potential, as well as limitations of the critique. Michael Doherty, in **Speculation in Legal Design? Ontological Concerns and Critical Alternatives**, addresses the criticism of human-centred design in law and justice (and elsewhere); this paper reasserts the value (and limitations) of affirmative design approaches (criticised as maintainers of the status quo) along with critical and speculative design approaches. This contribution invites us to think of the multiple approaches to designing in which critical and affirmative practices are along multiple points in the continuum. Jules Rochielle Sievert, in **Broadening the Scope of Legal Design**, engages with community work carried out at the NeuLaw Lab. This chapter shows how both affirmative as well as transformative legal empowerment are necessary to bring radical change.

A second theme is that of looking at what we are centering and decentering in LD. It examines the aspects of relationality that bring with it asymmetries in legal structures, resulting in the predominance given to some points of view over others. Ebru Metin, Nina Toivonen, and Jaana Kovalainen offer in **Bridging Paradigms: Comparing the Elements of Human-Centered Design in Legal Design and People-Centered Justice Frameworks** a comparative analysis, highlighting the common grounds between human-centred design in law and people-centred justice. These two approaches to law and justice have been developed from different places – independent practice and academia, and international policy-making bodies (i.e., the Organisation for Economic Co-operation and Development, OECD); however, they have much to benefit from each other. The chapter suggests impactful alliances between the two approaches. In **Legal Design with Silent Agents – Biomimicry as a Strategy to Understand the Rationales of More-than-Human in Legal Design,** Nina Toivonen begins with the provocation: what if you could design law with a forest or a herd of cows? The chapter explores further the role of legal designing in the relationship between humans and nonhumans. It offers an account of biomimicry as a strategy to design with other agencies, based on the design principles of resonance and harmony.

The third theme looks at the question of impact in LD. It explores the ways in which standardisation and scalability are needed to ensure that LD can have the necessary value for creating change in the legal profession. Dorra Harrar in **Does the Legal Design Lexicon Need to be Designed? A Theoretical and Critical Study** explores the need for a stable vocabulary in LD practice. The paper investigates the value of having boundaries in interdisciplinary, as well as the need for a LD lexicon to have rigour through discussions of LD in the MENA region. Kanan Dhru in **The Transformative Role of the Public Sector in the Evolving Practice of Legal Design** discusses the role that partnerships can play in scaling the promise of LD. The paper advocates for a multi-stakeholder approach through a case study of working with the Election Commission in India and discusses engaging with the public sector for LD work.

The fourth theme examines the role that lawyers and the legal profession have played in shaping society for the last centuries, defining certain ways of being and certain possibilities for change. Ade Mabogunje in **Weaving an Emergent Future from an Engineering Design Perspective: Law, Science, Engineering, and Indigeneity** begins from the premise that we cannot build a better future without the legal profession. The chapter offers the proposal of weaving an emergent future that seeks ways to turn lawyers into enablers using engineering design tools such as crowdsourcing and rapid prototyping. The chapter emphasises the critical role of legal education in facilitating the social transformations required to face the challenges of today. In **Designing against 'Self-Abandonment': A U.S. Law Student's Reflections on Legal Design,** Elena Kuran offers a first-person perspective on the legal education system in the United States. The chapter argues that designerly interventions can serve as an antidote against an alienating educational project, providing spaces for social and political change. Based on the author's experience as a law student, it reflects on the toll that the current legal education in the U.S. has on students of marginalized and minoritized identities. Bhawna Parmar, in **A Grounds-up View of Design: Making Meaning of Design in India Through Rooted Legal Design Interventions,** discusses the limitations of a human-centred design approach, and argues for examining LD through grassroots interventions. Grounded in a case study from India, it argues for a design that is culturally contextual and adopts principles from design justice to empower communities and counter oppression.

The fifth theme explores citizenship, participation, and epistemic justice. It examines the role that deliberation and democratic processes play in bringing forth a liberatory practice. In **Activating Imagination to Promote Epistemic Justice: Speculations on an Island-Wide Citizens' Assembly for Cyprus,** Amanda Perry-Kessaris discusses through a case study of a citizen assembly how designerly ways can help secure epistemic justice. The chapter argues for engaging with an imagination that is both empathetic and systemic to be able to capture a variety of different futures that are grounded in people's viewpoints. In **Legal Design as Movement Lawyering Methodology: Lessons Learned at the New Jersey Legal Design Lab,** Abdul Rehman Khan and Hallie Jay Pope ask what role can LD play as a tool towards democracy, solidarity, and liberation. Through a case study from the New Jersey Design Lab, the chapter discusses the role that links between law and design, and local movements to further housing justice, creating spaces for self-determination in challenging oppressive systems. In **Can Making a Law Be Playful? A Case for Designing for Democratic Deliberation in India,** Siddharth Peter de Souza, Varsha Aithala, Siddhi Gupta, and Saumya Varma discuss through reflecting on the development of a board game 'Sabha' to show how play can be a vital pedagogical tool to stimulate civic awareness, as well as create deliberative spaces to understand how democratic processes work in action. The chapter discusses how such spaces can create new groups of political actors, by democratising knowledge around government institutions.

The sixth theme discusses legal spaces and technologies, arguing for the criticality of going beyond the neoliberal experience when we explore justice reform. This raises the spectacle of the privatisation of justice, and the implications of this for people engaging with justice systems. In **Justice Beyond the User-Experience: Designing for the Sublime in Courts,** Pablo Hermansen and Joaquín Santuber, inspired by courts and judicial processes, propose Design for the Sublime, an approach renewing the interest in rituals and transcendence in our design practices. It is articulated as a reaction to the limitations of design as problem-solving and the focus on the individual in the legal field. The proposal is grounded in two cases in which the sublime in the form of sound plays a central role. Finally, in **Beyond the Problem-Solution Paradigm in Legal Design: Making the Cloud Rain in Bahrain,** Bader Alnoaimi discusses Bahrain's Cloud First Policy. This chapter problematises the adoption of cloud technologies and its government policy. It argues that technology policy and regulation is a socio-political process, and that the 'choices hold inherent value-laden assumptions about technologies' and society. The chapter sheds light on how regulating technology is not a neutral or just technical process left to the experts, but inherently political and social.

FROM LEGAL DESIGN TO *LEGAL DESIGNING*

The question of whether LD is a discipline or not pervaded the first years of the community – with some anxiety also formulated in the form of a question, 'Is Legal Design a thing?'.[9] The answer to both questions has concrete implications: if LD is a discipline, it can have its own conferences, journals, study programmes, and even departments within the established law schools. If LD were not a discipline, it would rather try to squeeze itself into the existing conferences or journals, and be just a module or a course in study programmes and be just another desk in different departments (public law, procedural law, etc). Michael Doherty argued that LD meets the criteria to be considered an emerging discipline, highlighting the unique opportunity that LD practitioners and researchers had/have to shape how this discipline might be. In this regard, all disciplines have been created – there is no such thing as a discipline to be discovered in the

[9] Legal Design as Academic Discipline: Foundations, Methodology, Applications, at the JURIX18 Conference, December 2018. Workshops JURIX 2018 (rug.nl).

wild nature, and thus with a design mindset, the LD community could intentionally produce an academic discipline to serve its users.[10] (The question that arises from that statement is: who are those users LD serves?)

The risks of producing a discipline were that LD would add to the isolation that law as a discipline already has, a sort of impermeability to other disciplines, and perhaps LD could be seen as a subset of design, the practice of designing applied to a specific area, such as law and justice.[11] Others have argued that law and the legal profession have already been designing our being for thousands of years[12] and that LD is better captured in light of post-disciplinary ways of doing and learning.[13]

Some years later, LD now has a journal on its own,[14] a specialised track on a design conference,[15] and a vibrant community gathering in the form of a summit – all three developed intentionally as participatory initiatives, in the pursuit of a stabilising discipline. However, it is important to raise the following question: is designing a discipline ever finished?

Like any other design project, we would argue, it is never finished. As an ongoing process of designing, in this workshop/book, we have raised the question about the socio-politics of LD and their epistemic consequences. From the contributions to the workshop, we have seen that plurality is there. However, 'to attain the multiple, one must have a method that effectively constructs it […]'.[16]

Inspired by design research literature, we propose to see our work as *nomadic practices*, which embrace a multiplicity of intentionalities and diverse ways of knowing.[17] As a first step, paraphrasing Deleuze and Guattari, to think of a method that effectively constructs the multiple, is to call our work *legal designing*.

Moving from the noun *legal design* to the verb *legal designing* emphasises the practices, and the doing of the community, instead of the requirements

[10] Doherty, M (2018) *Intentionally Designing 'Legal Design' as an Academic Discipline.* Paper presented at JURIX 2018, Groningen, the Netherlands.

[11] Allbon, E and Morgan, R (2021) 'Is Law Really That Special?' in Rossana Ducato and Alain Strowel (eds), *Legal Design Perspectives. Theoretical and Practical Insights from the Field* (Milan, Ledizioni).

[12] Bhatnagar, S (2022) 'What Legal Design Is as Opposed to Could/Should Be', DRS Biennial Conference Series, dl.designresearchsociety.org/drs-conference-papers/drs2022/researchpapers/239.

[13] Santuber, J and Edelman, J (2022) 'Designing with Theories: Producing Legal Design Diffractively in Courts of Justice', DRS Biennial Conference Series, dl.designresearchsociety.org/drs-conference-papers/drs2022/researchpapers/259.

[14] *Legal Design Journal* – The first online journal dedicated solely to Legal Design, www.legaldesign-journal.com.

[15] Jackson, D and others (2022) 'What Legal Design Could Be: Towards an Expanded Practice of Inquiry, Critique, and Action' DRS Biennial Conference Series, dl.designresearchsociety.org/drs-conference-papers/drs2022/editorials/32.

[16] Deleuze, G and Guattari, F (1987) *A Thousand Plateaus: Capitalism and Schizophrenia,* translated by Brian Massumi tr, 2nd Edition (Minneapolis, MN, University of Minnesota Press).

[17] Wakkary, R (2020) 'Nomadic Practices: A Posthuman Theory for Knowing Design' *International Journal of Design* 14(1), 117–136.

to include and exclude ways of knowing and creating, and ultimately who belongs and who does not to LD. Referring to our practices as legal designing is not just a grammatical nuance, but a powerful opportunity – and a call to action to redefine the ways in which this community can participate in the metabolism of giving shape to a broadening and plural epistemology. LD as a discipline and legal designing as practices are not in a binary opposition; they co-exist and nurture from one another. This co-existence can be seen in terms of the molar and the molecular.[18] Based on Deleuze and Guattari's characterization, LD as a discipline tends to represent the molar, which is 'punctual, highly organized, easily represented, and perceived as clearly demarcated and bounded assemblages'.[19] In contrast, legal designing practices can be seen as molecular, 'vital, incessant, and unruly [...] associated with becomings of innumerable kinds',[20] operating on the microphysics level of law and design. As seen in some of the contributions to this volume, these practices may align with 'minor political actions that traverse, cross-cut, and continually undermine molar imaginations [... embodying the potential to] "thwart and break through"'[21] dominant systems of ontological and epistemological injustices.

Talking about our work as legal designing implies focusing on our practices instead of subjects or disciplines. It allows us to welcome a plurality of ways of doing and their corresponding ways of knowing, freeing us from the categories, norms, rules, and expectations agreed upon.

With the risk of being repetitive, legal designing is about practices. Practices are ways of doing, highly context-dependent, shared by a community (see communities of practice[22]), in which the shared values of the community are reified by a constant commitment to 'doing together'. A community of practice was originally defined as 'groups of people who share a concern or a passion for something they do and learn how to do it better as they interact regularly'.[23] More recently, communities of practice have been characterised as 'groups of people informally bound together by shared expertise and passion for a joint enterprise, who interact regularly to learn about or improve their practice'.[24]

Following practice-oriented research, we characterise practices as relational, sociomaterial, situated, partial, open, messy, and fluid. Each of these aspects

[18] Deleuze and Guattari (n 17).

[19] Merriman, P (2019) 'Molar and Molecular Mobilities: The Politics of Perceptible and Imperceptible Movements' *Environment and Planning D: Society and Space* 37, 65–82.

[20] ibid.

[21] Deleuze and Guattari (n 17) 216.

[22] Lave, J and Wenger, E (1991) *Situated Learning: Legitimate Peripheral Participation* (Cambridge, Cambridge University Press).

[23] Wenger, E (1998) *Communities of Practice* (Cambridge, Cambridge University Press).

[24] Nicolini, D and Monteiro, PDN (2016) 'The Practice Approach: For a Praxeology of Organizational and Management Studies' in Ann Langley and Haridimos Tsoukas (eds), *The SAGE Handbook of Process Organization Studies* (London, Sage), vol. 3 uk.sagepub.com/en-gb/eur/the-sage-handbook-of-process-organization-studies/book243122#contents.

has implications in the epistemologies of legal designing, how knowledge is produced, stored, exchanged, published, censored, and so on, and most importantly by whom, for whom, from where, to where.

The Epistemologies of *Legal Designing* as a Practice

Relational: To consider legal designing practices to be relational, means that they are not seen as isolated actions, projects, or initiatives but as interactions (or intra-actions[25]) and connections among people, objects, environments, and other practices.[26] This perspective emphasises that actions, projects, and initiatives gain meaning and significance through their relationships and interdependencies with others. Understanding legal designing practices as relational encourages a holistic, adaptable, and ethically aware approach. It highlights the interconnectedness of actions within broader networks, fostering a deeper understanding of the complexities and dynamics involved in any legal designing effort.

Sociomaterial: When thinking of practices, it is important to note that it is not just what legal designing practitioners say and do, but all the social and material conditions that make this practice possible.[27] By this, we mean that a practice is not only the designing team carrying out, but also a range of stakeholders (think of clients, end users, students, assistants, etc), infrastructures (classrooms, studios, desks, software, etc), beliefs, cultural knowledge, and social traditions. Therefore, our practices' epistemologies, and ways of creating, storing, and distributing knowledge, are embedded in the extended sociomaterial networks we deploy our work.[28]

Consider the act of scientific research: it is not solely the intellectual pursuit of knowledge, but also a practice deeply embedded in the materiality of laboratories, the technology of instruments, and the social dynamics of research teams, like hiring. The precision of an experiment relies on the calibration of instruments, the protocols developed through collaborative effort, and the historical evolution of scientific methodologies. All of these define how and what kind of knowledge is produced.[29] The same is true for legal designing with its methods, instruments, and social dynamics.

[25] Barad, K (2007) *Meeting the Universe Halfway: Quantum Physics and the Entanglement of Matter and Meaning* (Durham, NC, Duke University Press).

[26] Darian-Smith, E (2013) 'Reimagining Legal Geographies', in *Laws and Societies Global Contexts Contemporary Approaches* (Cambridge, Cambridge University Press).

[27] Santuber, J and Krawietz, L (2021) 'The Sociomateriality of Justice: A Relational Ontology for Legal Design (La Sociomaterialidad de La Justicia: Una Ontología Relacional Para El Diseño Legal)' *RChD: Creación y Pensamiento* 6, 1–20.

[28] See Perry-Kessaris in this volume.

[29] Barad, K (1999) 'Agential Realism: Feminist Interventions in Understanding Scientific Practices' in M Biagioli (ed), *The Science Studies Reader* (New York, Routledge).

By viewing legal designing practices as sociomaterial, we appreciate the mutual constitution of the social and the material. This approach dismantles the dichotomy between human agency and materiality, revealing a more nuanced understanding of how our activities are enacted and experienced. It highlights that our practices are dynamic assemblages where social relationships and material conditions continuously interact, shaping and being shaped by each other, defining our possibilities of acting, knowing, and transforming.

Situated: Practices being situated means that they are context-dependent, as well as the perspectives and commitments. Haraway in Situated Knowledges,[30] emphasises that all knowledge is subjective. That is also true for the sciences, which eloquently claim their objectivity to sustain their power. However, all knowledge is produced by someone, from somewhere, in a *somewhen*, and it is bounded both in its potential and limitations by those circumstances. Each researcher or knowing body has a lens through which they see the world, and their worldviews define what is possible and not possible in that world.[31]

Practices are therefore not neutral. They have intentionality, which members of the community share.

Moreover, in line with situatedness, practices foreground the possibilities of certain standpoints[32] and perspectives[33] as forces to create knowledge otherwise. This means that certain groups marginalised and excluded by a system can provide vantage points about the questions and knowledge about that system. This perspective cannot be achieved when looking from the centre. Communities and users are therefore not informants or interview subjects, but they create knowledge through unique forms, only possible because of the places they occupy.[34]

Partial: Practices generate knowledge that is situated, and with that comes that it is always partial.[35] It is created from somewhere, by someone(s), at a somewhen. This means that legal designing practices do not have universality claims, nor do they claim to be objective. Instead, these practices reveal an aspect of an interwoven network of novel knowledge creation ways in legal-related matters. In Barad's words – how matter comes to matter – our practices disclose certain aspects of the world, they define what matters and what doesn't, what counts and what is left out.[36]

[30] Haraway (n 7). See Parmar in this workshop.

[31] See Bhatnagar and Kuran in this workshop about judicial cases as worlds.

[32] Harding, S (1992) 'Rethinking Standpoint Epistemology: What Is "Strong Objectivity?"' *The Centennial Review* 36, 437–470.

[33] Eduardo Viveiros de Castro, *Cosmological Perspectivism in Amazonia and Elsewhere* (HAU 2012) haubooks.org/cosmological-perspectivism-in-amazonia/.

[34] See Parmar and also Sievert in this volume.

[35] See Sievert, and also Kahn and Pope in this volume.

[36] Barad, K (2003) 'Posthumanist Performativity: Toward an Understanding of How Matter Comes to Matter' *Signs: Journal of Women in Culture and Society* 28, 801.

Since the knowledge our practices produce is partial, members of this community of practice are responsible for the kinds of knowledge we produce. This responsibility starts with understanding that there are many approaches to dealing with a legal issue, and deciding which to use is a political decision, as well as the choices we make in terms of tools, software, and platforms we use.[37]

Open: As practices can be more or less stable, seeing legal designing as a practice invites more creativity, innovation, and distributed initiative.[38] Talking about legal designing is at the same an invitation to embrace indeterminacy and resist the temptations of early closure. In terms of ways of creating knowledge, openness reaffirms the commitments of the community to embrace not only alternative epistemologies, but also new forms, mixed forms, and messy forms of knowing and being.

Messy: Practices are messy. Beyond the purity and hygienic imperatives of modern science (noise removal, data cleaning) in coalition with the law (the purity of the legal profession), there is a tendency to consider valid only those measurable and formal approaches to reality – rendering secondary or in most cases invisible the messy relationships and ways of making sense or reality we live by. The lived experiences of law (a sort of phenomenology of law) are encounters that are both transcendent[39] and domestic.[40] Talking about legal designing should refigure an interest in both the domestic and the magnificent aspects of our designing practices.

Fluid: We like to see practices in legal designing as part of a continuum, in which we can move across or within.[41] In this sense, practices are permeable and porous. Therefore, the boundaries of these practices, the knowledge they produce, and how they produce are blurry and multiple. As members of the legal designing community of practice, we ought to be familiar with our ways of doing and thinking, and develop a sensibility towards the ways of others, so we can transit and dialogue with other practices beyond our onto-epistemologies.[42] Moreover, the manifolds of legal designing can only be refigured in this plurality, as reality 'can only be glimpsed through a kaleidoscope of overlapping and even contradictory points of view'.[43]

[37] For a political economy perspective on designing the law see Alnoaimi in this volume.

[38] See Dhru and also Harrar in this volume.

[39] See Hermansen and Santuber in this volume on Design for the sublime, transcendence and rituality.

[40] On integrating messiness see de Souza, SP (2022) 'Epistemic Diversity and Voices from the Global South: Countering the Managerial Implications Of Measuring Justice', in *Designing Indicators for a Plural Legal World* (Cambridge, Cambridge University Press).

[41] See Doherty and also Metin et al. in this volume.

[42] Santuber, J and Hermansen, P (2024) 'Designing for Posthuman Legalities: Legal Design(Ing) and the Ontological Turn' in Rossana Ducato, Alain Strowel and Marique Enguerrand (eds), *Design (s) for Law* (Milan,Ledizioni), doi.org/10.5281/zenodo.10829515.

[43] Davis, E (2015) *TechGnosis: Myth, Magic, & Mysticism in the Age of Information* (Berkeley, CA, North Atlantic Books), 181.

In summary, imagine legal designing as a grand tapestry (or a mesh a lá Ingold[44]), each thread weaving through countless others (human and more-than human),[45] creating practices that are intricate, dynamic, and endlessly evolving. Practices, in this tapestry, are not isolated strands but vibrant connections that bring legal designing to life. They are the dance of relations – between people, environments, and tools – each step influenced by and influencing the other. Like when one sows a seed, hands are not merely executing a task; they are conversing with the soil, responding to its vibration, guided by traditions passed down through generations, and shaping new possibilities for the future. Thus, knowledge is not in the designer, but out there. In every practice, whether it's teaching, researching, consulting, or simply caring, there lies a web of interactions – a symphony of situated engagements that infuses our actions with depth and meaning. This invitation to see legal designing as practice is to see our work not as a collection of solitary acts but as an interplay in both harmony and tension where every gesture, every decision, resonates within the larger, interconnected community. Far from a romanticised view of legal designing, seeing it as practices implies that their meaning arises from resonances and frictions within, across, and beyond them.

SOCIO-POLITICAL COMMITMENTS FOR LEGAL DESIGNING

Legal designing's radical proposal is to open up possibilities[46] for the otherwise, where *the otherwise* means alternative imaginations, vocabularies, and conceptual ideas. In this vein, possibilities emerge for participation otherwise, for engaging with power hierarchies otherwise, for thinking of the political action of our methods otherwise, for narratives, plurality, scale, and sustainability to become otherwise.

What kinds of commitments do we need to move from LD to legal designing? As a process that is ongoing, iterative, and dynamic, what nature should such commitments take? Should they be tentative, open, or suggestive? Should they have some degree of certainty to ensure adherence to them?

The Legal Design Alliance took on the challenging task of writing a manifesto for the field.[47] In its work, it set about thinking of what would help increase the understanding of the field, as well as of its use. Our exercise is to explore what is required to shift the focus in the discipline to placing importance on practice, and alternative imaginaries of knowing and doing LD. We like to see

[44] Ingold, T (2022) *The Perception of the Environment : Essays on Livelihood, Dwelling and Skill* (London, Routledge), www.taylorfrancis.com/books/9780203466025.

[45] See Mabogunje, and also Toivonen in this volume.

[46] Possible is an adjective that means 'that may be, capable of existing, occurring, or being done' from www.etymonline.com/word/possible.

[47] The Legal Design Alliance, www.legaldesignalliance.org/.

this more as a series of propositions to which we could commit. A community of practice(s) that shares some values. The propositions were worked together with the workshop participants and authors of the chapters of this book at two moments. First, based on their contribution, we elaborated a list of propositions to serve as the basis for discussion at the workshop. Below are some of the propositions we discussed during the workshop.

- Legal designing should engage with the power hierarchies that are emerging in its field.
- Legal designing uses methods in a socio-political sense – how can we be equipped to make choices while addressing the political consequences?
- Legal designing is a political exercise; it can challenge existing narratives in legal systems.
- Legal designing is participatory – in how far are the voices of those under-represented included in practices of the field.
- Legal designing should be plural, in how far can it be scalable as well as plural?
- Legal designing should engage with economic interests openly but not be driven by them.
- Legal designing needs to offer sustainable alternatives; are designs made for time?

Second, during the workshop, at the beginning and end of each day, we allocated generous time to discuss the nuanced reactions and understandings of the workshop participants in smaller groups and in the plenum.

The general agreement was that while earlier attempts at definitions and manifestos were normatively written and tended to closure, ie, LD is human-centered. In our discussions, we all acknowledged that while legal designing includes practices that follow human-centred design approaches, it is not limited to it. A key component of legal designing is to think about, the 'co', ie, the community around the design intervention, which might influence, shape, or even transform ways of thinking. In a similar vein, practices are not exclusive; they are not either human-centred or critical, but can be both. In this regard, we celebrated the openness of legal designing, which offered spaces to dismantle the binaries and to imagine unusual possibilities: how legal designing for a law firm can also be participatory by bringing in voices not represented within the organisation, or can be radically critical, challenging power dynamics between client and lawyer. Likewise, community-driven legal designing can be transformative in offering immediate support for pressing issues like housing, while affirming current systems and structures of injustice. Aware of unavoidable economic interests in modern societies, legal designing offers possibilities to engage with them differently as context and goals require. In terms of plurality and the question of locality of scalability, instead of opposite concepts, legal designing understands them as different strategies suitable at different moments and in different contexts.

In summary, at the core of these commitments, it is the basic principle: where there is a dogma (legal, economic, spatial, temporal, etc), legal designing is there to offer possibilities for acting and doing.[48] In these commitments, there are no right or wrong ways of legal designing, but a repertoire of practices that are situated, relational, fluid, and messy. As such, there is no right way of legal designing; there are many practices that align more or less to certain goals depending on the context, time, people, and conditions.

REFERENCES

Allbon, E and Morgan R (2021) 'Is Law Really That Special?' in Rossana Ducato and Alain Strowel (eds), *Legal Design Perspectives. Theoretical and Practical Insights from the Field* (Milan, Ledizioni).

Barad, K (1999) 'Agential Realism: Feminist Interventions in Understanding Scientific Practices' in M Biagioli (ed), *The Science Studies Reader* (New York, Routledge).

—— (2003) 'Posthumanist Performativity: Toward an Understanding of How Matter Comes to Matter' *Signs: Journal of Women in Culture and Society* 28, 801.

—— (2007) *Meeting the Universe Halfway: Quantum Physics and the Entanglement of Matter and Meaning* (Durham, NC, Duke University Press).

Bhatnagar, S (2022) 'What Legal Design Is as Opposed to Could/Should Be' *DRS Biennial Conference Series*.

Code, L (1987) *Epistemic Responsibility* (Hanover, NH, Published for Brown University Press by University Press of New England).

Darian-Smith, E (2013) 'Reimagining Legal Geographies', in *Laws and Societies Global Contexts Contemporary Approaches* (Cambridge, Cambridge University Press).

Davis, E, *TechGnosis: Myth, Magic, & Mysticism in the Age of Information* (Berkeley, CA, North Atlantic Books).

De Souza, SP (2022) 'Epistemic Diversity and Voices from the Global South: Countering the Managerial Implications Of Measuring Justice', in *Designing Indicators for a Plural Legal World* (Cambridge, Cambridge University Press).

Deleuze, G and Guattari, F (1987) *A Thousand Plateaus: Capitalism and Schizophrenia*, translated by Brian Massumi, 2nd Edition (Minneapolis, MN, University of Minnesota Press).

Doherty, M (2018) 'Intentionally Designing 'Legal Design' as an Academic Discipline. Paper presented at JURIX 2018, Groningen, the Netherlands.

Doherty, M et al. (2021) 'A New Attitude to Law's Empire: The Potentialities of Legal Design' in Marcelo Corrales Compagnucci et al. (eds), *Legal Design: Integrating*

[48] The idea of design research as opposed to dogmas came from Prof. Larry Leifer, director of the Center for Design Research at Stanford University. In one of the Design Thinking Research Program community-building workshops hosted in Potsdam, he went to the board where "D.T." was written in big letters (in reference to Design Thinking), replaced D.T. with 'Dogma.Thinking', in clear critique to the path design thinking was taking as a method and set of rules (or dogmas) to be followed.

Business, Design and Legal Thinking with Technology (Cheltenham, Edward Elgar Publishing).
Escobar, A (2018) 'Introduction', in *Designs for the Pluriverse: Radical Interdependence, Autonomy, and the Making of Worlds* (Durham, NC, Duke University Press).
Etmyonline.com (Website)
Fricker, M (2007). 'Introduction' in Miranda Fricker (ed), *Epistemic Injustice: Power and the Ethics of Knowing* (Oxford, Oxford University Press).
Hagan, M (2021) 'Legal Design', *Law By Design*.
—— (2020) 'Legal Design as a Thing: A Theory of Change and a Set of Methods to Craft a Human-Centered Legal System' *Design Issues* 36.
Haraway, D (1988) 'Situated Knowledges: The Science Question in Feminism and the Privilege of Partial Perspective' *Feminist Studies* 14, 575–599.
Harding, S (1992) 'Rethinking Standpoint Epistemology: What Is "Strong Objectivity?"' *The Centennial Review* 36, 437–470.
Ingold, T (2002) *The Perception of the Environment : Essays on Livelihood, Dwelling and Skill* (London, Routledge).
Jackson, D, and others (2022) 'What Legal Design Could Be: Towards an Expanded Practice of Inquiry, Critique, and Action' *DRS Biennial Conference Series*.
Kolko, J (2011) *Thoughts on Interaction Design* (Waltham, MA, Elsevier).
Lave, J and Wenger, E (1991) *Situated Learning: Legitimate Peripheral Participation* (Cambridge, Cambridge University Press).
Legal Design Alliance (Website)
Legal Design Journal – The first online journal dedicated solely to Legal Design (legaldesign-journal.com)
Legal Design as Academic Discipline: Foundations, Methodology, Applications, at the JURIX18 Conference, December 2018. Workshops JURIX 2018 (rug.nl)
Merriman, P (2019) 'Molar and Molecular Mobilities: The Politics of Perceptible and Imperceptible Movements' *Environment and Planning D: Society and Space* 37, 65–82.
Moggridge, B (2007) *Designing Interactions* (Cambridge, MA, MIT Press).
Nicolini, D and Monteiro, PDN (2016) 'The Practice Approach : For a Praxeology of Organizational and Management Studies' in Ann Langley and Haridimos Tsoukas (eds), *The SAGE Handbook of Process Organization Studies* (London, Sage 2016), vol 3.
Norman, DA (1988) *The Psychology of Everyday Things* (New York, Basic Books).
—— (2013) *The Design of Everyday Things: Revised and Expanded Edition* (New York, Basic Books).
Perry-Kessaris, A (2019) 'Legal Design for Practice, Activism, Policy, and Research' *Journal of Law and Society* 46, 185–210.
—— (2021) *Doing Sociolegal Research in Design Mode* (London, Routledge).
Santuber, J and Edelman, J (2022) 'Designing with Theories: Producing Legal Design Diffractively in Courts of Justice' *DRS Biennial Conference Series*.
Santuber, J and Hermansen, P (2024) 'Designing for Posthuman Legalities: Legal Design(Ing) and the Ontological Turn' in Rossana Ducato, Alain Strowel and Marique Enguerrand (eds), *Design (s) for Law* (Milan, Ledizioni).
Santuber, J and Krawietz, L (2021) 'The Sociomateriality of Justice: A Relational Ontology for Legal Design (La Sociomaterialidad de La Justicia: Una Ontología Relacional Para El Diseño Legal)' *RChD: Creación y Pensamiento* 6, 1–20.

Santuber, J (2023) 'Designing for Digital Justice' (Doctoral Thesis, University of Potsdam).
Santuber, J, Refaie, RA and Meinel, C (2022) 'Interrogating E-Justice: Lessons from Digitalizing Courts in Chile' *EGOV-CeDEM-ePart 2022* 54–65.
Seitz, T (2020) *Design Thinking and the New Spirit of Capitalism: Sociological Reflections on Innovation Culture* (Cham, Springer International Publishing).
Simon, H (1969) *The Sciences of the Artificial* (Cambridge, MA, MIT Press).
Viveiros de Castro, E (2012) *Cosmological Perspectivism in Amazonia and Elsewhere* (New York, Hau Books).
Wakkary, R (2020) 'Nomadic Practices: A Posthuman Theory for Knowing Design' *International Journal of Design* 14(1), 117–136.
Wenger, E (1998) *Communities of Practice* (Cambridge, Cambridge University Press).

1

Speculation in Legal Design? Ontological Concerns and Critical Alternatives

MICHAEL DOHERTY[1]

INTRODUCTION

SPECULATION IN LEGAL design is having its first 'moment', with a number of legal designers arguing for the adoption of speculative approaches. Speculative critical design (SCD) is often presented as a counterpoint to 'affirmative design', a comparison that often seeks to contrast how speculative design is seen as more innovative, creative, free-spirited, progressive, and ambitious than its timid cousin. Speculative design seeks to boldly imagine new worlds that support and liberate ordinary citizens. Affirmative design, in this account, merely aims at making the pain of the status quo less acute or the inequitable society more efficient without undoing its inequity. The inequitable state of law as a social system is readily apparent, so this distinction in design concepts is felt particularly sharply in our domain.

This paper, framed as a methodological and conceptual contribution to the debate, takes aim at this characterisation in two ways. First, it seeks to challenge the ontological dualism inherent in most presentations of speculative design. As well as an unjustified appropriation of the word 'critical', this categorisation underappreciates the radicalism, imagination, and innovation in mainstream legal design. We should see the ontology of design not as a dualistic categorisation but as points along a spectrum that is largely defined by scale (time, geographic and demographic scope). Seeing design in this way opens up space to recognise and celebrate criticality (or to criticise its absence) along multiple points of the spectrum.

Second, it highlights some concerns about the place and usage of speculation in the legal design repertoire. These include its departure from the pragmatic

[1] Lancaster University, UK.

iterative development of solutions to problems that are grounded in present realities. Ultimately, speculative design has its place in a pluralistic field of practice in extending the imaginative reach of design. It is, though, often ill-equipped to leverage concrete practical change in the social systems it seeks to reimagine, including law, and the most defensible forms of speculative design are still reasonably closely connected to mainstream design mindsets and methods.

To clarify, the paper does not seek to criticise imagination, innovation, or radical ambition in legal design. It does not argue against trying to identify potentially reachable future states that would resolve or ameliorate present troubles in legal systems, even in relation to those problems that are currently emergent or on the horizon. It does argue that we do not need a separate category of design demarcated as 'speculative critical design' to do so, and that the tools and mindsets of what is called 'mainstream design' can be used in ways that are critical of the status quo.

SPECULATIVE CRITICAL DESIGN

The Workshop on the Socio-Politics of Legal Design and their Epistemic Consequences (Oñati International Institute for the Sociology of Law, 2024) invited us to think critically about legal design, and in particular to 'interrogate the emergence of vocabularies of the emergent field and unpack their epistemic consequences'. The legal design stream at the DRS 2022 similarly aimed 'to generate a shared language around what legal design could be'. It is useful, therefore, to connect our understanding of criticality with how this concept is understood in the wider design world.

The starting point is the work of Anthony Dunne and Fiona Raby. In the Design Interactions Department at the Royal College of Arts in the 1990s and early 2000s, they developed conceptions of critical design and speculative design, with a definition that 'critical design uses speculative design proposals to challenge narrow assumptions, preconceptions, and givens about the role products play in everyday life'.[2] They further explain that 'Critical designs are testimonials to what could be, but at the same time, they offer alternatives that highlight weaknesses within existing normality'.[3]

They take an expansive view of what speculative design is, including 'critical design, design fiction, design futures, antidesign, radical design, interrogative design, design for debate, adversarial design, discursive design, futurescaping, and some design art'.[4] For Dunne and Raby, at least, speculative design is *the key mindset and method* of critical design – the concepts are largely coterminous.

[2] A Dunne and F Raby, *Speculative Everything: Design, Fiction, and Social Dreaming* (Cambridge, MA, The MIT Press 2013) 34.
[3] ibid 35.
[4] ibid 11.

It is important to note that the origins of SCD were in counterpoint. Dunne and Raby describe how they began a list – the A/B list: 'In it, we juxtaposed design as it is usually understood with the kind of design we found ourselves doing. B was not intended to replace A but to simply add another dimension, something to compare it to and facilitate discussion'.[5] Contrasting pairs included …

A	B
Affirmative	Critical
Problem solving	Problem finding
Provides answers	Asks questions
In the service of industry	In the service of society
For how the world is	For how the world could be
Innovation	Provocation
Makes us buy	Makes us think

James Auger further explains that SCD:

> (i) moves away from the constraints of the commercial practice (steered by the market); (ii) uses fiction and speculates on future products, services, systems and worlds, thus reflectively examining the role and impact of new technologies on everyday life; (iii) and initiates dialogue between experts (scientists, engineers and designers) and users of new technologies (the audience).[6]

For Mitrović, speculative design is about creating space for considering alternative possibilities: 'Through its imagination and radical approach, by using design as a medium, it propels thinking, raises awareness, questions, provokes action, opens discussions, and can offer alternatives that are necessary in today's world'.[7]

It is hard to pick out a representative sample of SCD examples from those used by Dunne and Raby due to their diversity; however, it is important to have a picture of the sorts of things that were in their minds when they developed these conceptual categories – not least for when we apply the concept to the legal field. They talk, for example, of the conceptual designs of Jurgen Bey on social and political issues. In 2007, Bey created *Slow Car*. This is a motorised office chair and desk enclosure 'designed to question our use of time spent in cars in highly congested cities. It is not intended to be mass produced but to circulate through exhibitions and publications'.[8]

[5] ibid 1.

[6] I Mitrović, 'Introduction to Speculative Design Practice' (*Speculative*, 4 May 2016) speculative.hr/en/introduction-to-speculative-design-practice/.

[7] ibid.

[8] Dunne and Raby (n 2) 18.

Another example comes from the design studio Superflux, which created the *Song of the Machine* project in 2011. This is a video that:

> shows the world seen through a prosthetic device for people with reduced vision. Rather than simply replacing what has been lost, the proposal suggests technology could be used to enhance our vision, letting the wearer see parts of the light spectrum beyond human capability, infrared and ultraviolet, for example.[9]

The influence of SCD within the design world has grown since its initial development, and Lindley and Green talk of the 'burgeoning Speculative Design community'.[10]

For advocates of SCD, it stands in a different category to what is variously called affirmative design, or traditional/mainstream design: 'Its opposite is affirmative design: design that reinforces the status quo'.[11] This dualistic categorisation of speculative design is echoed in the way it is often presented as one of two possible positions on the nature and role of design. Mitrović, for example, says 'whereas traditional design actually legitimizes the status quo, speculative design envisages and anticipates the future, at the same time helping us to understand and re-think the world of today'.[12]

SCD and Legal Design

The ontology and methods of SCD are important to law because there has been recent enthusiasm for the potential of SCD in legal design. Perhaps the most fully formed speculative legal design project so far is Phoebe Walton's *James v Birnmann*, a speculative future scenario exploring the performativity of court processes and the potential impact of artificial intelligence.[13] Walton, a designer in an architecture studio at the RCA, refers to her approach more often as critical design but indicates that it uses 'speculative design proposals' and explicitly draws on Dunne and Raby's work. Karma Dabaghi proposes that legal design takes a more critical and speculative turn: 'a speculative legal design can engage in futuring that can help the legal profession develop strategies and methods for holding powerful institutions and powerful individuals to account'.[14] She speculates on the potential of forensic architecture to be applied

[9] ibid.

[10] J Lindley and DP Green, 'The Ultimate Measure of Success for Speculative Design Is to Disappear Completely' (2021) Interaction Design and Architecture(s) 32, 42.

[11] Dunne and Raby (n 2) 35.

[12] Mitrović (n 6).

[13] P Walton, 'James v Birnmann: The Potential of Critical Design for Examining Legal Issues' (2022) dl.designresearchsociety.org/drs-conference-papers/drs2022/researchpapers/106.

[14] K Dabaghi, 'Beyond Design Thinking and into Speculative Futures in Legal Design' (2022) dl.designresearchsociety.org/drs-conference-papers/drs2022/researchpapers/70.

in a future-looking proactive way to avoid regulatory failures such as the Beirut port explosion of 2020.

Emily MacLoud, a legal designer at Portable in Australia, gives a full and positive outline of speculative design and how it can be applied to legal design.[15] Barbara Pasa and Gianni Sinni of the University of Venice advocate for speculative approaches in law and describe how they use SCD methods, including 'provotypes', in their educational practice.[16] Provotypes have also been discussed by Jaana Kovalainen and Hilja Autto of the University of Lapland.[17]

We can see this speculative and critical turn in legal design reflected in conferences and events. The Legal Design Roundtable, Brussels 2023, encouraged designers to go 'beyond design thinking', and speakers like Monica Palmirani discussed extended reality, whilst **Joaquín Santuber** and **Pablo Hermansen** explored designing for posthuman legalities.[18] Mel Flanagan also discussed a beyond-human vision for legal design at the Legal Design Summit, Helsinki 2023.[19] The Oñati IISL workshop posited a very deprecatory view of how legal design has evolved: 'as a Trojan horse to impose the market values over those of democracy, justice and equality'. The legal design stream at the Design Research Society conference, Bilbao 2022, has been the deepest engagement, so far, between legal design and the wider design research discipline, and it asked us to consider 'what legal design could be' with a much greater focus on critique. It condemned existing approaches to legal design as 'largely affirmative [in] maintaining the status quo with proposals that are too narrow in scope, reductive in nature, or constrained in capacity" and invited us to learn from more speculative and critical approaches.[20] We return below to the question of just how 'affirmative' and uncritical mainstream legal design really is.

[15] E MacLoud, 'An Exercise in Speculative Legal Design' in Rossana Ducato, Enguerrand Marique and Alain Strowel (eds), *Design(s) for Law* (Milan, Ledizioni, 2024).

[16] B Pasa and G Sinni, 'New Frontiers of Legal Knowledge: How Design *Provotypes* Can Contribute to Legal Change' in Alain Strowel, Rossana Ducato and Enguerrand Marique (eds), *Design(s) for Law* (Milan, Ledizioni, 2024).

[17] J Kovalainen and H Autto, 'Do we legal designers dare to provotype?' *Legal Design Roundtable*, 2023 uclouvain.be/fr/instituts-recherche/juri/crides/evenements/legal-design-roundtable-2023-design-s-for-law-17-2-23.html.

[18] M Palmirani, 'Extended Reality and Legal Design' (*Legal Design Roundtable*, 2023) uclouvain.be/fr/instituts-recherche/juri/crides/evenements/legal-design-roundtable-2023-design-s-for-law-17-2-23.html; J Santuber and P Hermansen, 'Designing for Posthuman Legalities: Legal Design(ing) and the Ontological Turn' in Alain Strowel, Rossana Ducato and Enguerrand Marique (eds), *Design(s) for Law* (Milan, Ledizioni, 2024).

[19] M Flanagan, 'Visualising Laws for Clarity, Connection and Collaboration' (Legal Design Summit, 2023).

[20] 'What Legal Design Could Be: Towards An Expanded Practice of Inquiry, Critique, and Action' (2022) www.drs2022.org.

RATIONALE FOR DEVELOPMENT OF THE SCD CONCEPT

I have never seen this question posed: what problems were Dunne and Raby trying to solve by creating a label of speculative design? It might be because SCD explicitly moves away from problem-solving, but I think it is still a pertinent question in identifying the roots and aims of the categorisation. Looking at their published work and those of their former students, such as Auger, I propose that the intention was to address two problems in design practice, as they saw it. First, its commercial focus, and second, its limited scale.

Ivica Mitrović argues that design has primarily involved problem-solving in relation to problems identified by others. That is, it has **served the needs of industry**, and primarily addressed clients' needs.[21] It could be argued further that it is not so much clients as businesses who have benefited, by using design methods to increase sales, market share, customer satisfaction, shareholder value, etc.

Dunne and Raby said that design had been used so far:

> mainly to sell new ideas and future technologies to consumers. One of the things we were trying to do … was to relocate this way of designing from a strictly commercial context into one where it could be used for other purposes.[22]

Enfants terribles of design, such as Enzo Mari, have long berated the consumer 'pornography' of design.[23]

Dunne and Raby's background is mainly in product and technology design, and they acknowledge that there are different parts of the design world that do not have this same commercial context. They are keen, though, to *exclude most of this work* from the category of SCD:

> *It is different from social and humanitarian design, and design thinking too, which, although also often rejecting market-driven design, still operate within the limits of reality as it is. This is very important for us.* We are not talking about a space for experimenting with how things are now, making them better or different, but about other possibilities altogether.[24]

(I have added emphasis here to illustrate just how restrictive and exclusionary this initial formulation of the design categories was).

Just as significant as the move away from commercial client-centred briefs and projects is **the question of scale**. Dunne and Raby posit the need for SCD in global challenges such as 'overpopulation, water shortages, and climate change'. They question the traditional designer mindset and toolkit 'as though

[21] Mitrović (n 6).

[22] 'Interview with Antony Dunne and Fiona Raby' (*Speculative EDU*, 2 August 2019) speculativeedu.eu/interview-dunne-raby/.

[23] 'Icon (Profile of Enzo Mari, 2009)' (*ICON Magazine*, 18 December 2009) www.iconeye.com/design/enzo-mari.

[24] Dunne and Raby (n 2) 12.

[these problems] can be broken down, quantified, and solved'. They go on to argue: 'Design's inherent optimism leaves no alternative but it is becoming clear that many of the challenges we face today are unfixable and that the only way to overcome them is by changing our values, beliefs, attitudes, and behavior'.[25]

With respect, this does not make a lot of sense. It allows that mindsets and behaviours can be changed (or 'fixed'), and that this will allow us to overcome the problems ('fix them'), but that the problems are themselves 'unfixable'. If we speculate that Dunne and Raby are making a different point – that traditional (or affirmative) design with its emphasis on breaking down problems, quantifying them, and (trying to) solve them is incapable of successfully addressing global mega-challenges – then it makes more logical sense, but also opens the argument to empirical refutation.

We can use, as an example, an issue mentioned by Dunne and Raby themselves – overpopulation. This is not a speculative problem. It is a large-scale ongoing issue that will have future negative effects on sustainability, biodiversity, and human health. It is also an issue that seems to be not only fixable but is in the process of (slowly) being fixed, in part by policy interventions that draw on mainstream design.

'Peak child', the year in which the largest number of children were born, happened around 35 years ago in 1990. The peak in global population is estimated to arrive somewhere between 2060 and 2080 – at around 9.5 billion – before a projected decline.[26] Lower population growth rates appear to be tied, to a significant extent, to economic development, regardless of policy initiatives, but health and education policy interventions (often drawing on mainstream social design methodologies) have a record of success and impact.

These interventions are particularly those policies for the education and empowerment of women to control their fertility. Significant contributions have been made by processes of breaking down and quantifying problems, listening to people, understanding the reality of their current lives, developing ideas that might have traction with this reality, prototyping them with users, applying them, and iterating (eg, Bangladesh Ministry of Health, 2012).[27] The Gapminder Foundation have done important work in showing that the perception of population growth as an intractable problem is grounded in Western ignorance of the realities of life outside of the Western world – a wider criticism that is made of some forms of speculative design.[28]

[25] ibid 4.

[26] NV Bhattacharjee and others, 'Global Fertility in 204 Countries and Territories, 1950–2021, with Forecasts to 2100: A Comprehensive Demographic Analysis for the Global Burden of Disease Study 2021' (2024) 403 *The Lancet* 2057.

[27] 'Bangladesh Population Policy 2012', bangladesh.gov.bd/sites/default/files/files/bangladesh.gov.bd/policy/98896a22_df81_4a82_b70c_24125dec56d7/Bangladesh-Population-Policy-2012.pdf.

[28] 'A Paradox: Less People If More Survive' (*Gapminder*, 2023) www.gapminder.org/topics/typical-family-size/; J Thackara, 'Republic of Salivation (Michael Burton and Michiko Nitta)' (*Design and*

Dunne and Raby argue that:

> Although essential most of the time, design's inbuilt optimism can greatly complicate things, first, as a form of denial that the problems we face are more serious than they appear, and second, by channelling energy and resources into fiddling with the world out there rather than the ideas and attitudes inside our heads that shape the world out there.[29]

The first objection really does not flow from the inherent nature of design, even in the mainstream forms of service design or design thinking, although we can admit it might come from the lived experience of being an art/design school's 'classically trained designer' working in a commercial context on briefs set by clients. However, the design world is much wider and in places very different from this. It has been embraced by government services, academia (beyond art/design), civil society, and justice groups who would never think of design in this limited way. Engineering, social policy, and design efforts on issues like clean energy, etc, do not seem to deny or underestimate the challenges of the climate emergency, but rather than retreat to imagined future utopias, they offer concrete solutions to the problems of changing the carbon-based foundations of modern capitalism. This is important for why and how legal designers adopt SCD. Legal design has a very different (albeit short) background, trajectory, and scope to the worldview that the dualist ontology of '*SCD vs affirmative design*' came from. Discussions of speculative design in law need to be alive to this.

The second objection is also problematic. It denounces design interventions that make an impact on the world as 'fiddling', in favour of thought experiments that will either stay in our heads or have to be implemented in the world through design interventions. Dunne and Raby say that 'Designers start by identifying shortcomings in the thing they are redesigning and offer a better version'.[30] That is, mainstream design is not a fundamentally different approach. It is a question of scale. This is obliquely acknowledged when they write:

> The subject can vary. On the most basic level it is about questioning underlying assumptions in design itself, on the next level it is directed at the technology industry and its market-driven limitations, and beyond that, general social theory, politics, and ideology.[31]

Violence, 19 December 2013) www.moma.org/interactives/exhibitions/2013/designandviolence/republic-of-salivation-michael-burton-and-michiko-nitta/. Not all organisations are as sanguine as this about the continuing risks of overpopulation, eg, Population Matters populationmatters.org/ though such organisations also emphasise the (urgent) need for the sort of engaged human-centric public policy interventions that can be informed by design.

[29] Dunne and Raby (n 2) 2.

[30] ibid 35.

[31] ibid.

Scale can be measured on a different axis – that of time. It is here, rather than in the size of current problems, that speculative design seems to find its place. Mitrovic (n.d.) argues that design is based on:

> the observation and understanding of the world around us ... The problem arises when we want to expand the horizon of our observation in order to identify emergent themes. The question is how to begin with the design of concepts when we do not know what the design space itself will look like, let alone who its users will be.[32]

We explore some reservations about this future-casting form of SCD below.

THE ONTOLOGY OF SCD

The response to the challenges of commercial focus and scale, identified above, was an ontological one. It sought to establish two categories of design: one that draws on the repertoire of mainstream design, that is deeply concerned with 'the problem' and that (in this account) is affirmative of the status quo; and another that is critical of existing social ordering, that has a more ambitious scope in the timeline and scale of the issues it considers and that requires a speculative design approach. Malpass places speculative design as a particular mode within a wider umbrella of Critical Design. The critical approaches to design all 'serve to challenge orthodox conceptions of design and extend the agency of design and the matters of concern that design might typically engage'. I find this ontological dualism unrealistic and unhelpful, particularly when it co-opts the term 'critical'.

These taxonomies of design types are reductive, and paint what they label as 'affirmative design' into a corner. They deny the existence of critical approaches to forms of design – particularly those that provoke thought and strive for a better world – that do not involve the distinctive characteristics of speculative design.

We should acknowledge, and appreciate, the lack of fundamentalism in Dunne and Raby's conception of SCD, as well as their insistence that it is 'another dimension' of design. In this sense, the ontology is more dualistic than dialectic: 'We believe that some design should always question prevailing values and their underlying assumptions and that this activity can sit beside mainstream design rather than replace it'.[33] Lindley and Green also emphasise that it is not a panacea or a replacement for more 'scientific' approaches to design knowledge creation.[34]

[32] Mitrović (n 6).
[33] Dunne and Raby (n 2) 44.
[34] Lindley and Green (n 10) 36.

This distinction between what is variously called mainstream design, design thinking, and affirmative design on the one hand (Type A) and speculative and critical design (Type B) on the other is also reflected in the legal design scholarship. MacLoud defines design thinking as 'a problem-solving method that applies the creative design process to traditional business problems … Design thinking is not enough. … It maintains the status quo'.[35] Yet, design thinking is not necessarily so limited. It has been applied to a wide range of non-business social and humanitarian ends in legal and in other fields of design.

MacLoud follows the dualistic categorisation in contrasting design thinking with 'Speculative design [that] falls within the umbrella concept of critical design, which offers a way to confront and challenge existing power imbalances'.[36] In terms of ontological organisation she places speculative within the wider movement of critical design, but this is very much in contrast to 'the opposite of affirmative design'. Pasa and Simmi frame this as a distinction between 'backward-looking reference systems' of legal change as compared to 'speculative design and storytelling as tools for legal and policy change: what we have named forward-looking reference systems'.[37]

Does a Dualistic Categorisation of Design Work?

Cameron Tonkinwise is a noted critic of the ontological distinction between 'speculative and critical' design and a category of 'other' types of design: 'Designing that does not already Future, Fiction, Speculate, Criticize, Provoke, Discourse, Interrogate, Probe, Play, is inadequate designing'.[38] He explains 'Every time you qualify design with, or add design to, some other quality or practice, you are claiming that design does not already do that'. It is worse than mislabelling – it amounts to an appropriation of the qualifying term. This is particularly egregious in relation to the qualifier 'critical' in legal design.

There are signs that later authors have taken a more nuanced view of the categories of design approaches, including in legal design. In a legal context, the categorisation is not, in the main, adopted by Amanda Perry-Kessaris. Her work articulates the need for working with 'legal futures' and describes some of the projects referenced here (including, eg, Walton's court project), but she does not generally draw on the framework or terminology labels of SCD.[39] Indeed, much

[35] MacLoud (n 15).

[36] ibid 75.

[37] Pasa and Sinni (n 16) 46.

[38] C Tonkinwise, 'Just Design' (*Medium*, 21 August 2015) medium.com/@camerontw/just-design-b1f97cb3996f.

[39] A Perry-Kessaris, *Doing Sociolegal Research in Design Mode* (London, Routledge, Taylor & Francis Group, 2023).

of Perry-Kessaris's work in legal design can be seen as a call for criticality,[40] which (it is argued here) indicates scope for critical forms of legal design that do not draw on the mindsets, methods, or taxonomies of speculative design. Hallie Jay Pope through various papers and presentations has also expressed dissatisfaction with forms of legal design that affirm the status quo. Whilst she has drawn on some speculative future fiction methods, she presents her work using the language of liberation and solidarity more than speculation.[41]

Even MacLoud, whose has arguably been the strongest advocate of speculation in legal design, does not regard the categorisation as being A/B. Whilst retaining the concepts of critical and affirmative design, she sees particular methods as landing on a spectrum somewhere between the two concepts (along with other spectrums, eg, qualitative and quantitative), and that speculation is something that extends the capabilities, the imaginative reach, of designers.[42] This sense of additionality and adding to the existing repertoire is also seen in the design research fields. Lindley and Green, while providing a robust defence of speculation, emphasise that SCD should not 'alone – become the default means of making sense of our world' but rather hope that it should become 'a normal and not-unexpected tool in the box of available methods', and that it should 'augment' mainstream design methods.[43]

Does So-called Affirmative Design Maintain the Status Quo?

Much of what is called affirmative design does not support the status quo, certainly in the field of legal design. It changes it to a contingent and new existing state of affairs. We can highlight two examples of legal design projects that *could* conceivably, under the SCD ontology, be characterized as 'affirmative design'. Robert de Rooy and Creative Contracts reimagined the employment contract and presented it in a comic book format, eg, for fruit pickers in South Africa.[44] The Amurabi legal design agency has worked with large corporations on compliance with, eg, anti-corruption regulations.[45]

[40] A Perry-Kessaris, '"Unlimiting" Legal Conceptualisation in Designerly Ways' (Edinburgh Centre for Legal Theory Seminar, 16 November 2023) www.ssrn.com/abstract=4621423.

[41] H Pope, 'Liberatory Legal Design and Radical Imagination' (2022) dl.designresearchsociety.org/drs-conference-papers/drs2022/researchpapers/254; H Pope, 'Designing to Dismantle' in Amanda Perry-Kessaris and Emily Allbon (eds), *Design in Legal Education* (London, Routledge 2023).

[42] Personal correspondence, 16 June 2024.

[43] Lindley and Green (n 10) 43 & 47; Lindley and Green, above n 9, 43 and 47.

[44] 'Creative Contracts, Clemengold Comic Contract' creative-contracts.com/examples/; A Kletola, R de Rooy and H Haapio, 'Comic Contracts 2.0 – Contracts That Have (and Give) a Voice' in Alain Strowel, Enguerrand Marique and Rossana Ducato (eds), *Design(s) for Law* (Milan, Ledizioni, 2024).

[45] 'Compliance Design with Marie Potel-Saville and Elisabeth Talbourdet' podcasts.apple.com/us/podcast/episode-7-compliance-design-with-marie-potel-saville/id1556020090?i=1000516681436; 'Portfolio – Compliance Projects' (*Amurabi*) amurabi.eu/en/categorie_projets/compliance/.

Both series of projects work within existing paradigms – those of labour practices in the South African fruit-picking industry and the regulation of corporate activities under national and EU law. They do not explicitly seek to reform the substantive content of the legal frameworks or the overall justice of the socio-economic conditions of these facets of capitalism. In the dismissive terminology of SCD, they could be called 'affirmative design', or merely 'fiddling'.

Yet, neither of them *actually* accepts the status quo, particularly on the usefulness of legal documents or regulatory processes. They use imaginative and radical forms of innovation. They imagine different futures, albeit within the scope of the particular projects they were working on. They are connected to 'the problem' and aim to bring direct and tangible benefits to people, corporations, and society. They are also, to some extent, 'critical'.

A comic contract, for example, can have the effect of changing power dynamics in employment relations. This is more obvious when it effectively communicates employees' rights under the contract, but even where it clarifies the responsibilities of the employee, it allows them to exercise some agency. If employment relationships are not regulated, at least in part, by the legal contract, then they are governed by something else, ie, power, largely informational and economic, and often arbitrary.

A core element of criticality lies in examining power relationships in society and in questioning their fairness. We can do a similar 'critique of power in society' analysis of anti-corruption work. Anti-corruption laws are motivated by a range of factors. Corruption is economically inefficient, and it is also immoral. It degrades trust in institutions and society. In an international context, it often amounts to a colonialist abuse of power that leverages the effects of inequality. Making existing anti-corruption rules more efficacious changes the status quo and serves critical goals.

It is, of course, possible to imagine legal design projects that are not capable of being framed as 'critical' in this way. Such projects might adopt user research, ideation, prototyping, and better visualisation methods simply to sell more legal services – the sort of consumerism that alienated mainstream designers in the first place. This, though, has not been the mainstay, the dominant paradigm, of the legal design movement, and those who characterise that movement as largely affirmative need to be clearer on whose work they are basing this judgement on.

This section has criticised the ontology of SCD, particularly its dualism. This is on the grounds that it co-opts 'critical' and tries to make it coterminous with speculative design. This denies 'criticality' to the 'other'. It is reductive, and an ontology map of design really needs to be seen as a spectrum or more likely a series of spectrums. It affixes the rather derogatory label of 'affirmative design' to a wide range of work that is not just socially useful but that shows a deep understanding of power and equity in society and, by trying to address it (in what might be called piecemeal ways) change the status quo.

SCD METHODS

It is often said that speculative design is more of a mindset than a set of methods.[46] There are, however, some methods particularly associated with speculative design, often involving fictional scenarios and the use of 'what-if' questions. They draw on:

> the methodological playgrounds of cinema, literature, science, ethics, politics, and art … [embracing] fictional worlds, cautionary tales, what-if scenarios, thought experiments, counterfactuals, reductio ad absurdum experiments, prefigurative futures, and so on.[47]

They are often based in the near future and are 'informed extrapolations of existing product lineages'.[48]

Mitrović connects speculative design to science fiction: 'Imaginary worlds are an exceptional source of inspiration to designers in their re-thinking of the future'. She also includes in the palette of speculative design methods many things that are used in mainstream design such as storyboarding, user testing, and interviews/questionnaires.[49] MacLoud contrasts the problem-focused approach of design thinking with speculative design where 'instead of identifying problems, speculative designers identify hopes and fears, weak signals and insights generated from extrapolating data and projections'.[50]

Separated from the World

Dunne and Raby explain that 'The usual channels [for speculative design outputs] are exhibitions, publications, press, and the Internet. Each channel or medium creates its own issues of accessibility, elitism, populism, sophistication, audience, and so on'.[51] In a legal context, MacLoud argues that it is a benefit of SCD that it provides the 'opportunity to solve problems that may not yet be problematic'[52] and similarly, Dabaghi identifies the most potent drawback of design thinking in its focus 'on solving problems that already exist'.[53] It is argued here that SCD runs the risk that, as it does not draw on the experience of real problems in the current world, its outputs may have little to say to people facing those real problems. This can shade into speculation being a place of indulgence freed from the responsibility of direct contact with a group of people who need help in the present.

[46] Dunne and Raby (n 2); MacLoud (n 15).
[47] Dunne and Raby (n 2) 3.
[48] J Auger, 'Why Robot? Speculative Design, the Domestication of Technology and the Considered Future' (PhD Thesis, Royal College of Art, 2012) researchonline.rca.ac.uk/1660/.
[49] Mitrović (n 6).
[50] MacLoud (n 15) 77–78.
[51] Dunne and Raby (n 2) 139.
[52] MacLoud (n 15) 78.
[53] Dabaghi (n 14).

Speculative designers, including legal ones, have been alive to these criticisms. MacLoud says 'that scenarios should avoid straying into the zone of fantasy, nor should they present a world where everyone gets along or where technological silver bullets have saved the day'.[54] She highlights the work of organisations such as Mantis Systems, who within a speculative design project on global risk systems used desk research, ethnographic research, and interviews with experts: 'This highlights the rigour involved and the types of research that can be carried out to ensure the speculative designs focus on problems that are relevant and of concern to the audience of interest'.[55] It also shows that the forms of SCD that are more easily defended as robust and relevant draw on mainstream design methods. Pasa and Sinni agree that effective speculative design cannot be 'a mere exercise in futurology" and that it should "address the shortcomings of our current understanding of how legal change takes place and broaden our understanding of key aspects of the law'.[56] That is, effective SCD does not stray too far from the world of current problems.

Top-down and Designer-centric Concerns

The core strengths of mainstream design methods include rejecting assumptions in favour of research, seeking to understand the whole lived reality of users, and testing ideas and prototypes with the people who will be affected by them. This can lead us to a related criticism of SCD: since it does not seek to explore the lived reality of people facing current problems, it inevitably centres the designer.

Mitrović addresses this risk:

> Speculative practice may seem as a top-down approach at first glance, placing the designer at the centre of the process, offering her personal vision, without involving the target audience, [but] one of the main goals of speculation is the inclusion of the public in the re-thinking and dialogue on new technological realities and new social relations. Also, a successful speculative project is necessarily connected to the research of a social context and is fundamentally directed towards the individual needs and desires.[57]

This makes a lot of sense, but also reinforces the impression that SCD works best when it is closely aligned with the methods and aims of mainstream design: that it is best understood as being a little further along a spectrum rather than as a separate category.

[54] MacLoud (n 15) 89.
[55] ibid 107.
[56] Pasa and Sinni (n 16) 54.
[57] Mitrović (n 6).

Pasa and Sinni argue that SCD practices 'do not run the risk of distraction or self-indulgence' but rather focus on concrete legal change in moving us 'from where we are now to where we would like to be'.[58] They further explain, however, that their work is implemented through more mainstream participatory and social interaction practices – indeed, one of the key methods they use in their workshops with students is the standard mainstream design method of ecosystem mapping. This theme of participation and connection to current social realities is also found in MacLoud's legal argument for SCD.

'The Problem'

SCD disavows the centrality of 'the problem'. In design thinking, it is normally the privilege of the users (or potential users) of a service to define what the problem is. Mainstream design actually does ask us to speculate. We are invited to pause feasibility and take part in exercises like brain-writing to generate ideas free from constraints. These take place, however, within the context of a concrete and present problem, so that we can generate ideas that we immediately return to the touchstone of the problem. SCD does not have this anchor. MacLoud admits that choosing the right problem is challenging in SCD, because the issues it 'calls into question are often so nebulous and systemic'.[59]

We can find a difficulty with this shift away from 'the problem' in the political and social philosophy of Karl Popper. For Popper, 'All of life is problem solving', and this is reflected in his political philosophy of incremental rather than utopia-driven change. The task of social change:

> begins with the problem itself, and with the reasons for it being a problem. One learns to work hard and long on formulations of problems before one switches one's main attention to the search for possible solutions; and one's degree of success in the latter is often determined by one's degree of success in the former.[60]

Popper would also argue that 'grappling' with real problems means that 'one will be existentially committed to one's work … and the work will have what the Existentialists call 'authenticity' … It will be not only an intellectual interest but an emotional involvement, the meeting of a felt human need'.[61]

SCD is often portrayed as a bolder and braver version of design, compared to forms of design that are grounded in the world as it is. Popper would take issue with this characterisation and say that problem solving 'puts the greatest

[58] Pasa and Sinni (n 16) 48; Pasa and Sinni, above (n 15), 48.

[59] MacLoud (n 15) 105.

[60] Bryan Magee, *Popper* (London, Routledge 1975) 66.Popper is arguably *the* proto-design philosopher, even though his thought continues to be misunderstood in design circles, see, eg, Lindley and Green presenting his scientific philosophy as aspiring for theories to be 'fixed', when it rests entirely on knowledge being provisional.

[61] ibid 68.

premium of all on boldness of imagination' and is 'fundamentally at variance with all views of science or rationality which see these as excluding passion or imagination or creative intuition'.[62] The problem is also a strong provoker of innovation – if we go where it takes us. This is often beyond existing disciplinary boundaries and other manifestations of the status quo.

SCD AND EFFECTIVENESS

Perry-Kessaris, drawing on Manzini, argues that legal design mindsets should be 'practical-critical-imaginative'.[63] It is argued here that SCD appeals to the imaginative aspect of this triumvirate but is very weak on practicality, lacking a coherent theory of change. In part, Dunne and Raby do not see this as a problem: conceptual designs 'celebrate their unreality and take full advantage of being made from ideas', they 'emphasize imagination over practicality'.[64] They also argue that 'The project's value is not what it achieves or does but what it is and how it makes people feel, especially if it encourages people to question, in an imaginative, troubling, and thoughtful way, everydayness and how things could be different' and that speculation is more about 'providing complicated pleasure, enriching our mental lives, and broadening our minds in ways that complement other media and disciplines'.[65] They do reflect, however, that 'we feel that the privileged space of conceptual design should serve a purpose. It is not enough that it simply exists and can be used to experiment or entertain; we also want it to be useful, to have a sort of social usefulness'.[66]

Legal designers like MacLoud also emphasise the need for this bias towards action.

> Without this [commitment to action] a lack of control may start to set in and along with it, the preferable futures may become just another workshop relic, that's too distant, too fleeting and too hard to attain … As designers, there is a need to create things that have an impact and are useful. This last element gives speculative design its edge.[67]

MacLoud is insistent, however, that speculative design actually does catalyse action:

> The outputs of speculative design are created to make future possibilities tangible and to call into question aspects of the here and now. When these outputs are done

[62] ibid.
[63] Perry-Kessaris (n 40).
[64] Dunne and Raby (n 2) 12.
[65] ibid 189.
[66] ibid 139.
[67] MacLoud (n 15) 82.

> well, they have the potential to make the impact of the future possibilities compelling in a way that no amount of data can.[68]

Dunne and Raby similarly argue that speculative future scenarios can serve as inspiration for policymakers, but there is no detailed sense of how this might occur, or how it might be better in helping make laws and legal systems (and the experience of them) more effective than mainstream design.[69] It is outside of the scope of this paper, but the lens of immanent critique may be useful in evaluating the extent to which SCD has a theory of change. It could particularly highlight that many speculative exercises generate critiques that are 'transcendent' in nature. That is, they draw on values that are external to the system they are critiquing and can therefore be easier to dismiss and resist. It is unfortunate that Dunne and Raby explicitly reject the Frankfurt School notion of 'critical theory' that informs much of the social and political science conception of what critique involves. They are also sceptical about the need to evaluate the impact of SCD projects. There are obvious difficulties in undertaking such evaluations, but to reject attempts to evaluate the work abdicates responsibility for design creating change in the world.

CONCLUSION

Perhaps there were parts of the design world that needed the jolt of speculative design – a provocation to pay attention to the consumer consequences of design outputs and to see the products they designed as part of wider social, political, and ecological systems. The logical and ontological defects of SCD may have been a price worth paying for that disruption. Much of the work of the legal design movement over the past decade or so, however, does not have this context. A dualistic categorisation between critical/speculative design on the one hand and affirmative/mainstream on the other is not a useful ontology for our field. In co-opting the word 'critical' and linking it so closely to speculative design, it denies the deep social understanding and ambitions for change that mark many non-speculative legal design projects and hides the creative elements of future-thinking and status-quo-changing that they embody. It also categorises as 'critical' forms of speculation that have no real strategy for change.[70]

There is clearly a complementary role for speculation in legal design, particularly in creating design knowledge outside of 'society's dominant models of

[68] ibid 78.

[69] Dunne and Raby (n 2) 65.

[70] Interestingly Dunne recognises that speculation has been used in design often in strictly commercial contexts simply to sell 'more stuff', using the example of concept cars in the auto industry; as discussed in Lindley and Green (n 10).

knowing';[71] however, it is argued here that even these forms work best when they are reasonably closely connected to near-futures, to mainstream design methods and to (the multitude) of real and serious problems that people face in our legal systems.

REFERENCES

'A Paradox: Less People If More Survive' (*Gapminder*, 2023) <https://www.gapminder.org/topics/typical-family-size/> accessed 23 August 2024.

Amurabi (Portfolio – Compliance Projects) <https://amurabi.eu/en/categorie_projets/compliance/> accessed 23 August 2024.

J Auger, 'Speculative design: crafting the speculation', (2013) 24(1) Digital Creativity 11.

J Auger, 'Why Robot? Speculative Design, the Domestication of Technology and the Considered Future' (PhD Thesis, Royal College of Art, 2012) <https://researchonline.rca.ac.uk/1660/> accessed 23 August 2024.

'Bangladesh Population Policy 2012' <https://bangladesh.gov.bd/sites/default/files/files/bangladesh.gov.bd/policy/98896a22_df81_4a82_b70c_24125dec56d7/Bangladesh-Population-Policy-2012.pdf> accessed 23 August 2024.

NV Bhattacharjee and others, 'Global Fertility in 204 Countries and Territories, 1950–2021, with Forecasts to 2100: A Comprehensive Demographic Analysis for the Global Burden of Disease Study 2021' (2024) 403 *The Lancet* 2057.

'Compliance Design with Marie Potel-Saville and Elisabeth Talbourdet' <https://podcasts.apple.com/us/podcast/episode-7-compliance-design-with-marie-potel-saville/id1556020090?i=1000516681436> accessed 23 August 2024.

'Creative Contracts, Clemengold Comic Contract' <https://creative-contracts.com/examples/> accessed 23 August 2024.

K Dabaghi, 'Beyond Design Thinking and into Speculative Futures in Legal Design' (2022), in Lockton D, Lenzi S, Hekkert P, Oak A, Sádaba J, and Lloyd P (eds) *DRS2022: Bilbao*. <https://dl.designresearchsociety.org/cgi/viewcontent.cgi?article=2868&context=drs-conference-papers> accessed 23 August 2024.

A Dunne and F Raby, *Speculative Everything: Design, Fiction, and Social Dreaming* (Cambridge, MA, The MIT Press, 2013).

M Flanagan, 'Visualising Laws for Clarity, Connection and Collaboration' (Legal Design Summit, 2023).

'Icon (Profile of Enzo Mari, 2009)' (*ICON Magazine*, 18 December 2009) <https://www.iconeye.com/design/enzo-mari> accessed 23 August 2024.

'Interview with Antony Dunne and Fiona Raby' (*Speculative EDU*, 2 August 2019).

D Jackson, Sievert JR, Kim, M, and Bhatnagar S, 'What legal design could be: Towards an expanded practice of inquiry, critique, and action', in Lockton D, Lenzi S, Hekkert P, Oak A, Sádaba J, and Lloyd P (eds) *DRS2022: Bilbao*. <https://dl.designresearchsociety.org/drs-conference-papers/drs2022/editorials/32/> accessed 23 August 2024.

A Kletola, R de Rooy and H Haapio, 'Comic Contracts 2.0 – Contracts That Have (and Give) a Voice' in Alain Strowel, Enguerrand Marique and Rossana Ducato (eds), *Design(s) for Law* (Milan, Ledizioni, 2024).

[71] ibid 33.

J Lindley and DP Green, 'The Ultimate Measure of Success for Speculative Design Is to Disappear Completely' (2021) *Interaction Design and Architecture(s)* 32.

E MacLoud, 'An Exercise in Speculative Legal Design' in Rossana Ducato, Enguerrand Marique and Alain Strowel (eds), *Design(s) for Law* (Milan, Ledizioni, 2024).

B Magee, *Popper* (London, Routledge, 1975).

I Mitrović, 'Introduction to Speculative Design Practice' (*Speculative*, 4 May 2016).

M Palmirani, 'Extended Reality and Legal Design' (*Legal Design Roundtable*, 2023).

B Pasa and G Sinni, 'New Frontiers of Legal Knowledge: How Design Provotypes Can Contribute to Legal Change' in Alain Strowel, Rossana Ducato and Enguerrand Marique (eds), *Design(s) for Law* (Milan, Ledizioni, 2024).

A Perry-Kessaris, 'Could alternative econo-legal futures be made more possible and probable through prefigurative design? Insights from and for Cyprus', (2021) 72(4) NILQ, 623.

A Perry-Kessaris, *Doing Sociolegal Research in Design Mode* (London, Routledge, Taylor & Francis Group, 2023).

A Perry-Kessaris, 'Working with Legal Futures: Conceptualising, Investigating, Imagining and Making', <https://papers.ssrn.com/sol3/papers.cfm?abstract_id=4572756> accessed 23 August 2024.

——, '"Unlimiting" Legal Conceptualisation in Designerly Ways' (Edinburgh Centre for Legal Theory Seminar, 16 November 2023).

H Pope, 'Liberatory Legal Design and Radical Imagination' (2022), in Lockton D, Lenzi S, Hekkert P, Oak A, Sádaba J, and Lloyd P (eds) *DRS2022: Bilbao*. <https://dl.designresearchsociety.org/drs-conference-papers/drs2022/researchpapers/254/> accessed 23 August 2024.

——, 'Designing to Dismantle' in Amanda Perry-Kessaris and Emily Allbon (eds), *Design in Legal Education* (London, Routledge 2023).

'Portfolio – Compliance Projects' (*Amurabi*).

J Santuber and P Hermansen, 'Designing for Posthuman Legalities: Legal Design(ing) and the Ontological Turn' in Alain Strowel, Rossana Ducato and Enguerrand Marique (eds), *Design(s) for Law* (Milan, Ledizioni, 2024).

J Thackara, 'Republic of Salivation (Michael Burton and Michiko Nitta)' (*Design and Violence*, 19 December 2013).

C Tonkinwise, 'How We Intend to Future: Review of Anthony Dunne and Fiona Raby, Speculative Everything: Design, Fiction, and Social Dreaming' (2014) 12(2) Design Philosophy Papers 169.

C Tonkinwise, 'Just Design' (*Medium*, 21 August 2015).

P Walton, 'James v Birnmann: The Potential of Critical Design for Examining Legal Issues' (2022), in Lockton D, Lenzi S, Hekkert P, Oak A, Sádaba J, and Lloyd P (eds) *DRS2022: Bilbao*. <https://dl.designresearchsociety.org/cgi/viewcontent.cgi?article=2904&context=drs-conference-papers> accessed 23 August 2024.

2

Broadening the Scope of Legal Design

JULES ROCHIELLE SIEVERT

INTRODUCTION

THE WORLD IS currently grappling with an unprecedented convergence of crises: geopolitical instability, climate change, economic inequality, mass migration, and the erosion of democratic norms. These challenges are placing immense strain on legal and political systems that were never designed to handle such complexity. Law, as traditionally structured, often assumes a level of stability and predictability that no longer exists. In response, legal systems must evolve beyond policy reform or procedural adjustments through a fundamental rethinking of how law is experienced, designed, accessed, and practiced.

The socio-political dimensions of legal design shape not only the accessibility and functionality of legal systems but also how law itself is experienced, conceptualised, interpreted, and practiced. Legal design is inherently political, embedded within power structures that dictate who can meaningfully engage with legal processes and whose voices are marginalised. Traditionally, it has reinforced dominant epistemologies and institutional logics, prioritising efficiency and proceduralism over inclusivity and accessibility. These limitations underscore the urgent need for a reimagined approach that moves beyond conventional frameworks to actively centre alternative epistemologies and the voices of those historically excluded from legal processes.

Addressing these shortcomings requires a fundamental shift towards a transformative, transdisciplinary, and practice-based design research approach. This shift moves beyond critique to actively reimagine law in ways that embrace multiple ways of knowing, being, and engaging with justice beyond dominant legal traditions. It challenges legal design to move beyond static models and instead engage with law as a dynamic site of negotiation and co-creation.

Transformative transdisciplinarity in legal design strengthens a critical legal empowerment (CLE) framework by prioritising legal agency, participatory knowledge production, and bottom-up approaches to justice. This aligns with the principle that legal knowledge should not remain confined within elite institutions but must be accessible, co-produced, and mobilised by those directly impacted by the law.

By integrating insights from design research, the social sciences, and community-driven practices, this framework for legal design can foster more participatory and contextually grounded forms of knowledge production. This approach not only challenges existing hierarchies within the legal system but also expands its epistemic foundations, making legal structures more adaptable, equitable, and responsive to evolving societal conditions and needs because it offers a framework that includes the discourse and participation of other disciplines and stakeholders outside of the legal profession.

CHALLENGING THE NOTION OF THE END USER

Rethinking legal design requires a departure from a lawyer-driven model towards one that fosters collective agency. Achieving this shift necessitates cross-sector collaboration, bringing together design professionals, community organisers, social scientists, technologists, and other key stakeholders. By centring user agency and incorporating diverse knowledge systems, legal design can move beyond top-down, expert-driven paradigms. Instead, it can embrace a more equitable and transformative framework rooted in co-created solutions that reflect the lived realities of those it seeks to serve.

The concept of the '*end user*' in legal design and law is a reductive framing that oversimplifies legal subjectivity, agency, and participation. Borrowed from product and service design, this notion implies a passive recipient of a pre-structured system rather than an active co-creator of legal meaning and practice. It often aligns with neoliberal logics of efficiency, usability, and consumer-centred design, which can obscure deeper power dynamics and structural inequalities within legal systems.

This critique parallels debates in human–computer interaction (HCI), particularly those articulated by Pedro Ferreira, José Abdelnour-Nocera, and Hugo G. Nicolau in *User Oppression in Human-Computer Interaction: A Dialectical-Existential Perspective*, they argue that systemic oppression in HCI reduces opportunities for users to 'become-more' by limiting their agency through design practices that reinforce existing hierarchies.[1]

Rather than empowering users to actively engage with technology, many systems confine them to passive roles, perpetuating a 'user-as-object' paradigm. Freire's framework highlights how both designers and users are dehumanised: designers by maintaining control and users by being denied opportunities for creative and transformative participation.[2]

The authors highlight that systemic oppression in HCI stems from a profound power imbalance in which designers control the development and

[1] RF Gonzatto and FMC van Amstel, 'User Oppression in Human-Computer Interaction: A Dialectical-Existential Perspective' (2022) 74(5) *Aslib Journal of Information Management* 763–764.
[2] ibid 764.

creation technology development, leaving 'users' confined to passive roles with little opportunity to influence or modify the systems they rely on, asserting that this imbalance can be intensified by intersecting oppressions, including racism, sexism, and ableism, which are ingrained in systemic practices. In addition, they critique 'userism' as an ideological framework that perpetuates these inequalities by framing users as reliant on designers for technological progress, reinforcing a hierarchical structure that limits users' ability to actively engage in or contribute to technology production.

Transdisciplinary and transformative research (TTR) aims to address systemic injustices through participatory, justice centred methods. Mertens states that the transformative paradigm is grounded in understanding how power dynamics play out in research and practice, stating that this dynamic must be considered at every stage of the research process. One of the most critical early decisions is defining the research focus. Although researchers traditionally rely on scholarly literature to identify research problems, transformative mixed methods research incorporates both quantitative and qualitative approaches to shape the research direction, with a particular emphasis on addressing power imbalances. A key strategy within this paradigm is actively engaging community members in the initial discussions to ensure their perspectives inform the research focus.[3]

Mertens outlines the four foundational assumptions of the transformative paradigm, emphasising its commitment to social justice and power-conscious research practices.

- The ***ontological assumption*** asserts that reality is socially constructed and shaped by power dynamics, necessitating critical analysis of whose reality is privileged in research.
- The ***epistemological assumption*** stresses the importance of an interactive relationship between researchers and participants, acknowledging that knowledge is historically and culturally situated.
- The ***methodological assumption*** promotes the use of quantitative, qualitative, or mixed methods, ensuring that research is participatory and responsive to cultural complexity while explicitly addressing issues of power, oppression, and discrimination.
- Lastly, an ***axiological assumption*** integrates ethical principles of respect, beneficence, and justice, extending these to emphasise human rights and the advancement of social justice through research processes and outcomes.[4]

To challenge the deeply embedded power imbalances in design, where 'end-users' are often positioned as passive recipients rather than active contributors,

[3] DM Mertens, 'Transformative Paradigm: Mixed Methods and Social Justice' (2007) 1(3) *Journal of Mixed Methods Research* 212.

[4] ibid 215–216.

participatory and transdisciplinary methodologies seek to redistribute authority and power. This justice-based approach helps to ensure that design happens in ways that actively respond to the needs and lived realities of communities.

Method Insights: Trauma Informed Understandings

Using a trauma-informed justice lens is central to this type of community-engaged work. Because systemic injustices produce and perpetuate trauma, participatory design must move beyond inclusion to recognise and address the emotional, psychological, and historical wounds carried by marginalised communities. A trauma-informed approach ensures that participation does not become another site of harm, instead it aims to build spaces for agency, trust, and healing. Cayley Balser and Antonio M. Coronado argue for trauma-informed legal practices as a means of addressing systemic inequities in access to justice, they write about the value of an applied power-conscious perspective in legal advocacy and discuss how trauma-informed legal practices have become increasingly critical, as most individuals in the United States have encountered at least one traumatic event.[5]

Such experiences can have lasting effects on physical health, potentially disrupting the functioning of major bodily systems. In addition, trauma can significantly impact mental health, leading to behavioural changes, memory difficulties, challenges in completing daily tasks, struggles with interpersonal relationships, and symptoms commonly linked to post-traumatic stress disorder (PTSD).[6] Existing research explores the connection between past traumatic experiences and subsequent interactions with the civil justice system, highlighting the ways in which trauma shapes individuals' engagement with legal processes.[7] Trauma is defined as '*an event, series of events, or a set of circumstances an individual experiences as physically or emotionally harmful or threatening, which may have lasting adverse effects on the individual's functioning and mental, physical, social, emotional, or spiritual well-being*'.[8] It can be experienced at individual, generational, or community levels, with systemic and historical factors playing a role in its perpetuation.[9]

This awareness recognises the widespread impact of trauma, understands potential paths for recovery, and fully integrates trauma knowledge into

[5] C Balser and AM Coronado, 'Power-Conscious Legal Work: Building a Roadmap for Rural Access to Justice Through Trust, Accountability, & Trauma-Informed Practices' (2024) *Alaska Law Review* 146.

[6] ibid.

[7] ibid.

[8] Substance Abuse and Mental Health Services Administration (SAMHSA), *Practical Guide for Implementing a Trauma-Informed Approach* (SAMHSA Publication No. PEP23-06-05-005, 2023) 1.

[9] ibid.

the design of policies, procedures, and practices, while actively working to prevent re-traumatisation.[10] This approach is particularly crucial in fields like law, healthcare, social services, and education, where understanding trauma-informed principles can lead to better outcomes for affected individuals.[11]

This approach fundamentally challenges existing legal hierarchies and power structures, requires legal professionals, designers, activists, and community members, operate from a shared and continually reinforced set of values. This approach is discussed in *Making Power Explicit: Using Values and Power Mapping to Guide Power-Diverse Participatory Action Research Processes*, Littman and others explore how a participatory action research (PAR) team navigated power dynamics through a values-driven approach. The study highlights how the team, composed of university-based researchers and peer support specialists with lived experience of homelessness, used core values to guide their decision-making and interactions. These values are structured by centring lived experience, multiple truths, practicing humility, and person-first approach. Each play a crucial role in ensuring equitable participation and fostering meaningful collaboration. By making these values explicit, the team was able to address tensions, power imbalances, and challenges inherent in the PAR process.[12]

The process described by Littman's team requires both trauma-informed practices and values alignment, because it operates in a context where power imbalances, historical injustices, and lived experiences of trauma shape interactions and decision-making. To meaningfully engage individuals with lived experience of homelessness, the research team had to ensure that their process was not only participatory but also healing, empowering, and non-extractive. Trauma-informed practices and values alignment are interdependent in this context – one cannot be fully effective without the other.

I. Core Values and their Role in the PAR Process

Core values are agreements that are created and determined by a group; they can be modified over time and co-created through an open and intentional community discourse. Littman's team outlined how the use of core values, such as *centring lived experience, embracing multiple truths, practising humility, and adopting a person-first approach*, provided a guiding framework for collaboration and power-sharing across the participatory process.

Lived experience is a value that centres the embodied knowledge and wisdom of those with firsthand experience. The authors describe how their

[10] ibid.

[11] ibid 2.

[12] DM Littman, K Bender, M Mollica, J Erangey, T Lucas and C Marvin, 'Making Power Explicit: Using Values and Power Mapping to Guide Power-Diverse Participatory Action Research Processes' (2021) 59 *Journal of Community Psychology* 266.

team explicitly centred the lived experience of the peer support specialists, whose insights shaped coding decisions during data analysis and ensured that research categories accurately represented participants' realities.[13] The authors value and recognise that *multiple truths* coexist within any group. They describe a process of surfacing and navigating tensions between differing perspectives to ensure inclusivity and epistemic plurality.[14]

Practising humility enables teams to recognise mistakes and respond to power missteps through restorative dialogue. They describe a moment when university researchers unintentionally overstepped during a peer-led session, prompting reflection and adjustment. The safety created through the value alignment process allowed the peer leaders to address the overreach, leading the researchers to recognise their mistake, apologise, and adjust their approach.[15] In the research process, the authors suggest using a *person-first* approach that recognises each team member as an individual before their role as a researcher, accommodating personal needs, and valuing well-being over rigid deadlines.[16]

In summary, the values outlined above provided a structured foundation for addressing and mitigating power imbalances, supporting collective decision-making, and ensuring that collaboration remained equitable and anchored in shared purpose, regardless of positional authority. This values-based approach offers a model for other power-diverse teams engaged in participatory research, emphasising the importance of intentionality in cultivating the conditions necessary for a collaborative transdisciplinary and transformative inquiry.

BRIEF CASE STUDY: EAST BOSTON SPATIAL JUSTICE LAB

Tedeschi and Sievert (2024) define spatial justice as the recognition that *justice and injustice are always spatially situated*, occurring within the spaces people inhabit, not apart from them. They argue that space is not a passive background but an *active condition that shapes, mediates, and expresses justice and injustice.*[17] Highlighting how spatial justice is deeply embedded in the routines, interactions, and structures that shape everyday life. They emphasise that injustices are not merely abstract concepts but are experienced through spatial practices and social dynamics. They argue that design research plays a crucial

[13] ibid 272, 273–74.
[14] ibid.
[15] ibid 273.
[16] ibid 275.
[17] Miriam Tedeschi and Jules Rochielle Sievert, 'Spatial Justice in Design Research: A Transdisciplinary Discourse' in C Gray, E Ciliotta Chehade, P Hekkert, L Forlano, P Ciuccarelli and P Lloyd (eds), *DRS2024: Boston, 23–28 June 2024* (Design Research Society 2024) 1.

role in making these inequities visible, offering creative and transformative approaches to challenge and reconfigure unjust spatial conditions.[18]

In 2017, as part of NuLawLab's exploratory research into applied legal empowerment through community-engaged design, the team began its collaboration with Boston's housing justice movement through the *Stable Ground* project, supported by two grants from the Kresge Foundation's Arts & Culture programme. This initiative addressed the intersections of chronic housing insecurity, psychological trauma, and municipal housing policy through participatory, community-based arts and cultural programming. By embedding artists-in-residence, legal designers, and trauma specialists within neighbourhood settings, the project sought to inform the work of Boston's Office of Housing Stability (OHS) while cultivating resilience, solidarity, and community empowerment.

The artists-in-residence for *Stable Ground were* Ngoc-Tran Vu, L'Merchie Frazier, and Anna Meyer, each artist played a significant role in advancing this exploratory research effort, contributing distinct creative practices that deepened community dialogue and informed the project's justice-oriented approach. Their creative practices introduced fresh perspectives and innovative methodologies, engaging communities, and amplifying the voices of individuals and groups often excluded from policy discussions. Stable Ground also collaborated with key community organisations, including City Life/Vida Urbana, Violence Transformed, Dorchester Not for Sale, and Boston's OHS. Together, this network of grassroots activists, cultural workers, and policymakers worked collectively to address systemic inequities and envision a more equitable future for Boston's neighbourhoods.

In May 2019, a collaboration with artist Anthony Romero led to the creation of *Fight Displacement!*, a trivia board game designed to educate Bostonians about resisting displacement and influencing neighbourhood development. This project was part of Romero's broader work, "*… first in thought, then in action,*" exhibited at the Institute of Contemporary Art's *When Home Won't Let You Stay: Migration through Contemporary Art*. The collaboration demonstrated how institutions could meaningfully support residents while producing innovative art, connecting new audiences to exhibitions, and establishing long-term community partnerships.

The second phase of Stable Ground faced significant challenges due to the COVID-19 pandemic. In response, the coalition built on lessons learned during the initial phase to address the emerging housing crisis. With in-person arts and cultural programming suspended, the team redirected remaining funds to establish Stable Ground: Boston Housing Support Stations (BHSSC), focusing on eviction response support in East Boston. From 2020 onward, BHSSC

[18] ibid 2–4.

became a collaborative project designed to counter the wave of mass evictions resulting from COVID-19 economic instability and Boston's ongoing housing crisis.

The initiative provided residents experiencing housing insecurity with technological access and legal knowledge to defend themselves against eviction. Each *eviction defense terminal* was equipped with a laptop, printer, resources, and legal tools necessary to navigate the eviction process. In addition, the team organised direct action, supported Section 8 tenants at Maverick Landing, and provided weekly groceries, rental relief application assistance, and access to technology to empower residents facing economic hardship.

Emerging from the pandemic into the endemic phase of COVID-19, BHSSC received a Public Art for Spatial Justice Grant from the New England Foundation of the Arts in 2022. This grant facilitated ongoing collaboration with artists Gabriela Cartagena and Anthony Romero. The resulting initiatives included multilingual comic strips and life-sized public art installations; these creative and participatory efforts build solidarity and amplify diverse voices in the fight for housing justice. The collective efforts of *Stable Ground, Fight Displacement!*, and the *Boston Housing Support Station Coalition (BHSSC)* laid the foundation for the creation of the EBSJL. Each project contributed to a growing framework of participatory and arts-based approaches aimed at addressing systemic inequities. These efforts established a dynamic space where legal practitioners, artists, community organisers, and residents collaborated to tackle complex challenges and co-create sustainable, community-driven solutions.

Today, EBSJL stands as a transdisciplinary research practice committed to collective action, housing justice, coalition building, and equitable community development. At its core are guiding values that emphasise connection, equity, and solidarity, forming the bedrock of the Lab's initiatives. The NuLawLab, is situated at Northeastern University School of Law and through grant funding, it provides EBSJL with core ongoing organisational stability, institutional resources, and expertise in managing multidisciplinary teams. Partnerships with established, community-engaged artists anchor the Lab's work in neighbourhood-scale, resident-driven, and place-based practices. This collaboration also continued to deepen the relationship with Maverick Landing Community Services, City Life/Vida Urbana, and other community-based collectives and organizations.

Legal advocacy remains central to EBSJL's mission. Through past collaborations with the Northeastern University School of Law Housing Clinic and local partners, EBSJL has built an infrastructure that provides legal support and peer-driven legal information networks for residents facing displacement. This integration of legal empowerment and grassroots advocacy reinforces EBSJL's commitment to advancing systemic justice for marginalised communities.

Methods Insights: Building Core Values Through Collective Action and Collaboration

It is important to note that our core team had the necessary time to co-develop core values because we were supported by a trust-based, grant-funded structure that allowed and supported this form of community-based practice. The funding created conditions for sustained dialogue and participatory planning to support a long-term collaboration. This support allowed us to cultivate a set of values that supported collective decision-making, while deepening alignment among partners to ensure that our work was guided by shared principles rather than external pressures. More funders need to recognise that transformative, community-led initiatives require not only financial investment but also the trust, flexibility, and continuity needed to nurture genuine collaboration and systemic change.

To date, this core team includes Maverick Landing Community Services (Rita Lara and Maxwell Chezam), NuLawLab (Jules Rochielle and Dan Jackson), and our group of artists and community builders (Gabriela Cartagena, Paola Ruiz, and William Wallace). This sustained partnership has allowed us to expand community outreach, strengthen community networks, and provide economic support to a growing coalition of organisers and community builders committed to reclaiming equitable spaces while addressing systemic housing inequities. NuLawLab would not have been able to sustain this type of practice without our deep connection to our partners, artists, and local community builders.

Creating spatial justice is an active, collective process that unfolds through solidarity, collaboration, and sustained community action. It is not merely a theoretical construct but a lived practice, realised through participatory engagement, legal empowerment, cultural organising, and arts-based advocacy. This work demands community-driven solutions that integrate lived experience, legal advocacy, and creative intervention. By positioning communities as co-creators, spatial justice moves beyond theory to become a practice grounded in collective action, mutual care, and the radical reimagining of space as a site for equity, inclusion, and belonging.

As part of this collective process, the EBSJL operates through a set of core values and justice-oriented principles that guide its efforts to confront systemic inequities. When faced with conflict, disagreement, or complexity, the team returns to these shared values as an anchor – realigning intentions, rebuilding trust, and reaffirming its commitment to collaborative, community-led action. Over time, these values have evolved in response to the group's changing needs and contexts. The following table summarises several of the Lab's collectively held values (see Table 2.1).

Table 2.1 EBSJL Core Values and Justice Tenets

Category	Description
Solidarity	Fosters an environment where individual and community well-being are interconnected, addressing systemic power imbalances related to race, class, gender, and other oppressions.
Housing as a Human Right	Advocates for affordable, safe, and equitable housing as essential to human dignity and stability, combatting housing insecurity and displacement.
Research Justice	Ensures that community members are actively involved in all stages of research, reflecting their priorities and elevating their voices as key contributors.
Language Justice	Provides translation services and multilingual programming, ensuring inclusive participation and breaking down barriers for non-English speakers.
Temporal Justice	Enhances inclusivity by scheduling events at varied times, accommodating diverse needs of community members balancing work, family, and other commitments.
Spatial Justice	Spatial justice is rooted in daily interactions, social structures, and spatial practices. It examines how spatial arrangements influence social justice, promoting equitable urban development and strengthening community agency.
Procedural Justice	Ensures transparency and inclusivity in decision-making processes.
	Prioritises collaborative methods that allow all voices to meaningfully contribute and shape outcomes.
Epistemic Justice	Recognises the value of community knowledge in driving systemic reform.
	Elevates lived experiences and challenges traditional hierarchies of expertise, ensuring marginalised voices are amplified and respected.
Social Justice	Aligns with broader movements for housing, environmental, and workers' rights.
	Connects EBSJL's initiatives to larger justice frameworks to address intersecting inequities and strengthen advocacy efforts.
Environment	Focuses on addressing systemic environmental injustices, sustainability, equitable access to natural resources, and the mitigation of environmental harm in communities.
Health Equity	Centres on eliminating health disparities by addressing the social determinants of health, ensuring access to care, and prioritising the well-being of marginalised populations.

Through these values and approaches, our team centred the participatory process as a form of legal empowerment that included cultural organising, public education and arts-based advocacy. As a project, EBSJL illustrates how spatial justice can move beyond theory to become a lived practice, shaped through collaboration, sustained engagement, and the co-creation of knowledge.

EBSJL's work underscores the importance of funding structures that support long-term dialogue, shared decision-making, and coalition-building to ensure that community voices not only participate but actively inform legal, policy, and spatial transformation. By integrating these principles, EBSJL offers a flexible and context-responsive model for advancing equity, inclusion, and resilience. Through solidarity, justice-centred research, and cross-sector collaboration, the Lab continues to create spaces for community empowerment and systemic change, demonstrating how participatory research and collective action can be sustained over time.

Methods Insights: Participatory Practice-based Design Research Methodology

EBSJL's participatory *learning pods* were distinguished by their co-creative and community-embedded structure, centring those most affected by systemic injustices in the design and implementation of solutions. They operate as relational, iterative, and action-oriented frameworks that ensure legal, social, and spatial justice initiatives are informed and shaped by the very communities they aim to serve. Through this participatory model, the *learning pods* offer a scalable and adaptable methodology, providing a blueprint for integrating participatory design research within broader movements for systemic change.

The *learning pods were* intentionally assembled groups that engage in shared problem-solving through participatory methods such as story circles, arts-based inquiry, and workshops. Facilitated by cross-sector teams including legal experts, community organisers, and artists, their programming is multilingual, accessible, and deeply rooted in cultural organising. By incorporating arts-based advocacy, the *learning pods* provided a platform for local participants to build a dialogue about mutual aid, eviction defence, zoning policies, gentrification, and housing injustices.

EBSJL's approach acknowledges the psychological impacts of housing instability and systemic power imbalances, ensuring that community well-being remains central throughout the process. By positioning community members as co-researchers, the *learning pods* decentralise traditional hierarchies of expertise and create direct dialogue between legal, policy, and cultural knowledge and local lived realities. Community participation fosters trust-building and redistributes power, while transdisciplinary collaboration strengthens research outcomes and informs the design of various legal empowerment strategies. Trauma-informed practices centre healing through arts-based advocacy, restorative justice, and reflexive engagement, while the project's infrastructure sustains impact through education, mentorship, and interconnected advocacy ecosystems.

The following table illustrates how this model was implemented by the East Boston Spatial Justice Lab (EBSJL), outlining its key components, guiding principles, activities, and intended outcomes (see Table 2.2).

Table 2.2 Overview of Methods Implemented in EBSJL

Component	Description
Building Shared Knowledge and Trust	*Learning pods* are small, intentionally assembled groups of participants who come together to explore shared challenges, exchange knowledge, and co-develop strategies for collective action. *Circle practice* is a facilitated restorative justice technique that creates opportunities for individual voices to be heard in shared spaces; community ground rules are determined through the activation of this practice.
Guiding Principles	Grounded in Participatory Action Research (PAR) and Popular Education, prioritising *co-researchers*, inclusive dialogue, and community-driven inquiry.
Core Objectives	• Fostering social cohesion, trust, and a sense of belonging. • Enhance public wellness and address systemic challenges like housing instability. • Community members as co-creators in decision-making and problem-solving processes. • By integrating participatory methods, arts programming, and continual collaboration, learning pods lay the foundation for lasting community building, catalysing learning, legal empowerment, and advocating for policy and practice transformations responsive to local needs.
Partnership Implementation	Facilitated by a cross-sector team (EBSJL staff, community organisers, artists, community builders, legal experts, and partners like Maverick Landing Community Services), ensuring accessible, multilingual programming and creative engagement strategies.
Arts & Culture	Arts-based methods serve as a critical lens and platform for advocacy, enabling participants to critique zoning, gentrification, and housing policies while amplifying local voices. Story Circles capture lived experiences and help identify priorities. Workshops, speakers' series, and co-design sessions, create the opportunity for feedback loops, group reflection, education, and collective action.
Community Involvement	Community members are co-researchers, contributing firsthand experiences, setting priorities, and shaping decisions. This approach decentralises traditional power structures and brings legal, policy, and cultural expertise directly into dialogue with local realities.

(continued)

Table 2.2 *(Continued)*

Component	Description
Trauma-Informed Practices	Leveraging insights from past projects to address the psychological impact of housing instability, recognising how systemic power imbalances affect mental health and community well-being.
Long-Term Impact	Anticipated outcomes included community-driven strategies for housing justice and equitable community development, strengthened social support networks and increased capacity for grassroots advocacy, and the advancement of sustainable, community-led reforms to promote systemic change.

A transformative transdisciplinary research framework for legal design provides an analytical lens for examining the methodologies that contribute to structural reform and community empowerment. The following key methods and strategies illustrate how transdisciplinary approaches can effectively address systemic inequities.

Community participation focuses on engaging people in the planning, decision making, and design process. These choices help to build grass-roots ownership which helps to ensure that solutions reflect lived experiences. These efforts contribute to trust-building, power redistribution, education, mentorship, and research justice. This process stresses the importance of utilizing participatory methods in access to justice initiatives.

Transdisciplinary collaboration and trauma-informed practices further shape the framework by integrating knowledge across disciplines and centring restorative justice and healing in advocacy work. Legal empowerment, policy advocacy, and systemic reform emerge from interdisciplinary engagement, strengthening advocacy efforts, and ensuring long-term sustainability. Table 2.3 offers an overview of the key elements that emerged through EBSJL.

Table 2.3 Key Elements and Outcomes

Element	Focus	Outcomes
Community Participation	Engages people in planning, design, and decision-making to ensure lived experience informs solutions.	Builds trust, redistributes power, and strengthens access to justice.
Example of Transdisciplinary Collaboration	Bridges design, law, and community-based collaboration.	Advances legal empowerment, policy reform, and sustainability
Trauma-Informed Practices	Centres restorative justice, arts-based advocacy, and well-being.	Promotes inclusivity, healing, and reflexive research ethics.

(continued)

Table 2.3 *(Continued)*

Element	Focus	Outcomes
Coalition Building	Creates networks and advocacy ecosystems.	Supports scaling, mentorship, and policy impact.
Guiding Principles	Establishes shared justice frameworks.	Aligns actions with equity, accountability, and reflexivity.
Holistic Framework	Integrates all elements into a unified participatory justice model.	Enables systemic and sustainable transformation.

Next Steps

Building on our learning outcomes, the next phase of the project will begin with collective planning, visioning and a co-design process that seeks to strengthen and support a peer-driven local anti-eviction legal empowerment network. At the core of this approach is the recognition that legal empowerment must extend beyond formal legal services to include informal community justice workers. By reinforcing peer networks through community-led and co-designed legal trainings, this process ensures that participants have access to accurate legal information and practical resources that can be shared and mobilised through ongoing advocacy efforts.

Moving forward the project intends to include:

- Community-centred legal education that translates complex legal concepts into accessible knowledge for non-lawyers.
- Peer-led workshops that enable trained community members to disseminate legal knowledge and build local capacity.
- Collaborations with legal experts to verify the accuracy and relevance of shared information.
- Co-design of digital and physical legal resource hubs to provide communities with up-to-date materials and tools that support sustained engagement and advocacy.

These strategies support, build, and activate grassroots agency, enabling individuals to make informed decisions and advocate for themselves and their communities. A crucial issue in participatory legal empowerment is maintaining peer-to-peer legal education within the scope of legal information sharing, without crossing into unauthorised practice of law (UPL). While UPL regulations aim to safeguard individuals from inaccurate or misleading legal advice, they can also hinder community-driven legal empowerment initiatives.

To navigate this tension, the next stage of the project seeks to adopt a multifaceted strategy that balances community empowerment with regulatory compliance. The initiative will focus on training peer advocates to share legal information, not legal advice, ensuring that community educators are equipped to provide general legal knowledge while referring individuals to licensed attorneys for case-specific guidance. A team of community justice workers will collaborate closely with legal professionals, law clinics, supervised law students, bar associations, and public interest lawyers to ensure that all training adheres to established regulatory guidelines.

Through participatory legal design workshops, the project will emphasise legal literacy, popular education, and rights awareness rather than individualised legal representation. These efforts will support the development of community-based legal empowerment network that connects trained community leaders with pro bono legal services, tenants' rights groups, and legal aid organisations, fostering a sustainable and ethically grounded model of collective legal learning and local advocacy.

CONCLUSION

To fully embrace a transformative transdisciplinary research framework in the context of legal design, we must recognise that this work is inherently a collective action that requires co-creation, shared responsibility, and sustained engagement. Addressing systemic inequities in legal design, policy, and justice movements cannot be accomplished in isolation. Instead, it necessitates an ongoing process of building relationships, redistributing power, and fostering collective vision. The act of reimagining legal systems is not solely about institutional reforms but about creating dynamic, participatory spaces where communities, legal practitioners, designers, technologists, and activists work together towards more equitable futures.

The following collective design exercise provides a set of prompts that will allow the reader to envision ways to put these ideas into practice. It invites readers to explore methods and opportunities for co-creation, ensuring decision-making remains inclusive and grounded in lived experience. The exercise encourages dismantling hierarchies, rethinking access to law, and embedding shared ownership throughout processes of systemic change.

By prioritising participation, community agency, and long-term sustainability, transformative research models can extend beyond institutional funding cycles and academic constraints to build deeply embedded networks of resilience. This shift requires an ongoing commitment to imagining, designing, and implementing justice together, ensuring that legal and advocacy systems remain adaptable, inclusive, and responsive to the realities of those most affected. Rather than viewing justice as a fixed goal, this approach envisions it as a continually evolving practice co-created through collective vision, interdisciplinary collaboration, and a shared commitment to systemic transformation.

DESIGN EXERCISE FOR THE READER

This exercise invites readers to take an active role in designing a world where lawyers, activists, designers, technologists, and community members collaborate to co-create and sustain more equitable futures.

The exercise emphasises imagination, solidarity, and shared ownership in building systems that address systemic challenges through collective design. By participating in this brainstorming exercise, readers can adapt these prompts to their own contexts, whether in local neighbourhoods, service-based organisations, educational institutions, or organisational settings.

Table 2.4 offers the readers a series of design questions and reflections as an exercise in how they might become more deeply engaged in transformative and transdisciplinary legal design and research.

Table 2.4 Design Exercise for the reader

Action	Key Prompts and Considerations
1. Envision the Space – Visualise the collaborative environment. Space here is a conceptual framing.	• What does this space look like – virtual, physical, or hybrid? • How is collaboration fostered? • What elements (technology, art, tools) generate interaction?
2. Identify Stakeholders – Define who should be involved.	• Who are the key stakeholders (lawyers, designers, technologists, community organisers)? • Who might be missing, and how can they be included? • Ensure diversity across age, expertise, and lived experience.
3. Explore Issues – Brainstorm and align shared visions.	• What ideas or prototypes are emerging? • Are participants reimagining legal tools or advocacy strategies? • How can these ideas be visualised or modelled?
4. Roles & Contributions – Clarify participant roles and skills.	• What role will you play (facilitator, synthesiser, partner)? • What unique expertise do you bring? • What about other people, what do they offer?
5. Reflective Questions – Deepen analysis through critical inquiry.	• Who else needs to be involved? • What systems ensure equitable collaboration? • How can hierarchies be challenged? • How can diverse voices be amplified? • What design elements foster shared ownership? • What values anchor this vision?

(continued)

Table 2.4 *(Continued)*

Action	Key Prompts and Considerations
6. Partnerships & Evaluation – Identify partnerships and assess impact.	• What collaborations will sustain this work? • How can outcomes be measured through participatory methods?
7. Synthesis & Sharing – Consolidate and communicate your vision.	• How can reflections form a plan? • How can peer feedback refine the design? • What next steps support iteration?
8. Reflection & Commitment – Reflect on next steps and broader impact.	• What personal action can you take today? • How can this idea/vision inspire systemic transformation?

REFERENCES

C Balser and AM Coronado, 'Power-Conscious Legal Work: Building a Roadmap for Rural Access to Justice Through Trust, Accountability, & Trauma-Informed Practices' (2024) *Alaska Law Review* 146.

P Ferreira, J Abdelnour-Nocera and HG Nicolau, 'User Oppression in Human-Computer Interaction: A Dialectical-Existential Perspective' (2022) 74(5) *Aslib Journal of Information Management* 763–764.

RF Gonzatto and FMC van Amstel, 'User Oppression in Human-Computer Interaction: A Dialectical-Existential Perspective' (2022) 74(5) *Aslib Journal of Information Management* 763–764.

DM Littman, K Bender, M Mollica, J Erangey, T Lucas and C Marvin, 'Making Power Explicit: Using Values and Power Mapping to Guide Power-Diverse Participatory Action Research Processes' (2021) 59 *Journal of Community Psychology* 266.

DM Mertens, 'Transformative Paradigm: Mixed Methods and Social Justice' (2007) 1(3) *Journal of Mixed Methods Research* 212.

Substance Abuse and Mental Health Services Administration (SAMHSA), *Practical Guide for Implementing a Trauma-Informed Approach* (SAMHSA Publication No PEP23-06-05-005, 2023).

M Tedeschi and JR Sievert, 'Editorial: Spatial Justice in Design Research: A Transdisciplinary Discourse' in C Gray and others (eds), *DRS2024: Boston, 23–28 June* (London, DRS Digital Library, 2024).

3

Bridging Paradigms: Comparing the Elements of Human-Centred Design in Legal Design and People-Centred Justice Frameworks

EBRU METIN, NINA TOIVONEN AND JAANA KOVALAINEN

INTRODUCTION

THERE IS A clear trend among global policy circles adopting a people-centred justice (PCJ) approach in closing the access to justice gap.[1] Evidently, all measures are needed to improve access to justice globally. Realising access to justice is a tremendous challenge in many countries, 'bigger than law and lawyers'.[2] According to the United Nations Pathfinders' 2019 report, the global justice gap affects two-thirds of the world population, more than five billion people.[3] Therefore, addressing the issues of access to justice is also on the agenda of multinational organisations such as the United Nations,[4]

[1] The justice gap refers to the significant disparity between the legal needs of individuals globally and the capacity of justice systems to meet those needs. M de Langen, 'Delivering Justice and Fairness in People's Lives: Looking Beyond the Usual Suspects to Understand the Knowledge and Skills Required to Solve People's Justice Problems' (SSRN, 2023) ssrn.com/abstract=4587998 or dx.doi.org/10.2139/ssrn.4587998.

[2] RL Sandefur, 'Access to What?' (2019) 148(1) *Daedalus* 49; DB Maldonado, 'The Right to Access to Justice: Its Conceptual Architecture' 27 (2020) *Ind J Global Legal Stud* 15.

[3] The United Nations Pathfinders, 'Justice for All: Report from the Task Force on Justice' (2019) www.sdg16.plus/; World Justice Report, 'Measuring the Justice Gap' (2019) www.sdg16.plus/resources/measuring-the-justice-gap/.

[4] The United Nations promotes access to justice initiatives under the Sustainable Development Goal (SDG) 16 "Peace, Justice and Strong Institutions" with the adoption of the 2030 Agenda for Sustainable Development back in 2015. United Nations, 'The Sustainable Development Agenda' www.un.org/sustainabledevelopment/development-agenda/.

World Bank,[5] and Organisation for Economic Co-operation and Development (OECD).[6]

The concept 'people-centred justice' refers to redesigning the justice systems around the needs, experiences, and desired outcomes of the people affected by the systems, not the needs of the systems themselves.[7] Where past justice system reforms have traditionally been aimed at improving the existing structures, models and services, the PCJ approach is about creating fundamentally new solutions that put people at the centre of the system.[8] From the viewpoint of legal design, the global trend in adopting *a PCJ* approach instead of a *human-centred* legal design approach to justice innovation raises questions about the role of legal design in solving access to justice and other legal system-related challenges. Why has legal design not gained similar recognition? What is the role of legal design in improving access to justice? It seems that there are two, similarly defined approaches addressing the challenges of access to justice, but only the other is widely recognised as suitable for the job.

According to the OECD Framework and Good Practice Principles for People-Centered Justice, the human-centred design (HCD) approach should be distinguished from PCJ, primarily because it regards designing legal processes and systems for humans as 'users' or 'clients'.[9] The OECD principles do recognise the need for using design methods in justice innovation but warn that the HCD approach may lead to applying strategies and processes that are not helpful in transforming the justice system. According to OECD, 'Human-centered design may be used to improve certain formal justice system processes without first asking the question whether or not that process is appropriate for a people-centered justice system in the first place'.[10]

Legal design has many definitions that emphasise slightly different aspects of using design in the context of law and justice. This may explain some of the confusion related to the term legal design. Nevertheless, all the definitions share some similar elements to the idea of PCJ, such as the focus on human needs

[5] World Bank, 'Global Program on Justice and Rule of Law' www.worldbank.org/en/programs/global-program-on-justice-and-rule-of-law.

[6] R Hunter, A Olesen and R Sandefur, 'Lawyers and Access to Justice' in RL Abel, H Sommerlad, O Hammerslev and U Schultz (eds), *Lawyers in 21st Century Societies: Vol. 2 Comparisons and Theories* (Oxford, Hart Publishing, 2022) 303–326.

[7] S Muller, 'People-Centered Justice Goes from "How to Do It?" to "Let's Do It!"' (2022) www.hiil.org/news/people-centred-justice-goes-from-how-to-do-it-to-lets-do-it/.

[8] OECD, 'OECD Framework and Good Practice Principles for People-Centred Justice' (2021) doi.org/10.1787/cdc3bde7-en; UN Foundation, 'From Justice for the Few: A Model for High-Ambition Action to Deliver the SDGs' (2023) https://s3.amazonaws.com/media.unfoundation.org/2023/05/Justice-Paper-22May23.pdf.

[9] OECD (n 8).

[10] OECD (n 8).

and systemic improvement, particularly improvement of access to justice.[11] For example, Santuber and Krawietz have described legal design as an approach that combines 'multiple practices and studies concerned with the creation of novel – or the redesign of existing – legal related socio-technical systems (people, processes and technology) with a purpose driven by a public service bounded by agreed upon values such as access to justice, and the rule of law'.[12] According to the Legal Design Alliance, legal design 'applies human-centered design to the world of law to enable desirable outcomes and prevent the causes of problems from arising and developing into conflicts and disputes'.[13] Hagan has also called legal design as 'the marriage of a human-centered design approach to the challenges and structures of the legal system'.[14]

It seems that the understanding of the HCD approach and how it can support transformation and positive change in the context of access to justice is shifting. As similar concerns related to HCD have recently been raised within the design discourse, particularly in relation to the sustainability transition and the paradoxical role of HCD in it,[15] it is necessary to reassess HCD as a central paradigm of legal design. This paper takes part in this task by reviewing the elements of HCD, as standardised in the ISO standard 9241-210:2019 on Human-Centred Design for Interactive Systems,[16] in the legal design and PCJ frameworks as described in the OECD Framework and Good Practice Principles for People-Centered Justice and other relevant literature. With this exercise, we want to contribute to the discussion on what legal design is as a HCD approach and how it should be developed as a method for solving systemic justice problems. We hope that this paper helps articulate the objectives and relevance of legal design. We also want to build a bridge between the two approaches, legal design and PCJ, and develop the paradigm of putting people and true justice transformation at the centre of legal innovation.

[11] Legal design as an umbrella term for different approaches, see M Doherty, M Corrales Compagnucci, H Haapio and M Hagan, 'A New Attitude to Law's Empire: The Potentialities of Legal Design' in M Corrales Compagnucci, H Haapio and M Doherty (eds), *Legal Design: Integrating Business, Design and Legal Thinking with Technology* (Cheltenham, Edward Elgar Publishing, 2021) 1; A Perry-Kessaris, 'Legal Design for Practice, Activism, Policy and Research' (2019) 46(2) *Journal of Law and Society* 185.

[12] J Santuber and L Krawietz, 'User Research Methodologies in Legal Design Projects: Lessons from Practice' in Rossana Ducato and Alain Strowel (eds), *Legal Design Perspectives: Theoretical and Practical Insights from the Field* (Milan, Ledizioni, 2021) 94.

[13] Legal Design Alliance, www.legaldesignalliance.org/.

[14] M Hagan, 'Legal Design as a Thing: A Theory of Change and a Set of Methods to Craft a Human-Centered Legal System' (2020) 36(3) *Design Issues* 3–15. See also M Hagan, 'A Human-Centered Design Approach to Access to Justice: Generating New Prototypes and Hypotheses for Intervention to Make Courts User-Friendly' (2018) 6(2) *Indiana Journal of Law and Social Equity* 200.

[15] See e.g. D Norman, *Design for a Better World: Meaningful, Sustainable, Humanity Centered* (Cambridge, MA, MIT Press, 2023); D Jackson and others, 'What Legal Design Could Be: Towards an Expanded Practice of Inquiry, Critique and Action' (2022) *DRS Biennial Conference Series*.

[16] *ISO 9241-210:2019 Ergonomics of Human-System Interaction. Part 210: Human-Centered Design for Interactive Systems* (ISO 9241-210:2019).

A BRIEF ON HCD

Human-centred design focuses on creating solutions that ultimately seek to change the status quo for the better based on people's needs, behaviour, and experiences. In this sense, all design activities can be viewed as dynamic feedback relationships between designers and those to be served – customers, users, humans – to generate something that does not yet exist.[17] Design literature acknowledges two Western traditions of involvement behind this approach. The first is the *Scandinavian participatory design* (PD) tradition, which originally sought to increase the efficiency of industrial production through the expertise of designers, engineers, and the people whose work was to be affected. The second line of development is *user-centred design* (UCD), initially identified in computer sciences and industrial engineering back in the 1960s and 1970s.[18] These two development trends behind the HCD approach can be described as *designing for* end-users and the first steps of engaging the end-user to the design process.

Today, the HCD approach increasingly involves stakeholders as active participants in all phases of the design process. In other words, from designing *for* people to designing *with* and *by* people.[19] The shift from PDT and UCD towards co-design practices has also enabled creating solutions that fit better for people's purposes or societal needs. However, it has been noted that using terms 'user' or 'consumer' in the context of design may limit the roles of the people in the design process and alienate people's perspectives.[20] Design authors have recently raised the idea of shifting the design conversation from humans (or users) to the whole ecosystem of humanity.[21] This change responds to criticisms of human-centredness for taking a too narrow view of people and the relationship of individuals to social systems or regulations.

MAPPING THE ELEMENTS OF HCD IN LEGAL DESIGN AND PCJ FRAMEWORKS

Human-centred design method for interactive systems has been standardised in the ISO 9241-210:2019 standard Human-Centered Design for Interactive

[17] H Nelson and E Stolterman, *The Design Way. Intentional Change in an Unpredictable World* (Cambridge, MA, MIT Press, 2012) 37, 41.

[18] E Sanders and P Stappers, 'Co-Creation and the New Landscape of Design' (2008) 4(1) *International Journal of Co-Creation in Design and the Arts* 5–6; J Buur and B Matthews, 'Participatory Innovation' (2008) 12 *International Journal of Innovation Management* 255–273.

[19] Sanders and Stappers 2008 (n 18); Buur and Matthews (n 18).

[20] J Brush, 'How Design Contributes to Toxic Individualism, and What Can Be Done About It' (2024) *UX Collective* uxdesign.cc/how-design-contributes-to-toxic-individualism-and-what-can-be-done-about-it-4933b47b15cc.

[21] D Norman (n 15); T Gorichanaz, 'Toward Humanity-Centered Design without Hubris' in *Extended Abstracts of the CHI Conference on Human Factors in Computing Systems (CHI EA '24)* (ACM, New York, 2024) 1–7 doi.org/10.1145/3613905.3644060.

Systems.[22] This standardisation can be considered as one of the basic forms of HCD in current use, which makes it a suitable measuring tool for observing how the elements of HCD have been adopted in legal design and PCJ frameworks. It must be noticed, however, that like in any qualitative research, operating with concepts that are open to interpretation comes with caution. There are, and have been, many ways to conceptualise and practice HCD, as the above description of the evolution of the approach shows. The standardised version may thus not represent all the design actions that have been labelled as human-centred. The concepts 'legal design' and 'people-centred justice' are also still evolving, which only emphasises the paucity of research in this area. All this ambiguity makes this study and its results more or less tentative.

For the purposes of this paper, the ISO standard on HCD provides a clear and established definition of what HCD is about. According to the ISO standard, there are particularly six basic elements that make a design process human-centric. These elements are: (1) Focus on the needs of humans, (2) Involving the users in the design process, (3) User-centred evaluation, (4) Iteration, (5) Addressing the whole user-experience, and (6) Including multidisciplinary skills and perspectives. Design literature supports the idea that through the application of these elements, HCD can catalyse better understanding, learning, and improved decision-making, leading to changes in behaviours and systems.[23] How these elements are adopted in the legal design and the PCJ frameworks will be discussed next. An overview of this discussion can also be seen in Table 3.1.

Focus on the Needs of the Humans

According to the ISO standard on HCD, HCD focuses particularly on understanding and empathising the human needs, and on building a solution to meet those needs by addressing the root causes of problems and the whole user journey.[24] This focus on human needs is well articulated in various legal design sources.[25] Similarly, the first pillar of the PCJ framework of OECD,[26] 'Designing and delivering people-centered services', deals with 'identifying the legal and justice needs of society, the most vulnerable groups and the barriers they face to accessing justice'. Respectively, putting the needs of people/humans

[22] *ISO 9241-210:2019* (n 16).

[23] See, eg, D Norman, *The Psychology of Everyday Things* (New York, Basic Books, 1988); R Buchanan, 'Systems Thinking and Design Thinking: The Search for Principles in the World We Are Making' (2019) 5(2) *She Ji: The Journal of Design, Economics, and Innovation*; Nelson and Stolterman (n 17) 77.

[24] *ISO 9241-210:2019* (n 16) 2.

[25] See, eg, Hagan 2018 (n 14) 202; Doherty, Corrales Compagnucci, Haapio and Hagan (n 11) 2; Santuber and Krawietz (n 12) 95, 111; G Berger-Walliser, T Barton and H Haapio, 'From Visualization to Legal Design: A Collaborative and Creative Process' (2017) 54 *American Business Law Journal* 2.

[26] OECD (n 8).

at the centre of the design and delivery of services is a common element of both PCJ and legal design. However, the difference in the PCJ is that both the needs of the single individuals, as well as those of communities and other groups, are considered more clearly. One example is the open recognition of informal and customary justice practices in PCJ, while legal design seems to be more focused on discovering the user needs related to the tangible and practical, socio-technical elements of the existing legal systems, such as legal documents or processes.[27]

Involving the Users in the Design and Development

The ISO standard defines the role of the human-user as an active participant in the design process, both as a provider of information and as an evaluator and validator of the designed solutions, which happens throughout the design process.[28] Engaging the people whom the design seeks to influence is considered a central factor in designing for transformation, both in the frameworks of legal design and people-centred justice.[29] According to OECD, people centricity is about 'taking the needs and voices of people into account when designing, delivering, implementing and evaluating public policies and services'. In this regard, the PCJ approach seeks to actively involve people in the design process, which aligns with the participatory approach of the HCD. In the scope of the abovementioned OECD framework,[30] the third pillar promotes people empowerment: 'A people-centered justice system is one that seeks the involvement of the people in all phases of the justice system – from the making and reforming of laws themselves, through to providing real and effective means for ordinary people to actually participate in the legal processes and to enforce their rights'. In addition, this pillar also mentions community participation.

User-centred Evaluation

The ISO standard states that in HCD, the entire design process and its outcome are evaluated from the perspective of the user. This can involve user tests or

[27] See, eg, Doherty, Corrales Compagnucci, Haapio and Hagan (n 11); Santuber and Krawietz 2022 (n 12).

[28] *ISO 9241-210:2019* (n 16) 2.

[29] SP de Souza, 'Beyond Best Practices: How to Use Design Thinking in the Rule of Law Promotion' (PeaceLab-Blog, 13 March 2019) peacelab.blog/2019/03/beyond-best-practices-how-to-use-design-thinking; N Toivonen and S de Francisco Vela, 'Exploring the Dimensions of Participation in Legal Design' in Rossana Ducato, Alain Strowel, and Enguerrand Marique (eds), *Design(s) for Law* (Milan, Ledizioni, 2024).

[30] OECD (n 8).

long-term monitoring with users.[31] Both PCJ and legal design aim to ensure this as part of their frameworks with emphasising slightly different aspects. Due to its more systemic approach, PCJ particularly seeks to ensure that design solutions are inclusive, accounting for a wide range of human diversity, including age, gender, physical abilities, socio-economic status, and culture. This can happen by using key performance indicators and impact assessments to evaluate, ie, justice system reforms. Therefore, the goal in PCJ is to evaluate whether solutions are equitable, accessible, and valuable to as broad a user base as possible, especially for vulnerable populations,[32] whereas in legal design, the scope can be focused more on the targeted users and the impacted stakeholders depending on the design challenge.[33]

Iterative Process

The fourth element of HCD in the ISO standard is iteration, particularly by collecting feedback from users and making improvements based on that feedback.[34] Legal design implements this element particularly through the four or five-phased design process framework.[35] The process incorporates iterative feedback and response mechanisms in the Discover, Synthesise, Build, Test, and Evolve phases. Many legal design authors describe how particularly the prototyping and testing phase can provide new insights and understanding of the challenge, and thus work as the foundational basis for improvement and transformation.[36] PCJ incorporates iteration using people-centric methods such as justice need surveys that collect data on specific people and justice system needs 'to locate that need geographically and demographically', as well as focus groups and community meetings where it is possible to collect both data and feedback. PCJ also uses pilot programmes to test solutions before scaling, focusing on comprehensive evaluations.[37]

[31] *ISO 9241-210:2019* (n 16) 6–7.

[32] OECD (n 8) 15.

[33] Santuber and Krawietz (n 12) 103–104.

[34] *ISO 9241-210:2019* (n 16) 6–7; see also Y Cai, J Lin, and R Zhang, 'When and how to implement design thinking in the innovation process: A longitudinal case study' (2023) 126 *Technovation* 102816.

[35] M Hagan, 'Design Process' (*Law By Design*, 2013) lawbydesign.co/design-process/#1.

[36] M Hagan, 'Prototyping for Policy', in Marcelo Corrales Compagnucci, Helena Haapio, Margaret Hagan and Michael Doherty (eds), *Legal Design. Integrating Business, Design and Legal Thinking with Technology* (Cheltenham, Edward Elgar Publishing, 2021); Berger-Walliser, Barton and Haapio (n 25).

[37] OECD, 'Approach to the OECD People-Centred Justice Framework' (OECD iLibrary, 2024) www.oecd-ilibrary.org/sites/cdc3bde7-en/1/3/2/index.html?itemId=/content/publication/cdc3bde7-en&_csp_=34f65033a2a54df2f3bda223c22c4337&itemIGO=oecd&itemContentType=book#section-d1e2598; The Hague Institute for Innovation of Law (HiiL), 'Justice Needs Studies' (HiiL) www.hiil.org/research/?_sft_type=justice-needs-study; see also The Hague Institute for Innovation of Law (HiiL), 'Justice Needs and Satisfaction in Colombia' (HiiL, 2024) www.hiil.org/research/justice-needs-and-satisfaction-in-colombia/.

Addressing the Whole User Experience

In the ISO standard, HCD is about addressing the whole user experience, involving the user's prior experiences, attitudes, skills, personality, system experiences, as well as users' strengths, limitations, preferences, and expectations.[38] Both legal design and PCJ can be understood as approaches that seek to address all these aspects. Legal design authors emphasise the importance of learning as much as possible about the users' experience, their personalities, the circumstances when encountering the justice system, as well as their preferences and expectations about the desirable design outcomes.[39] This can happen through several design methods, such as user research, persona canvassing, empathy mapping, or user journey mapping.[40] Similar to legal design, PCJ highlights that designed justice solutions need to correspond to an empirical understanding of the diverse legal needs and capabilities of people seeking help, be appropriate, responsive, and inclusive.[41]

Including Multidisciplinary Skills and Perspectives

The ISO standard on HCD emphasises implementing design teams that have multidisciplinary skills and perspectives, which helps address the specific constraints and realities of different disciplines.[42] Legal design has been described particularly as an approach that 'recognises the value of interdisciplinarity' and which should openly welcome different professionals to solve legal design and access to justice challenges.[43]

PCJ also highlights multidisciplinarity, especially the need for participation of key stakeholders who represent different aspects of the justice challenge and who have the agency to make the necessary changes happen. This can be achieved, for example, by the application of the so-called 'multi-door' approach that requires state and non-state justice providers to work together in delivering the design outcomes.[44]

[38] *ISO 9241-210:2019* (n 16).
[39] Hagan (n 36); Santuber and Krawietz (n 12) 104.
[40] SP de Souza (n 29).
[41] OECD (n 8) 28.
[42] *ISO 9241-210:2019* (n 16).
[43] Doherty, Corrales Compagnucci, Haapio and Hagan (n 11) 2; Toivonen and de Francisco Vela 2024 (n 29) 281; S de Francisco Vela and L Guzmán-Abello, 'Systemic Design of Justice: Transdisciplinary approach to access to justice, in Rossana Ducato, Alain Strowel, and Enguerrand Marique (eds), *Design(s) for Law* (Milan, Ledizioni, 2024) 288.
[44] S Muller, 'Towards Utu-Centred Justice' (*HiiL*, 2024) www.hiil.org/news/towards-utu-centred-justice/.

Table 3.1 Mapping the elements of human-centred design in legal design and PCJ

Elements of Human-centred design	Legal design	People-Centered Justice
1. Focus on the needs of the humans (users, clients, citizens etc.)	Addressing human needs related to legal systems, legal services, products and processes etc. guides the design process.	Puts the needs of people/humans at the center of the design and delivery of justice systems, aiming to make them more accessible, fair, and effective for all people, particularly the vulnerable.
2. Involving the users in the design and development	Employs participatory methods and co-creation with users to provide elements for actual change and improvement.	Encourages innovation through cross-sector collaboration and the use of technology to meet user needs, uses broad consultation with users and stakeholders, often addressing systemic barriers.
3. User-centred evaluation	Evaluates design process and deliverables using user feedback.	Uses various assessment methods such as KPIs and impact assessments to evaluate justice reforms more broadly. Prioritizes inclusivity and equity in its evaluations, especially for vulnerable populations, with a strong focus on ethical practices.
4. Iterative process	Emphasizes rapid prototyping and iterative testing with users to collect feedback and improve solutions as part of the design process.	Uses different methods, such as surveys, focus groups and community meetings to collect data and feedback, and pilot programs to test solutions before scaling, focusing on comprehensive evaluations.
5. Addressing the whole user experience	Emphasizes the importance of learning about all aspects of the users' experience, which helps addressing the root cause and designing desirable outcomes.	Is based on wide empirical understanding of legal and justice needs and capabilities of those who seek access to justice.
6. Including multidisciplinary skills and perspectives	Interdisciplinarity is regarded as one of the defining concepts of legal design.	Emphasizes the importance of multidisciplinary and multi-stakeholder involvement in design and delivery of justice solutions.

DISCUSSION

Although both legal design and PCJ emphasise the principles and elements of HCD and aim to transform legal and justice systems to better serve people, there are some clear differences due to their focus and scope. PCJ has a broader focus on making justice accessible at a social-systemic level, also using structures, media, and mechanisms outside the existing judicial system. As described in the OECD framework and principles for PCJ, this enables transformation in the sense of creating completely novel solutions to access to justice issues. In contrast, based on the existing literature, legal design appears as having a more visible emphasis on improving the various artefacts (products, services, and processes) that represent the user-interface of the formal legal system. However, this approach can also be transformative in nature and give rise to larger systemic changes, for example, by discovering justice gaps.[45] The differences of the HCD approach and the PCJ approach to access to justice innovation are summarised in Figure 3.1.

Figure 3.1 Human-centricity vs. people-centricity in the context of access to justice innovation

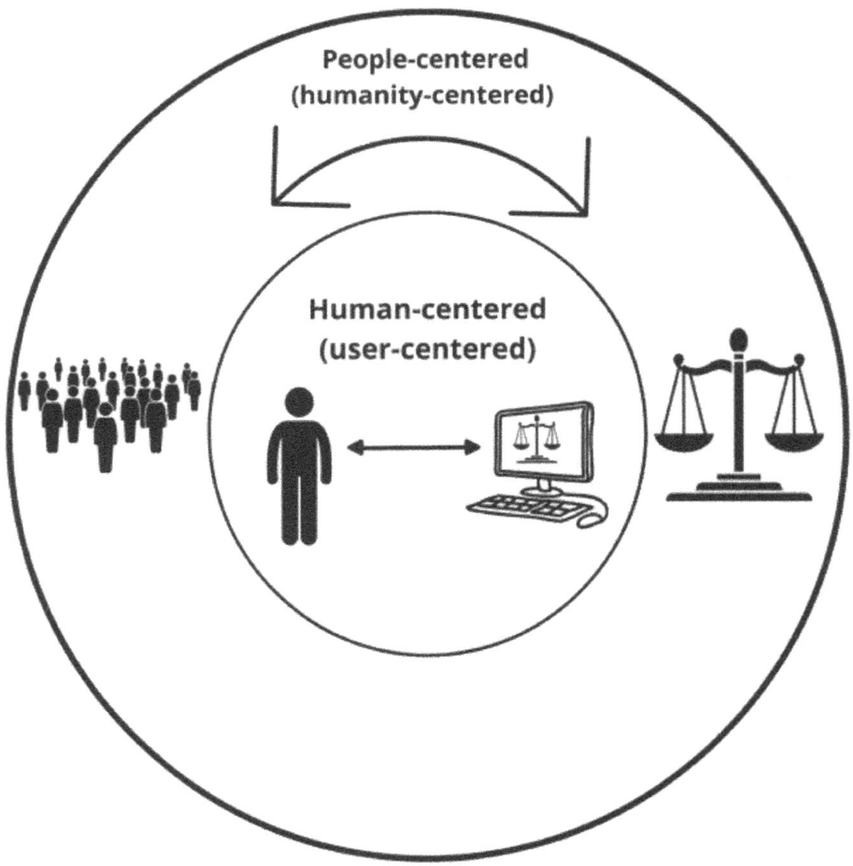

[45] Perry-Kessaris 2019 (n 11).

However, neither legal design nor PCJ is free from the inherited challenges of HCD.[46] A critical question is who should be involved in the design process and how. How to secure a sufficiently broad and a sufficiently human-centred view of the issue? This requires interpretation and value-based decision-making by those who lead the project.[47] Participation is therefore always based on some policy, strategy, or other circumstances in individual projects. One may therefore reasonably question if HCD, even in its current participatory emphasis, can ever be truly human-centred. HCD can easily be used as superficial rhetoric to promote something else than the interests of the people. This seems to be part of the OECD critique of the concept of HCD as well.[48] Therefore, perhaps HCD should be defined from the viewpoint of objective rather than subjective human interests.

It must also be noted that in practice, when developing solutions that aim to improve access to justice, it does not matter how the development project is labelled. What matters in the end is the actual transformativity of the solution. Does the solution provide a better way to satisfy an access to justice need, or is it just a new, shinier version of an existing solution? When talking about legal innovation and impact assessment, transformativity should be one of the quality standards guiding legal design work. The HCD approach, as described above, can be viewed as the foundational element in achieving it.[49]

Various theoretical frameworks can be used to support such a vision. An emergent theory of Transformative Law suggests an understanding of law as a form-giving exercise that transforms social phenomena.[50] The purpose of law would therefore be to transform and enable positive social change, which can happen through the application of practical, human-centred methods and tools.[51] Similarly, the more established Proactive Law approach emphasises the need to drive positive change through creating inclusive, empowering, and sustainable legal solutions that shift problematic power dynamics in contexts of traditional power imbalances.[52] There are also many other design approaches in addition to HCD that can support legal design and PCJ in their mission to transform legal and justice systems. For example, systems design can help

[46] Toivonen and deFrancisco Vela 2023 (n 29) 267.

[47] In earlier design trends, the role of users was to produce information and be the objects of observation for the designer. In other words, the designer defined how the design process was to be carried out and what was to be designed. As a result, the process reflected the use of power and the role of the designer. See more M Steen, 2011.

[48] OECD (n 8).

[49] Similarly Norman 2023 (n 15) 183.

[50] PF Kjaer, 'What is Transformative Law?' (2023) 1 *European Law Open* 760–780.

[51] H Haapio and A Ketola, 'From Rhetoric to Action: The Transformative Power of AI, Proactive Law and Legal Design' in D Sorin, N Mäntylä and JE Fountain (eds), *AI and Power in Government* (London, Palgrave Macmillan, forthcoming).

[52] ibid.

identify interconnected issues both within and outside the legal system and its environment.[53] Sustainable design paradigms ensure solutions that are viable and beneficial in the long term.[54] Furthermore, speculative design can help prepare the justice system for future challenges and opportunities.[55]

CONCLUSION

The global trend in adopting a PCJ approach to justice innovation has worked as the discussion starter of this paper. Despite their seeming similarities, legal design as a 'human-centred design' (HCD) approach has not been recognised in a similar way as PCJ to address the global access to justice challenges. This inspired us to ponder what is 'wrong' with the HCD approach in improving access to justice, and whether it is still a relevant framework in pursuing truly transformative legal innovation work.

To answer this question, we used the HCD elements standardised in the ISO 9241-210:2019 standard on Human-Centered Design for Interactive Systems as a measuring tool, to view how those conceptual elements are adopted in legal design and PCJ frameworks. Although our conclusions can be considered very generic and theoretical in nature, we can say that, based on the recent literature, HCD forms the basic elements in both frameworks. Both legal design and PCJ put humans at the centre of their design work, value participatory methods and multidisciplinarity, and trust in iteration, user-centred evaluation, and addressing the whole user-experience. However, it must be noted that it is another question and a topic for research whether and how the transformative elements of HCD are applied in practice.

To address the immense challenges of our time, such as the global justice gap, it is also necessary for the different approaches that aim at solving the same challenge to join their forces. We hope that this paper can work as a one humble bridge builder between the legal design and people-centred justice approaches.

[53] See, eg, P Hietanen-Kunwald, H Haapio and N Toivonen, 'Systems Theory as a Research Framework for Dispute Prevention and Resolution by Design' in R Ducato and A Strowel (eds), *Legal Design Perspectives – Theoretical and Practical Insights from the Field* (Milan, Ledizioni, 2021).

[54] See, eg, M Keitsch, 'Sustainable Design: A Brief Appraisal of its Main Concepts' (2012) 20 *Sustainable Development* 180, 180–188 doi.org/10.1002/sd.1534.

[55] See, eg, E Macloud, 'An Exercise in Speculative Legal Design' in Rossana Ducato, Alain Strowel and Enguerrand Marique (eds), *Design(s) for Law* (Milan, Ledizioni, 2024) 75; or C Fiesler, 'Innovating like an Optimist, Preparing like a Pessimist: Ethical Speculation and the Legal Imagination' (2021) 19 *Colorado Technology Law Journal* 1.

REFERENCES

G Berger-Walliser, T Barton and H Haapio, 'From Visualization to Legal Design: A Collaborative and Creative Process' (2017) 54 *American Business Law Journal* 2.

J Buur and B Matthews, 'Participatory Innovation' (2008) 12 *International Journal of Innovation Management* 255–273.

M de Langen, 'Delivering Justice and Fairness in People's Lives: Looking Beyond the Usual Suspects to Understand the Knowledge and Skills Required to Solve People's Justice Problems' (SSRN, 2023).

SP de Souza, 'Beyond Best Practices: How to Use Design Thinking in Rule of Law Promotion' (PeaceLab-Blog, 13 March 2019).

S de Francisco Vela and L Guzmán-Abello, 'Systemic Design of Justice: Transdisciplinary approach to access to justice, in Rossana Ducato, Alain Strowel, and Enguerrand Marique (eds), *Design(s) for Law* (Milan, Ledizioni, 2024) 288.

M Doherty, M Corrales Compagnucci, H Haapio and M Hagan, 'A New Attitude to Law's Empire: The Potentialities of Legal Design' in M Corrales Compagnucci, H Haapio and M Doherty (eds), *Legal Design: Integrating Business, Design and Legal Thinking with Technology* (Cheltenham, Edward Elgar Publishing, 2021).

C Fiesler, 'Innovating like an Optimist, Preparing like a Pessimist: Ethical Speculation and the Legal Imagination' (2021) 19 *Colorado Technology Law Journal* 1.

T Gorichanaz, 'Toward Humanity-Centered Design without Hubris' in *Extended Abstracts of the CHI Conference on Human Factors in Computing Systems (CHI EA '24)*, May 11–16, 2024 (Honolulu, HI, USA, 2024).

H Haapio and A Ketola, 'From Rhetoric to Action: The Transformative Power of AI, Proactive Law and Legal Design' in Dan Sorin, Niina Mäntylä and Jane E. Fountain (eds), *AI and Power in Government* (London, Palgrave Macmillan, forthcoming).

M Hagan, 'Design Process' (*Law By Design*, 2013).

——, 'A Human-Centered Design Approach to Access to Justice: Generating New Prototypes and Hypotheses for Intervention to Make Courts User-Friendly' (2018) 6(2) *Indiana Journal of Law and Social Equity* 199–239.

——, 'Legal Design as a Thing: A Theory of Change and a Set of Methods to Craft a Human-Centered Legal System' (2020) 36(3) *Design Issues* 3–15.

——, 'Prototyping for Policy' in M Corrales Compagnucci, H Haapio, M Hagan and M Doherty (eds), *Legal Design: Integrating Business, Design and Legal Thinking with Technology* (Cheltenham, Edward Elgar Publishing, 2021).

R Hunter, A Olesen and R Sandefur, 'Lawyers and Access to Justice' in RL Abel, H Sommerlad, O Hammerslev and U Schultz (eds), *Lawyers in 21st Century Societies: Vol. 2 Comparisons and Theories* (Oxford, Hart Publishing, 2022) 303–326.

ISO 9241-210:2019 Ergonomics of Human-System Interaction. Part 210: Human-Centred Design for Interactive Systems (ISO 9241-210:2019).

PF Kjaer, 'What is Transformative Law?' (2023) 1 *European Law Open* 760–780.

Legal Design Alliance (Website).

E Macloud, 'An Exercise in Speculative Legal Design' in Rossana Ducato, Alain Strowel and Enguerrand Marique (eds), *Design(s) for Law* (Milan, Ledizioni, 2024).

DB Maldonado, 'The Right to Access to Justice: Its Conceptual Architecture' 27 (2020) *Ind J Global Legal Stud* 15.

S Muller, 'People-Centred Justice Goes from "How to Do It?" to "Let's Do It!"' (2022)

——, 'Towards Utu-Centred Justice' (HiiL, 2024)

H Nelson and E Stolterman, *The Design Way. Intentional Change in an Unpredictable World* (Cambridge, MA, MIT Press, 2012).

D Norman, *Design for a Better World: Meaningful, Sustainable, Humanity Centered* (Cambridge, MA, MIT Press, 2023).

——, *The Psychology of Everyday Things* (New York, Basic Books, 1988).

D Norman and S Draper, *User Centered System Design: New Perspectives on Human-Computer Interaction* (Hillsdale, NJ, Lawrence Erlbaum Associates, 1986).

OECD, 'Approach to the OECD People-Centred Justice Framework' (OECD iLibrary, 2024).

OECD, 'OECD Framework and Good Practice Principles for People-Centred Justice' (2021).

A Perry-Kessaris, 'Legal Design for Practice, Activism, Policy, and Research' (2019) 46(2) *Journal of Law and Society* 185–225.

RL Sandefur, 'Access to What?' (2019) 148(1) *Daedalus* 49.

E Sanders and P Stappers, 'Co-Creation and the New Landscape of Design' (2008) 4(1) *International Journal of Co-Creation in Design and the Arts.*

J Santuber and L Krawietz, 'User Research Methodologies in Legal Design Projects: Lessons from Practice' in Rossana Ducato and Alain Strowel (eds), *Legal Design Perspectives: Theoretical and Practical Insights from the Field* (Milan, Ledizioni, 2021).

M Steen, 'Tensions in Human-Centred Design' (2011) 7(1) *CoDesign* 45–60.

The Hague Institute for Innovation of Law, 'Justice Needs Studies' (HiiL).

N Toivonen and S de Francisco Vela, 'Exploring the Dimensions of Participation in Legal Design' in Rossana Ducato, Alain Strowel, and Enguerrand Marique (eds), *Design(s) for Law* (Milan, Ledizioni, 2024).

The United Nations Pathfinders, 'Justice for All: Report from the Task Force on Justice' (2019).

UN Foundation, 'From Justice for the Few: A Model for High-Ambition Action to Deliver the SDGs' (2023).

United Nations, 'The Sustainable Development Agenda'.

United States Agency for International Development, 'USAID Rule of Law Policy' (April 2023).

World Bank, 'Global Program on Justice and Rule of Law'.

World Justice Report, 'Measuring the Justice Gap' (2019).

4

Legal Design with Silent Agents: Biomimicry as a Strategy to Understand the Rationales of More-than-Human in Legal Design

NINA TOIVONEN

INTRODUCTION

VARIOUS FIELDS OF art, science, and design have started to question the role of human-centrism in their paradigms. Serving human needs has inevitably led to social innovations, helped cure diseases, and catalysed the democratisation of information. However, it has also justified developments that have made using and consuming easier, normalising the idea of consumer-powered growth at the expense of the planet. Consequently, a growing trend in the design discourse is to decentre humans and to re-focus on the entire ecosystems of humanity, including all living things.[1] A similar shift of focus is also emerging in the legal space.[2] Environmental law scholars have long challenged the idea that only humans and their organisations can be regarded as legal beings, and more recently, to have exclusive legal rights, such as the right to property.[3] Arguments for rights of nature have often been justified by

[1] See, eg, M Tironi and others (eds.), *Design For More-Than-Human Futures. Towards Post-Anthropocentric Worlding* (London, Routledge, 2024).

[2] See, eg, J Santuber and P Hermansen, 'Designing for Posthuman Legalities: Legal Design(ing) and the Ontological Turn', in R Ducato and others (eds), *Design(s) for Law* (Milan, Ledizioni, 2024) 311, 321; E Cirkovic, 'The Next Generation of International Law: Space, Ice, and the Cosmolegal Proposal' (2021) *German Law Journal* 147, 162; F Capra and U Mattei, *The Ecology of Law. Toward a Legal System in Tune with Nature and Community* (San Francisco, Berrett-Koehler Publishers Inc., 2015).

[3] See, eg, K Birrell and D Matthews, 'Re-storying Laws for the Anthropocene: Rights, Obligations, and an Ethics of Encounter' (2020) 31 *Law and Critique* 275–292; C Stone, *Should Trees Have Standing? Law, Morality, and the Environment* (New York, Oxford University Press, 1972); DP Corrigan and M Oksanen, 'Rights of Nature: Exploring the Territory' in DP Corrigan and M Oksanen, *Rights of Nature. A Re-Examination* (London, Routledge, 2021) 1; K Bradshaw,

highlighting the ontological agency of more-than-humans. Animals, plants, rivers, and other natural entities deserve legal protection, because the way they exist in the world contributes to the ecological balance that forms the foundation for the existence of societies.[4] Ontological agency of more-than-humans can also be regarded as de facto legal agency.[5] Viruses, bacteria, and disease have shown how powerful that agency can ultimately be. Coronavirus not only passed through millions of human bodies but also caused those bodies to control others through the mechanisms of socio-legal systems. In a similar way, climate change may not only shift river courses through the effects of extreme events, such as floods, but also alter legal borders between nations or regions where watercourses have been used as jurisdictional boundaries.[6]

The notion that nature shapes society is not, of course, very new. Charles Darwin described how the 'cumulated effects' of 'small agencies', such as worms, can unpredictably contribute to human culture by acting together with other biological agents.[7] What is new is the increasing interest in intentionally including nature in shaping society. Regulatory institutions, such as national and global policymakers and courts, are creating the fundamental foundations for this ontological turn. Ecuador and Bolivia have adopted the rights of nature in their national legislations, and Courts in Colombia, India, and Bangladesh have declared that rivers have rights. New Zealand has also recognised legal personhood of rivers, a national park area, and a mountain.[8] Although these measures may be more symbolic than effective, they signal that the law can be changed radically. The European Union is following the path. A study for the European Economic and Social Committee recommends the implementation of the fundamental rights of nature at the legislative and policy level in the EU, to 'reframe rights from adversarial to synergistic' to foster 'a right relationship' with nature. According to the study, introducing the rights of nature to the EU legal system would not only require implementing the rights through legal acts but also adopting 'ecologically oriented' law-making strategies.[9] Integrating nature's perspective to regulation is also central to achieving the goals of the European Green Deal, aiming for climate-neutrality and a sustainable

Wildlife as Property Owners. A New Conception of Animal Rights (Chicago, The University of Chicago Press, 2020) 3.

[4] Birrell and Matthews (n 3) 278; S Vogel, 'The Silence of Nature' (2006) 15 *Environmental Values* 145–171, 145.

[5] A Philippopoulos-Mihalopoulos, 'Lively Agency: Life and Law in the Anthropocene', in I Braverman (ed.), *Animals, Biopolitics, Law. Lively Legalities* (London, Routledge, 2016) 202; Cirkovic (n 2) 163.

[6] S Grainger and D Conway, 'Climate Change and International River Boundaries: Fixed Points in Shifting Sands' (2014) 5(1) *WIREs Climate Change*, 835–848.

[7] C Darwin, *The Formation of Vegetable Mould, through the action of Worms, with Observations on Their Habits* (London, John Murray, 1881) 313; see also J Bennett, *Vibrant Matter. A Political ecology of things* (Durham, NC, Duke University Press, 2010) 96.

[8] Corrigan and Oksanen (n 3) 3.

[9] European Economic and Social Committee and others, *Towards an EU Charter of the Fundamental Rights of Nature: Study* 128 (Publications Office, 2020) data. europa.eu/doi/10.2864/25113.

economy,[10] and the Biodiversity strategy seeking to recover Europe's biodiversity by 2030.[11]

Establishing the concept of rights of nature and achieving the ambitious sustainability goals can hardly happen without seeking methods to integrate the more-than-human ways of knowing and being into the designs of law. The purpose of this paper is to contribute to this mission. By doing so, this paper participates in the ongoing discussion about developing design approaches to posthuman legalities and regenerative legal futures.[12] This exercise thus falls within the emergent, interdisciplinary domain of legal design, with acknowledgement that there are different definitions to the term.[13] This paper adopts a broad, and also a rather vague, understanding that builds on the idea of law as a particular type of design.[14] Framing law as design makes it possible to observe law both as a design activity and as an outcome of that activity.[15] It also allows better assessment of the quality of that design and suggests improvements using insights from various design approaches, such as participatory design, systems design, or speculative design. This broad understanding also acknowledges that designing as such is political and normative, and that law plays a role in regulating the designs of other types of artefacts too.[16] Therefore, legal protection, access to rights, and their fulfillment do not happen only through the design of formal legal artefacts, but also through the design of technologies, urban infrastructure, medicine, food products, trade agreements, or business models. The challenge in designing post-human legalities is to address the complexity and inherited human-centredness of all the socio-material things that, at the end of the day, make the visions for harmonious co-existence with nature come to life.[17]

[10] European Commission, *A Sustainable Finance Framework That Works on the Ground* (Strasbourg, COM 317 final, 13 June 2023).

[11] European Commission, *Biodiversity strategy for 2030*, environment.ec.europa.eu/strategy/biodiversity-strategy-2030_en.

[12] Santuber and Hermansen (n 2); D Jackson and others, 'What legal design could be: Towards an expanded practice of inquiry, critique and action' (DRS Biennial Conference Series, 2022).

[13] See, eg, M Doherty and others, 'A new attitude to law's empire: the potentialities of legal design' in M Corrales Compagnucci and others (eds), *Legal Design. Integrating Business, Design and Legal Thinking with Technology* (Cheltenham, Edward Elgar Publishing, 2021) 1; J Santuber and L Krawietz, 'User Research Methodologies in Legal Design Projects: Lessons from Practice', in R Ducato and A Strowel (eds), *Legal Design Perspectives – Theoretical and Practical Insights from the Field* (Milan, Ledizioni, 2021) 93; Amanda Perry-Kessaris, 'Legal Design for Practice, Activism, Policy and Research' (2019) 46 *Journal of Law and Society* 185.

[14] Any field that aims at discovering 'what ought to be' is concerned with design, I Niiniluoto, 'The Aim and Structure of Applied Research' (1993) 38 *Erkenntnis, An International Journal of Scientific Philosophy* 1–21, 8; see also H Nelson and E Stolterman, *The Design Way. Intentional Change in an Unpredictable World*. (Cambridge, MA, MIT Press, 2012) 11.

[15] R Koulu, 'In Search of Living Law: How Should We Design for (Digital) Legal Interaction?' (2024) 3(2) *Digital Society* 2.

[16] Koulu (n 15) 2. See also Santuber and Hermansen (n 2) 314; Niiniluoto (n 14) 1.

[17] Santuber and Hermansen (n 2) 314–315; Capra and Mattei (n 2) 178; Cirkovic (n 2) 162; European Economic and Social Committee and others (n 9).

In their manifesto for ecology of law, Capra and Mattei suggest an ecological approach to law where law mimics 'the natural strategies of long-term ecological survival, including the reduction of waste and consumption'.[18] Biomimicry, a design method that draws from natural phenomena, could help realise such a vision.[19] Although designers have always used analogies in the natural world to discover new possibilities, generate insights, and solve problems, yet mimicking nature as a design strategy for law is a field less researched. Biomimicry has been differentiated from other design disciplines by its particular focus and potential in cultivating more sustainable human–nature relations.[20] It is also recognised as a method that can support achieving the United Nation's Sustainable Development Goals (SDGs).[21] By using interdisciplinary literature, this chapter explores biomimicry as a possible strategy to integrate more-than-human perspectives to the design of law. The following sections will introduce biomimicry as a design approach, discuss its promises and tensions, as well as its applicability in socio-legal contexts. The article will also point out two natural phenomena, *resonance* and *harmony*, that have been used as biological analogies to describe social systems, but which could also inspire the design of more-than-human-centred law.[22]

BIOMIMICRY AS A DESIGN APPROACH

Biomimicry is perhaps the oldest method of design. Since the early versions of man-made tools, nature has provided not only materials but also ideas for human creation.[23] Biomimicry generally refers to studying the properties and models of natural organisms, elements, or environments and then imitating or taking inspiration from them as part of the design.[24] Examples of designs that mimic nature can be seen everywhere: fabrics that imitate the skin structure or colouring of animals, organisational patterns inspired by plant roots, and technologies that replicate the functions of neural networks.[25] Mimicking other species is also common among many plants and animals as a result

[18] Capra and Mattei (n 2) 14.

[19] D Baumeister and others, *Biomimicry. Resource Handbook: A Seed Bank of Best Practices* (Missoula, MT, Biomimicry 3.8, 2014); J Benyus, *Biomimicry. Innovation Inspired by Nature* (New York, Harper Collins Publishers Inc., 2002).

[20] L Ilieva and others, 'Biomimicry as a Sustainable Design Methodology – Introducing the 'Biomimicry for Sustainability' Framework' (2022) 7(37) *Biomimetics* 1.

[21] R Raman and others. 'Mapping biomimicry research to sustainable development goals' (2024) 14 *Scientific Reports* 18613.

[22] See, eg, N Luhmann, *Ecological Communication* (Chicago, The University of Chicago Press, 1989) 15.

[23] W Lidwell, K Holden and J Butler, *Universal Principles of Design* (Beverly, MA, Rockport, 2010) 156.

[24] Benyus 2002 (n 21) 3.

[25] The Biomimicry Institutes' website 'Ask Nature' provides a source with over 1700 biological phenomena that can serve as inspiration for human designs, Biomimicry Institute, *Ask Nature*, www.asknature.org.

of adaptations to their habitats, helping them to hide from or deter other organisms.[26]

In contemporary design discourse, biomimicry is framed as a method that holds potential in designing more sustainable outcomes. The potential centres around an insight that the 3.8 billion years of adaptive optimisation of life on Earth holds wisdom about what works, which, if studied and translated into human contexts, can help address the systemic challenges of our time. Biomimicry has gained increasing recognition since its introduction as a sustainable design approach in the late '90s. It has developed into a movement that seeks to balance the human–nature relationship, help restore ecosystems, and 'fundamentally transform' the way we think and exist 'by moving beyond anthropocentric narratives of human domination over non-human life'.[27] However, biomimicry literature shows that there is no collective understanding or vision amongst the biomimicry advocates, practitioners, and researchers about how, and to what extent, it is possible to apply nature's design strategies to solve human problems, and whether they truly lead to sustainable outcomes.[28]

Exploring all the nuances of the various biomimetic approaches is beyond the scope of this paper. To provide an overview of the biomimicry design discourse, the study draws on the synthesis by Ilieva and others in the article 'Biomimicry as a Sustainable Design Methodology – Introducing the 'Biomimicry for Sustainability' Framework' (2022).[29] The authors introduce a framework to analyse biomimicry designs based on how 'fixedly' or 'flexibly' they apply biomimicry. In biomimicry literature more generally, fixed or 'strong' approaches are characterised by their deep integration of biological knowledge to designs and narratives that highlight nature's ingenuity and human epistemic sufficiency to reproduce it. At the other end of the extreme, flexible or 'weak' approaches build on a view of nature as imperfect, emphasising human's ability to merely draw inspiration from biological phenomena rather than master them.[30]

Fixed biomimicry approaches often have a pragmatic, methodological orientation to what biomimicry is and how it should be practiced.[31] The biomimicry design process model proposed by Baumeister and others exemplifies this type of orientation (see Figure 4.1). A central element of the process is 'biologising' the design challenge. That means taking a human need or a

[26] WJH Wickler, 'The occurrence of mimicry among plants and animals' (*Encyclopaedia Britannica*, 2023) www.britannica.com/science/mimicry/The-occurrence-of-mimicry-among-plants-and-animals.

[27] Benyus 2002 (n 19); Ilieva and others (n 20) 2; RB MacKinnon and others, 'Promises and Presuppositions of Biomimicry' (2020) 5(33) *Biomimetics* 1; W Myers, *Bio Design* (New York, MoMa, 2021) 8.

[28] Ilieva and others (n 20) 2; MacKinnon and others (n 27) 1.

[29] Ilieva and others (n 20).

[30] M Fisch, 'The Nature of Biomimicry: Toward a Novel Technological Culture' (2017) 42(5) *Science, Technology & Human Values* 795–821, 807; Ilieva and others (n 20) 5.

[31] MacKinnon and others (n 27) 11. See, eg, Baumeister and others 2014 (n 19) 190.

desired function of the design and rephrasing it so that an analogy can be found in biology.[32] Once a possible solution is created, Baumeister and others suggest evaluating and improving the solution, particularly using six 'Life's principles':

- *Evolve to survive,*
- *Adapt to changing conditions,*
- *Be locally attuned and responsive,*
- *Integrate development with growth,*
- *Be source efficient, and*
- *Use life-friendly chemistry.*[33]

The principles are said to represent the overarching patterns and operating conditions of how biological organisms survive and thrive in nature. According to the authors, this makes them suitable standards to analyse whether biomimicry designs are 'truly sustainable', in other words, if the design is good or not.[34] The strong conceptualisation of biomimicry thus goes beyond the emulation of natural strategies by setting an eco-social ethic to the emulation process and outcomes.

Figure 4.1 Biomimicry design process as described by Baumeister and others (2014)

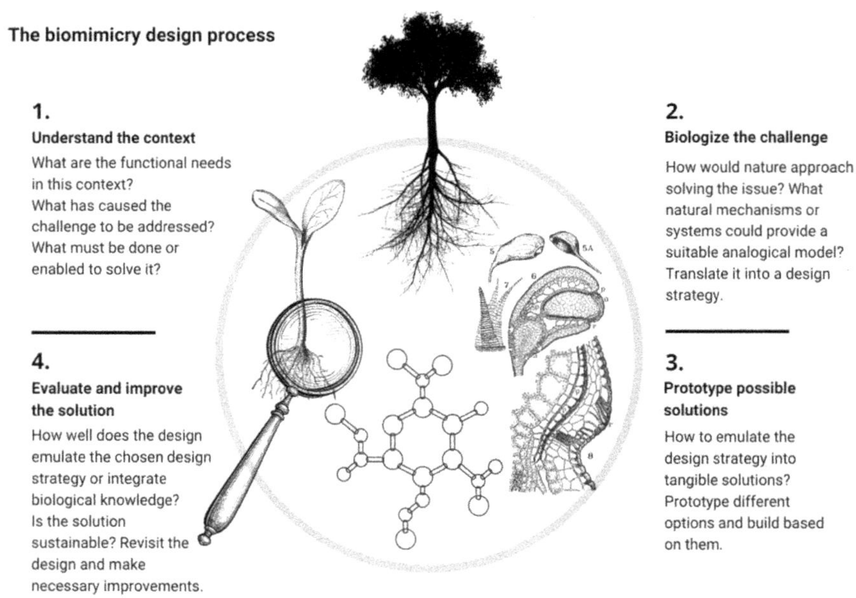

[32] Baumeister and others (n 19) 97, 109.

[33] Baumeister and others (n 19) 69–71.

[34] ibid 88; similarly, W McDonough and M Braungart, *Cradle to Cradle. Remaking the Way We Make Things* (New York, North Point Press, 2002).

Biomimicry literature highlights how adopting a fixed approach to biomimicry can be problematic. First, using ecological standards to normatively evaluate biomimetic (or any other type of) designs risks committing the naturalistic fallacy – arguing that something is 'good' simply because it is 'natural'.[35] This is also a critical aspect when considering the applicability of biomimicry in socio-legal contexts. It is tentative whether biological observations and theories of natural sciences can be used to 'scientise' or 'rationalise' social phenomena in the first place.[36] Second, applying a certain design method will not guarantee that the result is 'sustainable' – acknowledging that the term sustainability itself is open to interpretation. Even when using the advanced knowledge, tools, and methods of natural sciences that the successful application of biomimicry demands, the context and purpose of the design will nevertheless be saturated with cultural and societal norms and values, which will strongly influence the outcome.[37]

Third, it is useful to notice that if biomimicry is pursued without reflecting its underlying normative messages about the human–nature relationship, biomimetic designs may end up reinforcing anthropocentric narratives instead of moving beyond them. However, both the strong biomimicry approaches that view nature as a passive 'source of knowledge', as well as weak approaches highlighting nature as 'a mere source of inspiration', bear this risk. Using nature as any type of source can too easily be translated into valuing nature for what it can do to humans, rather than for what it is.[38] For example, patenting biomimicry solutions as inventions may not reflect 'a balanced relationship with nature'; rather, it highlights the deep-rooted disposition where capitalism relies on using nature as a resource, and where law, in turn, protects the private capitalisation of natural resources.[39]

Despite the constraints, there seems to be a consensus amongst biomimicry authors regarding biomimicry's potential in supporting the shift towards more regenerative, eco-literate societies. Particularly, biomimicry's bio-inclusive approach that assigns value to all different ways of knowing and being can work as a foundation for new social ethics, inspiring policy and profit-making.[40] Ilieva and others suggest that such a deeper level ontological turn is more likely to happen with a more flexible and reflective biomimicry approach, especially when looking for ways to incorporate ecosystem viewpoint in designing social interventions. The authors frame biomimicry as a process 'by which designers build upon natural inspiration with human analogical thinking', allowing 'a shift in the designer's focus from performance outcomes to process outcomes,

[35] MacKinnon and others (n 27) 10.

[36] G Teubner, *Law as an Autopoietic System*. A Bankowski and R Adler (trans.), Z Bankowski (ed). (Oxford, Blackwell, 1992) 25.

[37] Ilieva and others (n 20) 5; MacKinnon and others (n 27) 12; Myers (n 27) 11.

[38] MacKinnon and others (n 27) 10.

[39] Capra and Mattei (n 2) 169.

[40] MacKinnon and others (n 27) 11; Ilieva and others (n 20) 6; Baumeister and others (n 19) 21.

entering a more discursive and synergistic relationship with nature'.[41] In their view, this flexible approach can better support the application of biomimicry in social contexts, as it allows nature to 'redesign not only our commodities but also our own desires'.[42] What this could mean in the context of legal design will be hypothesised next.

SEARCHING FOR BIO-INCLUSIVE DESIGN INSPIRATION FOR LAW

Considering that legal issues, even those regarding more-than-humans, are inherently social phenomena, it may feel counterintuitive, and in a strict legal positivist sense also unorthodox, to 'biologise' or apply 'laws of nature' to address them. In the context of designing posthuman legalities, the potential of biomimicry may then be more inspirational in the sense of flexible mimicry, providing philosophical insights for bio-inclusive policy design and ideas on how the rights of nature and sustainability goals could be realised at socio-material level. Complementing other design approaches, biomimicry could be used as a method to shift the focus from humans to human–nature relationships and to empathise with more-than-human perspectives.

Biomimicry provides a means to discover often hidden or ignored more-than-human agencies, needs, and rationalities that, when exposed, could influence our thinking of what is 'right'. In a similar sense, Santuber and Hermansen propose 'a radically different approach' to designing posthuman legalities, such as prototyping forms of more-than-human relationships. Building on their proposition, particularly prototypes that mimic nature could 'test, reveal and become' 'the very conditions of that relationship and the entities that participate in it'.[43] For example, biomimicry prototyping, such as reconstruction of natural habitats together with artificial intelligence and machine learning, has been used to discover animals' behaviours and preferences in urban environments.[44] Creating biomimetic testing environments could help foster a more participatory approach to design with nature in general. Also, learning through biomimicry how more-than-humans operate in the world could make it easier to imagine or speculate alternative legal futures from their perspectives.[45]

[41] Ilieva and others (n 20) 5.

[42] ibid 9.

[43] Santuber and Hermansen (n 2) 339.

[44] Stanislav Roudavski and others, 'What makes a good tree? We used AI to ask birds' (2024), theconversation.com/what-makes-a-good-tree-we-used-ai-to-ask-birds-233281.

[45] I Farías and others, 'How would animals and architects co-design if we built the right contract?' in M Tironi and others (eds.), *Design For More-Than-Human Futures. Towards Post-Anthropocentric Worlding* (London, Routledge, 2024); M Bastian, 'Introduction: More-than-human participatory research: Contexts, challenges, possibilities' in M Bastian and others (eds), *Participatory Research in More-than-Human Worlds* (London, Routledge, 2016); European Commission Policy Lab, *Futures Garden*, www.futuresgarden.eu/artefacts/symbiotic.

Considering the need to generate deeper, more bio-inclusive social change, the flexible biomimicry approach advocated by Ilieva and others highlights the role of biological analogies, especially drawn from ecosystem-level functions and processes.[46] In other words, when we shift our analogies, the analogies can shift our paradigms.[47] However, using biological analogies to understand law and its objectives is not a new insight. Biological analogies are used particularly by different systemic and holistic approaches to law, such as Proactive Law.[48]

Systems theories more generally observe social phenomena through biological analogies.[49] For example, in Niklas Luhmann's theory of society as a social system, the resonance mechanism works as a metaphor to explain how operationally closed sub-systems, such as law and economy, can exchange information and support each other's functions.[50] Similarly, harmony as a natural phenomenon counterpart to resonance is used to describe an ideal society, where systems seek equilibrium (homeostasis, symbiosis) between contesting interests by embracing diversity and co-dependence.[51] The following will provide a brief overview of how such analogies could guide bio-inclusive legal design. What if posthuman law were *resonant*? What if we designed law to not only satisfy needs, but also *harmonise* them with the ecosystem?

Resonance

Resonance is a physical phenomenon recognised in various fields of natural sciences. In physics, resonance refers to a mechanism that produces amplification and synchronisation effects in oscillatory systems.[52] In biology, resonance mechanism enables mutual influence and adaptation, exchange of information, coordination of behaviours, and embodied cognition of biological organisms. In neuroscience and psychology, resonance describes how neurons and neural

[46] Ilieva and others (n 20) 10.

[47] Similarly Capra and Mattei (n 2) x.

[48] A common analogy used in Proactive Law is 'health', where the proactive approach 'promotes wellness' and 'prevents disease', see, eg, H Haapio and others, 'Legal design for the common good: proactive legal care by design' in M Corrales Compagnucci and others (eds), *Legal Design. Integrating Business, Design and Legal Thinking with Technology* (Cheltenham, Edward Elgar Publishing, 2021) 65.

[49] L von Bertalanffy, *General System Theory. Foundations, Development, Applications* (New York, Geroge Braziller Inc., 1968) 44.

[50] N Luhmann, *Law as a Social System*. Translated by KA Ziegert, Edited by F Kastner and others (Oxford, Oxford University Press, 2008) 381.

[51] JD Lomas and H Xue, 'Harmony in Design: A Synthesis of Literature from Classical Philosophy, the Sciences, Economics, and Design' (2022) 8(1) *She Ji: The Journal of Design, Economics, and Innovation* 5–64; in systems theories von Bertalanffy (n 49) 43; H Maturana and F Varela, *The Tree of Knowledge: The Biological Roots of Human Understanding* (Boston, Shambhala Publications, 1992) 199. See also McDonough and Braungart (n 34) 119.

[52] M Buchanan, 'Going into resonance' (2019) 15 *Nature Physics* 203.

circuits oscillate at certain frequencies, and support functions of perception, memory, and motor coordination, as well as amplification of shared feelings and experiences.[53] For example, when a person observes another person's behaviour, they can physically feel what the other person is feeling, because the observation activates neural representations of their own bodily experiences.[54] However, resonance theory suggests that the less there is similarity between the observer and the observed – such as is the case between a human and a plant, for example – the less there is also resonance.[55]

To design more ecologically sustainable and reciprocal human–nature relationships, resonance may provide a suitable analogy to how to increase empathy not only between two different life forms, but also between biological beings and machines.[56] As a design plan or pattern, resonance could help explore overarching interests between humans and natural entities and help integrate them into a design solution. This could mean, for example, exploring common denominators between humans and natural entities, such as similar elements of agency or causalities between ecological interests. The Indigenous perspective would offer a prominent lens for such explorations.[57] Research indicates that Indigenous communities may not only have better ecological knowledge, but also distinctive conceptual models of more-than-human agency and sophisticated insights, for example, when it comes to plant communication and behaviour.[58]

Harmony

In their comprehensive article 'Harmony in Design: A Synthesis of Literature from Classical Philosophy, the Sciences, Economics and Design', Lomas and Xue propose harmony as a guiding design principle for the more sustainable world.[59] Contrary to common belief, harmony does not mean pure agreement or 'sameness', but integration of diversity into a greater whole. As a biological term, harmony refers to cooperative interactions between organisms and their ecosystems, or within an individual organism's systems, which maintain system's resilience and balance. In the case of harmony within a single organism, the phenomenon is often expressed as *homeostasis*, the process by which

[53] JD Lomas and others, 'Resonance as a Design Strategy for AI and Social Robots' (2022) 16 *Frontiers in Neurorobotics* 1–28, 3, 8.

[54] S Hurley, 'The Shared Circuits Model (SCM): How Control, Mirroring, and Simulation Can Enable Imitation, Deliberation, and Mindreading' (2008) 31 *Behavioral Brain Science* 1–22. About observation, resonance and engagement, see Santuber and Hermansen (n 2) 345–346.

[55] Lomas and others (n 53).

[56] About resonance in human and artificial intelligence and social robots' interaction, see Lomas and others (n 54).

[57] Cirkovic (n 2) 164.

[58] See e.g. Bethany Ojalehto and others, 'Conceptualizing Agency: Folkpsychological and Folkcommunicative Perspectives on Plants' (2017) 162 *Cognition* 103–123, 115.

[59] Lomas and Xue (n 51).

the organism maintains a stable internal environment.[60] Harmonious states are achieved by co-evolving and are most evident in mutualistic relationships, where two organisms interact in a way that is beneficial to both. In this sense, harmony can also be a synonym for *symbiosis*.[61] Harmony emerges naturally in diverse ecosystems through various forms of dynamic adaptation and interlinked feedback mechanisms, such as food webs and nutrient cycles.[62]

In bio-inclusive legal design, the principle of harmony could guide designing mutually supportive, 'right relationships' among the diverse ecological needs within the human–more-than-human ecosystems.[63] Harmony would emphasise the critical role of diversity in creating balance in self-sustaining systems, which, in contrast, would also mean eliminating factors in the design that strive for sameness, including unnecessary human intervention. For example, in posthuman legal frameworks for food production, the principle of harmony would exclude monocultural farming methods and the use of chemicals that impoverish the soil, while promoting strategies that naturally eliminate weeds and pests, providing also habitats for a diversity of associated species.[64]

Lomas and Xue suggest that using harmony as a design principle could also help reduce dualistic views of the world in general, such as viewing capitalism and socialism, masculine and feminine, the east and the west, etc, as opposing forces.[65] Harmony would therefore challenge the human tendency to reduce information into binary heuristics, as well as fragmentated views of the world that this mechanism produces.[66] Harmony, as a principle that emphasises the whole over its parts, could support the reconciliation of various needs for equity, ecology, and economy, as stated in the United Nation's Sustainable Development Goals.[67] Harmony could also provide guidance for more reciprocal and generative application of biomimicry in the development of technology. Imagine a solarpunk utopia where technology is designed in harmony with nature: cities are vibrant ecosystems where lush green rooftops blend seamlessly with solar panels, and permaculture farms thrive alongside high-tech, sustainable infrastructure, designed by the community of all living beings.[68]

[60] von Bertalanffy (n 49) 43.

[61] Lynn Margulis, *Symbiotic Planet. A New Look at Evolution* (New York, Basic Books 1998) 5.

[62] Maturana and Varela (n 51) 199.

[63] European Economic and Social Committee and others (n 9).

[64] Lomas and Xue (n 51) 8, 11, 30.

[65] Lomas and Xue (n 51) 48.

[66] Capra and Mattei (n 2) 13.

[67] United Nations (n 21); McDonough and Braungart (n 34) 150. Some critical observations about intentionally "harmonizing" different social goals, Luhmann 1989 (n 22) 115–120.

[68] William Gillam, 'A Solarpunk Manifesto: Turning Imaginary into Reality' (2023) 8(4) *Philosophies* 73.

CONCLUSION

This chapter explored biomimicry, a design approach that emulates or draws inspiration from biological phenomena, as a possible method to engage nature to the design of law. As discussed above, such a proposition appears both as a radical, close to impossible idea, yet as something that has been done since the dawn of the humanity. However, the ongoing ecological crisis calls for radical solutions, an ontological turn that has new kinds of epistemic and methodological needs. In the case of law and the increasing recognition of more-than-humans as legal beings, these needs test the boundaries of our legal imagination:

- How can we design more-than-human centric law?
- How can a legal design process give agency to nature?
- How can we know what more-than-human beings consider as 'right'?
- How can we empathise with perspectives we are not able to sense?

Exploring legal territories beyond anthropocentrism presents an intriguing challenge for legal design. As an interdisciplinary, systemic, and practically oriented approach to law, legal design is equipped with suitable frameworks, methods, and tools for this task. Within this toolkit, biomimicry can provide philosophical inspiration and support the application of other bio-inclusive design methods. However, fully understanding the agents that silently weave the web of life may remain a mystery.

REFERENCES

M Bastian, 'Introduction: More-than-Human Participatory Research: Contexts, Challenges, Possibilities' in Michelle Bastian, Owain Jones, Niamh Moore and Emma Roe (eds), *Participatory Research in More-than-Human Worlds* (London, Routledge, 2016).

D Baumeister, R Tocke, J Dwyer, S Ritter and J Benyus, *Biomimicry. Resource Handbook: A Seed Bank of Best Practices* (Missoula, MT, Biomimicry 3.8, 2014).

J Bennett, *Vibrant Matter. A Political ecology of things* (Durham, NC, Duke University Press, 2010).

J Benyus, *Biomimicry. Innovation Inspired by Nature* (New York, Harper Collins Publishers Inc., 2002).

K Birrell and D Matthews, 'Re-storying Laws for the Anthropocene: Rights, Obligations, and an Ethics of Encounter' (2020) 31 *Law and Critique* 275–292.

Biomimicry Institute, *Ask Nature*.

K Bradshaw, *Wildlife as Property Owners. A New Conception of Animal Rights* (Chicago, The University of Chicago Press, 2020).

M Buchanan, 'Going into resonance' (2019) 15 *Nature Physics* 203.

F Capra and U Mattei, *The Ecology of Law. Toward a Legal System in Tune with Nature and Community* (San Francisco, Berrett-Koehler Publishers Inc., 2015).

E Cirkovic, 'The Next Generation of International Law: Space, Ice, and the Cosmolegal Proposal' (2021) *German Law Journal* 147.

DP Corrigan and M Oksanen, 'Rights of Nature: Exploring the Territory' in DP Corrigan and M Oksanen, *Rights of Nature. A Re-Examination* (London, Routledge, 2021).

C Darwin, *The Formation of Vegetable Mould, through the Action of Worms, with Observations on Their Habits* (London, John Murray, 1881).

M Doherty, M Corrales Compagnucci, H Haapio and M Hagan, 'A new attitude to law's empire: the potentialities of legal design' in M Corrales Compagnucci, H Haapio, M Hagan and M Doherty (eds), *Legal Design. Integrating Business, Design and Legal Thinking with Technology* (Cheltenham, Edward Elgar Publishing, 2021).

European Commission, *Biodiversity strategy for 2030.*

European Commission, *A Sustainable Finance Framework That Works on the Ground.* (Strasbourg, COM 317 final, 13 June 2023).

European Commission Policy Lab, *Futures Garden.*

European Economic and Social Committee and others, *Towards an EU Charter of the Fundamental Rights of Nature: Study* (Publications Office, 2020).

I Farías, T Sánchez Criado and F Remter, 'How would animals and architects co-design if we built the right contract?' in M Tironi, M Chilet, CU Marín and P Hermansen (eds.), *Design For More-Than-Human Futures. Towards Post-Anthropocentric Worlding* (London, Routledge, 2024).

M Fisch, 'The Nature of Biomimicry: Toward a Novel Technological Culture' (2017) 42(5) *Science, Technology & Human Values* 795–821.

W Gillam, 'A Solarpunk Manifesto: Turning Imaginary into Reality' (2023) 8(4) *Philosophies* 73.

S Grainger and D Conway, 'Climate change and International River Boundaries: fixed points in shifting sands' (2014) 5(1) *WIREs Climate Change.*

H Haapio, TD Barton and M Corrales Compagnucci, 'Legal design for the common good: proactive legal care by design' in M Corrales Compagnucci, H Haapio, M Hagan and M Doherty (eds), *Legal Design. Integrating Business, Design and Legal Thinking with Technology* (Cheltenham, Edward Elgar Publishing, 2021).

S Hurley, 'The shared circuits model (SCM): how control, mirroring, and simulation can enable imitation, deliberation, and mindreading' (2008) 31 *Behavioral Brain Science* 1–22.

L Ilieva, I Ursano, L Traista, B Hoffmann and H Dahy, 'Biomimicry as a Sustainable Design Methodology – Introducing the 'Biomimicry for Sustainability' Framework' (2022) 7(37) *Biomimetics.*

D Jackson, SJ Rochielle, M Kim and S Bhatnagar, 'What legal design could be: Towards an expanded practice of inquiry, critique and action' (DRS Biennial Conference Series, 2022).

R Koulu, 'In Search of Living Law: How Should We Design for (Digital) Legal Interaction?' (2024) 3(2) *Digital Society.*

W Lidwell, K Holden and J Butler, *Universal Principles of Design* (Beverly, MA, Rockport, 2010).

N Luhmann, *Law as a Social System.* Translated by KA Ziegert, Edited by F Kastner, R Nobles, D Schiff and R Ziegert (Oxford, Oxford University Press, 2008).

N Luhmann, *Ecological Communication* (Chicago, The University of Chicago Press, 1989).

JD Lomas, A Lin, S Dikker, D Forster, ML Lupetti, G Huisman, J Habekost, C Beardow, P Pandey, N Ahmad, K Miyapuram, T Mullen, P Cooper, W van der

Maden and E Cross, 'Resonance as a Design Strategy for AI and Social Robots' (2022) 16 *Frontiers in Neurorobotics* 1–28.

JD Lomas and H Xue, 'Harmony in Design: A Synthesis of Literature from Classical Philosophy, the Sciences, Economics, and Design' (2022) 8(1) *She Ji: The Journal of Design, Economics, and Innovation* 5–64.

L Margulis, *Symbiotic Planet. A New Look at Evolution* (New York, Basic Books, 1998).

W McDonough and M Braungart, *Cradle to Cradle. Remaking the Way We Make Things* (New York, North Point Press, 2002).

RB MacKinnon, J Oomen and M Pedersen Zari, 'Promises and Presuppositions of Biomimicry' (2020) 5(33) *Biomimetics.*

H Maturana and F Varela, *The Tree of Knowledge: The Biological Roots of Human Understanding* (Boston, Shambhala Publications, 1992).

W Myers, *Bio Design* (New York, MoMa, 2021).

H Nelson and E Stolterman, *The Design Way. Intentional Change in an Unpredictable World.* (Cambridge, MA, MIT Press, 2012).

I Niiniluoto, 'The Aim and Structure of Applied Research' (1993) 38 *Erkenntnis, An International Journal of Scientific Philosophy* 1–21.

B Ojalehto, DL Medin and SG García, 'Conceptualizing Agency: Folkpsychological and Folkcommunicative Perspectives on Plants' (2017) 162 *Cognition* 103–123.

A Perry-Kessaris, 'Legal Design for Practice, Activism, Policy and Research' (2019) 46 *Journal of Law and Society* 185.

A Philippopoulos-Mihalopoulos, 'Lively Agency: Life and Law in the Anthropocene', in I Braverman (ed.), *Animals, Biopolitics, Law. Lively Legalities* (London, Routledge, 2016).

R Raman, A Sreenivasan, M Suresh and others. 'Mapping biomimicry research to sustainable development goals' (2024) 14 *Scientific Reports* 18613.

S Roudavski, A Holland and P Gibbons, 'What makes a good tree? We used AI to ask birds' (2024)

J Santuber and P Hermansen, 'Designing for Posthuman Legalities: Legal Design(ing) and the Ontological Turn', in R Ducato, A Strowel and E Marique (eds), *Design(s) for Law* (Milan, Ledizioni, 2024).

J Santuber and L Krawietz, 'User Research Methodologies in Legal Design Projects: Lessons from Practice', in R Ducato and A Strowel (eds), *Legal Design Perspectives – Theoretical and Practical Insights from the Field* (Milan, Ledizioni, 2021).

C Stone, *Should trees have standing? Law, Morality, and the Environment* (New York, Oxford University Press, 1972).

G Teubner, *Law as an Autopoietic System.* A Bankowski and R Adler (trans.), Z Bankowski (ed). (Oxford, Blackwell, 1992).

M Tironi, M Chilet, C Ureta Marín and P Hermansen (eds.), *Design For More-Than-Human Futures. Towards Post-Anthropocentric Worlding* (London, Routledge, 2024).

United Nations. *Department of Economic and Social Affairs. Sustainable development goals.*

S Vogel, 'The Silence of Nature' (2006) 15 *Environmental Values* 145–171.

L von Bertalanffy, *General System Theory. Foundations, Development, Applications* (New York, Geroge Braziller Inc., 1968).

WJH Wickler, 'The occurrence of mimicry among plants and animals' (*Encyclopaedia Britannica*, 2023).

5

Does the Legal Design Lexicon Need to be Designed? A Theoretical and Critical Study

DORRA HARRAR[1]

INTRODUCTION

DOES THE LEGAL design lexicon need to be designed? From our point of view, the answer is a resounding yes. In fact, ambiguities exist in the practice of legal design yet and one must enquire about its epistemological foundations. Following a decade of literature, research, and practice in legal design, it is time to evaluate our practice of legal design in comparison with the design discipline that it emanates from, and the application by legal design practitioners to understand the relevance of this new approach.

Interdisciplinarity is the 'bringing together of at least two disciplines in order to develop an original representation of a concept, a situation or an issue'.[2] Based on interdisciplinarity, design is opening up to a new field of action – the law, where it acquires value and represents a new vision.

The practice of design is no longer limited to the creation and conception of an idea, a service or a product, or to the fitting out of spaces, etc. In order to enrich the practice of design, researchers are more interested in the new methods, strategies, and tools that it can generate as a result of its confrontation with other disciplines.[3] It is this creative power generated from the combination of strategic thinking and tools that is interesting about the design–law relationship.

[1] Business Lawyer, Expert practitioner in Legal design, Founder of Legal.D.

[2] Yves Lenoir, 'Fourez, G. (dir.), Maingain, A. et Dufour, B. (2002). Approches didactiques de l'in terdisciplinarité'. 29 *Revue des sciences de l'éducation* 211 (Bruxelles, De Boeck 2003).

[3] Rania Ghrabi, 'La Valeur Évolutive Du Design Vis à Vis de l'interdisciplinarité', *The How in Design? Introspective/Prospective Design* (Les publications de l'ESSTED, 2019).

Thus, we wish to reflect on the practice of legal design as an experience, to evaluate its user's satisfaction. It is interesting to approach design as a 'self-reflection and self-development strategy' for the discipline of law.[4]

This interdisciplinarity is beneficial for each discipline: it ensures its evolution and consequently enables the development of its values. How then can we assess the interdisciplinarity of design and law at the level of its lexicon? We will attempt to answer this question across three sections.

In the first part of this paper, we analyse the lexicon of legal design through its various sources and arrive at some conclusions (1). In the second part, based on a survey conducted among legal design practitioners (private practitioners and teachers), we arrive at conclusions drawn from their practice of legal design, specifically relating to the legal design lexicon and its accessibility (2). To enrich the discussion, we also address the issue of geographical accessibility of legal design and the questions surrounding its practice in African and Arab countries (3).

The objectives of our contribution are as follows:

1. Our contribution is an invitation to open a discussion or reflection on our legal design practice methodology and to assess whether the law has been able to absorb all facets of design and has benefited from them, to reduce the gap between the law and its users. This examination will be made through the use of the legal design lexicon.
2. Second, we seek the development of research around the practice of legal design in the countries of the South, and explore how the legal design practice could be made more inclusive and satisfactory.

THE SPECIFIC NATURE OF THE LEGAL DESIGN LEXICON: A MOSAIC OF CONCEPTS

Every discipline has its terminology and language.

What about legal design? Does it have its own custom lexicon, or does it draw from the broader design field? Does it encompass the entire design lexicon or only design thinking and a human-centred design approach? What effect does the legal design lexicon have on the elaboration of the theory of legal conceptions? Finally, it may be prudent to also check on the contributions by the design vocabulary to the legal vocabulary.

It could be argued that the lexicon of legal design is an accumulation of various conceptual currents that have influenced legal design, starting with design. Presented as a sub-discipline of design,[5] legal design has inherited many of the

[4] ibid.

[5] Michael Doherty, 'Disciplinarity and the Modes of Legal Design' (2022) dl.designresearchsociety.org/drs-conference-papers/drs2022/researchpapers/172.

concepts familiar to designers: graphic design, ideation, user, empathy, human centricity, needs analysis, etc.[6] Other terminologies have been added to this lexicon from outside the fields of design and law in their classic definition. These include terms such as innovation, legal tech, access to justice, access to dignity, and fair patterns.

Legal design has even helped to create new concepts, such as the proactivity of contracts,[7] contract design, comprehensibility in commercial contracting,[8] and other concepts such as visual law.[9]

This appropriation of new concepts in legal design is a key element in building the discipline of legal design and, according to some,[10] indicates a certain maturity of the subject, capable of creating its own vocabulary and gradually detaching itself from the parent discipline.[11]

In this way, multi-disciplinarity has contributed to enriching the lexicon of legal design and has even encouraged the creation of new terms specific to this approach. The result is a mosaic of concepts that have built the lexicon of legal design.

However, one of the limitations of the legal design lexicon is that it is mainly oriented towards the design thinking approach, to the detriment of other design approaches. The design thinking approach is commonly employed by legal design practitioners to practise or teach legal design.

Even so, 'There are different ways of doing legal design, and there are also various effects of legal design'.[12]

Indeed, there are four spaces of design other than design thinking that provide a broad understanding of design and the diversity of its practices.[13] It should also be noted that creative thinking through design thinking can only be effective if there is a shift 'from a common, analytical, purely intellectual, problem-solving approach to a dynamic one where the practitioner observes the environment to draw a problem to action'.[14]

[6] ibid.

[7] Helena Haapio, 'Introduction to Proactive Law: A Business Lawyer's View' in Peter Wahlgren (ed), *A Proactive Approach: Law Libraries* (Stockholm, Stockholm Institute for Scandinavian Law : Jure [distributör] : Almqvist & Wiksell [internationell distributör], 2006).

[8] Katri Nousiainen, 'Measuring the Impact and Value of Legal Design in Commercial Contracting within the Law and Economics Framework' (Economics and society; 374, Hanken School of Economics Svenska handelshögskolan 2023), /hdl.handle.net/10227/562065.

[9] Colette R Brunschwig, 'Visual Law and Legal Design: Questions and Tentative Answers' (2021) Editions Weblaw www.zora.uzh.ch/id/eprint/200875.

[10] Doherty (n 5).

[11] ibid.

[12] Marie-Sophie de Clippele, Vincent Couronne and Joachim Savin, 'A Critical Assessment of the Notion of Legal Design through the Case of "Les Surligneurs", a Legal-Checking Media Outlet' (2023).

[13] ibid.

[14] Apolline Le Gall, 'Legal Design Beyond Design Thinking: Processes and Effects of the Four Spaces of Design Practices for the Legal Field' in Rossana Ducato and Alain Strowel (eds), *Legal Design Perspectives: Theoretical and Practical Insights from the Field* (Milan, Ledizioni, 2021).

This limitation has strongly influenced the lexicon of legal design, which is largely made up of design thinking concepts (user, human-centred design methodology, needs, process of design) and has ignored other foundational design concepts, in particular the concept of co-creation, which is at the heart of any design project. This limitation impacts the unlimited potential of design to conceive innovative solutions in the field of law.[15]

Reducing the field of design in the legal sphere to design thinking only brings about superficial solutions that are far from effecting radical change and do not tackle the 'underlying problems or the defective framework itself'.[16] The author has quoted some projects that associate legal design only with its external result, as 'amateurism', ie, the form of the deliverable achieved without investing in the process of a design project according to the standards of this discipline, augmented by a lack of knowledge about design techniques and concepts.

If design has experienced a real evolution in its definition, it is due to its openness to other disciplines. This multidisciplinary approach has enabled it to retain its innovative character while opening up new fields of action.

The same applies to law when it meets design, which is an evolution in itself. It's just that this connection has not been made on the right foundations.

First, training lawyers in legal design does not include the basics of design theory. As we will see in the second part of the survey results, the majority of respondents are self-taught in legal design and have learned legal design on the basis of their own research. Very few have acquired a combined academic background in design and law. This lack of theoretical design knowledge can harm the management of legal design projects in the sense that, despite improvement, 'the fundamental aspects remain unchanged'.[17]

It is important to integrate legal design into a university law course, with particular attention to the history of design, to assimilate the basics of design theory and some central concepts, such as co-creation, co-design,[18] and participatory design, which need to be mastered before trying to define a legal concept or to detail its process, and to put it into practice quickly. Second, some have described limitations in the scope of design applicable to law, as a 'methodological rigidity' in design thinking only,[19] which would be counter-productive for legal design and also for design itself.

[15] de Clippele, Couronne and Savin (n 12).

[16] ibid.

[17] ibid.

[18] Co-design, is defined as 'a manoeuvre of self-reflection and communication which has participated in the development of working methods within a work group' and its distinction from participative design, which tends to involve the players in a collaboration in the design project chain, are the basis of the vocabulary of design and its working methods. Ghrabi (n 3) 80.

[19] de Clippele, Couronne and Savin (n 12).

In the next section, we explore how the legal design lexicon, influenced by the design lexicon, is accessible to practitioners and their audience.

THE ACCESSIBILITY OF THE LEGAL DESIGN LEXICON FROM THE POINT OF VIEW OF LEGAL DESIGN PRACTITIONERS AND THEIR USERS: A PRACTICAL STUDY

The idea of launching a survey to consolidate the experience of legal practitioners in design was certainly inspired by the writing of this article, but especially by my own experience. In my legal design practice since 2018, I have experienced a mean challenge in explaining what legal design means. Indeed, whenever I attempted to explain legal design to people in the ecosystem, I came across several definitions and approaches to the concept, and I have discovered that demonstrating examples is the most effective way to explain legal design. This observation is not limited to my experience alone. Similar feedback can be noted from the results of the survey with other legal professionals on legal design.

We chose to conduct a qualitative survey to extract feedback from legal design practitioners, particularly in relation to the use of the legal design lexicon. The answers help provide a better understanding of the challenges and perspectives related to using this lexicon in the field of legal design.

We also took into account the recommendations of the participants from the workshop, held at the International Institute for the Sociology of Law in Onati on 4 and 5 July 2024. The recommendations include additional and related questions to legal design professionals who practice legal design without proper awareness. The update will be completed by September.

The first version of the survey with 10 questions was posted on LinkedIn until 31 May, 2024.

The first part of the questions (from question 1 to question 4) relates to the identity of the legal design practitioner: Who is the legal designer today? From what region do they practice legal design? What is their training background?

The second part of the survey (from question 5 to question 7) questions the accessibility of the legal design vocabulary for the legal designer.

The last part of the survey consists of three open questions to seek feedback from legal design practitioners on the tools they use for explaining the legal design vocabulary, the challenges they face, and their ideas or suggestions to make the legal design vocabulary accessible.

In the last part, there are no graphical representations, only an analysis of the open-ended responses. Below are the results of the 31 responses received (Figures 5.1 to 5.7).

All figures are expressed in %

Figure 5.1 Where did you learn legal design?

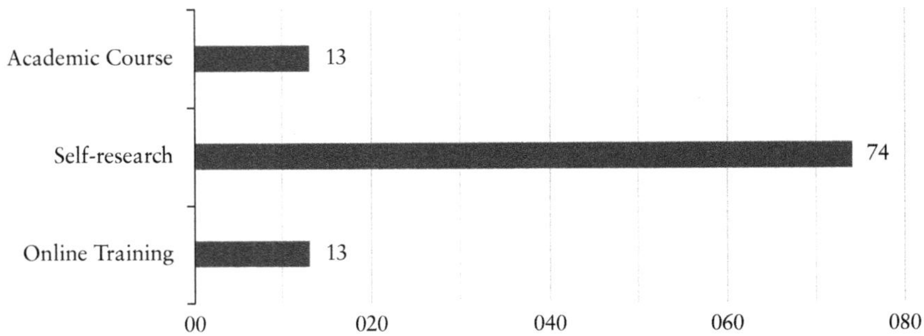

Figure 5.2 What types of legal design projects have you undertaken?

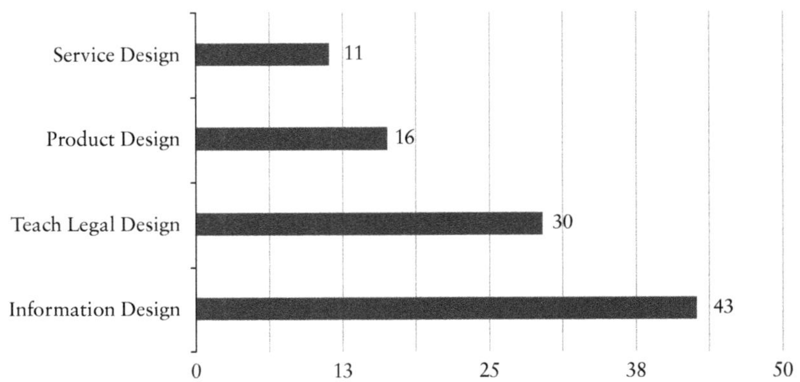

Figure 5.3 In which region of the world do you practise as a legal designer?

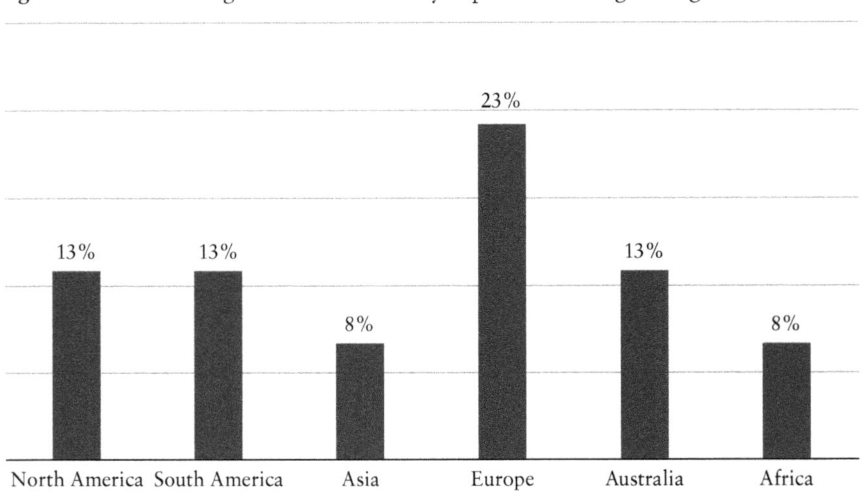

Figure 5.4 Do you have any prior experience in Design?

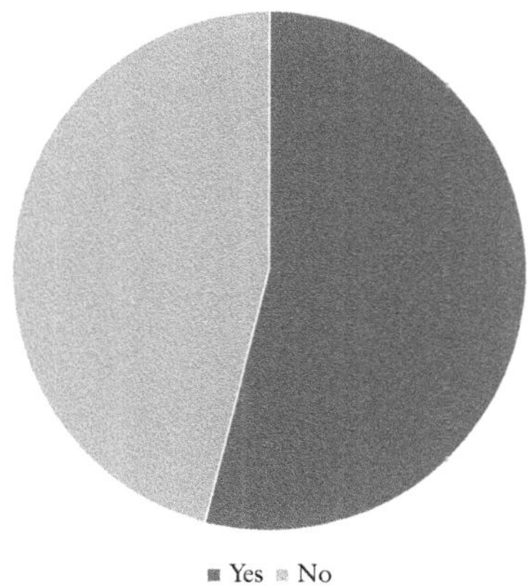

Figure 5.5 Difficulties faced in explaining legal design concepts to professional contacts?

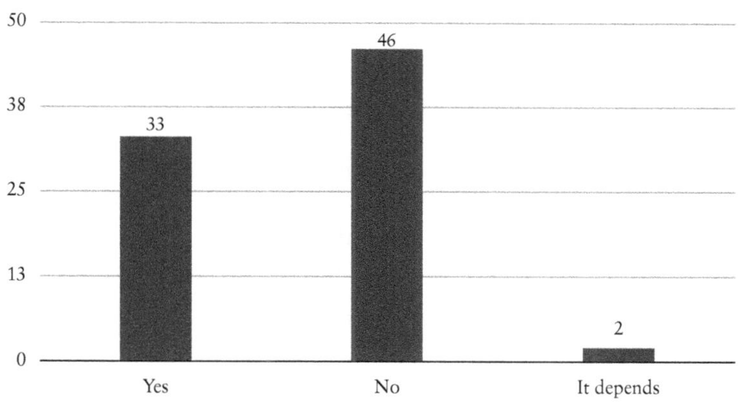

Figure 5.6 Do legal designers with a legal background understand design concepts used in legal design?

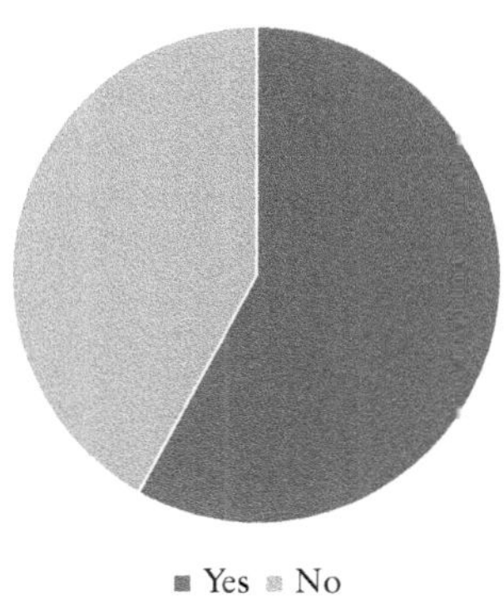

Figure 5.7 Is the legal design vocabulary accessible easily to aspiring students of legal design?

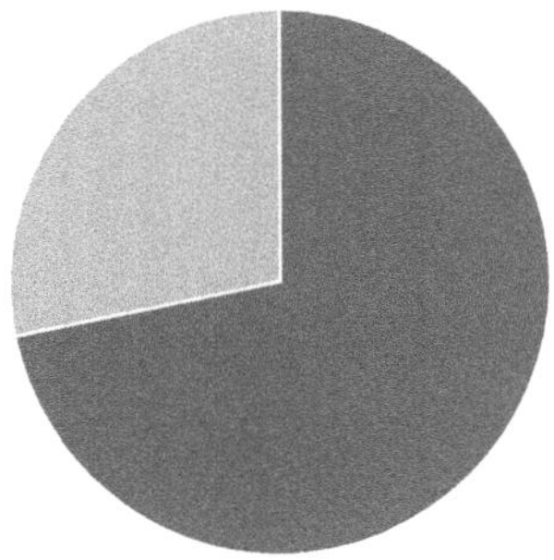

Broadly, the following results emerged from the responses:

1. The majority of respondents learnt legal design through their own research, with as many as 74 per cent of respondents being self-taught.
2. Academic learners are in the same proportion as those opting for e-learning from private training institutions.
3. At this stage, one could infer that legal design has not yet gained substantial momentum as an academic discipline taught in universities following a common legal design curriculum. Only a small minority of legal designers are university graduates.
4. As for the region where it is practiced, it was found that the majority hail from Europe, barring a few practitioners in Asia and Africa.

In the final part of our paper, we look at the practice of legal design in African and Arabian regions, as well as the history of design in those countries.

The survey also reveals that a key aspect of legal design practice remains information design, particularly contract design. This reiterates the approach presented earlier regarding the dominance of design thinking over the practice of legal design, with widespread application in the design of contracts. At second place is the activity of teaching legal design.

Another important finding from this survey is that a large proportion of respondents have prior knowledge of design. This explains why most of them do not find it difficult to understand design concepts used in legal design lexicons.

On the other hand, it was found that over half the respondents expressed concern in accessing the legal design lexicon for the target audience, and that they needed to explain design concepts even more.

To better understand this finding, we asked participants three open-ended questions about the accessibility of the legal design lexicon.

First, we looked at the various challenges faced with the accessibility of the legal design lexicon. Then, we examined the means used to overcome these difficulties. Finally, we invited suggestions to overcome these difficulties and make the legal design lexicon more accessible to new practitioners, especially those from the legal fraternity.

A majority of the respondents faced the following challenges:

1. People often tend to associate the term design with aesthetics and external elements like visuals alone, rather than a creative problem-solving approach and a mindset.
2. It was also noted that it takes time to persuade people to make legal services more user-centred. They also need guidance on why research and testing are necessary.

Other interesting outcomes include that:

3. Legal professionals do not seem to understand how they can use legal design themselves.
4. Legal design vocabulary can often seem superficial compared to legal concepts that are rich in interpretation and history. For example, if you consider user-friendliness as an objective in relation to human dignity, that sounds super social.
5. Some terms such as 'client', 'persona', and 'need' must be clearly identified by lawyers.
6. A respondent pointed out that the vocabulary of legal design is not consistent, as it transcends continents.
7. Another similar observation was the lack of standardisation, as design is often subjective, which explains the reason why legal professionals have yet to consider it among their working tools or have expressed scepticism about the efficiency and legality of visually enhanced legal documents.

Furthermore, legal design practitioners are challenged with the risk of over-simplification and the importance of maintaining legal accuracy while making documents more accessible.

In addition, legal design is often misunderstood as viewing legal documents. Participants may attend a legal design workshop expecting to rework a legal document, and if their expectations are not met when other activities are offered (such as empathy exercises, user persona work, user journey mapping, etc).

From these responses, one could infer that there is a lack of clarity in the concepts of legal design. Misunderstandings and the explanation of concepts, particularly in conveying their benefits, are among the main challenges.

Through this survey, we collected multiple propositions from respondents to overcome such misunderstandings:

- Explain concepts at least twice, giving examples.
- Explain that legal design is not just about externally looking good.
- Demonstrate and present articles for internal teams written in easy-to-understand language.

- Give concrete examples in workshops where time is taken to clarify design concepts.
- Practical, hands-on methods such as visual aids, real-world examples, and kinesthetic learning techniques are emphasised as effective ways to explain design concepts and methodologies.
- Use tools like Canva and AI to simplify contracts, as well as the use of plain language and design thinking frameworks.

It is interesting to report on the last part of the survey dealing with suggestions to make the vocabulary of legal design more accessible. Here is an overview of the key inferences that emerged:

1. Creation of Resources:

1. A legal design Dictionary or Terminology Glossary: Several respondents suggested the creation of a glossary or dictionary specifically for legal design terms, to serve as a fundamental resource for learners.
2. Expand Academic and Training Materials: Proposals include expanding academic production, incorporating legal design into law school curricula, and making more free resources available.

2. Training and Education:

1. Some suggestions also emphasise that legal design vocabulary should be part of every formal training program. This includes practical approaches such as webinars, live drafting sessions, and demo tools like the WorldCC Contract Design Pattern Library.
2. Focus on Plain Language and Avoidance of Jargon: Respondents recommend using plain language, avoiding jargon, and providing simple explanations for complex terms. Synonyms and simple terminology should be used to make concepts comprehensible.

3. **Practical Application and Examples:**

1. Real-world Applications: Many responses highlight the importance of connecting vocabulary and concepts to real-world legal problems and the day-to-day work of lawyers. Practical examples, case studies, and showing rather than telling are seen as crucial.
2. Standardisation and Consistency: There is a call for standardising terminology across the discipline, acknowledging regional differences, and striving for consistency to reduce confusion and misinformation.

4. Community and Ongoing Engagement:

1. Democratisation and Continuous Effort: The need to continually popularise legal design and make it a topic of ongoing discussion is emphasised. Engaging with broader communities, including design researchers and artistic communities, is seen to be beneficial.

2. Spaces for Discussion and Collaboration: Creating more spaces for discussion such as conferences and seminars and encouraging collaboration among professionals in the field are recommended.

5. Broader Learning and Adaptation:

1. Learning from Design Fields: It is suggested that those interested in legal design should not only focus on legal design courses but also learn from general design fields to discern the underlying principles.
2. Behavioural Change and Adaptation: Emphasising that practicing legal design requires a change in habits and a commitment to training, potentially guided by standards like ISO.

These responses make clear that it is important to create resources that clarify the meaning of the legal design lexicon through a glossary or a dictionary. Similarly, the integration of the legal design vocabulary into formal training programs, the use of plain language, and practical examples are essential to make the concepts more accessible and relevant to real-world legal practice.

Finally, creating collaborative spaces for discussion and learning in general design areas can further enrich practice. To do this, we need to bring together as many legal design practitioners, designers, and other professionals from different backgrounds as possible.

THE PRACTICE OF LEGAL DESIGN IN THE AFRICAN AND ARABIAN REGIONS: CHALLENGES AND OBSTACLES

I have observed that the representation of legal design practitioners from African and Arabian countries is often a minority or even non-existent in the international arena of legal design. This observation can be verified from various sources:

At an international legal design summit held in Helsinki, Finland, I participated as a speaker on a panel discussing the presence and development of legal design across different world regions, with a focus on the MENA region, which I represent. I started with a question addressed to the audience present (almost 300 people) to identify participants from the MENA region. Only three people raised their hands. The majority came from Europe and the Americas.

This under-representation is also confirmed by other resources, in particular the work of the legal design agency Amurabi entitled 'Legal Design around the World'.

This map indicates that legal design is almost absent in African and Arabian countries, while it is concentrated in Europe and the Americas (Figure 5.8).

Figure 5.8 Legal Design Around the World[20]

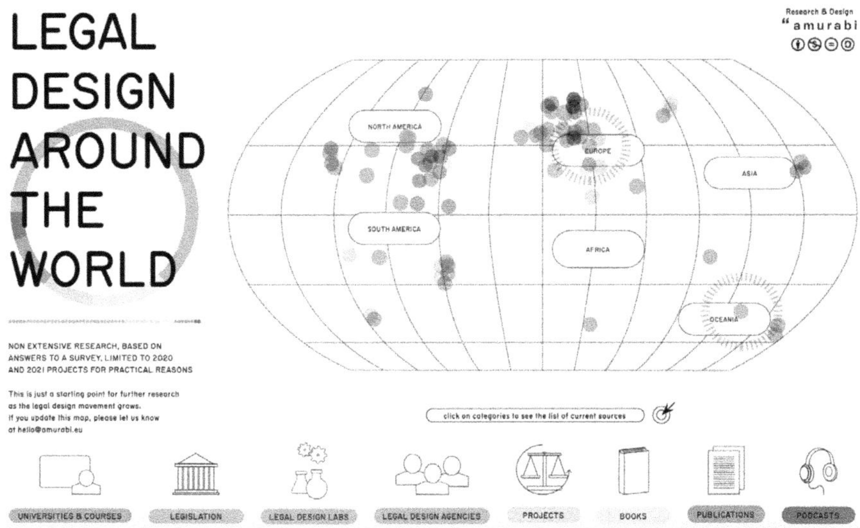

Even in terms of scientific resources and research, studies on legal design in this region of the world remain rare.[21]

With the exception of rare legal design practices in countries like South Africa, Tunisia, and Morocco, which are isolated personal initiatives, we cannot find a clear foundation for the practice of legal design in the African and Arabian regions.

Is this due to the accessibility of legal design, which remains, even in regions where it is well implemented, a vague notion that needs more guidance? Does this have anything to do with the place of design in African and Arabian countries and the reality of legal innovation in those regions?

From our point of view, the practice of legal design in the African and Arabian regions raises questions around the reality of legal innovation in this region and the integration of design. In discussing legal innovation, it is common to view technology and legal tech as the main forms of transformation. From the various experiments currently underway in the MENA region, it can be observed that all efforts are being directed towards digital transformation of the justice system. This process was accelerated by the COVID pandemic, resulting in a total shutdown of the courts. In East Africa, the use of technology to video conference hearings has become common practice.[22]

[20] 'Resources' (*Amurabi – Legal Design Agency*), amurabi.eu/en/ressources/.

[21] Karma Dabaghi, 'Beyond Design Thinking and into Speculative Futures in Legal Design' (2022) dl.designresearchsociety.org/drs-conference-papers/drs2022/researchpapers/70.

[22] In Tunisia, the legislature has adopted government decree-law no. 2020-12, which allowed criminal trials to be held by videoconference during the pandemic period and beyond. This innovation allows magistrates to judge remand prisoners from a room set up in the prison where they are being held.

In Tunisia, a strategic plan for the digitalisation of the judicial system has been drawn up, with its implementation from 2023 to 2025. Its aim is to link all Tunisian courts to an integrated computer network and to adopt electronic signatures, as well as to launch a digital platform enabling civil status documents to be exchanged between the courts and parties concerned, and to hold hearings remotely.

Similarly, the 'Egypt digital justice project' offers litigants digital services such as an e-notary, the holding of criminal trials by videoconference, and other services that avoid unnecessary travel by litigants to court. Another example of digitising the judicial system can be found in Lebanon, which includes cooperation between the IT Center and the Ministry of Justice on a project to automate the courts, archive data, and implement the use of electronic signatures. In the Gulf States, digitisation of courts project has achieved advanced levels of functionality compared with other countries. The adoption of a zero-paper policy is already operational. In the case of Kuwait, a ministry dedicated to artificial intelligence has been established. This is a reflection of the rapid achievement of high levels of technological innovation in these countries over a short span of time.

A review of experiences in the countries of the Maghreb and Arabian regions reveals that progress in access to justice is perceived as purely technological progress, focusing more on infrastructure and technical platforms than on education and training in accessing justice in all its forms.

Moreover, there is a profound alienation of the countries of the North, even in the implementation of this transformation. This is evident, both financially, given that most digital transformation programs in the justice sector are financed by the European Union or other Western international funds, and strategically.[23] Indeed, these solutions are exported without accounting for the socio-economic and political frameworks of the region. Innovation is only considered from a technological point of view, and not from a behavioural standpoint.

Yet what the MENA region needs today is to have its own development model and to adjust solutions to the specific characteristics of the region, particularly in terms of language; it is evident that a majority of the solutions offered to legal professionals are built in English, whereas the official language in the countries of the Maghreb and the Middle East is Arabic.

This is also true of design practice in these regions.

From our perspective, to understand the current experience of legal design in the African and Arabian regions, it is imperative to place it in the general context of the practice of design and specifically the history of design in the region. Moreover, an important critique of the legal design concept is that it

[23] Manuel Langendorf, 'The EU Needs to Expand Its Support for the MENA Region's Digital Transformation' (*Middle East Institute*, 19 August 2024) www.mei.edu/publications/eu-needs-expand-its-support-mena-regions-digital-transformation.

is notoriously blurry because it is disconnected from the historical roots of design.[24]

Studying legal design practice without contextualising it in general design practice would not be beneficial in identifying this lack of legal design integration in MENA countries. Understanding the history of design enables us to appreciate its evolution. This is also true for legal design. The practice of design in the MENA region is largely described as a practice dictated by the references of the Western countries that colonised Africa and the countries of the Middle East. For a long time, it was impossible to define African design or Arab design due to a paucity of references. The history of design may appear incomplete, or even reductive, because, in this version of history, there is only one possible trajectory for design, which is defined by industrialisation and European capitalism.

In his book 'World History of Design', Victor Margolin explains the context in which the history of design was structured, beginning in the 1970s.

Colonialism has shaped the way design is taught, valued, and practiced in the MENA region.

In the face of this reductive reading of design history, Elizabeth (Dori) Tunstall's research into the decolonisation of design is captured in her forthcoming work 'Decolonizing Design, A Cultural Justice Guidebook'. She also covers the concept of decolonised design on which various groups are working.[25]

The role of historians in revealing the history of art and design has now become crucial in shaping a design that is specific to the regions of the South. The recently published book on the history of visual arts in Tunisia[26] recounts the development of visual arts in the region over a decade. The book opens numerous avenues for reflection and work on the contemporary history of Tunisia. It provides essential material for research into the social practices associated with art, as well as the political and material aspects of artistic culture. This re-appropriation of the history of design is in progress and helps to develop a practice adapted to the reality of the region.

The same analogy holds good for legal design concepts. We need to consider concepts in a regional context: what meanings can be given to concepts such as product design, industrial design, graphic design, and service design in non-Western environments.

How can we think about design and legal design outside a Western frame of reference? How can legal design fit in with local legal practices, societal norms, and specific customer expectations?

[24] de Clippele, Couronne and Savin (n 12).

[25] 'Design Justice Network' (*Design Justice Network*, 11 December 2024), designjustice.org; 'Decolonising Design' (23 October 2017), www.decolonisingdesign.com/; ibid. see in particular https://designjustice.org/; https://www.whatdesigncando.com/stories/decolonising-design/; https://www.decolonisingdesign.com/.

[26] Alia Nakhli, *Arts Visuels En Tunisie* (Tunis, Nirvana, 2019).

Indeed, it is crucial to establish a legal design framework that arises from the specific needs of the region. We believe it is important to address these questions to find answers and solutions to proliferate legal design in these regions of the world.

The first step must therefore be to define the concepts of legal design and, of necessity, its design-inspired lexicon, before rushing headlong into implementing these tools to catch up with developed countries.

Second, creating bilingual or multilingual resources that include the original concepts and their culturally relevant translations.

In addition, documentation and research are essential to highlight projects that have been or are being developed in the region, but have not been identified as legal design projects, probably due to prevailing ignorance of their existence. At this level, building a local community remains the key to providing a local reference point for legal design practice in the region.

CONCLUSION

As with any design, legal design continuously evolves, both in terms of conceptualisation and practice.

The project of the legal lexicon deserves to be improved with respect to its impact and the consequences that its use may have on such evolution. The more we clarify the meaning of the legal design lexicon and establish a link with its origins in design, the more we remove ambiguity around the concept of legal design and expand the scope of possible legal design application.

This epistemological research should also be combined with studies and discussions on the practice of legal design in different countries around the world, particularly in emerging countries.

Working on the inclusivity of legal design practice by incorporating new regions of the world is a powerful driver for its evolution and certainly for a redefinition of the concept.

The survey conducted in the context of this article and its results also deserve to be developed and implemented in various action plans.

To aid the understanding of the legal design lexicon, it would be advantageous to conduct multiple studies and critically research the use of legal design vocabulary and its perception among legal design practitioners.

Signing off with a quote from Moholy-Nagy: 'The continuity of a culture comes from the fact that it has been able to attach more importance to quality than to novelty'.[27]

[27] László Moholy-Nagy, *Vision in Motion* (Chicago, IL, Paul Theobald, 1947) modernism101.com/products-page/art-photo/moholy-nagy-laszlo-vision-in-motion-chicago-theobald-1969-1947-duplicate-2/.

REFERENCES

Apolline Le Gall, 'Legal Design Beyond Design Thinking: Processes and Effects of the Four Spaces of Design Practices for the Legal Field' in Rossana Ducato and Alain Strowel (eds), *Legal design perspectives: theoretical and practical insights from the field* (Milan, Ledizioni 2021).

CR Brunschwig, 'Law Is Not or Must Not Be Just Verbal and Visual in the 21st Century: Toward Multisensory Law' in Dan Jerker B Svantesson and Stanley Greenstein (eds), *Internationalisation of Law in the Digital Information Society: Nordic Yearbook of Law and Informatics 2010-2012* (Stockholm, Ex Tuto Publishing, 2013).

——, 'Visual Law and Legal Design: Questions and Tentative Answers' (2021) Editions Weblaw.

M-S de Clippele, V Couronne and Joachim Savin, 'A Critical Assessment of the Notion of Legal Design through the Case of "Les Surligneurs", a Legal-Checking Media Outlet' (2023).

'Decolonising Design' (23 October 2017).

'——' (*What Design Can Do*, 17 June 2020).

'Design Justice Network' (*Design Justice Network*, 11 December 2024).

M Doherty, 'Disciplinarity and the Modes of Legal Design' (2022).

Helena Haapio, 'Business Success and Problem Prevention through Proactive Contracting' in Peter Wahlgren (ed), *A Proactive Approach: Law Libraries* (Stockholm, Stockholm Institute for Scandinavian Law: Jure [distributör]: Almqvist & Wiksell [internationell distributör], 2006).

——, 'Introduction to Proactive Law: A Business Lawyer's View' in Peter Wahlgren (ed), *A proactive approach: law libraries* (Stockholm Institute for Scandinavian Law: Jure [distributör] : Almqvist & Wiksell [internationell distributör], 2006).

K Nousiainen, 'Measuring the Impact and Value of Legal Design in Commercial Contracting within the Law and Economics Framework' (Economics and Society; 374, Hanken School of Economics Svenska handelshögskolan, 2023).

M Langendorf, 'The EU Needs to Expand Its Support for the MENA Region's Digital Transformation' (*Middle East Institute*, 19 August 2024).

Y Lenoir, Fourez, G. (dir.), Maingain, A. et Dufour, B. (2002). 'Approches didactiques de l'interdisciplinarité'. 29 *Revue des sciences de l'éducation* 211 (Bruxelles, De Boeck, 2003).

L Moholy-Nagy, *Vision in Motion* (Chicago, IL, Paul Theobald, 1947).

A Nakhli, *Arts Visuels En Tunisie* (Tunis, Nirvana, 2019).

Rania Ghrabi, 'La Valeur Évolutive Du Design Vis à Vis de l'interdisciplinarité', *The How in Design ? Introspective/prospective design* (Les publications de l'ESSTED, 2019).

'Resources' (*Amurabi – Legal Design Agency*).

6

The Transformative Role of the Public Sector in the Evolving Practice of Legal Design

KANAN DHRU

INTRODUCTION

'A PICTURE SPEAKS a thousand words'. It is widely believed that complex ideas and information can be conveyed more effectively by pictures than by written language.[1] Visuals are powerful communicators, and the human civilisation has used graphics to tell stories for thousands of years. The written language, in comparison, has its own use and significance on how and what we communicate on topics displaying a wide range of complexity.[2] The written language plays an important function, especially in the field of law to reflect the required intricacies and nuances.[3] This pattern of legal communication has eventually led to the creation of a complex system consisting of various institutions, actors, and 'systems'.[4] However, at times, these intricacies and complexities opaque the fundamentals hidden behind them and often make the legal information inaccessible for a large part of the population.[5]

[1] Pauline Dewan, 'Words Versus Pictures: Leveraging the Research on Visual Communication' (2015) 10(1) *Partnership: The Canadian Journal of Library and Information Practice and Research* doi.org/10.21083/partnership.v10i1.3137.

[2] 'Learned, fraternal, pellucid if not always stylish, efficient if not always concise, up-to-date in an old fashioned sort of a way'.; Lawrence Friedman, 'Law and its Language' (1964) 33 *George Washington Law Review* 563.

[3] Jamie Murray, Thomas E. Webb and Steven Wheatley, 'Encountering Law's Complexity' in *Complexity Theory and Law* (London, Routledge, 2018) 3–22 doi.org/10.4324/9781315158976-1.

[4] 'Interactive network of parts – actors, institutions and 'systems' that forms part of the law … gives rise to complex collective behaviour that can be observed in pattern of law communications'. Complexity Theory.

[5] Anna Harley, 'Language as a Barrier to Justice' (2014) *UNSW Law Society Court of Conscience* classic.austlii.edu.au/au/journals/UNSWLawSocCConsc/2014/8.pdf.

Across different parts of the world, the formal legal systems are observed to be falling short in addressing basic justice issues of citizens, silently creating an 'access to justice' gap.[6] Attempts are being made to improve the ease and access of legal information and processes for people by institutions across public and private sectors, as well as non-governmental bodies. Terms such as 'user-friendly justice' and 'people-centred justice' are gaining prominence, which stand for keeping the needs of the people in the centre of solution-creation.[7] And yet, these attempts lack a comprehensive and coordinated approach to address the existing gaps and inefficiencies in the legal service delivery. This is mainly owing to a vast array of complex and often interconnected reasons.[8]

Multiple research studies have established that the burden of injustice is heavy – for both the society and the individuals within it.[9] Lack of access to legal information and cumbersome processes exacerbate the existing injustice in the society. In addition, the delays and inefficiencies levy extra burden on the state resources and the exchequer, resulting in adverse consequences for the society.[10] The repercussions of lack of access to justice can include strained relationships at home and at work, eroding trust in public institutions, perpetuation of inequalities, and severe impacts on people's mental and physical well-being, among others.[11]

Legal systems are foundational to the stability of the society, which is one of the reasons why they are often traditional in their approach. However, in the fast-changing times, there is a need for the legal systems to innovate to keep pace. With rapidly evolving societal needs and technological progress, not only is the access to justice crisis growing, but a new set of legal issues is also emerging.[12] In times like these, legal systems are perceived as 'slow to change'

[6] The Hague Institute for Innovation of Law, 'Bridging the Justice Gap with "Gamechanging" Services' (19 January 2021) www.hiil.org/news/bridging-the-justice-gap-with-gamechanging-services/.

[7] 'A justice journey refers to the process by which an individual comes to feel a harm has been addressed and resolved personally'. Sarah Armstrong and others, '*Measuring Justice: Defining Concepts, Developing Practice*' (Scottish Centre for Crime and Justice Research 2020) No 6/2020.

[8] Peter H Schuck, 'Legal Complexity: Some Causes, Consequences, and Cures' (1992) 42 *Duke Law Journal* 1–52.

[9] World Justice Project and Taskforce on Justice, 'Measuring the Justice Gap' (World Justice Project, February 2019) worldjusticeproject.org/sites/default/files/documents/Measuring%20the%20Justice%20Gap_WJP%20Update_Feb2019_Final-updated_0.pdf. Also similar studies by other civil society organisations such as the Pathfinders and The Hague Institute for Innovation of Law.

[10] Task Force on Justice, *Justice for All – The report of the Task Force on Justice* (NYU, 29 April 2019).

[11] ibid.

[12] Elizabeth Penava, 'New Technology Will Raise New Legal Questions' *The Regulatory Review* (31 January 2023) www.theregreview.org/2023/01/31/penava-new-technology-will-raise-new-legal-questions/.

or 'catching up with the societal trends.'[13] Existing power structures, traditional framework of incentives, and the mindset of continuing the 'things as usual' serve as some of the barriers to reimagining the status quo in favour of people-centred approaches.

In fact, the issue of lack of access to justice presents a significant opportunity for innovation, particularly at a scale that could impact a broad population.[14] Among the numerous challenges that exist that need a novel solution, this paper particularly focuses on the challenge of accessing the legal information. Legal text is habitually obscured in dense, textual formats, and thus creates an interesting avenue for introducing newer, people-centred, legal design approaches in a systematic manner to ensure scale.

The field of legal design, with its commitment to autonomy and dignity, has the potential to transform access to justice gaps by simplifying the law for those for whom it is ultimately written, the people at large.[15] By adopting creative approaches, legal design can strike a meaningful balance between the necessary legal complexity and the use of people-centred approaches to generate powerful tools for addressing the access to legal information gap. This article looks at the epistemic consequences of legal design through the lens of an empirical case study of Lawtoons in India. It integrates a methodological framework and delves further into the research on scaling social innovations to establish practical lessons, while presenting the opportunities and challenges of introducing newer approaches in the field of law through different tools of legal design.

This paper starts by understanding the foundations of legal design within the legal systems and norms across countries that have been traditionally different in approach and practice. In addition, through the case study of Lawtoons that it showcases, it leverages a specific understanding of legal design – namely, visual depiction of the law, especially through elements of design such as comics, graphics, and storytelling. The case study being emphasised is that of collaboration of the startup Lawtoons with the Election Commission of India (ECI) to showcase how the method of collaboration or a public–private partnership can serve as an example of legal design addressing the issue of lack of legal awareness, particularly among populations such as those from the Global South.

[13] Gillian K Hadfield and Deborah L Rhode, 'How to Regulate Legal Services to Promote Access, Innovation, and the Quality of Lawyering' (2016) 67(5) *Hastings Law Journal* 1191.

[14] ibid.

[15] Kanan Dhru and Kelly Dhru 'Graphically Novel: The Role of Visuals in the Legal Design Movement' in *Legal Design: Dignifying People in Legal Systems* (Cambridge, Cambridge University Press forthcoming) ch 15.

MODERN LEGAL SYSTEMS

The inherently pluralistic[16] and geographically varied[17] nature of the legal systems needs the required attention in the literature and conversations on legal design. Jurisdiction and context play an important role in the field of legal practice.

Keeping the conversations about what constitutes legal design creates a universal narrative around the nature of law that helps in drawing the relevant attention to the idea of simplification of legal information. However, applying the concepts of legal design uniformly across diverse legal systems, with a singular understanding or epistemology, might inadvertently undermine the very pluralities these systems represent and should stand for.[18]

Legal systems and processes can be said to have evolved organically, albeit vastly differently across geographies and jurisdictions.[19] Customary and informal justice mechanisms (also known as 'community justice mechanisms'), which continue to thrive across many parts of the world, could provide us an important peek into this evolution.[20] Human-centred thinking has been inherent in the formulation and execution of legal norms and frameworks across various nations throughout history.

The jurisprudential scope of these systems may, for a large part of the recorded history, have been confined to a certain geography or region; however, evidence suggests[21] that they proved highly effective in integrating legal principles into everyday social norms. This integration was so seamless that it resonated intuitively with the majority of the local populace, profoundly influencing their daily lives and societal interactions.[22,23] Debate surrounding the efficacy and impartiality of local leaders in these societies has permeated Western discourse.[24,25] Nevertheless, it is indisputable that access to legal authorities and processes in customary and informal justice mechanisms

[16] Baudouin Dupret, 'Legal Pluralism, Plurality of Laws, and Legal Practices' (2007) 1(1) *European Journal of Legal Studies* 1.

[17] ibid.

[18] M Doherty, 'Speculation in Legal Design? Ontological Concerns and Critical Alternatives' (17–35) *The Socio-Politics of Legal Design and its Epistemic Consequences*, 2025.

[19] ibid.

[20] Werner F Menski, *Comparative Law in a Global Context: The Legal Systems of Asia and Africa* (1st edn, Cambridge, Cambridge University Press, 2000).

[21] ibid.

[22] Lisa Denney and Pilar Domingo, *Taking People-Centred Justice to Scale: The Role of Customary and Informal Justice in Advancing People-Centred Justice* (ODI and Pathfinders March 2023) CIJ_Taking_People_centred_Justice_to_Scale_paper_FINAL.pdf (cdn.ngo).

[23] Kanan Dhru, Manasi Nikam and Maurits Barendrecht, *Policy Brief on Community Justice Services* (The Hague Institute for Innovation of Laws, 2022) www.hiil.org/research/community-justice-services-policy-brief-2022-01/.

[24] ibid.

[25] See also: Janine Ubink (ed), 'Customary Justice: Perspectives on Legal Empowerment' in Thomas McInerney (series ed), *Legal and Governance Reform: Lessons Learned No. 3/2011* (Rome, IDLO, 2011).

remains markedly easier than it is within the complex frameworks of contemporary legal systems.

The societal and economic changes of the past century have necessitated the increased complexity of legal frameworks.[26] These unprecedented shifts have led to a marked transformation for the development and implementation of the law with a view to accommodating the growing multitude of stakeholders and entities that have attained jurisprudential significance. This includes entities such as the multinational corporation, civil society actors, and recently even the big technology companies.

Having first industrialised, the Western legal frameworks adapted to these transformations by cultivating complex legislation, case laws, and procedures. Bearing the marks of colonial influence, the legal systems in numerous nations of the Global South similarly evolved.[27] Regrettably, in pursuit of increased efficiency, this evolution occasionally departed from the human-centred processes intrinsic to these systems.[28]

These developments point to the fact that the progression of the heightened legal intricacies may have overlooked the needs of the most important stakeholder in the process, which is the user/customer of the system. The design thinking methodologies bring the focus back to this stakeholder.[29] This narrative sets the stage for the importance of legal design in deconstructing the non-essential complexities within the legal system and scaling the access to legal information to benefit the person at the last mile.

SETTING THE STAGE FOR LEGAL DESIGN

One way to make sense of legal design is through what it is understood to achieve. It is here that arguments have been made in the context of what legal design does to the role of law in the society itself. The misalignment of the law from the objectives it is set to achieve and functions it is supposed to perform in the society is highlighted prominently in the following definition, for example. The overarching goal of legal design, it says, is 'restoring the Law to its true strategic and its performative functions in society'.[30]

As for legal design itself, a singular definition does not exist. Different people have defined it differently. And while a case can be made for creating a more unified understanding, the flexibility has also aided in its evolution.

[26] Schuck (n 8).

[27] Leila Chirayath, Caroline Sage and Michael Woolcock, *Customary Law and Policy Reform: Engaging with the Plurality of Justice Systems* (Background paper for the World Development Report 2006: Equity and Development, July 2005).

[28] Insight arrived at during a large consultation of public sector officials from the legal domain in November 2021.

[29] Schuck (n 8).

[30] The White Paper. n.d.(a). 'Legal Design'. legaldesign-community.com/definition?lang=en.

Looking at some of the prevalent definitions, a few stand out. One of the popular definitions for legal design is 'the application of human-centered design to the world of law, to make legal systems and services more human-centered, usable, and satisfying'.[31] It is also understood as 'a methodology that allows to prioritise legal information and make it more accessible through a visual reading grid'[32] or even as 'visual communication from a cognitive perspective'.[33] According to these definitions, bringing human-centricity and visualisation to the field of law is what legal design is.

The discipline of legal design is now being equated with human-centred aspects of the systems and processes, as well as with the aspects of simplifying complex legal text through plain language and visualisation. Human-centred design methodology or design thinking process[34] that forms the basis for legal design has already influenced other service industries significantly.[35] The methodology has been widely influential and has produced considerably positive results in producing favourable outcomes and benefits across sectors and industries.[36] Its need has been felt for long now and is finally making in-roads into the legal system through movements such as legal technology, legal hacking, and access to justice reform.[37]

Given the broader context, the emergence of the field of legal design appears entirely indispensable, but not entirely unexpected or particularly innovative. And in the same light, the development of rules and norms in a manner that is comprehensible to their intended audiences is not a novel concept either. As argued earlier, human-centredness has been rooted in the organically evolved justice process. One can hardly argue against the fact that law and the society are inextricably linked, and human-centredness has served as one of the foundational pillars of the evolution and development of the legal system itself. Clarity, access, and ease of understanding are intuitive to its raison d'etre. What remains surprising, however, is the sluggish adoption of these imperatives for clarity and simplicity, and the fact that any convincing at all is needed for its adoption.

On a side note, many see the integration of technology as a significant opportunity to innovate in the direction of bringing more transparency and efficiency.

[31] Margaret Hagan, 'What is Legal, Design?' in *Law by Design* (2014) lawbydesign.co/legal-design.

[32] Shayan Remtoulah, 'What is Legal Design? Definition and Application Examples' (*Your-Comics*, 2021) Your-Comics your-comics.com/en/article/definition-legal-design-14.html.

[33] Deloitte, 'Legal Design: The Science behind Visual Design' (2021) www2.deloitte.com/content/dam/Deloitte/nl/Documents/legal/deloitte-nl-deloitte-legal-design-offering.pdf.

[34] Hasso Plattner Institute of Design at Stanford University, '*An Introduction to Design Thinking Process Guide*' web.stanford.edu/~mshanks/MichaelShanks/files/509554.pdf.

[35] Esther Han, '5 Examples of Design Thinking in Business' (*Harvard Business School Online*, 22 February 2022) online.hbs.edu/blog/post/design-thinking-in-business.

[36] Dutch MacDonald and others, 'Human-Centered Design Is More Important Than Ever' (*Boston Consulting Group*, 27 July 2020) www.bcg.com/publications/2020/the-importance-of-human-centered-design.

[37] Margaret Hagan, 'Legal Design as a Thing: A Theory of Change and a Set of Methods to Craft a Human-Centered Legal System' (2020) 36(3) *Design Issues* 3, 3–15.

However, even for this to be achieved, it is through the principles of legal design that this opportunity can be fully utilised effectively.[38]

This being said, the emergence of legal design as a discipline in recent years is encouraging and must be lauded. Strides are being made in the interdisciplinary work conducted in university labs, in government offices, in the initiatives taken by the civil society, as well as in the little efforts being made in private sector undertakings.[39] Compared to the situation a few years ago, there are now dedicated events and conferences on legal design.[40] Dedicated publications and courses on legal design are seen as a helpful addition to legal curriculum in universities.[41] The industry's demand for legal design as a crucial skill for job applications, and the expanding community of legal professionals advocating for its integration, in particular, speaks for its importance. Practitioners of legal design are increasingly being invited to law firms and legal departments to explore convergence and innovation opportunities. This growing demand is translating into the discourse for the public sector as well.[42]

Even with these encouraging developments, the conversion of entities to the discipline of legal design is steady but slow at best. This is especially acute in comparison to some of the other areas where legal services are being innovated and reimagined.[43] In contrast to the access to justice gap and the need for human-centred approaches to legal knowledge, the overall adoption of legal design has not yet achieved sufficient scale and convergence.

THE NEED FOR SCALING UP

According to a survey by the World Justice Project, 5.1 billion people – two-thirds of the world population – lack meaningful access to justice.[44] Many of these problems can be addressed adequately if relevant legal information is made easily accessible and understandable. Due to suboptimal ways of communicating legal information, people often feel vulnerable while seeking

[38] Siddharth Peter de Souza, 'The Spread of Legal Tech Solutionism and the Need for Legal Design' (2022) 13(3) *European Journal of Risk Regulation* 373–388.

[39] The Legal Design Lab in Stanford (law.stanford.edu/organizations/pages/legal-design-lab/), NULawLab in Northeastern University (www.nulawlab.org/) are two prominent examples.

[40] Legal Design Summit, Helsinki is one big example of this: legaldesignsummit.com/.

[41] *Legal Design Journal*, legaldesign-journal.com/.

[42] 'Nations Largest Trial Court Partners with Stanford Law School's Deborah L Rhode Center on the Legal Profession and Legal Design Lab to Identify Innovative Ways to Expand and Improve' (Stanford Law School, 24 January 2024) law.stanford.edu/press/nations-largest-trial-court-partners-with-stanford-law-schools-deborah-l-rhode-center-on-the-legal-profession-and-legal-design-lab-to-identify-innovative-ways-to-expand-and-improve/.

[43] Chris Metinko, 'Legal Tech Makes Its Case With Venture Capitalists, Tops $1B In Funding This Year' (*Crunchbase*, 23 September 2021) news.crunchbase.com/venture/legal-tech-venture-investment/.

[44] World Justice Project and Pathfinders for Peaceful, Just and Inclusive Societies, 'Grasping the Justice Gap: Opportunities and Challenges for People-Centered Justice Data' (Working paper, 2021) worldjusticeproject.org/our-work/publications/working-papers/grasping-justice-gap.

legal support and may end up relying on unreliable legal sources. To address this issue, fingers are often pointed at the public sector owing to its essential function of providing equal access to legal information to all. However, the bureaucracy and red-tape inherent in its functioning are some of the reasons that make it challenging for the public sector to innovate. Even with the best of the intentions and resources, the process of change is often prolonged and considerably difficult to achieve.

It is not much of a surprise, then, that the growing community of privately started-up initiatives dedicated to the fields of legal technology or legal design commonly caters to the law firms and in-house legal departments. Nonetheless, they frequently complain of slow adoption and the resistance of the legal firms to change. Survival of these initiatives has been mostly tough and all those who survive do not make it either. Either they stagnate at the pilot stages or, if successful, are acquired by an existing publishing or a conglomerate offering a variety of products.[45] Human-centredness in law cannot be achieved through piecemeal efforts or in silos and has to be imagined in a more holistic way. This has to happen at a scale at which the solutions start to matter, especially in the context of reaching a larger audience that deserves a better access to legal services.

Discussions on scale have started to gain prominence in conversations in addressing some of the most pressing challenges in the society.[46,47] The growing importance of scale in the context of solving social challenges suggests the need to develop solutions that move beyond pilot stage to a sustainable change for large populations.

Different methodologies and frameworks to understand scale in social innovation exist.[48,49] Scaling up is defined as:

> expanding, replicating, adapting and sustaining successful policies, programs or projects in a geographic space and over time to reach a greater number of people.[50]

[45] Kanan Dhru, Manasi Nikam and Maurits Barendrecht, *Use of Digital Technologies in Judicial Reforms and Access to Justice Cooperation* (The Hague Institute for Innovation of Laws 2021) HiiL-Use-of-digital-technologies-in-judicial-reform-and-access-to-justice-cooperation (1).pdf.

[46] Maria Y Rodriguez, Laysha Ostrow and Susan P Kemp, 'Scaling Up Social Problems: Strategies for Solving Social Work's Grand Challenges' (2017) 27(2) *Research on Social Work Practice* 139.

[47] Larry Cooley and Isabel Guerrero, 'The Broken Part of the Business Model in Taking Development Outcomes to Scale' (*Scaling Community of Practice*, 25 September 2023) scalingcommunityofpractice.com/the-broken-part-of-the-business-model-in-taking-development-outcomes-to-scale/.

[48] M van Lunenburg, K Geuijen and A Meijer, 'How and Why Do Social and Sustainable Initiatives Scale? A Systematic Review of the Literature on Social Entrepreneurship and Grassroots Innovation' (2020) 31 *Voluntas* 1013.

[49] Chiara Marradi, *A Design Tool-Box to Scale Social Innovations from One Context to Another: Unfolding the Scaling Journey of Designscapes Initiatives* (Delft University of Technology, 2021).

[50] Arntraud Hartmann and Johannes F Linn, *Scaling Up: A Framework and Lessons for Development Effectiveness from Literature and Practice* (Wolfensohn Center Working Paper No 5, Brookings Institution, 2008).

This can be made possible with adequate levels of customisation that can address individual needs to a required level of uniformity that can provide mass roll-outs.

Research suggests that there are 10 alternative methods or strategies, referred to as 'Pathways', through which social interventions can achieve scale (Figure 6.1).[51] The paper categorises the methods on scaling up approaches into three groups: Expansion, Replication, and Collaboration.

Table 6.1 Outline of "Scaling up approaches and methods of scaling up" by Cooley and Linn

Scaling up Approaches and Methods of Scaling up	
Type	**Method**
Expansion	• Growth • Restructuring • Franchising • Spin-off
Replication	• Policy Adoption • Grafting • Diffusion • Commercialisation
Collaboration	• Formal Partnerships and Strategic Alliance • Networks and Coalitions

As illustrated in the figure above, scale can manifest in different forms depending on the context. It can range from expansion, which may involve growing, restructuring, franchising, or spinning-off the initiative, to replication, achieved through policy adoption, grafting, diffusion, or commercialisation.

From these, the work on 'Collaboration' through formal partnerships and forming strategic alliances generates the most alignment with the existing case study on Lawtoons that this paper further examines. As a young startup using legal design to simplify legal information through visualisation, Lawtoons formed a partnership with the ECI to develop a series of stories to generate awareness on democracy, duties of citizens, and the importance of voting among others.

The nature of this partnership between a young startup with an innovative idea and approach and a government institution having a large outreach and

[51] Larry Cooley and Johannes F Linn, *Taking Innovations to Scale: Methods, Applications and Lessons* (Results for Development, 2014) www.msiworldwide.com/wp-content/uploads/2023/10/Taking-Innovations-to-Scale.pdf.

mandate to affect change provides a use-case of the nature of scale that is possible in the field of legal design by coming together of different stakeholders to address societal issues. A public–private partnership that was created to disseminate legal information to a large number of people in India is an example that is discussed below.

ACHIEVING SCALE THROUGH COLLABORATION

Figure 6.1 Cover of "Sentinels of Democracy," a comic book simplifying election-related laws for citizens of India

The collaboration of Lawtoons[52] with the ECI[53] emerged from the ECI's need to create a tool that could educate the vast Indian populace about their duties and responsibilities regarding voting. The Commission wanted to develop ways to easily and accessibly inform people about issues, including the voting process, important terminologies, and citizen duties. To that end, Lawtoons was commissioned to address this need owing to its expertise and focus in simplifying legal concepts through the medium of comics. The project brought together the innovative storytelling and comic design skills of the young startup Lawtoons with extensive reach and influence of a constitutional authority like the ECI.

Young adults, particularly first-time voters between 18 and 25 years, were the target audience for this comic book, which meant that the design and the content had to have a narrative that would appeal to them. Multiple consultations were held with this demographic to ensure the content was relatable. Stories and the characters were then developed with these audience members in mind and were created from the real-life experiences of Election Commission officials from across the nation. To represent the diversity of India, comic designers from various parts of the country were commissioned to contribute to this project, ensuring that their unique styles reflected the diversity in expression and design.

The stories came together as a comic book titled *Sentinels of Democracy*, a tool to empower and educate the Indian voters.[54,55] The election commission's efforts extend to the very last mile to ensure that every single vote in the country is collected. Their outreach and awareness programmes are designed to have the same extensive reach and impact.

Sentinels of Democracy was launched both online, via the ECI's website and other virtual platforms, and offline, through its various outreach programmes. It reached millions of users in its very first print run. In terms of scale, the design and storytelling developed by a startup were able to tap into the gigantic reach of the public sector.

[52] Lawtoons is a startup with the focus of simplifying legal information. It's pioneering project has been developing a comic book series simplifying laws for children in India. The comic book series has been successfully crowdfunded twice and has been featured across prominent publications and legal design conversations. The books are available in Hindi and English on Amazon for worldwide delivery and have sold thousands of copies to date. The work on Lawtoons started as part of our work at Research Foundation for Governance in India (RFGI).

[53] The Election Commission of India, one of the highest constitutional bodies in the country, is responsible for conducting elections in a diverse nation of 1.4 billion people – the world's largest democracy.

[54] Kanan Dhru and Kelly Dhru, '*Sentinels of Democracy*' (*Election Commission of India*, 2019) ceodelhi.gov.in/eLearningv2/admin/EnglishPDF/1.-Sentinels-of-Democracy.pdf.

[55] Avinash Nair, 'EC Comic on Poll Process Draws Out Lone Voter in Gir Forest, Other Tales' (*Indian Express*, 20 June 2017) indianexpress.com/article/india/ec-comic-on-poll-process-draws-out-lone-voter-in-gir-forest-other-tales-4712639.

This collaboration makes a strong case for how a public–private collaboration can bring an innovation of a small creative team to a large number of people. Affecting positive impact necessitates taking risks and channelising resources for ideas that can have the potential to bring about meaningful contributions. Through breaking of silos in which innovation usually takes place and going beyond small pilots, this project showcases the power of initiative and synergies that can drive a coordinated systemic change. In today's fast-changing times and rapidly growing need for better access to justice, there is a need for more public systems to innovate to keep pace.

BARRIERS TO SCALE

There are several reasons why more such examples are felt to be lacking. Unfortunately, the overall uptake of legal design as such remains low. Even the most well-funded and popularised examples have, at the very best, remained at the level of pilots or consulting projects. There are no significant investments in legal design startups, and it is not seen as a full-time occupation even now. A clear business case hasn't been made for legal design either, and it is considered more as a 'nice to have' addition to a firm's practice or as an academic course, but not a 'need to have' despite the ongoing efforts by its proponents. The inability to define a viable business model restricts their capacity to instigate a broader systemic change.[56,57] Civil society organisations that work towards addressing the issue of lack of legal awareness frequently grapple with donor dependencies. Academic institutions that play a considerable role in fostering the discourse on legal design are the ones predominantly located in the countries of the Global North.

Legal information across the world continues to style itself in bulky cumbersome text, desperately seeking simplification and yet sadly, failing the scale its needs or deserves. It is undeniable that a large portion of the world population currently lacks access to essential legal information, and human-centric approaches would be crucial for empowering individuals to make informed decisions and lead lives of dignity.[58] And yet, there are barriers to its scale.

Through conversations and owing to our own work at Lawtoons, the following are some of the broad reasons behind the limited prevalence of this discipline that come to light.

[56] This insight is formulated with consideration of the broader startup and civil society ecosystem of the legal technology and legal design sectors.

[57] Philippe Eiselein and Nikolay A Dentchev, 'Scaling Social Impact: What Challenges and Opportunities Await Social Entrepreneurs' in Deborah M Wasieleski and James Weber (eds), *Social Entrepreneurship* (Business and Society 360, vol 5, Bingley, Emerald Publishing, 2021) 145.

[58] Anne Ketola, Robert de Rooy and Helena Haapio, *Comic Contracts 2.0 – Contracts that Have (and Give) a Voice* (Milan, Ledizioni, 20 May 2024).

Interdisciplinary Nature of Work

The work of legal design remains interdisciplinary where the fields of law and design come together. However, these disciplines have their own distinct approaches, work methodologies, and require different forms of communication. Lawyers and designers have their unique requirements and interpretations, and there are times when enabling an alignment may not work successfully. Apart from this, the professionals who are open to these collaborative projects are also rare to find.

A lot gets lost in translation, and this does not result in good final outcomes. Although there are commonalities between these two disciplines,[59] law and design are also quite distinct from each other in terms of approaching nuances of legal communication. This remains one of the central challenges for the scale of legal design projects. A successful use case of legal design involves the right balance between simplification and keeping necessary nuance, which is not always possible owing to these differences. Despite sufficient resources and the best of intentions, there remains a gap in delivering quality products that can have a mass appeal.

Ad-hoc Nature

Even the most strategic and well-timed collaborations for scaling legal design remain ad-hoc in nature. For a solution to be sustainable, the scale has to be imagined across a longer-term timeframe.[60] For legal design initiatives, while pilots and short-term interventions have been garnering traction, a multi-year campaign with sufficient resources is needed to create the required impact. Pilots are oftentimes not converted into fully fleshed-out projects and partnerships that are formed to create change on the ground terminate after the completion of that goal. For scale to be achieved, collaboration on legal design initiatives needs a leadership with the right vision that can enable the implementation of these initiatives in a way that can systematically eradicate the issue of access to legal information.

Lack of Robust Business Model

As discussed above, the field of legal design lacks use-cases of scale – the examples where the products or services have reached a large number of people. Legal design is either championed within the premises of an academic institution or

[59] Margaret Hagan, 'Law by Design' lawbydesign.co/.

[60] Martin Geissdoerfer, Doroteya Vladimirova and Steve Evans, 'Sustainable Business Model Innovation: A Review' (2018) 198 *Journal of Cleaner Production* 401.

developed within the initiatives of donor-funded civil society organisations. Practical applications within the private industry exist; however, they remain few and far between. The cost of undertaking a legal design project remains high owing to the art of developing user-friendly design itself being expensive, and oftentimes there are questions as to return on investment. This makes private initiatives in this field either small-scale or project-based, without a robust business model that can display strong outreach figures to justify unit economics. Over time, many initiatives have ended up closing or pivoting to providing visualisation of other information, not legal information, to stay afloat.

CONCLUSION

The article demonstrates that although increasing social and economic complexities have necessitated more intricate and complex laws and legal processes, methods and frameworks to introduce simplicity and human-centred approaches to law are not new. These have been a part of organically developed legal processes for centuries. However, while legal design brings forth much-needed interventions in simplifying legal information for people through human-centred approaches, it often lacks scale.

However, scale is possible to achieve, for example, through collaboration and forging successful public–private partnerships. Through the case study for scale in social interventions with a particular focus on the collaboration between Lawtoons and the ECI in developing a comic book to empower first-time voters, the paper showcases one such example. Such a partnership combines the innovative and creative thinking of private individuals with the scale and impact of the public sector. Having said that, there are systemic and operational barriers that prevent the scale of the existing legal design initiatives, such as the need for better alignment across disciplines to create a robust business case and ultimately having the right visionary leadership that can develop a long-term agenda for legal design initiatives.

REFERENCES

A Armstrong and others, *Measuring Justice: Defining Concepts, Developing Practice* (Scottish Centre for Crime and Justice Research 2020) No 6/2020.

L Chirayath, C Sage and M Woolcock, *Customary Law and Policy Reform: Engaging with the Plurality of Justice Systems* (Background paper for the World Development Report 2006: Equity and Development, July 2005).

L Cooley and I Guerrero, 'The Broken Part of the Business Model in Taking Development Outcomes to Scale' (*Scaling Community of Practice*, 25 September 2023).

L Cooley and JF Linn, *Taking Innovations to Scale: Methods, Applications and Lessons* (Results for Development, 2014).

Deloitte, 'Legal Design: The Science behind Visual Design'. (2021).

L Denney and P Domingo, *Taking People-Centred Justice to Scale: The Role of Customary and Informal Justice in Advancing People-Centred Justice* (ODI and Pathfinders March 2023).

P Dewan, 'Words Versus Pictures: Leveraging the Research on Visual Communication' (2015) 10(1) *Partnership: The Canadian Journal of Library and Information Practice and Research*.

K Dhru and K Dhru, 'Graphically Novel: The Role of Visuals in the Legal Design Movement' in *Legal Design: Dignifying People in Legal Systems* (Cambridge, Cambridge University Press forthcoming) ch 15.

——, *Sentinels of Democracy* (*Election Commission of India*, 2019).

K Dhru, M Nikam and M Barendrecht, *Use of Digital Technologies in Judicial Reforms and Access to Justice Cooperation* (The Hague Institute for Innovation of Laws, 2021).

——, *Policy Brief on Community Justice Services* (The Hague Institute for Innovation of Laws, 2022).

B Dupret, 'Legal Pluralism, Plurality of Laws, and Legal Practices' (2007) 1(1) *European Journal of Legal Studies* 1.

P Eiselein and NA Dentchev, 'Scaling Social Impact: What Challenges and Opportunities Await Social Entrepreneurs' in Deborah M Wasieleski and James Weber (eds), *Social Entrepreneurship* (Business and Society 360, vol 5, Bingley, Emerald Publishing, 2021) 145.

L Friedman, 'Law and its Language' (1964) 33 *George Washington Law Review* 563.

M Geissdoerfer, D Vladimirova and S Evans, 'Sustainable Business Model Innovation: A Review' (2018) 198 *Journal of Cleaner Production* 401.

GK Hadfield and DL Rhode, 'How to Regulate Legal Services to Promote Access, Innovation, and the Quality of Lawyering' (2016) 67(5) *Hastings Law Journal* 1191.

M Hagan, *Law by Design*.

——, 'What is Legal, Design?' in *Law by Design* (2014).

——, 'Legal Design as a Thing: A Theory of Change and a Set of Methods to Craft a Human-Centered Legal System' (2020) 36(3) *Design Issues* 3, 3–15.

E Han, '5 Examples of Design Thinking in Business' (*Harvard Business School Online*, 22 February 2022).

A Harley, 'Language as a Barrier to Justice' (2014) *UNSW Law Society Court of Conscience*.

A Hartmann and JF Linn, *Scaling Up: A Framework and Lessons for Development Effectiveness from Literature and Practice* (Wolfensohn Center Working Paper No 5, Brookings Institution, 2008).

Hasso Plattner Institute of Design at Stanford University, *An Introduction to Design Thinking Process Guide*.

A Ketola, R de Rooy and H Haapio, *Comic Contracts 2.0 – Contracts that Have (and Give) a Voice* (Milan, Ledizioni, 20 May 2024).

D MacDonald and others, 'Human-Centered Design Is More Important Than Ever' (*Boston Consulting Group*, 27 July 2020).

C Marradi, *A Design Tool-Box to Scale Social Innovations from One Context to Another: Unfolding the Scaling Journey of Designscapes Initiatives* (Delft University of Technology, 2021).

WF Menski, *Comparative Law in a Global Context: The Legal Systems of Asia and Africa* (1st edn, Cambridge, Cambridge University Press, 2000).

C Metinko 'Legal Tech Makes Its Case With Venture Capitalists, Tops $1B In Funding This Year' (*Crunchbase*, 23 September 2021).

J Murray, TE Webb and S Wheatley, 'Encountering Law's Complexity' in *Complexity Theory and Law* (London, Routledge, 2018) 3–22.

A Nair, 'EC Comic on Poll Process Draws Out Lone Voter in Gir Forest, Other Tales' (*Indian Express*, 20 June 2017).

NULawLab in Northeastern University.

E Penava, 'New Technology Will Raise New Legal Questions' (The Regulatory Review, 31 January 2023).

S Remtoulah, 'What is Legal Design? Definition and Application Examples' (2021) *Your-Comics.*

MY Rodriguez, L Ostrow and SP Kemp, 'Scaling Up Social Problems: Strategies for Solving Social Work's Grand Challenges' (2017) 27(2) *Research on Social Work Practice* 139.

PH Schuck, 'Legal Complexity: Some Causes, Consequences and Cures' (1992-1993) 42 *Duke Law Journal.* 1–52.

Stanford Law School, 'Nation's Largest Trial Court Partners with Stanford Law School's Deborah L. Rhode Center on the Legal Profession and Legal Design Lab to Identify Innovative Ways to Expand and Improve' (24 January 2024).

Task Force on Justice, *Justice for All – The report of the Task Force on Justice* (NYU, 29 April 2019).

The Hague Institute for Innovation of Law, 'Bridging the Justice Gap with "Gamechanging" Services' (19 January 2021).

The Legal Design Lab in Stanford.

The White Paper, 'Legal Design'. n.d.(a).

J Ubink (ed), 'Customary Justice: Perspectives on Legal Empowerment' in McInerney T (series ed), *Legal and Governance Reform: Lessons Learned No. 3/2011* (Rome, IDLO, 2011).

M van Lunenburg, K Geuijen and A Meijer, 'How and Why Do Social and Sustainable Initiatives Scale? A Systematic Review of the Literature on Social Entrepreneurship and Grassroots Innovation' (2020) 31 *Voluntas* 1013.

World Justice Project and Pathfinders for Peaceful, Just and Inclusive Societies, 'Grasping the Justice Gap: Opportunities and Challenges for People-Centered Justice Data' (Working paper, 2021).

World Justice Project and Taskforce on Justice, 'Measuring the Justice Gap' (World Justice Project, February 2019).

7

Weaving an Emergent Future from an Engineering Design Perspective: Law, Science, Engineering, and Indigeneity

ADE MABOGUNJE

INTRODUCTION

THE DYNAMIC NATURE of society demands dynamic lawmaking designed to better help us navigate an unknown future. Here, we present a methodology called 'weaving' that, we argue, could make lawmaking both more inclusive and more agile. Weaving entails (1) crowdsourcing and integrating diverse perspectives to generate creative solutions (eg, policies and laws) and (2) rapidly prototyping those solutions using technologies such as virtual reality (VR) and artificial intelligence (AI). This methodology requires an interdisciplinary approach, combining the field of law with behavioural science, data science, and engineering. Though a radical departure from the law we know today, we believe incorporating weaving into legal education and practice might enable us to become more proactive as our social and physical environments evolve at ever-faster rates. That is, we envision a field of law that leads in innovation and is at the forefront of collective thought and imagination.

Recent developments give us a reasonable hope that this can happen:

First, the field of law, which codifies culture and protects the status quo, is being transformed as automation and AI technologies take over many tasks in that profession. This offers a tremendous opportunity to envision a new kind of law, one that is proactive and integrates insights from multidisciplinary knowledge sources.

Second, advancements in engineering and data science, including VR and AI, are poised to revolutionise the behavioural sciences. VR and AI can expedite and scale radical cultural changes by recording and immersing people in new situations, thereby facilitating the rapid prototyping and testing of social theories.

Third, there is increasing respect worldwide for diverse perspectives, including the traditional wisdom of Indigenous people, the critical consciousness of marginalised communities, and the unique perspectives of neuroatypical people. The preservation, revitalisation, and uplifting of these forms of knowledge are vital steps towards developing sustainable, global solutions.

In this paper, we first provide an overview of the field of law as it exists today, and as it could be. We next argue for a science that is honest, and inclusive of diverse ways of knowing, and expound on how this can engender the vast, rapid, and radical innovation required. Finally, we will describe how new technologies, such as VR and AI, can serve as catalysts for this endeavour – accelerating and scaling the positive impact of science and law on society while controlling for the negative effects, balancing progress, and safety.

LAW

> Bad behavior undermines our societies, our safety, our markets, our ecology, and our way of life. We have erected a complex legal code to address different forms of damaging behavior, and clearly the legal code is intended to shape behavior. Lawyers play a crucial role in all of this. As legislators, lawyers draft the language in our codified laws and choose what gets passed. As prosecutors and regulators, they make key decisions about if and how the law is enforced. Lawyers are hired to draw up contracts and design organizational rules, inserting the legal code into business transactions. Lawyers act as judges and apply the law to disputes, and in doing so interpret and shape the future meaning of the law. And as law professors and legal experts, they shape public debate about what the law is and what it should be. As such, we leave the design and crucial decision-making within our legal system to lawyers, yet they have hardly any knowledge of the social science underlying human behavior. Law school curricula have almost entirely ignored the behavioral revolution that has rocked fields like economics and ethics. Because lawyers who design and operate our legal code rarely receive any mandatory training in social and behavioral sciences, they are forced to rely on their own intuitions about human misbehavior, many of which have been proven false by empirical studies. We have left the most important coding of human conduct, the legal code, in the hands of behavioral novices.
>
> — Benjamin van Rooij and Adam Fine[1]

Except for incremental additions and despite numerous calls for reform, particularly from practitioners and students who say the curriculum is not helping them serve the needs of society, law school curriculum has not changed much since it was first conceived by Christopher Langdell in the 1870s.[2] See Exhibit 1 for an overview of the history of legal education and a sample of current curriculum.

[1] Benjamin van Rooij, *The Behavioral Code: The Hidden Ways the Law Makes Us Better or Worse* (Boston, Beacon Press, 2021).

[2] CC Langdell (ed), *A Selection of Cases on the Law of Contracts: With References and Citations* (Clark, NJ, Lawbook Exchange 1999).

Exhibit 1 A Brief History of Legal Education and Sample Outline of Curriculum

#1. Brief History of Legal Education

For a general history of legal education in America through the 1970s, see LAWRENCE M. FRIEDMAN, A HISTORY OF AMERICAN LAW (Friedman, 1973). Langdell's revolutionary changes in American legal education went beyond the case method of instruction, however, to encompass other educational standards. As explained by Friedman: [In the late 19th century] [t]he stage was ripe for reform or revolution. The first shot was fired in 1870. Charles W. Eliot had become president of Harvard the year before. He appointed Christopher Columbus Langdell a professor in the law school; and in September 1870, Langdell was made dean, a position new to the school. The duties of the dean, on paper, were not very awesome; he was to "keep the Records of the Faculty," prepare "its business," and "preside at its meetings in the absence of the President." But Langdell proceeded, with Eliot's concurrence, to turn Harvard Law School upside down.

First, he made it more difficult for a student to get in. If an applicant did not have a college degree, he had to pass an entrance test. The prospective student had to show his knowledge of Latin, translating from Virgil, or Cicero, or from Caesar; he was also tested on Blackstone's Commentaries. Skill in French was acceptable as a substitute for Latin.

Next Langdell made it harder for a student to get out. The L.L.B. course was raised to two years in 1871 and to three years in 1876 .... By 1899, the school had adopted a straight three-year requirement. The old curriculum had taken up matters subject by subject, as time allowed; it paid little attention to the relationship between courses; students entered and left at their own rhythm. Under Langdell, the curriculum was divided into "courses," of so many hour-units apiece. Courses were arranged in a definite order, some were treated as more basic, some as more advanced. In 1872, Langdell introduced final examinations. A student had to pass these exams after his first year, before going on to the second.

But Langdell's most far-reaching reform, the one for which he is best remembered, was the introduction of the case method for teaching law. This method cast out the textbooks, and used casebooks as teaching materials; these were collections of reports of actual cases, carefully selected and arranged to illustrate the meaning and development of principles of law. The classroom tone was profoundly altered. There was no more lecturer, expounding "the law" from received texts. The teacher now was a Socratic guide, leading the student to an understanding of concepts and principles hidden as essences among the cases.
The teacher showed how these concepts unfolded, like a rose from its bud, through a time series of enlightened cases.

Id. at 530-31 (footnotes omitted). Langdell had a theory for his emphasis on the case method. He believed that law was a "science;" it had to be studied scientifically, that is, inductively through primary sources. These sources were the printed cases; they expressed, in manifold dress, the few, ever-present, and ever-evolving and fructifying principles, which constituted the genius of the common law.

#2. Strawman outline of a typical law school curriculum

A foundation of compulsory first-year courses – Contracts, Torts, Civil Procedure, Property, and Criminal Law – to ensure complete doctrinal coverage, plus a few additions such as courses in Ethics, Legal Writing, and Appellate Advocacy.

Second-year curriculum might include a course in Constitutional Law and Evidence, a legal writing project; and a contextual course chosen from one or two of the following: American Legal History, Comparative Law, Law and Economics, Legal Process, and Legislation);

Third-year courses will include courses on the Legal Profession and Jurisprudence; a twenty-hour pro bono requirement; and a variety of elective courses, optional lectures, and clinical programs etc.

We posit that law school curriculum is a crucial challenge for society. Why? Because first, law is the bedrock of society, and second, people are who they are taught to be, act as they are taught to act, and think as they are taught to think. Looking at who has a law degree drives home the point: all judges, district attorneys and defence attorneys, many Senators, governors, mayors, legislators, lobbyists, Cabinet members and CEOs,[3] see also Figure 7.2. That incomplete roll call says all you need to know about why the education of lawyers must change if society is to change or better adapt to future challenges.

Figure 7.1 177th Congress (2021–2022) by education background

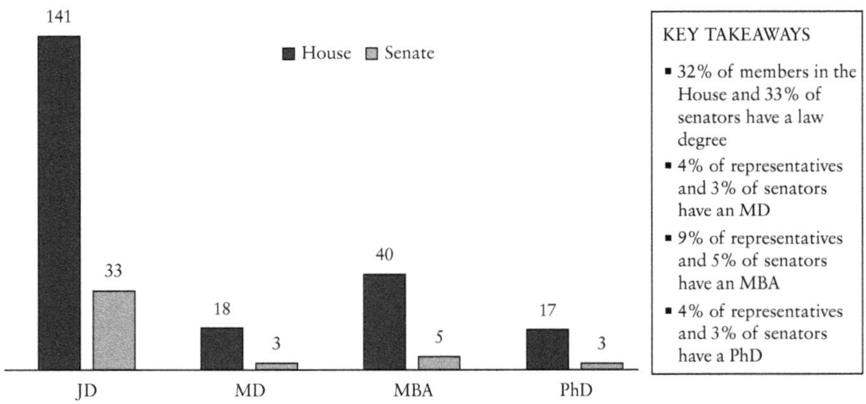

Given the out-sized influence lawyers have on society, particularly US society, we need to ponder more than how much power they wield. We also need to think deeply about what they know, and how they think.

We envision a law that empowers lawyers to be more than 'behavioural novices' by incorporating weaving – and therefore behavioural science, data science, and engineering – into their discipline. In the unique terminology of our proposal, to 'weave" is to gather the multiplicity of perspectives and ways of being in or across ecosystems and, with care, fold them into a pattern in which all may see themselves reflected. Weaving is not an end state, but an ongoing process of integration and adaptation.

[3] American Bar Association (ABA), 'Demographics and Composition of the 117th Congress' (*American Bar Association (ABA)*, 2021) www.americanbar.org/content/dam/aba/administrative/government_affairs_office/demographics-and-composition-117thcongress.pdf.

SCIENCE

The behavioural sciences, including psychology, economics, anthropology, and sociology, already inform policy, yet the challenges we face today will require a truly inclusive science – one that is honest about oppressive systems and proactive in incorporating marginalised perspectives. It was not so very long ago that many prominent cultural theorists advocated for eugenics and forced sterilisation, and only recently that the prominence of white supremacist ideologies has been widely acknowledged as a societal ill. Those who study behaviour and culture often obfuscate the role of violence and false narratives in establishing and protecting the dominant status quo. Psychology, for instance, has been particularly susceptible to ethnocentrism, focusing primarily on the minds and behaviour of people in the global North, but promoting their findings as universal, for example, Henrich et al.[4]

The potential for weaving to advance the relationship between the law, the behavioural sciences, science, and engineering is profound (see Exhibit 2). Incorporating weaving into the scientific process means researchers and practitioners can crowdsource hypotheses from a diverse audience, intentionally decentring the dominant narratives and including the perspectives of Indigenous people, communities of resistance, and neuroatypical individuals. We name these groups for the following reasons:

First, Indigenous people are the guardians of knowledge and practices accumulated over thousands of years, reminders that we are neither the first nor the primary agents operating on this planet and that there is wisdom encoded in the natural systems surrounding us. In the words of Robin Wall Kimmerer:

> In the Western tradition there is a recognized hierarchy of beings, with, of course, the human being on top – the pinnacle of evolution, the darling of Creation – and the plants at the bottom. But in Native ways of knowing, human people are often referred to as 'the younger brothers of Creation.' We say that humans have the least experience with how to live and thus the most to learn – we must look to our teachers among the other species for guidance. Their wisdom is apparent in the way that they live. They teach us by example. They've been on the earth far longer than we have been and have had time to figure things out."[5] Second, communities of resistance around the world have developed critical consciousness of oppressive systems that offer deep insight into what needs to change in society. These international perspectives are invaluable for charting a more equitable path forward.

[4] Joseph Henrich, Steven J Heine and Ara Norenzayan, 'The Weirdest People in the World?' (2010) 33 *Behavioral and Brain Sciences* 61.

[5] Robin Wall Kimmerer, *Braiding Sweetgrass: Indigenous Wisdom, Scientific Knowledge and the Teachings of Plants* (Minneapolis, Milkweed Editions, 2013).

Second, communities of resistance around the world have developed critical consciousness of oppressive systems that offer deep insight into what needs to change in society. These international perspectives are invaluable for charting a more equitable path forward.

Third, individual differences and the insights offered by neuroatypicality remind us of the creative or curious internal currents that drive some to deviate from what is deemed socially acceptable. Fresh and much-needed perspectives can be sought among these people, often labelled 'mentally ill', 'disordered', or 'mad', who have been forced to imagine a life beyond the status quo.

Incorporating these perspectives would reduce the reliance on researchers and status-quo practitioners' self-interests and biases, and create a channel for a more diverse and representative pool of ideas to flow into academia and practice. This would offer a more agile and robust law, acceptable to the many and not just the few. As Peruvian economist Hernando de Soto put it:

> Law is … not simply a set of spoken, written or formalized rules that people blindly follow. Rather, law represents the formalization of behavioral rules, about which a high percentage of people agree, that reflect behavioral propensities and that offer potential benefits to those who follow them (When people do not recognize or believe in these potential benefits, laws are often disregarded or disobeyed). The Romans and the English shared the idea that the law is something to be discovered more than to be enacted and nobody is so powerful in his society as to be in a position to identify his own will with the law of the land. The task of "discovering" the law was entrusted in their two countries to the jurist consult and to the judges respectively.[6]

The 'discovery' of law can be catalysed using data science and technology. SenseMaker™, a tool for data collection, analysis, and interpretation, can capture these diverse perspectives described above.[7] SenseMaker™ is typically used to collect micro narratives that the respondents then code and interpret themselves, thereby empowering the respondent to be their own ethnographer and limiting the introduction of researcher and expert bias.

Once perspectives are visualised and interpreted, hypotheses can be developed by lawyers about what laws and policies might be necessary to bring these perspectives to life. VR can then be used to rapidly prototype the laws and put the hypotheses to the test.

[6] Hernando de Soto, *The Mystery of Capital: Why Capitalism Triumphs in the West and Fails Everywhere Else* (1. paperback ed, New York, Basic Books 2003).

[7] Susara E Van Der Merwe and others, 'Making Sense of Complexity: Using SenseMaker as a Research Tool' (2019) 7 *Systems* 25.

Exhibit 2 Two Classes of Citizens within most Modern Societies: those struggling for survival, and those thriving and living the life

Consider the hypothetical chart below, showing the relationship between Survival and Well-being and Gross National Product (GNP) per capita. It can be re-interpreted to describe two different classes of citizens within a society, those still struggling for survival, and those who are thriving and living the life.

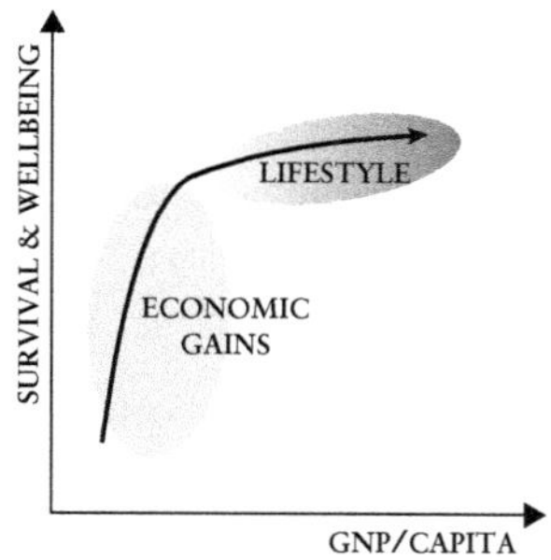

Now consider the same chart replacing the domains of behavioral sciences with the domains of law, AND sequencing the domains of law so that they are antecedent to the domain of the behavioral sciences. Close inspection of the two charts will show that in the absence of social justice and environmental justice, the volume of criminal activity in ***free society*** will swell, which in turn will overrun the criminal justice system.

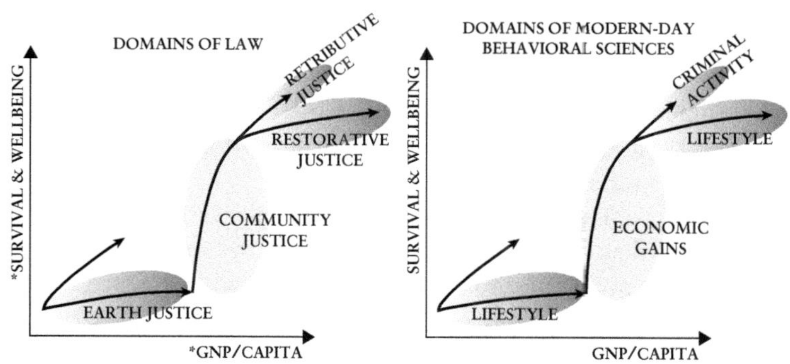

* axis label is borrowed and may be incorrect

** Earth Justice is not the same as Environmental Justice

** Community Justice is not the same as Social Justice

We have emphasized free society above, meaning that artificial restrictions have not been placed on the physical and social mobility of citizens. In case the comparison between law and the behavioral domains is still too abstract, one might replace the domain of law with the domain of health. Thus, during the COVID-19 pandemic, the absence of adequate environmental and social care would have increased the rate of infection (cf. criminal activity), and this would have overrun the health care facilities (criminal justice facilities) for all.

ENGINEERING

Testing Hypotheses in VR

> We must look ahead at today's radical changes in technology, not just as forecasters but as actors charged with designing and bringing about a sustainable and acceptable world. New knowledge gives us power for change: for good or ill, for knowledge is neutral. The problems we face go well beyond technology: problems of living in harmony with nature, and most important, living in harmony with each other. Information technology, so closely tied to the properties of the human mind, can give us, if we ask the right questions, the special insights we need to advance these goals.
>
> — Herbert Simon[8]

Testing hypotheses and theories of culture has traditionally been quite difficult – culture is complex and groups are dynamic. According to Paluck, Shepherd, and Aronow[9] 'one of the most elusive and important goals in the behavioral sciences is to understand how community-wide patterns of behavior can be changed'. Instead, much of the research has focused on individuals and modest ways to modify their behaviour. This means many theories are only tested in hypothetical scenarios online or in the lab, or remain at a purely conceptual level.

The testing of hypotheses entails researchers creating a new psychological landscape and witnessing how people process it and react. Using VR, a variety of media environments can now be created, individual responses can be tracked in real-time, and, most importantly, novel opportunities for self-reflection and introspection can be presented.

Being able to test policies and build worlds in VR will offer an extraordinarily rich preview into what laws may emerge, and what laws we need to create to meet new demands. Experimental worlds and societies could be created, involving all the practices of law – congress, bar, bench, companies, and citizens in the public and private sphere – and we could simulate alternative courses of conversation, decision, and action in a comprehensive and holistic way. In addition, the pace of progress in data science enables near real-time feedback of the impact of law and new technology on society.

Jeremy Bailenson, a leading researcher in VR, has suggested that VR can transform situations that are dangerous, impossible, expensive, or

[8] *Herbert Alexander Simon* 'Is it our Job to Forecast the Future or to Fashion it?' (the Newell-Simon Inauguration and Earthware Symposium, October 19, 2000) https://www.youtube.com/watch?v=EZhyi-8DBjc.

[9] Elizabeth Levy Paluck, Hana Shepherd and Peter M Aronow, 'Changing Climates of Conflict: A Social Network Experiment in 56 Schools' (2016) 113 *Proceedings of the National Academy of Sciences* 566.

counterproductive into ones that are much less fraught with negative experiences.[10] We would like to propose an additional set of criteria: complex (many elements and relationships), open-ended (no boundaries and solutions are emergent), dynamic (change over time, and solutions and prognosis are needed urgently), and exploratory (we are curious and want to explore) (CODE).

While the first three situations proposed by Bailenson are easy to understand, 'counterproductive' is more abstract. To contextualise the meaning, we offer three examples of counterproductive situations where VR has proven effective:

a) To demonstrate the effect of tree logging on climate change, we have people cut down trees. This is counterproductive because we are destroying what we are trying to protect.
b) To train medical doctors to perform a surgical procedure, we have them use live patients. This is counterproductive because we are harming patients whom we have sworn to cure.
c) To teach men on how to alter their behaviours towards women, let them practice with actual women. This is counterproductive because we will be subjecting the women participants to the very system that we consider abusive.

Therefore, beyond the danger, the impossibility, and the cost of translating social science findings into practice, the ethical dilemmas here have been insurmountable up until now. In the last part of this section, we will give six examples of current VR applications to illustrate this last point in its inclusiveness, variety, and concreteness of application areas.

Translating Scientific Findings into Practice

Ex 1. Social Defaults and Cultural Conditioning

People observe or are taught social roles, begin to enact those behaviours, and the differences between groups become further entrenched. Stereotypes form, in part, from people's observations of the world as it is (not as it could be). When people see women in predominantly home-making or caregiving roles, they begin to associate women with warmth and nurturing.

Along the same line of thought, it is said that we cannot be what we cannot see. This observation is often cited by those seeking to increase the representation

[10] Jeremy Bailenson, *Experience on Demand: What Virtual Reality Is, How It Works, and What It Can Do* (New York, WW Norton & Company, 2018).

of people of minoritised identities in government and media. Creating new worlds with alternative patternings is easy to do at scale with VR; people can be exposed to diverse people and environments and can engage with those people and be immersed in those environments. VR can capture the *feel* of different and better cultural norms in a way that words and video cannot. It can also create ways of interacting that are rare in mainstream spaces. Familiarity may breed contempt, but it can also breed empathy and help break down prejudices. By recording these types of encounters, we can teach participants more inclusive ways of interacting.

In this paper, VR is likened to a flight simulator used in training aircraft pilots. Many scenarios can be simulated to test the response of the pilot to various situations. Practice makes perfect, and a simulation can be run several times at minimal costs. These trials can be compared to moot courts currently used in legal education. VR can be used to reduce the cost of moot courts, while increasing the number of practices and scenarios to which each lawyer will be exposed. However, in addition to these moot courts, lawyers-in-training will have the opportunity to inhabit the spaces of various communities virtually, to get a lived experience of the people, and further understand the consequences of various legal decisions played into plausible futures.

Through VR, we can immerse people in new social defaults and disrupt common patterns of behaviour and implicit associations. In today's VR, any physical setting and event can be replicated. Avatars (real people) and agents (algorithmic re-representations) can be used to populate a setting. And because of the breakthroughs in how realistic these simulations have become, we can bring the likeness and mannerisms of anyone into the VR situation, for example, a bank robber or the President of the United States. VR can thus be a training ground in which people break down their cultural conditioning.

Ex 2. Post-traumatic Stress Disorder (PTSD) Therapy and Bias Training

Many therapists have used VR to treat patients with PTSD. The research has demonstrated how VR, through positively increasing levels of exposure, helps inoculate these people from their fears. Since it works for a condition like PTSD, we believe it can work for, say, antisemitism or racism.

Ex 3. Compassion and Rehabilitation

The Public Broadcasting Service (PBS) documentary *Tribal Justice* highlights the efforts of two tribal judges to bring more compassion into the legal system – to 'walk with' offenders and support them on their path through rehabilitation. Such efforts are often marginalised because it is hard to translate them to the mainstream, and scalability is uncertain. Through VR, however, solutions and insights from most traditions can be explored.

Ex 4. Collaboration and Authentic Self-expression

VR training grounds are also essential in developing collaboration skills, in part because these are skills most of us need to both witness and practise to master. In VR, people can be immersed in environments that promote authentic self-expression and collaboration.

Ex 5. Policy and Long-term Effects

VR can be used to prototype policy proposals. There are many ideas about how to improve society. Through VR, these can be piloted, because it is a cost-effective tool for iterating solutions too risky or costly to implement in real life. This avoids the short time-horizons of most current government actions, either because we, the citizens, want immediate gratification or politicians are only guaranteed two- or four-year terms in office (expediency).

Ex 6. Real Time Feedback

We can measure our effectiveness by drawing on advances in data science technologies, such as the Johns Hopkins Coronavirus Resource Center (CRC) Tracker[11] which was used for visualising the spread of the COVID-19 virus, the location of the interventions, and the response of local populations to those interventions.

INDIGENEITY

With a more inclusive law education and new technologies like SenseMaker, VR, and AI to test and translate new understanding into experience and practice, we believe it might be worthwhile to walk through an example before concluding the paper. Researchers and practitioners who do not have a bias towards action may skip to the conclusion.

The example will combine a practice from engineering design and the natural sciences with a framework from law and a theory from cultural sciences.

[11] Justyna Surowiec, '"We Had to Get This Right": How Johns Hopkins Built the Coronavirus Tracking Global Dashboard: An Oral History' (*Johns Hopkins University Applied Physics Laboratory*, 26 April 2021) www.jhuapl.edu/news/news-releases/210426-JHU-COVID-dashboard-oral-history.

This walk-through will be a visual one. It borrows from the disciplines of Science and Engineering, where drawings are used to represent and internalise complex and dynamic situations, to propose changes to those situations, simulate the consequences of those changes, and finally to implement those changes in a safe manner. It is too often said that a picture is worth a thousand words, and visual literacy will become increasingly important for efficient and effective multidisciplinary communication (see Figure 7.2). Granted, there are times when obfuscation is the intention.

Figure 7.2 A picture is worth a thousand words

Given the rapid transformations that have been occurring in the world and the necessity of responding to threats like climate change, we believe it is imperative that we use knowledge from all available disciplines to augment the practice of law in society.

Before going further, it is useful to reflect on the word indigeneity. The related word indigene comes from Latin indigena 'sprung from the land', 'in-born'. As a noun, 'one who or that which is native'. Similarly, the word gene has a root meaning 'give birth, beget', with derivatives referring to procreation and familial and tribal groups. In both cases, the reference is to nature and thus the earth sciences and life sciences. Whether we are talking about listening to the voices of indigenous people, climate change, the environment, the genetic revolution, and other new technologies we are yet to discover, or a new virus that springs from the land, indigeneity is our new ground state and reference point.[12] A framework

[12] 'Etymonline – Online Etymology Dictionary' www.etymonline.com/search?q=indigene.

we have found useful for incorporating nature, the land, and indigeneity into our thinking is Steward Brand's pace model of change.[13] The model is re-represented in Figure 7.3. Note how the diagram illustrates different layers and different rates of change within a society.

Figure 7.3 Components of the pace model of the order of civilisation. The fast layers innovate; the slow layers stabilise. The whole combines learning with continuity. Adapted from Stewart Brand – Clock of the Long Now. Brand, S., (2000)

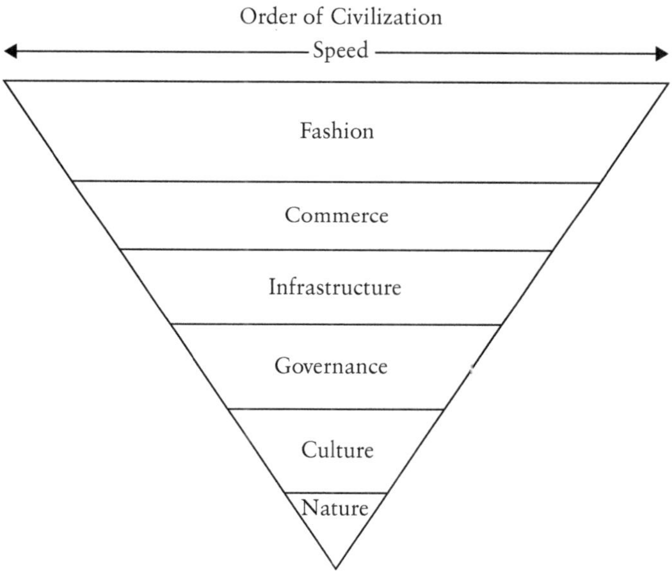

To create a cultural science that allows for experimentation and hypothesis testing, evolutionary adaptation, and positive change, we propose building on and extending a model from the field of cultural psychology. Building on a long line of work, Markus and Hamedani developed the Culture Cycle[14] (see Figure 7.4), a model that reduces culture to four elements, which they named the Four Is: Ideas, Institutions, Interactions, and Individuals.

[13] Stewart Brand, *The Clock of the Long Now: Time and Responsibility* (Paperback edition, London, Phoenix, 2000).

[14] Alan P Fiske and others, 'The Cultural Matrix of Social Psychology' in Daniel Todd Gilbert, Gardner Lindzey and Susan T Fiske (eds), *The Handbook of Social Psychology*, vol 2 (4th edn, New York, McGraw-Hill, 1998); Hazel Rose Markus and Shinobu Kitayama, 'Cultures and Selves: A Cycle of Mutual Constitution' (2010) 5 *Perspectives on Psychological Science* 420; Hazel Rose Markus and Alana Conner, *Clash! 8 Cultural Conflicts That Make Us Who We Are* (New York, NY, Hudson Street Press, 2013) behavioralscientist.org/clash-8-cultural-conflicts-make-us-excerpt/; Mar Yam G Hamedani and Hazel Rose Markus, 'Understanding Culture Clashes and Catalyzing Change: A Culture Cycle Approach' (2019) 10 *Frontiers in Psychology* 700.

According to this model, culture refers to the pervasive ideas in the society – such as conceptualisations about what is good, right, and moral – the institutionalisation of those ideas through law, education and media, and the enactment of those ideas in norms and everyday behaviours. Engaging with cultural systems, they argue, ultimately shapes the psychological processing of individuals, who in turn either perpetuate or challenge the status quo.

Figure 7.4 Components of the Culture Cycle (Adapted from Hamedani and Markus, 2019)

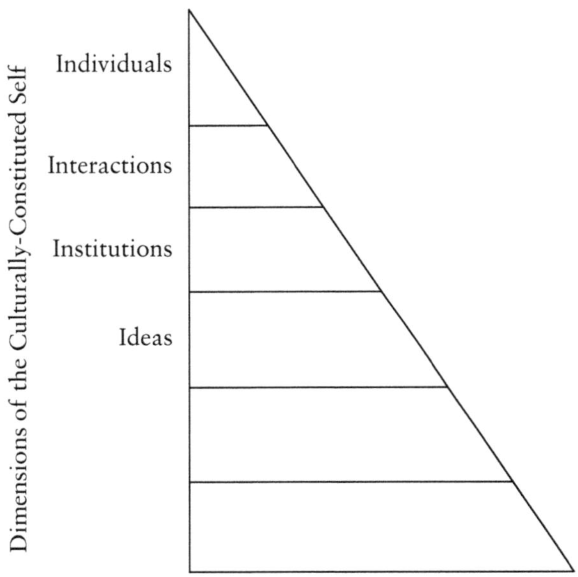

Comparing this model to Steward Brand's pace model, we can tentatively make the following mappings:

Individual = Fashion

Interactions = Commerce

Institutions = Infrastructure

Ideas = Governance

It is important to point out that the drawing of the culture cycle is similar to one by Lawrence Lessig, a professor of Law at Harvard University who has been exploring the role of technology in society (see Figure 7.5).[15]

[15] Lawrence Lessig, *Free Culture: How Big Media Uses Technology and the Law to Lock Down Culture and Control Creativity*, vol 2 (New York, Penguin Press, 2004) www.loc.gov/item/2019666613/.

Figure 7.5 Law and other dominant components constituting a society's interconnected system of regulation (Adapted from Larry Lessig, 2004)

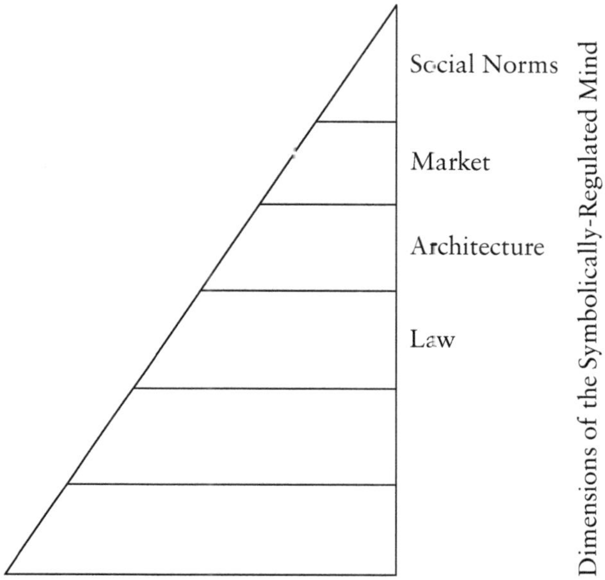

According to Lessig, Law is only a small component of a complex, interconnected system of regulation that depends on the market, cultural norms, architectural design (code), and finally, government. It is important to remember that this interconnection system of regulations maintains the status quo.

As before, we can map the labels here to the Cultural Cycle:

Individual = Behaviour

Interactions = Arrows pressing on behaviours

Institutions = Arrows linking law, norms, market, architecture

Ideas = Law

When we put all three models of rate of change of civilisation layers, culture, and regulation together, Figure 7.6, we can see how the nature/land/indigeneity and time are not explicit in the Hamedani & Markus's Cultural Cycle and in Lessig's interconnected regulation model. This absence makes it clear that what each society calls culture is, in reality, a variant of a more fundamental culture.

Figure 7.6 A comparison of three models: The Pace Layers of Change in Society, The Mutual Constitution of Self and Culture, and The Interconnected System of Regulation

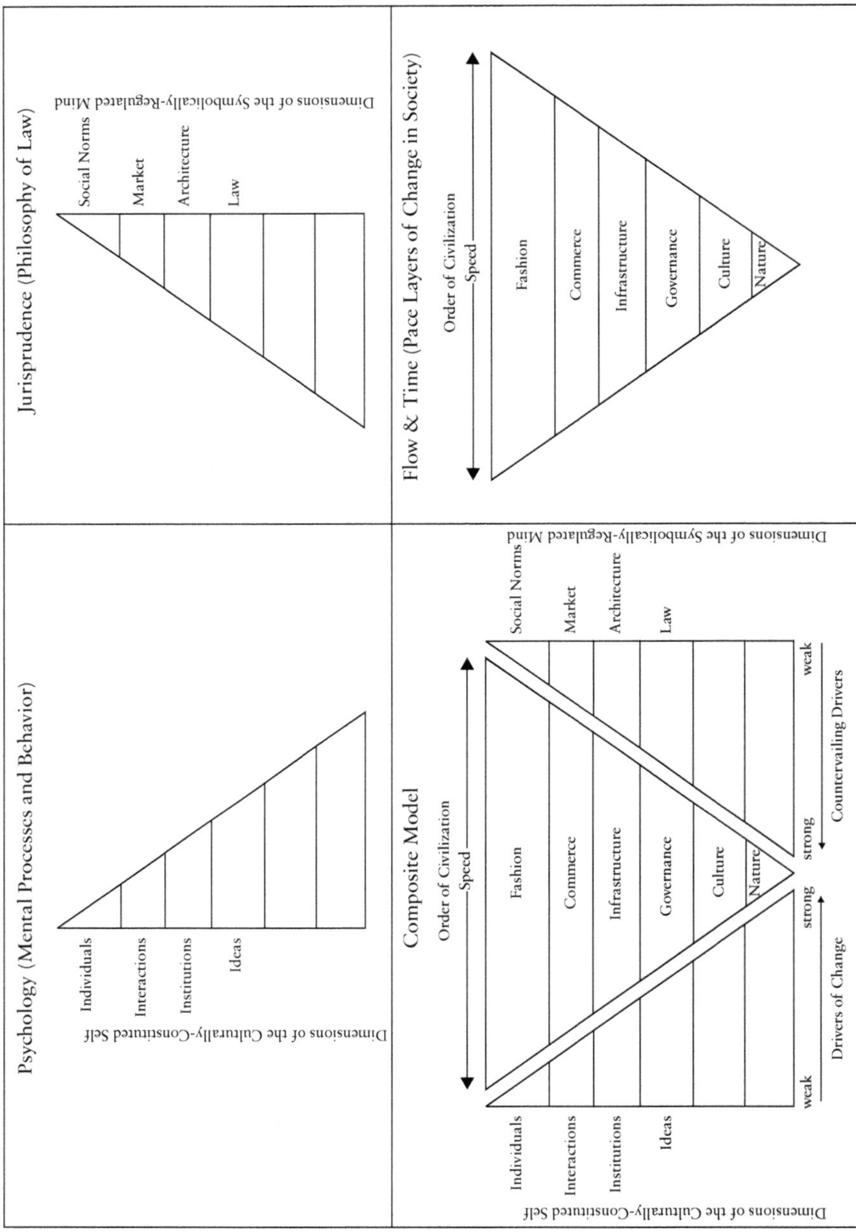

Furthermore, we can conceptualise a cultural chemistry where events like technology innovation, capital formation, and human migration cause changes to happen in their societies. The resulting picture, labelled Cultural Chemistry, appears to be a good framework for thinking of a given society's culture as a variant of a more fundamental culture, whose name we have not yet quite settled on, but it comes close to indigeneity. This conceptualisation is depicted in Figure 7.7.

Figure 7.7 Cultural Chemistry: Some cultures are more permeable than others. They have different shapes, sizes, and proximities

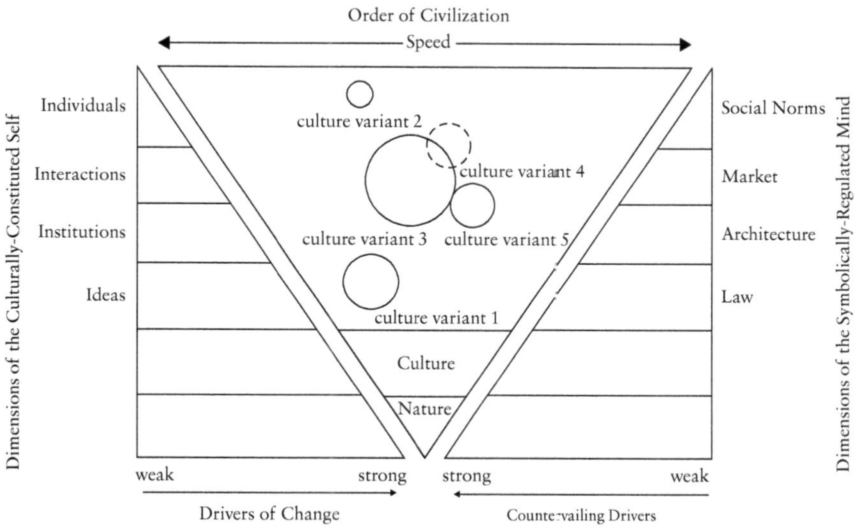

Thus, indigeneity appears to be a more fundamental science of culture, whereby what today is taken as culture is simply a variant produced by the mixture of other sub-variants and the chemistry of the interactions between a more fundamental and primordial human culture and nature. We believe VR, along with the disciplines of anthropology, can help in recreating this primordial world and thus expand the range of experiences and points of view we use in navigating and making laws for an unknown future.

Since Indigeneity demonstrates that culture can be treated like a science, and Law is the bedrock fundamental of every society, it holds that Law itself can be scrutinised and enhanced by scientific principles. In addition, Christopher Langdell's hope of giving legal education a scientific basis may have been given an important boost almost hundred years later, when Herbert Simon one of the early proponents of AI wrote:

> Historically and traditionally it has been the task of the science disciplines to teach about natural things: how they are and how they work. It has been the task of engineering schools to teach about artificial things: how to make artifacts that have desired properties and how to design.

> Engineers are not the only professional designers. Everyone designs who devises courses of action aimed at changing existing situations into preferred ones. The intellectual activity that produces material artifacts is no different fundamentally from the one that prescribes remedies for a sick patient or one that devises a new sales plan for a company or a social welfare policy for a state. Design, so construed, is the core of all professional training; it is the principal mark that distinguishes the professions from the sciences.
>
> Schools of engineering, as well as schools of architecture, business, education, law, and medicine are all centrally concerned with the process of design. … The proper study of those who are concerned with the artificial is the way in which [the] adaptation of means to the environment is brought about – and central to that is the process of design itself.
>
> — Herbert Simon[16]

The earth is evolving, ever-changing, just like the covid variants and man's capacity to confront challenges. Like mankind, GenAI is ever-learning, ever-changing. Trying to regulate a mutating system is foolhardy – it is like saying, let's regulate Covid! To survive, to thrive, we must adapt, evolve, and learn. And so must our legal system. We hope this partially visual walk-through gives readers a fair indication of the changes that will be required in legal education today and tomorrow. A more sensory, perceptual walk-through is not possible in the medium of an academic paper such as this one, but is readily available in a VR lab. We believe incorporating weaving into legal education and practice might enable us to become more proactive as our social and physical environments evolve at ever-faster rates.

CONCLUSION

When medical doctor and anthropologist Paul Farmer was distressed by the way tuberculosis was becoming an epidemic in the world, he did not call on politicians to fix it – he pointed out the responsibility his profession bore:

> Medicine is a social science and politics is nothing but medicine on a large scale. It is the curse of humanity that it learns to tolerate even the most horrible situations by habituation. Medical education does not exist to provide students with a way of making a living, but to ensure the health of the community. The physicians are the natural attorneys of the poor, and the social problems should largely be solved by them. (Paul Farmer expanding on Rudolf Virchow's statement, and quoted in Kidder, 2004[17])

We need a similar revelation in the legal profession. We need *lawyers* who are the 'natural attorneys of the poor'… and of the natural world. This requires

[16] Herbert A Simon, *The Sciences of the Artificial* (3rd ed, Cambridge, MA, MIT Press, 1996).
[17] Tracy Kidder, *Mountains Beyond Mountains* (New York, Random House 2004).

a radical re-conception of what role lawyers, law schools, and the law play in society. What our new world requires is more encouragement, better judgement, better advocacy, and better litigation. The goal is not to have a particular utopic end-state in mind, but rather to have the courage to co-create a future built upon mutual empowerment, experimentation, and compassion for each other and the natural world.

The organic development of this form of compassion and its eventual embodiment in law and institutions could easily take centuries to be realised if at all. Fortunately, organic processes can be catalysed. With technologies such as VR and AI, we are optimistic that we can immerse people in new ways of being that challenge the status quo and foster the creativity to imagine beyond what is.

Culture is a living phenomenon, and when we fossilise it in laws based on contexts that have changed significantly, we may be doing the opposite of what we intend, and what we need to do. Law, like the strands woven into a basket, creates a container for culture. If Poorly woven, the basket will leak, and certain populations will become vulnerable. Properly woven, it can reshape our culture to better meet the challenges we face, while serving all of us, rather than just a privileged few. We believe that weaving will open the discipline of law to lead society in innovation, as well as to protect society from extinction.

REFERENCES

American Bar Association (ABA), 'Demographics and Composition of the 117th Congress' (*American Bar Association (ABA)*, 2021).

J Bailenson, *Experience on Demand: What Virtual Reality Is, How It Works, and What It Can Do* (New York, WW Norton & Company, 2018).

S Brand, *The Clock of the Long Now: Time and Responsibility* (Paperback edition, London, Phoenix, 2000).

'Etymonline – Online Etymology Dictionary'.

AP Fiske and others, 'The Cultural Matrix of Social Psychology' in Daniel Todd Gilbert, Gardner Lindzey and Susan T Fiske (eds), *The Handbook of Social Psychology*, vol 2 (4th edn, New York, McGraw-Hill, 1998).

LM Friedman, *A History of American Law* (New York, Simon and Schuster, 1973).

MTG Hamedani and HR Markus, 'Understanding Culture Clashes and Catalyzing Change: A Culture Cycle Approach' (2019) 10 *Frontiers in Psychology* 700.

J Henrich, SJ Heine and A Norenzayan, 'The Weirdest People in the World?' (2010) 33 *Behavioral and Brain Sciences* 33(2-3): 61-83; discussion 83–135.

'Is It Our Job to Forecast the Future or to Fashion It' by Herbert Alexander Simon (2000).

T Kidder, *Mountains Beyond Mountains* (New York, Random House, 2004).

RW Kimmerer, *Braiding Sweetgrass: Indigenous Wisdom, Scientific Knowledge and the Teachings of Plants* (Minneapolis, Milkweed Editions, 2013).

CC Langdell (ed), A Selection of Cases on the Law of Contracts: With References and Citations (Clark, NJ, Lawbook Exchange, 1999).

L Lessig, *Free Culture: How Big Media Uses Technology and the Law to Lock Down Culture and Control Creativity, vol 2 (New York, Penguin Press, 2004).*

HR Markus and A Conner A, *Clash! 8 Cultural Conflicts That Make Us Who We Are* (New York, NY, Hudson Street Press, 2013).

HR Markus and S Kitayama, 'Cultures and Selves: A Cycle of Mutual Constitution' (2010) 5 *Perspectives on Psychological Science* 5(4), 420–430.

EL Paluck, H Shepherd and PM Aronow, 'Changing Climates of Conflict: A Social Network Experiment in 56 Schools' (2016) 113 *Proceedings of the National Academy of Sciences* 113(3), 566–571.

B van Rooij, and A Fine, *The Behavioral Code: The Hidden Ways the Law Makes Us Better or Worse* (Boston, Beacon Press, 2021).

HA Simon, *The Sciences of the Artificial* (3rd ed, Cambridge, MA, MIT Press, 1996).

HA Simon, "Is it our Job to Forecast the Future or to Fashion it" (the Newell-Simon Inauguration and Earthware Symposium, October 19, 2000).

H de Soto, *The Mystery of Capital: Why Capitalism Triumphs in the West and Fails Everywhere Else* (1. paperback ed, New York, Basic Books, 2003).

J Surowiec, '"We Had to Get This Right": How Johns Hopkins Built the Coronavirus Tracking Global Dashboard: An Oral History' (*Johns Hopkins University Applied Physics Laboratory*, 26 April 2021).

SE Van Der Merwe and others, 'Making Sense of Complexity: Using SenseMaker as a Research Tool' (2019) 7 Systems 7(2) 25.

8

Designing against 'Self-Abandonment': A US Law Student's Reflections on Legal Design

ELENA KURAN[1]

INTRODUCTION

> What is needed is to think about the law in a way that will allow students to enter into it, criticize it without utterly rejecting it, and to manipulate it without self-abandonment to an alien system of thinking and doing.[2]
>
> Duncan Kennedy, *Legal Education as Training for Hierarchy*

I WRITE THIS chapter as a dispatch from the belly of the beast. I am in my third and final year of law school in the United States. Since I began in fall 2022, the Supreme Court has razed reproductive health protections,[3] weaponised anti-discrimination principles to end affirmative action,[4] and undone decades of administrative law that helped to keep our air breathable and our drugs free of snake oil.[5] I have watched university administration deploy police in full riot gear against my classmates and faculty as they protested peacefully on our campus quad.[6] I have witnessed, with horror–rage–grief, the execution of an innocent man whose sentence even the prosecution opposed[7] – all of this, among the

[1] Northeastern University School of Law, NuLawLab Bronx Defenders, Civil Action Practice.

[2] Duncan Kennedy, *Legal Education as Training for Hierarchy* (first published 1983, New York, New York University Press, 2004) 42.

[3] *Dobbs v. Jackson Women's Health Organization*, 597 US 215 (2022).

[4] *Students for Fair Admissions, Inc. v. President and Fellows of Harvard College*, 600 US 181 (2023).

[5] *Loper Bright Enterprises v. Raimondo*, 603 US 369 (2024).

[6] Mark Herz, 'Northeastern students set up pro-Palestinian encampment' *WGBH News* (Boston, 25 April 2024) www.wgbh.org/news/local/2024-04-25/northeastern-students-set-up-pro-palestinian-encampment.

[7] Alyxaundria Sanford, 'The Injustice of Death Row: The Profound Tragedy of Marcellus Williams and the Fight to Save Robert Roberson' (*The Innocence Project*, 9 October 2024). innocenceproject.org/the-injustice-of-death-row-the-profound-tragedy-of-marcellus-williams-and-the-fight-to-save-robert-roberson/.

everyday and less spectacular, visible and invisible violence sanctioned by the US legal system. Importantly, I learned that these were not outcomes of a broken system in need of some well-intentioned reforms. Rather, these were outputs of a system that is working the way it is supposed to.[8] If I were considering attending law school at this moment, I am certain that I would decide against it. But now, the finish line is in sight, and I am both determined to reach it and confident in my ability to do so. How? And why? Part of it is due to my intentional decision to attend a public interest law school, one of just a handful in the United States. But even an environment that is committed to collaboration and is free of grades and hierarchy can only do so much to soften the blow of what is fundamentally an isolating and intellectually violent training. Rather, the way I have been able to resist the self-abandonment that Professor Kennedy warned of decades ago is by design.

By luck – or perhaps by the design of some merciful higher power – I learned at the end of my first year that my law school is home to one of the country's first legal design labs.[9] Prior to the NuLawLab, I had never studied design, let alone heard of legal design, but, following eight disorienting months of immersion in doctrinal law, I was eager (desperate) for something different. I sought to recover the familiar, generous ways of learning that had made me love school all my life. I enrolled in the Lab Seminar in Applied & Critical Design and began working as a research assistant for Sankalp Bhatnagar on his project, 'A Casebook for New Legal Imagination'. Since then, design has helped me to not only preserve but also develop a sense of self, leading me outside of the legal academy to design classrooms, museums, conferences, workshops, and even overseas, continually opening door after door, many of which I did not know even existed. Design continues to provide me with a vocabulary and way of working with law – one that is critical, hopeful, and sustaining.

From my position as a law student, I hope to offer something of a meta-reflection: my first-hand account of studying legal design and what I see as its liberatory potential, both for its students and for each person upon whom the law acts (that is, all of us). I hope to think through the ways we might use design – emanating from both outside and within law – to materialise legal practices, beginning with law school, that are committed to dignity not only for the beneficiaries of empire but also for those long and intentionally excluded. I write with a sense of urgency, as the veneer of justice around the US legal system is unmasked at alarming rates, sanctioning greater and unevenly distributed harm at home and abroad, and as one faction of Legal Design seems to replicate, rather than dismantle, these logics of empire.

[8] Paul Butler, 'The System Is Working the Way It Is Supposed to: The Limits of Criminal Justice Reform' (2020) 1(6) *Freedom Center Journal*.

[9] Dan Jackson, Jules Rochelle Sievert and Miso Kim, 'Mission + History' (*NuLawLab*) www.nulawlab.org/.

This chapter proceeds in three parts. First, I look to the ways that law schools, as the initial site of socialisation for future lawyers and judges, operate to produce foot soldiers of the status quo, which comes at a particularly high cost to students from historically marginalised and minoritised communities. My discussion draws from the work of critical scholars and movements, upon whose shoulders I graciously stand. I extend their critiques of law and legal education to legal design; specifically, to the ways the crystallisation of legal design as a professional field risks maintaining existing power structures. I rely on Professors Joaquín Santuber and Siddharth deSouza's call for a shift from Legal Design to legal designing.[10] I then turn to the liberatory potential of design in legal education, combining my own experience with insights from my colleagues and mentors at Northeastern and around the world. I explore the ways in which redesigning how future lawyers and judges are educated can increase the dignity of students, shift power to movements, and democratise freedom practices.

U.S. LEGAL EDUCATION AND WHITTLING DOWN THE SELF

When friends or classmates from college – particularly those interested in using law for social and political change – ask me for advice about applying to law school, I begin by sharing Dean Spade's 'For Those Considering Law School'.[11] Professor Spade offers several sharply articulated considerations, but here I focus on the fourth: 'Law school is a very conservative training and rarely a critical intellectual experience'.

> Law school is like a language immersion program, but one in which the language you are learning is the language of rationalizing white supremacy, settler colonialism, patriarchy and capitalism. The traditional pedagogy of law school relies on humiliating students if they bring in other ways of thinking or knowing about the world, thereby whittling them down to a shadow of their former selves and reshaping them to make them think inside a very narrow box.[12]

I myself had read this article before applying to law school, agreeing with Professor Spade's characterisation but confident in my ability to resist the experience, especially because I knew I would attend a law school with an articulated commitment to social justice. I now recognise that I had underestimated Professor Spade's warning; as he points out, 'no activist exits law school without having been changed and made more conservative'.[13] This is in part because

[10] Joaquín Santuber and Siddharth de Souza, *The Socio-Politics of Legal Design and its Epistemic Consequences* (Oxford, Hart Publishing, 2025) 8.

[11] Dean Spade, 'For Those Considering Law School' (first published 2010) VI *Unbound: Harvard Journal of the Legal Left* journals.law.harvard.edu/legalleft/wp-content/uploads/sites/81/2015/09/3.Spade_.final_.pdf.

[12] ibid 114.

[13] ibid 115.

people who end up in law school tend to be overachievers throughout their education. We are good students who read, internalise, and recite what is taught. However, in law school – 'ideological training for willing service in the hierarchies of the corporate welfare state' – this means that 'students act affirmatively within the channels cut for them, cutting them deeper, giving the whole a patina of consent, and weaving complicity into everyone's life story'.[14] The stakes of an unexamined legal education are high for groups far beyond the students.

The ideological and spiritual shaping of law school holds true even at Northeastern, where I had first-year professors who were committed to weaving missing or excluded perspectives into their doctrinal teaching, and classmates who were willing to co-create critical learning spaces outside of the classroom. To do well in law school and pass the bar exam (the ultimate barrier to becoming a lawyer in the United States), I felt pressured to suspend my moral intuitions – the same ones that had brought me to law school in the first place – or else fail to fully grasp the judge's reasoning or risk a shameful cold call. I watched my classmates, whom I admire greatly and who teach me so much, struggle to answer our professors' question: Did the judge get it right in this case? I could see them thinking, and occasionally voicing: *right in the legal or ethical sense?* What does the existence of this 'or' tell us about our legal system?

An early example continues to stick with me. *Ashcroft v. Iqbal* is one of the most important contemporary civil procedure cases, read by every first-year law student in the United States. The customary explanation of *Iqbal* is an interpretation of pleading standards in civil cases. Javaid Iqbal alleged that, in the wake of the September 11 attacks, he was deprived of various constitutional protections while in federal custody. He sued several federal officials, including Attorney-General John Ashcroft, for adopting an unconstitutional and discriminatory policy that subjected him to harsh conditions of confinement. The Court framed the question as narrowly and as procedurally as possible: 'Did respondent […] plead factual matter that, if taken as true, states a claim that petitioners deprived him of his clearly established constitutional rights?'[15] The Court found Mr. Iqbal's pleadings insufficient, ruling that a plaintiff must provide sufficient factual detail to make a plausible claim to survive a motion to dismiss. Ah! A sensible, operational procedural decision from the highest court.

As I struggled to make sense of what the Court's decision meant for the pleading standard, the dissonance set in – dissonance caused by the 'objective' framing of the majority's discussion, the stark xenophobia and Islamophobia animating its ultimate decision, and the utter absence of Mr. Iqbal's story beyond what the majority deemed to be 'legally relevant facts'. Mr. Iqbal's life was upended, and years later, we sat in a comfortable lecture hall performing an exegesis of a decision that affirmed it. The majority opinion begins with the

[14] Kennedy (n 2) 16.
[15] *Ashcroft v. Iqbal*, 556 US 662, 666 (2009).

following: 'Javaid Iqbal is a citizen of Pakistan and a Muslim. In the wake of the September 11, 2001, terrorist attacks he was arrested in the United States on criminal charges and detained by federal officials'.[16] As Shirin Sinnar points out '[a]lthough accurate and legally relevant, these opening lines also presented Iqbal, from the outset, as essentially a foreigner and possible terrorist suspect'.[17] One has to read only the opening line to predict the outcome.

Professor Sinnar's 'The Lost Story of Iqbal', which my civil procedure professor, Lucy Williams, had assigned as mandatory reading, contests the Court's narrative by telling the story of Mr. Iqbal and others like him who were subject to discriminatory investigations and detentions following the September 11 attacks. She also warns of the potential for facially neutral procedural decisions to affect substantive rights; to survive a motion to dismiss, a plaintiff must now meet some amorphous level of sufficiency determined exclusively by a judge. In doing so, the new interpretation of the pleading standard, though facially neutral, disadvantages injured plaintiffs seeking legal redress. Professor Sinnar's piece not only gave me the ability to comprehend and criticise the decision, but also assured me that I was not alone in feeling confused or borderline crazy upon reading the majority's racially and religiously biased yet carefully sanitised discussion. I suspect most civil procedure professors do not assign Professor Sinnar's article to their students. Who is assuring them? Who is telling Mr. Iqbal's story and the stories of countless other people rendered invisible by the law?

I use *Iqbal* as an example of what happens in all first-year classes and many upper-level doctrinal classes: students read decisions that present powerful and lopsided narratives carefully constructed out of a subjective set of legally relevant facts. Walls of text containing doctrine, legalese, and Latin phrases fashion law into an objective quasi-science – the enduring influence of formalism – insulating it from critiques of unfairness or judicial bias: it's simply what the law compels. It is insisted that judges are neutral umpires, calling balls and strikes as they apply the law to the facts. Students are discouraged from bringing in different ways of thinking and knowing about the world to respond to the reality that 'the traditional language of argument and opinion neither explains nor justifies court decisions'.[18] Cries of 'It's not fair!' are met with nervous nods of agreement from classmates and sympathetic smiles from the professors. While they may agree, there is simply too much material to cover; the doctrinal machine must barrel ahead. Thus, the content and structure of law school often require a division between our moral intuitions and the analysis we're expected to conduct in class, resulting in a fracturing of the self. This fracturing is disproportionately felt by outsider students who see, over and over, that people who resemble them

[16] ibid.
[17] Shirin Sinnar, 'The Lost Story of Iqbal' (2017) 105 *Georgetown Law Journal* 379.
[18] Felix S. Cohen, 'Transcendental Nonsense and the Functional Approach' (1935) 35(6) *Columbia Law Review* 809.

tend to be the losers in the cases we discuss with detachment in the classroom. The law school experience has been likened to hazing, hell, and indoctrination. Diagnoses of depression and anxiety, increased need for help with emotional or mental health, and suicidal ideation are accepted as part and parcel.[19]

Discouraging studies showing the effect of law school on students are not new. Generations of lawyers and activists have endured, identified, and critiqued the trouble with law school and the fallacies of law more generally, drawing from disciplines beyond law, including from personal experience. I take a moment to recognise and briefly trace these traditions of critical legal thinking because they have made legal education and the prospect of a life in law bearable and even aspirational for me.

I opened this chapter with a quote from Professor Kennedy's enduring self-published booklet, 'Legal Education and the Reproduction of Hierarchy'. Professor Kennedy belonged to Critical Legal Studies (CLS), a movement that emerged during the 1970s and which had its intellectual roots in legal realism of the late nineteenth and early twentieth centuries. Realism emerged near-concurrently as a response to the formalism of Classical Legal Thought, which was characterised by abstractions from simplified categories, binary bright lines, an adherence to law as a quasi-scientific process, and an intentional separation between social practices and the law. Early realists such as Holmes, Hohfeld, Cardozo, and Cohen attacked the formalist framing of law, arguing for the inductive rather than deductive nature of adjudication. They emphasised the indeterminacy of law and the role of social policy in producing decisions. Cohen went as far as characterising most mainstream jurisprudence as transcendental nonsense: '[I]n every field of law we should find the same habit of ignoring practical questions of value or of positive fact and taking refuge in 'legal problems' which can always be answered by manipulating legal concepts in certain approved ways'.[20] Nearly 100 years later, I see these critiques come alive in cases such as *Iqbal*.

Decades after the first waves of realism, a major branch of CLS attempted to recover their techniques of legal criticism. Critical legal realism also aimed to introduce modernist and postmodernist social and cultural theory into US legal thought. It 'was a place where contestation over various dimensions of power transpired', including class and labour, race and slavery, sex and gender, and legal history, practice, and pedagogy.[21] CLS was also 'influenced by and influenced other schools of the period, such as critical race theory, critical feminist legal thought, queer legal theory, and Third World approaches to international

[19] David Jaffe, Katherine Bender and Jerome M. Organ, '"It is Okay to Not Be Okay': The 2021 Survey of Law Student Well-Being' (2021) 60 *University of Louisville Law Review* 441.

[20] Cohen (n 18) 820.

[21] Dennis M. Davis and Karl Klare, 'Critical Legal Realism in a Nutshell" in Emilios Christodoulidis, Ruth Dukes, and Marco Goldoni (eds), *Research Handbook on Critical Legal Theory* (Cheltenham, Edward Elgar Publishing, 2019).

law'.[22] Critical Race Theory (CRT) 'accepted the [CLS] emphasis on how law produces and is the product of social power and crosscut this theme with an effort to understand this dynamic in the context of race and racism'.[23] CRT also expanded the methodologies and tools of critical legal analysis. Scholars such as Mari Matsuda and Patricia Williams wove the personal into discussions of law, culture, and history to reveal both the law's violence and emancipatory potential:

> It is my deep belief that theoretical legal understanding and social transformation need not be oxymoronic. I want this book to occupy the gaps between those ends that the sensation of oxymoron marks. What I hope will be filled in is connection; connection between my psyche and the readers', between lived experience and social perception, and between an encompassing historicity and a jurisprudence of generosity.[24]

CRT scholars were writing to my dissonance before I was born. In *When the First Quail Calls*, Professor Matsuda describes how outsider students can sharpen their dissonance into an analytical tool: 'This constant shifting of consciousness produces sometimes madness, sometimes genius, sometimes both'.[25] It is the ability to use the law, an imperfect but powerful tool for justice, by detaching it and seeing it as a system that makes sense only from a particular viewpoint.[26] Like CLS scholars, critical race theorists contested the dominant approach to adjudication: 'Abstraction and detachment are ways out of the discomfort of direct confrontation with the ugliness of oppression'.[27] The writings of Mari Matsuda, Patricia Williams, Kimberlé Crenshaw, Richard Delgado, and Derrick Bell, Jr. remind me, again and again, that there is another way to exist as a law student who is also a person with feelings, and who is trying her best to be both at the same time.

With the works of the Crits close to heart, I look to the current landscape of legal design with curiosity and concern. One approach emphasises practices with explicit political commitments. As the editors point out:

> to think of the socio-politics of legal design is to acknowledge that in the face of multiple approaches to change or renewal in the legal system, the decision of which approach we take is a political one and defines the possibilities and limits of the transformation we want to make in the world.[28]

[22] ibid.

[23] Kimberle Williams Crenshaw, 'Twenty Years of Critical Race Theory: Looking Back to Move Forward' (2011) 43(5) *Connecticut Law Review* 1289.

[24] Patricia Williams, *The Alchemy of Race and Rights* (Cambridge, MA, Harvard University Press, 1991) 8.

[25] Mari Matsuda, 'When the First Quail Calls, A Talk Presented at the Yale Law School Conference on Women of Color and the Law' (1989) 11(1) *Women's Rights Law Reporter* 8.

[26] ibid 8.

[27] ibid.

[28] Santuber and deSouza, 3.

However, another conflates legal design with technocapitalist innovation.[29] While attending the Legal Design Summit in September 2023, I was moved by presentations by scholars and activists such as Hallie Jay Pope, who discussed legal design's potential to shift power to movements and dismantle unequal systems. However, I began to experience a similar dissonance to that of my first-year law school experience. Following critical and hopeful presentations on how legal design could help make the world more free, counsel for large consulting groups and corporate law firms also took the stage. They spoke vaguely of innovation, law, and tech, and how design thinking could maximise efficiency and better understand the needs of their multibillion-dollar conglomerate clients. This was not the legal design that led me across the world. Rather, it was a version co-opted by corporate interests, the very same interests that had shaped legal education into such an undignified and alienating experience.

To combat the interconnected indignities of standard legal education and the corporate coopting of legal design, I believe the answer lies in design itself. Specifically, the project of employing design methodologies in law school would help to realise a more human-centred legal profession. The following section explores the ways this project could play out today, drawing on my own experiences as a student of legal design and proposals put forth by my mentors and colleagues.

REDESIGNING THE MEANS AND ENDS OF LAW SCHOOL

Before describing the ways in which design could interrupt traditional legal education, I take a moment to explicitly explain my own understanding of how law and design are related, and why their intentional combination in the education setting carries liberatory potential. First, I operate from the premise that law itself is 'a particular and consequential form of designing'.[30] It is a human-made thing, the invisible social infrastructure of our lives that acts on each of us. This framing shares principles of realism and its progeny: law is not some disembodied concept that can be accurately captured through a process of legal reasoning. Rather, it is made: decision by decision, statute by statute, argument by argument. Second, I understand law to be a form of ontological design. Anne-Marie Willis argues:

> 'that designing is fundamental to being human – we design, that is to say, we deliberate, plan and scheme in ways which prefigure our actions and making – in turn we are designed by our designing and by that which we have designed.[31]

[29] eg, Rachel Dooley, 'Innovate | Legal: McKinsey Legal Lab' *In The Balance* (New York, April 27, 2022) www.mckinsey.com/featured-insights/in-the-balance/innovate-legal-mckinsey-legal-lab.

[30] Sankalp Bhatnagar, 'What Legal Design Is as Opposed to Could/Should Be' in Dan Lockton and others (eds) *DRS2022: Bilbao* (2022).

[31] Anne-Marie Willis, 'Ontological Designing' (2006) 4(2) *Design Philosophy Papers* 69.

We design laws and they in turn design us: 'Both law and design are inherently social fields that stem from human actors and have recursive effects on them – their actions, interactions, and ways of thinking'.[32]

If law is a form of design – specifically a recursive ontological design which carries with it a politics – what are its ends, both purported and actual? Here I look beyond law because its purported ends have not produced lawful, right, or just outcomes in practice. Indeed, the US legal system has largely failed to embrace 'law as a special kind of design capable of bringing out marginal, forgotten, and overlooked practices of our own lives'.[33] I turn to the work of design scholars who ground design in dignity and a broad understanding of human rights. NuLawLab's Design Director Miso Kim argues that dignity is a fundamental principle of human-centred design.[34] While in Professor Kim's course, I was introduced to and further inspired by the work of Richard Buchanan: 'The quality of design is distinguished not merely by technical skill of execution or by aesthetic vision but by the moral and intellectual purpose toward which technical and artistic skill is directed'.[35] By extension, the quality of legal systems must be evaluated by the moral and intellectual ends towards which we adjudicate. Indeed, the current US legal system is an expansive and impressively organised feat of government-sanctioned racial capitalism. From an efficiency standpoint, it is a well-oiled, seemingly impenetrable machine. However, its disruption and perhaps dismantling is not only possible but urgently required.

Design offers itself as a promising intervention to disrupt the gatekeeping, obscuring, and detached rationalisation of violence that characterises much of the legal profession today and which begins in first-year law courses. For students, legal design approaches can help bridge legal theory and real-world application, materialising and unmasking 'objective' reasoning and instead centring the experiences of those most impacted by law. To do so, law students need not cast off law entirely. As Michael Doherty explains, 'legal design is not a turning away from the law'[36] Design is already at work within law, and contains virtues that direct us towards certainty, fairness, and justice. Thus, legal design 'involves a turning towards those virtues, but via a critique of existing legal methods'.[37]

What might progressive legal designing in law school curriculum look like in practice? For one, legal design courses with explicit political commitments to justice are emerging across the country and around the world. Universities

[32] Dana Altajem and others, 'A Legal Design Classroom: Reflections on Learning Through Legal Education' (2024) 1(1) *Legal Design Journal*.

[33] Bhatnagar (n 30).

[34] Miso Kim, 'A Study of Dignity as a Principle of Service Design' (2021) 15(3) *International Journal of Design* 87.

[35] Richard Buchanan, 'Human Dignity and Human Rights: Thoughts on the Principles of Human-Centered Design'(2001) 17(3) *Design Issues* 35.

[36] Michael Doherty and others, 'A New Attitude to Law's Empire: The Potentialities of Legal Design' in Marcelo Corrales Compagnucci and others (eds), *Legal Design: Integrating Business, Design and Legal Thinking with Technology* (Cheltenham, Edward Elgar Publishing, 2021).

[37] ibid.

have the advantage of institutional structure to support legal design labs such as the NuLawLab and its sister lab, the Amsterdam Law Hub at the University of Amsterdam. These labs split their efforts between pedagogy and projects with communities, providing more space to strengthen ties with movements; law students are drawn out of our ivory towers to work alongside communities bearing the unequal impacts of the law. In the classroom, legal design lab courses introduce law students to the design thinking process: empathise, define, ideate, prototype, and test. Students follow these steps to develop legal interventions – apps, services, and products – to increase access to justice and bridge the gap between the law and its end users. For example, in NuLawLab's Seminar on Applied & Critical Design, I created 'Missing Narratives', an AI-powered tool to chart missing and excluded narratives – such as Mr. Iqbal's – to challenge dominant paradigms in the classroom. In this way, Missing Narratives is an affirmative example of traditional design approaches combined with a commitment to a broader political project. During summer 2024, I co-taught the Amsterdam Law Hub's Justice Entrepreneurship course, where I guided second-year politics, psychology, law, and economics students through the same process. My own Gestalt switch of recognising designing in law was deepened by later helping other students to experience it as well.

Beyond seminars focused on designing new legal interventions, legal educators committed to social justice are finding other ways to draw in legal design. At Seton Hall University School of Law, Hallie Jay Pope and Abdul Rehman Khan lead the Housing Justice and Legal Design Clinic, which employs a legal design framework to understand and respond to housing inequity in New Jersey:

> Centering tenants and collaborating with organizers, students will use participatory design techniques to: (1) find and explore problems of housing injustice alongside impacted community members, (2) co-design, build, and test solutions that build tenant power, and (3) advocate for legal interventions that promote housing as a human right.[38]

Professors Pope and Khan's clinic is a model for how legal designing can better support the work of movements and provide social justice lawyers with concrete frameworks and tools to carry out our work.

In addition to the work of legal design labs and clinics, a radical reshaping of legal education requires extending legal design beyond these largely self-selecting settings into doctrinal classrooms. Indeed, the enduring value of legal design for me has been the way it changed how I navigate all of my law courses – with curiosity, criticality, and some level of irreverence for the spectacle of law. However, there is little room to implement the full design thinking process into a dense course such as first-year property law. Rather, there are transsubstantive ways to draw in/out design in the traditional legal curriculum.

[38] Abdul Rehman Khan and Hallie Jay Pope, 'Housing Justice and Legal Design Clinic' (Seton Hall Law School) law.shu.edu/clinics/housing-justice-legal-design.html.

Amanda Perry-Kessaris and Emily Allbon identify two such designerly ways to promote practical-critical-imaginative thinking in legal education ecosystems: visual and material communication strategies, and experimental processes.[39]

Walls of text and legalese remain the standard in legal communication. 'But by supplementing the textual with visual and material formats, and by encouraging experimentation, we can make legal communications more inclusive – that is, more meaningful, relevant and accessible'.[40] This holds true not only for nonlawyers navigating complex legal processes, but also for students of the law. Several of my professors would scribble flowcharts and maps on the chalkboard as they described concepts like impleader, race-notice statutes, and levels of judicial scrutiny. Almost always, these little impermanent drawings would clarify what 10 pages of our pricey casebooks could not, thereby maximising inclusion of different learning and processing styles. Furthermore, making ideas tangible 'can give students and teachers the confidence to draw on intuition to develop and explore a personal sense of a subject', promoting a deeper sense of empathy and a more critical, sophisticated sense of inquiry.

Relatedly, more experimental processes and strategies for studying law can help disrupt its hierarchical logics. Rather than rote memorisation of legal rules and doctrine, students should pursue, and professors ought to facilitate, iterative, divergent, and convergent thinking. Doing so will provide students with a deeper and more critical understanding of how a judge generated and defended their decision, expanding the scope beyond the legally relevant facts. As a study by Professor de Souza and LLM students found:

> Learning about new legal methodologies beyond the black letter legal methodology was a valuable experience and expanded understandings on making the law more accessible for individuals who interact with it on a day-to-day basis but are often excluded due to the assumptions and complexities of the law.[41]

Having outlined some ways legal design can be used in legal education, I turn to a brief discussion of some of their risks. Plainly, as big law firms rebrand their corporate litigation as user-centred lawyering and prosecutors begin to rely on experimental technology without transparency, legal design runs the risk of maintaining, rather than undoing, the unequal legal apparatus. As my professors and mentors argued as early as 2020: 'If we do not critically examine and correct the foundations, methods, and outcomes of the legal design process with enough care, we simply will enshrine long-standing racial and economic bias in a shiny new technologic or process wrapper'.[42] Legal designing ought only be done with a 'normative commitment to avoiding, exposing and remedying

[39] Emily Allbon and Amanda Perry-Kessaris (eds), *Design in Legal Education* (London, Routledge, 2022).

[40] ibid.

[41] Altajem (n 32).

[42] Dan Jackson, Miso Kim and Jules Rochielle Sievert, 'The Rapid Embrace of Legal Design and the Use of Co-Design to Avoid Enshrining Systemic Bias' (2020) 36(3) *Design Issues* 16.

biases and inequalities, whether they derive from law, from design or from legal design itself'.[43]

Where might these normative commitments come from, if we know we will not find them within standard jurisprudence? In the course of my studies, I have found that critical legal scholars and design justice practitioners have identified the same source, albeit using slightly different language. Professor Matsuda has called it 'looking to the bottom … adopting the perspective of those who have seen and felt the falsity of the liberal promise'.[44] The Design Justice Network includes as one of its 10 principles 'the centering of the voices of those who are directly impacted by the outcomes of the design process'.[45] The Design from Margins (DFM) methodology recognises that 'when those most marginalized are designed for, we are all designed for'.[46] By legal designing for the decentred and the displaced, using their lived experiences as a normative source, we are better situated to design a more equitable and dignified legal system for all of us.

CONCLUSION: PROCEDURE IS SUBSTANTIVE

As Professor Williams reminded us each week in first-year civil procedure, procedure is substantive. We recognise that facially neutral procedures are value-laden and outcome-determinative, tipping the scale further in favour of the historically favoured. Critical legal designing offers a promising way to transform the procedures and structure of law school. Sitting in the classroom, we cannot change what the black-letter law says – that people can be property, that no one has standing to challenge environmental crimes, that it is constitutional to lock someone in jail before a conviction of guilty beyond a reasonable doubt – but legal design can critically change how we study and interpret these words on the page. We can materialise the carceral, patriarchal, capitalist logics to better criticise them, to think in iterative, divergent, and convergent ways, and to draw in different ways of knowing about the world.

In doing so, my hope for legal designing in law schools is that it transforms what it means to be trained to 'think like a lawyer'. Rather than splitting hairs and demanding the legally relevant facts in an adversarial system, to think like a lawyer is to think like a conscientious designer. It requires centring the people in the cases – specifically those at the bottom – as well as the socio-political-economic context of each case. It is an embrace of the deductive and inherently creative, and thereby political, nature of lawyering. It is legal designing with,

[43] Amanda Perry-Kessaris, 'Legal Design for Practice, Activism, Policy and Research' (2018) 46(2) *Journal of Law and Society* 185.

[44] Mari Matsuda, 'Looking to the Bottom: Critical Legal Studies and Reparations' (1987) 22(2) *Harvard Civil Rights-Civil Liberties Law Review* 323.

[45] Design Justice Network, 'Design Justice Network Principles' (last updated 2018) designjustice.org/read-the-principles.

[46] The De|Center, 'What is dDesign From the Margins?' www.de-center.net/.

rather than for, communities[47] and is the source of courage for lawyers to use our elite training when moral clarity is urgent, rather than 'after the smell of death has dissipated'.[48] I know it is possible because I see it every day.

REFERENCES

E Allbon and A Perry-Kessaris (eds), *Design in Legal Education* (London. Routledge, 2022).

D Altajem and others, 'A Legal Design Classroom: Reflections on Learning Through Legal Education' (2024) 1(1) *Legal Design Journal*.

Ashcroft v Iqbal, 556 US 662, 666 (2009).

S Bhatnagar, 'What Legal Design Is as Opposed to Could/Should Be' in Dan Lockton and others (eds) *DRS2022: Bilbao* (2022).

R Buchanan, 'Human Dignity and Human Rights: Thoughts on the Principles of Human-Centered Design'(2001) 17(3) *Design Issues* 35.

P Butler, 'The System Is Working the Way It Is Supposed to: The Limits of Criminal Justice Reform' 1(6) *Freedom Center Journal*.

FS CohenS, 'Transcendental Nonsense and the Functional Approach' (1935) 35(6) *Columbia Law Review* 809.

KW Crenshaw, 'Twenty Years of Critical Race Theory: Looking Back to Move Forward' (2011) 43(5) *Connecticut Law Review* 1289.

DM Davis and K Klare, 'Critical Legal Realism in a Nutshell" in Emilios Christodoulidis, Ruth Dukes, and Marco Goldoni (eds), *Research Handbook on Critical Legal Theory* (Cheltenham, Edward Elgar Publishing, 2019).

De|Center, 'What is dDesign From the Margins?'.

Design Justice Network, 'Design Justice Network Principles' (last updated 2018).

Dobbs v. Jackson Women's Health Organization, 597 US ___ (2022).

M Doherty and others, 'A New Attitude to Law's Empire: The Potentialities of Legal Design' in Marcelo Corrales Compagnucci and others (eds), *Legal Design: Integrating Business, Design and Legal Thinking with Technology* (Cheltenham, Edward Elgar Publishing, 2021).

R Dooley, 'Innovate | Legal: McKinsey Legal Lab' *In The Balance* (New York, April 27, 2022).

R Eghbariah, 'The Harvard Law Review Refused to Run This Piece About Genocide in Gaza', *The Nation* (New York, 21 November 2023).

M Herz, 'Northeastern students set up pro-Palestinian encampment' *WGBH News* (Boston, 25 April 2024).

D Jackson, M Kim and JR Sievert, 'The Rapid Embrace of Legal Design and the Use of Co-Design to Avoid Enshrining Systemic Bias' (2020) 36(3) *Design Issues* 16.

D Jackson, J Rochelle Sievert, and M Kim, 'Mission + History' (*NuLawLab*).

[47] William P. Quigley, 'Ten Ways of Looking at Movement Lawyering' (2020) 5(23) *Howard Human & Civil Rights Law Review* 23.

[48] Rabea Eghbariah, 'The Harvard Law Review Refused to Run This Piece About Genocide in Gaza', *The Nation* (New York, 21 November 2023) www.thenation.com/article/archive/harvard-law-review-gaza-israel-genocide/.

D Jaffe, K Bender and JM Organ, '"It is Okay to Not Be Okay": The 2021 Survey of Law Student Well-Being' (2021) 60 *University of Louisville Law Review* 441.
D Kennedy, *Legal Education as Training for Hierarchy* (first published 1983, New York, New York University Press 2004) 42.
AR Khan and HJ Pope, 'Housing Justice and Legal Design Clinic' (Seton Hall Law School).
M Kim, 'A study of dignity as a principle of service design' (2021) 15(3) *International Journal of Design* 87.
Loper Bright Enterprises v. Raimondo, 603 US ___ (2024).
M Matsuda, 'Looking to the Bottom: Critical Legal Studies and Reparations' (1987) 22(2) *Harvard Civil Rights-Civil Liberties Law Review* 323.
M Matsuda, 'When the First Quail Calls, A Talk Presented at the Yale Law School Conference on Women of Color and the Law' (1989) 11(1) *Women's Rights Law Reporter* 8.
A Perry-Kessaris, 'Legal Design for Practice, Activism, Policy and Research' (2018) 46(2) *Journal of Law and Society* 185.
WP Quigley, 'Ten Ways of Looking at Movement Lawyering' (2020) 5(23) *Howard Human & Civil Rights Law Review* 23.
A Sanford, 'The Injustice of Death Row: The Profound Tragedy of Marcellus Williams and the Fight to Save Robert Roberson' (*The Innocence Project*, 9 October 2024).
J Santuber and S de Souza, *The Socio-Politics of Legal Design and its Epistemic Consequences* (Oxford, Hart Publishing, 2025) 8.
S Sinnar, 'The Lost Story of Iqbal' (2017) 105 *Georgetown Law Journal* 379.
D Spade, 'For Those Considering Law School' (first published 2010) VI *Unbound: Harvard Journal of the Legal Left*.
Students for Fair Admissions, Inc. v. President and Fellows of Harvard College, 600 US ___ (2023).
P Williams, *The Alchemy of Race and Rights* (Cambridge, MA, Harvard University Press, 1991) 8.
A-M Willis, 'Ontological Designing' (2006) 4(2) *Design Philosophy Papers* 69.

9

Grounds-up View of Design: Making Meaning of Design in India Through Rooted Legal Design Interventions

BHAWNA PARMAR

INTRODUCTION

RECENTLY, A FRIEND who runs a grassroots organisation asked me whether he should enroll in a design thinking course offered by Stanford. He asked me specifically because he knew I was trained in something called 'Social Design' and thought he had a great deal to learn from design as a discipline. Someone who is an advisor to his organisation and a mentor to him had suggested that he and the cofounder enroll in this course. His question caught me off guard. As a designer who is trained to design for and in the social, I felt he already was doing design, which was rooted in the Indian context. Only he or his organisation did not present it as such. This interaction stayed with me and led me to question the conventional understanding of design and its implications, particularly within the Indian context. I wondered whether grassroots' interventions, like my friend's, are better positioned to define what design means in the Indian context.

While design as a process predates humans, as noted by Ezio Manzini,[1] design as a discipline finds its name and meaning from the West. Design Thinking, popularised by IDEO, promises to solve complex problems creatively and efficiently through a five-step process: empathising, defining, ideating, prototyping, and testing. The notion of design thinking emphasises a systematic, often top-down approach to problem-solving. Design, human-centred design, and design thinking are synonymous and link creativity with innovation, promising innovative solutions if the process is followed diligently.

[1] Ezio Manzini (ed), *Design, When Everybody Designs: An Introduction to Design for Social Innovation* (Cambridge, MA, The MIT Press, 2015).

Tim Brown, the Chair of IDEO, while making a case for Design Thinking in 2008[2] mentioned 'Design thinking can feel chaotic to those experiencing it for the first time' positioning it as something novel, something that needs some getting used to. He[3] characterised design thinking as:

> a methodology that imbues the full spectrum of innovation activities with a human-centered design ethos. [...] Innovation is powered by a thorough understanding, through direct observation, of what people want and need in their lives and what they like or dislike about the way particular products are made, packaged, marketed, sold, and supported.

This novelty has been gaining ground in various industries. It has found its way into education[4,5] law,[6] gender,[7] health,[8] and other disciplines, which are working to solve complex social challenges where design is positioned as a tool for social transformation.

However, as design thinking gains traction, critics highlight its limitations. A growing conversation about the pitfalls of design as a tool for social transformation is gaining momentum. Practitioners point out the naivete and ungrounded recommendations that often reinforce the status quo due to the process's corporate foundations.[9,10] Many offshoots of design have now sprouted up which aim to remove its capitalistic foundations and redefine it to truly serve the people. These are being practiced under the terms – social design, co-design, participatory design, community-centred design, and design justice.

In much of the Global South, including India, design and design thinking have become a buzzword, adopted by many organisations to better understand their end users and design for them. Design thinking and human-centred design have now moved towards solving complex problems in India. The novelty and fascination with design thinking, understandably, is nudging social justice

[2] Tim Brown, 'Design Thinking' (*Harvard Business Review*, June 2008) hbr.org/2008/06/design-thinking.

[3] ibid.

[4] Rie Kijima, Mariko Yang-Yoshihara and Marcos Sadao Maekawa, 'Using Design Thinking to Cultivate the Next Generation of Female STEAM Thinkers' (2021) 8 *International Journal of STEM Education* 14.

[5] Lisa G Wyatt and others, 'Educational Change by Design: Creating a School of the Future' (2021) 24 *Journal of Cases in Educational Leadership* 55.

[6] Margaret Hagan, 'Introduction to Design Thinking for Law' in Daniel M Katz, Ron Dolin and Michael Bommarito (eds), *Legal Informatics* (Cambridge, Cambridge University Press, 2021).

[7] Karen Christensen, 'Design Thinking To Solve Gender Issues' (*Forbes India*, 2018) www.forbes-india.com/article/rotman/design-thinking-to-solve-gender-issues/51609/1.

[8] Mariana Oliveira, Eduardo Zancul and André Leme Fleury, 'Design Thinking as an Approach for Innovation in Healthcare: Systematic Review and Research Avenues' (2021) 7 *BMJ Innovations* 491.

[9] Rebecca Ackermann, 'Design Thinking Was Supposed to Fix the World. Where Did It Go Wrong?' (*MIT Technology Review*, 2023) www.technologyreview.com/2023/02/09/1067821/design-thinking-retrospective-what-went-wrong/.

[10] Lilly Irani, '"Design Thinking": Defending Silicon Valley at the Apex of Global Labor Hierarchies' (2018) 4 *Catalyst: Feminism, Theory, Technoscience* 1.

organisations to understand and employ it in the hopes that it will make them better equipped to address the socio-political issues they are attempting to eradicate. Just like in the West, design has percolated into the field of law, education, healthcare, livelihoods and others often without the consideration of context.

This paper attempts to problematise the uncritical adoption of Western design approaches in the Indian context by privileging the design processes of various organisations that are working on the ground. Although this research is a part of a larger project that seeks to build a decolonial grounds-up view of design, this paper concerns itself with legal design as a field. Legal design as defined by Hagan[11] is the application of human-centred design to the world of law to make it more human-centred. A design approach to legal services, according to her, 'puts people and their contexts as the focus and questions how their status quo could be improved'.

As design is being transplanted to the field of law, albeit at a nascent stage in India, it becomes imperative to study various organisations rooted in the Indian context working in the realm of legal design to learn from their methodologies and shape an understanding of legal design from their reflections. All the new offshoots of design have their own contributions to the field of design; however, design justice offers an important conceptual framework that looks at the relationship design has with power. Therefore, it becomes an important lens for this paper for analysis while designing for the social and building a liberatory approach to design.

This paper is not the first to explore and analyse interventions in the Indian context through a design lens. A few designers have attempted to contextualise various social interventions within design, such as Suchitra,[12] who studied the communication strategy of the Dandi March led by M.K. Gandhi, examining what communication designers can learn about building strategies for social causes from this historical event. This paper aims to build on decolonial design theory and add to the growing scholarship of the same.

While the methodology of human-centred design offers valuable tools and frameworks, it risks overlooking the nuanced, organic, and context-specific practices that grassroots organisations inherently develop. Through case studies of grassroots organisations, the paper will argue for an understanding of legal design and a design process rooted in the Indian context. This paper seeks to highlight how these organisations embody design principles in practice, often without formal recognition or validation from traditional design frameworks. Their interventions are not merely ad-hoc solutions but are deeply informed by lived experiences, cultural contexts, and a commitment to social justice.

[11] Hagan (n 6).

[12] Suchitra, 'What Moves Masses: Dandi March as Communication Strategy' (*Economic and Political Weekly*, 8 April 1995) www.epw.in/journal/1995/14/perspectives/what-moves-masses-dandi-march-communication-strategy.html.

This paper emerges from a desire to bridge the gap between traditional design frameworks and the rich, nuanced practices observed in grassroots interventions. It examines how organisations working at this intersection can build a methodology that not only integrates design justice principles but also shapes an indigenous approach to just and inclusive legal design. Furthermore, this research aims to bring to the fore certain methods and reflections that these organisations may have developed, which can be employed by legal designers, designers, and law practitioners while working in the field of law.

The case study that is provided in this paper is of one organisation, Zenith Society for Socio-Legal Empowerment, based in Madhya Pradesh. The methodology employed to document the case study is ethnographic in nature. I have spent time in the organisations immersing myself in the context and their work, combined with in-depth semi-structured interviews with various people who work in the organisations.

LEGAL DESIGN: THE INTERSECTION

Catherine MacKinnon[13] argues that when the state codifies social hierarchies into law, based on gender, race, and class, it effectively legitimises these forms of discrimination, making them invisible to recognize and challenge. By embedding these hierarchies within legal frameworks, the law not only reinforces existing social inequalities but also naturalizes them, making them appear as neutral, normal, and inevitable rather than as constructed forms of oppression. While these hierarchies are codified in the law, rendering it unequal for people from marginalised sections, legal design as a field attempts to humanise the law, working to make these invisible barriers visible and more navigable for those most affected by them.

Tim Brown in 2017 celebrated the increase of design thinking in law. He noted that although the field is not known for creative problem-solving, it is taking notice of design thinking in approaching the issues the field faces, just like other domains. Design thinking, since then, is getting embedded into the field of law, of which legal design is a product.

Hagan[14] defines legal design as 'the marriage of a human-centered design approach to the challenges and structures of the legal system'. It is a movement that aims to make the legal system work better for people and build a human centred, participatory approach to reforming the legal system, and looks at different ways of innovation, including technology. It wants to make the system more accessible to lay people as well as serve policy makers who use the system to set standards. Moving beyond legal tech solutionism and its association

[13] Catharine A MacKinnon, 'Toward Feminist Jurisprudence' in Alison M Jaggar (ed), *Living With Contradictions: Controversies In Feminist Social Ethics* (1st edn, London, Routledge, 1994).

[14] Hagan (n 6).

with productivity and efficiency, legal design offers a framework that includes user research, lateral and visual thinking, ideation, prototyping, and testing that places emphasis on the end user and their needs and contexts.[15] The focus is engagement with the end user, which theoretically addresses the questions of who is being excluded by technology and makes the intervention more inclusive.

Legal design is an emerging academic discipline.[16] The central methodology of legal design varies and is evolving. Doherty lays down the different processes various legal designers employ. As mentioned in his paper, NuLawLab uses a four-stage approach which includes inspiration, synthesis, ideation and experimentation, and implementation, whereas the model of Stanford d.school has five stages: empathise, define, ideate, prototype, and test. Lastly, the work of Stickdorn has four steps: discover, define, develop, and deliver. The steps, even though defined differently, are parts of a similar process which is derived from design thinking, something that Doherty also mentions.

The discourse surrounding legal design is now evolving beyond conventional design thinking towards more critical inquiry and provocative approaches, like speculative design. As explored by Karma Dabaghi,[17] speculative design in legal contexts enables practitioners to imagine and prototype alternative legal futures that prioritise justice and equity. This methodology moves beyond immediate problem-solving to questioning fundamental assumptions and foundations about legal systems and their impacts on marginalised communities' access to justice. Drawing from critical design, decolonial design, and feminist design theories, speculative legal design creates spaces for imagining radically different legal frameworks that challenge existing power structures. Through speculative design methodologies, legal design benefits from anticipating possible issues to come and may be well positioned to address systemic issues 'before they become too big to handle'. Combined with proactive law, which proposes using law to prevent things from going wrong, speculative design offers the creation of possible futures and alternate models.

Although global scholarship in legal design is increasingly being centred on these critical and speculative approaches, India stands at the nascent stage of incorporating design thinking into the legal domain. Organisations such as Manupatra and Justice Adda are spearheading efforts to integrate design thinking into legal practice, encouraging legal professionals to adopt a designers' mindset to give the users of law the best user experience that prevents the

[15] Siddharth Peter de Souza, 'The Spread of Legal Tech Solutionism and the Need for Legal Design' (2022) 13 *European Journal of Risk Regulation* 373–388.

[16] Michael Doherty, 'Disciplinarity and the Modes of Legal Design' in D Lockton, S Lenzi, P Hekkert, A Oak, J Sádaba and P Lloyd (eds) *DRS2022: Bilbao, 25 June–3 July, Bilbao, Spain.*

[17] Karma Dabaghi, 'Beyond Design Thinking and into Speculative Futures in Legal Design' (2022) dl.designresearchsociety.org/drs-conference-papers/drs2022/researchpapers/70.

perception of law as an obstacle.[18] Legal design is still finding roots in India, but this moment provides an opportunity to develop design approaches that honestly reflect Indian contexts and serve its diverse populace. This environment is particularly conducive to incorporating rooted knowledge and methodologies along with local perspectives into legal design methodologies, potentially creating more inclusive, community-centred and equitable legal frameworks.

DESIGN THINKING AND THE INDIAN CONTEXT

Matthew Wizinsky[19] elaborates on the history of design as a discipline. Design being a product of capitalism, he emphasises on how a designer as a specific kind of role only emerged during the industrial revolution. Intermingled inextricably with the rise of capitalism, design as a method historically worked to create products, services, and advertisements to increase profits for the capitalists. Initially, only limited to outcomes in terms of product, graphics, textiles, furniture, and similar domains, soon design as a discipline was adapted to also incorporate processes and systems. This change happened as the world moved towards creating services as manufacturing shifted to the Global South. The discipline of sesign began to incorporate the designing of services from end-to-end. With the boom of the service industry and the digital revolution, methods like design thinking, human-centred design, and UX–UI design started emerging. This shift brought in the aspect of understanding the consumers for whom the products and services were to be designed, and hence, putting emphasis on 'human needs'. As a result, design incorporated research in its process. The idea was to make products and services that are built after understanding what the target and potential consumers want, with the solutions that are creative, novel, and innovative that help the businesses stay relevant. Putting the potential customers at the centre and labelling it 'human-centred' became an important aspect of creating products and services to ensure that the businesses are distinguishable and are accepted and cherished by the consumers in the face of competition.

In an innovation age, design thinking inevitably found its way into the Indian subcontinent. Many Indian corporates quickly co-opted design to design user-centred solutions. Various design and innovation consultancies also started sprouting up in the late 2000s and early 2010s. This innovation process was soon embedded into startups with Indian companies like Lenskart, Oyo, and Ola implementing this process to gain a competitive edge.

[18] 'Manupatra, Legal Design Bootcamp and Competition.' www.manupatrafast.com/legal-design-workshop-competition/.

[19] Matthew Wizinsky, *Design after Capitalism: Transforming Design Today for an Equitable Tomorrow* (Cambridge, MA, The MIT Press, 2022).

Design thinking and human-centred design have now moved towards addressing complex problems in India. The allure of design thinking nudges social justice organisations to adopt it, hoping it will better equip them to tackle socio-political issues. Genpact,[20] for example, has published a primer on leveraging design thinking for social justice organisations to 'make bigger impacts on the beneficiaries or communities they serve'. Design thinking for social innovation is presented as a beacon of hope, capable of generating 'hundreds of ideas and, ultimately, real-world solutions that create better outcomes for organizations and the people they serve'. Development work is crowded with design thinking or human-centred design principles, advocating for better innovations through empathy and immersion in the problem contexts. In addition, design thinking has found a niche in policymaking,[21] ensuring user-friendly prototypes for better-designed policies.

While design thinking promises research, empathy, and collaboration, Ackermann[22] points out the loopholes in design thinking as it promotes the idea that anyone who follows a specific process can become a designer and solve a problem 'if we empathise hard enough'. The short-term focus on naive ideas results in ungrounded solutions which end up reinforcing the existing inequalities. Design thinking ends up reducing the complex systemic problems to mere 'pain points' which can be solved easily if one only follows the process. Moreover, the process is known to privilege ideas over implementation, beginner's mindset over expertise. Taking the example of the Diva Centres, Ackermann explains that while IDEO was able to design nail salons for teens in Zambiawhere they could learn about reproductive health but as the design neglected the world outside their walls 'a complex network of public health funding and service channels that made scaling the pilot prohibitively expensive and complicated'. The issue is that design thinking, in many instances, has failed to locate the challenges in the larger systems and societal orders which the 'users' find themselves in.

Having borrowed the design discipline from the West, how design is being done in India did not get much importance. Problem-solving as a skill is present in every population, as Manzini has noted, the urge to consider a situation, imagine a better situation and then act to create that better situation predates homo sapiens. By withholding design as an expertise and a discipline only performed by designers who have imbibed standardised design frameworks, notably design thinking, organisations run the risk of ignoring the rich design practices that already exist on the ground. Experts of design thinking who are invited by social justice organisations to make their interventions more 'design

[20] Neeta Kwatra, 'Design Thinking for the Social Sector' (Genpact 2020).

[21] R K Pattnaik and Ranjan Banerjee, 'Extending Design Thinking to Public Policy' (*Economic and Political Weekly*, 22 August 2020) www.epw.in/journal/2020/34/special-articles/extending-design-thinking-public-policy.html.

[22] Ackermann (n 9).

oriented' often lack contextual knowledge that is needed to address the complex challenges the particular intervention is embedded in. Moreover, there is a lack of acknowledgement by the expert designers and, in extension legal designers, of the vast knowledge that already exists in and about the subcontinent.

Design thinking as a process which was essentially concocted to serve businesses will inevitably have loopholes when trying to address the complex issues of caste, class, gender, sexuality, at a systemic as well as individual level plaguing the Indian society. For example, in the education context in India, building an understanding of careers is gaining momentum. Indian designers have flocked to build design apps and immersive experiences which enable young people to understand the various career options that they can avail. The solutions are built after a painstaking 'empathy' phase where the designers speak to young people to understand their challenges. Nevertheless, the solutions fail to acknowledge the unemployment crisis[23] India is going through. Furthermore, the reason why young people are not able to imagine or work towards building careers is not just because of lack of awareness alone. Factors like caste, gender, class, and disability contribute more towards gaining employment in a country like India, which these specific solutions fail to acknowledge.

In the Indian context, caste plays an important role in the very fabric of social life[24] and people belonging to the marginalised caste are often ignored by the government and discriminated against in the society. Yendge[25] asserts that caste as a system originated in the Hindu social order but has percolated to all faiths in the Indian social order. At its core ideological performance, it controls human capacity, creativity, and labour which is secured through a strict legal order, 'its strict division into five categorical instances organized in horizontal capacities is an archetype of legitimized apartheid'.[26] In India, Scheduled Caste (SC) and Scheduled Tribe (ST) minorities have historically been the most marginalised and have faced exclusion from mainstream economic, social, and legal spheres.[27] Access to the legal system is highly skewed for people from the marginalised castes and religions.[28] In this context importing the way legal design, with a focus on design thinking, is done in the Global North will insufficiently address the challenges faced by the communities in India. This design model is often blind towards the power dynamics and the resulting social oppressions unique to the subcontinent. This way of designing may not suffice and the designed interventions far too often run the risk of reinforcing the status quo.

[23] https://www.outlookbusiness.com/economy-and-policy/indias-job-crisis-youth-unemployment-jumps-to-161-in-q3-women-see-slight-relief.

[24] Suraj Yengde and Cornel West, *Caste Matters* (Gurgaon, Penguin Viking, an imprint of Penguin Random House 2019).

[25] ibid.

[26] ibid.

[27] Itishree Pradhan, Binayak Kandapan and Jalandhar Pradhan, 'Uneven Burden of Multidimensional Poverty in India: A Caste Based Analysis' (2022) 17 *PLoS One* e0271806.

[28] S Muralidhar, 'Appearing in Court in India: Challenges in Representing the Marginalised' (2022) 3 *CASTE/A Global Journal on Social Exclusion* 421.

Design as a discipline was brought to India after the first Prime Minister, Jawahar Lal Nehru, invited Charles and Eames Ray to research on the potential of design in India and Le Corbusier to design the city of Chandigarh. Charles and Ray Eames, as part of their visit, wrote a report on the prevalence of design in the subcontinent by undertaking a case study of lota (a metal vessel). While discussing the functional and aesthetic aspects of the lota, the authors completely ignored its fundamental casteist context in how it was produced through a caste-based occupation.[29] Design in how it's practiced in the mainstream in India is still very brahminised.[30] Designers working in India need to find a design process that understands the uniqueness of India, its diversity, its plural history, and the resulting oppressions. Many social organisations have, over the years, furthered ideas of equality and justice and have found unique solutions to the many challenges India faces. They understand how caste, class, and gender intertwine in the Indian context. They are known to work with the communities, build capabilities, and produce long-term change. The organisations working on the grassroots have acquired a unique problem-solving ability in the context they are rooted in, and offer great potential for learning for legal design practitioners.

DESIGN JUSTICE: A JUST CONCEPTUAL FRAMEWORK

As legal design gains traction in India, it is worthwhile to move away from design thinking and towards concepts like design justice.

Papanek positions design as a universal practice in human communities, 'Design is the conscious effort to impose a meaningful order. Designing is fundamental to humans'.[31] Everyone does design, but who gets to be called a designer is limited to a select few. Sasha Costanza-Chock[32] puts it eloquently, 'Design is professionalized, and that is how courses like design thinking are sold to people who are already designing'.

Design, according to Escobar,[33] is an 'ethical praxis of world-making'. He asks the designers to consider the ways that design today is reproducing 'the totalizing epistemology of modernity and in the process erase indigenous worldviews, forms of knowledge, and ways of being'. Design as a homogenised

[29] The Big Fat Bao, 'On Caste: The Roots of Discrimination in Indian Design' (*Futuress*, 2023) futuress.org/stories/on-caste/.

[30] ibid.

[31] Victor Papanek and R Buckminster Fuller, *Design for the Real World* (New York, Bantam Books, 1972).

[32] Sasha Costanza-Chock, *Design Justice: Community-Led Practices to Build the Worlds We Need* (Cambridge, MA, The MIT Press 2020) direct.mit.edu/books/book/4605/Design-JusticeCommunity-Led-Practices-to-Build-the.

[33] Arturo Escobar, *Designs for the Pluriverse: Radical Interdependence, Autonomy, and the Making of Worlds* (Durham, NC, Duke University Press, 2018) read.dukeupress.edu/books/book/2433/Designs-for-the-PluriverseRadical-Interdependence.

monopolised tool when applied to the Indian context erases various ways in which design in India is already happening. Sasha Costanza-Chock while making a case for Design Justice in their book mentions that it is important to acknowledge the importance of everyday, vernacular and often unrecognised design practices,

> alternative histories of [...] design help to recuperate and center people, practices, and forms of expertise that have long been erased by mainstream design theory and history, both in scholarly and popular writing.

Design justice, which tries to address the power between the designers and the designees in an attempt to make the process of design more democratic, becomes a crucial tool when designing for the social and the legal, where power is intertwined with the need designers are trying to solve. Design Justice as a way to rethink the design process and centre the people who are generally marginalised by design offers a just approach that legal design intervention in India can adopt.

Sasha Costanza-Chock defines design justice as,

> Design justice is a framework for analysis of how design distributes benefits and burdens between various groups of people. Design justice focuses explicitly on the ways that design reproduces and/or challenges the matrix of domination (white supremacy, heteropatriarchy, capitalism, ableism, settler colonialism, and other forms of structural inequality). Design justice is also a growing community of practice that aims to ensure a more equitable distribution of design's benefits and burdens; meaningful participation in design decisions; and recognition of community-based, indigenous, and diasporic design traditions, knowledge, and practices.

Design justice separates itself from social impact design or design for good and has developed principles that might help design practitioners avoid the reproduction of existing inequalities. It is conceptualised on two main components of Black feminist thought – intersectionality and the matrix of domination. Design justice holds that design that is not grounded in intersectional understanding of gender, caste, race, and class can never properly address or cater to the marginalised. The matrix of domination refers to race, class, and gender as interlocking systems of oppression. It is a conceptual model that helps think about how power, oppression, resistance, privilege, penalties, benefits, and harms are systematically distributed. Design justice urges us to explore the ways that design relates to domination and resistance. It brings to the fore how design may seem universal but is actually unequally distributed based on this matrix of domination.

The 10 design justice principles[34] are as follows:

1. Use design to sustain, heal, and empower communities, as well as to seek liberation from exploitative and oppressive systems.

[34] 'Design Justice Network Website' designjustice.org/read-the-principles.

2. Centre the voices of those who are directly impacted by the outcome of the design process.
3. Prioritise design's impact on the community over the intentions of the designer.
4. View change as emergent from an accountable, accessible, and collaborative process rather than as a point at the end of a process.
5. See the role of the designer as a facilitator rather than an expert.
6. Believe that everyone is an expert based on their own lived experience and that all people have unique and brilliant contributions to bring to a design process.
7. Share design knowledge and tools with communities.
8. Work towards sustainable, community-led and -controlled outcomes.
9. Work towards non-exploitative solutions that reconnect to the earth and each other.
10. Before seeking new design solutions, look for what is already working at the community level. Honor and uplift traditional, indigenous, and local knowledge and practices.

These principles provide a framework to practise legal design which upholds the values of liberation. It is worth noting that design justice as a framework will also not work perfectly in a context like India. To build on the framework, I along with a colleague have added another principle to this framework: 'We work consciously towards a design practice which dismantles systems of caste, religion, and gender based oppression'.[35] This principle actively acknowledges the larger oppressive systems at play and the role of the designer in dismantling them in the Indian context. Design justice offers a beginning to the conversation of the role of design in building just and inclusive worlds. It by no means should become the gospel that design thinking has become, as it runs the risk of reducing design again into neatly drawn steps which one can undertake to solve complex problems. Design justice is not supposed to be transplanted uncritically into the Indian contexts; however, it is to be engaged with, understood and built upon to find the way of designing that works in India. Many organisations have already been doing design in the Indian context, even though they do not label their practice as such nor are they trained designers in any of the design fields. It is pertinent to learn from their practice and see the similarities and divergences they have to the design justice framework. This will enable design practitioners in India to understand the ways in which just and inclusive design can be practiced in India.

Unlike Western contexts where digital accessibility and race-centred equity often dominate design discourse, the Indian landscape demands a focus on caste-based exclusion, legal illiteracy, and regional disparities.

[35] https://designjustice.org/news-1/2022/5/1/member-feature-rubina-singh-bhawna-parmar5.

For example, the implementation of digital legal services in India often overlooks non-English-speaking populations and those without internet access. A truly just and inclusive legal design methodology must, therefore, consider these structural barriers and work towards context-specific solutions. This includes leveraging local knowledge systems, community-based dispute resolution mechanisms, and participatory governance structures. The following case study of an organisation working in the grassroots can arguably be said to be practicing design justice in the Indian context in varying degrees even if they don't call themselves legal design organisations.

In a country like India where adivasis are constantly displaced for development projects and their lands are taken away from them, as well as, people from marginalised caste and religion are disproportionately imprisoned, what would a practice of legal design rooted in design justice look like? As India explores the intersection of law and design, can these organisations develop a methodology for legal designers that integrates the design justice framework while adapting it to the Indian context, giving rise to a distinctly Indian approach to just and inclusive design?

Before presenting the case study, it is essential to establish a framework for what constitutes 'legal design' specifically in the Indian context. Although Western legal design often focuses on user interfaces, document simplification, and technological solutions, legal design in India must address more fundamental structural barriers related to caste, class, religion, and language.

This paper proposes that legal design in the Indian context encompasses:

1. **Access mechanisms** that bridge gaps between formal legal systems and marginalised communities.
2. **Translation processes** that make legal language and procedures comprehensible across linguistic and cultural divides.
3. **Power redistribution tools** that shift agency from legal experts to community members.
4. **Navigation frameworks** that help communities traverse complex bureaucratic systems.
5. **Capacity-building methods** that develop sustainable legal literacy within communities.

Contemporary legal design must contend with the power hierarchy that persists in procedural complexity, linguistic barriers, and geographical centralisation of legal services.

CASE STUDY: ZENITH – LESSONS ON THE IMPORTANCE OF LONG-TERM ENGAGEMENT AND COMMUNITY EMPOWERMENT

Zenith, a socio-legal organization, is based in the Chambal region of Madhya Pradesh and operates out of Gwalior and Shivpuri. It was set up informally in 2013 and formally in 2018. Founded by two lawyers, Abhay and Swapnil, who have grown up in Shivpuri and Gwalior, respectively, the organisation primarily works in providing legal aid services and capacity building to the marginalised sections of the region. The origin of the organisation is interesting to say the least. Abhay engaged in 'back-packing lawyering' while pursuing his bachelor's degree to reach the remotest parts of his hometown to understand the issues people were facing. Having grown up in Shivpuri, a town known for its forest cover and greenery, he was privy to the marginalisation certain sections of the population were subjected to. He witnessed the systemic exclusion that Sahariya adivasis were facing and decided to address their issues as a lawyer.

Before delving into the work of Zenith, it is important to shed light on the socio-political context of this region. The Chambal region, namely, Gwalior, Bhind, Sheopur, Morena, and Shivpuri, fall under the Gird Agro Ecological Subregion (AESR) in the central Indian state of Madhya Pradesh. It is classified as a moist semi-arid region with average rainfall of 800–1000 m/year and is characterised by alluvial, loamy soil. The Chambal region, which includes Shivpuri and Gwalior, is home to Sahariya Adivasis. Sahariyas are a ST minority who are classified as a Particularly Vulnerable Tribal Group (PVTG) by the Indian government. They are one of the 75 tribes classified as such. Adivasis form 6% of population in the GIRD region. Sahariya villages are concentrated in the upland, in the forested and hilly tracts of the GIRD AESR and surrounded by large masses of non-adivasi population. The Sahariya Adivasi community constitutes an island of poverty, vulnerability, socioeconomic distress, political disempowerment, concentrated in the neglected rain-fed pockets of an otherwise agriculturally well-off AESR. Decades of neglect, official apathy, and lack of adequate investments by the state in the development of such rain-fed, semi-arid areas has resulted in a very high concentration of poverty and vulnerability in India's drylands.[36]

Sahariyas have been historically marginalised and Hartosh Singh Bal's[37] report on Sahariya deaths due to lack of rain and drought back in 2002 shows the failure of the governance system that went hand in hand to produce the resulting malnutrition due to droughts. Kabra[38] sheds light on the inadequate attention given to the livelihoods of the Sahariyas who were intricately linked to their ecological base as they keep being displaced from their homes in the name of development. The rehabilitation packages are designed with the state's neglect in mind. As a result, their material conditions deteriorate after the displacement. She highlights two reasons for this: one the loss of diversification of livelihood opportunities, and second, the alienation they face from their natural resource base. Hence, their integration into the national mainstream has been occurring at highly disadvantageous terms.

[36] Asmita Kabra, 'Conservation-Induced Displacement: A Comparative Study of Two Indian Protected Areas' (2009) 7 *Conservation and Society* 249.

[37] Hartosh Singh Bal, 'Killing Season' (The Indian Quarterly, 2002) https://indianquarterly.com/?p=2732.

[38] Kabra (n 36).

The Sahariyas of Shivpuri and Gwalior, specifically, are surrounded by the non-adivasi population. Landlessness, negligible literacy, lack of access to water and electricity, and no hospitals in the vicinity are some of the factors that inform their daily lives. The Sahariyas live in villages with the Gujjar community, a community which falls on a higher status than them on the caste ladder. The Gujjar community oppresses the Sahariya community and limits their access to resources. Gujjars are known to recruit Sahariyas to work in their agricultural fields or their illegal stone mines. It has been reported that this work may also become bonded labour as Sahariyas are prone to borrowing money from Gujjars in times of crisis. Many Sahariyas in Zenith's interactions with the community have noted that they 'live like slaves'. Gujjars are the head of the village, they are the police and the law for Sahariyas. They control their access to the forest as well. Apart from being socially dominated by Gujjars, Sahariyas are vulnerable to displacements due to development projects. In addition, because of working in the illegal stone mines, many Sahariyas develop silicosis, a fatal occupational lung disease because of the lack of protective gear.

Zenith works with Sahariyas to help them access their rights. I will outline the story of one village that Zenith has been working with around Shivpuri to provide legal aid and build the capacity of the Sahariyas. In their functioning and their reflections, there are important methodological aspects that legal design in the Indian context can incorporate.

In 2016, 25–30 Sahariya Adivasi families were relocated from their ancestral homes in Majhera, an ecologically sensitive zone, to the newly established Aamdar colony in Shivpuri. While the relocation was part of the Pradhan Mantri Aawas Yojna Scheme – intended to provide brick houses (pucca) to families living in traditional mud houses (kaccha) – the new colony was problematically situated along a national highway, far from essential resources.

When Zenith first encountered this community, they found the residents deeply distrustful of outsiders due to past negative experiences with Gujjars and government officials. Through consistent visits and gentle outreach, Zenith began building relationships with the colony's residents. They discovered that the settlement lacked basic amenities like electricity and water supply. Regular visits were arranged to slowly get the Sahariya acquainted with the Zenith team and start the discussion on their issues. The Zenith team filed an application at the Madhya Pradesh Madhya Kshetra Vidyut Vitaran Company Limited and after multiple applications, the electricity connection was established in the colony. Even though this was the first application that was filed solely by Zenith, the team kept the community informed throughout the process. Some of them came forward but were apprehensive about any change taking place. Dispirited by the system, they did not expect improvements to happen in their conditions of living. The successful installation of the electricity connection marked the beginning of building trust between the colony dwellers and the Zenith team.

After the establishment of the electricity connection, the Sahariyas started opening up to the Zenith team. The next task at hand was to get a water connection established, an ask that came from the community itself. The women complained that they have to walk 2–3 kilometers inside the jungles to fetch water. The application was filed at the Public Health Engineering Department of Madhya Pradesh. And the community was urged to attend a 'sunvai'(hearing) at the District Magistrate's office. They were asked to present their concerns to the DM while the Zenith team accompanied them. Raju, a person working in Zenith at the Shivpuri office explaining their process, said,

> First we encourage them and make them understand how to get their issue addressed. We write an application for them and tell them where to go to submit it. We tell them we will be there to support them but it's important that they go to file it themselves. This way they will feel a little less scared of the institutions and the system.

Zenith works on building the capacity of the Sahariyas to access justice on their own terms. Zenith realises that the task is enormous because of the multidimensional exclusion that Sahariyas face. Raju adds,

> The community is very vulnerable, they do not open up easily. If you go to them to ask them what their issues are, they will say everything is fine. They are scared of the state and the gujjars. They have seen oppression at the hands of outsiders.

After the application for water supply was filed successfully, three hand pumps were installed in the colony.

The people are originally from Majhera, a village called the widow village. Many men from the families have passed away due to silicosis leaving their wives behind. Illegal stone quarries are spread around the area and form one of the two main occupations that the people from the colony engage in. The presence of quarries lead to degradation of water and air in the surroundings. After the hand pumps were installed in Aamdar, the colony dwellers told Zenith that the water was red in colour and hence undrinkable. Due to mining, the iron content of underground water had increased and therefore the water quality had degraded. The colony members and Zenith wrote another application and a case was filed at National Green Tribunal to stop the illegal mining.[39] Currently, they are being supplied water from a nearby hotel on a temporary basis.

An exercise of slowly accessing what was rightfully theirs, some Sahariya Adivasis realised that this will be the roadmap to fight for their rights and demand what should be rightfully theirs – making their living conditions better. They became more active with the Zenith team and started bringing the issues

[39] Shuchita Jha, 'NGT Stops Mining in Ecologically Sensitive Madhav National Park in Madhya Pradesh' (*Down To Earth*, 2022) www.downtoearth.org.in/news/environment/ngt-stops-mining-in-ecologically-sensitive-madhav-national-park-in-madhya-pradesh-85290.

they were facing to their office. After getting acquainted with the legal system and realising it isn't a boulder they can't cross, they started actively chasing the relevant departments. Four men from the Aamdar colony are now connected with the Zenith office and work with them regularly to make the living conditions of the colony better. They have now demanded for an Anganwadi from the District Magistrate office and regularly attend meetings to make their case in front of the officials. Raju reports,

> Now they realize that they will have to raise their voices to make their living conditions better. Or else it will go on like this. Now they see that there's water, a better road, electricity, so they feel things can change. They have a seed of hope now and they want things to be better.

The caste-based hierarchy is very strong where the Sahariya community resides as they are surrounded by Gujjars. The Gujjars act as the livelihood providers and give microcredit in times of need which ensures that their exploitation of Sahariyas goes unchecked. Sahariyas in many cases have accepted the exploitation at the hands of Gujjars seeing no way out. The Zenith team reported that, in the process of building their capacity the Sahariyas filed a complaint against a gujjar who had illegally taken over a land in a nearby forest and would trouble the Sahariyas if they would enter that land. Their complaint is with the police department which they filed on their own.

The community after having their basic needs met are now demanding for education for their children, reported Abhay. Zenith identified a 19-year-old man, Ram Adivasi, who had studied till the 8th grade. He took up the task of providing tuition classes to the young kids in the morning before he started his work. Zenith is in the process of building a fellowship system to empower people like Ram Adivasi and provide them with compensation for the work they are doing. Ram Adivasi is prompt and is trying to understand the problems of the young to find better solutions for the community. The idea that the community is best suited to solve their own problems is something the Zenith team learned through the process.

The task of working with the community has not been easy because of the geographical and social location of the Sahariyas. Raju adds to this, 'We have been working with Aamdar for more than 5 years and even now we cannot say they are open to us. We are also still learning about them, trust building exercise is a continuous process'. The realisation of building internal leadership within the community was a gradual process where the Zenith team initially would file the cases and applications themselves and inform the community. But through working. they realised that they will always remain external to the community and it is important for the community to become self-reliant. Abhay, reflecting on the messiah complex, mentioned,

> Communities shouldn't rely on external actors to fight for their justice. We are here right now, we may not be here in the future. But the community needs to know the system and needs to know how to fight for their rights.

Reflecting on his work, and how he began, Abhay mentioned that the slowness of this work is a sobering experience.

> We try to create change immediately. We think in terms of innovation, that if we do this, everything will get better. Like when you file a case and get a bail it has immediate gratification. But this work is not like that. This work takes years on years, that was another learning. There is no linear approach like taking the court or capacity building – it needs a mix of strategies to see the change.

Zenith earlier thought of creating a people's movement in this area but soon realised that they don't have the necessary resources for it. The social realities and the Gujjar-Sahariya dynamic was another reason why this could not be possible. Reflecting on their own capabilities and rejecting ideas because they don't fit the context is a reflexive skill that many designers need. They tried to go through the route of the legal courts, but in filing cases, they soon realised that even after a favourable judgment, the implementation doesn't follow through. Through trial and error, community empowerment and community's access to justice were identified by Zenith as the most important tasks.

While raising the consciousness of the community and having them voice their needs, Abhay reflected on this,

> We only do what they tell us to do. If they are asking for something you think is wrong let them go ahead with it anyway. Who are we to tell them what is right and what is wrong? We give ourselves the chance to be wrong, to make mistakes, we don't give that many chances to the community who we are working with. They should get more chances than us. They themselves realize how they are going wrong and course correct if they feel there is a need to.

The process of iteration is something that the community should be given in the design process. Zenith designs strategies with the community to tackle their issues and is trying to be more community-oriented intentionally in their functions.

DISCUSSION

Zenith's work shows designers that immersion in contexts is important and understanding the caste dynamics is a slow process. Consistency and building a relationship to build trust is an important aspect for the community to take part in the design process and take ownership of the design. Abhay reflects on this,

> You have to take them on a journey because they are scared of the system. If they can learn how to engage with the system and how to participate in the system that is job half-done. They will not have to rely on lawyers completely but only ask them to draft applications. They will be prepared and the lawyers' role will diminish. Organizing community leaders and building their capacity is the most important task that any legal design intervention should do.

It is important to note here that Zenith's work isn't a utopia that legal designers must aspire towards. Zenith themselves are learning through trial and error. However, their learnings, reflexivity, community-orientedness, community-first mindset, and the importance of understanding the context are some methodological aspects that legal designers can learn from. Looking at themselves as facilitators and not problem-solvers, giving the community the space and tools to solve their own problems, providing safe spaces for the community to articulate their needs, are some principles that fall under the design justice paradigm that have proven to work in the Indian context. Zenith's work also showcases how design interventions can mitigate historical injustices albeit in a slow but sustained manner.

It is important to note that Zenith's work should not be considered as infallible and the only right way to approach design in the Indian context. The organisation officially is seven years old and is still finding its roots. They realise that their work is long-term and it will take years to see measurable impact. They are also learning from their mistakes through an iterative process. Nonetheless, Zenith's work offers several methodological insights for legal design practitioners:

1. **Immersion in Context:** Understanding the specific social and geographical context is essential for designing effective interventions. Understanding how caste, gender, and class are intertwined in the context you are working in helps implement interventions that are honest.

- **Trust Building:** Rather than imposing solutions as an outsider and an expert, working with the community and forming trust based relationships can ensure that the interventions last.
- **Community-First Mindset:** Centring the community's needs and voices in the design process is crucial for achieving meaningful and sustainable outcomes. Instead of imposing solutions, it is imperative to listen to the community and understand their perspectives.
- **Facilitative Role:** Designers should see themselves as facilitators, providing tools and support to empower the community to solve their own problems.
- **Iterative Approach and learning from the community:** Allowing the community and the designers themselves to iterate on the solutions helps hone the interventions.
- **Space to Make Mistakes:** Creating spaces for the community to learn from their mistakes will lead to self-reliance and agency.
- **Addressing Historical Injustices:** Design interventions should aim to mitigate historical injustices through sustained and community-driven efforts.
- **Reflexivity:** Understanding that designers can make mistakes and learn as they go instead of posing themselves as experts.

- **Long-term engagement:** Many designers see themselves as experts who helicopter into a context, solve problems, and then leave. For any meaningful intervention, long-term engagement with the community is crucial.
- **Capacity building:** Building the capacity of the community to inquire into their lived experiences and find their own solutions should be one of the main objectives of any legal design interventions.
- **Understanding the larger systems at play:** Navigating the various policy frameworks and systemic barriers and actively positioning the solutions within them is an important aspect of legal design.
- **Distributed Legal Expertise:** Zenith's work showcases the importance of empowering the community with legal expertise so they don't have to rely on legal experts to ask for their rights.
- **Power Redistribution:** Decolonial approaches fundamentally involve shifting power from colonial centres to marginalised communities. Zenith's methodology explicitly redistributes power in the legal domain through several mechanisms like diminishing their own role as experts, building internal leadership within the community, creating direct relationships between community members and legal authorities, and transferring legal skills rather than providing services.

CONCLUSION

The paper contributes to the building scholarship of decolonial design theory by understanding legal design interventions in Global South contexts. Although design thinking and human-centred design do offer structured approaches to creativity and problem-solving, its capitalist origins do not provide solutions to complex social problems as conventional design thinkers might hope. Moreover, their uncritical transplantation from the West runs the risk of producing unsustainable design outcomes. The case study highlighted in this paper demonstrates how interventions that are rooted in local practices and lived experiences offer insights into the design processes, even though the organisations may not be aware of design vocabularies.

The cases of the Zenith Society for Socio-Legal Empowerment illustrate that legal design is not simply about marrying law with design thinking. Instead, it is about understanding and intentionally integrating local socio-political contexts into legal design processes. These organisations, through their long-term engagement and participatory methods, embody principles of design justice rooted in the Indian context. The case study offers insights that emphasise the democratisation of design by centring the voices of those traditionally marginalised. It demonstrates the importance of the designer taking on the role of a facilitator rather than an expert, recognising that everyone is an expert of their own lived experiences. Capacity building and empowering the communities to raise their voices and demand justice are foundational in achieving sustainable, just, and liberatory outcomes.

In India, where marginalised groups such as Sahariya Adivasis historically have faced systemic exclusion and displacement, it is imperative to acknowledge the historical injustices and keep them into account while designing for them. Furthermore, learning from grassroots legal design interventions which do not necessarily borrow from conventional design thinking approaches opens up a new understanding of decolonial ways of doing legal design. The case of Zenith, a socio-legal organisation in the Chambal region of Madhya Pradesh, offers valuable insights into how legal design in India can be practiced. Through a sustained process of trust-building, and working with the community towards empowerment, Zenith has attempted to aid Sahariya Adivasis in accessing their rights and improving their living conditions. Zenith's work showcases the importance of a community-first mindset, where the role of the designer is to facilitate rather than dictate, and highlights the value of communities taking ownership of their design processes.

While we are quick to transplant the Western sensibilities of design to solve wicked problems that India has been facing, it may be worthwhile to pause and reflect on the already existing practices and learn from them. Other organisations like Zenith have much to offer to a decolonial design theory and legal design practices in India. 'Doing' is an inherent part of design but before jumping with both feet in to train organisations with design thinking or uncritically imposing design thinking methodologies to solve problems in India, it is beneficial to take a step back and reflect on the already existing design practices that have demonstrated achieving more equitable and sustainable outcomes.

REFERENCES

R Ackermann, 'Design Thinking Was Supposed to Fix the World. Where Did It Go Wrong?' (*MIT Technology Review*, 2023).

T Brown, 'Design Thinking' (*Harvard Business Review*, June 2008).

K Christensen, 'Design Thinking To Solve Gender Issues' (*Forbes India*, 2018).

K Dabaghi, 'Beyond Design Thinking and into Speculative Futures in Legal Design' (2022).

'Design Justice Network Website'.

A Escobar, *Designs for the Pluriverse: Radical Interdependence, Autonomy, and the Making of Worlds* (Durham, NC, Duke University Press, 2018).

M Hagan, 'Introduction to Design Thinking for Law' in Daniel M Katz, Ron Dolin and Michael Bommarito (eds), *Legal Informatics* (Cambridge, Cambridge University Press, 2021).

L Irani, '"Design Thinking": Defending Silicon Valley at the Apex of Global Labor Hierarchies' (2018) 4 *Catalyst: Feminism, Theory, Technoscience* 1.

S Jha, 'NGT Stops Mining in Ecologically Sensitive Madhav National Park in Madhya Pradesh' (*Down To Earth*, 2022).

A Kabra, 'Conservation-Induced Displacement: A Comparative Study of Two Indian Protected Areas' (2009) 7 *Conservation and Society* 249.

R Kijima, M Yang-Yoshihara and MS Maekawa, 'Using Design Thinking to Cultivate the Next Generation of Female STEAM Thinkers' (2021) 8 *International Journal of STEM Education* 14.

N Kwatra, 'Design Thinking for the Social Sector' (Genpact 2020).

CA MacKinnon, 'Toward Feminist Jurisprudence' in Alison M Jaggar (ed), *Living With Contradictions: Controversies In Feminist Social Ethics* (1st edn, London, Routledge 1994).

'Manupatra, Legal Design Bootcamp and Competition'.

E Manzini (ed), *Design, When Everybody Designs: An Introduction to Design for Social Innovation* (Cambridge, MA, The MIT Press, 2015).

S Muralidhar, 'Appearing in Court in India: Challenges in Representing the Marginalised' (2022) 3 *CASTE A Global Journal on Social Exclusion* 421.

M Oliveira, E Zancul and AL Fleury, 'Design Thinking as an Approach for Innovation in Healthcare: Systematic Review and Research Avenues' (2021) 7 *BMJ Innovations* 491.

V Papanek and RB Fuller, *Design for the Real World* (New York, Bantam Books 1972).

I Pradhan, B Kandapan and J Pradhan, 'Uneven Burden of Multidimensional Poverty in India: A Caste Based Analysis' (2022) 17 *PLoS One* e0271806.

R K Pattnaik, and Ranjan Banerjee, 'Extending Design Thinking to Public Policy' (*Economic and Political Weekly*, 22 August 2020).

Suchitra, 'What Moves Masses: Dandi March as Communication Strategy' (*Economic and Political Weekly*, 8 April 1995).

The Big Fat Bao, 'On Caste: The Roots of Discrimination in Indian Design' (*Futuress*, 2023).

M Wizinsky, *Design after Capitalism: Transforming Design Today for an Equitable Tomorrow* (Cambridge, MA, The MIT Press, 2022).

LG Wyatt and others, 'Educational Change by Design: Creating a School of the Future' (2021) 24 *Journal of Cases in Educational Leadership* 55.

S Yengde and C West, *Caste Matters* (Gurgaon, Penguin Viking, an imprint of Penguin Random House, 2019).

10

Activating Imagination to Promote Epistemic Justice: Speculations on an Island-Wide Citizens' Assembly for Cyprus

AMANDA PERRY-KESSARIS[1]

INTRODUCTION

THE TERM 'EPISTEMIC injustice' was coined by philosopher Miranda Fricker to draw attention to exclusionary dynamics in the everyday production, distribution, and consumption of knowledge. Most obvious are the injustices that arise from unfairness in the distribution of 'epistemic goods such as information or education'. Less obvious are the 'testimonial' and 'hermeneutical' injustices that arise from how we are treated in our 'capacity as a knower[s]'. Testimonial injustice occurs when we are not listened to – when 'prejudice causes a hearer to give a deflated level of credibility to a speaker's word'. Hermeneutical injustice occurs when we are not heard – when society at large lacks the 'interpretive resources' that they need in order to 'mak[e] sense of' our 'social experiences'.[2] Morten Fibieger Byskov argues that 'epistemic discrimination' of the kind identified by Fricker becomes a form of 'injustice' when it is associated with unfairness – an 'unfair outcome', 'judgement about epistemic capacity', 'denial of stakeholder rights', 'denial of knowledge, or 'existing vulnerability'.[3] Seen through a socio-legal lens,[4] epistemic injustice

[1] Professor of Law, Kent Law School, a.perry-kessaris@kent.ac.uk.

[2] Miranda Fricker, *Epistemic Injustice: Power and the Ethics of Knowing* (Oxford, Oxford University Press, 2007) 1. See further Ian James Kidd, José Medina and Gaile Pohlhaus (eds), *The Routledge Handbook of Epistemic Injustice* (London, Routledge, 2017).

[3] Morten Fibieger Byskov, 'What Makes Epistemic Injustice an Injustice' (2020) 52(1) *Journal of Social Philosophy* 116.

[4] Amanda Perry-Kessaris, 'Legal Design Could and Should Be More Sociolegal' in Dan Lockton, Sara Lenzi, Arlene Oak, Paul Hekkert, Juan Sádaba and Peter Lloyd (eds) *DRS2022: Bilbao, 25 June–3 July, Bilbao, Spain* (DRS, 2022).

is a problem not only because it harms those individual knowers who are not listened to or heard, but also because it undermines what Roger Cotterrell has termed 'the well-being' of law 'as a practical idea'. For law to be well, to be 'socially meaningful', it must accommodate and nurture all forms of social, including epistemic (not to mention epistemological), diversity.[5]

In this chapter, I consider how designerly ways might contribute to securing epistemic justice in a particular, speculative, 'proto-legal' context: an island-wide citizens' assembly for Cyprus. Cyprus is an extreme context in the sense that its status is contested, and this means that almost every (past, present, and future) thing about it is fundamentally contingent and multi-perspectival. I choose it both because it matters in its own right, and because extremes 'are good for thinking'.[6]

The chapter introduces citizens' assemblies and the history of the so-called Cyprus Problem. Next, it sets out a range of scenarios capturing possible futures for the island that have been generated by its inhabitants, one of which includes a possible citizens' assembly. It then identifies two types of imagination (empathetic and systemic) that seem to be crucial to the securing epistemic justice in any such assembly. Finally, it draws on an experiment run on behalf of the UK Government, the River Roding Interspecies Council, to suggest how designerly ways might prompt and facilitate both forms of imagination in the speculative context of a possible island-wide citizens' assembly for Cyprus.

CITIZENS' ASSEMBLIES

I use the term 'proto-legal' to refer to artefacts and processes that are directed towards law, but that are not yet, and may never be, formally legal. Applying designerly lens, we can think of such artefacts as legal prototypes, and such activities as legal prototyping.[7] They can be especially instructive for legal designers with an interest in epistemic injustice because they are sites of openness and of closure, of possibilities promoted and/or foreclosed, of legal-futures-in-the-making.[8] Here, latent epistemic injustice may become visible, and new epistemic injustices may be created. Policy-making is one important example of proto-legal activity. It is an especially productive site for lawyers

[5] Roger M B Cotterrell, *Sociological Jurisprudence: Juristic Thought and Social Inquiry* (New York, Routledge, 2018). On epistemological diversity see Margaret Davies, *Law Unlimited: Materialism, Pluralism and Legal Theory* (New York, Routledge, 2017).

[6] Yael Navaro-Yashin, *The Make-Believe Space: Affective Geography in a Postwar Polity* (Durham, NC, Duke University Press, 2012) 10–11.

[7] For another account of legal activity as prototyping see Davina Cooper, 'Crafting Prefigurative Law in Turbulent Times: Decertification, DIY Law Reform, and the Dilemmas of Feminist Prototyping' (2023) 31 *Feminist Legal Studies* 17.

[8] Here I am adapting Barbara Adam's concept of futures-in-the-making in 'Towards a Twenty-First Century Sociological Engagement with the Future' (2011) 4(11) *Insights, Institute of Advanced Study, Durham University* 6.

to explore how designerly ways can contribute to epistemic (in)justice for two reasons. First, recent decades have seen a turn towards 'open' policy-making – that is, an increasing tendency among governments to seek to improve their ability to surface and work meaningfully with the needs, wants, and broader insights of their peoples.[9] Second, this turn has been associated with a 'design turn' in policy-making – that is, an increasing tendency among governments to draw upon designerly ways to develop, implement, and/or disrupt policy.[10] For example, 'user-centred design' is now, along with service design and systems thinking, included in the Policy Profession Standards which 'describe the skills and knowledge required by policy professionals' within the UK Government.[11]

This chapter focuses on the proto-legal context of citizens' assemblies[12] because they bring together both of these turns. They are an open policy-making device, around which there is increasing interest in, and evidence of, the potential for designerly ways to contribute to creating the conditions for epistemic (in)justice. Citizens assemblies are a form of representative deliberative process in which a mini-public – 'a randomly selected group of people who are broadly representative of a community' – is proactively gathered to 'spen[d] significant time learning and collaborating through facilitated deliberation to form collective recommendations for policy makers'.[13] Through a distinctive combination of vertical engagement with experts with lived and professional experience, and horizontal engagement with each other, assembly members are prompted and facilitated 'to come up with meaningful solutions on the most challenging social and policy issues'.[14] Such processes are not new – they have their roots in Ancient Greece,[15] and 'the first contemporary wave started in the late 1960s'. What distinguishes the second contemporary wave, currently underway, is a 'greater experimentation in their purpose, design, combination with other forms of participation, and institutionalisation'.[16] Well-known examples of citizens' assemblies include the French Conseil Economique Societal et

[9] Sonia Exley, 'Open Policy Making in the UK: To Whom Might Policy Formulation Be Opening Up' (2021) 50(3) *Journal of Social Policy* 451–469; Lucy Kimbell and Jocelyn Bailey, 'Prototyping and the New Spirit of Policymaking' (2017) 13(3) *CoDesign* 214.

[10] Lucy Kimbell, Catherine Durose, Ramia Mazé and Liz Richardson, *Design and Policy: Current Debates and Future Directions for Research in the UK: Report of the AHRC Design|Policy Research Network* (London, University of the Arts London, 2023); Christian Bason (ed), *Design for Policy* (London, Routledge, 2014).

[11] 'Policy Profession Standards' (Gov.uk, 10 November 2021) www.gov.uk/government/publications/policy-profession-standards.

[12] See OECD, *Innovative Citizen Participation and New Democratic Institutions Catching the Deliberative Wave* (OECD, 2020); DemocracyNext 'Assembling an Assembly: A How-To Guide' (2023) assemblyguide.demnext.org/.

[13] ibid 24.

[14] *DemocracyNext* www.demnext.org/resources.

[15] Hélène Landemore, *Open Democracy: Reinventing Popular Rule for the Twenty-First Century* (Princeton, Princeton University Press, 2020).

[16] OECD (n 12) 25.

Environnemental, which has most recently produced propositions on assisted dying, to be considered by government; and the Citizens' Assembly of the Republic of Ireland, which has produced propositions on issues including abortion and climate change.[17] Less-cited examples include a citizens' assembly on energy justice held in Lebanon against the backdrop of the 'colossal explosion of a warehouse' in the Beirut port in 2020.[18]

Advocates of open policy-making initiatives such as citizens' assemblies often emphasise their practical benefits. For example, there is a growing consensus that 'collective intelligence' – that is, 'shared or group intelligence that emerges from the collaboration and collective efforts of many diverse individuals' – often produces more robust insights into problems and solutions than the kind of individual intelligence that can be gathered from surveys or interviews.[19] What is significant for the purposes of this chapter is that such initiatives also have the potential, if well designed, to offer the moral benefit of enhancing epistemic justice.[20]

THE CYPRUS PROBLEM

Communal divisions on the island of Cyprus began to emerge in the 1950s, as Cypriots began to contemplate what a postcolonial future might look like. For example, some in the majority Greek Cypriot community envisaged union with Greece; and some Turkish Cypriots, the largest minority community, envisaged union with Turkey, or a partitioned island with one side joining Turkey and the other Greece. These divisions were reflected in the constitution, which came into force on the island's independence in 1960, with Greece, Turkey, and the United Kingdom given the role of guarantors; and important positions, such as those of president and vice-president, were reserved for each community. However, amid inter-communal violence, Turkish Cypriots withdrew or (depending on your point of view) were expelled from power sharing. The constitutional order was suspended, the Republic of Cyprus became a de facto Greek Cypriot state, and in 1964, the island was physically divided by a United Nations-monitored Buffer Zone. In 1974, Greek Cypriot extremists, with the backing of the military junta in Greece, attempted a coup; Turkey invaded and occupied the northern

[17] Conseil Économique, Social et Environnemental, 'Convention Citoyenne sur la Fin de Vie' conventioncitoyennesurlafindevie.lecese.fr/; An Tionól Saoránach (Citizens' Assembly, Republic of Ireland) citizensassembly.ie.

[18] Ala'a Shehabi and Muzna Al-Masri, 'Foregrounding Citizen Imaginaries: Exploring Just Energy Futures Through a Citizens' Assembly in Lebanon' (2022) 140 *Futures* 102956, 1.

[19] Geoff Mulgan, *Big Mind: How Collective Intelligence Can Change Our World* (Princeton, Princeton University Press, 2017); Kathy Peach, Aleks Berditchevskaia and Theo Bass, 'Collective Intelligence Design Playbook' (*Nesta*, 2020) www.nesta.org.uk/toolkit/collective-intelligence-design-playbook/.

[20] Susan Dieleman, 'Epistemic Justice and Democratic Legitimacy' (2015) 30(4) *Hypatia* 795.

third of the island; and about a third of the island's population was displaced. In 1983, the, now Turkish Cypriot-majority, north of the island declared itself to be the independent Turkish Republic of Northern Cyprus – a status that has only ever been recognised by Turkey.[21]

In early 2003, the authorities in the north suddenly decided to allow Cypriots to move back and forth across the Island for the first time in decades.[22] Hopes were raised for a solution to the 'Cyprus Problem' and in 2004, referenda were held on each side on whether to adopt a reunification plan presented by UN Secretary General Kofi Annan. The plan failed, with 65 per cent voting in favour in the north, but 75 per cent voting against in the south. So when the Republic of Cyprus joined the European Union later that year, it joined as a whole island, but on the understanding that the northern third of the island is not under its control. Since then, multiple efforts by the United Nations to support the reunification of the island as a 'bi-communal bi-zonal federation' have also failed, most significantly in Crans-Montana in 2017.[23]

In recent years, disillusionment with the UN-sponsored process has led some civil society actors to go beyond promoting bi-communal contact and press for greater public involvement in peace-building.[24] In the words of one of the most prominent of these groups, Unite Cyprus Now: 'Surveys have demonstrated, over and over again, that Cypriots are ready to unite their country and build a common future together. It is time to hand ownership to citizens.'[25]

A CITIZENS' ASSEMBLY FOR CYPRUS?

Since early 2024, economist Fiona Mullen, who has a history of close involvement in the Cyprus negotiations, has advocated a highly participatory redesign of the peace process, with citizens' assemblies potentially playing a key role.[26] She envisages a 17-step co-design process centring on two stages of deliberation,[27] first by experts, then by members of the public, probably in the form of a

[21] See generally James Ker-Lindsay, *The Cyprus Problem: What Everyone Needs to Know* (Oxford, Oxford University Press, 2011).

[22] Mete Hatay, Fiona Mullen and Julia Kalimeri, *The Day After I: Commercial Opportunities Following a Solution to the Cyprus Problem* (PRIO Centre Cyprus, 2008) 9.

[23] See UN Cyprus Talks website www.uncyprustalks.org/.

[24] See Amanda Perry-Kessaris, 'Could Alternative Econo-Legal Futures Be Made More Possible and Probable through Prefigurative Design? Insights from and for Cyprus' (2022) 72(4) *Northern Ireland Legal Quarterly* 623.

[25] Unite Cyprus Now, 'International Community Should Stop Playing with Our Lives' (Press Release, 30 April 2021) unitecyprusnow.org/all-media/press-releases-statements/161-international-community-should-stop-playing-with-our-lives.

[26] Mullen is Director of Sapienta Economics and was involved in the negotiations between 2008 and early 2016, sometimes as a staff member in the UN Good Offices, and at other times as a consultant: sapientaeconomics.com/about-us/.

[27] Fiona Mullen, 'Steps to a New Cyprus Problem Process' (2024a) *Financial Mirror* (25 February 2024) www.financialmirror.com/2024/02/25/steps-to-a-new-cyprus-problem-process/.

citizen's assembly.[28] For Mullen, a deliberative citizens' assembly is appealing for the practical reason that it allows political leaders in Cyprus to 'share the burden of extremely difficult decisions with their voters', whilst also avoiding the high stakes of the 'big bang' all-or-nothing dual-referendum approach.[29]

As it happens, something akin to a citizens' assembly was advocated a year earlier by participants in the little-known Cyprus Futures project, run by social impact company Reos Partners. As we shall see, in this case, the body was seen as offering both practical and moral rewards. To put it in the terms of epistemic (in)justice, it seems that participants were drawn to the idea of a citizens' assembly in part because it might ensure that past, present, and future inhabitants of the island are listened to and heard.

Reos Partners specialise in a 'transformative scenarios' approach to peace building. Scenarios are evidence-based descriptions of different possible future worlds. They are designed to surface the complexities of the problem at hand, and of ways of approaching that problem; and they focus attention on possibilities which are plausible, even if they may seem remote. Adam Kahane, founder of Reos Partners, argues that scenarios are especially helpful in peace-building processes because, among other things, they focus the attention of participants on engagement over agreement, on the big picture and long-term horizons, and on the pragmatic scrutiny of ideas.[30]

The transformative scenarios approach has its origins in the South African Mont Fleur workshops, which occurred during the transition from apartheid to democracy, 1991–1992. The resulting Mont Fleur Scenarios are widely regarded as 'perhaps the clearest ever instance of a normative scenario project actually succeeding in its normative mission'. In that case, the mission was substantive – that is, to steer the African National Congress party towards a market-oriented policy programme.[31] By contrast, the mission of the Cyprus Futures project was more processual – to shift attention away from debates over the past, and towards the future; and to prompt and facilitate nuanced, evidence-based discussion about alternative possibilities, and the associated sense of empowerment. The emphasis is not only on identifying what might happen, but also on proactively

[28] Fiona Mullen, 'Deliberative Democracy: Only Way Out of the Cyprus Problem?' (2024b) *Financial Mirror* (8 January 2024) www.financialmirror.com/2024/01/08/deliberative-democracy-only-way-out-of-the-cyprus-problem/.

[29] Mullen (n 27). See also 'Nicosia Uncut – Episode 53: Special Guest Fiona Mullen: How Can We Revitalize the Solution Process?' (Island Talks, Podcast, 6 March 2024) islandtalks.fm/podcast/nicosia-uncut-episode-53-special-guest-fiona-mullen-how-can-we-revitalize-the-solution-process-6-3-2023/.

[30] Adam Kahane, *Transformative Scenario Planning* (San Francisco, Berrett-Koehler, 2021).

[31] Adam Vigdor Gordon, 'Limits and Longevity: A Model for Scenarios That Influence the Future' (2020) 151 *Technological Forecasting and Social Change* 119851. The process was repeated by the African Leadership Institute in 2004, a decade after the end of the apartheid regime: African Leadership Institute, 'SA 2020 Scenarios Project' alinstitute.org/our-programmes/grant-projects/scenario-projects/sa-2020-scenarios.

increasing the likelihood that particular, desirable futures will happen. So the project materials encourage civil society activists, businesses, educators, artists, and citizens more generally to 'us[e] the scenarios to inform and inspire individual and collective strategies, illuminate possible pathways, and clarify next steps'.[32]

The Cyprus Futures project centred on a series of workshops attended by 36 participants, selected to be broadly representative of the characteristics and opinions of the wider population of Cyprus. With the help of an editor, participants co-created four scenarios, each of which captures an alternative possible future for the island. Three of the scenarios were laced with negativity. First, the 'no way' scenario envisaged a future of 'stagnation and inaction' – a continuation of the status quo, meaning not stasis, but ever-increasing divergence between north and south, and of the conditions for peace. Second, the 'my way' scenario envisaged a future of 'divergence and opposition', with Turkish Cypriots moving away from a commitment to a negotiated settlement and becoming increasingly isolated from the international community. Third, the 'their way' scenario envisaged a future of 'peace under pressure' in which the international community presses for top-down negotiations, resulting in a superficial solution which lacks local ownership and resilience.

The fourth scenario, 'our way', was optimistic. It envisaged a future of 'resilient peace' in which the peace process is transformed to become more inclusive – that is, 'multi-track' and 'participatory', 'combin[ing] high-level talks between leaders with working groups, technical committees, and broad civil society engagement.' In this scenario, a solution becomes more likely because it is wanted and needed by those who use the physical and legal infrastructure of the island.[33] Citizens and elites are envisaged as engaging with each other, and with the Cyprus Problem, for practical reasons: as part of their wider mission to address a range of everyday island-wide problems such as energy shortages, waste management, and barriers to trade.

Most significantly for the purposes of this chapter, this scenario envisages much of that engagement occurring through a 'Civil Society Consultative Forum on the Future of Cyprus'. This body would be representative of the inhabitants of the island and would attend to traditionally marginalised voices. It would serve as a device through which the negotiating teams of the north and south can 'interact with diverse groups in society' and seek 'feedback on solutions being considered for specific issues.'[34] It sounds remarkably like a citizens' assembly.

[32] Cyprus Futures, *Possible Futures of Cyprus: Scenarios Report* (Cyprus Futures 2023) 59.

[33] Cyprus Futures (n 32) 13–14. Other scenarios, including that of a unitary state, as envisaged under the 1960 Constitution, and that of a negotiated two-state solution, were rejected by participants as being implausible.

[34] ibid 54.

DESIGNING FOR EPISTEMIC JUSTICE IN CITIZENS' ASSEMBLIES

Citizens' assemblies entail a wide range of design choices, from the logistics of inviting or compelling a representative sample of the population to participate, to the layout of the invitation letters and envelopes, to the process by which deliberation occurs, and the format in which recommendations are made; and designers are repeatedly credited in a recent major international survey of deliberative democracy practices.[35]

Some have criticised deliberative forums for tending to be what we might call over-designed – that is, 'top-down', 'overly prescriptive', insufficiently attentive to 'place-based considerations', and, therefore, 'exclusionary'.[36] Jan-Peter Voß and Nina Amelung attribute this to the fact that 'design knowledge' in the field 'was produced to be generic, mobile, and relevant across different contexts'.[37] It is important to note, given our focus on Cyprus, that Nicole Curato and Septrim Calamba have found that these problems can be amplified in 'fragile contexts', including those which are 'recovering from armed conflict'. For example, when running a deliberative forum in the Philippines, they encountered 'distrust' around the demographic data upon which selection processes are typically based, and a pervasive sense of economic precarity among participants that prevented them from devoting the time necessary for 'long-form' deliberation.[38]

The specific question that I want to address here is what designerly ways can do to ensure epistemic justice in citizens' assemblies. I use the term designerly ways, originally coined by design researcher Nigel Cross, to refer to three characteristics that are, in combination, distinctive of design-based disciplines: mindsets, processes, and strategies. A designerly mindset is simultaneously practical, critical, and imaginative.[39] That mindset is, in turn, activated and nurtured by processes that emphasise experimentation (both in the 'creative' sense of generating ideas and following where they lead, and in the 'scientific' sense of testing and discarding what does not work); and by strategies that emphasise making ideas visual and tangible in sketches and models (as part of experimental processes, as well as in more formal outputs such as diagrams). In

[35] Nicole Curato, David Farrell, Brigitte Geißel, Kimmo Grönlund, Patricia Mockler, Jean-Benoit Pilet, Alan Renwick, Jonathan Rose, Maija Setälä, Jane Suiter, *Deliberative Mini-Publics: Core Design Features* (Bristol, Bristol University Press, 2021); MADD LBP, *How to Run a Civic Lottery: A Guide and License* (2017) www.masslbp.com/resources; newDemocracy Foundation and UN Democracy Fund, *Enabling National Initiatives to Take Democracy Beyond Elections* (2019) 224; OECD, *Innovative Citizen Participation and New Democratic Institutions Catching the Deliberative Wave* (OECD, 2020) 5.

[36] Nicole Curato and Septrin Calamba, 'Deliberative Forums in Fragile Contexts- Challenges from the Field' (2024) *Politics* 1, 3–4.

[37] Jan-Peter Voß and Nina Amelung, 'Innovating Public Participation Methods: Technoscientization and Reflexive Engagement' (2016) 46(5) *Social Studies of Science* 749, 762.

[38] Curato and Septrin (n 36) 2, 8, 12.

[39] Amanda Perry-Kessaris, 'Legal Design for Practice, Activism, Policy and Research' (2019) 46(2) *Journal of Law and Society* 185.

combination, these ways generate 'enabling ecosystems' in which experts and non-experts can, individually and collectively, synthesise understandings of law as it is, as it was, and as it might yet be.[40] For example, we can find ourselves more able to 'disrup[t]' well-used concepts, 'surrender' to chance or change, and 'mov[e] beyond' the here and now.[41]

Given that the volume in which this piece appears is concerned with legal design, it is worth pausing here to note that the closest that most legal design projects tend to come to engaging with epistemic (in)justice is in seeking to be 'user'- or, more broadly, 'human-centred'.[42] When deployed with a user/human-centred orientation, designerly ways can render legal artefacts and processes more accessible by ridding them of traditional, jargonistic, and exclusionary, lawyerly ways.[43] To adapt Fricker's terminology, these examples demonstrate the potential of user/human-centred design to mitigate or compensate for distributive epistemic injustice. These projects can also reasonably be interpreted as prima facie support for the proposition that a user/human-centred orientation can contribute to epistemic justice of the broader, testimonial and hermeneutical, variety: If legal documents and processes are co-designed with users/other humans, and/or with their needs and wants in mind, then those users/other humans are more likely to be both listened to and heard. As one toolkit puts it: 'Being a human-centered designer is about believing that as long as you stay grounded in what you've learned from people, your team can arrive at new solutions that the world needs'.[44] However, upon closer inspection, it soon becomes clear that a user/human-centred approach is not only insufficient but also potentially damaging to the cause of promoting broader epistemic justice. Most notably, when we centre our own wants and needs, we necessarily peripheralize – do not listen to, do not hear--the wants, needs, and knowledge of other individuals and communities; as well as those of wider legal, not to mention planetary, systems.[45]

[40] Amanda Perry-Kessaris, *Doing Sociolegal Research in Design Mode* (London, Routledge, 2021).

[41] Yoko Akama, Sarah Pink and Shanti Sumartojo, *Uncertainty and Possibility: New Approaches to Future Making in Design Anthropology* (London, Bloomsbury, 2018).

[42] Elements of user-centred design can be traced back at least as far as the Arts and Crafts movement; and the notion of human-centred design is widely attributed to professor of mechanical engineering and business administration, John E. Arnold (1913–1963): John E Arnold, in William J Clancey (ed), *Creative Engineering: Promoting Innovation by Thinking Differently* (Springer, 2016). For (non-legal) designerly explorations of epistemic (in)justice see: Emilia Smeds and Ersilia Verlinghieri (eds), 'Seeing Like a Citizen: Rethinking City Street Transformations through the Lens of Epistemic Justice' (2023) 24(5) *Planning Theory & Practice* 697; Luce Beeckmans, 'Epistemic Justice in the Design Process' (2021) *ARCHINED*, no. 16/12/2021, 22–28.

[43] See, eg, Robert Waller and others 'Cooperation through Clarity: Designing Simplified Contracts' (2016) 21(1–2) *Journal of Strategic Contracting and Negotiation* 48; Grainne McKeever and others, *Using Human-Centred Design to Develop Empathy and Supports for Litigants in Person* (Belfast, Ulster University, 2023).

[44] IDEO, *The Field Guide to Human-Centered Design* (*IDEO* 2015) www.inist.org/library/1959.John%20E%20Arnold.Creative%20Engineering.pdf.

[45] See, eg, Donella H Meadows, in Diana Wright (ed), *Systems Thinking: A Primer* (Vermont, Chelsea Green Publishing, 2008); Kathryn Yusoff, 'The Inhumanities' (2021) 111(3) *Annals of the American Association of Geographers* 663.

The need to take a systemic approach to epistemic justice is emphasised by Fricker. She argues that, if we want to nurture testimonial and hermeneutical justice, we must begin, as individuals, by becoming 'virtuous hearers' – empathetically listening, sensitising ourselves to the social experiences of others, and actively correcting for our prejudices.[46] But we must also, she argues, work collectively to transform systems which are themselves sources, or reinforcers, of epistemic injustice.[47] We can interpret citizens' assemblies as having the potential to open up both of these pathways to epistemic justice: first, by promoting respectful and informed deliberation between individuals; second, by ensuring that participants and, through them, the policy-making system, are refreshed and challenged by collective, potentially transformative, insights. However, both of these pathways – being a virtuous listener and working to transform systems – require imagination.

Herein lies a problem. Cassie Robinson, a strategic designer who focuses on systemic transformation, has criticised collective intelligence and deliberative processes, including citizens' assemblies, for prioritising 'analytical and rational' thinking over imagination. In so doing, she argues, they 'hem things in by only offering choices against a narrow prescribed set of options'. She has also criticised co-design and participatory approaches more generally for failing to 'account for the unknown unknowns – the fact that communities don't know what they don't know, or can't imagine'. What 'we need', Robinson suggests, is 'something to pull us away from the status quo', and 'this comes from feeling and experiencing what else is possible.'[48] So she and others have called for a public programme of 'imagination infrastructuring'.[49]

Among those who promote deliberative methods, Lala Muradova and co-authors have highlighted the importance of imagination. For example, they have argued that in order to ensure 'careful consideration and integration of multiple and opposing perspectives',[50] and that one way of doing this is to ensure that members are prompted and facilitated to 'actively imagin[e]' the 'experiences, perspectives and feelings' of others.[51] Furthermore, a guide to

[46] Fricker (n 2) 5.

[47] ibid 8.

[48] Cassie Robinson, 'Change Happens If Our Collective Imagination Changes' (*Medium*, 9 January 2022) cassierobinson.medium.com/change-happens-if-our-collective-imagination-changes-7a1c0475a578. Robinson leads the Joseph Rowntree Foundation's work on Emerging Futures and Collective Imagination www.jrf.org.uk/society/emerging-futures.

[49] See, eg, presentations by Deb Chachra, Indy Johar and Anab Jain, 'What Is Infrastructuring? And What Is Imagination Infrastructuring?' (Imagination Infrastructuring, Notion, 10 June 2021) www.notion.so/13-35-What-is-Infrastructuring-And-what-is-Imagination-Infrastructuring-f5f07298e7ce43689ab7ab2fad50ced9.

[50] Lala Muradova and Kevin Arceneaux (2022) 'Reflective political reasoning: Political disagreement and empathy' 61 *European Journal of Political Research* 740–761, 741.

[51] Lala Muradova (2021) Seeing the other side? Perspective-taking and reflective political judgements in interpersonal deliberation. 69(3) *Political Studies*, 644-664, 647. See also Lala Muradova (2025). Empathy and Political Reasoning: How Empathy Promotes Reflection and Strengthens Democracy. Cambridge University Press.

citizens' assemblies produced by the research and action institute Democracy Next suggests in a section on 'innovative practices' that assemblies can be designed to include, among other things, collective imagination, and the perspectives of future generations and more-than-humans.[52] Drawing together Fricker's and Robinson's insights, we can be more specific and normative: if they are to promote epistemic justice, citizens' assemblies ought to be designed to activate imagination – individual and collective, empathetic and systemic. What might this look like in practice?

ACTIVATING IMAGINATION IN THE CONTEXT OF A CITIZEN'S ASSEMBLY FOR CYPRUS

What if an island-wide citizen's assembly for Cyprus could be constituted to contribute to the process of finding a solution to the problem of the island's division, as envisaged by Mullen, and/or to managing everyday island-wide problems, as envisaged by participants in the Cyprus Futures project? Of the many potential barriers to the success of such a venture, I am concerned with those associated with epistemic justice and imagination. Surveys consistently reveal that those living on each side of the island are open to interacting with the other, but that they hesitate, in part because they do not know, and cannot (empathetically) imagine, each other.[53] And it is rare anyone, let alone those entangled in the everyday one-sidedness of living on the island to (systemically) imagine it as a single, albeit sub-divided, unit.[54] So how might a citizens' assembly for Cyprus be designed to prompt and facilitate mindsets that are not only practical and critical, but also imaginative?

When considering how we might 'build and seed imagination infrastructures', Cassie Robinson speaks in terms of identifying and creating 'containers' in which we can 'work' with existing 'material'. Some of these materials exist in other times, such as 'future generations' and 'myths and histories of place'; some, such as 'civic spaces', exist in contemporary human relations; and some exist in the 'natural world'.[55] In this section, I explore how we might

[52] 'Assembly Guide Overview' (*English*) assemblyguide.demnext.org/.

[53] For example, the Centre for Sustainable Peace and Democratic Development (SeeD) produces the SCORE index of social cohesion and propensity to reconciliation among Cypriots by combining qualitative data from randomly administered questionnaires and follow-up face-to-face interviews: SCORE, *Predicting Peace Predicting Peace: The Social Cohesion and Reconciliation Index as a Tool for Conflict Transformation* (UNDP 2015). See also Shelley McKeown and Charis Psaltis, 'Intergroup Contact and the Mediating Role of Intergroup Trust on Outgroup Evaluation and Future Contact Intentions in Cyprus and Northern Ireland' (2017) 23(4) *Peace and Conflict: Journal of Peace Psychology* 392; and Hatay (n 22) 2.

[54] For a rare and effective attempt to make such imaginings possible, see: Cyprus Chambers of Commerce and Industry and Turkish Cypriot Chamber of Commerce (CCCI/KKTO), 'The Nine-O'Clock News in the Year 2030' (*YouTube*, 2011) youtu.be/Pbrk1i4xXBI.

[55] Cassie Robinson, 'Emerging Futures: Patterning the Third Horizon' (The Conference 2023, 22 September 2023) www.notion.so/13-35-What-is-Infrastructuring-And-what-is-Imagination-Infrastructuring-f5f07298e7ce43689ab7ab2fad50ced9.

work with one such natural material, 'the more-than-human', to enhance empathetic and systemic imagination (and, therefore, epistemic justice) within the 'container' of an island-wide citizens' assembly in Cyprus. I argue that this work might take place in a separate, pre-assembly, 'container': an inter-species council. To do this, I draw on the work of Policy Lab, a design-driven unit within the civil service in the United Kingdom.

In 2022, Policy Lab launched a new programme of work exploring 'experimental policy design methods' – that is, methods that go beyond user-centred design, service design, and systems thinking, which are already part of everyday practice across the civil service.[56] As part of that programme, they commissioned, together with the Defra Futures, which is part of the Department for Rural Affairs, an experiment focused on the River Roding in Barking, east London (Figure 10.1). The experiment was created by Moral Imaginations, a research and practice centre, which advocates the activation of collective imagination to achieve morally grounded systems change.[57] It combined aspects of deliberation and collective intelligence to ask: 'What if, in the future, we used our imaginations to represent more-than-human perspectives in decision-making?' It took the form of an Interspecies Council, the first ever held by the UK Government.[58]

The River Roding Inter-Species Council brought together 24 participants, including policy-makers and 'stakeholders with a professional or community interest … to imagine and empathise with the needs of some of the species living in and around the river Roding'.[59] Each participant was assigned in advance a species to inhabit for the event. Philip Tovey, Head of Futures at DEFRA, represented the tufted duck. 'Leading up to the event actually felt like a really special thing to do. To actually represent another people or another community. So I felt myself actually taking that really quite seriously'. During the event, Tickell asked participants to imagine they are 'actually looking through the eyes of this non-human creature … to look around and see a circle full of other non-human creatures … and share your concerns with this Council'. Participants reported that 'soil … was incredibly confident. It was like I've seen

[56] Sanjan Sabherwal and Neha Sharma, 'Launching Our Experimental Policy Design Methods' (*Policy Lab Blog*, 18 May 2022) openpolicy.blog.gov.uk/2022/05/18/launching-our-experimental-policy-design-methods/; See also 'MANIFEST: Artists, Policy and the Process of Making Change – Policy Lab' (26 March 2024) openpolicy.blog.gov.uk/2024/03/26/manifest-artists-policy-and-the-process-of-making-change/.

[57] 'Moral Imaginations' (*Moral Imaginations*) www.moralimaginations.com; Neha Sharma and others, 'Using Experimental Methods to Reimagine Decision-Making for the Freshwater System, Post 2043' (7 February 2024) openpolicy.blog.gov.uk/2024/02/07/using-experimental-methods-to-reimagine-decision-making-for-the-freshwater-system-post-2043/.

[58] The concept of an Interspecies Council has its roots in indigenous practices, and was popularised by John Seed, Joanna Macy, Pat Fleming and Arne Naess in the form of the 'Council of All Beings' (now often referred to as 'Deep Ecology' group processes) in their vol *Thinking Like a Mountain: Towards a Council of All Beings* (Gabriola Island, BC, New Society Publishers, 1988). Another example of its application, this time enhanced by live action role play (LARP), is the Treaty of Finsbury Park 2025 project: treaty.finsburypark.live.

[59] Neha Sharma and others (n 54).

it all before. I've seen the dinosaurs come and go'; whilst the grassnake was 'very low to the ground obviously very timid compared to humans which have a higher perspective'.[60]

To put the Moral Imaginations approach deployed in the River Roding project in the terms introduced above, it is about designing experiences which prompt and facilitate individual (empathetic) imagination, in order to open the door to collective (systemic) imagination, in order to create the conditions for systemic transformation. How might this approach be deployed to promote epistemic justice in a possible future island-wide citizens' assembly in Cyprus?

What if, as a prelude to participating in a citizens' assembly for Cyprus, assembly members held an Inter-Species Council for the Buffer Zone – an area in which the 'natural landscapes as well as endangered flora and fauna' has 'remained largely "untouched"' since 1974; and where first the United Nations, then local Turkish Cypriot and Greek Cypriot community leaders, have 'supported the development of co-management practices and institutions' such that 'ironically and paradoxically, new commons have been created in the very line of separation, such as common grazing grounds and mixed farming for both ethnic communities'.[61] What if each participant were asked to represent, to share the concerns of, a particular non-human element or inhabitant of the Zone – the Northern lapwing, the Cypriot mouflon, the Cyprus tulip, a pebble? Might such a process prompt and facilitate participants to be more willing and able to (empathetically) imagine the other, and to (systemically) imagine alternative futures for the island that they share? Might participants then be better placed to promote epistemic justice in the ensuing citizens' assembly?

Findings from the River Roding experiment are promising. Did taking the perspective of another species actually generate insights that could not be generated through traditional means? Yes. Participant Philip Tovey, Head of Futures at DEFRA, 'went into this like everyone else with quite a lot of scepticism'. But, he says, 'when we started getting into inter-species dialogue with each other, it really brought a new insights into the whole way we think about how decisions should be formed with those different ecological relationships.' Why? According to participant Paul Powesland, founder of the River Roding Trust, there was 'less friction' and that all participants of all kinds displayed 'more willingness to radically imagine' than is typical of traditional open policy-making ventures. As Phoebe Tickell, founder of Moral Imaginations, put it:

> We are short-termist in the way we see the future. We see ourselves as separate from nature. We see human beings as being above all other species. And this process can

[60] Policy Lab, 'River Roding Interspecies Council: Video' (*Vimeo*, 2023) vimeo.com/835341409.

[61] Costas M Constantinou and Evi Eftychiou, *The Cyprus Buffer Zone as a Socio-Ecological Landscape* Case Study (Tokyo, Satoyama Initiative, 2014). satoyama-initiative.org/case_studies/the-cyprus-buffer-zone-as-a-socio-ecological-landscape/.

> give policy-makers that deep, deep empathetic perspective on life so that they actually end up making decisions that are in the interests of all living beings.[62]

Using the terminology of this chapter, we can say that the experiment promoted empathetic and systemic imagination.

In an experimental workshop held in 2024, entitled 'What if a citizens' assembly were to design a future Cyprus peace process?', members of the island's peace-building community considered whether (a) a citizens' assembly might be used to design a future peace process for Cyprus; and (b) a pre-assembly inter-species council might help to activate the imagination of members of such an assembly. After completing a series of briefs designed to prompt and facilitate practical-critical-imaginative reflection, participants indicated that the answer to each question is broadly yes. However, they also emphasised the importance of careful, context-specific, locally-led design.[63]

Figure 10.1 The River Roding (top left), species labels (top right), the Inter-species Council in action (bottom). Images: Screenshots from Policy Lab (2023) River Roding Interspecies Council. Video. Available under Open Government Licence v3.0

[62] Policy Lab (n 58).

[63] The workshop was co-organised by the author and the Centre for Peace and Dialogue in the UN-controlled buffer zone in Nicosia, Cyprus, in November 2024. It was funded by a Socio-Legal Studies Association Impact Grant and governed by the University of Kent Research Ethics Policies and Practice framework. See further: Amanda Perry-Kessaris, Fiona Mullen and Meltem Onurkan Samani (2025) What if a citizens' assembly were to design a future Cyprus peace process?, *Global Social Challenges Journal, Early View*, DOI: 10.1332/27523349Y2025D000000061; and 'Figure It – Episode 17: Opening up Cyprob imaginations with an interspecies council'(Island Talks, Podcast, 18 February 2025) islandtalks.fm/podcast/ figure-it-episode-17-opening-up-cyprob-imaginations-with-an-interspecies-council-18-2-2025/.

CONCLUSION

Imagination is by no means the only thing required to promote epistemic justice. And designerly ways are by no means a panacea. For example, it is important to note that, for those who have historically been marginalised, being centred, 'being included', in a process designed by or in the image of a dominant group can be alienating and traumatic.[64] And design thinking and practice is itself, like law, pre-loaded with historical and contemporary biases such as ableism, sexism, and racism.[65]

To work for epistemic justice in the context of inter-communal division requires an enhanced capacity to (empathetically) imagine the other and (systemically) imagine how things might be otherwise. The example of the Roding River Inter-Species Council suggests that these capacities might be activated through carefully designed role-play experiences.

Whether the above speculations are credible is for the inhabitants of Cyprus to judge. Feedback from the 2024 workshop suggests that the answer is broadly yes. What is clear is that the island is home to a critical mass of activists and designers with the necessary drive and expertise to make this speculation a reality, should they so choose.[66]

REFERENCES

B Adam, 'Towards a Twenty-First Century Sociological Engagement with the Future' (2011) 4(11) *Insights, Institute of Advanced Study, Durham University* 6.

Adam K, *Transformative Scenario Planning* (San Francisco, Berrett-Koehler, 2021).

African Leadership Institute, 'SA 2020 Scenarios Project'.

S Ahmed, *On Being Included: Racism and Diversity in Institutional Life* (Durham, NC, Duke University Press, 2012).

Y Akama, S Pink and S Sumartojo, *Uncertainty and Possibility: New Approaches to Future Making in Design Anthropology* (London, Bloomsbury, 2018).

JE Arnold, in William J Clancey (ed), *Creative Engineering: Promoting Innovation by Thinking Differently* (Springer, 2016).

'Assembly Guide Overview' (English).

C Bason (ed), *Design for Policy* (London, Routledge, 2014).

[64] See, eg, Sara Ahmed, *On Being Included: Racism and Diversity in Institutional Life* (Durham, NC, Duke University Press, 2012); Irene Watson, 'Buried Alive' (2002) 13(3) *Law and Critique* 253.

[65] Ruben Pater, *The Politics of Design: A (Not So) Global Manual for Visual Communication* (Amsterdam, BIS, 2016); Caroline Criado Perez, *Invisible Women: Data Bias in a World Designed for Men* (London, Vintage Books, 2021); Bennett and Rosner 'The promise of empathy: Design, disability and knowing the "other"' in *Proceedings of CHI '19: CHI Conference on Human Factors in Computing Systems, May 04, 2019, Glasgow, Scotland UK. ACM, New York, NY, USA.* Arturo Escobar, *Designs for the Pluriverse* (Durham, NC, Duke University Press, 2017).

[66] Amanda Perry-Kessaris, 'Could Alternative Econo-Legal Futures Be Made More Possible and Probable Through Prefigurative Design? Insights from and for Cyprus' (2022) 72(4) *Northern Ireland Legal Quarterly* 623.

L Beeckmans, 'Epistemic Justice in the Design Process' (2021) *ARCHINED*, no. 16/12/2021, 22–28.

Bennett and Rosner 'The promise of empathy: Design, disability and knowing the "other"' in *Proceedings of CHI '19: CHI Conference on Human Factors in Computing Systems, May 04, 2019, Glasgow, Scotland UK* (ACM, New York, NY, USA).

MF Byskov, 'What Makes Epistemic Injustice an Injustice' (2020) 52(1) *Journal of Social Philosophy* 116.

Cassie Robinson, 'Change Happens If Our Collective Imagination Changes' (*Medium*, 9 January 2022).

——, 'Emerging Futures: Patterning the Third Horizon' (The Conference 2023, 22 September 2023).

D Chachra, I Johar and A Jain, 'What Is Infrastructuring? And What Is Imagination Infrastructuring?' (Imagination Infrastructuring, Notion, 10 June 2021).

Conseil Économique, Social et Environnemental, 'Convention Citoyenne sur la Fin de Vie'.

CM Constantinou and E Eftychiou, *The Cyprus Buffer Zone as a Socio-Ecological Landscape Case Study* (Tokyo, Satoyama Initiative, 2014).

D Cooper, 'Crafting Prefigurative Law in Turbulent Times: Decertification, DIY Law Reform, and the Dilemmas of Feminist Prototyping' (2023) 31 *Feminist Legal Studies* 17.

RMB Cotterrell, *Sociological Jurisprudence: Juristic Thought and Social Inquiry* (New York, Routledge, 2018).

N Curato and S Calamba, 'Deliberative Forums in Fragile Contexts- Challenges from the Field' (2024) *Politics* 1.

N Curato, D Farrell, B Geißel, K Grönlund, P Mockler, J Pilet, A Renwick, J Rose, MSetälä, J Suiter, *Deliberative Mini-Publics: Core Design Features* (Bristol, Bristol University Press, 2021).

Cyprus Chambers of Commerce and Industry and Turkish Cypriot Chamber of Commerce (CCCI/KKTO), 'The Nine-O'Clock News in the Year 2030' (YouTube, 2011).

Cyprus Futures, *Possible Futures of Cyprus: Scenarios Report* (Cyprus Futures 2023).

M Davies, *Law Unlimited: Materialism, Pluralism and Legal Theory* (New York, Routledge, 2017).

DemocracyNext 'Assembling an Assembly: A How-To Guide' (2023).

DemocracyNext (Website).

S Dieleman, 'Epistemic Justice and Democratic Legitimacy' (2015) 30(4) *Hypatia* 795.

A Escobar, *Designs for the Pluriverse* (Durham, NC, Duke University Press, 2017).

S Exley, 'Open Policy Making in the UK: To Whom Might Policy Formulation Be Opening Up' (2021) 50(3) *Journal of Social Policy* 451–469.

M Fricker, *Epistemic Injustice: Power and the Ethics of Knowing* (Oxford, Oxford University Press, 2007).

Gov.uk, 'Policy Profession Standards' (10 November 2021).

IDEO, *The Field Guide to Human-Centered Design* (IDEO 2015).

Island Talks, 'Nicosia Uncut – Episode 53: Special Guest Fiona Mullen: How Can We Revitalize the Solution Process?' (Podcast, 6 March 2024).

Kahane A, *Transformative Scenario Planning* (Berrett-Koehler 2021).

J Ker-Lindsay, *The Cyprus Problem: What Everyone Needs to Know* (Oxford, Oxford University Press, 2011).
IJ Kidd, J Medina and G Pohlhaus (eds), *The Routledge Handbook of Epistemic Injustice* (London, Routledge, 2017).
L Kimbell and J Bailey, 'Prototyping and the New Spirit of Policymaking' (2017) 13(3) *CoDesign* 214.
L Kimbell, C Durose, R Mazé and L Richardson, *Design and Policy: Current Debates and Future Directions for Research in the UK. Report of the AHRC Design|Policy Research Network* (London, University of the Arts London, 2023).
H Landemore, *Open Democracy: Reinventing Popular Rule for the Twenty-First Century* (Princeton, Princeton University Press, 2020).
MADD LBP, *How to Run a Civic Lottery: A Guide and License* (2017) MANIFEST: Artists, Policy and the Process of Making Change – Policy Lab' (26 March 2024).
G McKeever and others, *Using Human-Centred Design to Develop Empathy and Supports for Litigants in Person* (Belfast, Ulster University, 2023).
S McKeown and C Psaltis, 'Intergroup Contact and the Mediating Role of Intergroup Trust on Outgroup Evaluation and Future Contact Intentions in Cyprus and Northern Ireland' (2017) 23(4) *Peace and Conflict: Journal of Peace Psychology* 392.
DH Meadows, in Diana Wright (ed), *Systems Thinking. A Primer* (Vermont, Chelsea Green Publishing, 2008).
Moral Imaginations (Website).
F Mullen, 'Deliberative Democracy: Only Way Out of the Cyprus Problem?' *Financial Mirror* (8 January 2024).
——, 'Steps to a New Cyprus Problem Process' *Financial Mirror* (25 February 2024).
M Hatay, F Mullen and J Kalimeri, *The Day After I: Commercial Opportunities Following a Solution to the Cyprus Problem* (PRIO Centre Cyprus, 2008).
G Mulgan, *Big Mind: How Collective Intelligence Can Change Our World* (Princeton, Princeton University Press, 2017).
L Muradova (2021) Seeing the other side? Perspective-taking and reflective political judgements in interpersonal deliberation. 69(3) *Political Studies*, 644–664.
L Muradova and K Arceneaux (2022) 'Reflective political reasoning: Political disagreement and empathy' 61 *European Journal of Political Research* 740–761.
L Muradova (2025). Empathy and Political Reasoning: How Empathy Promotes Reflection and Strengthens Democracy (Cambridge, Cambridge University Press, 2025.
Y Navaro-Yashin, *The Make-Believe Space: Affective Geography in a Postwar Polity* (Durham, NC, Duke University Press, 2012).
Nesta, *Collective Intelligence Design Playbook* (2020).
newDemocracy Foundation and UN Democracy Fund, *Enabling National Initiatives to Take Democracy Beyond Elections* (2019).
OECD, *Innovative Citizen Participation and New Democratic Institutions Catching the Deliberative Wave* (OECD, 2020).
R Pater, *The Politics of Design: A (Not So) Global Manual for Visual Communication* (Amsterdam, BIS, 2016).
A Perry-Kessaris, 'Legal Design for Practice, Activism, Policy and Research' (2019) 46(2) *Journal of Law and Society* 185.
——, 'Doing Sociolegal Research in Design Mode' (London, Routledge, 2021).

——, 'Legal Design Could and Should Be More Sociolegal' in Dan Lockton, Sara Lenzi, Arlene Oak, Paul Hekkert, Juan Sádaba and Peter Lloyd (eds), *DRS2022: Bilbao, 25 June–3 July, Bilbao, Spain* (DRS, 2022).

——, 'Could Alternative Econo-Legal Futures Be Made More Possible and Probable Through Prefigurative Design? Insights From and For Cyprus' (2022) 72(4) *Northern Ireland Legal Quarterly* 623.

Perry-Kessaris, A., Mullen, F. and Samani, M.O. (2025) What if a citizens' assembly were to design a future Cyprus peace process?, *Global Social Challenges Journal*, Early View, DOI: 10.1332/27523349Y2025D000000061.

Policy Lab Blog, 'Launching Our Experimental Policy Design Methods' (18 May 2022).

——, 'Using Experimental Methods to Reimagine Decision-Making for the Freshwater System, Post 2043 –' (7 February 2024).

——, 'MANIFEST: Artists, Policy and the Process of Making Change – Policy Lab' (26 March 2024).

Policy Lab, 'River Roding Interspecies Council: Video' (Vimeo, 2023).

CC Perez, *Invisible Women: Data Bias in a World Designed for Men* (London, Vintage Books, 2021).

SCORE, *Predicting Peace Predicting Peace: The Social Cohesion and Reconciliation Index as a Tool for Conflict Transformation* (UNDP 2015).

J Seed, J Macy, P Fleming and A Naess, *Thinking Like a Mountain: Towards a Council of All Beings* (Gabriola Island, BC, New Society Publishers, 1988).

E Smeds and E Verlinghieri (eds), 'Seeing Like a Citizen: Rethinking City Street Transformations Through the Lens of Epistemic Justice' (2023) 24(5) *Planning Theory & Practice* 697.

The Treaty of Finsbury Park 2025 project.

Tionól Sauránach A (Citizens' Assembly, Republic of Ireland).

UN Cyprus Talks Website.

Ulster University, *Using Human-Centred Design to Develop Empathy and Supports for Litigants in Person* (2023)

Unite Cyprus Now, 'International Community Should Stop Playing with Our Lives' (Press Release, 30 April 2021).

A Vigdor Gordon, 'Limits and Longevity: A Model for Scenarios That Influence the Future' (2020) 151 *Technological Forecasting and Social Change* 119851.

JP Voß and N Amelung, 'Innovating Public Participation Methods: Technoscientization and Reflexive Engagement' (2016) 46(5) *Social Studies of Science* 749.

R Waller and others 'Cooperation Through Clarity: Designing Simplified Contracts' (2016) 21(1–2) *Journal of Strategic Contracting and Negotiation* 48.

I Watson, 'Buried Alive' (2002) 13(3) *Law and Critique* 253.

K Yusoff, 'The Inhumanities' (2021) 111(3) *Annals of the American Association of Geographers* 663.

11

Legal Design as Movement Lawyering Methodology: Lessons Learned at the New Jersey Legal Design Lab

ABDUL REHMAN KHAN[1] AND HALLIE JAY POPE[2]

INTRODUCTION

LEGAL DESIGN OFFERS a lens through which we can explore, critique, and reimagine more meaningful democracy, solidarity, and liberation. The New Jersey Legal Design Lab, an initiative of the Housing Justice Project at Seton Hall Law School's Center for Social Justice, is committed to fostering creative, collaborative, and community-driven approaches to local housing justice issues.[3]

Part I of this paper critiques the role of democratic participation within and beyond the legal profession, examining how legal design can lead to more inclusive processes. Part II investigates the roots of liberatory legal design, drawing on radical traditions of collective and creative sense-making that aim to foster self-determination in the grip of oppressive systems. We apply these lessons to our ongoing efforts at the Lab.

By co-creating solutions with our neighbours, we seek to dismantle unjust systems and ensure housing for all. This paper highlights the dual imperatives of participatory design and movement lawyering, demonstrating how they converge to form a tool for societal change.

DEMOCRACY, HOUSING, AND MOVEMENT LAWYERING

Exploring Democratic Participation

For framers of the American Constitution, their struggle against despotism yielded a liberal democracy characterised by a deeply embedded mistrust in

[1] Assistant Clinical Professor, Seton Hall Law School.
[2] Director, NJ Legal Design Lab, Seton Hall Law School.
[3] Seton Hall University, 'New Jersey Legal Design Lab' (2024) law.shu.edu/clinics/new-jersey-legal-design-lab.html.

the general populace's decision-making capabilities.[4] Despite their impressive education, the framers' conception of liberty was fundamentally predicated on human slavery.[5] These extreme binaries, based on control, continue to permeate every aspect of American life.[6] In particular, this paradigm has a significant influence in social research and design.[7]

This is the inherent conflict within the roots of American democracy: while it professes to champion equality and fairness, it is historically grounded in practices that systematically deny many the right to fully participate. In an attempt to address such biases, a Rawlsian 'Veil of Ignorance' framework requires theoretical participants to design society without knowledge of their future roles or capabilities.[8] This approach seeks to foster a fairer system. It, however, raises a pertinent question: How can individuals, unaware of various lived experiences, effectively design systems that fairly serve everyone? Often, our anticipations of social issues remain merely speculative.[9]

Moving from the ideals of the 'Veil of Ignorance' to the realities of societal design presents challenges. Transitioning from theory to practice requires us to rethink how we formulate questions to ensure they are grounded in reality and inclusive. Traditionally, social and political agendas have been set by those with systemic authority, who often overlook the nuanced and real needs of diverse communities.[10] This process has been dominated by institutional researchers.[11] In contrast, sourcing design questions directly from community input not only shifts focus but also ensures that transformative endeavors are relevant.[12] This paradigm shift is embodied in methodologies such as co-design, Participatory Action Research, and participatory design.[13] These methodologies promote democratic participation and, at their best, co-create knowledge by integrating

[4] Alexander Hamilton, James Madison and John Jay, in Clinton Rossiter (ed), *The Federalist Papers* (London, Penguin, 1961) Nos 10 and 51. See also Gordon S Wood, *The Creation of the American Republic, 1776–1787* (Chapel Hill, UNC Press, 1969).

[5] ibid.

[6] Richard Hofstadter, 'The Paranoid Style in American Politics' in *The Paranoid Style in American Politics and Other Essays* (New York, Alfred A Knopf, 1965) 4–5.

[7] Gordon S Wood, *The Radicalism of the American Revolution* (New York, Random House, 1992).

[8] John Rawls, *A Theory of Justice* (Cambridge, MA, Harvard University Press, 1971).

[9] Even the 'case and controversy' requirement in the United States Constitution restricts courts from speculative disputes. US Const art III, s 2.

[10] See, eg, Linda Tuhiwai Smith, *Decolonizing Methodologies: Research and Indigenous Peoples* (3rd edn, London, Bloomsbury, 1999); Paulo Freire, *Pedagogy of the Oppressed* (4th edn, London, Bloomsbury, 2018); Caroline Criado Perez, *Invisible Women: Data Bias in a World Designed for Men* (New York, Abrams Press, 2019).

[11] See, eg, Shawn Wilson, *Research Is Ceremony: Indigenous Research Methods* (Halifax, Fernwood Publishing, 2008); Alice McIntyre, *Participatory Action Research* (Thousand Oaks, CA, SAGE, 2008).

[12] See, eg, Meredith Minkler and Nina Wallerstein (eds), *Community-Based Participatory Research for Health: From Process to Outcomes* (2nd edn, San Francisco, CA, Jossey-Bass, 2008); David E Gray, *Doing Research in the Real World* (3rd edn, London, SAGE, 2013).

[13] Douglas Schuler and Aki Namioka (eds), *Participatory Design: Principles and Practices* (New York, Routledge, 1993).

cultural, political, and historical contexts into the design process.[14] They aim to dismantle traditional hierarchies between professionals and participants, creating a more equitable environment where knowledge flows mutually and multi-directionally.[15]

Sociologist Michael McQuarrie highlights an issue in participatory research: despite its theoretical appeal based on democratic involvement, community-based organisations may engage in participatory research more to secure organisational survival than to genuinely empower communities.[16] This issue is indicative of the broader challenges within the non-profit industrial complex,[17] which, when confronted with practical realities, can unintentionally legitimise the very power structures it seeks to dismantle.[18] This often leads to a perverse effect where efforts to achieve social progress inadvertently mask further exploitation, a scenario described as 'false consciousness'.[19] Overcoming false consciousness requires an ethos of true collaboration.[20] Barriers to true collaboration include hierarchical structures, ingrained biases, and power dynamics that hinder open and equitable dialogue between organisations and the communities they serve, as well as the pressure to secure funding that prioritises measurable outcomes over genuine empowerment.

In the context of knowledge production, like design research, this reorientation of power plays out as challenges to traditional frameworks of authority and governance. Legal designers, lawyers, researchers, and specialised professionals who receive institutional support must critically examine the 'fourth wall' of research – the implicit barrier that maintains the dichotomy between communities and researchers.[21] Rethinking this relationship allows communities to organically set their own research agendas, which is particularly vital for post-colonial practitioners striving to dissolve the stark binaries between researchers and communities.[22] This reorientation necessitates a thorough examination of what it means to ensure that legal designers truly enhance, rather than inhibit, the ability of communities to navigate and influence the issues that impact

[14] ibid.

[15] Jo Aldridge, *Participatory Research: Working with Vulnerable Groups in Research and Practice* (Bristol, Policy Press, 2015).

[16] Michael McQuarrie, 'No Contest: Participatory Technologies and the Politics of the Public Sphere' (2013) 25(1) *Public Culture* 143.

[17] INCITE! Women of Color Against Violence (ed), *The Revolution Will Not Be Funded: Beyond the Non-Profit Industrial Complex* (Durham, NC, Duke University Press, 2007).

[18] Rahnema and Leal showed, in fact, that PAR was adopted by neoliberal developmentalists in major global economic organisations as a means of ensuring local consent to interventionist and sometimes exploitative projects. Danielle Lake and Joel Wendland, 'Practical, Epistemological, and Ethical Challenges of Participatory Action Research: A Cross-Disciplinary Review of the Literature' (2018) 22 *Journal of Higher Ed Outreach and Engagement* 11.

[19] Letter from Friedrich Engels to Franz Mehring (14 July 1983) www.marxists.org/archive/marx/works/1893/letters/93_07_14.htm.

[20] Freire (n 10).

[21] Sonia Nieto, *Qualitative Research: Challenging the Orthodoxies* (New York, Routledge, 2009).

[22] Smith (n 10).

them.[23] Alice G. Abreu, for example, emphasises the need for legal scholars to draw on Latinx Critical Legal Theory scholarship to move beyond simplistic binary paradigms, especially the outsider/insider dichotomy.[24] She argues that individuals can hold both outsider and insider positions simultaneously, and urges a move beyond paradigms that essentialise one aspect of identity.[25] This can lead to a deeper understanding of how all participants in a discourse of human control and exploitation are, to some extent, controlled and exploited themselves.[26]

Moving beyond entrenched paradigms in research, legal design, and broader transformative efforts not only challenges conventional power dynamics but also prompts a deeper examination of our engagement with participatory democracy. It explores the essence of participatory democracy, where self-determination extends beyond mere participation, enabling communities to actively set their own agendas. It attempts to shift the spectrum from communities as receivers of information to communities as owners of decision-making processes. In this phase, 'communities have a direct say over what is needed to survive and thrive'.[27] Such a shift towards authentic community-driven decision-making challenges the foundations of traditional political systems, where decisions, though often labelled 'democratic', are frequently predetermined by a select few.[28]

Meaningful ownership over decision-making processes cannot be achieved if professionals set the initial agenda.[29] Participatory democracy, which seeks to 'democratise democracy'[30] by allowing citizens to directly participate in decisions without elected officials, encounters such challenges when those in power predetermine the substance and scope of the issues to be decided.[31]

To increase democracy, figures such as Aristotle, Plato, and Montesquieu have all advocated for sortition, a system that, much like jury duty, randomly

[23] Andrew H Van de Ven, *Engaged Scholarship: A Guide for Organizational and Social Research* (Oxford, Oxford University Press, 2007).

[24] Alice G Abreu, 'Lessons from LatCrit: Insiders and Outsiders, All at the Same Time' (1999) 53 *University of Miami Law Review* 787.

[25] ibid.

[26] Michel Foucault, 'Two Lectures' in Colin Gordon (ed), *Power/Knowledge: Selected Interviews and Other Writings, 1972–1977* (New York, Vintage, 1980) 78–108. This is evident in historical contexts such as the framers of the American Constitution, who, in seeking their own liberation, created a parasitic society dependent on the exploitation of its own mass. See, eg, Chris Hedges and Joe Sacco, *Days of Destruction, Days of Revolt* (New York, Bold Type Books, 2014).

[27] Movement Strategy Center, 'The Spectrum of Community Engagement to Ownership' movementstrategy.org/wp-content/uploads/2021/08/The-Spectrum-of-Community-Engagement-to-Ownership.pdf.

[28] Dimitrios Roussopoulos and C George Benello (eds), *Participatory Democracy: Prospects for Democratizing Democracy* (Montreal, Black Rose Books, 2004) 89–90.

[29] Patricia Maguire, *Doing Participatory Research: A Feminist Approach* (Amherst, MA, University of Massachusetts Amherst, 1987) 57–58.

[30] Carole Pateman, 'Participatory Democracy Revisited' (2012) 10(1) *Perspectives on Politics* 7.

[31] Marco Giugni, *Democracy and Participation: Popular Protest and New Social Movements* (Cambridge, Cambridge University Press, 2004) 142–43.

selects citizens to deliberate on public decisions.[32] Although sortition values the collective wisdom of the community and includes a broader cross-section of society in governance,[33] like participatory democracy, public issues are predetermined, raising again questions about community self-determination. It arrives too late in the decision-making process – after the framing of issues has already been established and does not address the foundational stage of problem construction.

Moreover, communities that have been stripped of meaningful agency due to power imbalances embedded in legal and social frameworks may lack the opportunity for full participation.[34] For individuals to engage genuinely in decision-making, it is essential to address the foundational conditions necessary for decolonisation and to acknowledge how and why their agency was undermined.[35] A community stripped of its collective wisdom might find itself perpetuating the tyranny it was subjected to, rather than fostering genuine self-determination.[36] The capacity of a community to shape its destiny is dependent on its ongoing process of decolonisation. Without addressing these foundational issues, efforts to increase participation may merely reinforce existing power structures.[37] In addition, the success of these efforts also depends on the time, bandwidth, and resources that communities can dedicate to addressing issues beyond mere survival.[38]

Nowhere is the challenge of addressing these principles of self-determination more evident than in the housing sector, where the struggle for control over one's living conditions directly impacts broader efforts for community autonomy. Housing becomes a battleground where the intersection of legal frameworks and power dynamics is starkly evident.

Property and Power

In the area of evictions, the severe consequences for tenants and society at large are extensively documented.[39] Indeed, there is a push to shift away from

[32] See also Amanda Perry-Kessaris, 'Activating Imagination to Promote Epistemic Justice', chapter 10 in this volume.

[33] Modern democratic republics, where people effectively hand off agency to those limited representatives exercising expenditures of time and resources not typically available to the masses, are far more susceptible to oligarchic influence. Bernard Manin, *The Principles of Representative Government* (Cambridge, Cambridge University Press, 1997).

[34] Smith (n 10) ch 2, 20–21; Freire (n 10).

[35] ibid.

[36] ibid.

[37] Scott G Chaplowe and J Bradley Cousins, *Community Capacity Building: Creating a Better Future Together* (Thousand Oaks CA, SAGE, 2016).

[38] ibid.

[39] Matthew Desmond, *Evicted: Poverty and Profit in the American City* (New York, Crown, 2017) 104–105. Compared to other industrial nations, American evictions often lack consideration

repeatedly detailing the brutality of evictions to prevent their normalisation.[40] However, the solutions that policymakers and institutional researchers propose and our capacity for radical ideas seem insufficient compared to the scale of the problem.[41] For example, many tenant services-based organisations primarily focus on securing legal representation for the vast number of tenants navigating eviction courts.[42] Incidentally, this approach typically aligns with increased resources for those same tenant services-based organisations.

Although a right to counsel in eviction proceedings is a significant step forward, housing injustice extends beyond the need for legal representation at eviction trials and touches on broader issues of housing instability.[43] The movement for housing equity clearly advocates for much more than merely the right to counsel in eviction proceedings.[44] Tenants require more than just a halt to evictions; they seek healthy living conditions with strong protections that prioritise human dignity over property rights, and they want a say in what that looks like.[45] Grassroots groups and community activists are supporting community-driven models such as tenant unions, cooperative housing, and mass rent cancellations (see part 1A Michael McQuarrie above).[46] If people were meaningfully involved in decisions that impact them, we could achieve radical change.[47] Instead, the agenda is typically set by a few with institutional authority who are secure in their own housing, leading to a narrow focus that treats the symptoms of racial capitalism manifest in housing.[48]

Andrew Scherer notes that in the late eighteenth century, 'White male property owners – the only people permitted to vote or hold office at the time – originally devised summary eviction proceedings to serve their own purposes,

for several critical factors; these include the presence of children, who are the most evicted demographic, the amounts owed, whether alternative housing has been secured, whether meaningful attempts at payment plans have been made, the duration of residence, and any other dimensions that contribute to the dignity of someone's home. See Andrew Scherer, 'The Case Against Summary Eviction Proceedings: Process as Racism and Oppression' (2022) 53(1) *Seton Hall Law Review*.

[40] See, eg, Matthew B Robinson, *Media Coverage of Crime and Criminal Justice* (2nd edn, Durham, NC, Carolina Academic Press, 2011) ch 7, 142–143.

[41] David J Erickson, *Housing Policy Revolution: Networks and Neighborhoods* (Lanham, MD, Rowman and Littlefield Pubs, 2009).

[42] Desmond (n 39).

[43] ibid.

[44] Rachel G Bratt, Michael E Stone and Chester Hartman (eds), *A Right to Housing: Foundation for a New Social Agenda* (Philadelphia, Temple University Press, 2006) 55–57.

[45] ibid.

[46] 'The overwhelming majority of New York City-based non-profit legal organizations did not come out in support of the demand to cancel rent'. Marika Dias, 'Paradox and Possibility: Movement Lawyering During the COVID-19 Housing Crisis COVID-19 Housing Crisis' (2021) 20 *CUNY Law Review* 173, 197.

[47] See, eg, bell hooks, *Outlaw Culture: Resisting Representations* (New York, Routledge, 1994) 105–107.

[48] Keeanga-Yamahtta Taylor, *Race for Profit: How Banks and the Real Estate Industry Undermined Black Homeownership* (Chapel Hill, University of North Carolina Press, 2019) 105–107.

to provide themselves the wherewithal to conquer, to vanquish – to evict – their tenants'.[49] Scherer reminds us that when those in power design systems, they are likely to craft them in ways that reinforce their own dominance, especially if they can only envision themselves on one side of a dispute.[50] This results in eviction courts presenting the choice as a zero-sum game:[51] to evict or not to evict. When rental arrears are involved, it results in a Hobson's choice – where the court primarily serves to execute the will of the petitioning landlord.[52]

The primary aim of property owners is not to provide housing but to derive profit. Property owners designed our legal system. Therefore, the design of eviction courts – and indeed, our legal system more broadly – prioritises financial interests over housing. Even after housing courts significantly expanded their jurisdiction more than half a century ago to include the implied warranty of habitability – a duty imposed on landlords to maintain safe and decent rental units – Nicole Summers found that 'approximately 73 percent of [New York City] tenants who had meritorious [habitability] claims and were represented by counsel still did not benefit from the law'.[53] In other words, the repairs necessary to bring their unsafe living conditions up to code were not made. By and large, it is a court that serves a single function: acting on behalf of landlords. This is why it is crucial to look beyond the courtroom. Tenant-led movements are already

[49] Scherer (n 39).

[50] 'When the people who have the power to design the system also have a dominant power relationship with the people most likely to be their adversaries and can only envision themselves on one side of a potential dispute, it stands to reason they will design a system that reinforces that dominance'. ibid. Scherer, aptly employing the word 'designed' dozens of times in his art, poses key questions:

> Is it any wonder, then, that the process to evict tenants was designed to serve the interests of the men who had exclusive control over the formulation of laws? Is it any wonder that the process was designed to achieve a specific remedy – eviction – and not, as with other civil litigation, to serve the orderly resolution of conflicts between presumed equals? ibid 50.

He contrasts this with other types of litigation, stating, 'Other than summary eviction proceedings, it is hard to imagine any form of litigation designed to give the instigator of the litigation the result sought, rather than designed to arrive at a just resolution. A contract dispute? A property dispute between abutting property owners? A marital dispute?' ibid.

[51] Housing is far from a zero-sum game, where one party's gain is exactly balanced by another's loss. In evictions, the broader implications include homelessness, increased demand on social services, and other societal costs that aren't accounted for just by the landlord gaining back their property or the tenant retaining their housing. Stout, 'Right to Counsel: The Nationwide Movement to Fight the Eviction Crisis' (2019) www.stout.com/en/insights/article/right-to-counsel-nationwide-movement-fight-eviction-crisis#whyarighttocounsel ('While the rate and vol of evictions varies by locality, the potential negative effects on evicted tenants are consistent, such as homelessness, unemployment, loss of child custody, and disruption to child education'.).

[52] ibid. By contrast, eg, in pre-modern Islamic societies, the concern in legal disputes was less about abstracted legal theory and more about maintaining social peace. This was done by avoiding zero sum situations. Wael B Hallaq, *An Introduction to Islamic Law* (Cambridge, Cambridge University Press, 2009) 57–60. Indeed, as al-Ghazali notes, the objective of economies is to balance providing for one's family and providing for those in need. Abdul Azim Islahi and Shaikh Mohammad Ghazanfar, *Economic Thought of Al-Ghazali* (Jeddah, King Abdulaziz University, 1998).

[53] Nicole Summers, 'The Limits of Good Law: A Study of Housing Court Outcomes' (2020) 87 *University of Chicago Law Review* 145, 214.

doing this, and legal designers must also expand their focus outside traditional legal frameworks.

The American legal system not only maintains housing instability but also overwhelms tenants, shifting their focus away from the underlying power dynamics that perpetuate their precarious situations.[54] This critique introduces the principles embodied by movement lawyering, an approach that emphasises aligning legal strategies with broader social movements.

Legal Design as a Method for Movement Lawyering

Communities under oppression can utilise a combination of direct legal strategy with broader social and economic strategies. These strategies not only aim to mitigate the immediate effects of injustice but also challenge the systems that perpetuate such conditions. They advocate for a reimagining of societal norms and legal frameworks.

Direct legal representation can be effective as long as it is contextualised within broader struggles. In the context of American slavery, Professor Daniel Farbman notes how abolitionist lawyers used the courtroom as a public stage, challenging the legality and morality of slavery.[55] These 'resistance lawyers' engaged in regular, direct service within a legal system they considered unjust and illegitimate, aiming to mitigate its worst effects while also working to resist, obstruct, and dismantle the system itself.[56] Abolitionist lawyers also educated communities to encourage more active participation in resistance against slavery, transforming their legal practice into a powerful tool for broader social change.[57] By purposefully delaying proceedings and exploiting every available legal loophole, these lawyers created time and space for abolitionist organisers to strategise and garner public support.[58] Eloise Lawrence illustrates how legal strategies that may seem purely defensive or reactionary – such as delaying eviction proceedings – are, in fact, part of a larger strategy to create space for community organising.[59]

Marika Dias reminds us that '[g]rappling with power, whether one is fighting against it or trying to build it, almost always involves encounters with the legal system', which she describes as '[t]he very powerful glue that holds together our many intersecting systems of oppression'.[60] Lawyers are pushed to transcend

[54] Richard Rothstein, *The Color of Law: A Forgotten History of How Our Government Segregated America* (New York, Liveright, 2017) 180–182.
[55] Daniel Farbman, 'Resistance Lawyering' (2019) 107 *California Law Review* 1877.
[56] ibid.
[57] Farbman (n 55).
[58] These lawyers also helped to shift public opinion by taking on high-profile cases and using the courtroom as a platform to highlight the brutal realities of slavery. ibid.
[59] Eloise Lawrence, 'When We Fight, We Win: Eviction Defense as Subversive Lawyering' (2022) 90 *Fordham Law Journal* 2125.
[60] Dias (n 46) 176.

traditional roles like 'advocate' or 'investigator' to become 'agents of social change' and 'mediums for greater democratic participation'.[61] As a result, the legal system becomes not just a backdrop, but a primary site 'itself [] of contestation and class struggle'.[62]

The Movement Law Lab defines movement lawyering as 'work[ing] in deep collaboration with social movements, leveraging every legal hook possible to build the collective power needed to transform our political and economic systems towards human dignity, multiracial democracy, and ecological harmony'.[63] Scott Cummings writes:

> [P]rogressive scholars have produced a rich new literature that places social movements at the center of legal and political transformation, pushing aside a focus on courts and lawyers that has long dominated scholarly analysis. ... By supporting and advancing the building and exercise of collective power, led by the most directly impacted, movement lawyering can contribute to systemic institutional and cultural change.[64]

The aim of movement lawyering is to have legal strategies fully aligned with the broader movement goals.[65] This requires ongoing communication and coordination with movement participants, community members, and organisers.[66]

The goal, in a sense, is to 'counteract the otherwise individualizing, disempowering, depoliticizing impacts of encounters with the law'.[67] Purvi Shah, Scott Cummings, and Gerald López, noted scholars in movement lawyering, articulate that lawyering itself must be a collaborative effort with communities.[68] They advocate for a model of lawyering that deeply engages with a community's experiences, needs, and objectives.

[61] Carrie Menkel-Meadow, 'The Legacy of Clinical Education: Theories about Lawyering' (1980) 29 *Cleveland State Law Review* 555.

[62] ibid.

[63] Movement Law Lab, 'About Movement Lawyering' www.movementlawlab.org/about/movement-lawyering#:~:text=Movement%20lawyers%20work%20in%20deep,multiracial%20democracy%2C%20and%20ecological%20harmony. First, movement lawyers may consider strategic litigation, including legal support for direct actions, protest observation, arrest defence, and rights training. Litigation strategy may involve challenging unjust laws and practices through precedent-setting court cases. Second, movement lawyers may explore transactional elements, including developing legal structures that support the sustainability and economic independence of the movement, such as food and worker cooperatives, as well as community land trusts. See, eg, John Emmeus Davis, Line Algoed and María E Hernández-Torrales (eds), *On Common Ground: International Perspectives on the Community Land Trust* (Amherst, MA, Terra Nostra Press, 2020). Last but not least, movement lawyers may deliver information, products, and services that catalyse the work of organizers and those who are primarily impacted by an issue. See, eg, Sasha Costanza-Chock, *Design Justice: Community-Led Practices to Build the Worlds We Need* (Cambridge, MA, MIT Press, 2020) 89–91.

[64] Scott L Cummings, 'Movement Lawyering' (2020) 27 *Indiana Journal of Global Legal Studies* 87.

[65] ibid.

[66] ibid; see also Dias (n 46).

[67] Dias (n 46) 176.

[68] Purvi Shah, 'Rebuilding the Ethical Compass of Law' (2018) 47 *Hofstra Law Review* 11; Cummings (n 64); George P López, *Rebellious Lawyering: One Chicano's Vision of Progressive Legal Practice* (Boulder, CO, Westview Press, 1992).

Compared to the robust literature on models of movement lawyering, its theoretical foundations, intersectionality, post-coloniality, and case studies, there is less scholarship on the methodological 'how' as opposed to the theoretical 'why'.[69] 'Movement Law', Amna Akbar, Sameer Ashar, and Jocelyn Simonson, is one attempt at providing a methodological focus.[70] They write: 'Our posture should not be to dismiss and relegitimate, but to listen and consider, learn, participate, and cogenerate'.[71] They highlight the lack of methodological focus in movement lawyering.[72] While movement lawyering considers the relationship between lawyers and social change, it does not provide a methodology of collaboration unto itself.[73] Contemporary movements, by contrast, employ a sophisticated array of method-based strategies in collective action, including intra-movement dissent and temporality.[74] There ought to be a method to the movement lawyers' madness too. Otherwise, as noted above, we risk perpetuating the inequalities we aim to abolish.

We cannot simply rely upon our own 'reflexivity' as a methodology.[75] Engaging in self-reflexivity requires a developed sense of mindfulness that must be cultivated over time, rather than something most of us naturally possess. Even if we did have the capacity to engage in constant self-reflexivity in 'identity, experiences, and positionality [and how it] contribute[s] to systems of power and oppression', it would not be sufficient.[76] Our peers have elucidated how law school pedagogy creates a perverse "professionalisation" effect that eventually limits law students' ability to conceptualise pathways to broad social progress.[77] The legal profession promotes risk-aversion, which often runs counter to the objectives of social movements and reinforces the belief that laws uphold civil society.[78] Law students yearn for a savior-oriented, mission-driven purpose while they deconstruct their own Atticus Finch dreams.[79] Bearing all this in mind, we

[69] Purvi Shah, 'Movement Lawyering Reading Guide' (2018) 47 *Hofstra Law Review* 99.

[70] Amna Akbar, Sameer Ashar and Jocelyn Simonson, 'Movement Law' (2021) 73 *Stanford Law Review* 821.

[71] ibid.

[72] ibid.

[73] See, eg, Cummings (n 64).

[74] Susan Carle and Scott L Cummings, 'A Reflection on the Ethics of Movement Lawyering' (2018) 31 *Georgetown Journal of Legal Ethics* 447.

[75] Lake and Wendland (n 18) 12 ('We suggest, for instance, that community-engaged scholars pursue more transparent and self-reflexive methods of engagement around the risks and challenges of this work ….'); Akbar, Ashar and Simonson (n 70) 830 ('While these risks are real, we believe scholars can overcome them with vigilance and reflexivity, and that movement law is a necessary form of legal epistemology in our current crisis'.).

[76] ibid.

[77] Menkel-Meadow (n 61).

[78] Anthony T Kronman, *The Lost Lawyer: Failing Ideals of the Legal Profession* (Cambridge, MA, Belknap Press, 1995) 210–212.

[79] Katie Rose Guest Pryal, 'American lawyers have an Atticus Finch complex, and it's killing the profession' *Quartz* (31 March 2016) qz.com/651270/the-american-legal-system-has-an-atticus-finch-complex-and-its-killing-the-profession.

need to be equipped with more than just our instincts. Our training and context as lawyers provide instincts that are contrary to movement lawyering. Even if we are able to critically examine those instincts within ourselves, that self-reflection alone will not suffice. It might reorient our values, but still may not provide us with the methods or tools necessary for effective movement lawyering. In short, a rigorous and transparent methodology of movement lawyering is required, which safeguards against our biases and instincts.[80]

While not inherently transformative, legal design has the potential to guide practitioners on how to shift power into local movements effectively, not merely relying on our reflexivity but instead building upon it.[81] Movement lawyers all agree that working people are the engines of social change, and our efforts should contribute to that collective capacity for transformation.[82] Co-creating understanding leads to solutions that are not only more relevant and grounded but also more just because of how they are produced.

The second half of this paper will examine legal design's roots as a flexible methodology for learning, engaging, and co-creating with social movements. This approach aims to reveal and engage with our biases and instincts, ensuring that movement lawyering not only challenges but transforms the systems of power and oppression we aim to dismantle.

LEARNING FROM LEGAL DESIGN'S HISTORICAL ROOTS

In Part I, we explored *why* lawyers, designers, researchers, and others with institutional power must shift that power to communities and movements in ways that value self-determination, dignity, and participatory democracy. But *how* might we do this, beyond self-reflection? Our work at the NJ Legal Design Lab hinges on the belief that we can employ 'designerly ways'[83] to implement movement lawyering principles and dismantle socio-legal systems of oppression. We have called this kind of design endeavour 'liberatory legal design'.[84] Liberatory legal design is aimed at 'designing to dismantle, in contrast to designing to reform, existing systems' of subordination, and in their place creating 'systems that cultivate and sustain our liberation'.[85]

[80] See, eg, Smith (n 10).

[81] See Joaquín Santuber and Siddharth Peter De Souza 'From Legal Design to Legal Designing', in this volume. Hallie Jay Pope, 'Designing to Dismantle' in Emily Allbon and Amanda Perry-Kessaris (eds), *Design in Legal Education* (London, Routledge, 2022). Alinsky's first rule in *Rules for Radicals* is 'Power is not only what you have but what the enemy thinks you have'. Saul Alinsky, *Rules for Radicals: A Pragmatic Primer for Realistic Radicals* (New York, Vintage, 1989).

[82] Austin Sarat and Stuart Scheingold (eds), *Cause Lawyers and Social Movements* (Stanford, CA, Stanford University Press, 2006) 123–125.

[83] Perry-Kessaris (n 32).

[84] See Hallie Jay Pope, 'Liberatory legal design and radical imagination' in Paul Hekkert et al (eds), *DRS2022: Bilbao* (Bilbao, Design Research Society, 2022).

[85] Pope (n 81) 4.

Liberatory legal design borrows from and de/reconstructs methods of human-centred design that currently dominate our field, particularly the 'double-diamond' process of engaging in collaborative, iterative cycles of convergent and divergent thinking. While such methodology offers a 'promising jumping-off point' for using designerly ways to dismantle unjust systems, it will more easily perpetuate the status quo than disrupt it if applied uncritically.[86] We have previously identified a few key ways to co-opt dominant design methods in the service of more radical ends, including: (1) constructing design problems in solidarity with broader movements, (2) using power and standpoint analysis to inform different approaches to different stakeholders (rather than remaining neutral among stakeholder viewpoints), and (3) deliberately amplifying counternarratives.[87] Now, we seek to build upon these strategies by engaging more deeply with related frameworks and traditions, in the hopes of further establishing liberatory legal design as a methodology for movement lawyering.

Liberatory legal design is developing alongside other critical, collaborative, and transformative frameworks within and across our parent fields of law, education, and design. These include Design Justice,[88] Participatory Law Scholarship (PLS),[89] Movement Law,[90] and the NuLawLab's spatial justice work.[91] It will be well worthwhile to explore the many overlaps and divergences between these emerging frameworks, and the authors hope to do so in future writings. But we believe we should start at the beginning, so to speak, by investigating our frameworks' shared roots.

Liberatory legal design and its contemporaneous sister frameworks draw from a rich ecosystem of radical sense-making and co-creation traditions. The rest of this part will explore two of these shared roots: liberatory education, as articulated and practiced by bell hooks and by the Highlander Folk School; and Scandinavian Participatory Design (PD), as implemented to promote workplace democracy in the 1960s and 70s. While neither of these traditions use the term 'legal design' to describe their work, both of them are concerned with transforming the socio-legal status quo through creative, participatory sense-making and decision-making. Both offer practical, historical insights into how we might combine law, design, and education for liberatory ends.

We draw four broad lessons from these two traditions: (1) that we must resist a dichotomy between theory and praxis, treating classroom as community and

[86] Pope (n 81). See also Perry-Kessaris (n 32) ('a user/human-centred approach is not only insufficient, but also potentially damaging, to the cause of promoting broader epistemic justice'.).

[87] Pope (n 81).

[88] Costanza-Chock (n 63).

[89] Rachel López, 'Participatory Law Scholarship' (2023) 123 *Columbia Law Review* 1795.

[90] Akbar and others (n 70).

[91] Sievert, 'Broadening the Scope of Legal Design', in this volume, chapter 2.

community as classroom; (2) that we must facilitate ways for people to experience, understand, and value their own agency to create conditions for meaningful democratic decision-making; (3) that we must intentionally embed our political values in our work; and (4) that joy and radical imagination are key ingredients for all liberatory endeavours. The rest of this part explores these lessons and describes and critiques our ongoing efforts to apply them to our legal design practice at the Lab.

Classroom as Community, Community as Classroom

In her book *Teaching to Transgress*, Black feminist scholar and teacher bell hooks reflects on education – both within and beyond the classroom – as a liberatory practice. In a series of essays, she articulates a feminist critical pedagogy through her personal experiences of teaching and learning. Growing up in Appalachia and attending an all-Black school, hooks experienced 'learning as revolution': she and her classmates learned from their Black teachers that their 'devotion to learning, to a life of the mind, was a counter-hegemonic act, a fundamental way to resist every strategy of white racist colonization'.[92] Only later, when schools underwent racial integration, did she experience education as domination and perpetuation of the status quo. hooks recalls that in her new educational setting,

> Knowledge was suddenly about information only. It had no relation to how one lived, behaved. It was no longer connected to antiracist struggle. Bussed to white schools, we soon learned that obedience, and not a zealous will to learn, was what was expected of us. Too much eagerness to learn could easily be seen as a threat to white authority.[93]

The combination of the theory and action – of knowledge and struggle – is ripe with liberatory potential. One of hooks's primary influences, educator and philosopher Paulo Freire, emphasises these two necessary and interdependent elements of transformation: *conscientização*, or conscientisation – the development of a critical and contextual understanding of oneself, others, and the world through reflection – and praxis, or action.[94] Only by both making sense of the systems around us *and* acting upon them with 'devotion to [continued] learning' can we change them.

Another Appalachian educator who was influenced by – and influenced – Freire was Tennessee native Myles Horton. Early in his career, Horton understood the importance of intertwining education and experience. As a young Bible school organiser in Ozone, Tennessee, Horton saw that the conventional

[92] bell hooks, *Teaching to Transgress* (New York, Routledge, 1994) 2.
[93] ibid 3.
[94] See Freire (n 10) ch 3.

church curriculum failed to connect with the lives and problems of the students and their families.[95] After his time in Ozone, Horton sought educational models rooted in local community life and aimed at social change, models that married theory and praxis. He found one such model in Danish folk schools, which writer and scholar Bishop N.F.S. Grundtvig had developed as a way to preserve Danish traditions and foster the conditions necessary for robust democratic participation.[96]

Grundtvigian theory emphasised several principles that resonated with Horton, including that 'learning is life-long', 'schools are responsive to the needs and struggles of ordinary people', 'wisdom of ordinary people is valued', 'learning is hands-on and experiential', and 'human identity is at the core of education'.[97] After visiting Denmark and experiencing folk schools firsthand, Horton returned to the United States ready to open a school where the questions and answers would come from the people, with teachers acting as facilitators and connectors to knowledge. In 1932, a 'school of freedom' known as the Highlander Folk School opened its doors in rural Tennessee.[98]

Freire's influence also extended to the Scandinavian Participatory Design (PD) movement.[99] Scandinavian PD emerged in the 1960s through 'industrial democracy' projects – efforts led by trade unions to promote democracy in the workplace and beyond.[100] While not as obviously tied to the classroom as hooks' critical pedagogy or the Highlander Folk School model, early Scandinavian PD shared these traditions' melding of theory and praxis: it critiqued 'expert' knowledge and instead emphasised collective sense-making. The PD framework articulated the 'development of alternative knowledge' as worker power.[101] Values of 'trust, reciprocity, and mutual learning' underpinned PD efforts, manifesting in the 'co-construction' of both knowledge and change.[102]

Highlander, hooks, and Scandinavian PD all stressed the importance of rooting sense-making in personal experience as a means of closing the gap between theory and praxis. As hooks notes:

> Personal testimony, personal experience, is such fertile ground for the production of liberatory feminist theory because it usually forms the base of our theory making.

[95] Frank Adams and Myles Horton, *Unearthing the Seeds of Freedom* (5th edn, Durham, NC, John F. Blair, 1998) 2.

[96] ibid 20.

[97] Vicky Eiben, 'Finding N.F.S. Grundtvig in the U.S.' in Mark Bradshaw Busbee and Anders Holm (eds), *Grundtvig-Studier* (Aarhus, Aarhus University Press, 2018) 99.

[98] Adams and Horton (n 95) 25.

[99] See Judith Gregory, 'Scandinavian Approaches to Participatory Design' (2003) 19 *International Journal of Engaging Education* 62, 64.

[100] See ibid 64; Eevi E Beck, 'P for Political: Participation is Not Enough' (2002) 14 *Scandinavian Journal of Information Systems* 77, 79.

[101] Gro Bjerknes and Tone Bratteteig, 'User Participation and Democracy: A Discussion of Scandinavian Research on System Development' (1995) 7 *Scandinavian Journal of Information Systems* 73, 85.

[102] Gregory (n 99) 62, 66.

> While we work to resolve those issues that are most pressing in daily life … we engage in a critical process of theorizing that enables and empowers.[103]

Unfortunately, dominant modes of education, law, and design privilege 'expert' knowledge over lived experience, and even critical modes fall into this trap (see, eg, the credentials of the attendees of this conference and of the authors of this paper). Highlander was constantly grappling with the tensions between operating as an effective educational institution and seeking to critique and move beyond traditional academic methods of knowledge production. Horton knew that '[e]ducation at Highlander had to be problem-centred, and the problem had to be the people's, not Highlanders'.[104] But both staff and students struggled with reimagining their roles: many teachers came to Highlander stuck in traditional 'expert' mode, and many students came ready to defer to such 'experts'.[105] Staff had to learn how to learn from their students, and students had to learn how to view themselves as teachers (more on that in Part II.b).

At the NJ Legal Design Lab, we strive to teach and learn these same lessons within the strict restraints of a law school bureaucracy and curriculum.[106] Law students, colleagues, and community partners alike are accustomed to rigid divisions between the roles of student and teacher, lawyer and client, expert and layperson, and classroom and experience. In the face of such challenges, we aim to use our Legal Design Clinic and our Community Co-Design Committee as vehicles to emphasise mutual learning that defies shibboleths of professional expertise, and to expand the contexts and spaces in which that learning takes place.

In Spring 2024, our Housing Justice and Legal Design Clinic collaborated with tenant organisers in a building in Montclair, New Jersey. During the semester, students travelled to the building to speak with tenants about their experiences, and tenants and organisers came to our classroom to share their knowledge and participate in key parts of the design process. In one such classroom meeting, participants collaborated to synthesise insights from a variety of sources, including: personal testimony from tenants, organisers, and other stakeholders; an organising handbook from a local organisation; observation of a town council meeting at which tenants voiced concerns; and scholarly readings. Participants' unique and varied perspectives enabled us to turn these disparate pieces of data into co-created knowledge – with one element of our shared understanding being the reality of persistent contradiction and ambiguity.[107]

[103] hooks (n 92) 70.

[104] Adams and Horton (n 95) 46.

[105] ibid 46.

[106] Fellow workshop participant Jules Sievert faces similar challenges in their work at the East Boston Spatial Justice Lab. See Sievert (n 91).

[107] See generally Hasso Plattner Institute of Design at Stanford University, 'Library of Ambiguity' (2024) dlibrary.stanford.edu/ambiguity.

The clinical setting posed hurdles to meaningfully combining theory and praxis. First, as professors, we maintained almost exclusive control over the clinic's agenda. We are now exploring ways to share that control with our co-designers and students. Ideas include asking co-designers to evaluate students, inviting co-designers to join student design teams, and co-creating our seminar curriculum with students and co-designers. Second, the classroom schedule and semester structure created burdens for tenant participation and curtailed our ability to sustain engagement. In an effort to expand and deepen participation opportunities, our next clinic will run for a full year instead of a single semester.

The Lab's new Community Co-Design Committee overcomes some, but not all, of these obstacles to merging classroom and community – and raises new ones. The Committee is:

> a group of creative New Jerseyans with a wide range of personal and professional experiences with housing injustice. [Committee members] work closely with each other, Lab staff, and Seton Hall students to shape the Lab's mission, values, priorities, and strategies.[108]

Unlike our clinic participants, who are stuck with a University-approved schedule, Committee members are able to set their own meeting cadence (we have currently landed on once every two weeks) and to continue their participation beyond the semester structure (a Committee term is four months, but members can elect to participate for multiple terms). In theory, Committee members will also exercise equal control over our meeting agendas and facilitation – in practice, although members have facilitated and planned parts of meetings, the authors of this paper remain the default leaders of the group. To further challenge this dichotomy, the Lab has hired a former Committee member – a longtime local organiser – to lead our collaborative endeavours, including the Committee. Hopefully, like participants at Highlander, our Committee members are learning to see themselves as teachers and leaders, and the authors are learning to redirect our institutional authority and make space for them to embrace those roles.

As Horton noted, 'Formally educated staff members have never been as effective in teaching as the people, once they saw themselves as teachers'.[109] But how do people come to see themselves as teachers and leaders? The next section explores the importance of facilitating ways for people to experience, understand, and value their own agency.

Reclaiming Agency Through Experience and Narrative

Emancipatory frameworks like movement lawyering affirm that the people impacted by a problem of injustice must be the ones to solve it. This theory of

[108] Seton Hall University (n 3).
[109] Adams and Horton (n 95) 47, quoting Horton.

social transformation requires 'ordinary people' – a term borrowed from sociologist Frances Fox Piven – to view themselves as agents of change and to act accordingly.[110] Liberatory education and Scandinavian PD both provide methods for people to make sense of their power as change-makers, whether by facilitating opportunities to experience that power directly or by sharing narratives that challenge conventional notions of power as being held exclusively by elites.

Horton saw an educator's role as 'helping people develop the capacity to make decisions and to take responsibility'.[111] Organisers trained at Highlander

> facilitated opportunities for community members to take on tasks 'they didn't think themselves 'qualified' to handle' – convincing others to vote, speaking at community meetings, engaging in demonstrations, and making decisions about the movement's direction and strategy – and 'creat[ed] an atmosphere in which people fe[lt] free to make mistakes and try again.'[112]

Horton suggests that nurturing self-determination is a role particularly suited to educators more so than organisers. Whereas an organiser's priority is to solve a problem, an educator's priority is to support people in developing their own solutions.[113]

Scandinavian PD also contemplates agency as a design output. It emphasises 'change and development, not only technological change and systems development, but change and development of people, organisations, and practices, occurring in changing socio-historical contexts'.[114] Scandinavian PD regards decision-making power as both a key element of participation in the design process, and as an outcome of that process.[115]

However, directly experiencing one's own agency is not the only way to build understanding of ordinary-people power. Storytelling – and specifically counter-storytelling – is another crucial way to make sense of individual and collective power. As Gerald López notes, humans 'see and understand the world through "stock stories"'.[116] Typically, our unexamined stock stories serve the status quo, acting invisibly as what legal scholar Richard Delgado describes as a 'bundle of presuppositions, received wisdoms, and shared understandings against a background of which legal and political discourse takes place'.[117] These

[110] See Hallie Jay Pope, 'Solidarity by Design: Generating Counternarratives About People Power' in Rossana Ducato, Alain Strowel, and Enguerrand Marique (eds), *Design(s) for Law* (Milan, Ledizioni, 2024) 148.

[111] Paulo Freire and Myles Horton, *We Make the Road by Walking* (Philadelphia, Temple University Press, 1990) 125.

[112] Pope (n 110) 146, quoting Charles M Payne, *I've Got the Light of Freedom* (2nd edn, Berkeley, CA, University of California Press, 2007) 331.

[113] Freire and Horton (n 111) 115–28.

[114] Gregory (n 99) 63.

[115] ibid.

[116] Gerald P López, 'Lay Lawyering' (1984) 32 *UCLA Law Review* 1, 3.

[117] Richard Delgado, 'Storytelling for Oppositionists: A Plea for Narrative' (1989) 87 *Michigan Law Review* 2411, 2413.

dominant narratives tell ordinary people that only elites can be leaders – that only exceptional people can change the world.[118] Practitioners of Scandinavian PD understood that facilitating meaningful participation includes revealing these invisible stock stories – 'working to bring forward tacit knowledge and shared knowledge that is taken for granted and therefore usually unspoken or invisible'.[119]

Horton compares sharing stories to planting seeds.[120] This method of foregrounding and challenging existing presumptions sets the stage for transformative experiences and new *understandings* of agency, and is itself an *exercise* of agency. As legal historian James Pope notes, 'Although elites might control the technical discourse of law, they do not and cannot control the generation of narratives about law'.[121] Ordinary people can collectively construct legal meaning by telling their own stories about the law – stories that provide frameworks for action in pursuit of socio-legal change.

The Lab seeks to facilitate ways for people to experience, understand, and value their own agency, both by exercising decision-making power and by sharing stories. In the clinic setting, law students, tenants, and organisers engaged in a '5 Whys'[122] exercise to interrogate their narratives about the roots of tenants' problems and tenants' roles in potential solutions. As one tenant leader told students, 'We are our own advocates. We need to speak for ourselves'. In a recent Community Co-Design Committee meeting, participants discussed ways to articulate and measure the Lab's impact: We agreed that one of the most important outcomes of the Lab's work has been the experiences and development of the Committee members. One member said that she had joined the Committee because she wanted to vent about her housing issues and be heard, but that she ended up finding her calling: fighting for housing justice.

The Lab also aims to guide law students in understanding their own agency and role in social justice movements. One Committee member, a tenant organiser, expressed the importance of developing law students into future lawyers who value collective decision-making and are equipped to support organising work. By including tenants and organisers as co-participants and clinic leaders, we hope to encourage law students to interrogate the narrative of lawyers and elites as sole holders of expertise, and to recast themselves as facilitators and collaborators alongside 'ordinary people' and social movements.

[118] Pope (n 110) 152.

[119] Gregory (n 99) 63.

[120] Freire and Horton (n 111) 99.

[121] James G Pope, 'Labor's Constitution of Freedom' (1997) 106 *Yale Law Journal* 941, 944. (Note: James Pope is the father of one of the authors and the former law professor of the other!).

[122] We thank Mike Sell and his team at the Digital Storytelling Project for introducing the Lab to this activity.

Explicitly Embedding Political Values

Designer, scholar, and activist Sasha Costanza-Chock warns would-be liberatory designers that 'under neoliberal multicultural capitalism, most of the time designers unintentionally reproduce the matrix of domination'.[123] As computer and society researcher Eevi Beck points out in her call for Scandinavian PD to return to its radical roots, '"participation" is not a sufficient condition for changing power relations'.[124] Rather, participatory sense-making fulfills its 'healing, liberatory, [and] revolutionary' potential 'only when we ask that it do so and direct our [efforts] towards this end'.[125] Liberatory legal designers must commit explicitly to our political agenda of dismantling oppressive systems.[126]

Highlander and Scandinavian PD both had the express political goal of building worker power. By facilitating worker participation in the design of systems for planning and performing their work, Scandinavian PD aimed not only to produce more effective systems: It also explicitly sought to increase workers' democratic participation in decisions affecting their working lives.[127] PD efforts endeavoured to foster not only '*workplace democracy*' – workers' control over decision-making in the context of their employment – but also '*working life democracy*' – workers' power and participation at a societal level.[128] It is this explicit embrace of worker power and democracy as guiding values that sets the early era of Scandinavian PD apart from other forms of participatory design and co-design. As designer Pelle Ehn writes, 'In the interest of emancipation, we deliberately made the choice of siding with workers and their organisations, supporting the development of their resources for a change towards democracy at work'.[129]

Similarly, at Highlander, '[n]othing was taught ... that would help workers become accustomed to exploitation'.[130] Horton notes that liberatory educators should not tell people what to think, but should openly share their ideas and values.[131] In a participatory classroom where students and professors are both teachers and learners together, this kind of sharing becomes possible.

Who constructs the problems of exploitation? Beck notes that a politically oriented PD must address 'the legitimacy of anyone not only to propose solutions, but to suggest what the problems are'.[132] As our fellow workshop participant Bader Alnoaimi observes, design problems are not 'identified' through neutral

[123] Costanza-Chock (n 63) 41.
[124] Beck (n 100) 82.
[125] hooks (n 92) 61.
[126] See Pope (n 81) 167–68.
[127] Bjerknes and Bratteteig (n 101) 74.
[128] Gregory (n 99) 64.
[129] ibid 73.
[130] Adams and Horton (n 95) 36.
[131] Freire and Horton (n 111) 105–07.
[132] Beck (n 100) 83; see also pt I.A.

examination, but rather are 'constructed' as problems requiring solutions.[133] In that construction lies the power to determine a design project's agenda.

One function of the Lab's Community Co-Design Committee is to co-construct the problems the Lab seeks to explore. Recently, the Committee decided to articulate a year-one vision. In that process, we also discussed our shared values and mindsets. The authors shared our initial description of the Lab's values – design democratically, design cooperatively, design critically – and then the Committee created their own expression of their values, which included:

- Dream big and get to the root of the problem.
- People-power is the catalyst for meaningful change.
- Policies can look good on paper, but ultimately, institutional power seeks to preserve itself.
- Act as a conduit for resources, knowledge, and power.
- Build community, build tenant power.
- This is a slow space, where we give ourselves time to dream past the crisis response.
- We come from a place of love.

At the end of the meeting, we had articulated the Lab's year-one priority: 'share knowledge to build people power'. The authors of this paper participated in the conversation, but mostly as listeners and facilitators. Still, we are cognizant of the power that facilitation and note-taking confer in terms of shaping and documenting conversations. Did the process of co-defining the problem with the community result in a genuine validation of our political and methodological agenda, or did we insert that agenda too aggressively into the process? This question highlights the importance of our ongoing efforts to cede facilitation responsibilities to Committee members.[134]

At times, a liberatory political vision may exist in tension with participatory methods, at least on the surface. Horton tells of one such anecdote: the people of Summerfield, Tennessee asked Highlander to help set up an employment agency.

> At first, it seemed like a pretty good idea. It came from the people. If it worked, it would be of help. But we refused, and told them our goal was to help workers unite with other workers for common strength and not to help some individuals rise above others.[135]

In this instance, had Highlander supported the people's idea, the school would have found itself in the position of using its limited resources to build a solution

[133] Alnoaimmi, 'Beyond the Problem-Solution Paradigm in Legal Design: Making the Cloud Rain in Bahrain', in this volume.
[134] See pt II.A.
[135] Adams and Horton (n 95) 36.

that ultimately replicated oppressive power structures (or at least, let's assume that conclusion for the purposes of this paper – one potential critique of Horton is that the people may have known better how to build community power).[136]

We have faced a similar tension in our Committee meetings. Several Committee members have voiced a desire to invite 'good' landlords into our design processes and projects. The authors have shared our hesitations about treating landlords as co-designers: namely, that 'it would be strategically incoherent to share power with those whose oppressive power we seek to eliminate'.[137] However, our tenant collaborators are not a monolith, and they hold a variety of perspectives on the root causes of housing injustice. This conversation remains open.

Such a disconnect between our Committee members' agenda and the Lab's political vision may stem in part from our failure to properly set the conditions of meaningful participation by illuminating dominant narratives that uphold the status quo. However, might it also be remedied by fleshing out the contours of a truly liberatory course of action that currently seems beyond reach – for example, housing as a public good rather than a vehicle for profit? The next section examines the importance of radical imagination and joy.

Radical Imagination and Joy

Articulating a political vision is important, but it is not enough: we must engage in collective dreaming to make that vision 'juicy'.[138] This is particularly true in contexts like housing that operate in constant crisis. 'Without the collaborative, joyful, reality-negating power of radical imagination, it is impossible to see beyond this harm that is so pervasive as to become grotesquely mundane'.[139] Organising solely around shared trauma is neither sustainable nor sufficiently transformative. We need space to dream to transcend the status quo.[140]

Joy is central to liberatory pedagogy; it is one way to 'subvert the classroom's politics of domination'.[141] One tenet of Danish folk education that Highlander strove to implement was 'first enliven, then enlighten'.[142] Highlander used music and plays about working-class struggles to bring joy to the community and transcend the realities of those struggles.[143] In *Teaching to Transgress*, hooks

[136] See Freire and Horton (n 111) 196.
[137] See Pope (n 81) 171.
[138] *See* Pope (n 81) 3–4, quoting Demita Frazier in Keeanga-Yamahtta Taylor (ed), *How We Get Free: Black Feminism and the Combahee River Collective* (Chicago, Haymarket Books, 2017).
[139] Pope (n 81) 5.
[140] See Perry-Kessaris (n 32) 7–8, citing Cassie Robinson, 'Change happens if our collective imagination changes' *Medium* (9 January 2022) cassierobinson.medium.com/change-happens-if-our-collective-imagination-changes-7a1c0475a578.
[141] hooks (n 92) 148.
[142] Adams and Horton (n 95) 72.
[143] ibid.

and educator Ron Scapp discuss how their colleagues view student enjoyment with suspicion and dismissiveness: 'Pleasure in the classroom is feared. If there is laughter, a reciprocal exchange may be taking place'.[144]

The Lab aims not only to nurture joyful experiences in our clinic and in the Community Co-Design Committee, but to discuss why joy and imagination are so important for sustaining our work. One way we articulate this value is our mantra of embodying a 'slow space': the Lab aims to support all participants in moving at the pace of deep dreaming rather than the typical flurry of crisis response. In our Committee meetings, we always take time to break bread together and check in on one another. Committee members often begin our meetings by sharing how they've missed the group and how happy they are to be with everyone. In our clinic, we draw silly drawings and co-create wildly unrealistic stories about how our little design projects will snowball into housing justice for everyone.[145]

CONCLUSION

At the New Jersey Legal Design Lab, we integrate participatory design and movement lawyering into our work, fostering a model of legal education that actively engages with community wisdom and creativity. We prioritise community-driven approaches that emphasise dignity, autonomy, and empowerment. Drawing on valuable lessons from radical traditions and participatory methodologies, our legal solutions are designed not only to respond to immediate needs but also to contribute to the self-determination of communities most impacted by housing instability.

We have described four lessons learned from liberatory pedagogy and Scandinavian PD; undoubtedly, we have many more lessons to learn, from these traditions and others. We see this paper as the beginning of an ongoing exploration of how legal design can facilitate collective endeavours for liberatory ends.

REFERENCES

A Abreu, 'Lessons from LatCrit: Insiders and Outsiders, All at the Same Time' (1999) 53 *University of Miami Law Review* 787.

F Adams and M Horton, *Unearthing the Seeds of Freedom* (5th edn, Durham, NC, John F. Blair, 1998).

A Akbar, S Ashar and J Simonson, 'Movement Law' (2021) 73 *Stanford Law Review* 821.

[144] ibid 145.

[145] See Pope (n 81) pt 4.

J Aldridge, *Participatory Research: Working with Vulnerable Groups in Research and Practice* (Bristol, Policy Press, 2015).
S Alinsky, *Rules for Radicals: A Pragmatic Primer for Realistic Radicals* (New York, Vintage, 1989).
B Alnoaimi, 'Making the Cloud Rain: A "Law and Political Economy" Reading of Bahrain's "Cloud First Policy"'.
E Beck, 'P for Political: Participation is Not Enough' (2002) 14 *Scandinavian Journal of Information Systems* 77.
G Bjerknes and T Bratteteig, 'User Participation and Democracy: A Discussion of Scandinavian Research on System Development' (1995) 7 *Scandinavian Journal of Information Systems* 73.
R Bratt, M Stone and C Hartman (eds), *A Right to Housing: Foundation for a New Social Agenda* (Philadelphia, Temple University Press, 2006).
L Brown and S Strega (eds), *Research as Resistance: Revisiting Critical, Indigenous, and Anti-Oppressive Approaches* (2nd edn, Toronto, Canadian Scholars' Press, 2015).
S Carle and S Cummings, 'A Reflection on the Ethics of Movement Lawyering' (2018) 31 *Georgetown Journal of Legal Ethics* 447.
CC Perez, *Invisible Women: Data Bias in a World Designed for Men* (New York, Abrams Press, 2019).
S Costanza-Chock, *Design Justice: Community-Led Practices to Build the Worlds We Need* (Cambridge, MA, MIT Press, 2020).
S Cummings, 'Movement Lawyering' (2020) 27 *Indiana Journal of Global Legal Studies* 87.
J Davis, L Algoed and M Hernández-Torrales (eds), *On Common Ground: International Perspectives on the Community Land Trust* (Amherst, MA, Terra Nostra Press, 2020).
R Delgado, 'Storytelling for Oppositionists: A Plea for Narrative' (1989) 87 *Michigan Law Review* 2411.
M Desmond, *Evicted: Poverty and Profit in the American City* (New York, Crown, 2017).
M Dias, 'Paradox and Possibility: Movement Lawyering During the COVID-19 Housing Crisis' (2021) 20 *CUNY Law Review* 173.
V Eiben, 'Finding N.F.S. Grundtvig in the U.S.' in MB Busbee and A Holm (eds), *Grundtvig-Studier* (Aarhus, Aarhus University Press, 2018).
Letter from Engels F to Mehring F (14 July 1983).
D Erickson, *Housing Policy Revolution: Networks and Neighborhoods* (Lanham, MD, Rowman and Littlefield Pubs, 2009).
D Farbman, 'Resistance Lawyering' (2019) 107 *California Law Review* 1877.
M Foucault, 'Two Lectures' in Colin Gordon (ed), *Power/Knowledge: Selected Interviews and Other Writings, 1972–1977* (New York, Vintage, 1980).
P Freire, *Pedagogy of the Oppressed* (4th edn, London, Bloomsbury, 2018).
P Freire and Horton M, *We Make the Road by Walking* (Philadelphia, Temple University Press, 1990).
DE Gray, *Doing Research in the Real World* (3rd edn, London, SAGE, 2013).
J Gregory, 'Scandinavian Approaches to Participatory Design' (2003) 19 *International Journal of Engaging Education* 62.
W Hallaq, *An Introduction to Islamic Law* (Cambridge, Cambridge University Press, 2009).
A Hamilton, J Madison and J Jay, in Clinton Rossiter (ed), *The Federalist Papers* (London, Penguin, 1961).

Hasso Plattner Institute of Design at Stanford University, 'Library of Ambiguity' (2024).
C Hedges and J Sacco, *Days of Destruction, Days of Revolt* (New York, Bold Type Books, 2014).
R Hofstadter, 'The Paranoid Style in American Politics' in *The Paranoid Style in American Politics and Other Essays* (New York, Alfred A Knopf, 1965).
b hooks, *Outlaw Culture: Resisting Representations* (New York, Routledge, 1994).
—— *Teaching to Transgress* (New York, Routledge, 1994).
INCITE! Women of Color Against Violence (ed), *The Revolution Will Not Be Funded: Beyond the Non-Profit Industrial Complex* (Durham, NC, Duke University Press, 2007).
A Islahi and S Ghazanfar, *Economic Thought of Al-Ghazali* (Jeddah, King Abdulaziz University, 1998).
A Kronman, *The Lost Lawyer: Failing Ideals of the Legal Profession* (Cambridge, MA, Belknap Press, 1995).
D Lake and J Wendland, 'Practical, Epistemological, and Ethical Challenges of Participatory Action Research: A Cross-Disciplinary Review of the Literature' (2018) 22 *Journal of Higher Ed Outreach and Engagement* 11.
E Lawrence, 'When We Fight, We Win: Eviction Defense as Subversive Lawyering' (2022) 90 *Fordham Law Journal* 2125.
GP López, *Rebellious Lawyering: One Chicano's Vision of Progressive Legal Practice* (Boulder, CO, Westview Press, 1992).
—— 'Lay Lawyering' (1984) 32 *UCLA Law Review* 1.
R López, 'Participatory Law Scholarship' (2023) 123 *Columbia Law Review* 1795.
B Manin, *The Principles of Representative Government* (Cambridge, Cambridge University Press, 1997).
M McQuarrie, 'No Contest: Participatory Technologies and the Politics of the Public Sphere' (2013) 25(1) *Public Culture* 143.
C Menkel-Meadow, 'The Legacy of Clinical Education: Theories about Lawyering' (1980) 29 *Cleveland State Law Review* 555.
A McIntyre, *Participatory Action Research* (Thousand Oaks, CA, SAGE, 2008).
M Minkler and N Wallerstein (eds), *Community-Based Participatory Research for Health: From Process to Outcomes* (2nd edn, San Francisco, CA, Jossey-Bass, 2008).
Movement Law Lab, 'About Movement Lawyering'.
Movement Strategy Center, 'The Spectrum of Community Engagement to Ownership'.
S Nieto, *Qualitative Research: Challenging the Orthodoxies* (New York, Routledge, 2009).
C Pateman, 'Participatory Democracy Revisited' (2012) 10(1) *Perspectives on Politics* 7.
CM Payne, *I've Got the Light of Freedom* (2nd edn, Berkeley, CA, University of California Press, 2007).
A Perry-Kessaris, 'Activating Imagination to Promote Epistemic Justice' (Chapter 10 in this volume).
HJ Pope, 'Designing to Dismantle' in E Allbon and A Perry-Kessaris (eds), *Design in Legal Education* (London, Routledge, 2022).
—— 'Liberatory Legal Design and Radical Imagination' in P Hekkert et al (eds), *DRS2022: Bilbao* (Bilbao, Design Research Society, 2022).
—— 'Solidarity by Design: Generating Counternarratives About People Power' in R Ducato, A Strowel and E Marique (eds), *Design(s) for Law* (Milan, Ledizioni, 2024).
JG Pope, 'Labor's Constitution of Freedom' (1997) 106 *Yale Law Journal* 941.

KRG Pryal, 'American lawyers have an Atticus Finch complex, and it's killing the profession' *Quartz* (31 March 2016).

J Rawls, *A Theory of Justice* (Cambridge, MA, Harvard University Press, 1971).

C Robinson, 'Change Happens if our Collective Imagination Changes' *Medium* (9 January 2022).

M Robinson, *Media Coverage of Crime and Criminal Justice* (2nd edn, Durham, NC, Carolina Academic Press, 2011).

R Rothstein, *The Color of Law: A Forgotten History of How Our Government Segregated America* (New York, Liveright, 2017).

D Roussopoulos and C Benello (eds), *Participatory Democracy: Prospects for Democratizing Democracy* (Montreal, Black Rose Books, 2004).

A Sarat and S Scheingold (eds), *Cause Lawyers and Social Movements* (Stanford, CA, Stanford University Press, 2006).

A Scherer, 'The Case Against Summary Eviction Proceedings: Process as Racism and Oppression' (2022) 53(1) *Seton Hall Law Review*.

D Schuler and A Namioka (eds), *Participatory Design: Principles and Practices* (New York, Routledge, 1993).

Seton Hall University, 'New Jersey Legal Design Lab' (2024).

P Shah, 'Rebuilding the Ethical Compass of Law' (2018) 47 *Hofstra Law Review* 11.

—— 'Movement Lawyering Reading Guide' (2018) 47 *Hofstra Law Review* 99.

J Sievert, 'Transforming Legal Inquiry and Design through Practice Based Research and Community Engagement'.

LT Smith, *Decolonizing Methodologies: Research and Indigenous Peoples* (3rd edn, London, Bloomsbury, 1999).

Stout, 'Right to Counsel: The Nationwide Movement to Fight the Eviction Crisis' (2019).

N Summers, 'The Limits of Good Law: A Study of Housing Court Outcomes' (2020) 87 *University of Chicago Law Review* 145.

K-Y Taylor, *Race for Profit: How Banks and the Real Estate Industry Undermined Black Homeownership* (Chapel Hill, University of North Carolina Press, 2019).

—— (ed), *How We Get Free: Black Feminism and the Combahee River Collective* (Chicago, Haymarket Books, 2017).

S Wilson, *Research Is Ceremony: Indigenous Research Methods* (Halifax, Fernwood Publishing, 2008).

G Wood, *The Creation of the American Republic, 1776–1787* (Chapel Hill, UNC Press, 1969).

—— *The Radicalism of the American Revolution* (New York, Random House, 1992).

12

Justice Beyond the User-Experience: Designing for the Sublime in Courts

PABLO HERMANSEN[1] AND JOAQUIN SANTUBER[2]

INTRODUCTION

IN 'FORCE OF Law: The "Mystical Foundation of Authority"', Jacques Derrida (1992) elaborates on the deconstruction of the law and its implications for the concept of justice. Derrida's notion of justice is dual. On the one hand, the measurable, concrete, finite; and on the other hand, an immeasurable, infinite justice that is impossible to achieve. We will refer to the first as justice, and to the second as Justice (Justice with a capital letter). In its constitutive tension, both justices are always in an incessant becoming. We argue that Justice – understood as the transcendent – becomes immanent only insofar as it engages the concrete conditions of justice. This is the radical proposal of designing for the sublime, to make a matter of design the conditions of possibility for the transcendent to become immanent.

The statement by Derrida prompts us to raise a challenge, one that we believe is inescapable for those who do justice and those who design their systems and material conditions of (re)production: to make Justice perceptible in justice. We will propose that, for this to happen, we must project the places and moments where justice occurs from the will (conviction) and the purpose (ideology) that the impossible concur in the concrete – that is, that what transcends the immediate participates in the perceptible. We will argue that it is not the mere presence of Justice in the judicial scene that gives meaning to acts of justice; it is the tension of this impossible encounter between the concrete and the transcendent that constitutes and gives movement to the metabolism of *doing* justice and constitutes it as a sublime act. Consequently, we will call Design for the Sublime, which proposes to create rituals whose vitality comes from the generative tension between the transcendent and the perceptible.

[1] School of Design, Pontificia Universidad Católica de Chile, Chile.
[2] Linz Institute for Transformative Change, Johannes Kepler University, Austria.

By *concrete*, we mean the set of sociomaterial dimensions of our life together, that is, the perceptible part of our coexistence in the world. By *transcendent*, we refer to entities, forces, and beliefs, ungraspable from scientific epistemology, but which concur and affect our daily experience in the world and are apprehended[3] both through art and from non-modern epistemologies. Following de la Cadena,[4] we understand transcendent as all that exceeds the limits of modern epistemology. Specifically, of the multiple empirically indemonstrable existences, we will focus on Justice, as an incorporeal and ungraspable entity that constitutes the horizon of meaning of every judicial act. Its non-modern origin and indirect agency make up the imaginary and animate the rituals of the judicial process. Rituals in courts constitute the tension between the private autonomy of the individuals and the common public interest, in which the parties are bound to follow certain forms and manners, to occupy certain spaces and be restricted to others.[5]

Our approach has a Nietzschean antecedent. Art or creation that moves towards the sublime, such as tragedy, is the one that manages to put the Apollonian and the Dionysian in tension, that is, idea and excess. Doing Justice is a creative act that aims at the sublime. We do justice with every rite in which we invoke Justice. Justice does not pre-exist the rite; it is recreated as a sublime act every time we propose to make the transcendent orient the perceptible. The trivialisation of justice by problem-solving interfaces reduces the re-production of justice to service. We have to distinguish between everyday practices – things we do periodically – and rituals. Derrida describes justice as a ritual when he raises its duality or constitutive tension between the concrete and the impossible.

However, many of its cultists and executors tend to understand the judicial system as an eminently modern and scientifically supported practice, neglecting other traditional, highly ritualistic practices.[6] It is precisely from this biased understanding of justice that, in recent decades – with special force since the restrictions on mobility and assembly during the pandemic – the judicial systems of many countries have undertaken to update it following technological imperatives. Consequently, new infrastructures and interfaces are designed and implemented to provide an *efficient service*, trivialising Justice by excluding its transcendent and ritual dimensions (ie, user-friendly justice). This trivialisation, achieved through problem-solving interfaces, reduces the re-enactment of justice to the mere production of a service, commodifying the more-than-human binding of Justice's rituality into mere interactions-transactions.

[3] Judith Butler, *Frames of War: When Is Life Grievable?* (London, Verso, 2009); Judith Butler, 'Precarious Life, Vulnerability, and the Ethics of Cohabitation' (2012) 26 *The Journal of Speculative Philosophy* 134.

[4] Marisol De La Cadena, in Robert J Foster and Daniel R Reichman (eds), *Earth Beings: Ecologies of Practice across Andean Worlds* (Durham, NC, Duke University Press, 2015) read.dukeupress.edu/books/book/142/.

[5] Linda Mulcahy, *Legal Architecture: Justice, Due Process and the Place of Law* (Abingdon, Routledge, 2011).

[6] Diego López Medina, 'La Historia de Otros: Ideología Del Derecho Procesal Europeo y Su Trasplante a América Latina' (2020) *Via Iuris* 1.

In what follows, we will argue that, although the practice of justice requires the agency of Justice (transcendent entity), those who currently project their operation tend to design their production conditions focusing only on their transactional dimension, efficiency, cost reduction, and speed. In other words, in the redesign and digitalisation of judicial systems, the question of what material and relational conditions favour the presence and agency of Justice has not been considered yet.

In this paper, we will advocate for the relevance of non-human agencies, such as Justice, the rites by which it deploys its agency, and the material and organisational conditions in which justice is produced, captured in the following question:

How can we design a form of justice whose movement has a vital metabolism, grounded in the constitutive tensions between the two forms of justice? In other words, a design practice that makes the tension between these two justices a constitutive engine of their metabolism. This leads us to overcome the problem-solution duality as an articulator of design processes and leads us to think of these relationships as part of a constitutive tension.

On the other hand, this has to do with the humility assumed by those who design, in the sense of being an articulator of conditions, leaving open spaces for the emergence of other types of creative agencies. When the centre is not on the needs of the users but on the tension between the two justices, the agencies of those who are part of the socio-material fabric can resonate. This constitutive tension between the agency of the transcendent and the socio-material conditions of those of us who co-exist in the world is in the relationship between these two justices.

Thinking and making justice systems from the critical design of the more-than-human offers us a substantial contribution from the field of law and justice to design. In this sense, studying courts demands us to consider the ritual, the transcendent, and the sublime in our design research practices. Although law has appropriated design methodologies to meet the challenges of innovation and digitalisation, in these pages, we offer an example of what law as a field of study has to offer to design. However, more than seeing this as an exchange, a give and take, we believe that the possibility to think beyond each discipline's assets is due to the fundamental disposition to entangle, to *enmarañarse*.[7] If we think of this process linguistically, it would be something like *legaldesigning*, with no space in between, no dash that keeps the purity of each discipline intact by keeping them apart. In terms of our methodological contribution, there are two questions that we will address in the following part of this work:

How can we apprehend the transcendent to incorporate Justice into the design's metabolism? What methodologies and epistemologies emerge from *legaldesigning* for the Sublime?

[7] Pablo Hermansen and José Guerra Solano, 'Furrowing the Maraña: Designing to Sail out of the Anthropocene' in Martin Tironi and others (eds), *Design for More Than Human Futures* (New York, Routledge, 2023); Pablo Hermansen and Martín Tironi, 'Interspecies Design for Co-Existence', *Routledge Handbook of Sustainable Design* (2nd edn, New York, Routledge, 2024).

The horizon of this constitutive tension is the (re)generation of the common, not the mere correction of contingent and practical problems in transactions between individuals. Design focused on solving problems of users trivialises the practice of justice, reducing it to a problem-solving technique. Thus, the invitation is to look at creative practices whose rituality allows 'third minds'[8] to manifest themselves. To understand creation and creativity as the embodiment of entities and forces that exceed modern epistemology. Creating justice as a generative process capable of making and reinforcing the social fabric beyond contingency requires embodying or embracing these transcendent more-than-human entities and forces.

Given that modern scientific epistemology does not have the tools to apprehend and register the agency of the transcendent, designing for justice implies looking beyond the scientific repertoire and innovation.[9] In this way, Designing for the Sublime seeks to resist the dominance of scientific epistemology and opens up to other non-modern and more-than-human epistemologies. In other words, Designing for the Sublime means decentring the human-individual as a creator of knowledge and *legaldesigning* in terms of relationships between humans and more-than-humans.[10]

To shed light on these questions, we will visit events and experiences in which the transcendent is manifested and becomes part of the generative process: the Chilean pavilion at the London Design Biennial and a *Machiluwün* ritual in Mapuche territory in southern Chile. From these situated experiences, we explore sound as a speculative path to begin applying *Designing for the Sublime* to Chilean courts' digitalisation. We position this prototyping exercise as a cosmopolitical action – one that expands cosmopolitics from a matter of concern to a matter of design.[11]

PROBLEMATISING: WHAT ARE THE SCOPE AND LIMITATIONS OF USER-CENTRED DESIGN?

Following the proposal addressed by the convenors of the workshop in Onati, we critically analyse the current methodological trends in design for law and justice. The central argument of our problematisation is that a dominant and

[8] William Burroughs and Brion Gysin, *The Third Mind* (New York, Viking Press, 1978).

[9] Joaquin Santuber and Jonathan Edelman, 'Designing with Theories: Producing Legal Design Diffractively in Courts of Justice' (2022) *DRS Biennial Conference Series* dl.designresearchsociety.org/drs-conference-papers/drs2022/researchpapers/259.

[10] Joaquin Santuber and Pablo Hermansen, 'Designing for Posthuman Legalities: Legal Design(Ing) and the Ontological Turn' in Rossana Ducato, Alain Strowel and Marique Enguerrand (eds), *Design (s) for Law* (Milan, Ledizioni, 2024).

[11] Pablo Hermansen and Martin Tironi, 'Cosmopolitical Interventions: Prototyping Interspecies Encounters for More than Human Futures' in Jennifer Roberts-Smith, Stan Ruecker and Milena Radzikowska (eds), *Prototyping across the Disciplines: Designing Better Futures* (Bristol, Intelect Books, 2021).

totalising methodology neglects and excludes fundamental aspects of justice systems that, in our view, go beyond the experience of the user.

The predominant notion of design in Legal Design is human-centred design, in which problem-solving is a fundamental aspect of its practice.[12] Following the design thinking method, the goal of the process is to create solutions to a user's need identified during a problem-finding phase. The focus on finding and solving transactional problems acts as a bias that disfavours the manifestation of Justice – it dissolves the constitutive tension inherent in co-existing in society (problem dissolving).

Illustrious representatives of reductionist ways of designing are *human/user-centred design, service design, interaction design (IxD)*, and, in short, the set of approaches inscribed in *Design Thinking* that propose that, by reducing the complexities of coexistence to a series of transactional and measurable problems, solutions to all social problems can be designed.[13] However, not everything in life can be solved, or is meant to be solved, especially those matters – such as justice – where more-than-human relationships are constitutive.[14]

By brandishing abstract and general models that would be used to design almost anything – from interfaces to celebrations, from judicial systems to corkscrews – and presenting them as successful methodologies limited to efficiency in the provision of services, these *problem-solving* designers tend to make invisible the homogenising effect of their approach – designing access to justice is developed with the same steps as designing access to fast food. Therefore, in this form, design lacks a reflexive epistemological and methodological stance that would allow its practitioners to critically understand the epistemological and ontological transformations precipitated by their design approach in justice and Justice.

Uncritically inscribed in *Design Thinking*, insofar as they do not problematise its belonging or the consequences of its praxis, these approaches inoculate logics and microphysical modes of production, reproduction, and understanding of justice – and *Justice* as a Brand. At the same time, by embracing – also uncritically – these methods of innovation centred on the user and their practical problems, justice systems incorporate the mercantile logic in which these approaches are

[12] Alan Cooper, *The Inmates Are Running the Asylum* (Indianapolis, IN, Sams, 1999) archive.org/details/inmatesarerunni000coop; Nigel Cross, *Design Thinking: Understanding How Designers Think and Work* (Oxford, Berg, 2011); Jon Kolko, *Thoughts on Interaction Design* (Amsterdam, Elsevier, 2011) linkinghub.elsevier.com/retrieve/pii/C20090613489; Bill Moggridge, *Designing Interactions* (Cambridge, MA, MIT Press, 2007); Donald A Norman, *The Psychology of Everyday Things* (New York, Basic Books, 1988); Herbert Simon, *The Sciences of the Artificial* (Cambridge, MA, MIT Press, 1969).

[13] Don Norman, *The Design of Everyday Things: Revised and Expanded Edition* (New York, Basic Books, 2013).

[14] In the chapter on the designing for more than human worlds, Hermansen and Guerra (2023) elaborate on the story of Alexander the Great and the Gordian knot in which man imposes his will and exceptionality by cutting the knot – instead of untying it. In this sense, that act has an ontological character.

inscribed.[15] The bias in user satisfaction, transaction efficiency, and cost reduction is not innocent: it tends to homogenise justice systems with market products that also organise their offer by applying the Design-Thinking ways of worlding, trivialising the judicial experience and, by extension, depreciating the ritual and transcendent dimensions that Justice provides – that is, extinguishing the power of the sublime through the deployment of the prosaic. With its transcendent dimension made invisible, justice becomes de-ritualised, that is, it is experienced as one of the many services with which, daily, we acquire or sell goods and experiences.

This trivialisation of rites to their merely transactional aspects – the resolution of conflicts between natural or juridical persons – and the invisibilisation of the agency of entities such as Justice dilutes what the collective does. The absence of entities and agencies that at the same time exceed, bind, and understand us undermines our ability to narrate and build the common beyond the contingent problems that, rather than uniting us, separate us. We will argue that the agency of Justice is indispensable to making a common world, to give meaning to our coexistence, to think of ourselves as a collective beyond our differences and frictions as *private*.

By deproblematising materialities through *problem-solving design* and eliminating the agency of Justice as a transcendent entity, justice changes ontologically. Now, the invisibilisation of the ritual and transcendent dimensions of an institution such as justice can imply its *disappearance, trivialisation, and displacement*.[16] Justice can disappear, transforming its images into empty signifiers; as such, they tend to trivialise, that is, to serve as logos or graphic icons (eg, Che Guevara), but lose all their capacity to be indices of the transcendent and, therefore, to precipitate the sublime. On the other hand, making the transcendent invisible trivialises the rituality of justice and shifts it to another centre, namely, the prosaic cult of services and their technologies of interaction. In all cases, justice ceases to be a centre of social gathering, leaving in its place the worship for satisfactory services and the conflicts that separate us – since Justice is not done, but a problem is solved. Without the agency of Justice, it is becoming increasingly obvious that the resolution of conflicts and differences between private parties in the judicial system will be tilted in favour of those who have better techniques and more resources. It is not the same for everyone to suspect that the powerful tend to achieve a justice more favourable to their interests than for it to be explicit that without capital there is no justice. If groups with fewer resources lose hope of being able to invoke Justice in the judicial system, since it will act in collusion with the forces of public order in favour of the powerful, then Justice will seek to be invoked in extrajudicial rites. The rise of citizen uprisings and the establishment of narco-authority in recent decades seem to have progressed in parallel with the exile of Justice from the State.

[15] Tim Seitz, *Design Thinking and the New Spirit of Capitalism: Sociological Reflections on Innovation Culture* (Cham, Springer International Publishing, 2020) link.springer.com/10.1007/978-3-030-31715-7.

[16] Joaquin Santuber, 'Designing for Digital Justice: An Entanglement of People, Law, and Technologies' (Doctoral Thesis, University of Potsdam, 2023).

RITUALS AND THE SUBLIME

This section will dive into the treatment that has been given to rituality and the sublime from an analysis of diverse literature, drawing lines from anthropology, sociology, philosophy, and theology, and certainly critical approaches to Law. To substantiate our argument, we turn to the works of prominent Latin American scholars who have explored the power of ritual and transcendent dimensions in strengthening social bonds and political resilience.

Silvia Rivera Cusicanqui's exploration of Aymara cosmology and rituals demonstrates how these practices offer a counter-narrative to colonial and modern epistemologies.[17] Rivera Cusicanqui highlights the concept of 'ch'ixi', a term that signifies the coexistence of multiple, contradictory elements. Through this lens, she shows how Aymara rituals create a space where diverse historical and cultural elements – ancestral and modern, spiritual and commercial – can coexist, fostering communal bonds and resilience. These practices disrupt the linear, homogenising narratives imposed by colonial and modern frameworks, instead promoting a form of knowledge that is deeply rooted in local, indigenous traditions and collective memory. This approach underscores the potential of ritual to act as a form of resistance and resilience against oppressive structures.[18] Similarly, María Galindo's activism with Mujeres Creando in Bolivia exemplifies how ritual acts and performative protest can reclaim public spaces and challenge patriarchal structures.[19] Galindo discusses the power of symbolic actions, such as public performances and graffiti, to disrupt the everyday normalcy of patriarchal oppression. These acts serve as rituals that not only reclaim space but also create a sense of collective empowerment and belonging among participants. By integrating feminist critique with creative protest, Galindo illustrates how ritual can be a powerful tool for social transformation, challenging both gender norms and broader societal structures.

Eduardo Viveiros de Castro's concept of perspectivism in Amazonian cosmologies[20] highlights the importance of understanding multiple ontologies' coexistence and the role of rituals in maintaining these diverse worldviews. Perspectivism posits that different beings (humans, animals, spirits) perceive reality in fundamentally different ways, and rituals are key to navigating these varied perspectives. Marisol de la Cadena's work on indigenous practices in the Andes[21] illustrates how rituals involving earth-beings transcend the human-nature divide. These rituals foster a sense of interconnectedness and mutual respect among community members, recognising the agency of

[17] Silvia Rivera Cusicanqui, *Ch'ixinakax Utxiwa: Una Reflexión Sobre Prácticas y Discursos Descolonizadores* (Retazos, Tinta Limón Ediciones, 2010).

[18] ibid.

[19] María Galindo, *No se puede descolonizar sin despatriarcalizar: teoría y propuesta de la despatriarcalización* (La Paz, Mujeres Creando, 2013).

[20] Eduardo Viveiros De Castro, *Cannibal Metaphysics* (Minneapolis, MN, University of Minnesota Press, 2014).

[21] De La Cadena (n 5).

non-human entities such as mountains and rivers. De la Cadena's original use of Stengers' notion of 'cosmopolitics', in dialogue with Viveiros de Castro's concept of perspectivism, allows us to challenge the modern, anthropocentric view of justice by recognising the fundamental agency of other-than-human entities and the complex interplay of multiple realities. Both perspectives support the argument that rethinking justice systems to include the viewpoints and agencies of these non-human entities fosters a more holistic and interconnected approach to justice – one capable of recognising what 'exceeds' modern epistemology.[22]

Rossana Reguillo's studies on youth cultures and urban rituals in Latin America reveal how these practices create spaces of resistance and community.[23] Reguillo examines how urban rituals, such as graffiti and music festivals, serve as forms of resistance against neoliberal and exclusionary urban policies. These practices not only challenge dominant power structures but also create spaces for communal belonging and political expression. Reguillo's work highlights the potential of ritual to foster resilience and solidarity in the face of social and economic marginalisation. For its part, Gastón Gordillo's research on the materiality of ruins in postcolonial landscapes[24] uncovers how rituals of memory and mourning can reclaim history and resist erasure by dominant narratives. Gordillo explores how communities engage with ruins through rituals that commemorate past events and losses, thereby maintaining a connection to their history and resisting the homogenising forces of modern development. These rituals create a sense of continuity and identity, reinforcing social bonds and collective memory. These urban rituals, by celebrating marginalised practices and territories, establish their own centrality by counteracting their trivialisation, which often precedes erasure.

Santiago Castro-Gómez and Ramón Grosfoguel's examination of coloniality and modernity in Latin America[25] emphasises the importance of decolonising knowledge and recognising the epistemic violence inherent in modern institutions. They argue for a way of being and knowing that accounts for and integrates diverse epistemologies, challenging the dominance of Western, scientific paradigms. Their work allows us to propose that incorporating ritual and transcendent dimensions into justice systems can improve the design of legal frameworks and infrastructures capable of recognising and integrating non-modern and local knowledge systems.

The ritual dimension has been approached not only from Latin America but also from other perspectives from the global minority, including the

[22] ibid.

[23] Rossana Reguillo Cruz, *Culturas Juveniles: Formas Políticas Del Desencanto* (Ed rev y aum, Mexico City, Siglo Veintiuno Editores, 2012).

[24] Gastón R Gordillo, *Rubble: The Afterlife of Destruction* (Durham, NC, Duke University Press, 2014) read.dukeupress.edu/books/book/289/RubbleThe-Afterlife-of-Destruction.

[25] Santiago Castro-Gómez and Ramón Grosfoguel (eds), *El giro decolonial: reflexiones para una diversidad epistémica más allá del capitalismo global* (Bogotá, Siglo del Hombre Ed [u.a], 2007).

modern one, despite its epistemological propensity to deny or depreciate the ritual. In European epistemology, ritual with van Gennep's Rites of Passage, the anthropologist conceptualised rite as an element of the transition between two incompatible states in a person's life – ie, childhood and adulthood.[26] In Liberating Rites, Driver argues on 'the work that rituals can and should perform in the liberation of humankind from enslavement to powers that diminish freedom and bring more death than life'.[27] However, in a society dominated by scientific and rational ways of knowing, the transformative power of rituals has been seen as unwelcome and negative.[28] Moreover, rituals play a fundamental role in becoming a community, becoming a society,

> to lose ritual is to lose the way. It is a condition not only painful and pathetic but also dangerous. Some people it destroys. As for the whole society, sooner or later it will find rituals again, but they may be of an oppressive rather than a liberating kind. Rituals have much to do with our fate.[29]

The sublime, since ancient Greece, was understood as the ability of the speaker to go beyond the persuasion of the audience, inciting passion and moving it (Longinus). The translator of Longinus's work, Nicolas Boileau-Despréaux (seventeenth century), wrote of the sublime: 'The sublime is not strictly speaking something which is proven or demonstrated, but a marvel, which seizes one, strikes one, and makes one feel'. The sublime experience as the experience of being part of something greater than the individual is a constant tension between the finite and the infinite (Tolstoy), it is this relationship 'established and extended between the physical and the otherworldly, the modern and the archaic, the personal and the communal, the profane and the divine, the routinized and the ecstatic'.[30] No wonder why the Enlightenment and their project of rational modernity could not handle it, and with that 'the West's mystical heritage of occult dreamings, spiritual transformations, and apocalyptic visions crashed on the scientific shores of the modern age'.[31] Yet, this did not attain the extinction of rituals, transcendence and the sublime, it just made them invisible, excluded them from the bright side of knowledge, and exiled them to the undergrounds of modern society, to the dungeons of its Science and its States.

For that reason, we do not need to reinvent the sublime, the sublime is out there, we just need the conditions for it to be part of our worlding. In what follows, after a brief reference to our design research context, we explore two ritual experiences of accessing the sublime.

[26] Arnold van Gennep, *The Rites of Passage* (Abingdon, Psychology Press, 1960).

[27] Tom F Driver, *Liberating Rites: Understanding the Transformative Power of Ritual* (Abingdon, Routledge, 2019) xi–xii (first published 1998).

[28] ibid.

[29] ibid 4.

[30] Georgios Sakellariou, 'Composing the Sublime: Rituals in Electroacoustic Music' (PhD Thesis, Coventry University, 2017) pureportal.coventry.ac.uk/en/studentTheses/composing-the-sublime.

[31] Erik Davis, *TechGnosis: Myth, Magic, & Mysticism in the Age of Information* (Berkeley, CA, North Atlantic Books, 2015) 5.

THE DESIGN RESEARCH CONTEXT

We look at the Chilean judiciary's experiment of moving the physical courts amidst the COVID-19 pandemic mobility restrictions.[32] Born out of exceptional circumstances, the practices rehearsed have continued way beyond the conditions that justified conducting judicial hearings online. The abrupt digitalisation of the Chilean judiciary prompts us the question:

How can we design systems, interfaces, and infrastructures that promote collective rituals capable of making Justice perceptible, a transcendent dimension of justice and constitutive of the (re)production of the commons?

How can we design to foster the embodied participation of the transcendent in justice?

Figure 12.1 A capture of a recording of the Chilean Supreme Court plenary before the pandemic stored in the judiciary's official YouTube channel. Link: Audiencia de solicitud de remoción del fiscal de O'Higgins, Emiliano Arias (24 de enero de 2020) – YouTube

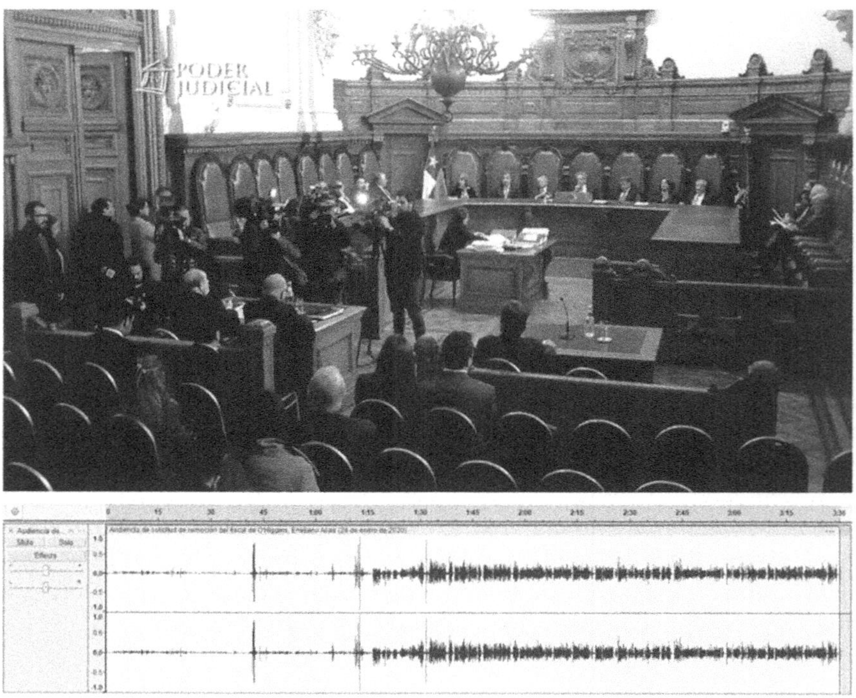

[32] Jenni Hakkarainen and Joaquín Santuber, 'Come in and See: Translating a Design Pattern from the Courtroom into an Online Environment' (2024) 3 *Digital Society* 27; Reem Abou Refaie and Joaquin Santuber, 'Risks and Challenges to E-Justice Principles: Governing Remote Work, Online Hearings and the Use of Social Media in Chilean Courts' (2023) 15 *JeDEM – eJournal of eDemocracy and Open Government* 118; Joaquin Santuber, Reem Abou Refaie and Christoph Meinel, 'Interrogating E-Justice: Lessons from Digitalizing Courts in Chile' (2022) *EGOV-CeDEM-ePart 2022* 54.

Figure 12.2 A capture of a recording of the Chilean Supreme Court hosting a hearing online via videoconference stored in the judiciary's official YouTube channel

INSPIRATION

As a reference, we present two research projects in design where the sublime is present. In this way, we seek to highlight that it is not necessary to invent the sublime, but that the sublime is out there, only that the scientific ways of knowing prevent us from accessing them. In this section, we introduce three design research projects as examples of how the sublime, the rituality, and the transcendent can be part of designing. We see these examples as a source of inspiration to practising Design for the Sublime.

Tectonic Resonances: Becoming with Stones

Resonancias Tectónicas, Chile's pavilion at the 2021 London Design Biennale and winner of the competition, is part of a broader project of experimentation and expansive thinking. For over a decade, this political agenda, inspired by cosmopolitical thought,[33] has extended discussions on design as a discipline beyond its traditional boundaries, engaging with networks of collectives, creators, and thinkers who challenge the hegemony of Modern epistemology and Capital flows in shaping and producing the worlds we inhabit. The pavilion's approach coincided with its creation under the influence of a non-human, planet-scale agency: COVID-19, which made evident the need to rethink the links and interdependencies between humans and more-than-humans. *Resonancias Tectónicas* makes explicit the conversation with many others that shape our socio-ecological life. When asked, 'How can we stage coexistence?' we responded by attempting to listen to some of the stones of Chile, in order to feel and ritualise the geological echoes of our territories.[34] Moreover, Marco Chilet adds that

> the curators were very aware of the work of authors such as Jussi Parikka, who talks about geology as a medium. […] Due to our interest in archaeology and anthropology, we began to investigate the enormous material, conceptual and political depth of the stones, and we decided to make the sounding stones the key to open a complex web of questions about contemporary design.[35]

Resonancias Tectónicas was located in the west wing of Somerset House, just steps from the River Thames. As shown in the images (Figures 12.1, 12.2, and 12.4), visitors were greeted by a deep blue space. Its windows, also tinted blue, allowed light to filter through, cut by the silhouettes of rocks. At the centre of the room, occupying the main focal point, were 17 stones arranged on two lightweight steel structures that formed the ritual centrepiece. These stones had travelled from various locations in Chile, transported in diplomatic suitcases to Heathrow Airport, then to the Chilean Embassy, and finally to the halls of Somerset.

Why create a contemporary design pavilion organised as a ritual space marked by simple stones? Given the primacy of the discourse on technological innovation, the dematerialisation of culture, virtual interfaces, and databases, isn't it counterintuitive to represent the design of a developing country by displaying a collection of stones? When we think about the conditions of production, distribution, and consumption of contemporary design, the stone appears as a material lacking exchange value, a remnant of primitive technologies and cosmologies, a residue of mining exploitation. However, from the Global South, this story must be told outside the extractivist-developmentalist narrative.

In Chile, rocks resonate, intertwining with memory. Situated between the Andes and the meeting of tectonic plates, earthquakes erupt with planetary reach, fusing rock and our imagination. At the same time, the thunder of mining dynamite shakes stones, strata, and sediments, along with spirits, communities,

[33] De La Cadena (n 5); Marisol de la Cadena and Mario Blaser (eds), *A World of Many Worlds* (Durham, NC, Duke University Press, 2018); Isabelle Stengers, 'La propuesta cosmopolítica' (2014) *Pléyade* 17.

[34] Martin Tironi, M Chilet, P Hermansen and C Ureta Marín (eds), *Resonancias Tectónicas: Del Diseño Centrado En El Usuario a Un Diseño Orientado En El Planeta* (Santiago, Ediciones UC, 2024).

[35] Revista Minga, Quintana, '"Resonancias tectónicas": La instalación que puso al diseño chileno en el mapa global' (*Revista Minga*, 2 July 2021) www.revistaminga.cl/2021/07/02/resonancias-tectonicas-la-instalacion-que-puso-al-diseno-chileno-en-el-mapa-global/.

and economies. In the pavilion, the resonance of the rocks vibrates through lithophonic stones. This ritual of stony sounds reverberates through our bodies, echoing the original strata that have been violated in the Anthropocene. By making these 17 resonant stones – arranged as lithophones – the protagonists, each with its own distinct timbre, the apparent geological silence is broken.

On each lithophone, there were strikers – made from a small stone connected to a copper rod, a mineral extracted from the stone – that invited visitors to strike the stones. The stones, struck by another stone, created a sonic ritual that filled the room, turning Somerset House into its resonating chamber. Each stone was different, with its own place of origin, mineral composition, and morphology, shaped by both millennia of geological movements and human intervention. Striking one rock with another is a primordial gesture that connects seemingly distant strata and meanings, reminding us of the obvious: design is geological, planetary, historical, and political.

On the north wall of the room, visitors could see a large infographic narrating four stories: first, the story of earthquakes in Chile as geological resonances; second, the history of mining extractivism that cuts across our communities and territories; third, stories of ecological resistance communities currently fighting for their rights; and finally, the narrative of the supposed immateriality of the global information economy. All these stories speak of Earth's resonances, situating design within the entanglement of the biographical with the geological, the future with the ancestral, and the local with the planetary. These four narrative threads intertwine to give meaning to the operations of the pavilion.

On the east wall of the room, alongside the windows, six screens were installed, alternating images of the stones, texts, people, and territories that formed the foundation of the pavilion. Among the texts, verses from Raúl Zurita's poem *Saludan las piedras de Chile* stood out:

> … at least you will feel my hand searching for yours here, in the hardest night of the stones.

This verse, resonating in our memories, perhaps guided the decision to darken the room and bathe it in blue light, creating the atmosphere of a hard, nocturnal cave in which the ritual would unfold.

On the south wall, three large-scale screens were set up like a triptych. These screens displayed the vibrations of the stones through specially designed software. Using a network of microphones, the software detected only the frequencies at which the stones resonated. Each time a stone was struck, the visualisation on the screen responded to its frequency, disregarding any other sound.

Resonancias Tectónicas is to design in order to explore situated ways of knowing and transforming,[36] fostering coexistence through correspondence[37]

[36] Patricia Sanchez and Pablo Hermansen (eds), *Reconocer(Nos) y Transformar(Nos)* (Independent, 2021).

[37] Tim Ingold, 'On Human Correspondence' (2017) 23 *Journal of the Royal Anthropological Institute* 9.

and multispecies alliances[38] with the creations and vitalities of organic and inorganic, material and incorporeal entities. While design has historically participated in the instrumentalisation and homogenisation of the planet in the name of progress, this pavilion ritually invites us to embody and imagine pluriversal,[39] cosmopolitical worlds;[40] to create practices and narratives that help vitalise the worlds we inhabit.

The rocks displayed in *Resonancias Tectónicas* serve as catalysts for this museographic reflection. First, because geological elements and processes have politically and economically shaped Chile's role on the planet. The substrate of this landscape, traded on international stock exchanges, forms the imaginaries of future splendour and prosperity in Chile. Lithium or copper, saltpeter or iron, are deterritorialised syntheses that, rooted in the North's technological utopias, tell stories of colonisation while omitting the fact that socio-environmental crises are endured with particular intensity in the South.

Figure 12.3 Tectonic Resonances, Chilean Pavilion in the London Design Biennale. Captured from youtu.be/VKqL27lAB_M?feature=shared

[38] Emanuele Coccia, *Metamorfosis: la fascinante continuidad de la vida* (Pablo Ariel Ires tr, Madrid, Siruela, 2021).

[39] Arturo Escobar, *Designs for the Pluriverse: Radical Interdependence, Autonomy, and the Making of Worlds* (Durham, NC, Duke University Press, 2018).

[40] Martín Tironi and Pablo Hermansen, 'Cosmopolitical Encounters: Prototyping at the National Zoo in Santiago, Chile' (2018) 11 *Journal of Cultural Economy* 330.

Figure 12.4 Tectonic Resonances, Chilean Pavilion in the London Design Biennale. Captured from youtu.be/VKqL27lAB_M?feature=shared

Figure 12.5 Tectonic Resonances, Chilean Pavilion in the London Design Biennale. Captured from youtu.be/VKqL27lAB_M?feature=shared

Machiluwün: Becoming Machi with the Spirits

Through an autoethnographic narrative, Salvador Abarzúa and Pablo Hermansen[41] recount their journey from Santiago de Chile to the Huilliche and Lafkenche territories. Their route included two stops: Fundo Huite, where a *Palín* tournament was held during the meeting of the Mapuche National Ancestral Authorities, and Isla Lican, the site of a *Machiluwün*, a ritual to consecrate a new *Machi*. The authors describe this journey as a process of enmeshment and bodily friction between the urban whiteness of Santiago – an epicentre of appropriation and capital production – and the vital, immanent Mapuche force, manifested in two ritual spaces. Along this trajectory between worlds, they gradually shed modern-capitalist technologies[42] as the agency of the territories, more-than-human entities, and the rituals they participated in became more intense. This exercise in nomadism constitutes a metamorphosis, inviting us to a becoming where the tension between Equilibrium and Transgression is constitutive.[43]

In the *Machiluwün* ceremony, eight island communities converge, bringing together a total of 60 to 70 people. Pablo was the only *wenüy* (non-Mapuche friend) present at the ceremony. The participants wear ceremonial attire and perform predefined roles. A dozen young men serve as *Kona*, tasked with protecting the *Machi*. They accompany her with their *guiños* (bamboo sticks) and spears, shielding her from hidden forces (negative energies, *wekufes*) that attempt to sabotage the process and prevent her consecration. Five other *Machi* and a *Machin* (*Machi* apprentice) also support her, while the ceremony is led by Ernesto Huenchulaf, the *Lonko Gñiatufe*, who acts as a translator (*zungun machife*) or diplomat with the spirits of the *Pu Logko* and the *Machi*, assisted by a young *Ñempin* (ceremonial priest). The rest of the participants position themselves in an outer circle, delineating the ceremonial centre where the *Machi* enters a trance. They dance the *purrun*, walking with small jumps around the *rehue* and the *Machi*, to the rhythm of the *kuktrunes* (shamanic drums), *cascahuillas* (silver bells), and their *trapalacuchas* (silver chest plates, serving as energetic protection). The *pifilcas* (wooden whistles), *ñolkin* (trumpets), and *trutrucas* (wind instruments) signal the *wenu mapu* (the land above) that Mapuche are performing a ceremony here. It is an intense, beautiful, profound, and complex ritual. White and blue flags adorn the *rehue* as symbols of peace and medicine (*lahuén*), qualities that distinguish the new *Machi*. Two

[41] S Abarzúa and P Hermansen, 'Transitando hacia el machiluwün de Isla Lican en lago Budi, Puerto Saavedra, región de la Araucanía: Autoetnografía situada en un entorno más-que-humano' (2025, forthcoming) *Diálogo Andino*.

[42] JJ Bautista, *Dialéctica del fetichismo de la modernidad: Hacia una teoría crítica del fetichismo de la racionalidad moderna* (La Paz, Editorial Autodeterminación, 2015).

[43] R Foerster González, Introducción a la religiosidad mapuche (Santiago, Editorial Universitaria, 1993); J Ñanculef Huaiquinao, *TAYIÑ MAPUCHE KIMÜN. EPISTEMOLOGÍA MAPUCHE: Sabiduría y conocimientos* (Santiago, UChile_Indígena, 2016).

animals are tied a few metres from the *rehue* (*a cow and a ram*), painted with symbols in blue and white, appearing calm, almost hypnotised. The animals have a special role; they are protected offspring that the Machi must care for throughout their life.

Throughout the ceremony, which lasts two nights and two days, a group of women is in charge of preparing food, while another group arranges the artefacts and performs actions based on the requests and commands of the *Pu Logko*, an ancestral Mapuche spirit that inhabits the *Machi's* body during the ceremony to deliver messages to the community. The community's interaction with the *Pu Logko* manifests in two ways. On one hand, there are the demands of the spirit embodied in the *Machi*, whose body, although not its own, allows it to corporealise: the *Machi's* spirit leaves her body to make room for the *Pu Logko*. On the other hand, the embodiment of the *Pu Logko* in the *Machi* is a gradual process, requiring adaptation and adjustment, which in turn affects the rhythm and flow of the ritual. As a relational moment between human and other-than-human entities, a series of ritual artefacts must be present. While the *Machiluwün* follows established conventions, the unpredictable agency of the *Pu Logko* creates uncertainty, as there is no clarity about what will happen next. Ernesto Huenchulaf, the *Lonko*, tells us that before our arrival, the ceremony was disordered and confusing, and the authorities felt a conflict between immanent forces. Each of the five *Machi* possesses their own *Newen* – vital force – and these are not always compatible. Each of these forces has its own quality, personality, and temperament, governed by an element of nature (earth, fire, water, air), as well as by an animal, plant, or a *pillan* (volcano). 'When you combine a fire newen with a water one, they can eventually generate friction and disturbance', says the *Logko*. Gradually, these forces begin to align, and the intensity of the ceremony channels the flow of cosmic forces in their splendour.

This intensity is followed by a more restful phase when the Machi's spirit returns to her body, the Lonko shares the Pu Logko's message with the Machi, and then she sits before her *rehue* and sings the message to those present in a lamenting tone. It is striking that almost everyone, if not all, speaks *Mapudungun*; there is no translation of the messages from the Pu Logko. The *Machi* conveys the Pu Logko's demands for actions that mobilise the political-spiritual agency of the entire community to halt neoliberal and extractivist transgressions against the equilibrium of the *Mapu*. Despite Salvador's efforts, he cannot fully and spontaneously translate the content of the message. Broadly speaking, the Pu Logko called for respect for the ethical principles of the *Mapu*, urging those with *Kimún* (knowledge) to defend and preserve the Mapuche world. Even without fully understanding the content, the *Newen* (vital forces) generated by this collective act are inevitably deeply felt.

How predictable is the rite? How much trial and error occurs during the ceremony? More importantly, to what extent is uncertainty inherent in the *Michiluwün*, and does attempting to answer these questions as researchers risk transgressing its mystery? Salvador and Pablo reject the idea of probing the mystery with a spotlight. Salvador and Pablo adopt an ethics of care that embraces recalcitrance and incomprehensibility, celebrating excess. To paraphrase Wittgenstein, they describe this ritual environment by accepting that it is better to remain silent about what cannot be said.

During the night, during the last *purrún*, Salvador approaches to check on Pablo.

Salvador:

> At one point during the early morning, I don't see Pablo, so I leave the *purrún* to look for him. Suddenly, in the shadows, with a dark windbreaker and hood on, I spot him dancing the *purrún* silently. I approach, put my hand on his shoulder, and ask, 'What do you think?' – he is in ecstasy. Pablo lifts his gaze and says, 'This is incredible, this is indescribable.' His body moves, hypnotized by the rhythm and intensity of the rite. This was around 3:00 am, the time when the ceremony pauses for the first night.

Pablo:

> I was struck by the flow of energy from the *Machi*, who by then had already endured at least 20 hours of intense physical and spiritual exertion. I couldn't believe she climbed the *rehue* at night, blindfolded, demonstrating the trance with the strength and agility of her body. As an observer, I tried not to interfere with the rite, but despite the physical fatigue, it was impossible not to become part of its energy flow.

Figure 12.6 The Michiluwün is a complex more-than-human ecosystem. Diverse entities become enmarañadas in the rite, a constitutive dimension of being Mapuche: without ceremony, the Mapuche cosmos ceases to exist. The rite makes clear that the Mapuche body is inseparable from the Mapuche cosmos

Figure 12.7 The Michiluwün is a complex more-than-human ecosystem. Diverse entities become enmarañadas in the rite, a constitutive dimension of being Mapuche: without ceremony, the Mapuche cosmos ceases to exist. The rite makes clear that the Mapuche body is inseparable from the Mapuche cosmos

The images (Figures 12.6 and 12.7) correspond to cartographic sketches of the ceremony record. In the first one, the lonko ñguillatufe and the Ñempin are seen together with the Machi performing a rogation, in which the actors feed the rehue with seeds and toasted flour. They also place jugs of water and muday (water with wheat). The arrows indicate the direction in which the purun is performed – counterclockwise – which is the direction of the water in the whirlpools and the direction in which climbing plants adhere to other plants.

In the second image, the Machi is seen on top of the rehue, blindfolded, in a full trance, holding bunches of sacred and medicinal plants (lahuen) in her hands. To the rhythm of the kuntrun (shamanic drum) and pifilkas (wind instrument), she continues her dance on the rehue, which is about 4 to 5 metres high. At no time does she show any doubt or fear, nor any sign of vertigo. Below, the heads of the community members are seen giving their energy to the machi through their dance, shouts, and songs. In this image, the third trance of Sunday is observed. The machi is drawn as the shadow beneath the wiños (wooden sticks), which are struck against each other forcefully without touching the machi's body. This is to give collective newen to the machi but also to protect her from the bad energies that are always lurking (weza newen).

DESIGNING FOR THE SUBLIME: JUSTICE AS A RITUAL FOR EMBODIED PARTICIPATION

If people cannot feel democratic participation in their bodies, why would they care?[44]

The works mentioned above highlight that distancing ourselves from the modern epistemological matrix, especially the scientific one, and observing other ways of creating the commons, reveals the power of ritual and transcendent dimensions in strengthening belonging and social bonds. From these non-scientific, non-modern ways of creating the commons, we can extract keys to redesign our justice systems without banalising them or inscribing them into neoliberal consumer logics, which ultimately homogenise justice and consumption with all the resulting consequences of the erosion of the commons. If this erosion occurs, the judicial system will collapse without us being able to transform it into something better for the Buen Vivir, pertinent to our times, social realities, and territories. This would leave this important flank open to the onslaught of capital flows driven by neoliberal logic.[45]

The pavilion was organised as a ritual space to rethink the potential of designing situated in the South, aiming to redefine our modes of relating to the geological as a more-than-human entity. The simultaneous forces of ecological devastation and the digitalisation of life make it urgent to reconsider the praxis, logics, and alliances of design as it connects with the planet. This transition requires distancing ourselves from modern design, envisioning worlds beyond its disciplinary limits, and thus apprehending and embodying relational and ecological approaches that allow us to restore conditions for habitability. This curatorial experience sought to stage a rituality capable of revitalising a decolonial way of *sentipensar*[46] that expands the possibilities of design in confronting environmental unsustainability. The hypothesis is that if the future of design is confined by the logic of transactional capitalism, then the question of its future becomes meaningless, as it loses its potential to imagine and create worlds for Justice to become.

As long as the origin myth of design remains rooted in the European Industrial Revolution and its epic, its practice will adhere to a modernising narrative of infinite and linear progress, fueled by the instrumentalisation and exploitation of the planet to serve a select group of humans. In this sense, design is marked by its role in accompanying and productivising the modernisation project, universalising this specific way of understanding, delineating, and therefore exploiting the Earth. Situated at the antipodes of the centres of power in capitalist modernity, we could argue that the ecological crisis is as much a matter of ideological principles as it is

[44] A statement motivated by a rich discussion with Prof. Joel Bakan during the lunch break in Onati while he was on a research stay at the Institute.

[45] Joaquin Santuber and Pablo Hermansen, 'Shifting Identities: New Materialities of Power and Control' (2023) *IASDR Conference Series* dl.designresearchsociety.org/iasdr/iasdr2023/fullpapers/185.

[46] Martín Tironi, 'Introduction: Design for More-than-Human Futures' in Martín Tironi and others (eds), *Design For More-Than-Human Futures* (1st edn, London, Routledge, 2023) www.taylorfrancis.com/books/9781003319689/chapters/10.4324/9781003319689-1.

of particular design practices, where non-modern entities are objectified and used as mere resources for production.[47]

In contrast to this perspective, *Resonancias Tectónicas* aims to expand the reflection on design through a ritual space where the resonances of invisible actors and entities can be apprehended, seeking consonance with the other-than-human designers who sustain and continue our existence. The pavilion was thus conceived as a challenge aimed at situating design within a horizon of interdependencies that exceed the limits of human coexistence, entangling biological, ecological, and technological agencies.

The dominant narrative on digitalisation and innovation, which is found on human-centred, people-centred,[48] works as a form of criticism of the old system and has thinned and reduced our judicial systems and access to justice to user-friendliness, speed gain, and cost reduction. By means of efficiency and agility, it leaves Justice, the transcendence element of the judicial practice out of the equation of innovation. Because under this logic what cannot be captured by this equation, does not exist.

As an alternative, by embracing these rituals and transcendent dimensions, we advocate for recognising the relevance of non-human agencies, such as Justice and the material and organisational conditions in which justice is produced and socialised. Designing for a justice whose movement (pistons, magnetic motors, nuclear fusion) has a metabolism based on the constitutive tensions between these two justices (the concrete and the transcendent) is essential. This leads us to overcome the duality of problem-solution as the articulator of design processes and instead consider these relationships as part of a tension constitutive of a Design for the Sublime exercise.

A Cosmopolitical Prototype of Sounds for Justice

As observed in the physical courtroom of the Supreme Court in Chile, and the two examples from Tectonic Resonances and the Machiliwün, the audience is not just an observer but actively participates in the performance. In a time when innovation imperatives and market logic permeate all private and public spaces, the seek of seamlessness, the experience of the user being as frictionless as possible, removes any possibilities of embodied participation from the public. However, as we have argued earlier, embodied participation is not just an add-on, a nice to have, but constitutive to the rituals of justice. While participation in the physical courtroom was limited but possible, public participation in online hearings was mediated by social media live streamings, confining participation to clicking likes, writing comments, and resharing a link.[49]

[47] Tironi and others (n 33).

[48] For a focused treatment of human-centred and people-centred approaches to judicial systems, see Ch 3 in this volume, Metin, Toivonen and Kovalainen 'Bridging Paradigms: Comparing the Elements of Human-Centred Design in Legal Design and People-Centred Justice Framework'.

[49] Hakkarainen and Santuber (n 31).

Similar to the object of our design research, during the COVID pandemic, music concerts were performed in empty halls, or from the living rooms of the artists, and the claps were silenced. The clapping at the end of a concert, far from being a transaction – eg, the artist receiving a reward – is part of the performance in which the audience makes hearable, audible, and explicit that they have been listening attentively. In a way, the audience reveals itself, removing the cover of silence carefully observed. It is the sublimation of the experience, crowned with the intensity of the clapping.

Traditionally, the audience takes part in a judicial hearing when the audience stands up as the judges make their entrance to the courtroom. As a form of showing respect to the authority of the court, in that embodied participation, the audience enacts the court's authority. They could resist it, by staying seated or shouting out loud something inappropriate, or throwing a shoe. Judges direct the attention of the court by hitting a wooden mallet called gavel. In a virtual courtroom, the possibilities of the embodiment of that participation are limited to clicks or taps, enclosed in the private environments of the audience, outside the public space.

Figure 12.8 Machitún ritual of the Mapuche people. Captured from youtu.be/Y-DkkV72Rso?feature=shared

Figure 12.9 Screen capture of the sound waves from the recording of a Machitún ritual. Captured from youtu.be/Y-DkkV72Rso?feature=shared

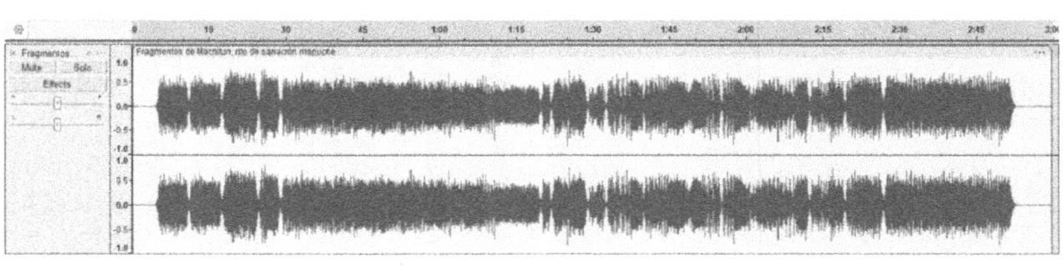

Participation in the tectonic resonances, visitors hit lithophones – stones – and create sounds, establishing the relationship between them and the stones, the soil, and the minerals. In the Machiliwün, while some are drumming, others participate by hitting sticks of wood, to one another or the ground, to the soil, sand, and stones under their feet.

We take the sound of the stones and the sticks and bring them into a virtual courtroom, creating an artefact in which we subvert the modern institution of the courts, by bringing in elements from elsewhere, a design pavilion and an ancestral ritual. Moreover, we counter-subvert the physical courtroom, subverted by the videoconferencing platform interfaces and functions, by adding layers of sounds that otherwise do not belong to that space, giving it a sense of rituality to a space dominated by an aesthetic of Zoom's corporate vision: 'frictionless communication'. In our speculative prototyping in designing for the sublime, we take audio clips from the two situations and transpose them to the recordings of the judicial hearings, both in the courtroom and online (see Table 12.1).

As such, we re-arranged the material conditions of a judicial hearing, by transposing the sounds of a curated artistic space and an ancestral ritual, to enact the perceptible dimension of rituality – sensible by questioning where the engine of the action is. In a film, the narrative is in the director who creates the sequence; in photography, it is in the observer. Our prototype allows us to shift the engine of action from the court and judges to the public.

In a sense, we work with ruins,[50] digital ruins in the form of video and audio recordings of judicial hearings that already happened, years ago. Their results are already known, and the consequences have already been forgotten. After all, the banal, the banalisation of justice is not remembered; it is disposable, like the other millions of videos stored on YouTube waiting to be seen. The thousands of video recordings of judicial hearings, stored on YouTube, are the recording of a past, which works as a sediment, a mineral layer, sustaining the hegemony of the ways of doing justice. We subvert those digital ruins of judicial processes, in the form of digital media pieces, and we reassemble them to see what happens. The 'what if' is not a light-taken attitude to this topic, but it is prototyping for the emergence of possibilities. These artefacts open up worlds, possibilities, by turning the digital ruins from matters of concern to matters of design. These prototypes are, in this sense, cosmopolitical.[51]

[50] Gordillo (n 23).

[51] Pablo Hermansen and Martin Tironi, 'Cosmopolitical Interventions: Prototyping Interspecies Encounters for More than Human Futures' in Jennifer Roberts-Smith, Stan Ruecker and Milena Radzikowska (eds), *Prototyping across the Disciplines: Designing Better Futures* (Bristol, Intelect Books, 2021).

Table 12.1 An overview of the transposition of audio recordings from the Tectonic Resonances and the Machitún onto the recordings of judicial hearings of the Chilean Supreme Court in both physical and online environments

We transposed the audio recording of the tectonic resonances and Michiliwün into the hearing of the plenary of the Supreme Court, both physical and online.		
	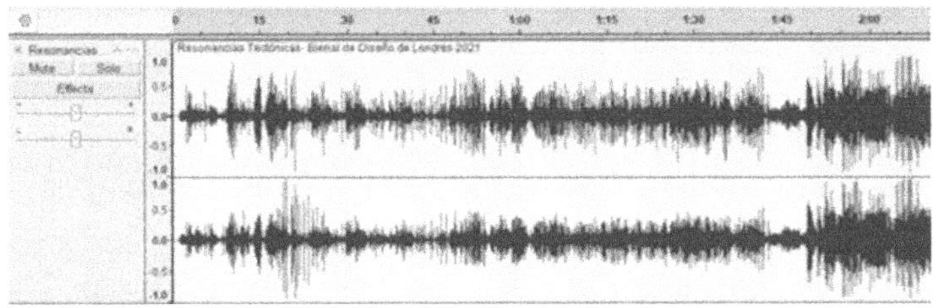	
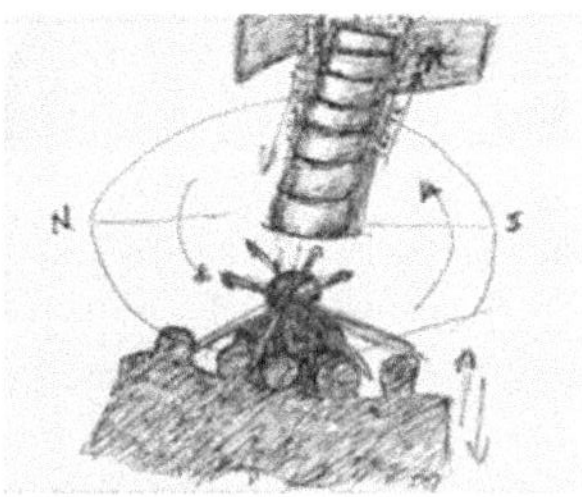	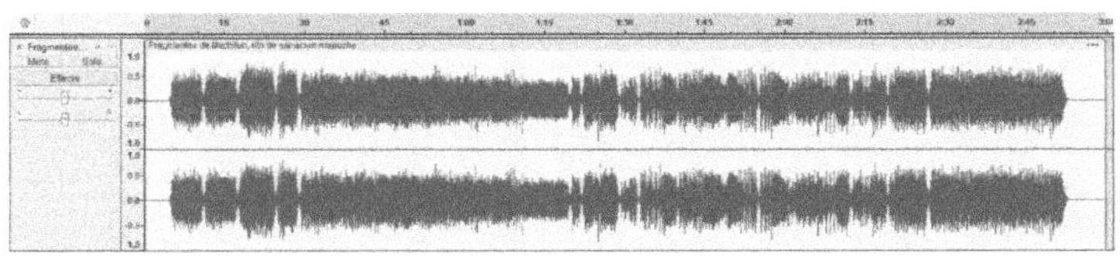	

Following Silvia Rivera Cusicanqui, designing for the sublime directs its efforts to hybridisation, mixtures of the traditional and the new, to achieve that commonness that transcends the individual. A plurality in the origin of the references is itself a subversion of linear, totalising worldviews that reduces them to the user, the individuum, an instrument of the transactions. Marisol de la Cadena, reference to cosmopolitics[52] as a way of allowing the emergence of both human and non-human agency in enacting a world.[53] In terms of prototyping as a cosmopolitical place[54] in Designing for the Sublime, we put forward a cosmopolitical device in the form of audiovisual scenarios in which the conditions are provided for transcendent agencies to become part of the ritual. In the specific case, in the form of sound waves, we prototyped not only a presence of transcendence but also a form of resistance to dominant ways of delivering justice. In line with Rossana Reguillo's[55] role of music in juvenile circles, we bring the sounds from stones and drumming as a form of resisting hegemonic forms of power and politics. Moreover, sound as an aesthetic experience is a transformative one, directed towards the openness to feel what exceeds the one, one's own one-ness.

Like in other rituals, the sound comes to symbolise the moment in which the individual becomes part of the collective, in the becoming of society, to then become a changed subject. In an ontological sense, in the ritual, the sound represents the moment in which transcendence becomes part of a world, it is present and becomes immanent. The sound symbolises the intensity of the ritual and guides our experiences to the moment and situation in which the transcendent is becoming immanent.

Designing rituals that awaken planetary consciousness means opening the design project to the diverse elements, agencies, scales, and modes of relation that the modern civilisational programme has chosen to ignore. Recognising the intelligence of materialities in mutual correspondence presents a significant challenge for design. It requires displacing the modern social contract that underpins its self-comprehension and relationship with 'nature' – a mere external resource – to embrace the more-than-human mystery of coexistence in interdependence.

In this sense, Design for the Sublime builds on *Resonancias Tectónicas*, which as a ritual space, invites us to traverse ancestral paths – excluded from modern design – staging a ritual of interdependence, where the multiple entities that make worlds are intertwined. Thinking about bodies and collectivities,

[52] Stengers (n 32).

[53] Marisol de la Cadena, 'Cosmopolítica Indígena En Los Andes: Reflexiones Conceptuales Más Allá de La «política»' (2020) *Tabula rasa* www.revistatabularasa.org/numero33/cosmopolitica-indigena-en-los-andes-reflexiones-conceptuales-mas-alla-de-la-politica/.

[54] Martin Tironi, Pablo Hermansen and José Neira, 'The Prototype as a Cosmopolitical Place: Ethnographic Design Practice and Research at the National Zoo in Santiago, Chile' (2016) *DRS Biennial Conference Series* dl.designresearchsociety.org/drs-conference-papers/drs2016/researchpapers/46.

[55] Reguillo Cruz (n 22).

politics and technique, through situated rituals serves as a drive to transcend the transactional logics that have dominated modern development and shaped our subjectivities. Resonating together affirms these interdependencies, an aesthetic experience that could help us navigate beyond the Anthropocene.[56]

Justice is constituted by conflicts and frictions between agents of all kinds: human interests, capital, property, power, materialities, ideas, words, prestige, the commons (water, air, space, time), non-humane living entities, and incorporeal beings. Design for the Sublime is the prefiguration and co-creation of a generative justice as becoming with the other – human and more than human. As such, Design for the Sublime involves the humility that designers must assume, acting as articulators of conditions while leaving spaces open for the emergence of other types of agencies. When the focus is not on user needs but on the tension between the two justices, the needs of those who are part of the sociomaterial fabric can resonate. This constitutive tension between the agency of the transcendent and the sociomaterial conditions of those who coexist on this planet is the relationship between these two justices.

Exploring the ritual and transcendent dimensions of contemporary Latin American practices offers a rich terrain for reimagining justice. It provides a framework for designing spaces and relationships that honour the complexity and interconnectedness of human and non-human entities, fostering a more holistic and sustainable approach to justice that transcends mere transactional efficiency. The presence of transcendent entities in the resolution of our daily frictions makes it possible for conflicts to be settled by maintaining a greater and common good on the horizon, thus strengthening the vitality of the social metabolism. In the extreme, when Justice is imposed, it is neither won nor lost; instead, it is a tendency to re-establish the balance (Mapuche balance and transgression).

FINAL REMARKS

To address the challenges of a solution-driven society, designing in the field of justice and the courts invites us to reconsider our practices beyond the user experience and articulate the material conditions for the emergence of the sublime. We have explored this in the form of embodied participation via sound. Addressing these challenges requires overcoming – transcending – the human individual exceptionalism and accepting that not everything is meant to be solved, like the Gordian knot. Inspired by the rituality of courts and the more-than-human agency of Justice, we are prefiguring an alternative approach, an alternative way of dealing with the pressing issues of a highly techno-digitally mediated, late-capitalist society.

[56] Hermansen and Guerra Solano (n 8).

We have introduced this approach, which we have called Design for the Sublime. Building on rituals, transcendence, and the sublime, we seek a way out of the individual ontology of dominant transactional narratives in law and design, and project ways in which we can support the emergence of the common, a being together. While the emphasis in design has been on the user/individual experience, we argue that there is no such thing as an individual experience, as all experience is collective. In this sense, Design for the Sublime seeks through rituals for ways in which the transcendent (what is beyond the immediacy of the human individual) has a greater agency in justice systems.

Because rituals, transcendence, and the sublime are neglected by the scientific epistemologies, Design for the Sublime solicits our practices to embrace alternative ways of knowing, ways of producing, storing, and exchanging knowledge, as a fundamental disposition to entangle with other knowing bodies – human and more-than-human. Although law has appropriated design methodologies to meet the challenges of innovation and digitalisation, in these pages, we offer an example of what law as a field of study has to offer to design.

In designing for law and justice, where the legal discipline has appropriated design practices (as Design has done before from elsewhere), the question is about what law has to contribute to Design. In this sense, the context of justice, its history, architecture, spaces, etc, served the authors as a space of inspiration to develop their proposal of Design for the Sublime.

However, more than seeing this as an exchange, a give and take, we believe that the possibility to think beyond each discipline's assets is to surrender to the fundamental disposition to entangle, to *enmarañarse*. If we think of this process linguistically, it would be *legaldesigning*, with no space in between, no n-dash (–) that keeps the purity of each discipline intact by keeping them apart.

In this regard, our contribution, Design for the Sublime, challenges the monopolistic hegemony of dominant practices of design at three levels: the ontological (beyond the human individual), the epistemological (beyond the scientific knowing), and the methodological (beyond the problem-solving design). It is clear that designing for the sublime exceeds law and justice and can be applied to other design projects. The authors thus recognise the resources provided by justice to rethink design from other perspectives. In this sense, the perspectives we refer to are plural perspectives in which the ways of creating knowledge, storing, and distributing it go beyond the hegemonic forms of scientific production. The epistemological reflection of design for the sublime invites us to look beyond common sources, as well as invites us to ask the question for whom legal design is designing. And not only for whom, but with whom.

The distinction between designing for the sublime and designing with the sublime is important to highlight. On the one hand, designing for the sublime refers to the objective of the practice of legaldesigning, in the sense that it encompasses beyond the immediate needs of the so-called human being, but aspires and intentionally seeks to create the conditions for the emergence of the sublime in the services, products, and systems that are being designed – in this case, justice. Designing with the sublime implies not only seeking the possibility of creating the material conditions that make the sublime experience possible in justice but also asking how to integrate sublime elements into creative practices, into the participatory process, transcendent entities that are part of designing with more-than-human agencies. In the case of designing with the sublime, these agencies – more-than-human – are represented by transcendent entities that become part of the design process; they become part of the creative process to generate alternatives of knowledge and production of socio-material reality beyond the imperatives of the capitalist market. In this chapter, we have argued and experimented with the first notion, designing for the sublime. Future design research should explore the role of the transcendent in the practices of legaldesigning.

On this point, it is important to emphasise that the proposal we develop in this article seeks to extend that for whom and with whom to transcendent entities that are part of the design proposal as well as of the practice of design. We grounded our proposal of Design for the Sublime on three cases where more-than-human rituality and transcendence comprise and give meaning to the immediate: the courtroom of the Supreme Court in Chile (both in its physical and virtual environment), the winning installation at the London Design Biennale 2021 'Tectonic Resonances', and a Mapuche ritual in the *Wellmapu* (south of Chile). The examples provided in this article show us the need to transcend the modern scientific paradigm, because knowledge is often outside the study room, outside the laboratory, and outside the faculty. While it is invisible to modern science and its epistemology, no doubt the sublime is out there, within and beyond.

REFERENCES

S Abarzúa and P Hermansen, *Transitando hacia el machiluwün de Isla Lican en lago Budi, Puerto Saavedra, región de la Araucanía: Autoetnografía situada en un entorno más-que-humano* (2025, forthcoming) *Diálogos Andinos*.

JJ Bautista, *Dialéctica del fetichismo de la modernidad: Hacia una teoría crítica del fetichismo de la racionalidad moderna* (La Paz, Editorial Autodeterminación, 2015).

W Burroughs and B Gysin, *The Third Mind* (New York, Viking Press, 1978).

J Butler, 'Precarious Life, Vulnerability, and the Ethics of Cohabitation' (2012) 26 *The Journal of Speculative Philosophy* 134.

——, *Frames of War: When Is Life Grievable?* (London, Verso, 2009).

S Castro-Gómez and R Grosfoguel (eds), *El giro decolonial: reflexiones para una diversidad epistémica más allá del capitalismo global* (Bogotá, Siglo del Hombre Ed [u.a], 2007).

E Coccia, *Metamorfosis: la fascinante continuidad de la vida* (Pablo Ariel Ires tr, Madrid, Siruela, 2021).

A Cooper, *The Inmates Are Running the Asylum* (Indianapolis, IN, Sams, 1999).

N Cross, *Design Thinking: Understanding How Designers Think and Work* (Oxford, Berg, 2011).

RR Cruz, *Culturas Juveniles: Formas Políticas Del Desencanto* (Ed rev y aum, Mexico City, Siglo Veintiuno Editores, 2012).

S Rivera Cusicanqui, *Ch'ixinakax Utxiwa: Una Reflexión Sobre Prácticas y Discursos Descolonizadores* (Retazos, Tinta Limón Ediciones, 2010).

E Davis, *TechGnosis: Myth, Magic, & Mysticism in the Age of Information* (Berkeley, CA, North Atlantic Books, 2015).

EV De Castro, *Cannibal Metaphysics* (Minneapolis, MN, University of Minnesota Press, 2014).

M De La Cadena, 'Cosmopolítica Indígena En Los Andes: Reflexiones Conceptuales Más Allá de La «política»' (2020) *Tabula rasa*.

——, in Robert J Foster and Daniel R Reichman (eds), *Earth Beings: Ecologies of Practice across Andean Worlds* (Durham, NC, Duke University Press, 2015).

M De La Cadena and M Blaser (eds), *A World of Many Worlds* (Durham, NC, Duke University Press, 2018).

J Derrida, 'Force of Law: The "Mystical Foundation of Authority"' in Drucilla Cornell, Michel Rosenfeld and David Gray Carlson (eds), *Deconstruction and the Possibility of Justice* (Hove, Psychology Press, 1992) 27.

TF Driver, *Liberating Rites: Understanding the Transformative Power of Ritual* (Abingdon, Routledge, 2019).

A Escobar, *Designs for the Pluriverse: Radical Interdependence, Autonomy, and the Making of Worlds* (Durham, NC, Duke University Press, 2018).

R Foerster González, *Introducción a la religiosidad mapuche* (Santiago, Editorial Universitaria, 1993).

M Galindo, *No se puede descolonizar sin despatriarcalizar: teoría y propuesta de la despatriarcalización* (La Paz, Mujeres Creando, 2013).

AV Gennep, *The Rites of Passage* (Abingdon, Psychology Press, 1960).

GR Gordillo, *Rubble: The Afterlife of Destruction* (Durham, NC, Duke University Press, 2014).

J Hakkarainen and J Santuber, 'Come in and See: Translating a Design Pattern from the Courtroom into an Online Environment' (2024) 3 *Digital Society* 27.

P Hermansen and J Guerra Solano, 'Furrowing the Maraña: Designing to Sail out of the Anthropocene' in Martin Tironi and others (eds), *Design for More Than Human Futures* (New York, Routledge, 2023).

P Hermansen and Martín Tironi, 'Interspecies Design for Co-Existence', *Routledge Handbook of Sustainable Design* (2nd edn, New York, Routledge, 2024).

P Hermansen and M Tironi, 'Cosmopolitical Interventions: Prototyping Interspecies Encounters for More than Human Futures' in Jennifer Roberts-Smith, Stan Ruecker and Milena Radzikowska (eds), *Prototyping across the Disciplines: Designing Better Futures* (Bristol, Intelect Books, 2021).

T Ingold, 'On Human Correspondence' (2017) 23 *Journal of the Royal Anthropological Institute* 9.

J Kolko, *Thoughts on Interaction Design* (Amsterdam, Elsevier, 2011).

D López Medina, 'La Historia de Otros: Ideología Del Derecho Procesal Europeo y Su Trasplante a América Latina' (2020) *Via Iuris* 1.

B Moggridge, *Designing Interactions* (Cambridge, MA, MIT Press, 2007).

L Mulcahy, *Legal Architecture: Justice, Due Process and the Place of Law* (Abingdon, Routledge, 2011).
DA Norman, *The Psychology of Everyday Things* (New York, Basic Books, 1988).
——, *The Design of Everyday Things: Revised and Expanded Edition* (New York, Basic Books, 2013).
J Ñanculef Huaiquinao, *TAYIÑ MAPUCHE KIMÜN. EPISTEMOLOGÍA MAPUCHE: Sabiduría y conocimientos* (Santiago, UChile_Indígena, 2016).
RA Refaie and J Santuber, 'Risks and Challenges to E-Justice Principles: Governing Remote Work, Online Hearings and the Use of Social Media in Chilean Courts' (2023) 15 *JeDEM – eJournal of eDemocracy and Open Government* 118.
Revista Leal Quintana, '"Resonancias tectónicas": La instalación que puso al diseño chileno en el mapa global' (*Revista Minga*, 2 July 2021).
G Sakellariou, 'Composing the Sublime: Rituals in Electroacoustic Music' (PhD Thesis, Coventry University, 2017).
P Sanchez and P Hermansen (eds), *Reconocer(Nos) y Transformar(Nos)* (Independent, 2021).
J Santuber and J Edelman, 'Designing with Theories: Producing Legal Design Diffractively in Courts of Justice' (2022) *DRS Biennial Conference Series.*
J Santuber and P Hermansen, 'Designing for Posthuman Legalities: Legal Design(Ing) and the Ontological Turn' in Rossana Ducato, Alain Strowel and Marique Enguerrand (eds), *Design (s) for Law* (Milan, Ledizioni, 2024).
——, 'Shifting Identities: New Materialities of Power and Control' (2023) *IASDR Conference Series.*
J Santuber, 'Designing for Digital Justice: An Entanglement of People, Law, and Technologies' (Doctoral Thesis, University of Potsdam, 2023).
J Santuber, RA Refaie and C Meinel, 'Interrogating E-Justice: Lessons from Digitalizing Courts in Chile' (2022) *EGOV-CeDEM-ePart 2022* 54.
T Seitz, *Design Thinking and the New Spirit of Capitalism: Sociological Reflections on Innovation Culture* (Cham, Springer International Publishing, 2020).
H Simon, *The Sciences of the Artificial* (Cambridge, MA, MIT Press, 1969).
I Stengers, 'La propuesta cosmopolítica' (2014) *Pléyade* 17.
M Tironi and P Hermansen, 'Cosmopolitical Encounters: Prototyping at the National Zoo in Santiago, Chile' (2018) 11 *Journal of Cultural Economy* 330.
M Tironi, P Hermansen and J Neira, 'The Prototype as a Cosmopolitical Place: Ethnographic Design Practice and Research at the National Zoo in Santiago, Chile' (2016) *DRS Biennial Conference Series.*
M Tironi, M Chilet, P Hermansen and C Ureta Marín (eds), *Resonancias Tectónicas: Del Diseño Centrado En El Usuario a Un Diseño Orientado En El Planeta* (Santiago, Ediciones UC, 2024).
M Tironi, 'Introduction: Design for More-than-Human Futures' in Martín Tironi and others (eds), *Design for More-Than-Human Futures* (1st edn, London, Routledge, 2023).

13

Beyond the Problem-Solution Paradigm in Legal Design: Making the Cloud Rain in Bahrain

BADER ALNOAIMI

INTRODUCTION

In April 2017, Bahrain's Information and e-Government Authority published the 'Cloud First' Policy, affirming the government's commitment to 'lead by example' by adopting cloud computing technologies 'to reduce costs, increase security, increase productivity, and to develop excellent citizen services'.[1] The policy was formulated in the context of the government's efforts to encourage Amazon Web Services (AWS) to invest in Bahrain and to establish a regional data centre. Yet, the enactment of the policy was one of AWS's demands during the negotiations for entering the Bahraini market,[2] which highlights how technology policy is primarily a product of compromise and contestation,[3] rather than the outcome of technical assessments and strategic planning.[4]

This paper seeks to problematise the notion that technology policy can be insulated within a technocratic framework that makes it distinct from other areas of policymaking. It argues that governance of emerging technologies should be seen as part of a socially embedded process of co-production,[5] and that social public interests should play a bigger role in shaping the direction

[1] General Directorate of Governance and Operations, 'Cloud First Policy' (Information and eGovernment Authority, 2017) www.bahrain.bh/wps/wcm/connect/f6cbcc73-18a1-4c5e-b50d-51579230338b/Cloud+First+Policy.pdf?MOD=AJPERES.

[2] Manish Ranjan, 'Cloud Strategy and Its Impact on Bahrain's Economy' (International Data Corporation in collaboration with Amazon Web Services and Bahrain EDB 2023) 11.

[3] Anke Sophia Obendiek, 'What Are We Actually Talking About? Conceptualizing Data as a Governable Object in Overlapping Jurisdictions' (2022) 66 *International Studies Quarterly* 2.

[4] Lyria Bennett Moses, 'Regulating in the Face of Sociotechnical Change' in Roger Brownsword, Eloise Scotford and Karen Yeung (eds), *The Oxford Handbook of Law, Regulating and Technology* (Oxford, Oxford University Press, 2016) 576–582.

[5] Obendiek (n 3) 3–5.

of technology policy, especially as technology policy becomes an area of high importance for governments. Legal design has been proposed as a way to introduce democratic practices into public policies. The turn towards public participation in technology policy is both a response to criticisms of technocratic governance and perhaps an indication of the influence of legal design principles of accessibility and inclusivity on technology policy. But legal design can fall short of achieving these lofty goals when legal design as a field, and legal designers as practitioners, fail to recognise the assumptions embedded within the field and its methodologies, and the subjectivity of the legal designer. Where it sees issues of accessibility and inclusivity in technology policy, it has proposed public participation mechanisms to resolve them. But legal design is too focused on 'problem-finding' and 'problem-solving' and fails to recognise that legal design is a practice of problem-constructing. Indeed, if we understand technology policy as an outcome of contestation between different normative commitments, then viewing technology policy from the perspective of legal design can help raise questions about the values that society wants to be governed by. Does society want to be competitive or efficient or innovative or something *else*?

Governments are competing with each other in the digital technologies space,[6] and seek to maintain and increase their competitiveness by emulating the perceived successes of other governments.[7] This convergence of interests has led to treating specific technologies as key policy priorities – and one of these technologies is cloud computing, which refers to a method of delivering computing resources over a network that may be scaled up and down according to needs. It is deployed as a service, in which customers contract with service providers to 'rent' computing resources that are managed from multiple infrastructures in multiple locations simultaneously and these resources are dynamically assigned to customers through an algorithm for purposes of resource optimisation.[8] When compared to other examples of 'policy priority' technologies such as artificial intelligence, fintech and blockchain, cloud computing emerges as a particularly critical priority because it underpins the technical infrastructure which makes these other technologies possible. It would be difficult to imagine the widespread adoption of fintech and the blockchain without the innovations in networked computing resources.

Yet, at the same time, the assumed benefits of digital technologies are not always questioned by policymakers, who continue to promote certain

[6] Dana Polatin-Reuben and Joss Wright, 'An Internet with BRICS Characteristics: Data Sovereignty and the Balkanisation of the Internet' (Usenix, 2014) 4.

[7] Ilias Alami and Adam Dixon, 'Uneven and Combined State Capitalism' (2023) 55 *EPA: Economy and Space* 73.

[8] Christopher Millard and W Kuan Hon, 'Cloud Technologies and Services' in Christopher Millard (ed), *Cloud Computing Law* (1st edn, Oxford, Oxford University Press, 2013) 3–6; W Kuan Hon, *Data Localization Laws and Policy: The EU Data Protection International Transfers Restriction Through a Cloud Computing Lens* (1st edn, Cheltenham, Edward Elgar Publishing, 2017) 2–3.

technologies as the key to 'unlocking' innovation, and 'unleashing' economic potential.[9] This approach leads to policies that are designed with these assumptions already built-in, and that accept the existing technology as a given. These assumptions mean that policymakers never question why *this* technology and not another, and why *this* form and not another. These rationales accept a technology's existing design as an inevitable outcome of market-based innovation, with the role of public policy constrained to regulation and minimisation of risks, coupled with the attempt to maximise the benefits of these technologies. Innovation becomes the deployment of 'techno-fixes' that emerge ready-made from the market as designed solutions to already assumed problems.

Legal design is thought of as a way to re-orient the legal system towards more inclusion and 'smarter' results,[10] but legal design's focus on 'solutions'[11] plays into the tendency to promote techno-fixes as solutions rather than critiquing the framing of the problem itself, especially when the problems they propose to solve are not clearly identified or even agreed upon. This 'solutionism' is inadequate for addressing systematic asymmetries in the law and holds a bias towards economic rationalities that do not question paradigms of 'efficiency' and 'innovation',[12] and which only serve to obscure the embedded interests of policymakers, or even design practitioners themselves. Instead, legal design should become more critical and orient itself closer to the critical legal studies (CLS) and critical design schools, in a way that can help legal design reveal inequalities by questioning our assumptions about reality. By centring critiques from CLS, science and technology studies (STS), and critical design scholarship, this paper seeks to problematise the unquestioned assumptions about the urgency and benefits of adopting cloud technologies as part of government policy, while also critiquing the response of legal design in proposing public participation mechanisms as a solution designed to address criticisms of technocracy. This paper understands technology policy as a process built on making political choices about which technologies to regulate and how, and in doing so, policymakers construct specific technologies as objects of governance and imbue them with particular characteristics. These choices hold inherent value-laden assumptions about technologies that make neither the design of policy nor the regulation of technology a neutral or technical process, but inherently political, and so should be subject to social interests. Through this

[9] 'How Bahrain's "Cloud-First" Philosophy Will Accelerate Digital Innovation' (*Economic Development Board – Bahrain*, 26 October 2023) www.bahrainedb.com/bahrain-pulse/how-bahrains-cloud-first-philosophy-will-accelerate-digital-innovation; Kathleen Garnett, Geert Van Calster and Leonie Reins, 'Towards an Innovation Principle: An Industry Trump or Shortening the Odds on Environmental Protection?' (2018) 10 *Law, Innovation and Technology* 4–6.

[10] Siddharth Peter de Souza, 'The Spread of Legal Tech Solutionism and the Need for Legal Design' (2022) 13 *European Journal of Risk Regulation* 378.

[11] Phoebe Walton, '*James v Birnmann*: The Potential of Critical Design for Examining Legal Issues' in D. Lockton and others (eds), *DRS Biennial Conference Series* (Bilbao, DRS Digital Library, 2022) dl.designresearchsociety.org/drs-conference-papers/drs2022/researchpapers/106.

[12] de Souza (n 10) 376.

interdisciplinary approach combining concepts from CLS, STS, and critical design, the paper aims to make a methodological contribution to legal design by arguing that it should move away from 'solution-oriented' methodologies, which are (a) inadequate for addressing systematic asymmetries in the law,[13] (b) possess a bias towards economic rationalities that do not question paradigms of 'efficiency' and 'innovation', and (c) only serve to obscure the embedded interests of policymakers, and design practitioners. Instead, legal design should become more critical, and orient itself closer to the CLS and critical design schools, and should be more concerned with raising questions of *why* and *for whom*, which can help reveal inequalities by questioning our assumptions about reality.

Furthermore, this paper emphasises that technology policy should be seen as part of a wider struggle to determine a society's social and technological future(s) – rather than be a tool to reproduce neoliberal categories of citizen-users and economic rationalities. Bahrain's adoption of cloud computing technologies is a relevant case study for highlighting the transformations that are negotiated and struggled over. The first section of the paper will discuss the problem-solution paradigm in legal design and the influence of linear design methodologies on the field. The second section critiques how the problem-solution paradigm aligns with techno-solutionism in technology policy to reduce avenues for introspective and purposeful decision-making that centres the most vulnerable in society. The third section analyses Bahrain's Cloud First Policy in light of solutionist rationales. Finally, the fourth section brings these debates together using the example of public participation to show how a critical legal design approach should address upstream considerations for technology policy, challenge the assumptions embedded within technology policy, and help constitute self-determination for society to determine social and technological futures.

SECTION I

Beyond the Problem-solution Paradigm

Solution-driven legal design is based on a linear methodology,[14] in which the first step is always the identification of the problem. However, problems first need to be constructed *as* problems before they can be identified. Solution-driven methodologies do not critically examine how problems are constructed and accept the process of problem identification as a neutral practice of applied rational thinking,[15] rather than one with implicit and explicit biases and perspectives as to what constitutes and defines 'problems'. Critical design theory holds the implication that the solution-oriented focus of design is itself problematic, because

[13] Walton (n 11) 3.
[14] ibid.
[15] ibid.

it requires the construction and framing of specific issues as problems which are in need of solutions – and often times, these solutions can only be offered by particular professionals or institutions. Walton highlights how design thinking emerged out of the corporate context with the intention to make organisational practices, systems, and products more competitive and more efficient[16] and legal design has incorporated this logic of competitiveness and efficiency, to the detriment of other values such as fairness or justice.[17]

Walton makes a distinction between 'legal design' and 'critical design', ascribing to the former conservative attitudes focused on problem solving, and the latter more open-ended and introspective attitudes focused on 'problem-finding,'[18] arguing that legal design should become more critical and offer more systemic solutions, but acknowledges the shortcomings of the environment in which legal design is practiced which is concerned with providing solutions as 'products'[19] which can be reproduced and exchanged in the legal services market. Part of this shortcoming is linked to the fact that legal design is still practiced in a traditional corporatised design environment which itself favours particular issues and solutions. But even critical design's 'problem-finding' outlook should be appraised, because any problem-finding practice requires issues to be framed as problems, and the frame should emerge from a methodology that is aware that problems are constructed, and that they are not 'discovered'. The discursive construction of problems also entails the production of a normative-epistemic framework that helps actors understand what the problem is, what the response to it should be, and justifications for why this response was chosen. The justifications could range from effectiveness, efficiency, promotion of justice, etc. A critical method also needs to be aware that not all problems are problems for everyone, so the critical method needs to be selective in terms of what its priorities are, or else it may find itself go the way of design thinking and legal design, which tend to define problems which are really only problems for corporations, rather than the problems faced by the most vulnerable in society.

Legal design should move away from problem-finding rationales to problem-constructing, in such a way that legal design practitioners are aware of the inherently constructed nature of the problems that they seek to solve. Problem constructing outlooks allow for more space to see the multitude of choices available in constructing the problem to be solved, and what the objectives of any solution should be.

[16] ibid.

[17] ibid; Sankalp Bhatnagar, 'What Legal Design Is as Opposed to Could/Should Be' in D Lockton and others (eds), *DRS Biennial Conference Series* (2022) dl.designresearchsociety.org/drs-conference-papers/drs2022/researchpapers/239.

[18] Walton (n 11) 3; original citation, Anthony Dunne, *Speculative Everything: Design, Fiction, and Social Dreaming* (Cambridge, MA, MIT Press, 2013) vii.

[19] Walton (n 11) 4.

The Role of the Legal Designer in Problem-construction

The subjectivity of the legal designer or other professional actors plays a key role in facilitating the process of problem-construction. The lawyer's toolbox involves applying legal principles and tests, and likewise, the designer's toolbox promotes the use of design thinking. The epistemic background that most lawyers and designers possess as a result of their institutional training encourages adopting rationales that understand problems as naturally existing phenomena, and the role of lawyers and designers is to unearth these problems and apply a set of rational, linear techniques that serve to unpack the problem, communicate it to others, and devise responses to it.[20] Far from adopting an introspective examination of problems as socially constructed, lawyers and designers act as specialist service providers that offer clients an expert perspective into the issues that they face, and propose solutions that (apparently) only they can offer, in such a way that obscures the interests of lawyers and designers in reproducing their status as specialist service providers.

Under a critical problem-constructing framework, the role of the lawyer-designer would have to change. No longer would the lawyer-designer be at the centre of the legal design process, they would have to take a step back and understand that everyone is capable of problem-constructing. As opposed to linear design methodologies that may require specialist training to unearth and identify problems, a critical problem-constructing framework requires no such specialist training. This means that the lawyer-designer needs to become more self-reflexive precisely because institutional training tends to condition lawyers and designers to see themselves as possessing a unique set of tools that allow them to act as 'saviours'.[21] The saviour-oriented subjectivity of lawyers and designers obscures their own interests in perpetuating problem-finding and problem-solving frameworks, the construction of certain issues as problems, and others as normal social reality.

To go beyond the problem-solution paradigm, legal design methodologies should start asking different questions; the most important are questions of purpose and intention. *Why* is this a problem? Questions of purpose and intention can reveal what is obscured, and open opportunities for speculative and introspective investigations,[22] which can help expose biases in the presentation of problems and solutions, and reveal the asymmetries in the legal system's priorities.[23] To be critical means to not accept what already exists as the only choice, or the only path that could have been taken, but requires us to take a few steps back to understand *why* something – be it a legal system, a form of technology, or an idea – is the way it is today, and how it could have been

[20] For more on lawyerly ways of 'seeing' the world, Khan and Pope, 'Legal Design as Movement Lawyering Methodology: Lessons Learned at the New Jersey Legal Design Lab', ch 11 in this volume.

[21] Khan and Pope (n 20) 12–13.

[22] Walton (n 11) 5–6.

[23] Ibid 24–26.

different. To be critical also means that lawyer-designers should understand their own subjectivities and biases and be aware that problem-construction is not the exclusive purview of lawyer-designers but should be an open social dialogue.[24] A 'critical legal design' may have the potential to destabilise the law's hegemony,[25] but more importantly, it invites us to imagine different possibilities for change. The implication for continuing an uncritical legal design would be the continuation of a status quo that only raises questions that we are told need answers, and to continue delivering solutions to problems that may only be problems for elites. Legal design needs to ask *itself* why; *why* is it performing this practice, and *for whom*.

SECTION II

Constructing Techno-solutionism as a Policy Response

Technologies as they exist today are not the outcome of a linear path dependency, but the product of a multitude of choices made by humans in a given social context.[26] Each contested choice represents a different normative and epistemic vision for that technology, what it is, what it should be used for, and who should benefit from it.[27] The law is also about making choices – choices over what to regulate, how to regulate it, and for what purpose.[28] Law and technology gain meaning when they are embedded within social worlds.[29] Humans discursively articulate what the law is, what it should be, and why it should be the way that it is, as they do the same for technology. However, at the same time, people have interests in advancing competing but overlapping visions for both law and technology and therefore have to make certain choices about how to advance these interests. Ultimately, these choices have distributive and political effects and are not merely technical,[30] which is why technology policy can become such a hotly debated issue of public interest, despite policymakers' attempts to keep technology policy within a technocratic space.[31]

In the midst of all this emerges the notion of techno-solutionism, which refers to the belief that technology is uniquely positioned to solve the myriad issues

[24] Khan and Pope (n 20) 14. I thank the authors for their feedback and for highlighting the term 'problem co-constructing'.

[25] Walton (n 11) 24–26.

[26] Sheila Jasanoff, 'The Idiom of Co-Production' in Sheila Jasanoff (ed), *States of Knowledge: The Co-Production of Science and the Social Order* (London, Taylor & Francis Group, 2004).

[27] Obendiek (n 3) 2–5.

[28] ibid 2–5.

[29] ibid 3–5.

[30] Roxana Vatanparast, 'Data Governance and the Elasticity of Sovereignty' (2020) 46 *Brooklyn Journal of International Law* 33.

[31] Melanie Smallman, '"Nothing to Do with the Science": How an Elite Sociotechnical Imaginary Cements Policy Resistance to Public Perspectives on Science and Technology through the Machinery of Government' (2020) 50 *Social Studies of Science* 597–600.

faced by society.[32] Techno-solutionism's appeal is both a result of the ignorance of the complexity of issues faced by society, and individual interests that push for technological solutions.[33] Importantly, techno-solutionism requires technology to be discursively constructed not only *as* a solution for a variety of issues, but also as a means to obscure the availability of other choices. Techno-solutionism feeds into the interests of policymakers who actively want to construct particular normative-epistemic visions for emerging technologies as social net positives and better placed to address issues than other choices.[34]

Policymakers co-produce technologies through these techno-solutionist rationales that construct a legal conception of technology and its regulation. A particular technology does not become a 'technology' until someone articulates a normative-epistemic framework for defining what it is, how it should be used, and who should benefit from it. In the case of cloud computing technologies, policymakers first articulate that it is a solution for improving efficiency, and that it should be adopted across the public and private sectors as a way to transform operations and services, and that this adoption would benefit the whole of society. Policymakers produce a normative-epistemic framework for the governance of cloud technologies that expects the cloud to solve problems in efficiency and competitiveness for a state trying to outpace its competitors.

Techno-solutionism closes the door on debates about the nature of the issues that society faces or the values that people want to be governed by. Similarly to how the problem-solution paradigm in linear design methodologies closes the door on discussions of purpose and intent, techno-solutionism cancels out opportunities for speculation and introspection because it is concerned with the deployment of an already-designed technology as a product into a market, without raising questions about why this specific technology was chosen, and who would benefit or lose from its adoption.

Techno-solutionism gains even more appeal as it is presented as the best choice to maintain the competitive edge necessary to stay relevant in a fast-paced global economy.[35] States fear 'lagging behind' other states in a global economy in which technological advantages play a key role.[36] In response, these states adopt competitive emulation strategies in a context of risk and uncertainty,[37] so

[32] Mahak Nagpal, David De Cremer and Alain Van Hiel, 'Is Technology Uniquely Placed to Solve Our Problems? An Examination Into Technosolutionism, What It Entails and What It Predicts' (2024) 0 *Business & Society* 2–3; Britt S Paris, Corinne Cath and Sarah Myers West, 'Radical Infrastructure: Building beyond the Failures of Past Imaginaries for Networked Communication' (2024) 26 *New Media & Society* 6384; de Souza (n 10) 377.

[33] Nagpal and others (n 32) 5–6.

[34] de Souza (n 10) 377; Nagpal and others (n 32) 7.

[35] 'Bahrain's "Cloud-First" Philosophy' (n 9).

[36] Alami and Dixon (n 7) 72.

[37] Jeffrey M Chwieroth, 'Fashions and Fads in Finance: The Political Foundations of Sovereign Wealth Fund Creation' (2014) 58 *International Studies Quarterly* 755–756; Frank Dobbin and others, 'The Global Diffusion of Public Policies: Social Construction, Coercion, Competition, or Learning?' (2007) 33 *Annual Review of Sociology* 449.

policymakers can either rely on revered models, which may or may not succeed in their specific context,[38] or seek to emulate the successful policies of other 'peer' states that they see themselves comparable to.[39] States assume the role of 'promoter, supervisor, and owner of capital'[40] by promoting the adoption of emerging technologies across the public and private sectors. But competitive emulation is always mediated by the state's own institutional context and political economy, which can lead to substantively distinct policies that carry their own legal, political, and epistemic consequences.

States see the adoption of cloud computing in both the public and private sectors as evidence of progress and innovation, considering it key to digital transformation efforts as part of a wider push to create dynamic market-led economies. At the same time, states perceive the investment by global cloud computing service providers in the country as further evidence of their competitiveness.[41] However, in a context in which cloud computing service providers are private multinational companies, based primarily in the United States (and to a much lesser extent, China), then 'adoption' of cloud computing is in effect a privatisation of public IT resources in favour of US companies – a fact that is obscured by its presentation as a state-led effort to enhance economic growth and support the local economy.[42] Techno-solutionist rationales, at best, fail to question these underlying assumptions, and, at worst, actively construct problems that suit the interests of technologists and elite policymakers.

SECTION III

The Cloud First Policy

In Sections I and II, I examined how legal design should move away from problem-finding solutionism, and how technology policy should similarly move away from techno-solutionism. In Section III, I bring these ideas together in analysing Bahrain's 'Cloud First' Policy as a particular choice of technology policy that carries its own set of rationales that should be questioned and critiqued.

Bahrain's 'Cloud First' Policy affirms the government's commitment to 'lead by example' by adopting cloud computing technologies 'to reduce costs, increase security, increase productivity, and to develop excellent citizen services'.[43] It was

[38] Chwieroth (n 37) 755–756; Dobbin and others (n 37) 449.
[39] Chwieroth (n 37) 752, 755.
[40] Alami and Dixon (n 7) 73.
[41] 'Bahrain the 1st in Region to Implement Multi-Cloud and Hybrid Cloud System in Government Sector' (*Bahrain News Agency*, 4 December 2023) www.bna.bh/en/Bahrainthe1stinregiontoimplementmulticloudandhybridcloudsystemingovernmentsector.aspx?cms=q8FmFJgiscL2fwIzON1%2BDuifwoHe0Fmxa66okKjOXz0%3D.
[42] 'How Bahrain's "Cloud-First" Philosophy' (n 9).
[43] 'Cloud First Policy' (n 1) 3.

formulated in the context of the government's efforts to encourage AWS to invest in Bahrain and establish a regional data centre. Notably, the policy was also one of AWS's demands during the negotiations for entering the Bahraini market,[44] which suggests that AWS negotiated the public sector's IT infrastructure migration to a cloud computing model as a condition of its investment, highlighting how technology policy is a product of compromise and contestation. Indeed, if we understand technology policy as an outcome of contestation between different normative-epistemic frameworks, then viewing technology policy through the lens of legal design helps raise questions about the values that society wants to be governed by.

The Cloud First Policy suggests that the benefits of cloud computing technologies outweigh any potential costs, and that these benefits would materialise for a multitude of stakeholders. It does not question the motivations behind adopting cloud technologies, implicitly treating them as serving overall objectives of innovation, efficiency, and economic improvements. Moreover, development of the policy preceded the COVID-19 pandemic (2019–2022) but the policy's inclusion as part of Bahrain Economic Recovery Plan (2022–2024)[45] is indication that the pandemic has led to acceleration of the policy's implementation. The adoption of cloud computing technologies, and the increased penetration of so-called 'pandemic tech' into new sectors are part of the same trajectory.[46]

Efficiency as Value and Objective

'Efficiency' is treated as a core value and appears in the policy text six times.[47] Its operationalisation would entail the deployment of a set of organisational and financial fixes to governmental organisations that redistribute the arrangement of risks, benefits, and responsibilities between society, public institutions, and private entities. Notably, the policy does not question the fact that the operationalisation of the Cloud First Policy would require widespread privatisation of IT resources, as neither Bahrain nor most other governments operate their own cloud computing infrastructure and instead rely on services provided by

[44] Ranjan (n 2) 11.

[45] 'Economic Recovery Plan' (*Government of Bahrain*) www.bahrain.bh/wps/portal/en/BNP/HomeNationalPortal/ContentDetailsPage/!ut/p/z0/lY9BT8JAEIX_ynroeZciBY4iidUEQQ8G90Km7bgd2M6W7VLl37uCMUa9eJvJvPfme1LLtdQMPRkI5Bhs3J91thncjlQ-uVZqNb9M1cPT9DGbLQZqcTOUd1J_F-T3q7nKlvlknI5nw-U0_Uig7X6vr6QuHQd8C3JdcLtBThQU7hBEqFHsiE3lmkQVUHsgFhUZCmCFcT16bpCD2LqDZzwmyqOFgJUIrqWyizGWzFnySqEW_AkvgCthXRmnCnu0rj1puuCj2xB2P-F_t_sn_AsxcImnx18UGJ2u-QP7fKBS-DjFlkfRWmDZ7nQxsubiHYdGB7E!/.

[46] 'Bahrain's Pandemic Response and Cloud-First Policy Highlighted at 23rd GCC e-Government Executive Committee Meeting' (*Information and e-Government Authority*, 22 June 2021) www.iga.gov.bh/en/article/bahrains-pandemic-response-and-cloud-first-policy-highlighted-at-23rd-gcc-e-government-executive-committee-meeting.

[47] 'Cloud First Policy' (n 1).

private cloud computing service providers, the majority of which are US-based companies.

The policy makes multiple mentions of the need for governmental organisations to become more 'agile' – a term typically used in the IT services sector which refers to a particular project management methodology focused on being responsive to change and prioritises deploying functioning software quickly over perfected software slowly.[48] However, the policy mostly associates being agile with reducing the amount of IT infrastructure that the government owns and manages, and shifting responsibilities for infrastructure to the cloud computing service provider.[49] According to the policy, this 'greater agility' would allow the government to focus on the delivery of services.[50] This redistribution of responsibilities and priorities is intrinsic to privatisation as it re-orders institutions by introducing market discipline and corporate logics. For example, one of the policy's core principles is its affirmation that organisational IT should focus on 'delivering higher business value',[51] without defining exactly what business value means for a governmental entity whose purpose is to provide public services.

'Efficiency' is constructed both as a value and an objective for governmental organisations to strive for. In its capacity as a value, efficiency is meant to serve as a test for how organisational decisions are made. The policy calls for governmental organisations to consider shifting to the cloud when assessing the launch of new major hardware or software projects, for example.[52] The decision of whether to shift to the cloud is to be made based on how efficient the project would become as a result. The policy aims for service delivery and organisational operations to become more efficient, which would then lead to overall better outcomes for citizens. The appeal to the cloud also comes with its own set of rationales, often linked to the concept of the 'network society' in which power and resources are dispersed across networks and more easily accessible.[53] These underlying rationales about the efficiency of distribution of resources in cloud computing – which can be scaled up or down based on needs – trickle down into the rationales behind technology policy and cloud adoption as itself being an exercise in efficiency. The idea is premised on the notion that overall resource distribution will become more efficient, because IT resources are shifted to an efficient infrastructure. The assumptions policymakers make about technologies translate into techno-fixes that are expected to produce certain outcomes once the technology has been situated within a normative-epistemic framework. Under a critical legal design, problem-constructing framework, a key question

[48] 'Manifesto for Agile Software Development' agilemanifesto.org/.
[49] 'Cloud First Policy' (n 1) 6.
[50] ibid 6.
[51] ibid 3.
[52] ibid 7.
[53] See generally, Manuel Castells, 'Materials for an Exploratory Theory of the Network Society' (2000) 51 *The British Journal of Sociology* 5; Philipp Staab, 'The Consumption Dilemma of Digital Capitalism' (2017) 23 *Transfer: European Review of Labour and Research* 281.

to ask would be why efficiency, and not another value like accessibility or fairness or justice?

Making the Cloud Rain

The adoption of cloud technologies is a top-down, centralised, and elite-driven project as evidenced by the position of the two key institutions leading efforts for cloud adoption – the Economic Development Board (EDB) and the Information and e-Government Authority (IGA). The EDB is an investment promotion agency headed by Bahrain's Crown Prince/Prime Minister, tasked with attracting foreign direct investment into the country. And the IGA is the governmental entity responsible for designing and implementing the government's IT policy and has supervisory authority over governmental entities' IT departments. The IGA established the National Cyber Security Centre, tasked with national oversight over cyber security matters, a development that was deemed necessary to ensure the 'centralisation' and 'unification' of data governance across the government.[54] The National Cyber Security Centre has since been placed under the jurisdiction of the Supreme Defence Council, which is headed by the King and composed of the heads of all security and military entities.[55]

Much of the rhetoric surrounding these developments is linked to the idea of inter-state contestation, particularly between Bahrain and other states in the region that have rapidly internationalised and modernised their economies. The Cloud First Policy and the Cloud Services Law[56] are presented in economic, rather than political, human rights, or security terms. Similarly, the EDB Chief Executive stated in a press release that these new data regulations show investors that Bahrain 'continues to take solid steps towards a data-driven economy by adopting robust and transparent regulation to support digital transformation at all levels'.[57] Even routine announcements about the conclusion of data sovereignty agreements with foreign governments, which are a regulatory requirement stipulated in the Cloud Services Law, are presented as proof of the 'favourable environment'[58] for foreign investment in Bahrain.

[54] Ranjan (n 2) 11.

[55] 'Royal Order No. (30) With Regards to Transferring Dependency of the National Cyber Security Centre to the Supreme Defence Council' (8 May 2024) legalaffairs.gov.bh/Legislation/HTM/O3024.

[56] Legislative Decree No. 56 of 2018 In Respect of Providing Cloud Computing Services to Foreign Parties 2018.

[57] Bahrain Economic Development Board, 'A New Law for the Digital Economy: Data Protection in Bahrain' (*Bahrain Economic Development Board*, 30 September 2018) www.bahrainedb.com/bahrain-pulse/a-new-law-for-the-digital-economy-data-protection-in-bahrain.

[58] 'Bahrain Grants US Sovereignty of US Users' Data in Kingdom's Cloud Computing Centres' (*Bahrain News Agency*, 3 April 2022) www.bna.bh/en/BahraingrantsUSsovereigntyofUSusersdatainkingdomscloudcomputingcentres.aspx?cms=q8FmFJgiscL2fwIzON1%2BDr346zzruLa%2Be2ZcIvqTJU4%3D.

The adoption of cloud technologies is presented as being in-line with the country's economic strategy, and as an avenue for attracting foreign investment.[59] The EDB claims that the cloud industry will result in economic diversification and new jobs for nationals.[60] The benefits of foreign investment are unquestioned, and ignore the fact that pursuing foreign investment is a political choice that precludes the option for developing domestic cloud technologies, and instead relies on purchasing services from foreign private corporations. This policy continues unabated as both IGA and EDB are currently in advanced talks with cloud computing companies to invest in Bahrain's cloud infrastructure,[61] and have recently agreed with the Chinese company, Tencent Cloud, to establish its first-ever data centre in the West Asia and North Africa region to be based in Bahrain.[62]

Not only is the adoption of cloud computing technologies a form of privatisation by another name, but the fact that it is privatisation in favour of private American capital reveals the coloniality involved in this model of technology transfer. When policymakers choose to privatise IT resources in favour of foreign American service providers, they not only preclude the choice of privatising in favour of local service providers but also preclude the choice to develop a home-grown national cloud computing service provider whose interests can be better aligned with national economic development objectives. This choice is not a coincidence, but the result of a technology policy that is firmly positioned within the techno-solutionist problem-solving rationale, which discursively constructs particular technologies as uniquely positioned to fulfil certain objectives like enhancing efficiency, productivity, and 'business value' through reduction in labour and capital costs. The result is continued dependence on purchasing ready-made techno-fixes as products provided by a foreign company, which itself has interests in perpetuating techno-solutionist rationales.[63] If the whole point of promoting the adoption of cloud computing technologies is constructed to be the reduction of labour and financial burdens on organisations, then privatising these resources becomes the most straightforward option.

Today, more than 80% of the government's data and operations have migrated to the cloud.[64] But this was not easy and was rife with challenges,

[59] Yousef Saba, 'Bahrain in Talks for Cloud Computing, FDI Deals' *Reuters* (23 June 2022) www.reuters.com/markets/rates-bonds/bahrain-talks-cloud-computing-fdi-deals-2022-06-23/.

[60] Economic Development Board – Bahrain, 'Tencent Cloud Deploys Its First MENA Region Internet Data Centre Hub in Bahrain' (*Bahrain Economic Development Board*, 1 March 2021) www.bahrainedb.com/latest-news/tencent-cloud-deploys-its-first-mena-region-internet-data-centre-hub-in-bahrain; Ranjan (n 2).

[61] Saba (n 59).

[62] 'Tencent Cloud Deploys Its First MENA Region Internet Data Centre Hub' (n 60).

[63] Kudakwashe Muzoriwa, 'Exclusive: Here's How AWS Is Supporting MENA's Cloud Journey' (7 December 2023) gulfbusiness.com/how-aws-is-supporting-menas-cloud-journey/.

[64] '85% of Government Data Transfer to Amazon More than 300 Sites Connected to the Government Data Network.' (*Information and e-Government Authority*, 4 August 2023) www.iga.gov.bh/en/article/85-of-government-data-transfer-to-amazon-more-than-300-sites-connected-to-the-government-data-network.

both organisational and epistemic. A report published by the International Data Corporation[65] highlights how governmental entities were sceptical of cloud computing's security adequacy and cost effectiveness[66] and the Ministry of Finance was also sceptical of the idea of spending on IT that did not result in the acquisition of assets, nor was it comfortable with the idea of spending public money for illiquid rights of access to network resources that were not owned by the government.[67] The report's findings[68] make it clear that a great deal of effort was necessary to bring governmental entities on board, and to make cloud computing a tangible and inescapable facet of organisations across the country.

To encourage adoption of cloud computing in the business sector, the Tamkeen Labour Fund started offering financial support to small and medium enterprises for cloud computing services, reaching up to covering 100% of their costs.[69] It also offered to pay companies for training employees to obtain cloud computing certifications (all of which were offered by AWS, Microsoft, or Google).[70] The two national universities, the University of Bahrain and Bahrain Polytechnic, established 'Cloud Innovation Centres' in partnership with AWS.[71] The University of Bahrain also introduced a new cloud computing degree programme at the bachelor's level as part of the government's efforts to create a skilled workforce trained in cloud computing.[72] The IGA also launched programmes which targeted governmental entities and management officials in order to shift the negative 'perception bias' against cloud computing as being less secure or more expensive than on-premises IT infrastructure.[73] The Central Bank of Bahrain also removed the data residency requirements for bank financial data,[74] which AWS proudly exhibits on its website.[75] Clearly, it takes a great deal of effort to make the cloud rain.

[65] Ranjan (n 2).

[66] ibid 8.

[67] ibid 7.

[68] I use the term 'findings' cautiously, as the report's language and style indicates that it may have been drafted by IGA officials given similarities to an article published by employees of the IGA, or at least relied heavily on press statements and material directly provided by the government. It should also be noted that the report was sponsored by AWS, so it should not be considered much more than an extension of AWS and Bahraini government public relations. See referred article here, Harikrishnan Sugumaran and Khalid Ahmed AlMutawha, 'Bahrain Cloud Transformation: Cloud First in eGovernment'.

[69] 'Tamkeen Reveals the Launch of Its Cloud Computing Services Support Program for Businesses' (*Tamkeen*, 29 September 2018) www.tamkeen.bh/en/tamkeen-reveals-the-launch-of-its-cloud-computing-services-support-program-for-businesses/.

[70] ibid.

[71] Ranjan (n 2) 7.

[72] 'University of Bahrain Introduces Cloud Computing Degree Program in the Middle East with AWS Educate' (*University of Bahrain*, 15 September 2019) www.uob.edu.bh/university-of-bahrain-introduces-cloud-computing-degree-program-in-the-middle-east-with-aws-educate/.

[73] Ranjan (n 2) 8.

[74] Ranjan (n 2) 10.

[75] 'Bahrain AWS Compliance Center – Financial Services for Cloud' (*Amazon Web Services*) aws.amazon.com/financial-services/security-compliance/compliance-center/bh/.

SECTION IV

The Case for Public Participation from the Perspective of Critical Legal Design

The institutionalisation of the problem-solution paradigm and techno-solutionism results in technology policies that reproduce coloniality and authoritarianism by actively shutting down opportunities to ask introspective questions like *why* and *for whom*, because these questions have the potential to challenge solutionist rationales. When these institutional discourses are challenged, this is seen to be a result of irrationality and lack of awareness about the real benefits,[76] which requires policymakers to deploy several organisational and financial fixes aimed at removing challenges to implementation of the desired policy (or to make the cloud rain). To gain legitimacy for these policies, dissuade accusations of technocracy, and increase engagement of various stakeholders, policymakers turn to public participation mechanisms,[77] with specific roles in mind for these publics.[78] Public participation is an example of legal design already put into practice and operation, even if it is not called legal design.

Legal design practices align with the turn to public participation by developing a number of productised services aimed at engaging various publics in the policymaking process, but these practices fall short of actually providing publics with real power to influence and affect decisions because they tend to focus on downstream concerns, like how and when an emerging technology is to be implemented, while ignoring upstream questions about *why* and *for whom* the technology is going to be used for. An uncritical legal design methodology

[76] Brian Wynne, 'Risk and Environment as Legitimatory Discourses of Technology: Reflexivity Inside Out?' (2002) 50 *Current Sociology* 463–465; Maria Lee, 'The Legal Institutionalization of Public Participation in the EU Governance of Technology' in Roger Brownsword, Eloise Scotford and Karen Yeung (eds), *The Oxford Handbook of Law, Regulation and Technology* (Oxford, Oxford University Press, 2016) 623.

[77] James Wilsdon and Rebecca Willis, *See-through Science: Why Public Engagement Needs to Move Upstream* (London, Demos, 2004) 16; Arlena Jung, Rebecca-Lea Korinek and Holger Straßheim, 'Embedded Expertise: A Conceptual Framework for Reconstructing Knowledge Orders, Their Transformation and Local Specificities' (2014) 27 *Innovation: The European Journal of Social Science Research* 409; Dario Bevilacqua, 'A Democratic Expertise? Public Participation in Science-Based Decision-Making' (2019) 19 *Global Jurist* 2; Wynne, 'Risk and Environment' (n 76) 463–465; Patrick Sturgis, 'On the Limits of Public Engagement for the Governance of Emerging Technologies' (2014) 23 *Public Understanding of Science* 38–39; Mark L Flear and Martyn D Pickersgill, 'Regulatory or Regulating Publics? The European Union's Regulation of Emerging Health Technologies and Citizen Participation' (2013) 21 *Medical Law Review* 42–43, 50, 59; Alfons Bora and Heiko Hausendorf, 'Introduction: Governing Technology through Public Participation' in Alfons Bora and Heiko Hausendorf (eds), *Democratic Transgressions of Law: Governing Technology Through Public Participation*, vol 112 (Leiden, Brill, 2010) 2, 7; Chris Degeling, Stacy M Carter and Lucie Rychetnik, 'Which Public and Why Deliberate? A Scoping Review of Public Deliberation in Public Health and Health Policy Research' (2015) 131 *Social Science & Medicine* 114.

[78] Lee, 'The Legal Institutionalization of Public Participation' (n 76) 623; Degeling and others (n 77) 119.

that does not recognise its practice as a process of problem-construction will fail to shift power asymmetries in favour of the most vulnerable in society, which should be the goal of a critical legal design.[79]

Public participation is often linked to democratic values[80] and seen as a way to produce new opportunities for conflict resolution and reduce tensions between state and non-state actors in the context of a knowledge society,[81] using specific mechanisms that seek to expand the available knowledge about an emerging technology by including a variety of stakeholders at different stages of regulatory governance.[82] But public participation that does not take seriously the objective of constituting the self-determination of society at large will only reproduce power asymmetries and binary dichotomies between public and private, government and society, experts and lay people, the Global North and the Global South. People want self-determination, not just to be asked their opinion and feedback about a technology policy that has already been decided.

Critical legal design can ascribe new meanings to public participation as a vessel to contest complex knowledge claims and the values upon which society should be governed.[83] It offers an opportunity to raise questions about why *this* technology and not another, and who will benefit and who will lose, and what the risks will be.[84] Scientific knowledge is 'generated in relation to social worlds'[85] and is not only constructed by categories of 'nature'. The 'natural sciences' is a socially constructed category, and any values of objectivity and neutrality are themselves discursively constructed to give meaning to the 'natural sciences'.

[79] Where I use the term critical legal design, others may use liberatory legal design, see Khan and Pope, 'Legal Design as Liberatory Dialogue'; or legal design justice, see Sasha Costanza-Chock, 'Design Justice: Towards an Intersectional Feminist Framework for Design Theory and Practice' (2018) dl.designresearchsociety.org/drs-conference-papers/drs2018/researchpapers/38; or transformative legal design, see Sievert, 'Broadening the Scope of Legal Design', in this volume. My use of a critical legal design does not necessarily mean that I see a 'critical' approach to be substantively different to liberatory, justice or transformative approaches, nor do I mean to blur any potential differences there may be between them. What I mean to show are the similarities and connections between legal design approaches that take seriously the normative objective of legal design as a social practice which centres vulnerable and oppressed peoples in its approach.

[80] Lee, 'The Legal Institutionalization of Public Participation' (n 76) 623; Sturgis (n 77) 39; Degeling and others (n 77) 115; Gabriele Abels, 'Participatory Technology Assessment and the "Institutional Void": Investigating Democratic Theory and Representative Politics' in Alfons Bora and Heiko Hausendorf (eds), *Democratic Transgressions of Law: Governing Technology Through Public Participation*, vol 112 (Leiden, Brill, 2010) 239.

[81] Bora and Hausendorf (n 77) 2; Flear and Pickersgill (n 77) 46.

[82] Bora and Hausendorf (n 77) 5.

[83] Bevilacqua (n 77) 6; Wilsdon and Willis (n 77) 16; Degeling and others (n 77) 115; Marloes Dignum and others, 'Contested Technologies and Design for Values: The Case of Shale Gas' (2016) 22 *Science and Engineering Ethics* 1172–1173.

[84] Lee 'The Legal Institutionalization of Public Participation' (n 76) 623–624; Wilsdon and Willis (n 77) 28.

[85] Brian Wynne, 'Uncertainty and Environmental Learning: Reconceiving Science and Policy in the Preventive Paradigm' (1992) 2 *Global Environmental Change* 127.

The reification of science and the total confidence in its ability to answer even the most complex questions[86] give rise to policymaker bias towards scientific modes of knowledge production, and against other forms of knowledge production such as the perspectives of so-called lay publics. Critical legal design should deconstruct dichotomies such as facts/values and science/politics,[87] and should problematise the notion that technocratic expertise produces 'hard facts' and publics produce 'soft values'.[88] The desire for society to have self-determination over its resources is not a 'soft value' or politicisation of technology, nor is a policymaker's assessment that adoption of cloud technologies leads to increases in efficiency and productivity a piece of 'hard facts' or the result of scientific rationality. What is so irrational about a society wanting to choose how to use its resources and how to govern itself?

If public participation mechanisms are tacked on to technocratic processes without critical examination of the underlying values and assumptions within the governance process, this will only limit the scope of public participation and its potential for enhancing self-determination.[89] Moving public participation 'upstream' is one way to achieve this change.[90] Shifting public participation to an earlier, more strategic stage in the regulatory process can have a range of benefits, including redistributing the power relations between politicians, technocrats, market actors, and citizens, by prioritising questions of why and who,[91] and produce a governance framework based on collaboration rather than adversity.[92] It offers the opportunity to raise questions like: why has this technology solution been chosen over another? And who will it benefit or harm? The status quo in public participation activities tends to overemphasise downstream concerns, which reflects the false assumption that participating publics are only concerned with the practicality of emerging technology,[93] thereby restricting participating publics from engaging with questions about the purposes and meaning of innovation.

Choices, not Necessities

Decision-makers must acknowledge that all matters of technology policy are choices and not necessities, no matter how 'critical' certain technologies

[86] Wynne 'Risk and Environment' (n 76) 469.
[87] Jasanoff (n 26); Wynne 'Risk and Environment' (n 76) 462.
[88] Abels (n 80) 241.
[89] Lee 'The Legal Institutionalization of Public Participation' (n 76) 635; Wynne 'Risk and Environment' (n 76) 463.
[90] Lee 'The Legal Institutionalization of Public Participation' (n 76) 636; Wilsdon and Willis (n 77) 17–19.
[91] Maria Lee, 'Beyond Safety? The Broadening Scope of Risk Regulation' (2009) 62 *Current Legal Problems* 251.
[92] Flear and Pickersgill (n 77) 46.
[93] Wilsdon and Willis (n 77) 27.

and developmental projects may seem or be presented as such to the public.[94] Critical legal design should facilitate the integration of ethical concerns in the decision-making process, to shift the conversations towards values and not just mechanisms of implementation.[95] Vulnerable segments of society are key to the knowledge production process because knowledge is co-produced through every social interaction.[96] Critical legal design should value this knowledge the most. Over the long term, embedding these values in the design of emerging technologies itself contributes to improving justice and self-determination in technology policy – it helps society determine where it wants to spend its resources, for what purpose, and for whom.[97] Critical legal design should aim to embed social values at the upstream stage to lead to more just and socially oriented technologies and institutions.[98] People want to shape the direction of their society over the long term, not just to be brought on to provide soft values and legitimacy to an already-designed marketised product that someone else decided is the solution to a problem that they decided was a problem.

People want self-determination to decide their social futures, of which technology policy is only one part. Critical legal design should help facilitate the realisation of these self-determined futures, so that people are not dependent on what 'the market' or techno-solutionist policymakers tell them their future should be.

CONCLUSIONS

There is a lot at stake in the struggle to determine technology policy because it is part of a wider struggle to determine the values that society wants to be governed by. It is no coincidence that technology policy follows a technocratic approach that is resistant to democracy, because in Bahrain, all matters of public policy follow this approach. The critique of technocracy in STS and critical legal scholarship is premised on the idea of a public/private divide where a distinction is made between what's "political" and what's "economic", and technology policy is placed in the latter camp. Not only is this distinction false, but it also emerges from a particular historical and political context of European and American liberal democracies, where technocracy is seen as a circumvention of democratically accountable institutions. But this does not necessarily play out the same in a context where democratically accountable institutions are non-existent and

[94] Lee, 'Beyond Safety?' (n 91) 255.

[95] Mariachiara Tallacchini, 'Governing by Values. EU Ethics: Soft Tool, Hard Effects' (2009) 47 *Minerva* 291–292.

[96] Jung and others (n 77) 403.

[97] Dignum and others (n 83) 1173.

[98] ibid 1181.

all issues of public policy are shaped by relations of coloniality with those same liberal democracies.

The struggle over technology policy is a struggle over the future of society. This is why adoption of cloud technologies is presented in such dire ways – either we adopt this technology or be relegated to the past – it is an attempt to hide the fact that it is a choice, not a necessity. Bahrain has spent enormous resources, time, and effort to make the cloud rain; it has fully subsidised adoption of the cloud in the private sector, changed its laws and regulations, created new institutions, and introduced new roles and responsibilities, all just to force the policy to work. Contrary to the stated goal of efficiency and productivity, one has to question whether these efforts actually achieved the stated goals or only served to increase the costs – both social and financial. The roll-out of neoliberalism is rarely an easy task – it requires an enormous effort. Critical legal design can and should play a role in challenging these rationales and assumptions, with the responsibility to enhance social control over society's future(s).

REFERENCES

'85% of Government Data Transfer to Amazon More than 300 Sites Connected to the Government Data Network' (*Information and e-Government Authority*, 4 August 2023).

'A Conversation with H.E. Zayed R. Alzayani, Bahrain Minister of Industry, Commerce, and Tourism' (*Arab Gulf States Institute in Washington*, 17 October 2017).

G Abels, 'Participatory Technology Assessment and the "Institutional Void": Investigating Democratic Theory and Representative Politics' in Alfons Bora and Heiko Hausendorf (eds), *Democratic Transgressions of Law: Governing Technology Through Public Participation*, vol 112 (Leiden, Brill, 2010).

I Alami and A Dixon, 'Uneven and Combined State Capitalism' (2023) 55 *EPA: Economy and Space* 72.

'Bahrain AWS Compliance Center – Financial Services for Cloud' (*Amazon Web Services*).

Bahrain Economic Development Board, 'A New Law for the Digital Economy: Data Protection in Bahrain' (*Bahrain Economic Development Board*, 30 September 2018).

'Bahrain the 1st in Region to Implement Multi-Cloud and Hybrid Cloud System in Government Sector' (*Bahrain News Agency*, 4 December 2023).

'Bahraini High Court on Choice of Court and Choice of Law Agreements' (*Conflict of Laws*, 23 February 2024).

'Bahrain's Pandemic Response and Cloud-First Policy Highlighted at 23rd GCC e-Government Executive Committee Meeting' (*Information and e-Government Authority*, 22 June 2021).

D Bevilacqua, 'A Democratic Expertise? Public Participation in Science-Based Decision-Making' (2019) 19 *Global Jurist* 1.

A Bora and H Hausendorf, 'Introduction: Governing Technology through Public Participation' in Alfons Bora and Heiko Hausendorf (eds), *Democratic Transgressions of Law: Governing Technology Through Public Participation*, vol 112 (Leiden, Brill, 2010).

S Costanza-Chock, 'Design Justice: Towards an Intersectional Feminist Framework for Design Theory and Practice' (2018).

N Couldry and UA Mejias, 'Data Colonialism: Rethinking Big Data's Relation to the Contemporary Subject' (2019) 20 *Television and New Media* 319.

——, 'The Costs of Connection: How Data Is Colonizing Human Life & Appropriates It for Capitalism' (London School of Economics – Department of Media and Communications, 25 February 2021).

J Daskal, 'The Un-Territoriality of Data' (2015) 125 *The Yale Law Journal* 326.

C Degeling, SM Carter and L Rychetnik, 'Which Public and Why Deliberate? A Scoping Review of Public Deliberation in Public Health and Health Policy Research' (2015) 131 *Social Science & Medicine* 114.

M Dignum and others, 'Contested Technologies and Design for Values: The Case of Shale Gas' (2016) 22 *Science and Engineering Ethics* 1171.

A Dunne, *Speculative Everything: Design, Fiction, and Social Dreaming* (Cambridge, MA, MIT Press, 2013).

Economic Development Board – Bahrain, 'Tencent Cloud Deploys Its First MENA Region Internet Data Centre Hub in Bahrain' (*Bahrain Economic Development Board*, 1 March 2021).

'Economic Recovery Plan' (*Government of Bahrain*).

ML Flear and MD Pickersgill, 'Regulatory or Regulating Publics? The European Union's Regulation of Emerging Health Technologies and Citizen Participation' (2013) 21 *Medical Law Review* 39.

A Fraser, 'Curating Digital Geographies in an Era of Data Colonialism' (2019) 104 *Geoforum* 193.

'G42 and Microsoft Unlock New Opportunities for Digital Transformation with Joint Sovereign Cloud and AI Offering – Middle East & Africa News Center' (9 May 2023).

General Directorate of Governance and Operations, 'Cloud First Policy' (Information and eGovernment Authority, 2017).

WK Hon, *Data Localization Laws and Policy: The EU Data Protection International Transfers Restriction Through a Cloud Computing Lens* (1st edn, Cheltenham, Edward Elgar Publishing, 2017).

'How Bahrain's "Cloud-First" Philosophy Will Accelerate Digital Innovation' (*Economic Development Board – Bahrain*, 26 October 2023).

S Jasanoff, 'The Idiom of Co-Production' in Sheila Jasanoff (ed), *States of Knowledge: The Co-Production of Science and the Social Order* (London, Taylor & Francis Group, 2004).

A Jung, R-L Korinek and H Straßheim, 'Embedded Expertise: A Conceptual Framework for Reconstructing Knowledge Orders, Their Transformation and Local Specificities' (2014) 27 *Innovation: The European Journal of Social Science Research* 398.

Kathleen Garnett, Geert Van Calster and Leonie Reins, 'Towards an Innovation Principle: An Industry Trump or Shortening the Odds on Environmental Protection?' (2018) 10 *Law, Innovation and Technology* 1.

D Lambach, 'The Territorialization of Cyberspace*' (2020) 22 *International Studies Review* 482.

M Lee, 'Beyond Safety? The Broadening Scope of Risk Regulation' (2009) 62 *Current Legal Problems* 242.

——, 'The Legal Institutionalization of Public Participation in the EU Governance of Technology' in Roger Brownsword, Eloise Scotford and Karen Yeung (eds), *The*

Oxford Handbook of Law, Regulation and Technology (Oxford, Oxford University Press, 2016).

M Leiser and A Murray, 'The Role of Non-State Actors and Institutions in the Governance of New and Emerging Digital Technologies' in Roger Brownsword, Eloise Scotford and Karen Yeung (eds), *The Oxford Handbook of Law, Regulation and Technology* (Oxford, Oxford University Press, 2017).

J López and others, 'Digital Disruption or Crisis Capitalism? Technology, Power and the Pandemic' (Global Data Justice Project 2022).

'Manifesto for Agile Software Development'.

R Mogielnicki, 'Sovereign Data: The Development and Marketing of Bahrain's Digital Domain' (The Arab Gulf States Institute in Washington, 2020) 11.

LB Moses, 'Regulating in the Face of Sociotechnical Change' in Roger Brownsword, Eloise Scotford and Karen Yeung (eds), *The Oxford Handbook of Law, Regulating and Technology* (Oxford, Oxford University Press, 2016).

'Mumtalakat Leads Kingdom's Cloud Migration Drive'.

K Muzoriwa, 'Exclusive: Here's How AWS Is Supporting MENA's Cloud Journey' (7 December 2023).

M Nagpal, D De Cremer and A Van Hiel, 'Is Technology Uniquely Placed to Solve Our Problems? An Examination Into Technosolutionism, What It Entails and What It Predicts' (2024) 0 *Business & Society* 2–3.

'Notes on the Main Issues of Cloud Computing Contracts' (UNCITRAL 2019).

AS Obendiek, 'What Are We Actually Talking About? Conceptualizing Data as a Governable Object in Overlapping Jurisdictions' (2022) 66 *International Studies Quarterly* 1.

SA Paco, 'Data Colonialism, the Danger It Poses to India's Democracy, and the Effectiveness of Data Localization Laws as Resistance Notes' (2021) 48 *Rutgers Computer and Technology Law Journal* 254.

BS Paris, C Cath and SM West, 'Radical Infrastructure: Building beyond the Failures of Past Imaginaries for Networked Communication' (2024) 26 *New Media & Society* 6366.

M Ranjan, 'Cloud Strategy and Its Impact on Bahrain's Economy' (International Data Corporation in collaboration with Amazon Web Services and Bahrain EDB, 2023).

'Royal Order No. (30) With Regards to Transferring Dependency of the National Cyber Security Centre to the Supreme Defence Council' (8 May 2024).

Y Saba, 'Bahrain in Talks for Cloud Computing, FDI Deals' *Reuters* (23 June 2022).

Sankalp Bhatnagar, 'What Legal Design Is as Opposed to Could/Should Be' in D Lockton and others (eds), *DRS Biennial Conference Series* (2022).

J Santuber and L Krawietz, 'User Research Methodologies in Legal Design Projects: Lessons from Practice' in Rossana Ducato and Alain Strowel (eds), *Legal Design Perspectives. Theoretical and Practical Insights from the Field* (Geneva, Zenodo, 2021).

SP de Souza, 'The Spread of Legal Tech Solutionism and the Need for Legal Design' (2022) 13 *European Journal of Risk Regulation* 373.

A Stirling, 'Precaution in the Governance of Technology' in Roger Brownsword, Eloise Scotford and Karen Yeung (eds), *The Oxford Handbook of Law, Regulating and Technology* (Oxford, Oxford University Press, 2016).

P Sturgis, 'On the Limits of Public Engagement for the Governance of Emerging Technologies' (2014) 23 *Public Understanding of Science* 38.

H Sugumaran and KA AlMutawha, 'Bahrain Cloud Transformation: Cloud First in eGovernment'.

M Tallacchini, 'Governing by Values. EU Ethics: Soft Tool, Hard Effects' (2009) 47 *Minerva* 281.
'Tamkeen Reveals the Launch of Its Cloud Computing Services Support Program for Businesses' (*Tamkeen*, 29 September 2018).
'University of Bahrain Introduces Cloud Computing Degree Program in the Middle East with AWS Educate' (*University of Bahrain*, 15 September 2019).
R Vatanparast, 'Data Governance and the Elasticity of Sovereignty' (2020) 46 *Brooklyn Journal of International Law* 1.
MF Vila Seoane, 'Data Securitisation: The Challenges of Data Sovereignty in India' (2021) 42 *Third World Quarterly* 1733.
S Viljoen, 'A Relational Theory of Data Governance' (2021) 131 *Yale Law Journal* 573.
P Walton, '*James v Birnmann*: The Potential of Critical Design for Examining Legal Issues' in D Lockton and others (eds), *DRS Biennial Conference Series* (Bilbao, DRS Digital Library, 2022).
'Welcome to Cloud Nation' (*Invest in Bahrain*).
J Wilsdon and R Willis, *See-through Science: Why Public Engagement Needs to Move Upstream* (London, Demos, 2004).
B Wynne, 'Uncertainty and Environmental Learning: Reconceiving Science and Policy in the Preventive Paradigm' (1992) 2 *Global Environmental Change* 111.
——, 'Risk and Environment as Legitimatory Discourses of Technology: Reflexivity Inside Out?' (2002) 50 *Current Sociology* 459.
Legislative Decree No. 56 of 2018 In Respect of Providing Cloud Computing Services to Foreign Parties 2018.

14

Can Making a Law be Playful? A Case for Designing for Democratic Deliberation in India

SIDDHARTH PETER DE SOUZA, VARSHA AITHALA, SIDDHI GUPTA AND SAUMYA VARMA

INTRODUCTION

THE INDIAN PARLIAMENT acts as the most visible institution of Indian democracy and as the country's highest legislative authority,[1] it serves to enhance governance through informed debates and deliberations. However, Parliament is still an imperfect institution, and the manner of its functioning has been increasingly up for debate. In the 17th Parliament, one-third of the legislative bills were passed without discussions, members were suspended in record numbers, and there were lengthy disruptions to parliamentary proceedings.[2] These numbers suggest that the functioning of Parliament as a space for democratic deliberation has been increasingly affected.

Despite its symbolic and actual importance, trust in the Indian Parliament is on the wane. A 2024 IPSOS IndiaBus 'Most Trusted Institutions' annual survey places institutions like the army, the Prime Minister, the Supreme Court, and others above the Parliament in terms of institutions trusted by the public.[3]

Many Indians feel disconnected from the legislative process due to the perceived complexity and inaccessibility of Parliament. Political scientist Subhash Kashyap described this phenomenon several years ago:

[1] MN Kaul and SL Shakdher, in *Practice and Procedure of Parliament*, in Anoop Mishra (ed) (7th edn, New Delhi, Lok Sabha Secretariat, 2016).

[2] Anjishnu Das, 'How 17th Lok Sabha performed: One-third of Bills passed under an hour, record suspensions, lengthy interruptions' (*Indian Express*, 17 February 2024) indianexpress.com/article/political-pulse/lok-sabha-performed-bills-passed-suspensions-lengthy-interruptions-9164669/.

[3] Madhurima Bhatia, 'Defence Forces (army, navy & air force), PM of Country, RBI, Supreme Court of India and Election Commission emerge most trusted Institutions – Ipsos IndiaBus Most Trusted Institutions 2024' (*Ipsos*, 24 June 2024) www.ipsos.com/en-in/indiabus/defence-forces-army-navy-air-force-pm-country-rbi-supreme-court-india-and-election-commission.

> People talk of happenings in Parliament and of the Members of Parliament as things quite remote and different from themselves ... It is necessary to establish a new rapport between the people and the Parliament. The two must be brought closer to each other.[4,5]

Respect for parliamentary conventions, practices, and procedures and adherence to them are important measures to understand the functioning of the Parliament, enhancing the effectiveness of this institution.[6] An effective Parliament represents the political will and social diversity of its population, is transparent, accessible, and accountable to citizens, and manages its legislative and oversight functions at the national and international levels effectively.[7]

In this paper, we reflect on the ways in which it is possible to build an effective parliament by strengthening citizen engagement with it as an institution. To do this, we take a legal design approach, which prioritises empathy, collaboration, and being responsive to the evolving needs of the end user. In this approach, our intention is to look at the problem of the effectiveness of Parliament through an inherently dynamic, collaborative, and multidisciplinary approach. We reflect on the development of a board game titled 'Sabha', which is a design intervention that aims to bring the Parliament closer to the people.

The game focusses on how the Indian Parliament passes a bill. It offers insights based on years of analysing the functioning of the Parliament. As a game, it responds to the informational challenge of understanding the intricacies of how the Indian Parliament functions, and at the same time, offers an approach that is grounded in play as pedagogy to build inclusive learning, as well as discussion spaces. We reflect on how we implemented a legal design approach in this project, and discuss different steps that involved ideation, iteration, and co-creation with end-users to ensure that the final output is practical, inclusive, and tailored for diverse audiences.

This project was an outcome of a multi-year project by Justice Adda (of which the authors are a part), a law and design social venture in India, developed in partnership with the Hanns Seidel Stiftung.[8] Justice Adda focusses on designing interventions that tackle legal information asymmetries primarily in the Indian context. As an organisation, we work towards tackling the consolidation of informational power, which it sees as being critical to denying people access to justice.[9] These informational barriers reside in terms of who is producing

[4] Subhash C Kashyap, 'Working of Parliament and Need for Reforms' in Subhash C Kashyap, D D Khanna and Gert W Kueck (eds), *Reviewing the Constitution?* (New Delhi, Shipra Publications, 2000).

[5] Inter-Parliamentary Union 'Evaluating Parliament – A self-assessment toolkit for parliaments' (2008) archive.ipu.org/PDF/publications/self-e.pdf.

[6] Kaul and Shakdher (n 1).

[7] Inter-Parliamentary Union (n 5).

[8] 'SABHA' playsabha.com/.

[9] 'Law + Design | Justice Adda | India' www.justiceadda.com/.

legal information, what kinds of audiences this information is being produced for, and how such information is being consumed.

This paper is organised as follows. The second section studies as well as problematises what a well-functioning Parliament is, and the role that we see for citizenry in India. The third section describes our intervention, and outlines how we designed 'Sabha'. It also discusses our reflections from the game, and also more generally on what this means for designing for deliberative democratic spaces. In reflecting on the project, we argue for how legal design affords the opportunity to bring in play into the way in which the law is produced and understood.

THE CASE CONTEXT: THE PARLIAMENT IN INDIA, AN INSTITUTION FOR THE PEOPLE, AND YET FAR FROM THE PEOPLE

India's size and diversity led the makers of the Indian Constitution to turn to representative democracy.[10] This allows citizens to indirectly participate in governance through their elected representatives, who bring local and regional issues to the national platform. As a result, engagement between citizens and Parliament has typically occurred through the electoral process. Citizens vote in elections, which determines who represents them in Parliament, and in turn these representatives elect the head of the government.[11] Beyond elections, citizens have a few notable but limited means to engage with the Parliament. The Constitution and the legal framework avoided formal mandates that enshrined people's participation in the process of law-making directly, such as referendums or recalls.[12] It can be argued that the absence of direct forms of deliberation frequently disrupted the social and political climate of the country and led to mass mobilisation for reform. This was witnessed in the movement for the Right to Information Act, amendments to the criminal law in the aftermath of the heinous gangrape and murder of a paramedical student in 2012 in the country's capital, and the anti-corruption movement which called for an ombudsman to examine cases of corruption at the national level.[13]

To correct the limitations to means for people's participation, the Pre-Legislative Consultation Policy was introduced in 2014.[14] This policy sought

[10] Rajamanickam Srinivasan, 'Representative Democracy, Identity Politics, and Participatory Governance: The Indian Experiment' in Adluri Subramanyam Raju (ed), *Understanding Governance in South Asia* (Abingdon, Routledge, 2020).

[11] The Constitution of India, 1950, Part V.

[12] Prashant Bhushan and Atishi Marlena, 'Initiatives and Referendums: The Next Step in Indian Democracy' (2012) 47(34) *Economic and Political Weekly* 53.

[13] Centre for Democracy and Social Action, *New Citizens' Activism In India: Moments, Movements, and Mobilisation* (New Delhi, CDSA, 2014).

[14] Government of India, Ministry of Law and Justice, *Pre-Legislative Consultation Policy* (New Delhi, Government of India, 2014).

to institutionalise public consultations on proposed legislation and incorporation of public input. The policy has seen varying levels of success and has not been effective mainly owing to its non-obligatory nature. The government need not adhere to the prior public consultation requirement and is not required to justify why a given suggestion from the consultation was excluded from the final draft of the bill.[15]

Over the years, think tanks and consultancies have catered specifically to parliamentarians, industry bodies, and the private sector, providing information about the inner workings of Parliament. These information sources are often gate-kept, or if available to the public, are dense and not written for a wider audience, in particular, young people. This creates "distance" between the Indian Parliament and its people. This can take the form of not only physical distance[16] but also an institutional one.

Technological advancements have sought to enhance opportunities for citizen engagement with Parliament. Live telecast of all parliamentary proceedings since 2006,[17] online portals for accessing legislative documents, and platforms for submitting feedback on draft bills have made it easier for people to stay informed and involved.[18] For instance, Civis is a user-friendly platform that aggregates different bills, policies, rules, and regulations that are open for public comment and feedback, and provides citizens with an easy-to-use avenue to submit their feedback.[19] Despite this, there is a severe dearth of useful information resources about Parliament that speak directly to citizens.

An effective Parliament is important for good governance, accountability, and participation. The Inter-Parliamentary Union evolved a toolkit for Parliamentarians to self-evaluate the democratic functioning of the parliament against the following criteria: (i) representativeness; (ii) oversight over the executive; (iii) legislative capacity; (iv) transparency and accessibility; (v) accountability; and (vi) parliament's involvement in international policy.[20] The World Bank Institute has also published a study on legislative oversight and budgeting that provides metrics to assess the effectiveness of legislatures that includes special committee hearings and parliamentary questions, as

[15] PS Arun, 'The need for a proper Pre- Legislative Consultation Policy' (*The Hindu*, 26 November 2021) www.thehindu.com/news/national/the-need-for-a-proper-pre-legislative-consultation-policy/article37677558.ece.

[16] Saumya Varma and Manisha Shastri, 'Whose Parliament is it Anyway?' (*The Citizen*, 12 September 2020) www.thecitizen.in/index.php/en/NewsDetail/index/9/19348/Whose-Parliament-is-it-Anyway.

[17] Lok Sabha Secretariat, *Lok Sabha Television Channel* (New Delhi, Lok Sabha Secretariat, 2014).

[18] Shachi Nelli and Shonottra Kumar, 'How to be an active citizen in India' (*IDR*, 13 October 2022) idronline.org/article/rights/how-to-be-an-active-citizen-in-india/.

[19] Civis www.civis.vote/.

[20] Inter-Parliamentary Union (n 5). Parliamentarians are required to answer questions under each of these heads listed above and rate their responses on a scale of 5 (very high/very good) to 1 (very low/very poor).

well as extra-parliamentary accountability institutions like audit institutions and ombudsmen, and informal and formal institutional incentives like party discipline, and parliamentary committee monitoring of government policies.[21] The Commonwealth Parliamentary Association's recommendations on benchmarks reflecting good parliamentary practice include elections to the house, eligibility of members, freedom of speech immunity, organisation of the legislature, parliamentary committees and their powers, political parties – their funding, rights and responsibilities in the legislature, and values associated with the parliament such as accessibility, openness and engagement with citizens and media, ethical governance including accountability, transparency, responsibility and propriety in the conduct of legislators.[22] Adapting from these reports, a PRS study evolved a set of metrics covering each of the four main functions of the Indian Parliament: legislation, oversight, representation, and budgeting. Under each of these functions, these metrics cover several qualitative and quantitative aspects of the Parliament's functions, discussed in detail below.[23]

Relevant to the Sabha project were two of the functions of the Parliament as highlighted by the PRS study: 'legislation' and 'representation'. The study explains that the 'legislation' function measures both the 'quantity' and 'quality' of laws. Quantity estimates the time spent by Members of Parliament (MPs) on debating bills and legislative business, and includes the types of legislation introduced by the government and by private members, time spent in discussions of private member bills, etc. 'Quality' evaluates aspects such as the overall quality of speeches made during legislative debates, laws enacted versus struck down by courts, laws amended, effective implementation of laws and delegated legislation, evaluating the operations of the Parliamentary Standing Committees and ad hoc committees on bills, etc. It expands on the 'representation' function which the PRS study describes as looking at the amount of time spent by MPs in monitoring government activities that affect their constituencies. This includes matters of urgent public importance raised by members (Rule 377), questions asked by Lok Sabha MPs during Question Hour that have a bearing on their constituencies, etc.

Considering these different insights, the game design was focused on the role of the key players in the Parliament, called MPs, elected by citizens who are eligible

[21] Rick Stapenhurst, Riccardo Pelizzo, David M Olson and Lisa von Trapp, *Legislative Oversight and Budgeting: A World Perspective* (Washington DC, World Bank Institute, 2008) documents1.worldbank.org/curated/en/545851468313500246/pdf/456270PUB0Box3101OFFICIAL0USE0ONLY1.pdf.

[22] Commonwealth Parliamentary Association, *Recommended Benchmarks for Democratic Legislatures* (December 2006) www.cpahq.org/media/l0jjk2nh/recommended-benchmarks-for-democratic-legislatures-updated-2018-final-online-version-single.pdf.

[23] In summary, the other functions mean: 'Oversight' ensures that the executive remains responsive and accountable, through the use of the committee system, oversight of issues discussed, questions discussed, session interruptions by members, etc. 'Budgeting' examines various aspects of the government's financial budget such as time spent on budget discussions, Parliamentary Standing Committees sittings on budgets, line items in the budgets etc.

voters from various constituencies across the country, directly and indirectly.[24] MPs are entrusted with the responsibility of advocating for the interests and concerns of their constituents.[25] The passage of a law is one of the foremost responsibilities of the MPs. The MP is both a representative and a leader and is responsible for bringing to the forum of Parliament, the aspirations of their constituency. The MP must also make numerous decisions on behalf of their constituents and act in their best interests.[26] In the arena of Parliament, MPs engage in debating and voting on legislation, scrutinising the government's policies and actions, and ensuring that the executive branch remains accountable. Given that parliaments are frequently being disrupted, we were keen to examine the role that such deliberation plays in passing bills and determining legislation.

OUR INTERVENTION: DESIGNING SABHA

In order to develop this project further, we drew from legal design approaches. We see legal design as an approach that revisits how the law is developed, understood, and circulated.[27] While at one level, legal design focusses on reimagining the form of law, in terms of its aesthetic, we are interested in how it contributes to democracy and freedom.[28] We particularly found it useful as it emerged counterpoint to more doctrinal, institutional, and managerial ways of imagining as well as constructing legal systems.

Furthermore, we saw design as a discipline that offers ways of thinking, doing, and imagining, and, drawing from Di Salvo, we were interested in how designing can tend towards care.[29] This was particularly relevant, as the challenge of designing spaces that can further democratic inquiry and deliberation in a multicultural and multiparty context that is India, requires this. It was critical that in our design, we could tackle the wicked problem of the distance of

[24] The Rajya Sabha (or the Upper House) is indirectly elected through a system of proportional representation. The elected members of the Legislative Assembly of a state elect the representatives of that state.

[25] The Constitution of India (n 11).

[26] Lok Sabha Secretariat, *The Indian Parliament* (New Delhi, Lok Sabha Secretariat, 2012).

[27] Margaret Hagan, 'Legal Design as a Thing: A Theory of Change and a Set of Methods to Craft a Human-Centered Legal System' (2020) 36 *Design Issues* 3; Michael Doherty and others, 'A New Attitude to Law's Empire: The Potentialities of Legal Design' in Marcelo Corrales Compagnucci and others (eds), *Legal Design: Integrating Business, Design and Legal Thinking with Technology* (Cheltenham, Edward Elgar Publishing, 2021); Justice Adda, 'The Not So Secret Life of Your Data' www.justiceadda.com/datarights; 'Graphic Law Library' (*Justice Adda*) www.justiceadda.com/graphiclawlibrary; Justice Adda, 'Illustrated Cases of the Supreme Court of India' (2018) www.justiceadda.com. See also Bhawna Parmar and Kanan Dhru in this book.

[28] Hallie Pope, 'Liberatory Legal Design and Radical Imagination' (2022) *DRS Biennial Conference Series* dl.designresearchsociety.org/drs-conference-papers/drs2022/researchpapers/254; Joaquin Santuber and Lina Krawietz, 'The Sociomateriality of Justice: A Relational Ontology for Legal Design: A Relational Ontology for Legal Design' (2021) 6 *RChD: creación y pensamiento* 1.

[29] Carl Disalvo, *Design as Democratic Inquiry: Putting Experimental Civics into Practice* (Cambridge, MA, MIT Press, 2022).

parliament, a problem which does not have clear solutions, is interrelated, and complex.[30]

Design as Play

Games have been shown to have strong pedagogical properties for learning. Here, learning is not limited only to inside the classroom for curricular purposes but is more focused on transacting information in an interactive and engaging manner. UNESCO Mahatma Gandhi Institute of Education for Peace and Sustainable Development's Games for Learning is a testimony to this, along with the market for knowledge-based games, which has always existed.[31]

With the advent of modern digital communication tools, the concept of 'play' has increasingly become digitalised. Pratham Foundation's Annual Status of Education Report found that 90% of young people surveyed in rural India (ages 14–18) reported having a smartphone at home and being on social media.[32] While it is pertinent to recognise the role of the digital in empowering children, experts are highlighting the importance of recognising the ill-effects of excessive screentime[33] and promoting the deployment of board games for a child's cognitive development in addition to digital media already being utilised.[34]

Physical board games, in particular, in the past, had a particular cultural receptivity in India, as an intrinsic part of most people's childhood, across regions. The board game market in India, for the most part, was a niche market, dominated by traditional children-oriented games like Ludo, Snakes and Ladders, Monopoly, Business, and so on. In the last decade or so, driven by the purchasing power of millennials, the board game market has seen a diversified uptick. This was further accelerated by the COVID-19-induced lockdown.

People of older age groups, in fact, are turning to board games as an activity for leisure, socialising, team building, and much more. The notion that board games are solely for children has been upended, with growing communities of board game clubs, cafes, and so on. In 2020, the Bored Game Company, a

[30] Johanna Lönngren and Katrien van Poeck, 'Wicked Problems: A Mapping Review of the Literature' (2021) 28 *International Journal of Sustainable Development & World Ecology* 481.

[31] 'Games for Learning' (*UNESCO MGEIP*, 25 April 2022) mgiep.unesco.org/games-forlearning#:~:text=UNESCO%20MGIEP%2C%20through%20its%20Games,achieve%20the%20UN%20SDG%204.7.

[32] Pratham, *Annual Status of Education Report (Rural) 2023: Beyond Basics* (Mumbai, Pratham, 2024).

[33] GS Charan, R Kalia, MS Khurana and GS Narang, 'From Screens to Sunshine: Rescuing Children's Outdoor Playtime in the Digital Era' (2024) 20(1) *Journal of Indian Association for Child and Adolescent Mental Health* 11–17.

[34] G Fatima, Shirly Anitha and Udayakumar Narasimhan, 'Coronavirus Disease 2019 and the Inevitable Increase in Screen Time Among Indian Children: Is Going Digital the way Forward?' (2020) 29(1) *Industrial Psychiatry Journal* 171–175.

Pune-based seller of board games, saw a 30% increase in board game sales.[35] Industry estimates value the Indian market for board games at $45 million.[36] According to a 2021 study conducted by Statista, a provider of market and consumer-related data, the board games market in India is expanding rapidly, with projected annual growth of around 11.5% in the next five years.[37] This uptick has also been accompanied by a growing demand for India-centric board games. Some experts have pointed to the government's push for 'Made in India' toys and games.

Noting the manner in which people's ideas about board games and play are ever evolving, we carried out a survey with 126 responses to understand the needs and preferences of our target audience, which included high school students, college students, and young professionals. One of the main questions we asked respondents was what type of board game they like to play. The results showed a 68% preference for strategy games, followed by games of chance, skill, and knowledge/trivia in that order. We asked respondents on how much trivia they like in board games that they play. Majority of respondents (73%) stated that they would like 'Lots' or 'Moderate' amounts of trivia. This enabled us to assess how much information about Parliament should be a part of the game and whether it would be palatable to the audience.

This research was complemented by a market study of existing games to identify gaps and opportunities. While other games in the market touched on political themes, none focused specifically on the Indian Parliament and its legislative process. Moreover, many existing games were relatively expensive, making them inaccessible to a large portion of the population.

At our end, we wanted to create a tool that would demystify the Indian Parliament and make the law-making process accessible to everyone, regardless of their background. We recognised early on that existing educational tools often failed to meaningfully engage people in civic processes. Traditional methods were either too abstract or too passive, leading to a disconnect between citizens and their understanding of how their government functions.

With all these considerations, we decided to develop an open-access board game as our chosen format, because of the evolving understanding of games and play and their role in learning, whereby young adult students learn by doing rather than by passively receiving information.[38] This was crucial for our

[35] Rashmi Menon, 'How pandemic gave a boost to the Indian board game industry' (*Mint Lounge*, 9 February 2021) lifestyle.livemint.com/news/bigstory/how-pandemic-gave-a-boost-to-the-indian-board-game-industry-111612772224435.html.

[36] Remya Lakshmanan and Aarushi Aggarwal, 'India plays: Time to realise domestic potential of boardgames' (*Indian Express*, 10 January 2021) indianexpress.com/article/technology/opinion-technology/india-playstime-to-realise-domestic-potential-of-boardgames-queens-gambit-chess-7140483/.

[37] Statista, 'Mobile gaming market worldwide' (*Statista*, 2024) www.statista.com/study/87396/mobile-gaming-market-worldwide/.

[38] Chris Crowell, 'Why Games can be Effective Pedagogy?' (*MGEIP*) mgiep.unesco.org/article/why-games-can-be-effectivepedagogy#:~:text=Critical%20Thinking%20and%20Problem%20Solving,further%20toward%20his%2F%20her%20goal.

objective of promoting civic participation, as we wanted to create an interactive experience that would allow players to engage with the processes and responsibilities of the Indian Parliament in a hands-on manner.

Designing for Democratic Participation

Sabha was the product of a collaborative effort by a diverse team of parliamentary experts, graphic designers, lawyers, and social scientists. Our team was a combination of those with expertise in the workings of the Parliament, those with more than above-average knowledge, and those with basic information. As we developed this game together, we were able to exchange notes and get insights into how different people understood Parliament and take decisions consciously. It allowed us to ground ourselves in the different learning abilities and knowledge levels of our users.[39]

As a game, Sabha encourages the players, acting as MPs, to facilitate good governance through prompt and high-quality decision-making. We understand governance as the 'government's ability to make and enforce laws and deliver goods and services to the satisfaction of the public, so as to generate required faith and confidence on the effectiveness in the working of the government institutions'.[40] Retaining the focus on ensuring the maximisation of social welfare contributes to greater faith and confidence of the public in the government, and finally, to their trust in the institution.

Building awareness: In our design, it was critical to define the problem statement before we could proceed and ideate. For Sabha, the main objective was to evoke in the players, a familiarity with the fundamental process of passing a bill in the Parliament so as to explain to people how it works in action. This familiarity would be the first step in bridging the distance between the institution and the people it represents. It was important to define this focus clearly and ensure that the player would walk away with a nuanced understanding of this process. In creating a game that leads with the objectives of education, increasing civic awareness, and enhancing democratic participation, communicating information was not an option but a mandate. For example, we decided to give the instructions manual as much attention and importance as the main game board itself. The instructions manual is equal in size to the game board and, more importantly, is as designed as the game board. The players refer to this manual not just at the onset of the game but throughout the gameplay. It not only facilitates the playing of the game but also roleplays as an actual facilitator of the learning experience by providing succinct pieces of information at every stage. This ties the mechanics and communication strategies together to ensure

[39] Design kit (n.d.). web.archive.org/web/20221204130633/https://www.designkit.org/mindsets/.

[40] F Fukuyama 'What is Governance?' Centre for Global Development Working Paper N.314 (2013) www.cgdev.org/sites/default/files/1426906_file_Fukuyama_What_Is_Governance.pdf.

we achieve our objectives subtly while employing the tools and methods of playing a game.

Creating immersions: Once the problem statement was defined, it was important to prioritise the user experience. Would players experience suspense in the game, or would there be an underlying anxiety to get to the finish line? What would be the emotional trajectory of the players? Are we building this game for the experience of community building, tolerance, humour, negotiation, or is it something else? The group was clear that the experience was first and foremost educational, followed by that of building camaraderie between the players, excitement, inquisitiveness, creativity, and so on. McLuhan in his seminal work, 'The Medium is the Message',[41] points out that the best education is delivered through entertainment, and this is what we wanted to hold onto. We wanted to create an entertaining experience that was driven by the objectives of education. In our case, the curriculum for this education was the procedure of passing a bill.[42] The gameplay was designed to be dynamic and interactive, allowing players to assume the roles of MPs and navigate the challenges of passing legislation. We incorporated real-world scenarios and obstacles to make the experience as realistic as possible, helping players make connections between the procedures/actions that the game prompts with actual events they would have come across in the news. For instance, players might face opposition from other MPs, need to build coalitions, or deal with time constraints – reflecting the pressures and negotiations that occur in actual parliamentary sessions. This also pushes players to articulate ways in which they would navigate/respond to such situations, which they otherwise are not called upon to engage with.

Ensuring drama: The game was aimed as an edutainment tool for young adults (16+ years of age). The aim was to keep the game simple, while allowing for space and scope within the game design for the players to personalise the game based on their experience. We also aimed to build entertainment visually and in the game mechanics. The process of how the bill is passed is somewhat agnostic to the content of the bill. We made it entertaining and individualistic by giving the players the option to imagine and propose their own bills. This allowed for the game to become contextual and expressed our empathy for each and every player who may play the game. Empathy[43] is a key step in the design process, and it was important that we incorporate this in our design. The Parliament is an institution for each and every citizen of India, and it is important that we ensure this diversity to be acknowledged and celebrated in the game. Proposing unique and individualistic bills was one way to ensure we

[41] Marshall McLuhan, Quentin Fiore and Jerome Agel, *The Medium is the Massage: An Inventory of Effects* (Berkeley, CA, Gingko Press, 2001).

[42] Ibid.

[43] 'The role of empathy mapping in the process of design thinking' (May 15, 2023) www.qed42.com/insights/how-empathy-works-in-design-thinking.

celebrated this diversity. As a team designing the game mechanics, we realised that opportunities for fiction where the game could go beyond reality would also add lightness and relatability. The part where players write their own bills offered this. This served to make the game customisable for each player.

Facilitating playful learning: Sabha also aligns with the broader global trend of gamification in education, which seeks to make learning more engaging and effective.[44] As a tool of learning, gamification can make seemingly dull and complex procedures and information far more interesting and comprehensible. We wanted to ensure that the game had an element of 'play' – that it was not only informative but also enjoyable. By simulating a parliament in action, Sabha aims to demystify the functioning of Indian democracy for many. It has made abstract concepts more tangible and accessible, particularly for those who may have previously felt disconnected from the legislative process. For example, the game consists of a simulation of a 'No Confidence Motion' where players engage in defending their position and voting on other players' positions, with consequences of the vote in motion.

Furthermore, at different points, players are rewarded with 'votes' for following the right parliamentary procedure or securing support from external stakeholders like the media and civil society.

Enhancing access: It was also important to make the game 'look like a game'. We built this keeping in mind our own experiences of playing popular board games in India like Ludo, Snakes and Ladders, and Monopoly. Each of these games has an in-built sequence in their mechanics. The player moves ahead either based on the rolling of the dice or by completing certain tasks. This worked very well for our narrative, which was also organised as a sequence of stages that followed one another. Incorporating this sequence as the border, similar to Monopoly, embedded the design with symbols and metaphors of a game board. All other graphic design decisions followed this decision. This included where and how the cards were placed. Clear and legible labels for each shape on the game board were essential, which was achieved through the many rounds of testing with different audiences.

Furthermore, the rapid rise of digital literacy and social media usage in India has created new avenues for civic engagement, particularly among younger generations.[45] Sabha is motivated by the desire to tap into this potential by offering an educational and informative experience that resonates with this growing digital-savvy population. By making Sabha available online, we have aimed to reach as wide a digitally engaged audience as possible. Yet, by adopting a

[44] Nikolas Kairisnos, 'Why gamification means motivation in the future of education' (*We Are Tech Women*, 18 February 2022) wearetechwomen.com/why-gamification-means-motivation-in-the-future-of-education/.

[45] TOI Online, 'How e-learning is contributing to Digital Literacy in India' (*Times of India*, 21 September 2022) timesofindia.indiatimes.com/education/online-schooling/how-e-learning-is-contributing-to-digital-literacy-in-india/articleshow/94350600.cms.

print-and-play model, Sabha is built on the understanding that digital tools have limitations.

Figure 14.1 Image of Sabha board

Figure 14.2 Game components available for download on the Sabha website

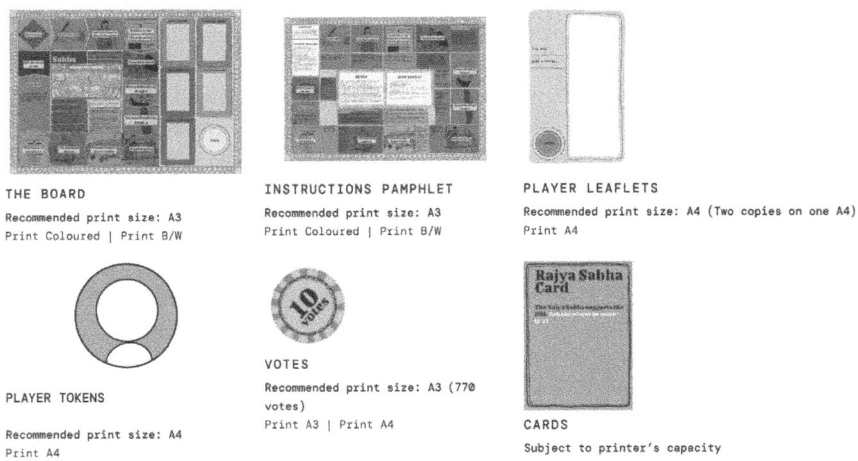

Playing Sabha

After we put together a prototype, we organised focus group discussion sessions in multiple cities across India, including Delhi and Bengaluru, to test the game in real time. These groups consisted of high school students, college students, young professionals, and other interested individuals.

One of the key findings from the testing phase was differences in how the game was received based on players' varying educational backgrounds, familiarity and comfort with the English language, and exposure to board game cultures. While those still in school gave feedback on the drama of the game, working professionals provided insights into the technicalities of the game, and what was lacking thereof.

Many participants expressed that they had gained a better understanding of how the Indian Parliament functions and felt more confident in their ability to engage with civic processes. However, younger players and/or those who did not frequently play boardgames tended to find the rules to be too complex.

The final version of the game was launched in January 2023, in a format that allows easy access and setup. Players can download high-quality images of the game components from the specific website we designed for the game, www.playsabha.com, print them, and start playing within their own spaces with minimal effort. This was a deliberate choice aimed at diffusing costs for the game, while also encouraging ownership of setting up the game. This has admittedly seen less uptake than we expected, in part due to the effort required to set up the game. We noted that those participants with relatively higher disposable incomes expressed a desire to buy the game board rather than use the 'print and play' version available on Sabha website. Participants felt that more time and effort would be required to set up the game from scratch and expressed doubts on the quality of output that a home/college printer could achieve.[46]

We also distributed 100 physical iterations of the game to schools, colleges, civil society organisations, and children's charities to further extend its reach and conducted game sessions in formal and civic education centres as well as in community centres across several Indian cities, including Delhi, Bengaluru, and Panaji.

In the three-year period since its launch, the game has been played by a mixed profile: undergraduate students, graduates, and professionals across disciplinary backgrounds. Players showed different degrees of interaction with the game based on the stages of the game. At the start, when several concepts, practices, and procedures of the Parliament were explained to the players, which they were expected to internalise quickly, players' reception to these varied. As the game progressed, however, a marked difference was observed, with players getting more comfortable with the rules and therefore being able to strategise and plan their moves. By the end of the game, players were immersed in the game play and offered several suggestions to improve the game experience for the next set of players.

In its conception, we aimed for players of various backgrounds – from school/college students to working adults – to play the game. While students from educational institutions in urban spaces have participated in game play sessions that we have organised, so far, we have been unable to actively track

[46] Impact report on file with authors.

the game experience from working adult populations in cities, and more generally, from participants living in semi-urban or rural areas of the country. The game is currently available in English, Hindi, and Kannada with the objective of expanding the range of participation.

In our experience with young students and professionals engaging in live game plays, we find that Sabha has not only succeeded in educating players about the legislative process but has also ignited meaningful debates about governance, policymaking, problem-solving about everyday issues, as well as macro -level challenges, democratic participation, and more.

The game encourages players to engage in meaningful discussions and actions, not just as a means to an end but as a core part of the experience. For instance, Coalition Cards, which form part of the game, give players the opportunity to think through potentially varying approaches to a policy problem and how they can be unified towards a common goal. These cards urge players to join forces, putting aside their differences, and to think strategically about emerging victorious.

What we noticed after nearly all of our live gameplay sessions was that the game did not just end when a winner was declared. Participants picked up themes brought up during the gameplay and continued discussing and debating them long after the game was over. There was a sense of reflection about mistakes that could have been avoided, strategies that could have been deployed, and compromises that could have been made. This post-game reflection is where we see the real potential of Sabha to have a life beyond a game session and permeate into different facets of critical thinking and civic engagement in one's communities.

CONCLUSION

Through discussions on developing the board game Sabha, this paper has aimed to reflect on choices we made to deploy design to create democratic spaces. In this process, we aimed to address the challenge of how to close the distance between the Parliament and its people. In our approach, this involved addressing the goal of building awareness through creating immersive learning experiences that facilitated play and enhanced access to knowledge.

Imagining the making of law as a playful exercise is a challenging process, and in our design process, we recognised the criticality of looking at various forms of interventions that were necessary. This involved making thoughtful choices in every aspect of the process. From the core objectives of the game to the visual design of the game, how it will be published and distributed, and lastly, the outreach strategy with educational institutions.

We explored the visual aesthetics of how to make the game feel, the product aspects of how to package such a learning outcome in a translatable way, the liberatory dimensions of how to make people feel empowered through greater agency, and the epistemic dimensions of ensuring that the game also has elements where the narratives of the gameplay are from the world view of the players themselves.

To us, the value of using legal design in this process was to not only think beyond the typical form of the law but also to free ourselves of the typical spaces of the law and to find new communities that can shape and engage with legal questions in their own contexts.

REFERENCES

M Bhatia, 'Defence Forces (army, navy & air force), PM of Country, RBI, Supreme Court of India and Election Commission emerge most trusted Institutions – Ipsos IndiaBus Most Trusted Institutions 2024' (*Ipsos*, 24 June 2024).

P Bhushan and A Marlena, 'Initiatives and Referendums: The Next Step in Indian Democracy' (2012) 47(34) *Economic and Political Weekly* 53.

Centre for Democracy and Social Action, *New Citizens' Activism In India: Moments, Movements, and Mobilisation* (New Delhi, CDSA, 2014).

GS Charan, R Kalia, MS Khurana and GS Narang, 'From Screens to Sunshine: Rescuing Children's Outdoor Playtime in the Digital Era' (2024) 20(1) *Journal of Indian Association for Child and Adolescent Mental Health* 11–17.

Civis (Website).

Commonwealth Parliamentary Association *Recommended Benchmarks for Democratic Legislatures* (December 2006).

C Crowell, 'Why Games can be Effective Pedagogy?' (*MGEIP*).

C Disalvo, *Design as Democratic Inquiry: Putting Experimental Civics into Practice* (Cambridge, MA, MIT Press, 2022).

M Doherty and others, 'A New Attitude to Law's Empire: The Potentialities of Legal Design' in Marcelo Corrales Compagnucci and others (eds), *Legal Design: Integrating Business, Design and Legal Thinking with Technology* (Cheltenham, Edward Elgar Publishing, 2021).

'Games for Learning' (*UNESCO MGEIP*, 25 April 2022).

Government of India, Ministry of Law and Justice, *Pre-Legislative Consultation Policy* (New Delhi, Government of India, 2014).

G Fatima, A Anitha and F Narasimhan, 'Coronavirus Disease 2019 and the Inevitable Increase in Screen Time Among Indian Children: Is Going Digital the Way Forward?' (2020) 29(1) *Industrial Psychiatry Journal* 171–175.

M Hagan, 'Legal Design as a Thing: A Theory of Change and a Set of Methods to Craft a Human-Centered Legal System' (2020) 36 *Design Issues* 3.

Inter-Parliamentary Union 'Evaluating Parliament – A self-assessment toolkit for parliaments' (2008).

N Kairisnos, 'Why gamification means motivation in the future of education' (*We Are Tech Women*, 18 February 2022).

SC Kashyap, 'Working of Parliament and Need for Reforms' in Subhash C Kashyap, D D Khanna and Gert W Kueck (eds), *Reviewing the Constitution?* (New Delhi, Shipra Publications, 2000).

R Lakshmanan and A Aggarwal, 'India plays: Time to realise domestic potential of boardgames' (*Indian Express*, 10 January 2021).

'Law + Design | Justice Adda | India' (Website).

Lok Sabha Secretariat, *Lok Sabha Television Channel* (New Delhi, Lok Sabha Secretariat, 2014).

Lok Sabha Secretariat, *The Indian Parliament* (Lok Sabha Secretariat, 2012).

J Lönngren and K van Poeck, 'Wicked Problems: A Mapping Review of the Literature' (2021) 28 *International Journal of Sustainable Development & World Ecology* 481.

R Menon, 'How pandemic gave a boost to the Indian board game industry' (*Mint Lounge*, 9 February 2021).

S Nelli and S Kumar, 'How to be an active citizen in India' (*IDR*, 13 October 2022).

H Pope, 'Liberatory Legal Design and Radical Imagination' (2022) *DRS Biennial Conference Series*.

Pratham, *Annual Status of Education Report (Rural) 2023: Beyond Basics* (Mumbai, Pratham, 2024).

PS Arun, 'The need for a proper Pre- Legislative Consultation Policy' (*The Hindu*, 26 November 2021).

'SABHA' (Website).

J Santuber and L Krawietz, 'The Sociomateriality of Justice: A Relational Ontology for Legal Design: A Relational Ontology for Legal Design' (2021) 6 *RChD: creación y pensamiento* 1.

R Srinivasan, 'Representative Democracy, Identity Politics, and Participatory Governance: The Indian Experiment' in Adluri Subramanyam Raju (ed), *Understanding Governance in South Asia* (Abingdon, Routledge, 2020).

R Stapenhurst, R Pelizzo, D Olson and L von Trapp *Legislative Oversight and Budgeting – A World Perspective* (Washington DC, World Bank Institute, 2008).

Statista, 'Mobile gaming market worldwide '(*Statista*, 2024).

The Constitution of India, 1950, Part V.

TOI Online, 'How e-learning is contributing to Digital Literacy in India' (*Times of India*, 21 September 2022).

S Varma and M Shastri, 'Whose Parliament is it Anyway?' (*The Citizen*, 12 September 2020).

Index

www.ingramcontent.com/pod-product-compliance
Ingram Content Group UK Ltd.
Pitfield, Milton Keynes, MK11 3LW, UK
UKHW020241290926
15470UKWH00002B/667

9 781509 990061